RUGER & HIS GUNS

A History of the Man, the Company and Their Firearms

R. L. Wilson

**Photographs by
Peter Beard and G. Allan Brown**

CHARTWELL
BOOKS, INC.

Other books by R. L. Wilson:

Steel Canvas: The Art of American Arms
The Peacemakers: Arms and Adventure in the American West
Winchester: An American Legend
Colt: An American Legend
The Book of Colt Firearms
Winchester Engraving
Colt Engraving
Winchester: The Golden Age of American Gunmaking and the Winchester 1 of 1000
Samuel Colt Presents
The Arms Collection of Colonel Colt
L. D. Nimschke Firearms Engraver
The Rampant Colt
Colt Commemorative Firearms (two editions)
Theodore Roosevelt Outdoorsman (two editions)
Antique Arms Annual (editor)
The Book of Colt Engraving
The Book of Winchester Engraving
Colt Pistols
Colt Handguns (Japanese)
Paterson Colt Pistol Variations (with Philip R. Phillips)
The Colt Heritage
The Deringer in America (with L. D. Eberhart, two volumes)
Colt's Dates of Manufacture

This edition published in 2007 by
CHARTWELL BOOKS, INC.
A division of Book Sales, Inc.
276 Fifth Avenue Suite 206, New York, New York 10001
Published by arrangement with R. L. Wilson
Copyright © 1996 R. L. Wilson.
Designed by Martin Moskof
Design Assistant: George Brady
Editorial assistance provided by K&N BOOKWORKS.
Library of Congress Cataloging-in-Publication Data
    Wilson, R. L. (Robert Lawrence), date.
    Ruger & His Guns : a history of the man, the company and their firearms / R. L. Wilson : photographs by Peter Beard and G. Allan Brown.
      p.   cm.
    Includes bibliographical references and index.
    1. Ruger, William, B., 1916 - 2002 2. Ruger Corporation—History. 3. Firearm—United States—History. 4. Gunsmiths—United States—Biography.
    I. Title.
    TS533.62.R84W57   1996
    338.7'683'0092—dc20
      ISBN-13: 978-0-7858-2103-8   95-26287 CIP
      ISBN-10: 0-7858-2103-1
Printed in China   Reprinted 2009, 2010 twice, 2011 twice, 2012

The Great Trees, Mariposa Grove, California. Albert Bierstadt, oil on canvas, 118⅜" × 59¼". Painting exhibited at The Metropolitan Museum of Art as well as at the Museum of Modern Art and elsewhere. In front of the giant sequoias, on top of nineteenth-century books on the American West, Sharps sporting rifles, both customized by acclaimed Frontier gunsmiths the Freund Brothers. At *bottom*, Model 1874 Sharps, engraved on the right lockplate:

    Freund Bros. Cheyenne Wyo. / U.S.A.

On right side of receiver: AMERICAN FRONTIER. Engraved on left side of receiver: FREUND and IMPROVD. .40 caliber; engraved on upper tang: *Pierre Lorillard* Engraved on the left side of the frame: AMERICAN/ FRONTIER; on lockplate: *WYOMING ARMORY/FREUND'S PATENT/ Wyo. T. U.S.A.*
Indian warrior on right side of receiver. Buttplate checkered steel with scroll engraving.
At *top*, another Freund Model 1874 Sharps, engraved on the right lockplate, in script: *Freund Bros. Cheyenne Wyo. / U.S.A.* On right side of receiver: AMERICAN FRONTIER. Engraved on left side of receiver: FREUND and IMPROVD. Checkered steel buttplate, .40 caliber.

Front endpaper: The Ruger saga from the nineteenth century through the 1960s. Camp scene at *left* painted by Grandfather Julius Ruger, during Civil War service; *beneath*, sister Betty with "Bud" (Ruger's nickname, coined by family) on outing; nearby their father on horseback; *above*, German heritage family heirloom pistol from matched pair. "Blue Boy" style portrait at *left center* painted on ivory by young Ruger's Aunt Emma. Lodge to *right* of Schoeverling, Daly & Gales catalogue was on father's Long Island duck-hunting property. Drawings of technical designs from youth and into 1950s. Wife Mary Thompson Ruger in several pictures, formal portrait to *left* of prototype Ruger .22 pistol, and *above* Ruger in college dormitory at University of North Carolina. First patent next to photograph of the Rugers on their wedding day, April 26, 1938. Mother May Batterman Ruger on passport, *above* first yacht, the *Island Waters*. Coveted Shaw & Hunter trophy, at *far right*, awarded to Ruger by East African Professional Hunters Association, for record reedbuck taken with Ruger .44 Magnum Carbine on 1961 safari to Uganda. Family picture, to *left* of *Queen Mary* postcard, published in *Life*, August 11, 1947, had been taken at Fairfield County fair. Sons Billy and Tom, and daughter Molly, to *right* of Ruger standing in safari clothes, in Uganda bush. Original Southport, Connecticut, factory at *top right center*, next to Ruger with light machine gun he designed for Auto-Ordnance, during World War II.

Back endpaper: Continuing the Ruger saga from the 1950s through the mid-1990s. Old friend Bill Lett (*at right*) in whitetail deer-hunting scene at *bottom left*, next to outdoor writer (in green jacket) Larry Koller, car and shotgun specialist Lyle Patterson, and yawning cat Keto. Shooting champion Jim Clark, with favorite Ruger .22 Standard pistol, at *far left*. *Left center*, company directors in session on board yacht *Titania*, black-hulled vessel at *top center* and *bottom left*. Southport factory at *upper left*: Newport factory at *far right*; Prescott factory at *top right*. President Carter with his new Ruger Red Label shotgun, with Executive Vice President John M. Kingsley, Jr., and President Bush with his new Red Label, with then Sturm, Ruger President William B. Ruger, Jr., in Oval Office. *Top left* and *at center*, Ruger family home in Southport, purchased 1958. Beneath Ruger Sports Tourer prototype cars at *left center*, Stan Terhune and Lenard Brownell, instrumental in establishing Newport factory. Writer Skeeter Skelton on horseback next to Ruger on safari, with trophy zebra. Ruger daughter Molly in library of her home, Fasnacloich (listed in National Register of Historic Places) with extensive collection, primarily of children's books. Ruger with granddaughter Victoria above Cape Buffalo trophy. Grandson Charlie with his sisters Amy, *left*, and Adrienne, *above* Ruger's daughter Molly with niece Cameron Wesselhoft Brauns, *above* Charlie with Ruger great-grandsons Terry and Stephen. Ruger secretary Margaret Sheldon next to poster celebrity Kelly Glenn on brochure; *above* Sam and Sylvia McAllister—Sylvia was with the family from 1958–66, and again from 1993. Race car (The Ruger Special), driven by Johnny Unser, at Loudon, Indianapolis car race, September 1994. Beneath Ruger P85 pistol on *Time* cover, Mary in garden of Southport home, with factory employee Ken Siwy and standard poodle Sophie. Partial interior of Ruger Prescott factory *to left of* Blackhawk in service with U.S. Special Forces; both pictures beneath "Forge of Vulcan" ambiance photographs from Pine Tree Castings foundry. Other Prescott and Pine Tree factory photographs to *left* of Tom Ruger with industry advertising executive Dave Crosby; Maynard Dixon's celebrated "Cloud World" painting *beneath*. Tom with exhibition shooter Joe Bowman *beneath The New York Times* article on Christie's auction. Robert Delfay, Executive Director, National Shooting Sports Federation, interviewing Ruger for NSSF publication. 1950s group of gun writers, with Ruger on New Hampshire whitetail deer hunt; *below* antique arms dealer Herb Glass at bench with No. 1 Rifle. Reeves Callaway standing behind Ruger's Stutz engine (turbocharged and fine-tuned by Callaway Cars). At *left*, Ruger longtime friend and fellow gun and car collector Hunting World founder Bob Lee, on Marco Polo sheep hunt in the Pamirs, China, 1980. Coterie of celebrated gun writers and publishers *above* the original advertisement for Ruger firearms, the .22 Standard pistol, from *The American Rifleman* issue of August 1949.

Contents

. . . Man is a Tool-using Animal. . . . Weak in himself, and of small stature, he stands on a basis, at most for the flattest-soled, of some half-square foot, insecurely enough; has to straddle out his legs, lest the very wind supplant him. Feeblest of bipeds! Three quintals are a crushing load for him; the steer of the meadow tosses him aloft, like a waste rag. Nevertheless he can use Tools, can devise Tools: with these the granite mountain melts into light dust before him; he kneads glowing iron, as if it were soft paste; seas are his smooth highway, winds and fire his unwearying steeds. Nowhere do you find him without Tools: without Tools he is nothing, with Tools he is all.

Thomas Carlyle, *Sartor Resartus*

. . . the Ego *has steadily tended to efface itself, and, for purposes of model, to become a manikin on which the toilet of education is to be draped in order to show the fit or misfit of the clothes. The object of study is the garment, not the figure. The tailor adapts the manikin as well as the clothes to his patron's wants. The tailor's object . . . is to fit young men, in universities or elsewhere, to be men of the world, equipped for any emergency; and the garment offered to them is meant to show the faults of the patchwork fitted on their fathers.*

At the utmost, the active-minded young man should ask of his teacher only mastery of his tools. The young man himself, the subject of education, is a certain form of energy; the object to be gained is economy of his force; the training is partly the clearing away of obstacles, partly the direct application of effort. Once acquired, the tools and models may be thrown away.

The manikin, therefore, has the same value as any other geometrical figure of three or more dimensions, which is used for the study of relation. For that purpose it cannot be spared; it is the only measure of motion, of proportion, of human condition; it must have the air of reality; must be taken for real; must be treated as though it had life. Who knows? Possibly it had!

Henry Adams, *The Education of Henry Adams, An Autobiography*

Preface

This book began as the story of William B. Ruger, Sturm, Ruger & Co., Inc., and Ruger firearms. But the project became much more than that, as it revealed the widespread dedication to firearms and their positive aspects—their art and craftsmanship, history, mechanics, performance, and romance.

In 1995, the overall impact to the U.S. economy from sport hunting alone has been estimated at about $40 *billion*. Add to that figure the billions collectively spent—directly and indirectly—on target, skeet and trap shooting, action pistol shooting, home gunsmithing, handloading, engraving, custom metal and stock making, collecting, historical reenactments, magazines and books about firearms, ammunition and accessories, and on the nonhunting shooting sports. Sixty million American households have firearms, and the number of guns in America now exceeds 250 million, a figure that's rising steadily.

In Ruger's career, one can clearly see the evolution of expertise and achievement in the history of firearms, from their inception as an invention through their engineering, tooling up, manufacturing, marketing, collecting, and use. No one has done this better, more comprehensively, more convincingly, or more successfully.

William B. Ruger and Alexander McCormick Sturm, 1950.

At the same time, the Sturm, Ruger & Co., Inc., financial history serves as a model for any businessperson, especially a manufacturer who deals with endless details, from the smallest on up to the most complex: purchasing, marketing, cost and manufacturing analyses, distribution, product liability, planning, investing, dealing with the government, *ad infinitum*.

When Ruger started he was told that his gun and his company would fail. Colt, Winchester, Smith & Wesson, and Remington were the big four of American gunmaking.

Today Ruger makes more firearms in a single year than any of them. And he has had the opportunity to acquire all of these famous old firms, but has, in each instance, decided against it—as this book will reveal.

Even before meeting the founder in 1960, the author had been intrigued by Ruger guns, beginning with Ruger's first revolver, the Single-Six, purchased in 1954. In 1970 it was the writer's rare good fortune to have successfully hunted a lion in fair chase with a Ruger No. 1 Single Shot rifle while on safari in Zambia. That rifle rests with such prized Rugers as a .22 Standard pistol serial 203—originally bought by heavyweight boxing champion Gene Tunney, who gave it to his friend adventurer-filmmaker Peter Gimbel—

and several low serial numbers of various models. As the book evolved, adding more guns to the collection became irresistible.

Researching Ruger's career has proven to be an adventure in itself. Although "The Chief" suffers from the ravages of diabetes and rheumatoid arthritis, the author found that trying to keep up with him at his Southport (Connecticut), Newport (New Hampshire), and Prescott (Arizona) factories—and wherever else he might be—was daunting and exciting at the same time.

Whenever I ventured to ask him a question, there was always an answer: straightforward, to the point, presented with piercing clarity and often with total recall. Genuinely self-effacing, more often than once Ruger remarked to the effect that "I don't have 'saint' in front of my name. I'm not a saint; be as critical as you can." Ruger's personal photographs proved to be the key to many recollections, and proved nothing short of extraordinary. Quickly it became evident the story was so complex that only a collage-style approach for many of the illustrations could touch on the multifaceted subject's breadth and scope. This technique also allowed a pivotal theme to

come across: Ruger is the mainspring to his company, but the fulfillment of his dreams increasingly has depended on the dedicated teamwork of his employees. That team spirit was obvious from the day this project began, and was in constant evidence as the story unfolded.

Research was augmented by interviews with William B. Ruger, Sr. and Jr., the Ruger family, numerous present and past employees, friends (many of them journalists), acquaintances, and even gun enthusiasts who have never met the man himself, but know Ruger through his firearms.

This is a project which has no end. As Ruger himself has said, we should "save some of the story for future editions." Therefore, it is a story which is not yet complete, and perhaps never will be.

Unfinished or not, the Ruger story is one that is all too rare in contemporary manufacturing in America—a story with an abundance of romance, adventure, excitement, humor, struggle, pathos, and unending fascination.

Despite the enormous publicity given Ruger and his guns over the years, few really know

William B. Ruger, the legend or the man. And fewer realize that the man not only lives up to his legend; he surpasses it.

Sadly, in spite of the many fields of interest in which he is truly successful—guns, cars, art, entrepreneurial business, and manufacturing—Ruger has not been accorded the recognition he deserves. Had his major accomplishment been in any domain other than guns, he would be a darling of the media, a recipient of honorary degrees, national and international design awards, and much, much more.

It is the author's fervent wish that those who read this work may come away with an understanding and appreciation of this one facet of the American dream: a career of truly heroic proportions. This is the story of one company and its products, with a unique contemporary dynamic, the telling of which could not be more timely than *right now.*

R. L. Wilson, Castle View
Hadlyme, Connecticut

RUGER & HIS GUNS

CHAPTER I

"We've Got to Learn Sometime"

The Education of William B. Ruger
1916–1949

World War II was over. Bill Ruger, in the vanguard of the nascent American firearms industry, had left his wartime employer, Auto-Ordnance, and set up a small machine shop in Southport, Connecticut. It was something to do while he sorted out his future.

Elegant and exquisite family heirloom pistols, the first guns seen by Bill Ruger, with which he played pirates as a boy. Made in Germany by Wolff & Hinrichs, and signed in gold on top of the multi-groove rifled barrels. Snapshots from his youth and family: his grandfather Julius (at wheel of sports convertible), his parents, aunts Clara and Emma Batterman, his sister Betty, and other relatives, the Brooklyn Stuyvesant Avenue apartment building and some of the other family residences. "I first went to Sunday school at a famous old brownstone Dutch Reformed Church at the corner of Flatbush and Albemarle Terrace." Ship model was an exhibit in one of Adolph's trials. Although in these snapshots his riding was for pleasure, Ruger remembers that in his youth, "There were still horses used for conveyance, delivery vehicles, and so forth. Once, on my bicycle, I skidded on some horse manure!" *Lower right* shows Bill shooting, with his mother watching. In those days, Brooklyn was a "marvelous environment, often compared to Paris. My mother's uncle, Henry Batterman, was on the Board of Trustees of the Brooklyn Museum of Art, and he saw to it that all of the children were life members. My mother seemed to be always going to concerts and art exhibitions, sometimes with Betty and me in tow."

"Auto-Ordnance was giving up the manufacture of machine guns in favor of the consumer products which were in great demand once the war ended," recalls Ruger. "One of their first big postwar projects was an automatic changing record player. I went in and made a bid on producing some of the components, and I got a big order from them."

The Ruger Corporation, all 1,500 square feet of it, was off and running.

Almost.

There was the small matter of the equipment to be overcome. Ruger had outfitted his shop with a variety of used machine tools, and when he and his handful of employees were ready to begin turning out their first job, they were in for a shock.

"I started the milling machine and had to shut down immediately because the cutters were chattering and squealing terribly. We didn't know what the hell was the matter. Everything checked out. We tried it again—more squealing.

"Solitary trees, if they grow at all, grow strong; and a boy deprived of a father's care often develops, if he escapes the perils of youth, an independence and vigour of thought which may restore in after life the heavy loss of early days."
—Winston Churchill, *The River War*

"This shop represented all my capital. I was broke, and I was thinking, 'I really don't need this.'"

Bill Ruger, who was to become one of America's foremost industrialists, needed help.

He went looking for it in Bridgeport, where an old-time mechanic named Burt Barns was living.

"He ran a beat-up looking little shop with automatic screw machines in it. He was seventy-five years old in those days, I guess, and usually needed a shave."

Ruger persuaded Barns to stop work and come to Southport. Barns walked around the machine, pushing here and pulling there, trying a number of moves as Ruger and his staff watched anxiously.

"Finally, he took a wrench, gave a couple of twists to a nut—one nut—and said, 'Okay, now try it,' and it worked.

"It was going at a slow speed, so I said, 'All right, let's try it a little higher,' and the guys in the shop were sort of reluctant. They said, 'Yeah, this is great. But why risk damaging the cutters?' I said, 'We've got to learn sometime.'"

So they cranked it up. No problem. When Ruger said to keep pushing it higher, the men thought he was nuts and told him so.

"I'll never forget the battle those guys put up; they just didn't want to take a chance, and I made them do it. That machine was really using some of its power by *then, but it sailed right through, and we were in business."*

Burt Barns went home to Bridgeport, and Bill Ruger went on to make history.

The Early Years

William Batterman Ruger was born on June 21, 1916, in the elegant Cathedral Arms apartment house on Ocean Avenue, Brooklyn, the first of two children of Adolph and May Batterman Ruger.

His father's family was from northern Germany, and his paternal great grandfather Julius, who had been a drummer boy in von Blücher's army at Waterloo in 1815, had immigrated to America in the 1840s. His grandfather, also named Julius, had fought in the Civil War and lived to become a portrait painter in Brooklyn, while his great uncles became worldwide clipper ship entrepreneurs known as the Ruger Brothers. His mother, May, was from a wealthy New York family of department store magnates.

Adolph Ruger was a fairly successful trial lawyer who became a heavy drinker when he started having problems in his law practice. In 1918 he moved with his family to a house in Albemarle Terrace, in the then-fashionable Flatbush section of Brooklyn. He also purchased a farm farther out on Long Island, where the family stayed off and on. Inevitably, however, his alcoholism had a terrible effect on his finances, and when the economy sagged, on the eve of the Great Depression, Adolph was unable to keep up with payments on an office building he had financed with his brother and law partner, Julius. His home was also heavily mortgaged, and the bank foreclosed. When his parents' marriage ended, Bill and his mother moved into his grandfather Karl William Batterman's comfortable house, also in Brooklyn, where he spent the remainder of his childhood.

Bill's schooling during this period was as chaotic as the rest of his life. He attended two different Brooklyn elementary schools and spent several months attending a two-room country schoolhouse on Long Island.

To complicate matters further, Bill was plagued with chronic health problems. He developed severe respiratory symptoms as he was about to start seventh grade, and his mother, fearing tuberculosis, took him out of school and sent him to live with family friends who had a farm in northeastern New York.

"It was a real working farm," he says, "and a very basic, wholesome life. I ate in the kitchen with the farmhands, and I ate like a horse, with a marvelous table set every day."

He fell in love with the outdoors. Still recuperating, he was given few chores to do and was free to wander and explore the countryside. "I had a rifle, and there were woodchucks. . . . I was out all day long, climbing those Catskills hills." It was the best possible therapy; he put on some much-needed weight, and his pleurisy and nagging cough began to diminish.

When he finally returned to Brooklyn, Bill entered Alexander Hamilton High School. He also joined Boy Scout Troop 225, which was featured in an early writing venture: *Stork Patrol in the Congo*. Written in the tradition of the boys' adventure series that were popular then, it was a tale of young Bill Ruger and his Scouts friends, off on a fictional African adventure. Authored and edited primarily by Bill, the story was self-published in mimeographed form, complete with an illustration showing him saving the day by firing his .30-06 Springfield rifle, foreshadowing African adventures still many years away.

A Passion for Mechanics

One thing Bill Ruger had absorbed during his early years was a love for the outdoors, for hunting, and for the purposeful beauty of the guns he used. Adolph Ruger had owned a duck hunting lodge in Shinnecock, on Long Island, and by age six, Bill was accompanying his father on hunting trips, where he learned to shoot with a Stevens single shot .22 rimfire rifle. His father gave him a Remington Model 12 pump-action .22 rifle for his twelfth birthday, when he was recuperating from scarlet fever, and Bill went on to join the rifle team in high school, becoming an excellent shot.

Firearms became more and more of an interest. "I remember seeing them in the store windows and they looked so beautiful, particularly the Savage 99 and the Winchester lever action. The mechanics were so artistically designed—they absolutely thrilled me. I associated them with great adventure and great art."

It was during the year spent on the farm upstate that Bill encountered his first high-powered rifle. "I was out in the hills and I heard a gun go off. It was a tremendous explosion. I ran and walked for half a mile until I saw two men in a meadow. One was sighting-in for the fall hunting season and the other was down by the target, spotting. The rifles were .30-06 bolt actions, probably the Springfield sporters which were very popular in those days. When that rifle went off, I was stunned. What a racket! I thought, 'Boy, that's something fantastic!' And it was."

Back in Brooklyn, his school friend William J. Lett, who lived around the corner, was "a real gun crank." Ruger talked Lett into ordering a Spanish-American War surplus .30-40 Krag bolt-action rifle from an ad in *Popular Mechanics*. When the Krag arrived, Lett wanted to take it down to his basement to fire on a range they had rigged up for their .22s. Ruger said, "Dammit, Bill, you can't do that—it'll make too much noise!"

Instead, they tucked the rifle into a canvas bag, taking turns carrying it, and took the Fulton Street Elevated Railroad (for a nickel) to the end of the line in Brooklyn. They built a fire in a patch of woods, fantasizing grandly about camping out, set up a target, and began shooting. "We were still way inside the city limits, but we did arrange an excellent backstop. We had an unfor-

Toy dog and letters from childhood accompanied by sardonic print of baby (illustrating what not to do with a revolver), and two boyhood inventions. At *right* a semaphore, weighted at one end with a taped-on piece of lead, the other end broken off long ago. At *left* an engine, bearing Ruger's own penned-on markings: "RUGER STEAM-ENGINE. MADE BY W.B. RUGERs CO. 8000 H.P. 1731 Pat applied for (AND REFUSED)." On the driveshaft is written: RUGER. On the left side, visible in the photograph, is: "RUGER & CO., INC. SHIPYARDS." Identically positioned, on the right side, the marking: "FOR STEAMER ALEX. HAMILTON 1000 R.P.M." On the bottom, Bill marked his initials, and drew a heart, with an arrow going through it, with the initials J.R. and W.R. and an illegible inscription; below that: "IF SHE COULD ONLY COOK." The Ruger sense of humor was already evident at an early age. The Mannlicher rifle in the umbrella stand was a Ruger favorite, acquired in the 1950s. Photographed in the entrance hallway of Ruger's Southport, Connecticut, home, purchased in 1958.

gettable afternoon learning what a full power .30 caliber rifle was like. Lett had bought a marvelous Krag—not the $9.75 one, but the special $15.00 version, just like new. We put it back into the canvas case and went back to his house, two of the happiest kids you've ever seen."

Not long afterward, Bill sold an old Reming-ton shotgun of his grandfather's for $20.00 and went to Francis Bannerman's famous military surplus emporium in New York City.[1] There he found a Sedgley-Springfield service rifle irresistible and purchased it. This was a well-constructed 1903 model, built up from surplus parts, and it shot perfectly. "I had no trouble with it at all; it didn't blow up in my face. I'm pretty sure that it was that old type—case-hardened—frame and receiver; Reginald F. Sedgley was knowledgeable enough and conscientious enough to re-heat-treat those receivers to withstand the chamber pressures of most .30-06 cartridges."

Once Bill Lett had his Krag and Bill Ruger had his Springfield, they set about trying to convert them into "really elegant sporters." "Making a stock was a gargantuan undertaking for us, but we got right at it. Bill Lett made one out of a pine plank first, and once he saw it was possible, he made a better one. Our rifles slowly evolved into homemade sporters."

His experiences with hunting, shooting, and design gave early direction to Bill Ruger's exploding interests. In these early teen years, most of his spare time was devoted to learning about guns. While still in high school, he bought two deactivated machine guns, an 11mm Vickers and a .30-40 Model 1905 Colt "Potato Digger,"[2] to take them apart and learn how they operated. He haunted the hunting and firearms section of the New York City Public Library, and by the time he was thirteen or fourteen, he had worked his way through the stacks.[3] "Nobody else was reading these books. You could see that some of them hadn't been off the shelf in fifteen or twenty years. Many of them were covered with dust."

One day he saw a copy of *The American Rifleman* in the school library. "I was thrilled to realize that there was a whole magazine on the subject of firearms and shooting." Once again, Ruger got Bill Lett to spend some of his money, this time to join the National Rifle Association, the magazine's publisher. "Every month I'd be there knocking on his door, asking if *The Rifleman* had come in yet."

One series of *Rifleman* articles, published in 1932, would never be forgotten by Ruger. Major Julian S. Hatcher of U.S. Army Ordnance had written a four-installment essay on self-loading ri-

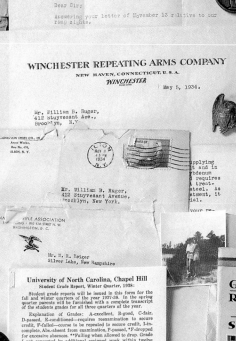

MACHINISTS · CONTRACTORS

Mrs. May J. Ruger
412 Stuyvesant avenue,
Brooklyn, N. Y.

The REVOLVER

Board of Education
of the City of New York
Alexander Hamilton High School of Commerce

This Diploma is awarded to

William Ruger

who has satisfactorily completed the

General Course of Four Years

and by proficiency in scholarship and by integrity of character
has merited graduation   January 1936

President Board of Education   Superintendent of Schools

Acting Principal

May 8, 1934.

Mr. William B. Ruger,
412 Stuyvesant Avenue,
Brooklyn, New York.

Dear Sir:
This refers to your letter of April 27th which our Bridgeport,
Conn. office has referred to us for attention as regards supplying you
with a block of steel 7" by 3-1/2" by 3" ...

Field & Stream
578 MADISON AVENUE
NEW YORK, N. Y.
January 31st, 1931.

ARMS & AMMUNITION DEPT.
Capt. PAUL A. CURTIS, Editor

ELTINGE F. WARNER
PUBLISHER

Showing
STATE and MAIN TRAVE
HIGHWAYS, RAILRO
AND AIRPORTS

"Old Man of the Mountain"
Franconia Notch

NEW HAMPSHIRE
STATE PLANNING & DEVELOPMENT COM
246 SCHOOL STREET
CONCORD, NEW HAMPSHIRE

1935

ALEXANDER HAMILTON
HIGH SCHOOL
FALL - 1931 - TERM

ROOM
IS A MEMBER OF THE GENERAL ORGANIZATION FOR
THE TERM ENDING JANUARY 31, 1932.

EDWARD F. TAYLOR
Faculty Adviser

W. J. Sutton,
Vice Pres & Fact. Supt.

R. J. Miller,
Pres. & Mgr.

Robt. S. Miller,
Secy. & Treas.

PACIFIC GUN SIGHT CO.
682 24th. AVE.
MAIN OFFICE & FACTORY
424 BALBOA STREET
SAN FRANCISCO, CALIF.

November 20, 1931.

William B. Ruger
412 Stuyvesant Avenue
Brooklyn, New York

Dear Sir:

Answering your letter of November 13 relative to our
ramp sights.

STATEMENT OF ACCOUNT
OF MAY J. RUGER AND
WILLIAM E. SCHRAMEK
AS TRUSTEES UNDER THE
LAST WILL AND TESTAMENT
OF MARY E. BATTERMAN FO
THE BENEFIT OF WILLIAM
RUGER AND ELIZABETH
RUGER.

APRIL 1st, 1936 to
MARCH 31st, 1937.

WILLIAM E. SCHRAMEK
Attorney at law,
Two Rector Street,
Borough of Manhat
City.

Book of Fine Guns

AMERICAN ARMAMENT CORPORATION

DAVID T. L. VAN BUREN   SIX EAST FORTY-FIFTH STREET
NEW YORK, N. Y.

RULES
FOR
HIGH POWER
RIFLE
MATCHES
. . . . .

JULY, 1938
PRICE, 10 CENTS

WINCHESTER REPEATING ARMS COMPANY
NEW HAVEN, CONNECTICUT, U.S.A.
WINCHESTER
May 5, 1934.

Mr. William B. Ruger,
412 Stuyvesant Ave.,
Brooklyn, N. Y.

REMINGTON ARMS CO., IN
Arms Works,
Box No. 676,
ILION, N. Y.

Mr. William B. Ruger,
412 Stuyvesant Avenue,
Brooklyn, New York.

NA   RIFLE ASSOCIATION
ING · 910 TTH STREET N. W.
WASHINGTON, D. C.

Mr. W. R. Reiger
Silver Lake, New Hampshire

...pplying
...nt in
...bdenum
... requires
... treat-
...steel. As
...atment, it
...rial.

...your re-

Schoverling · Daly & Gales
202-304 Broadway · New York

Salisbury School

The Headmaster and Mrs. Quaile request the pleasure of
...
Your company on the
Thirteenth Anniversary Day of the School
Saturday, June the eighteenth

Please reply if accepting

FIALA OUTFITS Inc.
NEW YORK
47 WARREN STREET
NEW YORK, N.Y.

Mr. William B. Ruger
Salisbury School
Salisbury, Conn.

FIALA SCHOOL OF FIREARMS
& SMALL ARMS RANGE

47 WARREN STREET
New York City

Telephone — COrtlandt 7-4725

NATIONAL RIFLE ASSOCIATION
OFFICIAL

ANNIVERSARY DAY
1938

FRIDAY, JUNE 17th

2:15 P.M. Inter-Club Tennis
4:30 P.M. Crew Races and Water Sports
7:00 P.M. Buffet Supper
8:30 P.M. Dancing
Reception at Headmaster's House
for Old Boys, Parents, and Friends

SATURDAY, JUNE 18th

8:30 A.M. Inter-Club Track Events
2:00 P.M. Luncheon
3:15 P.M. Address by the Headmaster and
Distribution of Prizes

The invitation is extended to any of your
friends and family who may be interested.
There is ample room. In accepting please
say how many.

University of North Carolina, Chapel Hill
Student Grade Report, Winter Quarter, 1938:

Student grade reports will be issued in this form for the
fall and winter quarters of the year 1937-38. In the spring
quarter parents will be furnished with a complete transcript
of the students grades for all three quarters of the year.

Explanation of Grades: A-excellent, B-good, C-fair,
D-passed, E-conditioned—requires reexamination to secure
credit, F-failed—course to be repeated to secure credit, I-in-
complete, Abs-absent from examination, P-passed, *F-dropped
for excessive absences. **Failing when allowed to drop. Grade
I not converted by additional assigned work within twelve
months becomes F. N.R.-No report. Graduate grades—P-sat-
isfactory, F-failed.
T. J. WILSON, Jr.
Registrar.

Gun Sights
Reloading
Tools
Supplies

PACIFIC GUN SIGHT COMPANY

University
-of-
North Carolina
Quiz

B—

Griffin & Howe

Rear view of G & H new, low, quick-
detachable, micrometer wind gauge
mounting, fitted on a Winchester M/51,
showing clearance between scope and re-
shaped bolt-handle when fully raised; also
clearance available when scope is in its
clearance available with safety raised to the
"on" position.

LYMAN ALASKAN AND
WEAVER TELESCOPE
SIGHT MOUNTS

A J. Griffin & Howe telescope rifle sight mounts are of modern design, reliable, and accurately
adjustable. A telescope sight with our standard double-lever type mount can be attached to
the rifle, ready for aiming, in five seconds. These mounts are notable for permitting sighting in
the rifle with the minimum of shots, and doing their part in holding the rifle's zero. If desired,

FEC

PRECIS
TELESCO
SIGH

"SEDGLEY" MANNLICHER TYPE SPORTER

26-inch Barrel, 5-shot Magazine, Lyman No. 48 Micrometer Windgauge Receiver Sight.
Gold or Ivory Bead Front Sight mounted on Matted Ramp, with Guard. Finely checkered Forend and Stock, Sling Swivels, Steel Pistol Grip Cap.

PHONE: WORTH 2-3839   ENTIRE PLANTS

MODERN

PHONES CANAL-6 5386
2644

LIQUIDATION OF PLANTS
OUR SPECIALTY

Alliance Machinery Exchange
DEALERS IN
METAL AND WOODWORKING
MACHINERY

GRAND MACHINERY EXCHANGE

fle and machine gun development, recounting the entire effort by Springfield Armory and other arms design centers to develop autoloading rifles and fully automatic infantry weapons.[4] It was Bill's introduction to the subject of self-operating gun mechanisms. "I started making drawings of how I would incorporate these principles. Of course, it was all very limited, because you can't design a thing if you have no idea how it is manufactured."

His level of understanding and expertise was evident when he wrote a letter to his mother in August 1934, describing the impression he made

---

Memorabilia and papers reflect Ruger's early fascination with firearms and machine tools. "Guns are interesting and there's just something about a thing like a firearm or a boat that anyone can really develop a genuine enthusiasm about or interest in. I should say that when I was a boy and when I was in my teens I just loved to shoot, and part of the reason was I liked the firearms themselves. It wasn't just shooting to hit something, but it was to hit something with that particular firearm. And there were some I thought were better than others, for one reason or another. It should take a natural fascination for someone with some mechanical basis on a subject of this sort, and then, assuming they have some technical and background information, to attempt their own designs." Drafting kit from boyhood proved vital in early development, and the set continued in use for many years.

Correspondence with gun writers and gunmakers reveals depth and scope of dedication. Ruger kept up such a steady stream of correspondence with shooting editors and gun factories that he worried that they wouldn't always reply, so he occasionally wrote letters under Bill Lett's name.

High school diploma reflects fact that New York then had the finest school system in the U.S., and his alma mater was considered the equivalent of a private school in quality of education. "Good marks there would get you into the Ivy League schools without any question." Letters to mother source of detailed information on much of period, well into the 1940s. At Salisbury School, Ruger is the robust oarsman, second from right. Photo at desk with pipe, from University of North Carolina days. Lovely young woman, his wife-to-be Mary Thompson.

---

when he visited the Marlin Firearms Company in New Haven:

> . . . spent all . . . morning at Marlin Firearms Co. —discussing machine gun with their chief engineer.
>
> Ha! You should have seen me. I was giving him lessons in firearms design. After awhile, there were about ten of the company's elders, standing around listening. . . . I never knew I knew so much about guns until then. When I was going they invited me to use their shops in which to build my model. I didn't say much just enough to tantalize them.

Learning About Machines

Bill Lett came by the house one day and said, "Boy, I've just seen something that you ought to know about. It's an amazing place. They've got machines in there that actually carve steel!"

He took Ruger to a machine shop in the second story of a big garage nearby. The equipment was old and crude by modern standards, but "These shapers, planers, lathes, milling machines, and drill presses were stunning. . . . I realized there were specialized machines to make holes, to make smooth surfaces, to cut slots—to do all kinds of things. I began to comprehend that if you used your head and understood the proper use of these machines, you could sculpt out a working mechanical component, no matter how complicated. I kept asking this old machinist, who was also named Bill, 'If I wanted to make this piece, could I do it this way?' He was a kindly fellow and let Bill Lett and me watch him work. His shop might not have been fancy, but the machinery he had there was typical of the commonly used machine tools. It was the most marvelous introduction for us."

Ruger returned to the library. "I began to study engineering textbooks every afternoon, reading on all these engineering subjects. Some were grossly obsolete, but still a good grounding in the basic principles. Looking back, I realize that, even though I was self-taught, I was a well-educated engineer by the time World War II

---

came along. The war was quite a motivation. The only thing I lacked was a strong mathematical background. I had studied algebra, and knew logarithms and a little trigonometry, but I didn't really know higher mathematics."

Bill went to the Salisbury School in the Connecticut Berkshires for his senior year, where the active schedule and required athletic participation further strengthened his body. Leaving Salisbury in June 1935, just short of the credits needed for a diploma, Bill returned to Alexander Hamilton High for a half year, graduating in January 1936.

College held little allure for Bill at this point. He was restless, ready for adventure, and he decided to conquer Wall Street. He sought and landed a job there. "I was a runner for a very exclusive brokerage house. They wanted kids with certain types of backgrounds. I thought that this would be my start to becoming the 'wolf of Wall Street.' But I was kidding myself."

Jobs were drying up everywhere, and the young dropout found himself spending the summer doing maintenance work at a children's camp in Connecticut. "It was hard work all summer long, but I guess it was good for me."

It was at the camp that he met Bill Budden, a co-worker and a student and football player at the University of North Carolina. His influence, and the remembered advice of a teacher at Salisbury ("Ruger, the University of North Carolina at Chapel Hill is a goddamn good school!") pushed Bill toward the college education he had rejected. In September 1936, at age twenty, he entered UNC.

Older than most of his classmates, and without a family business waiting for him upon graduation, Bill spent the usual amount of time partying, raising hell, and "worrying about getting started in a job—and what was I going to get for a job."

His mother's older sister, Aunt Emma, had left him a trust fund of $10,000. This helped finance his two years at UNC, plus a small set of machine tools. Bill convinced the University to let him set up an experimental machine shop in an empty room in the chemistry building, where he pursued his experiments in gun design, usually at the expense of his other studies. It's worth stopping here to note the drive and powers of persuasion Ruger brought to bear in his pursuit of his goals, qualities that would serve him well in years to come.

One of his first serious projects was a belt-fed machine gun, one of the most sophisticated of all firearms to design. Unlike most machine guns, Ruger's had the barrel blow *forward* upon firing, with a spring to return it after a new cartridge was positioned for reloading. This system permitted the use of an unlocked breech.

I made a rough prototype, a thing that would shoot and had a barrel which could slide forward. I discovered that if you had a bottlenecked cartridge, it moved maybe one eighth or three sixteenths of an inch while the pressure was still high. As a result, the cartridge case shoulder was deformed, which can cause jamming.

I quickly realized that I had to have some sort of delay mechanism. My solution was to have the barrel temporarily held in place by a toggle that was close to, but not on, dead center. This mechanism functioned exactly the same way as the famous Austrian Schwarzlose machine gun. That weapon, a true blowback with the breech going back, not the barrel going forward, proved the toggle could do a good job. The Pedersen rifle, which had been a competitor to the John Garand rifle, was based on the same principles.

I worked on this gun design for a while and put some money into it, but I never achieved good results. I was just a beginner and my mechanical design skills were still very underdeveloped. I didn't even know proper drafting room procedure. All my drawings were still being done on crude wrapping paper.

Ruger was interested in obtaining a patent for his design. On a trip to New York City, his mother's lawyer introduced him to Thomas Howe, a respected patent attorney. Howe prepared Ruger's very first patent application (over seventy more would follow during the next six decades) for Bill at a reasonable cost, and introduced him to the intricacies of patent searches. Ruger discovered that he could go to the Patent Office and read the firearms patents then in existence.

He began to make regular trips to Washington, D.C., staying at the historic Willard Hotel across the street from the old Patent Office library. He spent days reading and thinking about the patents that had been granted for gun designs. He was especially fascinated by the Gatling gun, and after a while he felt he knew more about its different feed mechanisms than anyone in the world. "I could tell you all about how to make feed systems, not only for Gatling guns, but for all of those hand-cranked guns, and even the completely automatic machine guns."

A Job in the Industry

Near the end of his sophomore year at UNC, Bill met Mary Carolyn Thompson, the strikingly beautiful daughter of a prominent Greensboro, North Carolina, family. After a brief engagement, they were married at the Greensboro First Presbyterian Church on April 26, 1938. Bill dropped out of school at the end of the spring term and the couple spent a glorious three-month honeymoon traveling through Europe. On his return, he began looking in earnest for work in the firearms industry.

One of his first jobs was in Hartford, Connecticut, but not at Colt's Patent Fire Arms Mfg. Co., Inc. From October 1938 to March 1939 the Rugers lived in Hartford.[5] Colt's apparently didn't offer any prospects, for in November Bill wrote his mother, "It dawned on me that I would be a nobody at Colt's, and I couldn't do any of my own work. . . . I am with a small shop that specializes in guns, and working part of the time on my own rifle. I make just enough to pay for the

April 17, 1939: Bill Ruger to His Mother from 302 Parkway, Greensboro, North Carolina, on His Hartford "Gunsmith-Machinist" Stationery

I haven't got a job yet, but I seem to have a pretty definite offer from a firm out of town. It is some sort of engineering job, in response to an ad I put in the paper. There were two other responses I turned down. I put another ad in over the weekend and am going downtown now to see if it brought any responses.

This afternoon I am leaving for Washington, D.C., to see one of the best-known firearms patent attorneys in the country. I have just found out about him. However, I *did* prepare the patent application complete, myself, drawings and all. It was the toughest job I ever did, but I did it well, even if it did take a month. At least I tested my own ability, and it may save me a lot on the attorney's fee. In a couple of days now, I ought to know pretty definitely what the outcome of all this will be.

Did you get my corsage for Easter? . . .

groceries."

The rifle he was working on was one he had admired as a teenager—the Savage Model 99

The first machine gun patent model, design for which Ruger began at the age of 16, although he had started designing guns as early as age 15. Ruger styling is evident already, in the economy of parts, the compactness and strength, the elegant breech, the purposeful profile, handsome front sight, and the mechanical ingenuity (the front sight band and rotary feed mechanism will appear again). Father with child is his future father-in-law, James F. Thompson, holding daughter Mary. At the time the wedding photo of Bill and Mary was taken, Ruger had already been engaged for six years in the developmental designs for his machine gun. Government $.10 check result of failed Southeastern Auto Repair business; the only time Ruger received assistance from the federal government.

THE RUGER MACHINE GUN

lever action. He converted it into a gas-operated self-loader. Half a century later, he is critical of his early work, saying it "lacked elegance." But this altered rifle, which is still in his gun collection, was a sign of things to come, displaying the original thinking and unique style of a true artist.

With characteristic self-assurance, Ruger was certain that Savage Arms would be interested in his invention and demonstrated it to management at their office in New York City. To his amazement, they responded politely but unenthusiastically, and summarily concluded that they had no need for a self-loader.

"So there I was, married and nearly busted. I'd

Bill Ruger on his conversion of the Savage 99 (*bottom*) from a lever action to a self-loader:

The Savage 99 conversion is pretty crude gunsmithing done sometime during 1938 or '39 by the hacksaw and file method, primarily. Functioning, as might be expected, was very mediocre and the gun illustrates nothing but an idea. The essential effect of these alterations is simply that the original finger-lever is discarded as the means for operating the bolt and is replaced with a reciprocating, gas-actuated rod which passes through the center of the magazine rotor. This rod forms a piston at its forward end, and is connected to the bolt at its rearward end. The strength of the action is unimpaired, and the design of the firing pin is such that it is mechanically impossible for the gun to fire unless it is properly locked. [shown with bolt slightly unlocked].

The rifle was test-fired with several hundred rounds, but Ruger regarded the extractor as needing improvement, something that time and effort would resolve. Article on rifle from *The American Rifleman*. Patent drawing from the Ruger 10/22 rifle, and patented Ruger rotary box magazines from the 10/22 (*bottom*) and the 77/22 Magnum bolt-action rifle—innovative designs inspired by the Savage 99 rotary system. Deluxe Savage Model 99 from the Ruger collection, as are all the illustrated antique and collectors' firearms.

Savage turned down Ruger's offer of selling them the rights to his design. "This family needs a little more luck—Savage turned down my gun. Why, I don't know, but I think I will write them and try to find out. The way they worded their refusal was so ambiguous that they may possibly be thinking of trying to shut me out of the deal. . . ."

The doctor had thought it would be a girl, or at least he got me ready to expect one, so you can imagine how pleased I was when it turned out to be a boy. He weighed almost eight pounds and is perfect in every way. He looks beautiful and healthy and cool and seems head and shoulders above all the other squalling brats in the nursery. He sleeps most of the time, and when he is awake he just lays there and looks around, and seldom cries, as far as I can make out. His jaw sticks out like a battleship, his mouth is an exaggerated Cupid's bow, and his head [is] round and full. His ears are perfect and lay right up against his head and he has a real high forehead. His chest sticks out like Walter Budden's. . . . We named him William B. Ruger Jr., but everyone calls him 'Little Bunnie.' I sure am proud of him. . . .

—June 12, 1939, in Greensboro,
writing his mother

used up most of my inheritance, and we were now living on money borrowed from Mary's family. I was really quite baffled about how to find employment. . . . How the hell do you find a decent way to make a living? I was way out on a cliff, teetering!"

Mary was pregnant with their first child, and the Rugers decided to move back to Mary's family home in North Carolina. Bill was still hoping for some recognition of his invention, and on the way they stopped at the Army Ordnance office in Washington, where he met some of the engineers. One was Lt. Colonel Sidney P. Spalding. Ruger showed him the gas-operated Savage conversion, and they discussed the pros and cons of the concept, but he left without any sort of formal offer from the Army. Bill and Mary drove on to Greensboro, where their son, William Batterman Ruger, Jr., was born on June 4, 1939.

A telegram from the War Department soon arrived. It read, "Would you be interested in a position designing machine guns with Springfield Armory?" Ruger remembers it well. "I was stunned, and flattered." His immediate one-word answer was, "Yes." The job, as a laboratory assistant, paid $32.50 a week. It was a civil service position, and the service rules had been bent to get Ruger qualified.

Leaving his family in Greensboro, Bill went to Springfield, Massachusetts, to work at the Armory. There he gained more insight into the American firearms industry by spending as much time as possible studying the Armory museum which, then as now, housed the most extensive collection of military small arms in America. The custodian, after recognizing Ruger's fascination and learning of his mechanical abilities, would point out a complex gun and challenge him: "I'll bet you can't take that one apart." But Ruger always could, and, when time allowed, always did. Among these astonishingly complex mechanisms was the original, hand-built model of the first M1 Garand rifle, in .276 caliber.

The Army was looking for a new light machine gun at this time, and had just published its requirements. Bill began thinking about how to achieve their esoteric design goals. At the same time, he knew he'd never be satisfied with what the government was willing to pay a civil service employee. In the spring of 1940 he boldly quit the Armory to return to North Carolina and work on his own light machine gun for the Army. Reflecting on the decision years later, he says, "I could have stayed with the government and had a career like that of John Garand. Garand lived through thirty years of designing guns at the Armory, was paid a very mediocre salary, and was always treated like some sort of an in-house genius mechanical toy. I thought I could do much better than that."

Working at his in-laws' house, he drew a complete concept for an extremely compact light machine gun. The Thompsons' dining room was his work center, and an old bread board served as his drafting table. He labored over the details for the Ruger Machine Gun, first as rough sketches, then

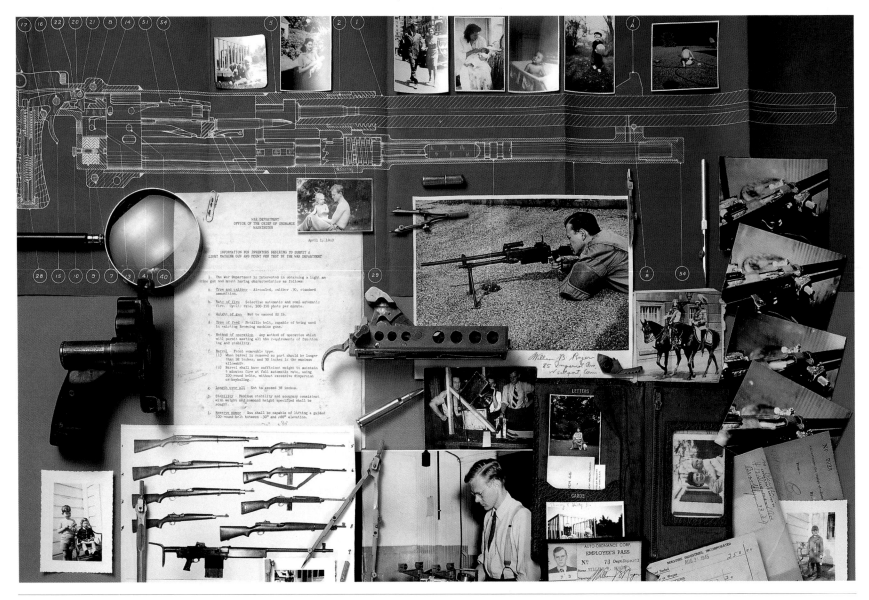

The Auto-Ordnance years; the gun was designated by the company as "The Ruger Machine Gun." Photograph beneath Ruger's adjustable cyclic rate trigger mechanism shows the young inventor (*right*) with his friend Bill Lett, and with pioneer stop-motion photographer, Harold Edgerton—some of the high-speed pictures at right. *Bottom center* shows Ruger and his sophisticated computing aircraft machine gun sighting device, a project undertaken in the latter months of his work in Bridgeport. Candid shot of the Rugers in New York City taken by a sidewalk photographer.

Working at Auto-Ordnance "was really, at that point for me, a great triumph. I was in complete charge of my whole program and I was doing exactly what I wanted to do. It was just fascinating and a challenge and the possibilities were unlimited."

as finished mechanical drawings. He even undertook the difficult task of building a functioning prototype, traveling to New York to have the major working components fabricated by Fred Goat and Company of Brooklyn.[6] This "old-time, super quality, fine type of experimental machine shop" made packaging machinery (like that used to make the Chiclets gum box) and engineering prototype models for clients such as the makers of the famous Norden bomb sight.

Ruger showed the finished components to his contacts at the Ordnance Department, but got a predictably cool reception from the officials there, who felt he should have stayed at Springfield and done his prototype engineering directly for the government. Unfazed, he returned to North Carolina, finished the machine gun by himself, and started looking for a company to produce his invention.

Ruger went from one gun company to another through the New England-based firearms industry. Several firms offered him respectable engineering positions on the strength of his prototype. At Smith & Wesson's old Springfield plant he talked to two of the owners.

> I remember going there on a cold fall night and meeting Victor Wesson and his older brother. . . . They were just amazed at my machine gun. "How did you do this? Who are you?" Arms engineering in the late thirties was at a very low state, and to find someone who could undertake the conception and execution of a whole new design was rare. Victor said, "Bill, we don't want this gun; we can't do anything with it. But we'd like to have you in the company here. We'd be willing to pay you $75 a week." That was just about double what I'd been making the year before and was unusually generous at the time. I went out to the car where Mary was waiting and told her about the offer.

History might have been very different if Bill Ruger had embarked upon his firearms design career at Smith & Wesson, a firm later to become one of his most serious competitors. Instead, he decided to try a few more firms. He went next to a small company called High Standard, in Hamden, Connecticut, where he met the founder, A. W. ("Gus") Swebilius.[7] Swebilius looked over Ruger's machine gun and commented, "Well, this is pretty good, but we don't want it. We've got our hands full with our current line of products." Another rejection, but this one concluded with some helpful suggestions, including a recommendation that Ruger talk to the Auto-Ordnance Corporation, a company with big military contracts. "They've got tons of cash from selling all those tommy guns. Go down there and show them your design, and if they like it, remind them that you don't work for nothing. Demand a lot. Demand $100 a week." Ruger said, "You think I could get that?" Swebilius insisted, "Demand it!"

Ruger took his advice and met with Auto-Ordnance Vice President Ray Koontz.[8] The interview went well. Ruger showed the prototype and Koontz asked him about the type of business arrangement he had in mind. Ruger said that he would sell his patent rights in exchange for a royalty on sales of production machine guns, plus a regular salary while employed by Auto-Ordnance in perfecting the weapon. "What sort of a salary do you want?" asked Koontz. Ruger answered, "I want $100 a week."

The interview ended with a noncommittal "All right, we'll talk this over among ourselves and be in touch with you." Somewhat perplexed, Ruger asked, "Well, what will I do?"

"Call us back in a couple of days."

"How about Wednesday?"

"Okay."

On Wednesday, the Rugers were in an uptown Manhattan hotel. When they woke, at about 9:00 A.M., Bill picked up the telephone, looked at his wife, and said, "Well, here goes." When Koontz came on the line he got right to the point.

"We're ready to talk business. When can you come down here?"

Auto-Ordnance and the Thompson

The Auto-Ordnance Corporation that Bill Ruger joined in 1940 was a bustling firm, flush with recent orders. Contracts with the French and British governments for .45 caliber Thompson submachine guns had created a positive cash flow. It was an excellent place for a young gun designer to learn volume manufacturing techniques.

The company was established in 1916 by the gun's designer, General John T. Thompson, and financed by a man named Thomas Fortune Ryan, with production carried out by Colt. Approximately 2,000 finished guns had been produced by the early 1930s, and orders were small and infrequent. The Federal Firearms Act of 1936 imposed a heavy fee on the sale of submachine guns, virtually destroying the market. Colt, the first major Thompson producer, had already decided to bow out of the Thompson business for two reasons: the weapon's association with gangsters in the public mind, and Colt's preoccupation with contracts for large quantities of Browning machine guns.

Ruger recalls, "This all took place just before the Germans invaded Norway. During that exercise, the Germans taught the world that submachine guns had a very real tactical role in warfare. Up to that time they had only been considered a weapon for prison guard use or police."

Russell Maguire, a Wall Street broker and investor, bought the firm in 1939, and shortly thereafter he negotiated a contract with the French government for 3,000 Thompson submachine guns. With a substantial British order pending, Auto-Ordnance approached Savage Arms Corporation to manufacture 10,000 of the Model 1928 Thompsons. Savage agreed, but their terms were breathtaking. They demanded that Auto-Ordnance pay for all the manufacturing equipment, all the raw materials, and all the necessary quality assurance costs. Furthermore, they insisted that Auto-Ordnance deposit in escrow a

percentage of all expected costs before they would even begin work. Finally, Auto-Ordnance was to pay Savage the equivalent of the full contract price from the final customer as each gun came off the assembly line. This meant that Savage would get their full payment by the time only half the order had been built.

It was a daunting prospect, but Maguire, a risk taker with limited capital to risk, agreed to these road-agent terms. He signed the production contract with Savage on December 15, 1939.

Maguire had Colt send their mothballed Thompson tooling to Savage's factory in Utica, New York. Most of it was in good shape, and after a quick refurbishing program, Savage got into production. The first Thompsons were delivered in April 1940.

By this time, the European military scene had worsened dramatically; Germany had overrun Norway, Denmark, and Poland, and France and Britain had declared war. The French military had ordered 3,000 more guns in March, and the U.S. Army contracted for 20,450 Model 1928s in December of 1940, with formal U.S. standardization of the Thompson on February 6, 1941.

As one writer noted, "For almost twenty years the Tommygun [*sic*] had scandalized its inventors and distressed its investors. Then, almost over-

night, it turned into a vital, highly profitable piece of military ordnance."[9]

Ruger Joins Auto-Ordnance

Even before Savage began production in April 1940, Maguire had decided to open up a new factory in Bridgeport, Connecticut. In August, Auto-Ordnance purchased and occupied an entire block on Railroad Avenue.[10] It was here that Bill Ruger, all of twenty-four, came to pursue his career as a firearms designer.

The site needed major rehabilitation before production could begin: new flooring, new electric utilities, and a complete plumbing overhaul. By January 1941, the plant was ready for the engineering department, and manufacturing moved in a short time later. Ruger watched the factory evolve, and filed away what he'd learned for future reference.

As manufacture of the Thompson got under-way, the Bridgeport factory concentrated on fabricating the larger and more complex components, while jobbing or subcontracting out most of the smaller parts. Initially, final assembly was performed outside the Railroad Avenue plant, and the first "tommy" guns were completed in this fashion in August 1941. By mid-1942, however, most key components, like the barrel, were made totally at Railroad Avenue.

Maguire and Koontz knew that the Bridgeport factory would never get into production quickly if they had to stand in line waiting for new machine tools. All the big companies were clamoring for everything on the market and pulling every string to get it.

Auto-Ordnance went to the secondhand market instead. Approximately 75 percent of the company's equipment was purchased used—either "rebuilt and guaranteed" or "as is" to be rebuilt in their own in-house machine repair department.

On the lookout for skilled machinists and toolmakers, Maguire had snapped up one of the best

From the Ruger, Batterman, and Thompson family scrapbooks: Most of the pictures of girls and of young women are of Mary and her younger sister, Fran. Bill's parents on their honeymoon in Palm Beach (*lower left*). Some shots from Bill and Mary's honeymoon tour to Europe; they sailed aboard the *Bremen*. Other pictures show the Ruger children growing up; at *far right* the family at the Fairfield Fair, published in *Life* magazine. Some of these shots also include relatives and friends. Picture of Bill and Mary on their wedding day (*above* Springfield Armory visitor's pass) includes Fran and her husband, Carl Wesselhoft. At *left center*, Betty dancing with her husband, then–U.S. Air Force officer and pilot George Hamilton. Both Wesselhoft and Hamilton were destined to be associated with their brother-in-law, in the firearms business, for many years.

tool rooms in the Bridgeport area, the Willard Tool Company. The famous old firm employed some one hundred first-rate craftsmen, and Maguire set them up in a tool room and repair facility on the top floor at Railroad Avenue. In this beautifully lit work area, with new floors, new benches, and new everything else, the dirty and often heavily rusted old machines were overhauled. They went in looking more like museum artifacts than equipment for making modern weaponry, and emerged gleaming.

Auto-Ordnance also used the former Willard staff to make all of its own tools, fixtures, jigs, cutters, and gauges. As a result, with the exception of easy-to-acquire standard items, the Bridgeport facility was self-sufficient; a vital management decision that enabled the firm's quick entry into full-scale production, and another lesson that was not lost on Bill Ruger.

The four years Ruger spent at Auto-Ordnance, where innovation in production processes was the rule rather than the exception, proved to be an on-the-job tutorial in firearms manufacture as well as design. When he later began his own firm, he applied many of the lessons learned there, such as the economic wisdom of making do at first with rehabilitated machinery. He had also observed that staying on the cutting edge of new production technologies could give him an advantage over competitors who let their processes grow obsolete.

Compared to the dingy workshops and confined working environment at Springfield Armory, the newly rehabilitated Auto-Ordnance facility was an exceptionally exciting place to work for Ruger, and he enjoyed the sense of entrepreneurial adventure. He liked working in the company of men who possessed vision, enthusiasm, and competence.

Although the factory's first priority was filling the Thompson contracts, the company was also supporting an active research and development program. Designer and engineer Grant Hammond was assigned to direct the development of

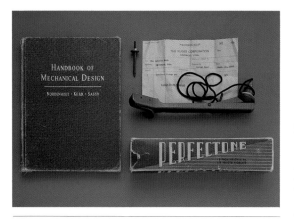

Book which played a key role, along with his practical work experience under trained eyes, in the education of Ruger as a draftsman and designer; published 1942. Record player arm and part was sent to the fledgling Ruger Corporation for quoting on a high-quantity production run, in late 1946.

prototypes to compete in the Army Ordnance "Light Rifle" program—the search for what would eventually be the M1 Carbine—in 1942. One of these .30 caliber rifles was designed by a man named Bergmann; the other was the work of Doug Hammond, best known for his design of self-loading pistols earlier in the century.

Hammond also had responsibility for developing a simplified .45 caliber submachine gun, to which the Army assigned the experimental designation T2. That program, which led to the M3 submachine gun, plus the M1 Carbine project, would ultimately end the demand for the Thompsons.

Although neither of these projects was continued beyond mid-1942, their existence demonstrated Auto-Ordnance's interest in putting profits back into projects that supported the nation's war effort.

Bill Ruger was given a substantial workspace, alongside other experimenters, to set up his own design and prototype studio. There, again with the help of Bill Lett, he began preparing the .30 caliber light machine gun he'd conceived in

North Carolina to compete successfully in government trials scheduled for October 1941. He had only nine months, and they were filled with twelve- and fourteen-hour days as he sought to eliminate some design shortcomings and directed the manufacture of a second prototype.

In September 1941, the Light Machine Gun Subcommittee of the Army Ordnance Committee held a series of planning meetings in Washington. Six competing teams from Auto-Ordnance, Colt, Rock Island Arsenal, Schirgun Corporation, R. F. Sedgley, Inc., and Springfield Armory were called to show their weapons and answer questions for the assembled board of officers.

Bill Ruger and Lawrence E. de S. Hoover, representing Auto-Ordnance, attended a meeting held at the Social Security Building on October 10th. Lieutenant Colonel Rene R. Studler, the most influential member of the Subcommittee, aimed most of his questions at Ruger, who stated that the first prototype had successfully fired between 4,000 and 5,000 rounds, and that several design improvements had been made in developing the new prototype.

Minutes from the meeting put it this way:

The gun is a very clean looking weapon with a welded receiver, connected to the trunnion by seamless tubing. Locking members are welded to the receiver. Mr. Ruger did not have a tool for removing the barrel but one could be easily adapted. It was easily removed by a threaded collar. No gas fouling has been noted to date.

The gun was stripped before the committee and the operation seemed very simple. A special tool is required at present but modifications can be made so that all components can be removed or replaced with a cartridge point. The gun will require a special adapter so that it may be mounted on the standard Caliber .30 tripod mount. The gun is considered ready for test at Aberdeen although Mr. Ruger needs a little more time to reduce the rate of fire. Mr. Ruger has studied the manufacturing costs quite carefully and apparently the production costs would be relatively low.

After the presentations were completed, tests

were scheduled. Springfield Armory and Rock Island Arsenal were slated for October 13th, Colt and Sedgley for the 20th and 27th, and Auto-Ordnance and Schirgun for November 3rd and 10th respectively. The competitors would be told how their own gun performed, but none would know how they compared with the other entrants.

Ruger arrived at Aberdeen for the test of the "Auto-Ordnance Cal. .30 Light Machine Gun," as it was officially designated. It was a gas-operated, belt-fed, air-cooled weapon in which the operational gas was taken from a barrel port located seven inches from the muzzle. The gun had a total of just seventy-four parts (including ten coiled and six flat springs and excluding the standard M1918A2 BAR rear sight)—about fifty fewer than the Colt, Rock Island, and Springfield lightweight versions of the standard Browning LMG.

The heart of the Ruger/Auto-Ordnance LMG was a beautifully designed heavy block of steel upon which all of the complicated machining operations for the receiver were performed. The rear portion of the gun's receiver housing was made of pressed sheet steel that was welded to the forward block. The hand grip was attached to the receiver housing by means of threaded dowel pins. A threaded collar was employed in fastening the barrel and for adjusting headspace. The gun's barrel was relatively easy to remove, but the testing officers noted that "no protection against a hot dismounting collar has been provided." The gun alone weighed 19.46 pounds, or 20.75 pounds with the special pintle mount required to attach and shoot it from the standard M2 machine gun tripod—considerably less than the then-standard 33-pound M1919 Browning machine guns.

After five days of tests, the board noted that Ruger's design had a cleverly simple mechanism, though its general functioning was not yet acceptable. Its basic cyclic rate of firing needed to be reduced to improve reliability of performance and to extend parts life expectancy. Nevertheless,

"this gun is considered to offer excellent possibilities, but it will require considerable further development."

The results of the tests of all six guns were summarized by Colonel Studler at a meeting on November 27, 1941. He stated that none of the guns tested had shown "sufficient promise to justify service test." The committee concurred. However, since a new LMG was still needed, they decided to give "moderate encouragement" to further development of the Auto-Ordnance gun. They noted that the Schirgun entry was still in the design stage, and that of the three modified Brownings, Rock Island's was the best, although it did not offer anything new except for weight reduction.

Major John Claybrook, the Cavalry member of the Subcommittee, was concerned that the specifications had been developed nearly five years earlier and significant tactical changes had occurred in Europe and Asia since then. He thought the Army should reevaluate its requirements. They agreed and sent out requests for ideas, to be submitted by January 1, 1942.

Ten days after the Subcommittee adjourned, the Japanese attacked Pearl Harbor, catapulting the United States into World War II. The search for improved military small arms became urgent. Ruger was to fight on the home front, where his abilities as a designer were critical to the war effort.

Back in Bridgeport, Ruger continued to improve his design. In June 1942, he again submitted his LMG for shooting tests at Aberdeen. Unfortunately, the gun still didn't perform well enough, and when twenty-three malfunctions occurred in the first five hundred shots attempted, the rest of the test was suspended. Auto-Ordnance was advised that the weapon should be made easier to load, disassemble, and reassemble.

For the next twelve months, Ruger conducted a major rework of the gun's design. While he kept the basic operating principles (locking

When I first learned the principles under which machine guns functioned, I was just fascinated. It was almost like a little kid finding out how a steam engine or internal combustion works. I almost immediately started making drawings of how I would incorporate these principles; and, of course, it was all very limited because you can't design a thing if you have no idea how things are manufactured. I could remember even that at one point I was just astonished to learn that there were such things as machine tools, that there was a thing called a lathe that could turn steel, that I could drill steel with drill presses and mill steel, and shape it with old-fashioned shapers and planers. I mean, to me this was, "*That's* how these hard steel parts are formed." To some child that's been used to making things with a hammer and a saw, it was a revelation. You put a little insight of that sort together with some other little insight, like Julian Hatcher's *Rifleman* article about World War I machine guns; then you see if you've got any inspiration to try to put this very form of know-how together.

I must say that guns weren't the only things I tried to design at first, but they have always been a thing that I came back to most strongly and urgently. I just loved guns, loved the outdoors, and hunting experiences. I always wanted to be an explorer, and the source of all the irony of my life has been that there is nothing much left to explore. People can talk about exploring space and exploring with a microscope and all these sublimations, but that's not tramping through the jungle and seeing a river for the first time in recorded history, and that is what I would have loved to have done.

mechanism and feed system), his third version featured a redesigned exterior housing to accommodate a quick change barrel latch, and a completely modified trigger mechanism, incorporating an ingenious rate-reducing mechanism

When at Alexander Hamilton High School, there was a teacher who took a particular interest in his students. He would ask me about how my plans were coming at being an explorer; had I made any contact with one of my boyhood heroes, Roy Chapman Andrews; and asked about my dreams of going on an expedition to the Gobi Desert. I told this teacher how I'd gone over to Andrews' office at the American Museum of Natural History, but no one was there, and the door was locked. This teacher encouraged me to go back again. He said: "Do you want to be known as 'Ruger, the explorer of the Gobi Desert,' or 'Ruger, the pants manufacturer?'"

Selection of Ruger Corporation tools, with photographs of the factory, the work force and managers, the founder at *left*. Notes on card are in his left-handed penmanship. Sheet metal halves for drill grips were supplied in stamped form by Worcester Pressed Steel, of Worcester, Massachusetts, and were then welded at the Ruger Corporation factory. Prototype pistol of later date, shown for comparison with pistol grip drill handles. The founder remembers: "Every so often a collector will show the early Ruger tools to me. The little spiral ratchet screwdriver [*top center*] is very nearly a well-made tool; some of the manufacturing equipment to produce those spiral ratchet shafts was absolutely beautiful. As I look back on it, they worked like a charm. The machines made six pieces at once.

"The business that we then formed was just to get some sort of manufacturing business for subcontracting started, and get it well established. Perhaps then we felt we would be able to consider making a firearm. We were profitable at one point, but then made some general misjudgments on certain programs and some things we tried to do proved to be profitless. I can't help but say that when 1949 rolled around, Sturm, Ruger was poised to become the next successful company. We were better qualified than we realized."

which engaged the hammer through notches in a hammer extension and a cog wheel. He hoped this would satisfy the government's requirement for a high and slow rate of fire (500–600 and 250–300 shots per minute). Ruger also added a simple and easily detached tubular buttstock assembly, and he adapted a BAR bipod so it could be mounted on the exterior of the gas piston housing.

As Ruger worked on the gun, major changes were taking place at Auto-Ordnance. In addition to contracting for work on the Springfield/Colt T10 light machine gun, Auto-Ordnance became one of IBM's major subcontractors for M1 Carbine bolts and slides. In 1943, the demand for carbines increased and contracts for the Thompson submachine gun, which had been replaced by the M3 "grease gun," ceased. Auto-Ordnance struggled with fabrication of carbine components, finally solving their problems by the end of October.

At the end of June 1943, Ruger made his third and, as it turned out, last trip to Aberdeen with his machine gun. The testing officer noted with approval the bipod-mounting and the metal shoulder rest. They reported that the firing pin was activated by a spring and a hammer controlled by a double sear, and the new rate-reducing selector allowed the gun to be shot at a fast or slow automatic rate, in addition to permitting the user to fire single shots.

The board had criticized Ruger's earlier model for firing too fast (630–750 shots per minute). They now decided that the newer model's fast rate of 400 shots per minute was too slow! The test results were still less than satisfactory, and First Lieutenant W. C. Forcey, the testing officer, ultimately recommended that "no further consideration be given this gun in its present form."

Ruger and Auto-Ordnance were disappointed. But the war was winding down and the need for a new light machine gun was rapidly diminishing. Bill was assigned to work on the top secret design of an elaborate computing sighting mechanism for use by airplane machine gunners, intended to compensate for rapidly moving enemy fighter aircraft. He recalls:

> In the last year or so of my time with Auto-Ordnance I was working on a variety of other programs. I did some of their production planning for electronic components and .30 caliber carbine components, and so on. Then I began to find my position in the company was more ambiguous than it should be. I began to feel I would be more successful working privately.

The Ruger Corporation

With the Allied victory in 1945, Bill Ruger left Auto-Ordnance. He had five years of design and manufacturing experience under his belt, and wanted a company of his own. In 1946, he and a partner named Clements set up a small factory in Southport, Connecticut; later, he bought Clements out. The company's letterhead stated that their intent was to supply small parts to industry, develop a hardware tool line, and introduce a ".22 Automatic Pistol."

The Ruger Corporation, as it was called, produced two parts needed by Auto-Ordnance, now heavily involved in meeting postwar consumer

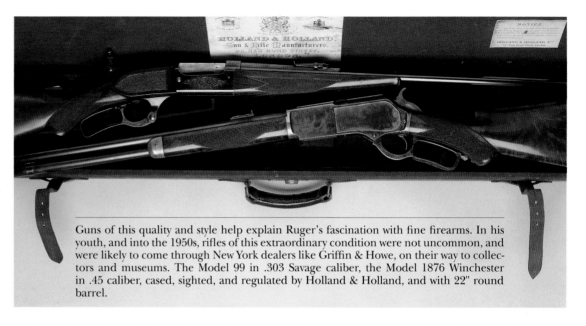

Guns of this quality and style help explain Ruger's fascination with fine firearms. In his youth, and into the 1950s, rifles of this extraordinary condition were not uncommon, and were likely to come through New York dealers like Griffin & Howe, on their way to collectors and museums. The Model 99 in .303 Savage caliber, the Model 1876 Winchester in .45 caliber, cased, sighted, and regulated by Holland & Holland, and with 22" round barrel.

product demand. With Ruger's experience, resources, and skill, this part of the venture was profitable. Not so profitable was a government hardware contract his partner brought in. Running short on money, the firm had to borrow heavily to make ends meet.

The final blow came with production of a set of carpentry tools Bill had designed. A major hardware jobber in New York, one of the largest in the country, had assured Ruger that this would be a good, solid business. Bill tooled up and began manufacture, but the well-made line proved too expensive for the public. "The harder we worked, the poorer we got, until finally the company went bankrupt and into receivership and that was the end of it," he says now.

An ironic footnote to the tale is that the dozen or so marked drills and other hand tools he made are now collectors' items and fetch prices higher than many of the firearms he later produced.

The Ruger Corporation closed, but it was far from the end for Bill Ruger. By now he was an experienced first-class gun designer, machinist, and

> Our young son develops into a bigger prize package every day. He weights 15½ lbs., and is 1½" taller than the usual baby his age. You can see by his expression that he has his father's genius. . . .
> —September 14, 1939,
> writing his mother

modern manufacturer. He knew how to organize a plant, knew something about cost accounting, and had learned some hard lessons in sound financial management.

He also had an ace up his sleeve which would change the game completely: a .22 caliber pistol. He had originally hoped to produce it through his corporation, and it even shared some basic components, such as the grip, with his hand drills. However, his partner had resisted taking the chance, and the design was not complete. But in 1949 a crucial collaboration with the singular Alexander Sturm would bring Bill Ruger to the forefront of firearms manufacturing.

He was ready.

"A Clean Sheet of Paper"

Ruger Creates a New Pistol, Single-Action Revolvers, and Two Factories
1949–1959

Bill Ruger is addressing the Carl Eller School of Business, University of Arizona, in the late 1980s, giving his grandson Kurt's classmates the benefit of a firsthand account of Sturm, Ruger & Company, Inc. In an age of junk bonds and astronomical business debt, Ruger's company has an unbroken history of no long-term debt whatsoever. The class has already studied the company's casebook, pre-

---

Earlier years of the Southport factories: the "red barn" complex, and the main plant. Polaroid at *upper left* a rare depiction of the founder in office he used for a few years in the red barn. At *far right*, Ruger, Sr., watching as trademark sign lowered into position. Sturm, Ruger staff c. 1970, at *top center: front row left to right*, Chris Cashavelly, Imre Kohut, comptroller Walter Berger, and Robert E. Dearden; *back row left to right*, John Polonetz, Matthew De Mezzo, Larry Larson, Randle Gillespie, William B. Ruger, shop superintendent Michael Horelik, assembly department foreman Walt Sych, and master toolmaker Rex King. Hunting knives short-lived program in 1960s; made from castings. Bill, Jr., with his father at *far left*, discussing a Farquharson single shot rifle; picture *above* of Pete Kuhlhoff and Ruger, Sr., sitting on Bentley running board. Engineer Harry Sefried on phone to *right* of nineteenth-century picture of "red barn." Export manager Steve Vogel to *left* of "Ruger Team" recruiting advertisement, Walter Howe (with glasses) sitting in front of pinwheel of Rugers. Jack Behn and Ed Nolan by early NRA Show display, to *left* of Little League team.

---

1. 1949
.22 Standard Pistol
2. 1953
Single-Six
("Old Model") Revolver
3. 1955
Blackhawk
("Old Model") Revolver
4. 1958
Bearcat
("Old Model") Revolver
5. 1959
Super Blackhawk ("Old Model") Revolver

---

pared by the Harvard Business School. The graduate students are transfixed by the stentorian voice and the distinctive Ruger-speak; extemporaneous, simple, straightforward, and no-nonsense—just like the founder-inventor-entrepreneur's guns:

Our strategy was to carve out a niche, combining quality with low cost. Our company would be strong on expertise, service, uniqueness, simplicity, and strength of design; our marketing based on gut instinct and keeping in touch with the consumer and the distributor/jobber/dealer. Our advertising would be relatively minimal, there would be virtually no sales staff, and a top-thin management.

Our advertising would emphasize safety and the responsible use of firearms, support the concepts of wildlife and habitat conservation, and training of new gun owners. We would counter the environmental issue with a head-on campaign rightfully equating the hunter with conservation. Our advertising and marketing goal would be to take more and more of the market share.

A dedication and interest in your product is critical: It is a genuine interest in the product that counts. In this company, I feel like an artist, not merely a businessman. Business is the art of the possible, or let us say, avoiding the impossible. A basic law of business: When you borrow money, you have to pay it back. The best technique of manufacturing: Make the

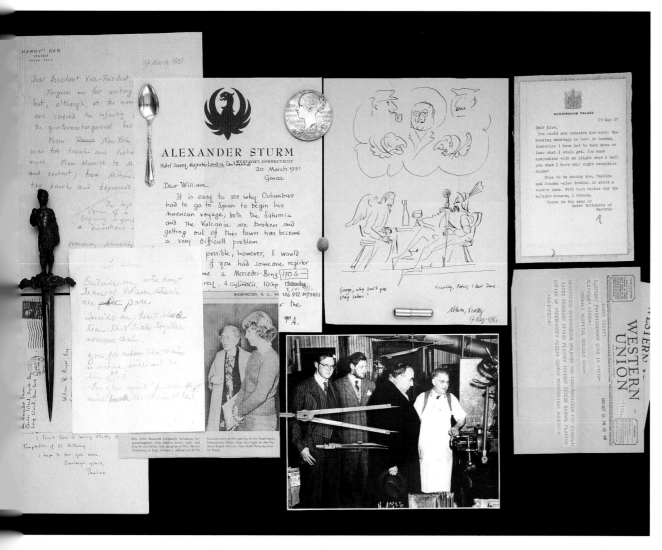

Partners Bill Ruger and Alex Sturm in 1950, giving a tour of the factory to the Ambassador from Brazil. The *Bridgeport Telegram* quoted the Ambassador as saying the factory "represented the American spirit of free enterprise. . . . It is in the small manufacturing shops like this that I see the greatness of your country."

Sturm was a cartoonist with the flair of a James Thurber, and his work was published by *Saturday Review*, as well as Scribner's. Poem written by Mary Ruger, in tribute to Sturm.

product the best you can, in every way.

On the subject of quality, our products have to be made to a standard so I would want them even if they were made by our competitors. In our case, product engineering is the fundamental factor in our success.

Business is a creative, patriotic process, and I am offended by the "if it wasn't for the regulatory agencies, we'd all steal from the public" attitude.

"Not failure, but low aim, is the crime."
—James Russell Lowell, *Under the Willows*

The Founding of Sturm, Ruger and Company

By 1949, when The Ruger Corporation went into receivership, Bill Ruger had developed a friendship with Alexander McCormick Sturm, a graduate of Yale University. An accomplished writer, artist, amateur film maker, actor, and a keen firearms enthusiast, Sturm was also a potential investor with the wherewithal to back a viable idea.

Friend and Yale classmate Norwick R. G. Goodspeed remembers Alex Sturm:

The Sturms were very prominent people in Westport, and Alex's father, a football star from his Yale days, was friendly with VIPs, including the likes of boxing champion Gene Tunney.

Alex's lifestyle was truly bizarre. When we were undergraduates at Yale, he would dine at the best hotel in town (while the rest of the students would eat at the school dining room). He would go to New York regularly on weekends, his clothes were all custom-tailored, and he was a Renaissance type, with all kinds of talent. An artistic sense, a true brilliance, were in his genes. Alex was a voracious collector: guns, canes, swords, heraldry. But Alex was not a hunter; in fact, he didn't really like to go outdoors, and when indoors, he liked to have the shades pulled, so that the ambiance was always after hours. He was, however, accomplished at polo, and I used to go over to the Fairfield Hunt Club to watch him play.

Definitely a car enthusiast, after the war Alex

22

had the first Mercedes ever in Fairfield County, a four-door open touring car, though it was of prewar date. Both Bill and Alex had highly refined senses of humor, and they got along superbly.

Sturm's investment opportunity came in the form of a strikingly handsome .22 caliber pistol Ruger had designed in his spare time and completed after the machine shop business had closed down. It had a profile somewhat like the popular German Luger, which appealed immensely to Sturm's aesthetic philosophy. Ruger was convinced that the pistol could be manufactured with high enough quality and a reasonable enough price to provide a strong challenge to both the popular Colt Woodsman and its close competitor, the High Standard .22. Ruger's description of Sturm hints at his future partner's complexity:

> We started off with tremendous enthusiasm. At that time, Alex was about twenty-eight. His background was essentially artistic. At Yale he had majored in art and had many literary interests. He had published a highly acclaimed book, had been published in the *Saturday Review*, was a very accomplished easel painter, and a student of history. His house was handsomely decorated, mostly with his own paintings. During World War II he had been an OSS officer stationed in Washington, D.C. He had a top secret assignment as a liaison with the ex-Hitler associate, Baron Hafstengel, trying to predict Hitler's wartime behavior.
>
> While in Washington, Alex met and later married socialite Paulina Longworth, "The Valentine Baby." Paulina's mother, Alice Roosevelt Longworth, was the eldest child of Theodore Roosevelt, and the grande dame of Washington society. Alice married Nicholas Longworth, who had been a Congressman for twenty years and was Speaker of the House of Representatives [1925–31]. Alex's own mother was from the McCormick mercantile family, so he had a distinguished pedigree of his own.

Bill Ruger says of his initial talks with Alex Sturm:

> Our meeting was one of people having some com-

mon interests. At that time, I had developed the entire concept for the new company and had a product in mind, but I had no capital. Alex was willing to invest. Frankly, this company was a kind of last-ditch effort; I was beginning to wonder if I had some kind of seeds of failure built into me. I said, Okay, we're starting with a clean sheet of paper, and this time there will be no borrowing—makes it harder to go bankrupt that way. Sturm agreed with me. I said, "I want to run this thing. It's your money, but I want to run it so that we can put a key in the door and walk away anytime we want." By that time I was better trained than I could ever have been if I'd gone to some business school. I had the actual experience, and that's really the final test.
>
> The entire Sturm, Ruger and Company plant operation was conceived on the basis of a $50,000 investment, which sounds like a ridiculously small amount now. Today, we spend more than that on a single machine tool. Back in those days it wasn't such a small amount of money, but the businessmen I talked to still said, in effect, "You can't do it." That included Gus Swebilius, president of High Standard. John H. Graham, head of the foremost hardware distribution company in New York, said that I was "a damned fool." Colt scoffed at us. Now, maybe it's true that a normal business couldn't have done it. But we had a way of doing things very economically.

The former Ruger Corporation was now in receivership. With Alex Sturm's investment, which entitled him to preferred stock ownership in the new Sturm, Ruger & Company, Sturm bought out the few assets of the old company and moved into its premises in the "red barn" complex on Station Street, in Southport, Connecticut. Ruger continues:

> At first there was no administrative staff. I was working on the drawing board, designing the parts and so on. I was actually making the tooling drawings, and was talking every day with the chief toolmaker. We had this small shop which we rented at a low cost, and had one or two toolmakers. Every day there would be another drawing peeled off the drawing board, and the toolmakers would be building that certain fixture.

We got to the factory early in the morning, and the usual routine was to come back after dinner to see if we could complete yet another drawing. This kept us up until about 11:00 at night. Then I'd often go back to Sturm's house and have a drink or two, and make some plans for the next day.

In the course of confirming all our plans and so forth, I recall saying to Alex, "What we've got to have is a trademark, something that can be rolled onto the firearms, something we can have on our letterhead and in our advertising, something that ties together all our products so the identity is there." And he is the one who then designed the eagle, which we've used all these years, and I think it has been very appropriate.

The Sturm, Ruger "Red Eagle" has become one of the most instantly recognized business trademarks in the world today. Sturm's lifelong interest in heraldry is clearly evident in the stylized rampant bird. At first a brilliant red, the device as marked on the firearms was changed to black upon his untimely death, by order of his partner. Ruger continues:

> The way in which we approached the tooling for the automatic pistol was to run a sample of 2,500 parts through each operation as the tooling was completed. The result was that by the fall of 1949 we had run every operation and had something like 2,500 sets of parts. We could see that we were coming to the stage where we could actually begin assembling and shipping, and we had a little assembly area set up. By this time we had hired a couple more people and were ready to go. We even had orders, from a small advertisement in *The American Rifleman* magazine.
>
> Julian Hatcher [the former head of U.S. Army Ordnance] had given us a very good write-up in the "Dope Bag" [a regular feature of *The American Rifleman* which highlights new developments in the firearms field; also the term for an old-time shooter's equipment pouch], and we got a tremendous bunch of letters, each with a money order or check enclosed.
>
> Alex Sturm came around for lunch one day in late 1949 as I was writing out the check to cover our

payroll. I said to him, "Alex, this is the last of that $50,000." But fortunately, that day we had a hundred pistols ready to ship and Alex took a hundred $37.50 money orders to the bank. Now we were really in business.

It was a little tight for a few months more, but then the picture began to brighten. Our bank balance began to grow and we were able to stop selling to individuals. The retailers and wholesalers were sending us substantial orders that demanded all our production. It was great! For a year or two, we were living the good life: Alex was happy and I was happy.

I remember Sturm and I going to New York. We invited Warren Page of *Field & Stream* magazine to join us for lunch so we could tell him about the pistol. Page was looking forward to meeting Alex; he expected an impressive person, which Alex was, but not in the way Page expected him to be. Alex was an odd fish in those days. He had a beard, wore green suits with all sorts of bells and whistles on them—cuffed sleeves and so on—and he had a marvelous manner. He gave you the general impression of being a prewar German baronial type. He was actually a very artistic and sensitive person, but he also looked like a bull in the woods and was quite strong.

Then, in the fall of 1951, I went off on a hunting trip to Quebec with Warren Page, then down to the King and Bartlett hunting camp in Maine. When I got back, Alex was in the hospital with hepatitis and the situation was very bad. He died about ten days later. That changed everything.

Paulina Sturm

Alex's wife Paulina had personally helped launch Sturm, Ruger & Co., stuffing envelopes with Alex on Sunday afternoons, and giving moral support to the two partners. She had faith in Bill Ruger's vision, and was wary of the attempt by Alex's father, Justin, to take control of the company after his son's death. Alex and Paulina, with their infant daughter Joanna, had been living in a house on the estate of Justin and Katherine Sturm in Westport. The elder Sturm, a Yale graduate, former football star, and a would-be playwright and

Faux "Gothic" panel painting of twelfth-century style, by Alex Sturm, for the town clerk of Fairfield, Connecticut. Discovered by the present owner in a flea market. Style, draftsmanship, colors, perspective, heraldry, humor, and the car among the clues to Sturm's artistry. The party comfortably seated, at *left*, may be Sturm, possibly enduring a tax assessment or simply registration of his new automobile by the town clerk. Letters at the *lower left* and *right* have yet to be deciphered. Tempera on board. 8⅜" x 10¾".

novelist, proved aggressive and combative. He even threatened Ruger: "If I ever catch you seeing Paulina, I'll kill you!" It was apparent that a management crisis was inevitable.

The crisis came to a head at a meeting between Paulina, Nick Goodspeed (her lawyer), Justin and Katherine Sturm, and Bill Ruger. As the talk progressed, Ruger began to realize that Justin Sturm didn't know that the $50,000 start-up money for Sturm, Ruger had actually come from his wife. The Sturms left the meeting for a discussion, and Katherine gingerly broke the news to Justin, adding that she, too, wanted Ruger to have control of the company. Justin's hostility toward the young gun designer began to soften, and he never again attempted to dominate the company.

The first prototype .22 Ruger pistol at *left*, with 1949 production prototype, the latter with wooden grips. Flat sheet of steel was press-formed to make one half of the grip, which was welded to a mirror-image stamping to form the pistol's grip frame. Partially finished bolt at *bottom right*. Ruger remembers the euphoria he felt on completion of the design of the .22 Standard pistol:

> After finishing the engineering drawings of the .22 pistol, there was an enormous pleasure and satisfaction of knowing that I had created an object which was handsome, functional, and practical; and that this pistol would have a ready market, and its creation was something that I wanted to do. I was bursting with pleasure and delighted in every way. The future looked promising, and I was ready to tackle any challenge. How wonderfully satisfying, the prospect of being able to make a living at something one thoroughly and genuinely enjoyed.

Hardware distributor John H. Graham had advised Ruger that he should talk to the Mossbergs, Connecticut gunmakers, about making the .22 Automatic pistol. He did so, and was advised that it was something that couldn't be done at the $50,000 figure. Ruger had been told to expect failure by such experienced hands as Swebilius ("You can't do it"), one of the Mossbergs, and others. Their chorus was, "It can't be done for a capitalization of only $50,000." Today that kind of investment wouldn't even cover the tooling costs for the pistol's magazine.

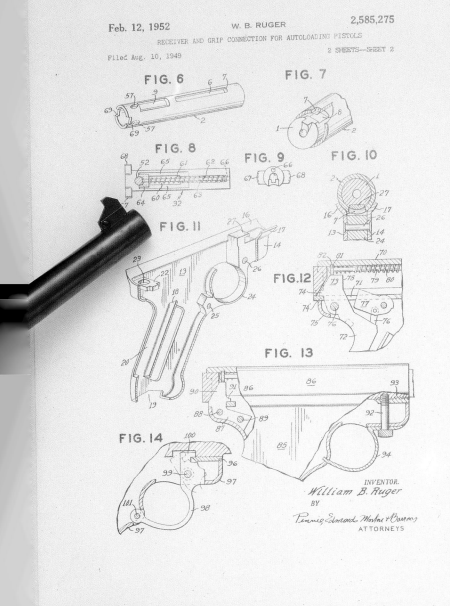

Feb. 12, 1952   W. B. RUGER   2,585,275

RECEIVER AND GRIP CONNECTION FOR AUTOLOADING PISTOLS

Filed Aug. 10, 1949   2 SHEETS—SHEET 2

FIG. 6   FIG. 7

FIG. 8 FIG. 9 FIG. 10

FIG. 11   FIG. 12

FIG. 13

FIG. 14

INVENTOR.

William B. Ruger

BY

Pennie, Edmonds, Morton & Barrows

ATTORNEYS

RUGER
MUZZLE BRAKE
FOR MARK 1 PISTOLS ONLY
STURM, RUGER & CO., INC.
SOUTHPORT, CONN.

RUGER MAGAZINE
FOR STANDARD & MARK 1 PISTOLS
STURM, RUGER & CO., INC.
SOUTHPORT, CONN.

Paulina agreed to retire her shares of preferred stock, and—recognizing that the company would succeed only if Bill Ruger was at the helm—assigned management control to him. For a $75,000 fee, paid out over the next few years, and other considerations, Bill Ruger emerged as the controlling stockholder. Paulina, victim of an unfortunate childhood, dominated by strong-willed parents, depressed and in weakened health, would die on January 27, 1953, of a sleeping pill overdose. She was thirty-one.

Advertising and Marketing

Ruger knew from his years of experience that a small company could easily go under from any number of costly errors. He was determined that, this time, everything would work. When in doubt, he sought out expert advice. One person he went to, late in 1949, was John Orr Young, a friend of Alexander Sturm's family and a founder of the highly respected and successful Young and Rubicam advertising agency.

Alex and I had a long luncheon with John Young, and he answered a lot of specific questions, such as, "Considering the size of our company, would you say that small advertisements were useful, or should we have big ones?" He said that if these small ads were properly done and designed, they could be just as effective as a big one. Our first ad was designed by Al Bury, who was with Sturm, Ruger and Company until approximately 1958. Sturm wrote the copy, and I may have changed a word or two in consultation with him. But the woodcut and proportion had a little professional touch that suggests Bury was involved in it. He had a little office in New York that he set up for himself. He had been with the firm that represented The Ruger Corporation, and had then been advertising manager with another company.

After a succession of small agencies, we established Hawkeye Communications, our own in-house agency, to facilitate our program and to place our ads directly. I wanted to call it "Tom Tom" but that name was too raffish for everybody. The agency was a success. People used to say, "Bill, I like your ads. There's no B.S.!"

Stationery

It was Alex Sturm who designed our stationery, and when he first designed it, that eagle took up about the top third of the page. Warren Page said, "Who the hell designed that stationery? It looks like something from the German embassy!" I said, "That's Sturm. The design is part German heraldry, and part Japanese." Page said, "I'll say one thing for it; you know where the letter comes from!"

As with the eagle logo, we tried to develop a design sense that would last, and it has carried us through to today. There's a very distinctive style to our advertising and our use of artwork. There's always been that artistic element. I've always been interested in the advertising side of it, and at that lunch with John Orr Young, we got some of our theories. I used to be a regular reader of *Printer's Ink* magazine, a marvelous publication in those days for the ad industry, and I learned a little bit about how advertising is remembered. There were ten rules published in the magazine on the characteristics of an ad that gets high ratings. I tried to follow them. Our ads were dignified, truthful, important, and also tended towards the technical. We assumed that people wanted to know the facts. With a product like a gun, it was important to speak technically.

Aesthetics and Functionality

I still don't necessarily assume that anybody sees it the way I do, but to me, guns have great lines or no lines. I used to think Winchesters were not especially good-looking rifles, but even so, one of my favorites, one I wanted badly, was the Model 1894 carbine. I always thought the Savage 99 was marvelous, and of course, the Luger was a handsome pistol.

The [Colt] Woodsman was the first influence on our .22 pistol, and also the Luger. What I did was to conceive our .22 as a low-cost equivalent to the Woodsman, which is exactly what High Standard had done previously. But there was something about the High Standard that wasn't as neat as the Colt; they didn't get it right. It looked too much like a product of the '50s, with plastics and things. We really murdered High Standard with our guns. The world probably isn't fully conscious of that. It was High Standard, high, wide, and handsome after the war and up through the very early '50s. Then all of a sudden this pistol of ours took command, and in about six months the only .22 anyone was interested in was the Ruger.

Another reason people buy a particular gun is its mechanism. Understand the mechanism, understand the product. You see this in anyone who loves machines. It's a mixture of art and mechanics. It is an aesthetic for guns. Some think the only thing that makes a gun handsome is the engraving; that is simply not true. A gun has to be beautiful on its own; the engraving can only add surface beauty to what's already artistic.

Design Consciousness

Everything I look at is an example of product design, a mixture of the technical and the functional. One day, around 1953, I was killing an afternoon in New York before going somewhere on a company mission—to Detroit or Chicago—to see a casting company about working for us. I was kicking around the Museum of Modern Art and began talking to a distinguished-looking man, well groomed and beautifully dressed, who was also by himself. He was a designer or some kind of professional man, and we talked about "design consciousness." In fact, that's where I picked up that concept and phraseology. This man admired the sculpture of Alexander Calder, and we continued talking about design matters at the Stork Club over dinner. I forget now who that was, but this design consciousness has been an integral part of every gun we've made.

Materials

In the early 1950s, the federal government required allocations for materials, particularly steel, classified as "strategic." As a gunmaker, Sturm, Ruger was subject to these restrictions:

During the Korean War we found it necessary to go to Washington three or four times. The bureaucracy was pathetic; you couldn't find anyone who could give you any straight answers. We were just a start-up company and hadn't even reached a targeted or intended level of output, so criteria like "last year's consumption" (which they invariably used when calculating how much steel you'd be al-

Norwick Goodspeed on Alex Sturm

Although they had much in common, I'm sure that, sometimes, Bill wondered what to do with Alex.

I believe Alex would have lived much longer if he had only taken vitamins, and eaten from time to time. You wouldn't see him eat anything. He used to say that he never expected to live to the age of forty, and he was right. I know that if something happened to him, his intention was that Bill should carry on the business, and have controlling interest in it.

Quite a few of us attended the memorial service for Alex, at the Congregational Church in Southport, near the factory. Among others, the entire factory work force was there.

---

lowed) had hardly any bearing on our situation. I had to continually try to get around all those factors that didn't apply to us, and somehow or other I finally got an allocation.

Someone noted that these allocations were just like hunting licenses: Next thing you had to do was go find somebody who liked you that would sell you the steel. One way or the other, we got it, but it was really a struggle!

The Competition

In the early days I really didn't think of myself as a competitor of most of the gun companies. We didn't make rifles, and my only close friend among other handgun firms was Dan Wesson at Smith & Wesson. We had plenty to talk about without anything that could ever be criticized as conspiratorial or anything of that sort. Single-actions of the type we made really were not competitors of Smith's police-type double-actions in any event. It was the same way with Savage, but again, Savage wasn't in the

---

Julian S. Hatcher's favorable *American Rifleman* review of the ".22 Ruger Pistol," an endorsement that helped significantly in recognizing the new product, which came to be known in firearms circles as representing "real value."

NRA TECHNICAL SERVICE

Maj. Gen. J. S. Hatcher, Director

Edwards Brown, Jr. ● A. H. Barr ● J. S. Rose ● M. D. Waite

Dope Bag

EDITED BY *Al Barr*

.22 RUGER PISTOL

Some months ago W. B. Ruger showed us the designer's model of his new pistol, and he asked for criticisms and suggestions. Since that time Mr. Ruger and Alexander Sturm have formed the firm of Sturm, Ruger & Co. Their factory at Southport, Connecticut is now completely tooled for production and is turning out guns in quantity. We have just seen and fired two production-line samples of the .22 Ruger.

Shaped like the Luger pistol, the gun looks good and handles splendidly. It hangs and balances just right, and points naturally, which is a great aid in quick shooting. The fixed sights are well shaped and easy to see. Mr. Ruger said the trigger pull would probably not be to our liking, as the guns were taken right off the production line and not dolled up at all for our tests. Actually, one of the two samples had an excellent pull, while the other had a slight creep, but even that was not too bad.

While we have not done much firing as yet, we know that the gun has accuracy and is capable of tight groups. One very desirable feature is that the front and rear sights are both on the same piece of metal, so that there is no chance of relative motion between them, as is the case when one sight is on the barrel and the other on the moveable breech block.

Both of our sample guns grouped a little low for us, which means that the front sight is just a bit too high. That is, however, a good fault with fixed sights, for it can be corrected easily by filing the front sight.

The gun, chambered for the .22 long rifle only, weighs 36 ounces, has a 4¾-inch barrel and a nine-shot magazine. It has a thumb safety, and a quick and easy take-down. The finish is excellent, with Butaprene grips and an excellent bluing job.

One can readily see that the designer of this gun knows something about shooting as well as designing; W. B. Ruger has been a shooter all his life, was captain of his high school rifle team, and has been an NRA member since he was old enough to read.

Mr. Jack Boudreau of the Ruger factory has used a Ruger in several local matches. He placed high in several of them, and won at least two medals in September alone.

We like this new gun a lot and at the very moderate price of $37.50 it represents real value.—J.S.H.

Despite a strong resemblance to the Luger, the Ruger is American in design and manufacture

handgun business. Only after quite a while, when we'd begun producing our .44 Magnum carbine, did Remington and Winchester begin to see us as a growing company in the arms industry and possible competition.

Of course, Colt and High Standard knew we were around very early on, because I can tell you that within a year of offering our pistol, their sales had fallen off drastically. Bill Donovan, sales manager for High Standard, became a pretty good friend of mine. He used to try to needle me a little: "If you amateurs are all through, we can teach you something about guns." But the truth was, one day (and I got this story straight from someone who was there) Donovan was talking to the purchasing agent at E. K. Tryon in Philadelphia; they were the biggest gun jobber in America, and Donovan was asking why High Standard wasn't getting more business. The buyer had no reason to pull any punches. "People aren't buying your guns now; they're buying Rugers." Donovan tried to argue that it couldn't be true. So this man opened the file drawer in his desk, brought out a big stack of orders, all for Rugers, put them on his desk and said, "Listen, when High Standard produces a volume of business like this, we'll be ordering at that volume."

Then High Standard produced an automatic shotgun which was engineered and made all wrong. The story was that Sears, Roebuck got interested in High Standard and placed huge orders for what they thought would be their "J. C. Higgins" shotguns. A carload of guns was shipped to Sears in Chicago. The guns worked just fine if you kept them horizontal, but when you pointed them up-

---

Blued pistols are prototypes, the earliest at *top left* (outside marked only RUGER on the tubular receiver; with profile like Colt Woodsman, and used its magazine; Franzite grips; overall length 8½"), followed by the first .22 Standard with the conventional profile, and two pre-production run-through pistols at right. The chrome-plated pistol, number 15886, was built for display purposes, and is a Mark I Target Model. Ruger's penciled notes an estimate of production costs. Patents issued to Ruger apply to the .22 pistol. Brochure prepared by Sturm, assisted by Ruger. Magazines based on High Standard designs, known for reliable functioning.

---

ward, they didn't work at all! The whole carload had to come back, and High Standard effectively disappeared not long after.

Executives and Guns

Early on, Ruger recognized that a knowledge of and love for guns was a distinct advantage, and a vital element in realizing success in the firearms field:

I think Remington or Winchester or both had a member or two that went to Camp Fire [a historic private club in Chappaqua, New York]. But their top management, I don't remember a single one of them at the time ever had the slightest interest in going on a long pack trip or something. The man I knew there quite well was the president. He had been sales manager when I first met him and induced him to listen to my plan for selling the Ruger pistols.

I knew a little bit about how hardware and sporting goods were sold and distributed because I'd had that experience in the tool business earlier, but I had figured out some variations on it. I wasn't going to be strictly a jobber-oriented manufacturer. I was going to offer the jobber's price only to qualified jobbers, and I was going to offer a higher price directly to established dealers. A jobber price, a dealer price, and a retail price, all rigidly adhered to according to what type of firm you actually were. Of course, in those days you also had this fair trade law, and it was really beneficial to us because it prohibited the kind of discounting you see today, which you now can't do a thing about.

Another industry executive I got quite friendly with put out this dictum that his management team

---

Norwick Goodspeed on the Ruger Pistol and on Bill Ruger

There was a third original director of Sturm, Ruger & Co., Norwick R. G. Goodspeed, whose involvement with the firm ceased soon after Alex Sturm's death. Goodspeed had been asked by Sturm to check out the business potential of the .22 Standard pistol. Accordingly, for several

---

weeks he showed the prototype to competent gunsmiths, machinists, and others whom he felt would have real insight into the pistol's potential, among them Griffin & Howe, Folsom Arms, and Stoeger's:

After Alex and Bill had met, Alex approached me as a friend and lawyer. He had the prototype of the Ruger .22 pistol, and he gave it to me: "Is this something I could put my mother's money into?" His parents wanted desperately to have something Alex could do. I reported back to Alex that everyone I showed the pistol to felt it had merit, found it intriguing, liked the looks, and thought it would sell. However, what I did had a further importance as to whether or not the gun would fly: Every bit as important was my own impression of Bill Ruger. If I had gone back to Alex and said I had no confidence in Ruger, I am sure Alex would have said "so be it," and that would have been the end of it.

But I was impressed by Bill as a human being, he was very straightforward, honorable, conscientious, and an obviously creative talent. There was a dedication to what he wanted to achieve. You could see that intensity, and how focused he was. Ruger sufficiently impressed me, despite his recent emergence from a failed business, that I encouraged Alex to get the funds and go ahead. It was Bill Ruger's character, intellect, and talent, as much as the merit of the pistol, that made me say that this is something worthwhile, and something that Alex should be a part of.

In the course of my experience as a lawyer, and later as a banker, there have been many times in which I had the opportunity to put people together, and there were many times that I advised not to do something. I had no doubts whatsoever about this business venture.

After Alex's death, Goodspeed was replaced by Norman Parsells, representing Paulina Sturm's interests on the board of directors. Goodspeed eventually became the chairman of People's Bank of Connecticut, which grew under his stewardship from a half dozen branches in 1967, to sixty at the time of his retirement in 1987.

The Ruger .22 Standard Pistol

First production .22 Standard Pistol, number 0012; left grip removed to show "red eagle" trademark medallion.

Number 13-40371 Mark I Target Pistol.

Number 0012 .22 Standard Pistol, with its original "salt cod" box, and Ruger cardboard carton of somewhat later vintage, circa 1954–1960.

Introduced: 1949. "The first overall improvement in automatic pistol design since the Browning patent of 1905."

Production of original series completed December 31, 1981; succeeded by the Mark II Standard Model.

Serial Numbers: Began with four-digit numbers, customarily preceded by zeros. Numbers 0661 to 1999 not produced. Standard .22 range from 1 to 301500; Mark I Target Pistol from 300000 to 337962.

Prefix first used c. 1969 (began with 10-00000 to -99999), and the following employed sequentially thereafter 11-, 12-, 13-, 14-, 15-, 16-, 17-. Last serial number before introduction of New Model Mark II Automatic: 17-80344. **D** prefix or suffix marking was to avoid duplication of serial numbers. **S** or **U** *see tables, page 310–311.*

Total Made Through 1981 (including Target): In excess of 1,250,000.

Caliber: .22 Long Rifle.

Magazine Capacity: 9 in spring-fed detachable box.

Barrel Lengths: 4¾" and 6". Crowned muzzle changed to flat configuration at approximately serial range 9101 to 9124. 6⅞" barrels introduced with Target Model pistols at serial range 15000.

Rifling: Six grooves, right-hand twist, one turn in 14 to 16".

Markings: See Table of Markings, pages 330–35.

Receiver maker marking changed on some specimens by addition of **, INC.** at approximately serial number 286360; by the number 430841, the new marking was standard.

Serial number die size was of small configuration (1/16" high) from 1 to 259200, with some production marked with large size dies (⅛" high) from number 255478, and standard after 259201.

Die struck metal red eagle trademark inlaid on left grip, changed in 1951 to black.

Warning marking on left side of receiver, from serial number 14-84935 (approximately January 12, 1978).

BEFORE USING GUN—READ WARNINGS IN *INSTRUCTION MANUAL* AVAILABLE FREE FROM —STURM, RUGER & CO., INC. SOUTHPORT , CONN. U.S.A.—

Sights: Square notch rear sight measuring ¼" thick, dovetailed onto breech of receiver; at approximately serial 10793 to 10850 range a ½" thick contoured sight adopted. Front sight of Patridge style, wide blade, precision machined. Sight radius of first model: 7½".

Overall Length and Weight: 9", 36 ounces (4¾" barrel). 10", 38 ounces (6" barrel).

Grips: Black hard rubber with red trademark (often termed "red eagle") medallion inlay. At serial 34369 the trademark changed to black, honoring the memory of Alexander Sturm (a few specimens with red trademarks have been observed with higher serial numbers). Checkered walnut grips introduced on some specimens midway in 1963. Grip variations as follows: red trademark with screw escutcheons, same without escutcheons, black trademark hard rubber, black trademark with walnut thumbrest, black trademark walnut with escutcheons located on lower panel, silver trademark walnut, silver trademark plastic, and walnut with high polish silver trademark.

Finish: Blued, with chrome-plated trigger. A very few with full chrome finish, an available option from late 1950 (extremely rare in "Red Eagle" model).

Materials, Construction, and Innovations: Two-piece stamped steel frame; welded. Machined steel barrel, tubular steel receiver. Broad, grooved trigger.

Simplicity of design and construction, built-in strength, handsome form and line, superb balance. Rear sight mounted on receiver, and thus remains stationary. Cylindrical bolt cycles within tubular receiver. All barrel and receiver assemblies utilize same grip frame, permitting ready manufacture of both standard and target models. Steel cross pin in receiver walls arrests rearward motion of bolt. Unbreakable steel music wire springs (no flat springs) throughout. Positive safety catch. Two-stage trigger pull. Solid, non-moving sights. Dismantling achieved in five seconds; only screws in construction used for securing grips.

Issue Price: $37.50 (1949). Reached price of $126 in 1981 catalogue, before being replaced by MK II series, 1982.

Engraving: Engraved examples extremely rare. Number 3161 gold inlaid for Milt Klein, publisher, *Gun Digest,* and pictured page 127 of the 1951 edition (only factory-engraved "Red Eagle" pistol). Serial number 47698 was presented by William B. Ruger to Vice President Richard M. Nixon, at the National Rifle Association show, Ambassador Hotel, Washington, D.C., spring 1954. Number 109000 engraved and gold inlaid as a 1956 NRA show display sample, by Charles H. Jerred. Serial number 1000000 embellished by Ray Viramontez, 1979, and donated to the International Shooter Development Fund. Serial number 17-23222, also by Viramontez, and presented to William B. Ruger by company employees. Numbers 1000001 to 1000004 lightly gold inlaid, and fitted in deluxe casings; gold work by Viramontez. Numbers 1000000 through 1000004 fitted with ivory grips, with red eagle medallions. Number 17-02953 Signature Series pistol engraved and sculpted in relief for William B. Ruger by Paul Lantuch.

Packaging: First shipments were in hinged-lid boxes (of red, white, and black colors) wrapped in paper within pine boxes with sliding lids, the latter known to collectors as the "salt cod" style; *or* contained within a shipping sleeve of cardboard. Salt cod boxes discontinued at about serial range 9101.

Price Sheet Listings:

RST4: 4¾" barrel, composition grips.

RST6: 6" barrel, composition grips.

RST4W: 4¾" barrel, walnut grips.

RST6W: 6" barrel, walnut grips.

Major Production Variations: Approximately 30 variations have been determined for the Standard Model .22 production, predating the MK II. These are primarily based on such features as the following:

Ejection Port: Changed from rectangular shape to contoured end design by serial range 10062 to 10206.

Safety Button: Changed from .255" diameter to .285" at range 9399 to 9411.

Bolt: With or without recoil spring support.

Tapered Ear Bolt: Serial range 43181 to 82850.

Bolt Stop Pin: Angled type used through serial range 75000; overlap with round style from range 30000, continuing to end of production; rare tapered type only in range 13-15884 to 13-55719.

Specific Models Include:

Armamex, Mexico: A rare variation, examples were made in 4¾" and 6" barrel lengths, using parts supplied by the factory, and assembled in 1955–57 by the Armamex factory in Pachuca (located north of Mexico City), an operation headed by Colonel Rex Applegate. Total built: 250, with the assembled pistols shipped by Sturm, Ruger & Co. to the American Firearms Company, Brownsville, Texas. 50 pistols had 6" barrels, the balance of 200 had 4¾" barrels. The pistols were then disassembled, and exported to Mexico. At Armamex the pistols were marked, finished in blue, and reassembled, and sent to Cia Compania Importada Mexicana, for distribution to the Mexican market. Pistol number R1054 was sent to William B. Ruger by Colonel Applegate. **Markings:** on right side of receiver HECHO EN MEXICO. On left side of receiver: RUGER-CAL .22 L.R.-ARMAMEX, MEXICO. On right side of receiver of most specimens, below the standard marking: ODIN-ALEX.-VA. **Serial Number:** appears on right side, forward of the ejection port, in a special range different from the Ruger factory serials, and believed to be R1001 to R1200 (4¾" pistols), and R1201 to R1250 (6" pistols).

Duplicate Pistols: D323351 to D324283 (1966), with **D** prefix.

Liberty Series: Pistols made in 1976 (including some finished early in 1977), roll marked on the receiver: MADE IN THE 200TH YEAR OF AMERICAN LIBERTY. Note: There are variations within the overall Liberty category.

Warning Series: Introduced approximately January 1978, in serial range and with receiver "warning" marking as above.

Ruger Collectors Association "Chamber Seal": 6" pistol within serial range 15-45602 to 75740; 301 made, hand engraved RCA logo on top of breech of receiver (near barrel), with special numbers RCA 1500 to 1599, or RCA 01400 to 01600.

Signature Model: Serial range 17-00000 to 17-05000. First .22 Rugers of stainless steel construction. *William B. Ruger* signature roll marked on left side of receiver. **1 OF 5000** roll marked on right side of barrel.

California Freedom Series: Made within the Signature Model serial series, specifically 17-03379 to 17-04792. Hand engraved CAL. FREEDOM '82 on top of receiver near barrel breech. Donated by Sturm, Ruger & Co. to the California "Citizens Against the Gun Initiative," 1982, and used in drawings which raised substantial sums to help defeat Proposition 15 (a total handgun freeze).

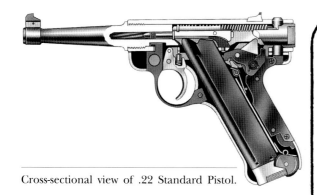

Cross-sectional view of .22 Standard Pistol.

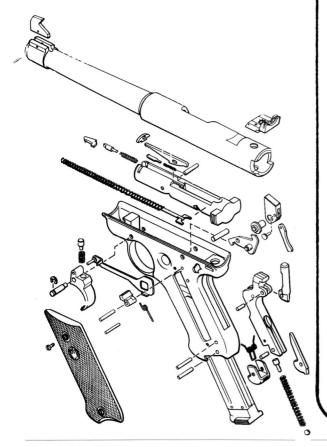

Exploded view of .22 Mark I Pistol.

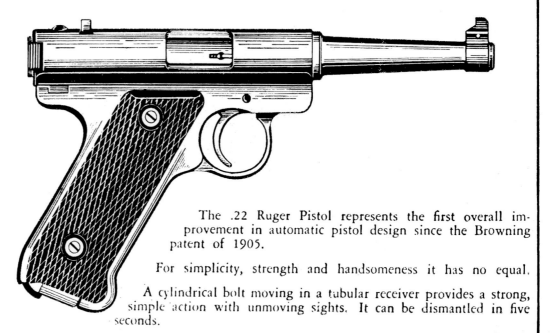

the .22 RUGER pistol

The .22 Ruger Pistol represents the first overall improvement in automatic pistol design since the Browning patent of 1905.

For simplicity, strength and handsomeness it has no equal.

A cylindrical bolt moving in a tubular receiver provides a strong, simple action with unmoving sights. It can be dismantled in five seconds.

The Ruger Pistol weighs 2¼ pounds and measures 9 inches with a 4¾ inch barrel. It fills a man's hand fully and comfortably. The grips are sharply checkered hard rubber; the trigger is broad and grooved. It has a positive safety catch and detachable magazine holding nine .22 caliber long rifle cartridges.

The reader is invited to send for a free leaflet describing the Ruger Pistol in detail.

STURM, RUGER & CO., INC.
SOUTHPORT, CONNECTICUT

The first Ruger advertisement, in *The American Rifleman* magazine, August 1949.

IN THEIR SOUTHPORT GUNSHOP
WILLIAM B. RUGER (SEATED) AND
ALEXANDER STURM OF STURM,
RUGER AND CO., INC.

THE .22 CALIBRE AUTOMATIC,
SOMETHING NEW IN THE
WAY OF HANDGUNS.

MR. STURM COACHING HIS WIFE, THE
FORMER PAULINA LONGWORTH, IN
THE ART OF SHOOTING.

JOHN SMITH, PLANT SUPERINTENDENT
WATCHES JULIUS ENHAUSER CUT
THE MAGAZINE SLOT IN THE
BARREL OF A RUGER.

IN THE ASSEMBLY DEPARTMENT (LEFT TO RIGHT)
JACK BOUDREAU, IN CHARGE OF ASSEMBLY;
LOUIS HASSELMAN, TEST-FIRING; AND
WALTER SYCH ASSEMBLING A RUGER.

ADDRESSING RUGER CIRCULARS, MRS. STURM,
ALEX STURM (STANDING) AND
NEIGHBOR-PARTNER BILL RUGER.

would be expected to quit playing golf every time they did any business entertaining, and go out to do some shooting instead. Remington had this marvelous shotgun shooting installation near Bridgeport, a little place called Lordship, on a peninsula sticking out into Long Island Sound. Quite a few Remington managers did get out to the trap or skeet fields there. I always felt that, if nothing else, you should be using your own company's products—not hitting around a golf ball. Remington, in those days, was a well-managed company, no question about it. They did everything right. In that postwar period I was expecting to see prewar

---

Illustrations from the first press exposure given to Sturm, Ruger and Co., published in the *Bridgeport Sunday Post*, November 20, 1949, headlined RUGER AUTOMATIC IS NO PLAYTHING FOR PISTOL-PACKIN' MAMAS. "Resembling a Luger and hanging like a Luger, it handles like a breeze . . . . Rugers selected at random have been shot up to 11,000 rounds with no signs of wear. . . . The [Sturm] home on Cranberry Road, Westport . . . is a small arsenal. Sturm's collection includes everything from early American arms (all in shootable condition) through modern European guns. . . . At high school Bill was on the rifle team, and when he went to Salisbury where guns are verboten, he defied the authorities to the extent of secreting his favorite firearm in a tumbledown shack in the nearby woods. . . . Sturm went into the service before the ink was dry on his sheepskin, serving in and around Washington with the OSS, and meeting in the Capitol City, the gay, dark-haired daughter of Washington's most distingushed hostess. . . . After the war Sturm drew and wrote for the *Saturday Review of Literature*. . . . For eight months after taking over the red frame buildings formerly occupied by Rolock, the new concern was busy tooling up. Last Oct. 1 they started shipping, and today have so many orders they don't know what to do with all of them. The current staff comprises a flexible fifteen employees, and total floorspace isn't over 3,000 feet. But the plant is capable of turning out 10,000 Rugers a year. Sturm, Ruger & Co., Inc. have no sales force nor are they planning any in the near future. To date the response their product has met has precluded the necessity. Letters have poured in, literally in the high thousands, requesting circulars (Paulina, the volunteer addresser, is almost up to the 10,000 mark), and orders have exceeded Sturm-Ruger's wildest dreams. . . . 'For better shooting it's a Ruger.'"

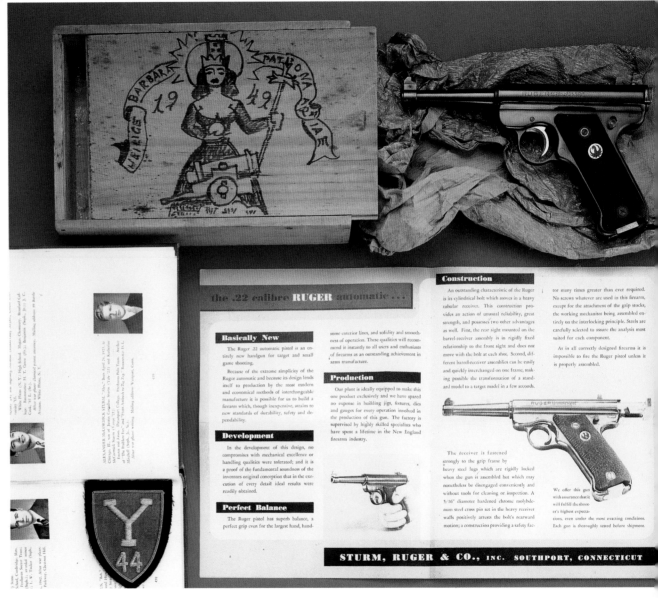

The wood box lid of this early production .22 Standard pistol was decorated by Alex Sturm, with a drawing of St. Barbara, patron saint of arms and armaments. The pistol is still in its original paper wrapper. Accompanying the set is the Yale *Class Book* for 1944, and a blazer patch for that year. Brochure reveals the inside spread of the first company flier.

firearms reintroduced with a slide action model and the semiautomatic rifle, but instead they brought up a new 700 series that's marked their style ever since. It was a really well-engineered, integrated line of different products. They invented the first really good-looking, low-cost bolt-action rifle with a tubular receiver.

Product engineering, marketing—both were models; nobody did it better. I think you could say much the same about Winchester, although Winchester was not as decisive and creative in bringing a product line forward. It took them a long while. They spent a lot of money, talked about it a lot, and when the products did appear, they were not unqualified successes like Remington's. Winchester postwar lever-action and semiautomatic rifles, the Models 88 and 100, were pretty good but not quite as good as they could have been, and they never really caught on. You hardly ever see them anymore.

I always thought that shooting fast with some of their lever actions was a hard thing anyway, because that iron loop, the lever, could take off the thin skin on the back of your fingers. Of course, the Model 70 rifle and the old 94 carbines were unbeatable, so they had some really strong products. But they couldn't seem to improve on those.

Staffing Sturm, Ruger & Co.

Ruger's skill at consistently hiring some of the best talent in gunmaking and manufacturing was further enhanced by his capacity for inspiring, cajoling, challenging, demanding, and expecting his staff to excel. Not infrequently, some found themselves reaching heights of accomplishment which they might have considered beyond their individual reach. The resultant euphoria of achievement has been partially a result of the feedback and input which is inherent in any assignment one does for Ruger.

Writing to his friend and sometime gun writer, Judge Don Martin of Salmon, Idaho, Ruger revealed the results of careful and judicious hiring:

I don't think that I have ever worked so hard as during the first three or four months of this year [1953]. Fortunately, we have a new man in the company, Nick Brewer, who has about 20 years of expe-

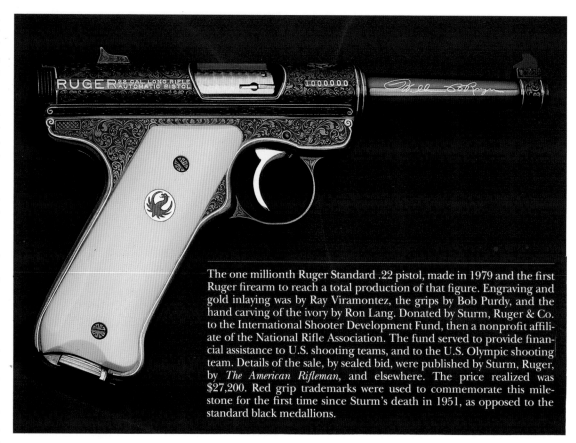

The one millionth Ruger Standard .22 pistol, made in 1979 and the first Ruger firearm to reach a total production of that figure. Engraving and gold inlaying was by Ray Viramontez, the grips by Bob Purdy, and the hand carving of the ivory by Ron Lang. Donated by Sturm, Ruger & Co. to the International Shooter Development Fund, then a nonprofit affiliate of the National Rifle Association. The fund served to provide financial assistance to U.S. shooting teams, and to the U.S. Olympic shooting team. Details of the sale, by sealed bid, were published by Sturm, Ruger, by *The American Rifleman,* and elsewhere. The price realized was $27,200. Red grip trademarks were used to commemorate this milestone for the first time since Sturm's death in 1951, as opposed to the standard black medallions.

rience in designing and manufacturing firearms. He was the designer of Savage's low priced .22s and during the war was chief engineer of their machine gun program. After the war he . . . retired, but we got him up here last September, and without him [the Ruger Single-Six] would still be in the talking stage. He completed all the component part drawings, establishing every tolerance, and just recently finished up all the tool drawings.

Bill Ruger would be the first to state that "nobody does it alone."

Gun Writers

From the beginning, Sturm, Ruger & Co. was recognized as innovative and knowledgeable regarding how to invent, design, engineer, make, and market popular firearms. They had the kind of savvy that captured the loyalty of people who liked guns and shooting. Coincident with the rise of Ruger, a solid corps of writers began specialized features in new magazines which concentrated on firearms and related subjects. This cadre was recognized by Ruger early on:

We were either lucky or had the right instincts there, too, because even after the pistol was well launched and the company was running like a machine, there were marketing efforts that began to cultivate these new gun writers. I think I was the first gun manufacturer to really exploit this source of marketing. Firms like Winchester and Remington would loan a gun to a writer so he could write something about it, but they didn't cultivate any friendships. I became really friendly with Warren Page just about the time he was getting started, and he didn't know a hell of a lot about guns. He wanted to go to *Field and Stream* as a fishing editor, and the publisher said, "Hell, I don't need a fishing writer, I need a gun writer. Can you write about guns?" Page said yes right away, and he went right out, got some books, and started reading. He ended up spending his life on guns.

Then there was Pete Kuhlhoff, who was writing a gun column for *Argosy* magazine, and there was Peter Barrett doing the same thing for *True*. And then there was *The American Rifleman*. Old Major General Julian Hatcher from the Army was reviewing guns for them, and he really helped us with his article in the "Dope Bag" section about the .22 pistol. In those days the *Rifleman* was the preeminent publication on firearms, and the best place to advertise or be featured in. *Field & Stream*, *Outdoor Life*, and *Sports Afield* were the big three hunting and fishing magazines, but they really didn't get into the technical gun field anything like the *Rifleman*.

I met Jack O'Connor rather early on and knew him many years until his death. I went hunting with him a lot, and bought him expensive dinners in New York—that's what he enjoyed most, after hunting.

In addition to the publications I've mentioned, we occasionally contacted *Fur-Fish-Game* or that five-cent magazine called *Hunting and Fishing*. Lucian Cary was a gun writer and a novelist working for *True* magazine. He came up with a story about us which was very important in spreading our reputation. This was later, after we began making revolvers.

None of what I'm speaking about happened all at once. It was a kind of evolution. The company, the postwar cadre of outdoor writers, and the expansion of interest in the shooting sports by returning World War II and Korea veterans, all coincided beautifully.

The Single-Six

Ruger's first revolver was an improved Colt-type Single Action, always one of his favorites. The exterior looked much like the classic Colt, and its mechanism functioned identically. But inside it contained significant mechanical improvements. And it was slightly smaller, being a .22.

The appeal of the classic Single Action is the stuff of which legends are made. Of all Colt revolvers, none earned greater fame than the Single Action Army—the Peacemaker—accepted by most connoisseurs as the *ne plus ultra* of Colt firearms. In design and performance, no more beautiful and practical Colt was ever created. The proliferation of Western movies and television shows became a constant reminder of the role this "equalizer" had played in the winning of the West. Ruger recognized all this, while Colt would not until Ruger had solidly captured the market—a market which remains dominated by Sturm, Ruger & Co. to this day.

Through Ruger's recollections, the evolution of the single-action models can be traced, from early prototypes to production models.

When I went up to Quebec with Warren Page [in 1951—when Sturm died], our first single-action revolver, the .22 caliber Single-Six, was just getting into development; we were just beginning the tooling design. In trying to decide on a name, we both agreed that "Peacemaker" was an absolutely beautiful name, but there was no doubt that it would infringe on Colt patents or trademarks. I remember raising the question with Hal Seagraves, another figure with a significant history with the company. He was a first-class patent attorney with a New York firm called Pennie, Edmonds, Morton and Barrows. I met Hal during World War II and he filed a few patent applications for us. I think he was the patent attorney for the original automatic pistol patents. About the time the Single-Six idea came along, I remember raising this question: If the gun looks that way, we don't need to use the names Colt had used, but can I make a gun that looks and operates like that Peacemaker? Pennie and Edmonds did not try to answer that question right off the cuff. They thought about it long and hard, and in due time said there was absolutely no question,

Colt no longer had a way of legally objecting to it. On the strength of that we went forward.

Colt, in fact, had paved the way for us, because in *The American Rifleman*, around 1947, there had appeared a little box, a notice from Colt's Manufacturing Company, in which they formally announced that they would not be resuming postwar manufacture of the Single Action Army model. Colt suggested there was insufficient demand for the gun to justify replacing the tooling they had scrapped during the war to make room for machine gun production. They wound up saying that they were abandoning the classic American sidearm! I recall perfectly my shock and amazement at the obtuseness of some of those old men who were managing that grand old company. They really saw no fun in the gun. To them it was a chore and a bore; they just loved to play golf.

Ben Connor, Colt's president, was a man who had been the founder and head of a fairly good-sized plastic molding firm in New Jersey. Colt had bought him out just before World War II. He was Colt's president all through the war and into the postwar era, but he was utterly oblivious and indifferent to firearms, and said so publicly on more than one occasion. We were sitting at a meeting at one of the very first industry get-togethers, engineered by a talented old veteran of *Argosy* magazine who thought that he could act as an ambassador to propose a kind of industry trade association. So there we were at a hotel in Hartford, and I remember Colt's sales manager, then really rather elderly, remarking that the market for the type of gun we're talking about was essentially a market for "toys." He thought the only real handguns were double-action police-type revolvers and automatics. He turned to me and said, "You'll find that out."

Ironically, Colt later just blew away their police market—lost it to Smith and Wesson. When I was a kid, every policeman had a Colt. In the pre-war period, during the thirties, there was no question that Colt dominated. Smith was a poor second, ranked equally on quality but definitely second in sales. Eventually it was Smith & Wesson president Carl Hellstrom who really did in Colt in the police market by the late 1950s.

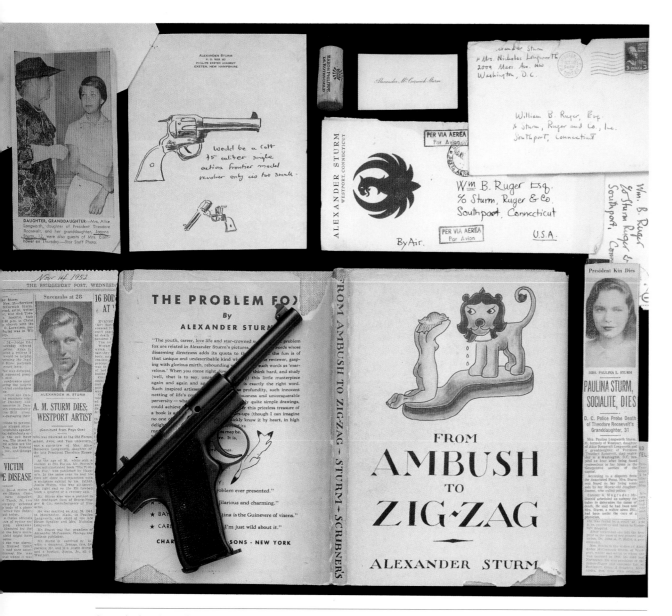

Sturm's drawing of a cap pistol was accompanied by humorous note to Bill Ruger, describing this discovery. Caption for the cover art of Sturm's children's alphabet book was: "Quail: Though a man would strive to win her, To a lion she's just dinner." Critic Edna Ferber said of *The Problem Fox*, "I am going to buy it in lumps," and Westbrook Pegler remarked, "I'm afraid it's wonderful." *The New York Times* reviewer said the book was "marvelous," a "little masterpiece," and a "priceless treasure."

Precision Investment Castings

When I was at Auto-Ordnance, I remember distinctly the day I was in the office of the metallurgical consultant. He said, "You know, there's a very interesting process, investment casting, the so-called 'lost wax' system. It's an ancient technique; you can find little objects cast by this means several thousand years ago. Dentists use the method today." He gave me a book about investment castings, and it proved to be a striking and new kind of thinking for a machinist. I didn't have much time to spend then, but after the war I learned that several people were already experimenting with the process.[1]

Winchester at one time had constructed an experimental investment casting facility. I've forgotten what they were trying to make, but they were really interested in the process. Then the man who got High Standard's big contracts put some money into a fledgling investment casting foundry, which proved a failure. At first, we tried to have them make the sear component of the .22 pistol, but in spite of many assurances, they just couldn't do it. We were getting ready to assemble the .22 pistol but we had no sears. I changed the design a bit and adapted it to be made from this special section, cutting off pieces of pre-formed bar stock. In those days every penny counted and it was a perfectly functional, yet economical sear—you can still see it in the Mark II pistols today.

A jewelry company called Arwood was the earliest commercial foundry that I knew of and actually made our first investment cast part. I think it was a trigger or the hammer for the Single-Six. I had asked them if they could cast the frame, because the machining for it was absolutely beyond us. They had a very engaging man, Lester Gott, and he said, "No, that's too big for us." But a year later he said they'd like to take another look at that frame. Their engineering had progressed enough so that casting a part of that size was feasible.

The concept of precision investment casting something as big as a Single-Six frame was all brand new at that point. The truth is, even today there are some significant limitations upon casting. If you still have to do a lot of machining on a part after casting it, you haven't gained much. A simple unimaginative casting, one that doesn't have any real complexity, costs just as much as a real SOB of a casting that's the same size. The key is complexity of the component you are considering to make as an investment casting. If it isn't complex, the casting process is hardly beneficial. You can make it some other, less involved way. However, complexity isn't absolutely free. It does require more involved mold cores and so forth, with more engineering details. And there's not a hell of a lot to write the casting dies off against.

Arwood went ahead, casting the frame, but for a long time their scrap rates were unacceptable. They were located in Brooklyn, where they had a foundry, but they also had a foundry in Groton, Connecticut. That's where Stan Terhune was working when he was introduced to our company through the Single-Six frame. As the volume of castings Arwood was making for us grew year by year, Stan became the man in charge of that work.

One time we were having some trouble with a new part for the .44 Magnum Carbine—it was a hammer, which was experiencing some breakage. I was pretty sure we knew what to do with it, but I was very pleased when Stan came down to Southport and said, "Bill, you've got a bad radius in this corner; you want to do this and do that." And I knew that Stan understood the stress factors and how parts become heavily loaded and how to overcome the problems. [Terhune says the solution was classic textbook, right out of his education at Rensselaer Polytechnic Institute and his background experience at Watervliet Arsenal and Arwood.]

So that was the beginning, really, of our single-actions. The frame had to be an investment casting or there never would have been a successful product. Not at that stage. This was a classic case where machining the complex frame the old way, out of a solid block of steel, in hundreds of machine operations, would have required too much factory, too

Ruger on the Mystique of the Single-Action Revolver

During the period just before the war the Colt was absolutely the only single-action. I don't think anyone for a generation ever had a thought of reproducing it. That all came after the war when a great market for them ultimately developed.

I think the appeal of the single-action lies in its extreme simplicity, its appearance, its nice feel in the hand, and the fact that, generally speaking, it's a great strong revolver capable of handling the heaviest cartridges. Double-actions are much more complex things. The average owner wouldn't dare take one apart, unless, of course, it's a Ruger. And double-actions seem to associate themselves with a more utilitarian world.

In contrast, the single-action has always related itself to the old West, to an outdoor tradition, and so on. Although the truth is, of course, that after the double-actions came in, particularly in the 1890s, a great many of them were used on hunting trips and by people living in the open. So, in reality, even that explanation of the single-action's appeal isn't completely understandable. It's really a mystique, much like the dedication to classic cars and single shot rifles, which exploded right after World War II. But, unlike the great motor cars of the late 1920s and early 30s, which are now easily outperformed by modern cars of the same class, these older types of firearms don't necessarily concede anything in sheer performance when you compare them to the more modern types. An automatic pistol isn't necessarily going to give you any better performance in terms of accuracy or power than an old single-action.

The sales of the Colts before the war were small but that could partially be accounted for by the Depression. After the war, by 1950, things were quite different and there was evidence that a significant number of shooters wanted single-actions. Enough to interest us because, with our very small company and small resources, we weren't going to attempt to produce them in any vast quantities.

Considering the size of our company, even the manufacture of a single-action seemed like a rather formidable undertaking!

We were a very small organization, say, probably twenty-five people. And these mainly engaged in the manufacturing and assembly of the Mark I automatic. I had a drawing board right there in my office and also one at my house and I spent a lot of time over them. By instinct I am a mechanical engineer and I'd been designing mechanisms and guns for many years by that time. I was thirty-four years old and had been seriously working on the design of firearms, or trying to design firearms, which is almost the same thing, for maybe fifteen years. And I had had an immense amount of experience during the war, developing machine guns, and at that time, I didn't really ever think of designing a revolver.

But I had always loved the old single-action Colt. I can remember yearning for one when I was just fourteen years old and living in New York City, where there was no chance of my owning one. But I had the Colt catalog and I used to open it up and look at that gun and say to myself, "Someday that's what I'm going to have."

The first announcement of our gun was in a tiny little box Pete Kuhlhoff ran in *Argosy* magazine. A few days later we got a phone call from the post office in Southport wanting to know what was happening. They were absolutely inundated with our mail. We went down there and they had it in cardboard cartons and bushel baskets! I suspect our single-action revolver made a first-class post office out of that station! As I look back on it, I don't think there has been a case where so much interest was engendered so instantaneously. The same sort of thing had happened with the announcement of our first .22 pistol but not to quite the same degree. I suppose that because shooters were so well-satisfied with that first effort of Sturm, Ruger & Co. they now had even greater confidence in this young company.

much infrastructure, too much organization for a small firm to produce in significant quantity. Investment castings made the Single-Six a whole different story. Getting the cylinder frames from outside casting vendors went on for a long while, from when we first began making single actions in 1952 to 1953 up until the early '60s when we established our own foundry.

One day Gott called me to say that Stan Terhune was leaving Arwood. They were trying to transfer him out of Groton to another plant, and he got into some rhubarb with the top management. Gott had a proposal for us. He owned some sort of mold-making business, and he proposed using Stan half-time if we could use him the other half, and we'd split his salary. I agreed to it and we went along that way for a while, until Stan eventually came to work with us full time. I don't know whether we'd begun thinking at that time of starting our own foundry; most likely we had.

When our own foundry finally began to evolve, Stan felt we shouldn't try to set it up in Southport. I had bought a place in Newport, New Hampshire, where I went mainly to hunt, and I learned about a little shop in town that was on the market. The building, about twelve thousand square feet, had been erected as a machine shop. We negotiated the purchase. Stan liked the idea of being up there, feeling it was an ideal location. We had to add a little space to allow for the high headroom needed for the melting furnace, and that was completed during the summer. And that was the very beginning of Sturm, Ruger, Newport, now one of the largest firearms manufacturing facilities in America.

Then Arwood surprised us. When we told them we wouldn't be doing any more business with them, I'm sure they were disappointed, but they were also very realistic, saying, "Okay, let's keep in touch because we might be able to function for you as consultants and plant engineers." We really needed that, and they were very broad-minded. They let us have drawings for their wax injection machines and other specialized equipment. They had a marvelous chief engineer named Parenchief—the grand old man of Arwood—and he was the designer of these specialized little foundries. He developed a floor plan for us in our new building. Bill Lett fabricated some of this equipment for us to

---

Taking the Initiative: Rex King Remembers

When we first started making the Single-Six, with investment casting of the cylinder frame, the hammer slot at the rear of the recoil shield would be closed in, from the casting, and it required machining it out so the hammer would pass through it freely. I took it upon myself to make up a drawing on a yellow pad, to draw up a set of vise jaws to hold this part. Ruger came into the shop and he didn't realize that I had these jaws probably 75 percent completed. But seeing the drawing on my bench, he was upset because he didn't want it done that way. He wanted to design something with adjustable jacks in it. The problem was that we needed this tooling. So I took it upon myself to go ahead and complete what I was doing, against his wishes—something normally not recommended! We then proceeded thereafter to machine the frames from that fixture. I'm not so sure, it may well be the same tools are being used today.

Approximately two years later, Ruger came over from his office and visited in the plant. He and I were walking around looking at various things. When we came to the machine with these vise jaws functioning in machining the parts, he made the remark that, on reflection, "I have to admit, you were right."

---

make wax injection molds. It was all there was available. Now the world is full of machine tools that make this kind of equipment, but in those days it was sort of "every man for himself."

Stan and his wife Carolyn were just kids then, their children were all babies. They were thrilled to come to New Hampshire and found a little house to move into. There was plenty of work to do and the small town environment was perfect for raising a family.

Selling the Single-Six

A master at arousing the curiosity of others,

Ruger hinted in a September 4, 1952, letter to Major General Julian S. Hatcher that "we're now preparing to put a little extension to our facilities; and to add a little news in confidence—on the few occasions when I have discussed the matter, I have received a very favorable reaction to the idea of making the .22 caliber single-action revolver. We are doing a great deal more engineering on this and although it is not 100% settled, I really think we may start tooling soon."

In January, Ruger wrote Jack O'Connor, of *Outdoor Life:*

We are finally on the home stretch toward production of our single-action revolvers and enclose photographs and specifications as a preliminary announcement for whatever news value it has. Although it will be around the end of March before we are able to send a production sample of the gun for your testing and etc., the enclosed photographs show the external appearance of the gun in its final form. There are internal differences, however, which no existing samples have and which cannot be incorporated until certain tooling is completed.

We have put a great deal of thought into this gun with the hope of making it as nearly perfect as a firearm can be. Our idea has been to preserve the style of the older single-action guns and, at the same time, to adapt the design to the latest and most efficient manufacturing methods, and I personally am very gratified with the degree of success that has been attained in this objective.

The selling price will be in the neighborhood of $50.00; the exact amount dependent on the result of some cost studies we have in progress now.

That Ruger had shown a prototype to Major General Hatcher is evident from a letter written the same day as that sent to O'Connor:

At the time of our last meeting I sent you a preliminary model and although we have made subsequent models which look exactly as the production guns will look, we have not yet been able to fabricate any complete samples made entirely from production components. Full production samples will probably be available around March 15th and from these you should be able to obtain a definite idea of the gun's performance and internal design. . . . I look forward to . . . periodic visits with you.

In May, Ruger sent writer and former professional guide Elmer Keith a Single-Six, and wrote that he hoped Keith "might be interested in trying it out and . . . letting us have . . . [your] reaction to it . . . The article you wrote many years ago called 'Six Gun Improvements' was very helpful to me in designing this new gun. . . ." By February 1, 1954, he advised Hatcher that the factory had completed "100 guns of an original pilot run of 175 which were in the assembly run last December. There has been a great deal of trouble in bluing the chrome-molybdenum frames and a large percentage of this original run has had to be kept here for various bluing experiments. [See illustration, page 44, Single-Six serial number 28.] An initial production run of 1,000 guns is now almost entirely through the final polishing operations and bluing has been started." Already Ruger was planning for a new factory:

We really must have a larger plant and will get it as soon as this expansion can be financed without borrowing and without jeopardizing our present very healthy working capital position. Our engineering is months ahead of our production and we have several very exciting new low-cost products completely drawn up. Our Federal Income Taxes are taking about two thirds of our 1953 profit. If it were not for this, we would probably have a new plant already. This may sound as though I am blaming Uncle Sam for the delay in the Single-Six deliveries, but I'll be damned if there isn't a lot of truth in it, and any businessman will agree.

The Blackhawk Single Action

The .22 caliber single-action, while a great success, still wasn't a full-sized "Colt." Demand was high for a more powerful, larger single-action revolver that felt like the Colts that shooters loved. It was decided that the most versatile and useful cartridge for the bigger revolver would be the .357 Magnum, since all the plentiful .38 Special cartridges could also be used in it. Drawing upon

his love for automotive lore, Ruger christened his first centerfire revolver the "Blackhawk," after a favorite Stutz of the same name. By then, the Ruger trademark "hawk" was also black, and the association was a natural.

By the end of January 1955, Ruger had written about his new .357 Magnum Blackhawk to Major General Hatcher, and stated: "I am very pleased personally the way our 'line' of single-action revolvers has shaped up and feel that we have done the right thing in having the smaller frame gun for .22 caliber and the larger frame for the centerfire. A single frame for all calibers results in a .22 that is absurdly heavy." A month later, Ruger sent Jack O'Connor advance information on the Blackhawk, in the form of a single sheet:

A one paragraph news leak would be harmless provided no mention of price and delivery date is made and I believe that *Argosy* is going to run a mention of this kind in their April issue. If you would like to have one of those models for try out I can send you one very shortly or if time is not too much of a problem and you would rather have it that way I will send one of the very first production guns when they come through.

Ruger went on to say:

I am really very anxious to get this Magnum gun started because it seems to be an indispensable addition to our line, and until it has been made a reality I cannot get on with a couple of other projects which I have already begun and which I think [are] equally interesting. You can see from all this that we have a very heavy program, and it is a fortunate thing that I enjoy this work as much as I do, because it would certainly be an exasperating burden in any circumstance.

Ruger vs. Colt

The "Preliminary Announcement" stated that the new gun will undoubtedly be the finest we have ever built, and the two samples which have been completed to production drawings are 100% perfect in every detail of functioning and performance. Each gun was fired with six 50% overload proof cartridges, one in each chamber and the guns handled these "blue pills" as though they were

gallery loads. Mechanically the gun is built to be very similar to the Single-Six and many component parts are common to both guns. The Magnum is of course considerably larger through the cylinder and frame, the cylinder having a diameter which is substantially the same as that of the old Colt Single Action. The hammer is somewhat taller to go with the larger frame. . . . The price is expected to work in the $85.00 range but no definite figure has been reached as we have not yet assembled adequate cost information.

A month later, O'Connor received a three-page letter from Ruger, with the latest information. The steel, frame, and springs warranted special detail:

The frame and cylinder of this new gun will be made of 4140 (chrome-moly) steel; in fact we use chrome-moly quite extensively—it is used for the hammer, loading gate, trigger, and pawl. None of these parts require such good material but it only costs a few mills extra and makes for added prestige. I do not know whether you are acquainted with the mechanism of the Single-Six as compared with that of the Colt and at the risk of being repetitious would like to point out some differences. The most notable is the use of music wire coil spring in the hammer spring, in place of the old flat leaf. This gives us a far more velvety action in that the hammer does not get harder to draw as it is moved toward full cock. Furthermore, all other leaf springs in the original Colt design have been replaced by music wire coil springs. It was the springs which broke in the old Colt and these springs of ours are as near to being unbreakable as any physical structure on this earth. . . . In our revolver everything has been beefed-up considerably—the sear made wider and thicker and the notches of a more rugged contour. The old cylinder bolt (or cylinder latch as we call it) was a particularly delicate component, prone to break even when fitted by an expert. Our cylinder latch is solid, instead of being slotted as the Colt's was and we have been able to make this change because of our patented system of actuating a latch by a spring plunger in the hammer.

These differences have evidently been of practical value as well as theoretical value because our

Ruger Single-Shot XP Pistol prototypes instrumental in evolution of the Single-Six. .22 Hornet, *top*, and .22 Long Rifle. Bill Ruger remembers:

We had our automatic pistol in full production with the plant running very smoothly, so I suppose it's only natural in that position to begin thinking about another world to conquer. One of the thoughts we had at that time was to make a nice little single shot pistol. I got into that quite thoroughly and built a couple of prototypes.

It was a tip-up. In fact it was supposed to be somewhat on the order of the old Stevens. I always had a great affinity for the single shot type. I had thought that I was going to use a single-action type grip on this single shot pistol. Kind of a unique configuration. I don't believe there's ever been a single shot made with that grip, even since then.

In the course of designing that single shot the thought had obviously occurred to me we had many of the components of a single-action revolver . . . the grip and grip frame, the panels, the hammer, the main spring and so on, a trigger, and a barrel. As I looked it all over and reflected, I did say to myself, "Well, it isn't really a great deal more to make it into a revolver." Then, one day, I recall showing this prototype to the buyer from California Wholesale Hardware Company, a firm that was one of our main customers. He seemed to be sort of unenthusiastic and finally said, "You know, if it was a real single-action revolver, then you'd be talking about something that really intrigues us. The single-action is something people really want." The situation at that time was that everybody, including myself, was lamenting the apparent demise of the Colt Peacemaker. After World War II, when Colt announced that they were no longer going to produce that model, everyone began rushing to find a good specimen . . . or even a rough one! The prices began to climb and no one could quite see the logic of Colt's decision . . . but there it was and everyone was absolutely keen to have a single-action.

I realized that in the single shot we had already committed ourselves to building many of the components of a single-action revolver . . . and approaching the whole concept of building a revolver on this basis I had developed a certain conviction that we could, even with our small company, then only about twenty-five people, actually get the tooling together and manage the production so as to produce these guns very reasonably. So that was our first insight and perhaps the most significant early step in actually coming out with the revolver and winding up, as we subsequently did, as a very large manufacturer of them.

Single-Six has now been on the market for over a year and in spite of the fact that many thousands of them are in service we are having [a] negligible number of service calls and virtually never a complaint [of] mechanical functioning . . . the loading gate of the Magnum will be the solid style, thereby obviating one of the few criticisms we have had of the Single-Six (which was flat in contour).

We are at the moment getting ready for our exhibit at the NRA convention next week. Is there any possibility that you will be in the East soon enough to at least take in the last couple of days in Washington? Every shooter and gun crank I have heard of is apparently going to be on hand.

The Importance of Testing

To Judge Don Martin of Salmon, Idaho (another renowned gun experimenter and a friend of Elmer Keith), Ruger was outspoken about the importance of testing and experimenting:

I have been trying to work around into a position which would permit me to do more research with all our guns and also to spend a good deal more time on the engineering end of our affairs. We are very nearly up to that point, having completed a program aimed at increasing our manufacturing capacity, and in the very near future I expect to be down to brass tacks on a great many different mechanical questions. My plan is to research the whole question of revolver accuracy as far as I can, with the general objective of establishing some relationship between performance and the mechanical characteristics of individual guns. So far, we have not been able to establish any very close relationships of that sort. We find that some guns which seem notably inaccurate from the point of view of barrel-cylinder alignment or in other mechanical ways turn in very good groups and then, mysteriously, guns which appear to be perfect do not group as well. There are unquestionably a great many variables involved and it is going to take a considerable amount of work to find out just what is what.

The .44 Magnum Blackhawk

The .357 Ruger Blackhawk proved to be ex-tremely popular, with demand far exceeding supply. Many of the original Colts were made in .44 caliber and interestingly, the brand-new .44 Magnum cartridge was about to revolutionize the sporting application of handguns, particularly for hunting.

Ruger remembers:

Sitting in my little office one day I learned about the existence of a thing called the .44 Magnum. A man came in and he said, "Bill, what do you think of this?" And he had five shells. The headstamp said "REMINGTON UMC-.44 MAG." I was stunned! It was like a .44 Special, but longer—just as the .357 Magnum is longer than a .38. I immediately called a friend at Remington, Gerard Peterson, and inquired. But he would tell me nothing.[2] I think I designed that .44 Magnum pistol without even seeing a fully loaded cartridge.

On the basis of that cartridge casing we were able to make a chamber design drawing. As to the cylinder, it was the same as what we already had in production for the .357. The rest of it was the standard grip frame and grips, and so on. And there it was.

Or so Ruger thought at the time. Pre-production testing later would reveal that it was not *quite* that simple. Ruger continues:

Remington made that .44 Magnum in cooperation with Smith & Wesson. Remington wouldn't talk to me because they had some sort of a promise with Smith & Wesson; a promise which I assumed would be in operation at all times. They fought tooth and nail to keep the .44 Magnum a secret for Smith & Wesson.

Remington wouldn't tell me a damn thing. I got ahold of Dewey Godfrey, their director of marketing, and by this time, he knew goddamn well their silence wasn't going to prevent us from getting into the .44 Magnum business. So, I went up to see him at Remington's offices, which (for some reason I could never understand), were located in the Stratfield Hotel in Bridgeport.

I walked in and there was Dewey Godfrey, this marvelous old Southern gentleman type. He had a big Southern accent and told me to come in, "Set down right there." And then we talked a bit, and I told him some of the things that I had been doing to market our pistols. And of course, the success of our company, by this time, was an industry conversation piece. We had really done what nobody else had done in the arms industry since time began. Since the turn of the century, there'd been no new, successful, gun companies started, and certainly none since the war.

High Standard could be thought of as a solitary exception. You could say they did start, in their own way, in the late 30s. World War II gave them their big manufacturing plant and the resources to extend their product line during the late 40s and early 50s, but you could see that they had already levelled off and were beginning a steady decline. Whereas, at that point, we were just starting, very successfully, and it astonished everyone and thrilled a lot of people besides just us owners.

Godfrey talked about that a little bit, and I told him some of the things I'd been doing. One of them particularly intrigued him and has always fascinated me. I said, I did something none of those guys ever thought of doing, and that was to send out a big mail poll of the leading firearms retailers throughout the country. This nice magazine, *Hardware Age*, had kept lists of that sort, and they handled the mailing for me. My questionnaire for these retailers was very simple and it just said, 'Who is your favorite firearms jobber?' or 'When you buy firearms, who do you like to buy them from?' And that's all I asked—not just our firearms, anybody's firearms. And that was all phrased very clearly.

We got about a 90% return on that poll, and we collated returns very quickly. You could see the size of the market in various states by the number of retailers responding. You know, we learned then about what California represents in comparison to New Hampshire, and New York State in comparison to Texas, and so on—all very interesting. But the big thing is that we were able to take their votes on the various jobbers and make a list in order of popularity. E. K. Tryon in Philadelphia was clearly the world's leading gun jobber in those days. Then there were other great ones, you know, the big wholesalers in the Midwest and so on. So I knew

The Ruger Single-Six Revolver "Old Model"

Number 200001 Lightweight Single-Six Revolver.

Number 28 Single-Six Revolver; note purple color of the blued cylinder frame.

Introduced: 1953, succeeded by New Model, 1973. "The time honored virtues of the single-action revolver are combined with improvements resulting from present day metallurgy and precision manufacture."

Serial Numbers: *Single-Six:* 1 to 196942; D181600 to D182597; 200000 to 212534; in 1959, began at 300000, ran through 499999 with a few skipped blocks of serial numbers in the 300000 range. Mid-year in 1969 serial numbers began with 800000 and ran to 824407. Introduction of prefix in 1969, with 20-00000 to -99999, and 21-00000 to -56105.

Lightweight Single-Six: 200000 to 212534.

Super Single-Six: 500000 to 572012; 60-00000 to -99999; and prefixes similarly numbered to 61-, 62-, 63-, 64-, 65-, 66-, 67-, 68-, 69-, 260-, 261-, 262-.

Single-Six Magnum: 300000 to 824407.

Note: Three size classifications of serial numbering employed:

1st type, from earliest Single-Six, measuring $\frac{1}{16}$" in height.

2nd type, from 1963 (serial range 370000), measuring $\frac{1}{8}$" in height.

3rd type, from February 1969, measuring $\frac{1}{8}$", and using the two or three number prefix system, e.g., 20-00000.

Total Made Through 1972: In excess of 700,000.

Caliber: .22 Short, Long, and Long Rifle; .22 Magnum introduced 1959.

Number of Chambers in Cylinder: Six.

Barrel Lengths: $4\frac{5}{8}$", $5\frac{1}{2}$", $6\frac{1}{2}$", $9\frac{1}{2}$" *Super Single-Six convertible,* $5\frac{1}{2}$", and $6\frac{1}{2}$".

Lightweight Model, $4\frac{5}{8}$".

Magnum Model, $6\frac{1}{2}$" and $9\frac{1}{2}$".

Rifling: 6 grooves, right-hand twist, one turn in 14".

Markings: See Table of Markings, pages 330–35.

Marking on left side of barrel: **INC.** added to marking in October, 1965 (serial range 425000).

On left side of barrel of Magnum revolver, in late production, the trademark and **R** *present.*

Lightweight Model barrel marking (*see below, under Variations*).

Serial numbers *on right side of forward section of frame.*

D marking as prefix or suffix with serial number indicates duplication of number at the factory.

S marking as suffix with serial number indicates use of revolver as a sample or with a surface blemish (Single-Six); found on Lightweight Model, on lower section of frame forward of trigger guard.

* star marking on bottom of frame, forward of trigger guard, indicates single cylinder revolvers.

Sights: Square notch rear sight dovetailed onto top of frame; Super Single-Six models have rear sight adjustable for windage and elevation. Patridge style front sight blade set into muzzle of barrel. $6\frac{1}{8}$" sight radius on $5\frac{1}{2}$" barrel.

Overall Length and Weight: *Standard model:* $10\frac{7}{8}$", 35 ounces ($5\frac{1}{2}$" barrel). *Lightweight model:* 10", 23 ounces ($4\frac{5}{8}$" barrel), 27 ounces (with steel cylinder).

44

Magnum Model: 11⅞", 36 ounces (6½" barrel).

Grips: Checkered hard rubber, with inlaid trademark medallion. Varnished walnut grips with trademark medallion inlay available as an option until 1960, when they became standard. Stag grips with trademark medallion inlays available as factory option from 1953–61; ivory grips with trademark medallion inlays available from 1954–57.

Finish: *Single-Six:* Blued steel; anodized aluminum grip frame.

Lightweight Model: blued steel barrel and ejector assembly. Aluminum alloy frame and cylinder (later option of blued steel cylinder), anodized; black anodized aluminum grip frame.

Note: experimental case color finish on cylinder frame of Single-Six offered in 1953; very rarely encountered.

Materials, Construction, and Innovations: Chrome-molybdenum steel cylinder and frame, one-piece aircraft-quality aluminum alloy grip frame, unbreakable cylinder latch, alloy steel precision frame-mounted firing pin, deep cylinder locking notches, machined steel ejector housing (later replaced by aluminum), non-loosening nylok screws (introduced 1959), all springs made of unbreakable coiled steel music wire, patented locking system, low sighting plane, smooth action, finely polished and finished.

Lightweight Model with investment cast cylinder frame of ALCOA 218 aluminum alloy. Cylinder machined from 7075T6 aluminum alloy stock; the chambers sleeved with steel sub-chambers; then finished in Martin Hard Coat (file-hard and comparable to chrome plating and case-hardened steel).

Issue Price: $57.50 (Single-Six, 1953); $63.25 (Lightweight, 1955); $63.25 (Magnum, 1959).

Engraving: 20 Single-Six revolvers initially engraved in Spain (nos. 5100 to 5119). Charles H. Jerred embellished Single-Six revolvers, dating from c. 1954 to 1958, during which time he engraved approximately 238. These revolvers fitted with varnished walnut grips. Revolvers were sold in single cases, or as cased pairs (catalogue code numbers **RSSE** and **RSSEC**).

Price Sheet Listings (adopted over the period c. 1957 through c. 1961): **RSS:** 5½" barrel, first model Single-Six offered.

RSS4R: 4⅝", hard rubber grips.
RSS5R: 5½", hard rubber grips.
RSSMR: 6½", hard rubber grips.
RSS4W: 4⅝", walnut grips.
RSS5W: 5½", walnut grips.
RSSMW: 6½", walnut grips.
RSS9R: 9½", hard rubber grips.
RSS9W: 9½", walnut grips.
RSSE: 5½", engraved, walnut grips, cased.
RSSEC: engraved, cased pair, consecutive serial numbers.
RSSMX: 6½", .22 WMR, extra .22L.R. cylinder.
RSS4X: 4⅝" barrel, with extra .22WMR cylinder.
RSS5X: 5½" barrel, with extra .22WMR cylinder.

RSS9X: 9½" barrel, with extra .22WMR cylinder.
LWAC: Lightweight, with aluminum frame and cylinder, 4⅝".
LWSC: Lightweight, with aluminum frame and steel cylinder, 4⅝".

Listings adopted in 1965 Price Sheet:
Super Single-Six Convertible
SC-5: 5½", with .22 WMR cylinder, adjustable rear sight, ramp front sight.
SC-6: as above, with 6½" barrel.

Major Production Variations:

Pre-Production: Some early Single-Six revolvers serial numbered with **X, A, B, C,** and other alphabet letters. Flat configuration for loading gate; early cylinders with rounded terminus to flutes, as compared with standard tapered flutes on later revolvers; grip frames of two-piece construction; flat mainsprings; checkered wood grips. Square front sight of target type. Marking on top of barrel.

Catalogue code: **RSS.**

1st Variation: Flatgate Model, 5½" barrel, round profile front sight, small and square ejector rod thumbpiece, steel ejector housing; thin trigger, with noticeable curve; blued and anodized finish.

2nd Variation: same as above, but with 2nd type ejector housing.

3rd Variation: made with larger rounded style ejector housing (about 61,000 made from 1953 to early 1957). Last model with flat loading gates.

4th Variation: contoured loading gates; new barrel lengths added of 4⅝" and 9½". Gradual change in ejector rod housing, trigger, and ejector rod thumbpiece.

5th Variation: straight rod ejector housing gradually comes into production (known as Type 3). Flat-faced ejector rod thumbpiece. Convertible (extra cylinder) models introduced.

Changes of 1962: Aluminum ejector rod housing; increase in serial number size; redesigned XR3-RED grip frame; oil-finished walnut grips. 1963 was the final year of ALCOA as subcontractor for the grip frames. The new contractor was Dohler-Jarvis. XR3-RED grip frame began in serial ranges 342000, 196000, and 244000.

D-Stamped Duplicates: noticeable block with serial range 500000D to 505140D.

Single-Six in .22 Magnum: Catalogue code RSSM, began to appear in the serial range 173400; rifling changed to accommodate the new cartridge. Eight experimental revolvers made in the serial range 110600 and 113600, with **X** prefix. Production models began to be shipped late in 1959, with advertisements indicating 6½" and 9½" barrels. Revolvers further distinguished by details of bore, frame marking, and cylinder chambering. Assigned serial range in production beginning with 300000, and continuing through 342450; thereafter frames

made without magnum markings, through serial 344019. The CONVERTIBLE SINGLE-SIX, code RSSMX, appeared at serial range 318800; the last three digits of serial number marked on front of the extra cylinder. Another catalogue code was RSSMW.

Super Single-Six: Introduced November 1964, distinguished by its integral sight rib frame, ramp style front sight, .22 L.R./.22 WMR chamberings, XR3-RED grip frame, aluminum rear sight, and aluminum ejector rod housing. Discontinued 1972.

4⅝" Barrel Model: Barrels shortened from 5½". Only approx. 200 made, March 1965.

Nickel-Plated 6½" (with and without extra cylinder): Only 100 made. The plating had been applied to cylinder frames which could not be properly blued. From August 1965, and July 1968.

Lightweight Variation: Experimented with in 1954–55, and production shipments began in December 1955. Catalogue code LWAC. Top of barrel marked:

STURM, RUGER & CO.,
SOUTHPORT, CONN. U.S.A.

XR-3 pattern grip frame. Type 2 offset ejector rod housing.

1st Variation, the "Tri-Color" or "Two-Tone": silver-gray anodized color frame; reddish-brown cylinder; flat loading gate, small Type 1 ejector rod thumbpiece, thin trigger, with noticeable curve.

2nd Variation, Transition Model: as above, except with contoured loading gate, larger round and concave-faced ejector rod thumbpiece (serial range about 204500 to 206000, with overlapping to preceding and succeeding variations).

3rd Variation: as above, except with blue-black anodized color frame, and anodized finish on cylinder to match blue and blue-black color on balance of revolver.

4th Variation: as above, except with blued steel cylinder. Began in serial range 205500. Catalogue code LWSC.

5th Variation: within serial range 200000 to 205000, and stamped **S** following serial number, or on bottom of frame forward of trigger guard. Built from silver-color frames (August 1964, April 1965). Approximately 226 made, and had minor surface finish irregularities of white splotches on frames, from the anodizing process.

S-Marked Lightweights: 242 revolvers assembled in August 1964, with XR3-RED grip frames, and oil-finished walnut grips, aluminum ejector rod housings, contoured loading gates, large round ejector thumbpiece, steel cylinder, with **S** marking after the serial number (denoting "surface blemishes"). 26 additional like revolvers assembled, April 1965, but with the **S** marking on bottom of the frame, forward of the trigger guard. Curiously, some of the total of 268 arms had flat loading gates, square ejector thumbpieces, thin curved triggers, steel ejector rod housings or XR3 grip frames with black hard rubber grips.

The Ruger Blackhawk Single-Action Revolver "Old Model"

Number 1 Blackhawk Revolver.

Exploded view of Blackhawk Revolver.

Number 100000 Blackhawk Revolver.

Introduced: 1955, succeeded by New Model, 1973. "In the design and production of the . . . Blackhawk, it has been our intention to exceed the expectation of the enthusiasts who want revolvers of this caliber. The specialized design of this gun, its handsome appearance, and its fine finish will certainly be admired by every experienced user of firearms."

Serial Numbers: *.357 Magnum or 9mm:* 1 to 108764; introduction of prefix in 1969, 30-00000 to -99999; and similarly numbered prefix 31-00000 to -45190.

.41 Magnum: 1 to 15967; 40-00000 to 40-22906.

.44 Magnum: 1 to 29860.

.45 Colt or .45ACP: 45-00000 to 45-23031.

.30 U.S. Carbine: 1 to 9304; 50-00000 to -23700.

Total Made Through 1972: In excess of 300,000.

Calibers: Introduced in .357 Magnum (.38 Special interchangeable); later calibers of .30 Carbine, 9mm, .41 Magnum, .44 Magnum (and .44 Special, .44 Russian), .45 Long Colt, .45ACP.

Number of Chambers in Cylinder: Six.

Barrel Lengths: Introduced in 4⅝"; subsequent lengths of 6½", 7½", 10", varying by caliber.

Rifling: .357 Magnum and .45 Long Colt: 6 grooves, right-hand twist, one turn in 16".

.30 Carbine, .41 and .44 Magnum: 6 grooves, right-hand twist, one turn in 20".

Markings: See Table of Markings, pages 330–35.

On left side of barrel:

STURM, RUGER & CO.
SOUTHPORT, CONN. U.S.A.

on early revolvers, until August 1963, at which time marking changed to:

STURM, RUGER & CO., INC.
SOUTHPORT, CONN. U.S.A.

On left side of frame:

Serial number on right side of frame, above trigger guard; note evolution of digit height difference, from 1/16" to 1/8" (at approximately serial range 51000 of the .357 Magnum revolvers), followed by the prefix system, which remained at 1/8" height.

D serial prefix indicates duplicate number.

S marking after serial number, indicating show gun or sample, sold with minor surface wear or marks; abbreviation for "surface blemishes."

S marking on cylinder serves as proof marking.

Sights: Micro rear, click adjustable for windage and elevation. Baughman style ramp front blade, approximately 1/8" wide. Some variation in sights will be noted, including a group of approximately 25,000 purchased from Micro, which had been originally made for the Colt company. 10,000 of these were used on the .357 Blackhawk (August 1963). Sight material changed from steel to aluminum, in 1963, and Ruger's own sights succeeded the Micro on Blackhawks at that time.

Overall Length and Weight: 10½", 2 pounds 6 ounces (4⅝" barrel, .357 Magnum).

Grips: Black butaprene-rubber, checkered, with trademark medallion insert; used through 1960. American walnut, stag or ivory grips available at extra cost (only for pre-1962 XR-3 grip frame); walnut became a standard grip from c. 1960, with trademark insert. Variation noted in these walnut panel contours, particularly in area of trademark, and slight variations have been observed in the medallion inlay (with or without neck feathers or SR monogram).

Finish: Blued; black anodized grip frame.

Materials, Construction, and Innovations: Chrome-molybdenum steel; one-piece aluminum alloy grip frame, rather than conventional Colt Single Action backstrap and trigger guard strap. Unbreakable steel music wire coil springs; frame-mounted firing pin; thick and wide topstrap for frame strength; non-loosening nylok screws used throughout.

Cylinder frames for the .357 somewhat smaller than those for the other caliber Blackhawks.

Flattop frame changed late 1962 by addition of the patented integral frame ribs at rear sight area.

Blued steel ejector rod housings informally known as Types 2 (slot offset and allows for increased ejector stroke over housing used on Single-Six) and 3 (straight slot; introduced 1963). Type 4 (of anodized aluminum) introduced 1963, and has straight slot. Ejector rod thumbpieces of Types 1 (small and square, with serrations; used through mid-1956), 2 (concave faced, through 1958), and 3 (flat-faced).

XR-3 marked grip frame used through late 1962; succeeded by re-designed XR-3RED grip frame, in use through 1972. Some few grip frames of both XR-3 and XR-3RED finished in a gold-toned anodize.

Issue Price: $87.50 (1955).

Engraving: Engraved by Charles H. Jerred, for the factory, serial numbers 100 and 3203 of the .357, and numbers 225, 500, 60, 1967, 2165, and 7498 of the .44 Magnum.

Price Sheet Listings (introduced c. 1957–73):

.357 Magnum (and 9mm):

BKH-3: 4⅝" barrel, hard rubber grips, first listing.

BKH-34: above revolver, revised code, walnut grips (from 1959).

BKH-34X: 4⅝", walnut grips, with extra 9mm cylinder (from 1967).

BKH-36: 6½", walnut grips (from 1959).

BKH-36X: 6½", walnut grips, with extra 9mm cylinder (from 1967).

BKH-30: 10" barrel, walnut grips (from 1959).

.41 Magnum:

BKH-41: 4⅝", walnut grips (from 1965).

BKH-42: 6½", walnut grips (from 1965).

BKH-41B: as above, but brass grip frame.

BKH-42B: as above, but brass grip frame.

.44 Magnum:

BKH-4: 6½" barrel, walnut grips, first listing 1956 (codes introduced in 1959 Price Sheet).

BKH-46: 6½", walnut grips.

BKH-47: 7½", walnut grips.

BKH-40: 10" barrel, walnut grips.

.45 Colt (and .45ACP):

BKH-44: 4⅝" (from 1971).

BKH-44B: as above, but brass grip frame.

BKH-44X: 4⅝", with .45ACP extra cylinder (from 1971).

BKH-45: 7½" (from 1971).

BKH-45B: as above, bur brass grip frame.

BKH-45X: 7½", with .45ACP extra cylinder (from 1971).

.30 Carbine:

BKH-31: 7½" (from 1968; not available with brass grip frame).

Major Production Variations:

.357 Magnum:

From number 1 through 42689 had "flattop" frame; frame changed to "protected sight" variation thereafter (1962). Rare group of case-hardened frame revolvers (serial numbers 5784 to 5791). Approximately 1,000 10" revolvers built in the 18000 to 30000 and 36000 to 37000 serial ranges. Of the first 1,600 .357s, the majority of numbers under 100 were not built and shipped until 1957, and thus exhibit features of four years after introduction of the Blackhawk. Approximately 760 Type 1 revolvers (in 14000 and 15000 serial range) assembled, in 1956 (preceding their serial range by two years).

1st Variation: hard rubber grips, 4⅝" barrel, 6-groove rifling, narrow front sight base (and wavy line matte finish), Type 2 ejector rod housing, Type 1 ejector rod thumbpiece, narrow groove cylinder pin.

2nd Variation: same as above, but with barrel lengths added of 6½" and 10"; Type 2 ejector rod thumbpiece, wide base front sight, wide groove cylinder pin.

3rd Variation: as above, but with Type 3 ejector rod housing. Walnut grip panels gradually become standard by 23000 to 25000 serial range.

4th Variation: as above, but with Type 3 ejector rod thumbpieces, 8-groove barrel.

.44 Magnum:

1st and 2nd Variations: 1st with XR-3 grip frame, hard rubber or walnut grips, Type 2 ejector housing, 6½" barrel, and Type 1 ejector thumbpiece. 2nd variation with Type 2 ejector thumbpiece.

3rd Variation: as above, but with walnut grips, Type 2 ejector housing, larger Type 3 ejector rod thumbpiece, and collared head to cylinder pin. Serial range of approximately 9000 to 16000.

4th, 5th, and 6th Variations: as above, but with Type 3 ejector rod housing, and in 6½", 7½", or 10" barrel lengths (6½" length by far the most common). Serials from about 16000 to 29660. Model discontinued 1963.

Note: Numbers 5000 and 5001 fitted with 15" barrels.

Brass Grip Frame: Available as an option, 1965–72. Majority built on Blackhawks date from September to December 1972. Total of about 4,290 factory-built revolvers with brass grip frames; these parts do not fit New Model revolvers, and are found only on Blackhawk "Old Models" in .357 Magnum, .41 Magnum, .44 Magnum, and .45 Long Colt calibers.

who the top jobbers in America were, right down to that part of the list at the bottom where the votes were just onesies and twosies. When I told Dewey about this, he said to me, "You did that? What a triumph you are!" He couldn't wait to get some answers, and he asked me a few more questions and said, "Yep, that's right. That's the way it is, Bill." He may have done all this, you know, by the seat of his pants.

He knew this information, but then that I knew, too. So, I said, "Well what about some of the same ammunition, Dewey?" He said, "Now, Bill, just take it easy 'cause when you leave, you just take that paper bag with you and just walk on out." It was full of loaded .44 Magnum ammunition!

So, I guess that way he excused himself from our friends up the river.

Elmer Keith and the .44 Magnum

Maintaining the momentum, Ruger wrote author, hunter, and experimenter, Elmer Keith, in January 1956:

We are now preparing to produce our Blackhawk in .44 caliber and it will be the .44 Magnum which I presume you are acquainted with. I am still in the process of gathering data regarding the cartridge itself and on the strength of what I now know it seems to me that the external dimension of our Blackhawk as made for the .357 will be o.k. for the .44 Magnum. . . . I have already ordered barrel blanks and am planning to use .429" to .431" groove diameter and .416" to .418" bore diameter. The rate of twist has me a little bit up in the air and while we are going to try one turn in twenty inches it may be that one in sixteen or eighteen will be better. . . . Incidentally, I should imagine that you would be very happy about this new caliber and I am pretty sure that it will be very popular and that it will vindicate the position you have taken on the subject of .44s. We are also working on some interesting Single Shot pistols which I will show you in Washington—maybe sooner if they are ready.

In the February issue of the *Rifleman* we will run our announcement of our engraved Single-Six revolvers and in April the *Rifleman* will carry the announcement of the new aluminum version of the Single-Six. . . . I personally believe it is the most in-

Ruger describes designing of the Ruger "Baby Nambu" Pistol, seen here for the first time:

Back in the Station Street days, I did a lot of work on a beautiful little pistol that was a copy of the Japanese Baby Nambu, a staff officer's pistol. From two Baby Nambus in my own collection, I derived a design in .22 caliber, which was almost exactly like the original 7mm. It was a nice little pistol. Two prototypes were made in our tool room by Rex King, a master toolmaker of real skill and ingenuity. It was the second of these that was really much more thought out. I never fired either of these personally. But I did lend one to our patent attorney, Hal Seagraves. And he said, "I like that little pistol. I fired it, and fired it, and fired it, and fired it. I never had a jam or malfunction."

How's that!—from the tool room to a completely outside-of-the-company shooter without ever malfunctioning, and never even tested by anybody in the company! It worked perfectly.

I think really in those days, I was a little bit of a wimp, in the sense that I was so anxious not to have any guns in the line that would be accused of being "concealable." And this is a pretty small gun. You might call it a "pocketbook" size. On top of that, it had quite a complicated little receiver. Everything that was designed was in that frame piece. I suppose that might have been made as a casting, although I don't believe we even dreamed of having our own foundry in those days. Who knows what might have happened if we had it to do over again?

teresting gun we make and that it will be our most popular model. We have done an enormous amount of testing and find that the durability and safety of the gun is equal to that of our steel Single-Six.

Writing to author Charles Askins in February, Ruger dealt with the challenge of the .44 Magnum:

> Producing this gun is going to involve a great deal more than simply reaming out our present Blackhawk, and to do the job the way we want to do it will involve virtually complete redesign and retooling. We have three .44 Magnum revolvers at hand which have been based on the use of Blackhawk components, these being guns which we put together in a hurry to gather a little experience with the cartridge. In external appearance they are probably indistinguishable from the .44 as we will ultimately make it, but nevertheless I cannot say that at this moment these initial samples can be photographed as accurate representations of the production guns. Our plans are developing on a daily basis and should be frozen in another couple of weeks and by that time we may know definitely what the production guns will look like.
>
> So far we have been unable to obtain proof loads and, of course, this is a considerable nuisance when you are trying to develop a new product.... Our production cylinders will be somewhat larger and longer in diameter.... The sudden appearance of this caliber has come as sort of a challenge to us and the whole crowd here is enthused with the opportunity to produce a really sensational firearm.

A few days later, Ruger told Elmer Keith that, "After making a couple of revolvers in .44 Magnum caliber we decided [that although] a new frame and larger and longer cylinders will take us longer to produce, there is no doubt that this is the proper way to proceed. Our new cylinder will be .053" larger in diameter and ⅛" longer."

At the end of June, Ruger advised Keith that "our first lot of twelve hundred .44 Magnum frames [is] well into the works and [the factory is

expected] to be assembling finished guns before the end of August. However, we are processing a dozen guns on a rush basis in order to be able to have a batch available for distribution to gun writers on the various magazines and I hope to send you a gun to keep before the end of July. . . . Someday, maybe we will bring out this .44 Magnum with a grip like the old Colt Dragoon model, wide trigger and Bisley hammer, but until we have more plant space such variations cause road blocks in the production line."

To the *Rifleman*'s Technical Editor, M. D. "Bud" Waite, Ruger described the effect of .44 Magnum test revolvers on their machine rest equipment:

> We have never been able to run machine rest groups with the .44 Magnum because the recoil is too great for our Potter rest. We did, in fact, try it but could not get definitive results and after very few shots, cracked the aluminum carriage casting of the Potter rest. However, we are well satisfied as to accuracy on the basis of our offhand shooting and to illustrate what I mean, I am enclosing a couple of targets shot by Herb Glass. We will, ultimately, have to design a machine rest which will handle the .44 Magnum but up to the present time have been unable to make a start on that project.
>
> In our new .44 as well as our original .357 Blackhawk, we fire a full cylinder of proof loads in every gun. We obtain our proof ammunition from Remington but I know exactly what pressures it is supposed to develop. I have only been able to obtain the pressure of the service loads via a grapevine and this information, which I am sure is reliable, states that the service loads develop approximately 36,000 pounds per square inch, so presumably the proof cartridges are in the neighborhood of 50,000 pounds.

The following October, Ruger wrote to Keith, reporting that the .44 Magnum performance "has been uniformly marvelous and I am delighted with the status of the program as it now stands. . . . I have never been busier and it seems impossible to keep abreast of the work here. We have recently acquired a new Sales Manager and that is

going to make a great deal of difference. His name is Ed Nolan—I am sure he will do a great deal for us, as he did for Winchester until he left them to come down to Sturm, Ruger & Company. . . ."

The Bearcat

In June of 1958, Ruger proudly wrote to second-generation gun writer Charles Askins, Jr., about "our latest development—our Bearcat model which is now going into production and which will be announced during the last week of July."

> We have worked on this gun for almost a year and it goes into production with detailed refinements both as to the mechanism and external appearance, which we think will make it rate as a little jewel among American handguns. As you can see, it represents the "kit gun"[3] idea applied to a single-action. The integral one piece frame, with only the trigger guard detachable, is of course reminiscent of the old Remington revolvers and after a good deal of study and tool development, we found that this consideration was the key to a considerable saving in production costs. Hence the price of $49.50, although the gun has the looks and mechanical quality of something in the $60.00 bracket.[1958 prices]
>
> I am sorry that we do not have a sample to send to you immediately, but in view of our rush for actual production, we have assembled just one specimen to check our drawings and for photography. . . . Ever since coming back from Africa, I have been busy with this project—it seems that there have been thousands of details. I hate to think of what a shotgun would involve, but some day soon we may take a serious look at that idea. After all, the bigger the job, the more interesting it is.

Ruger's shotgun idea would surface again, two decades later.

The New Factory and the Super Blackhawk

On February 1, 1959, the *Westport Town Crier* announced, "Sturm, Ruger, Gun Maker, Move to

The Ruger Bearcat Single-Action Revolver

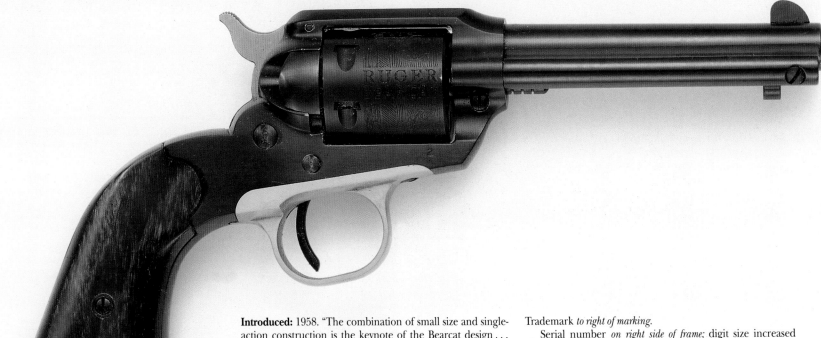

Numbers 2 and 91-00001 Bearcat Revolver.

Introduced: 1958. "The combination of small size and single-action construction is the keynote of the Bearcat design . . . No other handgun possesses the characteristics which give the 'Bearcat' its special utility and appeal . . . a jewel among firearms."

The steel frame "Super Bearcat," listed as available May 1971. "Compact single-action revolver that sportsmen find ideal on hunting and fishing trips. Reliable, accurate and handsome."

Serial Numbers: 1-999; A001 to A999; B001 to B999, etc. (using all letters of the alphabet as prefix except O), through Z999. Numbering resumed at 1000 to 114730. From 1969, 90-00000 to -25622 (end of aluminum frame).

Super Bearcat serial numbers began in 1971, from 91-00000 to -64417.

Total Made Through 1973: Approximately 229,769.
Note: New Bearcat introduced 1993.

Calibers: .22 Short, Long, and Long Rifle.
Number of Chambers in Cylinder: 6, non-fluted cylinder.
Barrel Length: 4$\frac{1}{16}$".
Rifling: 6 grooves, right-hand twist, one turn in 14".
Markings: See Table of Markings, pages 330–35.
On left side of barrel:

STURM, RUGER & CO.
SOUTHPORT, CONN.

Trademark *to right of marking.*

Serial number *on right side of frame;* digit size increased from $\frac{1}{16}$" to $\frac{1}{8}$" (serial range 35000).
Sights: Fixed, open.
Overall Length and Weight: 8$\frac{13}{16}$", 17 ounces.
Grips: Two-piece plastic impregnated; changed to oil-finished walnut, with trademark medallion inlay (serial range approx. 30000).
Finish: Anodized aluminum frame, steel parts blued; aluminum trigger guard anodized in a brass finish. Super Bearcat with steel frame, blued rather than anodized.
Materials, Construction, and Innovations: Frame and action more similar to Remington than Colt single-action revolvers. One-piece grip frame and cylinder of aluminum alloy. Super Bearcat frame of investment cast chrome-molybdenum steel.

Roll engraved cylinder. Ejector rod housing changed to aluminum alloy in 1963. Detachable trigger guard made of brass-colored anodized aluminum, later changed to black. Finally changed to blued steel on last Super Bearcats.
Issue Price: $49.50 (1958).
Engraving: Cylinder roll engraved with a bear and cougar motif, and the legend RUGER/BEARCAT. One hand engraved revolver built, serial number 43813.
Price Sheet Listings and Major Production Variations:
Bearcat: **BC-4**

50

Super Bearcat: SBC-4

1st Variation: serial range 1 to 999; 4" barrel, steel ejector housing, impregnated walnut grips, anodized aluminum frame, roll engraved cylinder, brass-finished trigger guard.

2nd Variation: as above, but with serial number preceded by a letter of the alphabet (known as "Alphabet" guns).

3rd Variation: as above, but in serial range 2000 to 30000.

4th Variation: as above, but with blue-finished (anodized) trigger guard; date from c. 1966.

5th Variation: grips changed to oil-finished walnut, with trademark medallion inlay.

6th Variation: ejector housing changed to anodized aluminum.

Note: Last of the aluminum frame series bore serial number 90-25622.

D Bearcat: Duplicate serial series, marked with D suffixes: 80000D to 80265D, and 97960D to 98325D.

Super Bearcat: Blued steel frames, approximately half of production having gold-tone anodized aluminum trigger guard, and the balance with blued steel guard. Ejector rod housing of anodized aluminum. Serial numbers 91-00000 to -64417.

Exploded view of Bearcat Revolver.

The Ruger Super Blackhawk Revolver "Old Model"

Number 2 Super Blackhawk Revolver.

Introduced: 1959. "A masterpiece of power and precision . . . represents a logical advance in the construction of high-powered single-action revolvers. . . . The shape, size and mechanical design of this magnificent firearm have been perfected with the object of taking full advantage of the power of the .44 Magnum cartridge and the result is a sporting and defensive weapon of capabilities that have never previously been possible in a handgun."

Serial Numbers: 1 to 40916; 80-00000 to -64750.

Total Made Through 1972: In excess of 96,000.

Calibers: .44 Remington Magnum (.44 S & W Special interchangeable).

Number of Chambers in Cylinder: 6 non-fluted cylinder.

Barrel Length: 7½".

Rifling: 6 grooves, right-hand twist, one turn in 20".

Number 2 Super Blackhawk Revolver.

Markings: See Table of Markings, pages 330–35.
On left side of barrel:

STURM, RUGER & CO.
SOUTHPORT, CONN. U.S.A.

on early revolvers, until August 1963, at which time marking changed to:

STURM, RUGER & CO., INC.
SOUTHPORT, CONN. U.S.A.

On left side of frame:

RUGER *SUPER BLACKHAWK*
.44 MAGNUM CAL.

Serial number on *right side of frame, above trigger guard.*
Sights: Micro open square notch rear sight, click adjustable for windage and elevation. Baughman style ⅛″ front sight blade, on ramp mount.
Overall Length and Weight: 13¼″, 49 ounces.
Grips: American walnut with distinctive grain, and trademark insert. Varnished through 1962, and oil-finished thereafter.

Letter **C** stamped on back of first imported grip panels, slightly longer than later production (c. 1959–60). Popularly known as "Long Dragoon" grip panels.
Finish: High polish blue; sides of hammer polished bright.
Materials, Construction, and Innovations: Differentiated from the standard .44 Blackhawk as follows: integral sight rib on top of rear of frame, steel "Dragoon" style grip frame (with squareback trigger guard), non-fluted cylinder, wide spur target hammer, and wide serrated trigger.
Issue Price: $120 (1959), including cloth-lined mahogany case for the first 4,000 revolvers (discontinued 1961).
Engraving: Serial numbers 1806 and 4806 engraved for the factory by Charles H. Jerred.
Price Sheet Listings and Major Production Variations:
  S47: first code used, 1959 Price Sheets, 7½″ barrel.
  S47B: second code, added 1965–67 Price Sheets only, with brass grip frame.
  Standard Frame: (with or without mahogany case).

Long Frame: (with or without mahogany case).
  Approximately 300 to 500 early revolvers fitted with ³⁄₁₆″ longer grip frames and with larger profile at lower section; usually found within the first 700 revolvers produced. Grip frames marked with part number MR-3D. Within range of approximately 196 to 3111.
  Barrel Without Trademark Marking.
  Barrel with Trademark Marking.
  Brass Grip Frames: Available from the factory as an option, from c. 1965–67, 1971–72. Some "Old Model" Super Blackhawks built with brass grip frames (24000 serial range).
  6½″ Barrel Variations: A limited number of 6½″ barrel early revolvers produced (**S46**, not used in Catalogue or Price Sheets), within the serial number range approximately 24000 to 26000.

$250,000 Building" and stated, "This past Thursday the firm officially marked its move into its new $250,000 building on Lacey Place, Southport, by holding open house for its customers from all across the country, with more than 100 attending, including a dealer from California,

one from Chicago and others from cities along the Atlantic seaboard. In addition there were gun editors and outdoor writers from national publications."

On the verge of moving into the new factory at Lacey Place, Ruger wrote to Elmer Keith:

We are about to move into our new factory building and, of course, we are all very much preoccupied with the problem of transferring our operations without undue production delays. Our new plant has been custom built for our operations and will be completely and perfectly equipped practically regardless of cost to provide everything for precision manufacture and super quality products. It will be a small plant compared to the old-timers in the industry, but much more efficient and will give us double the floor space we have now so that we have every prospect of making more and better firearms.

In June, Ruger advised Keith of a trip:

. . . to Europe where [I] canvassed the firearms industry pretty thoroughly. My purpose was to see if they could make gun parts more advantageously than we can and also to pick up information if possible. I went through several of the big plants and I am convinced now that our methods and standards are probably better than anyone, anywhere, and taken in the aggregate.

We are sending today . . . a prototype of the "Super Blackhawk" showing it as it is to be built in production and I think you will like it tremendously. . . . You will note that the grip on this new sample is a little different and in my opinion a little better than the one on the first sample we sent to you; in any event, I think it looks considerably better. . . . We expect to price the new "Super Blackhawk" very moderately . . . [and] there is a definite limit as to how many of these big steel grip frames we can make. . . .

The Super Blackhawk, the first product of the new factory, was quite unlike any previous revolver. It answered the criticisms that some had leveled at the original .44 Magnum Blackhawk (that it "kicked too much" and was unpleasant to shoot) in exemplary fashion. An all-steel longer squarebacked trigger guard grip frame, unfluted

cylinder, longer barrel, and frame reinforcement around the adjustable rear sight went a long way toward taming the powerful .44 cartridge. Resembling the huge pre-Civil War Second Model Colt Dragoon revolvers it seemed an answer to many shooters' prayers, including those of Elmer Keith, then the dean of American revolver students and practitioners:

The "Dragoon" Ruger arrived. My hat is off to you. This is just about what I have wanted and worked for 40 years now in a single-action and is by far the finest single-action sixgun ever produced to my way of thinking. It embodies all my ideas of what such a gun should be for the cow puncher, hunter guide or old hill billy. . . . It's the culmination of a lifetime of dreams for me. . . . I tried to get Colt to bring out such a gun as this for over 30 years with no luck at all, 'simply could be no improvement over their old 1872 model' they thought; now we will show them what a single-action should be and what they could have done years ago, only they did not have the gray matter of one Bill Ruger. . . .

TO PRESIDENT JIMMY CARTER
WITH BEST REGARDS FROM
BILL RUGER
January 1981

TO FRITZ MONDALE
FROM YOUR FRIEND
JIMMY CARTER
JANUARY 1981

"The Risks of Competition"

On Safari in Africa and the Newport Factory
1958–1967

Geerge and Joy Adamson, soon to be famous in America for their conservation work with lions and featured in the best-selling book and equally popular motion picture Born Free, are at home in Isiolo, Kenya, hosting Bill Ruger, friend George Rowbottom, and professional hunters Tony Henley and Glen Cottar. The date is February 1958, and the hunting party is taking some time off in the midst of a six-week safari, relaxing from the strenuous regime of stalking game, moving campsites, and dealing with the tropical sun, heat, and humidity.

They had already stopped for a respite at actor William Holden's Mt. Kenya Safari Club, on the way to seeing the Adamsons. Ruger and Adamson, a for-

---

The Newport, New Hampshire, factory, from 1963 to date. At *center*, the main building in early years of development; *beneath*, complex with most recent addition sketched in. To *left* of wax injection machine (*top right*), 20-year service guns being presented by Plant Manager Al Scribner and Stan Terhune, by then Pine Tree Castings Vice President. Controller and Vice President Erle Blanchard presents shotgun at *left center*. I.D. badges are of retired employees, as of December 1994. Bill Lett, Sr. (green jacket), on deer hunting trip, at *bottom left*. At *bottom center*, George Hamilton and Stan Terhune, with some family members, enjoying the New Hampshire sunshine. Shotguns inscribed to President Carter and Vice President Mondale in January 1981, at *bottom right*, were manufactured in Newport.

6. 1960
.44 Magnum Carbine
7. 1963
Hawkeye
Single-Shot Pistol
8. 1964
10/22 Carbine
9. 1966
No. 1 and No. 3
Single-Shot Rifles

mer professional hunter, became friends, and Ruger bought some of Adamson's sporting rifles.

Another hunting party is there as well, and the two groups trade stories ranging from the African veldt to fresh news from New York. In the other safari group is a widely experienced hunter and champion marksman, destined to figure with increasing prominence in the fortunes of Sturm, Ruger & Co. The redoubtable Charles Askins, Jr., is on his first Kenya safari—and is now about to meet William B. Ruger. Askins remembers, as quoted from his autobiography, Unrepentant Sinner:

In Isiolo was George Adamson and his Austrian wife, Joy. They had captured a lioness, as a wee cub, and had named her Elsa. George was the game warden for the Northern Frontier and was a most pleasant person. He and [my hunter Tony Dyer] were quite friendly. . . . While at the Adamson quarters [we met] another safari party. The white hunter was Glen Cottar, grandson of the famous Bwana Cottar. Of more importance one of the clients was Bill Ruger. It was my first meeting with this remarkable man. Bill these days suffers from arthritis and his hunting is severely curtailed but this was 25 years ago and he was as hale and hearty as any man in the group. He had with him a personable cuss named Rowbottom.

They were on a [45] day safari and were in camp about 30 miles from our camp site. Their successes had been quite as good as our own and maybe better for Bill had taken a good lion. That chance meeting was the first of many since. Bill has a fabulous place above his plant in Newport [New Hampshire], and like an old feudal lord he holds forth in truly baronial splendor. To be invited there is a royal treat.

Ho! Get to lair! The sun's aflare
Behind the breathing grass:
And creaking through the young bamboo
The warning whispers pass.
By day made strange, the woods we range
With blinking eyes we scan;
While down the skies the wild duck cries:
"The Day—the Day to Man!"

—Rudyard Kipling,
"Morning Song in the Jungle"

From time to time Ruger would leave the Southport factory for some much needed rest and relaxation, and this often was timed to coincide with the hunting season. In the early 1950s, he made an important trip across the country, particularly to the West, Midwest, and Southwest, visiting jobbers, writers, and shooters, and showing off samples of the Single-Six and Blackhawk revolvers. To a great extent these trips helped crystallize Ruger's understanding of his market, strengthening his contacts with his customer base.

His hunting experiences through the late 1960s were the subject of correspondence with writer Clyde Ormond (August 6, 1969):

My first hunting began in 1927 when I was twelve years old, and received a Remington pump-action .22 as a reward for recovering from scarlet fever. I became a menace to squirrels, crows, and woodchucks on eastern Long Island.

When I was fourteen or fifteen, I became pretty good at killing woodchucks with a Springfield army rifle. However, I really didn't do much hunting until the postwar period. Until then, I was always in school during hunting season or involved with firearms design and development.

Since 1950, I have hunted in northern Quebec, this being the country of big lakes, canoes, and moose. For many years, we always had a gang together for deer hunting in Maine—this was typical Maine northwoods still hunting out of a very remote camp at King and Bartlett Lake.

I have had two very fine safaris, the first in Kenya, the second in Uganda, before the British left. In Kenya we hunted in the south on the Mara escarpment and Loita hills, and in the north along the Tana. In Uganda we have hunted the plains country, south and west of Mt. Debasien. This was the locale of W.D.M. Bell's *Karamojo Safari*. We also hunted without benefit of Land Rovers, along the south Uganda shore of Lake Albert, having traveled with our gear and safari boys in a chartered launch. On the same safari, we also had a fine camp in the Semliki Valley, south of Lake Albert. This was at a time when the valley was populated with thousands of kob [antelope], buffalo, and elephant.

I have also had a few trips in the Rockies, in Wyoming, Alberta, and Yukon territory. I have also made a few occasional visits to Wyoming for the antelope hunting. My last good hunt was the pack trip in the Yukon. Since then, I have had some trouble with arthritis, but seem to be coming out of it now and [am] beginning to think about a long trip somewhere.

In any event, I always spend a few weeks away every fall hunting in various areas of New England—the best of that hunting happens to be not far from our New Hampshire factory.

I think you have to do a lot of hunting to really enjoy it. Something is generally wrong on most hunts—either the game is scarce, you don't feel well, the weather is bad, somebody you were counting on didn't show up, you shot the little head instead of the big one, or any one of a dozen other things that you know about. But, if you have to work in the city, it is still the best part of life.

"The Poor Man's Burl Ives—Very Poor" and Other Engineers and Designers

Ruger needed to hire a topflight engineer and designer, and in the 1950s he had met the brilliantly talented Harry Sefried.

Hunting in Kenya with George Rowbottom, Tony Henley, and Glen Cottar, 1958

Ruger's first safari was from January 10 to early March 1958. For a bit of luxury before and after hitting the bush, the clients stayed at the Savoy Hotel, in London.

Among the Ruger-Rowbottom battery of firearms was a Ruger .44 Magnum revolver, allowed in the country by special dispensation. It was among the first handguns designed specifically for hunting, which always comes as a surprise to those who feel that such firearms have no "sporting purposes." Hunters Henley and Cottar soon fell in love with the powerful handgun. They were then ranked as two of the leading professional guides in Africa, and both have remained active.[Henley passed away in 1995.]

Game taken by Ruger on the 1958 safari included the "big five" of lion, leopard, black rhinoceros, Cape buffalo, and elephant, as well as warthog, impala, kongoni, waterbuck, oribi, bushbuck, klipspringer, duiker, Grant's gazelle, Thomson's gazelle, steenbok, reedbuck, greater kudu, eland, oryx, Grevy's zebra, gerenuk, hartebeest, and baboon. Some birds were also taken.

In those days the hunters ran a real risk of getting such exotic diseases as bilharzia, sleeping

---

Snapshots and memorabilia from Ruger's 1958 and 1961 African safaris accompany oil painting of waterbuck by Wilhelm Kuhnert, 1865. Mary and Tom Ruger bidding farewell to Ruger at Southport train station. Glen Cottar, with Ruger .44 Magnum Carbine and trophy waterbuck, *lower left*. Pete Kuhlhoff with zebra. Tragedy at *upper right* of native poacher, killed by Cape buffalo, which also died in confrontation. Massive black rhinoceros horn measured 24". Ruger stands on the historic Tsavo Bridge, at *right*. .450 cartridges used by Ruger in Evans double rifle, for elephant, Cape buffalo, and other large game. Bill, Jr., was working on experiments with the early Polaroid Land cameras, and his father is believed to have had the first Polaroid in Africa. The pictures had a hypnotic effect on the natives.

sickness, or malaria, but the fresh air and sunshine did both men good. At that point Ruger had already endured the pain of two years of rheumatoid arthritis, then mainly in his hands.

Among the seemingly unending sightings of the adventure, Ruger remembers being transfixed watching a male elephant down in a gulley near the Tana River, the sides of which were deeply eroded. Eventually the elephant decided to climb out of the place, and managed to claw his way to the top. There he was met by a hyena. The two faced each other for awhile, "the elephant looking rather irritated." Finally the hyena ambled off in the species' curious, slinking, yet menacing, shuffle.

While Ruger and Rowbottom were on safari, memories of the Mau Mau difficulties were still fresh, and the stories told by Henley and Cottar, formerly with colonial British Army Intelligence, were unforgettable. Ruger described some of his safari's highlights in a letter to Judge Don Martin:

I had a forty-day trip in Africa and got back here on March 5th or 6th. . . . Everything about the safari was a complete success meaning that we not only filled our licenses, but that we had excitement every day, magnificent country and climate and luxurious camps. Ours was the hunting sport as it should be with plenty of shooting as well as plenty of hunting. . . . The most sublime hunting was that which produced my 51" kudu. . . .

My battery included a Lancaster .470 nitro [double rifle]—one of the early ones with sidehammers which I prefer for its Edwardian elegance. I also had a magnificent side-hammer Holland & Holland double rifle for the .450-3 ¼" blackpowder express cartridge. Then for more utilitarian type equipment, I had a Model 70 .375 H & H, which was nothing but the factory standard gun equipped with Griffin & Howe mounts and Lyman Alaskan [scope]. I also had with me the Mannlicher Schoenauer .30-06. . . . All these rifles performed beautifully. . . . the old .470 killed one [Cape buffalo] instantly with one shot through the base of the neck and on another occasion dropped a rhinoc-

eros right where he was standing. . . . When it comes to shooting elephant, it seems to me that shot placement is more critical than in any other African game and although I am far from an expert, I think that bullet placement and penetration are the really important factors. The steel jacket is apparently indispensable. Unless they are hit in the brain, I cannot imagine any rifle bringing them down quickly. My elephant was standing broadside to me at about thirty yards and in accordance with our plan (or nearly) I fired. . . . As I was reloading, my . . . hunter had him covered. When I got the gun up to my shoulder, the elephant had taken a couple of steps forward and was facing a little away from us. Both Henley and I fired simultaneously and he then went down. That shot of Henley's annoyed me, but Henley had no idea of how long I would be in reloading and he did not want the elephant to move into the bush. I hated to have him shoot at any of my game; he knew this and was very good at not interfering. There was only one other case when he fired a shot—one time when I was slow about getting a shot off at a buffalo which was really done for, but was about to get into the thick stuff.

Actually, I could go on describing the details of this hunting for hours. The antelope hunting was, for me, the most fascinating part of the whole trip—there was so much opportunity to observe the animals and to be selective. . . . As we came close in the Land Rover, we saw [a] lion sitting in a small clump of trees nearby. We drove around the trees to look him over, while he nonchalantly had a look at us. We then drove away and stalked back [on foot], found him sitting right where we left him and fired with a .375 at about seventy yards. . . . he came bounding out of the trees more or less towards us, but not really at us and I remember that I seemed to have an endless amount of time as I watched him through the scope and put in two more shots before he disappeared into some nearby bush. We found him dead there a couple of minutes later just inside the edge of the bush. I can tell you that the first sight of a lion and the approach to him, even when he isn't looking at you, is plenty exciting.

Everyone over there was tremendously en-

thused about the .44 Magnum, particularly Tony Henley who seized every opportunity to practice with it. He is a tremendously experienced young white hunter and has been living in the African bush ever since he was a boy, and for many years was one of the game wardens in Uganda. One day he said, 'I have absolutely no doubt that if a man was knocked down by a buffalo, but could pull out this gun from his holster, he could save his life.'. . .

He came to us from Jefferson Mfg. Co.; something was going sour over there. Harry's penchant was to see what he could do in the way of neat little ideas, such as a bent wire spring performing the function of several other springs or even the role of several working parts, making things that could significantly cut costs, and were eminently practical. That had been Harry's principal sideline at High Standard, inventing economical products—like the Sentinel revolver (of which over 1,000,000 were made), getting the costs down, while keeping quality up through innovative engineering.

Harry's first work for us was on our first rifle, the .44 Magnum Carbine, very soon after we moved to the Southport plant at Lacey Place in 1959. He stayed with us some twenty years, working through several major projects and was, in fact, the lead designer. After the .44 Magnum Carbine he had a great deal to do with the rotary magazine of the 10/22 Carbine; it was Harry who designed the subtly complex rotor which turned out to be the key to the way those cartridges lie in there so that the rims can't catch on each other and the top cartridge is nicely pointed toward the mouth of the chamber. Later, Harry was the chief designer of our Security-Six double-action revolver and was heavily involved with our New Model Single-Actions and many other products.

And then we had other people working of course. There was Doug McClenahan, who later founded Charter Arms Corp., Larry Larson, Henry Into, Roy Melcher, and Jim Sullivan. After Sullivan left, Harry had a great deal to do with the Mini-14 rifle. When we ran into serious problems and the rest of us were out of ideas, Harry often came into the picture to see what could be done to refine something or to perfect the drawings for it and so on.

That was also true of the No. 1 Single-Shot rifle. Harry also had some work to do on the various layouts we were trying on the Over-and-Under Shotgun, and the M77 bolt-action rifle. The M77 was largely Jim Sullivan's, and he also worked on the Mini-14.

Among Sefried's many talents, he had been a professional country-and-western singer, performing on stage with top-notch bands. At picnics and parties, Harry would perform at the slightest hint or request. Bill Ruger called him "the poor man's Burl Ives—very poor!" Sefried, with his innocent, cheery-good-fellow demeanor, genuine character, and intense knowledge and experience, proved to be one of Ruger's most competent designers and engineers, and played a key role in two decades of creative engineering at Sturm, Ruger.

Harry Sefried Remembers

My work when at Winchester was mainly on long guns, but I was also interested in and had experience with pistols and revolvers, especially through assisting Marsh "Carbine" Williams (made famous by a James Stewart movie of the same name), and building a couple of interesting revolvers there (these were side exercises, not done with official Winchester approval). I went from Winchester to High Standard in 1950, where works manager George Wilson hired me

Best quality double rifles from the Ruger collection, *left to right*, a .470 Nitro Express by Charles Lancaster (Ruger's elephant and Cape buffalo rifle), a William Cashmore, two rifles by John Rigby & Co., an Army & Navy C.S.L., a Robert Schuler (German), a John Rigby & Co., an Alexander Henry, four Holland & Hollands, and a William Evans. At *bottom*, a John Rigby & Co. All British, except the Schuler, and representing the pinnacle of handcrafted British firearms craftsmanship of the late 1800s and early 1900s.

Hunting in New England and Canada. Elmer Keith (*left*) and Larry Koller, at *far right*. Pete Kuhlhoff photographing Harry Sefried, shooting the new Ruger Hawkeye single-shot pistol in 1963. At *lower left,* Jack Behn with a wild boar, taken with a Ruger .44 Magnum Carbine; and Lenard Brownell sighting-in two rifles. By comb of one of Ruger's favorite Mannlicher rifles, publisher-conservationist Robert E. Petersen.

away from Winchester's grandson-in-law Edwin Pugsley, because of my interest in handguns.

Besides designing the Sentinel revolver, I took out a half dozen or more patents on the re-design of High Standard's automatic pistol line. Also during that period I met Bill Ruger, probably at Pete Kuhlhoff's; later on we hunted together, up at the King and Bartlett property in Eustace, Maine. We got along quite well, even though at High Standard I was designing competitive models to Ruger's, both the Olympic and Supermatic model .22 pistols and the Sentinel. Later, I left High Standard and went to the Jefferson Corporation, where we were making high-powered bolt-action rifles for Montgomery Ward, and a single barrel shotgun of my design.

I kept in touch with Bill, and at the end of my association with Jefferson, Bill offered me a job. In 1959 I went to Southport and joined Sturm, Ruger. The plant at that time was just moving into the new building on Lacey Place. My first visit to the factory had been when it was in the little red building complex near the railroad station. Engineers Gene Geber and Chris Cashavelly were then finishing up the drawings for the Bearcat. Bill was then tied up with designs for the .44 Magnum Carbine. Of course, one of the other guns in my background at Winchester was a modified M1 Garand Rifle, making it into a semi- and a full-auto, and building a box magazine for it for possible Army trials.

Bill and I set up drawing boards right next to each other at Lacey Place, and hammered away on the .44 Carbine from the first day I came into the company. This project went on for quite some time—until the design was satisfactory. Bill had started the .44 Carbine project, which was proving very complex, considering the components. Bill did not want the breech profile sticking up as it does on the Garand rifle, or a bolt with studs sticking out as on the M1 Carbine. Bill wanted this entire mechanism within the walls of the enclosed, beautifully shaped receiver, with its silhouette absolutely elegant, and that's the only word to describe it. "Elegant" is one of Bill's favorite words, and it's something he seeks in every design.

The system was like a shotgun, where the shells load into the bottom of the receiver. We did not want a button on the side of the receiver, like the Winchester Model 50 shotgun (a Marsh Williams design), which you had to push for loading. So we worked out the lifter latch underneath, in which you put the shell in and automatically dislodge the latch when pushing the shell against it, feeding the shell into the tubular magazine.

Then I got into dealing with quite a bit of feed work, because when you fire the gun, the shock of the recoil makes the shells go forward up the magazine tube. We had to arrange for the bolt to move to the rear, while the cartridge lifter waited for the shell to fall on top of it from the magazine. The bolt would not be allowed to come forward until the shell was completely out of the magazine. When the shell hit the lifter, then the mechanism would complete the operating cycle. The timing system needed to wait for the shell, and then go past the latch as the shell fed past. Otherwise you would get a double feed.

We pretty basically adapted a shotgun system, and had to miniaturize it to work with the .44 Magnum cartridge. The system also had to be rugged, a typical feature of Ruger designs. The mass of those parts hitting each other was the worst punishment you could give a telescopic sight, an increasingly common sight system in the 1960s. When the mechanism was first designed, the shock would wipe out scope crosshairs at a rapid rate. The scope makers just had to build a better scope, since that 250-grain bullet created a lot of recoil in a light little carbine. However, the jarring of the bolt helped to make the feed work well. Functionally, we wanted the bolt to hit pretty hard, so if the shooter used a lighter load the rifle would still work.

The real secret to correcting the .44 Magnum's scope problem was to anchor it better. The rifle's recoil was such that it could actually shear some of the scope bases off. It was a matter of making bases which were sturdy enough, and had clamps to anchor the scope. If the recoil didn't knock the crosshairs out, it would tend to slide the scope forward in the scope mounts. So the mounts had to be equally as sturdy.

About ten test Carbines were taken, along with cases of .44 ammunition, up to Newport, firing them in the Blue Mountain Forest. The testers were Bill and me, Walt Sych, Ed Nolan, Mike Horelik, Rex King, and others. We had a ball because we went to a wasteland part of the complex, with a lot of scrub trees, about four or five inches in diameter. Each shooter had someone behind him loading, and we'd take turns shooting. We fired thousands of rounds in these guns. Any malfunction would be noted, so that we could sort out any possible performance problems. We literally cut down a section of woods with bullets, which were flying like in a pitched battle. Once a scrub tree was just about cut off, we'd vie with each other to see who could cut down that tree with the hail of .44 Magnum slugs. We shot all day and burned up tens of thousands of rounds of ammo.

We really wrang out those guns, and gave them a hell of a test. Then we went back to Southport, disassembled each gun, to check them out, and made whatever changes and improvements we felt were necessary.

The funniest thing that ever happened with that gun: Bill and I were walking through the forest, and we had one of the Carbines with us. We saw some elk, deer, and other game, but they were out of season so we couldn't take one of those. All of sudden, we spotted a big porcupine in a tree. These beasts can be very destructive, causing a lot of havoc. I called Bill's attention to this creature, and thought this could allow a test of the performance of the Carbine, and get rid of an unwanted, irascible varmint at the same time. Bill told me, "You shoot him and I'll watch to see what that .44 does." He moved over to the side so he could have the best angle. I raised the .44, and Bill said, "Okay , let him have it."

Bam! It looked like a bomb had gone off! The quills blew out in a ball of about seven feet in diameter. Along with the quills, a great deal of porcupine showered down, mostly in Ruger's direction. It looked like the porcupine completely blew up. We were satisfied as far as the .44's power was concerned, but I didn't quite anticipate that result. Little did I realize, but Bill was downwind of all this, and a lot of it landed on him! Rather indignantly, he said, "You could have warned me about that." I was quick to say that I didn't realize the mushroom cloud would land on him! I very carefully refrained from saying, "My God Bill, you are full of s—t," but he really was!

A few years later, we decided it would be nice to have a hotter cartridge for the .44 Magnum Carbine. Bill asked me to look into that; so I necked the .44 down into a .357 bullet, into something you could fit into a Model 1892 Winchester. This special cartridge (called the ".38-44 Magnum") was something very similar to the old .38-40. It could be loaded a little hotter, but we didn't have enough cartridge case capacity to do anything spectacular. We ended up making two special carbines, one chambered in a .44 cartridge necked down to .357, and the other a .44 necked down to .40 caliber (to take a .38-40 bullet, which is actually .40 caliber). For the case, I took the brass from a .45-70, and cut the rim off in a lathe, turning it down to be compatible with the .44 Magnum rim diameter, so I could use the same bolt, extractor, and everything else, though it had a bigger chamber by quite a bit.

We found the .40's muzzle energy above and beyond the .30-30 Winchester. Bill and I went to a meeting with the fellows from Winchester-Olin, and we tried to get them to manufacture the cartridge. I was using Hercules 2400 powder, and about 100 percent filling the case, which gave us reasonable pressures, and beautiful energy. It had the advantage that you couldn't overload it with 2400.

They decided they couldn't possibly load it to that capacity, and would have to do only 90 percent, which would make it less powerful than the .30-30. Bill, Jr., took a bighorn sheep with either the special .357 or the .40 cartridge. The hot one was the .40 caliber. We were on the verge of something really spectacular, but Winchester didn't want to compete with their own .30-30.

We proof-tested the .44 Magnum Carbine, but decided we really should have an independent evaluation. Two sample Carbines were sent to Burt Munhall, of the H. P. White Laboratory, in Bel Air, Maryland (a few miles from Aberdeen Proving Ground), for testing. I told Burt, "We want you to see what it takes to blow them up." He called and said, "What are you doing, pulling my leg? I'm using a compressed case full charge of Bullseye powder (about the fastest burning powder available), and all I'm doing now is putting a ring in the chamber. We're already at over 100,000 pounds per square inch pressure!" Bill and I found that the only damage to the gun was in the threads on the barrel, as we had a recess cut there, which was normal. When the proof load went off, it created a little ring around the brass case up toward the mouth, where this had bulged the barrel at that point, but couldn't blow it because the receiver was a solid hunk of steel, and there was no way it was going anywhere.

Even though any firearm can be blown up if you try hard enough, we had created a damn near indestructible gun. We were very happy about its amazing strength. The Carbine's locking lugs gave one solid breeching.

This was also at the exact time of the expansion of the company into the new building. We had beautiful offices there, right next to the tool room with Rex King checking on tooling and making the .44 Carbine models. He was literally right outside the door. That Carbine involved some extremely interesting geometry on its locking cams and methods of manufacture, because we carved that .44 Carbine receiver the "old-fashioned" way, out of a solid chunk of steel. The camming cuts for the locking lugs and the takedown bits were keyed in like an old-fashioned Kentucky rifle. The barrel and receiver could easily be removed from the stock, like the M1 Carbine. Also, there was some very intriguing tooling, complex machining, and the use of both die casting and investment casting. We had a lot of fun with that project. It was a very satisfying job, and we learned a lot that would stand us in good stead on many later projects.

When we got the .44 Magnum Carbine going, we had even more fun when we had a lot of experimental work to do on barrel rifling pitches, twist, and accuracy. That got us into working with Remington and Winchester to get a jacketed bullet made up so we could get some decent accuracy at rifle ranges. Up to this time it was considered just a pistol cartridge. The .44 Magnum was really a beautiful cartridge, particularly for brush shooting, up to 150 yards, and the handy semiautomatic .44 Carbine allowed for a few quick shots at short range—a perfect combination for Eastern whitetail deer.

The .44 Magnum Carbine

Launching the .44 Magnum Carbine was a signal event in the history of Sturm, Ruger & Co. This was the company's first entry into the long gun line, and it was conveniently chambered for the same cartridge as the most powerful of Ruger revolvers. Unlike most of the rest of the company's line, major components were not precision investment castings. Due to the size and complexity of the Carbine's receiver, it was machined out of a billet of steel. At this point, Ruger's designs had outpaced casting technology.

Sales were enhanced by articles run by Ruger's growing legion of supporters, writers like Pete Kuhlhoff, Charles Askins, Jr., Warren Page, John Amber, and Jack O'Connor.

The "Deerstalker" name used on the first Carbines was soon changed because the Ithaca Gun Company had a "Deerslayer" shotgun. Ruger says he "wasn't even thinking about their trade name when we named ours. The name Deerstalker occurred to me because of some interest in stag hunting, in Scotland. In fact, I was at that point wearing those double-ended hats of the same name. I even gave a few away as Christmas presents. But to avoid any bad feelings, we changed our rifle's name to simply "the Ruger .44 Carbine."

.44 Magnum Performance

The .44 Magnum's performance elicited quite a positive reaction at the time, and the company's testing program was awesome. A widely distributed flyer was headlined "A Progress Report from Sturm, Ruger & Co., Inc.," and noted:

1. All final and exhaustive tests now completed on RUGER Carbine.
2. Carbine shipments to begin week of September 4th, 1961.
3. We're on two shifts to provide better deliveries of all RUGER firearms.
4. "Single-Six" with interchangeable [.22 Magnum] cylinder now appears to be most popular sporting revolver in the world.
5. We're planning a new model for .256 Winchester in January.

The remainder of the flyer listed Ruger distributors, and referred to "Some RUGER 'Proof-Marks'":

1. We've never increased a price—proof positive of RUGER's modern engineering and alert designing.
2. We still have a one-man Service Dept.—proof

Adventures with Bill Ruger:
Rex King Remembers

We were testing the new .44 Magnum Carbine up in Newport, out in a private forest preserve, and we thought we'd see how the bullet would look if we shot a few straight up in the air, and recovered them from a nearby pond. There was no danger, we thought, to doing this where we were, which was miles from human activity. We had experienced poor results trying to recover fired bullets from a test box, because the bullet mushroomed substantially only about 18" into the sawdust filler, even though we had built a box about eight feet long.

We fired about a dozen shots and all of sudden, *kerplunk!* One of the bullets came down hard and with real velocity only a few feet away. We got the message that the .44 Magnum on the way down could do almost as much damage as when it was headed up! That was the end of that! Imagine if it had landed on Bill's head! Or on one of ours!

We never did recover a good, non-deformed .44 Magnum bullet.

positive of RUGER quality—both in material and workmanship.

Ruger's letter to Gale Bennett, an enquiring shooter, was typically thorough in describing the .44 Magnum's performance and potential:

Ballistic tables suggest that the .44 Magnum might be inadequate for some game. We have recognized this from the outset and I have on many occasions

Lefever double barrel rifle, in .45-70 caliber, with early production Ruger .44 Magnum "Deerstalker," specially stocked in mesquite; with peep-sight and the aluminum furniture left bright. Classic nineteenth-century boar hunting scene, "Canadian Winter," by American artist Regis François Gignoux. Both rifles perfectly suited for the game. Painting given to Ruger as Christmas present, c. 1958, by Southport employees.

Bill Ruger's Demand for Perfection: Rex King Remembers

Ruger's got a pretty tough temper, I can tell you that. He can really be temperamental; though he never was with me. I never had a problem with him. But I've seen him stomp some guys out in pretty good shape; up one side and down the other.

While he's always been a generous, thoughtful guy, he can get mad over something that might seem trivial. That's largely due to the fact [that] he is an absolute perfectionist, and simply will not tolerate sloppy work or lack of preparation and dedication. On the whole, he was all business. He was also the kind of a guy that if he liked you, he really liked you. But if he didn't like you, he didn't like you, *period*!

One thing he learned was that just because somebody had a degree from an Ivy League school, or pedigrees from some major big companies, GE, Westinghouse, or even some of the gun companies, that didn't mean they would fit in at Sturm, Ruger. Sometimes they didn't have the smarts to go with their background. We learned a lesson or two on buying machinery; some of these characters would try to sell us a bill of goods on equipment that, long term, just wouldn't work out.

I loved my job; couldn't wait to get to work in the morning.

---

advanced the argument that on the basis of actual personal experience, the .44 Magnum is far more effective than the paper ballistics would indicate. This experience embraces dozens of heads taken here in the U.S.A. and in Africa, either personally or by hunting companions. My professional hunter in Africa was always immensely enthused about the .44 Carbine's performance and regarded it in his non-technical way as amazingly powerful for its light weight. I remember on one occasion that he killed a fully grown hyena at a full 100 yards with

one shot. The hyena did not go 10 feet after being hit. On another occasion, he borrowed the rifle while he tried to drive a lion out of a thickly wooded draw. I killed many head of African antelope—little ones like reedbuck and big ones such as waterbuck and hartebeeste. In the U.S.A., I have killed boar and deer on many different hunts and far from ever having an animal get away, the stopping power seemed in every case to be better than what I was previously used to, hunting with a .243 or .30-06.

However, I will not really claim that the .44 Magnum is better than the .30-06. I will merely say that what this experience proves is that both are more than adequate for the type of game I have referred to in this letter. Incidentally, I have also killed a leopard, instantly, at 100 yards with one shot offhand, using the .44 Magnum. I will also say that I think the .44 Magnum ought to be regarded as basically a 100-yard rifle for this kind of game, although if the shooter can really place his shots accurately, this can be stretched to 125 or 150 yards. We have many letters on file from owners who are genuinely enthusiastic about this Carbine.

So thorough were Ruger and his staff in engineering the Carbine that in February 1961, Ruger draftsman Chris Cashavelly wrote all the major gun sight manufacturers seeking advice on the sights for the new gun. He contacted Maynard P. Buehler, Bushnell, Leupold & Stevens Instruments, Original Sight Exchange, W. R. Weaver Company, Redfield Gun Sight Company, and Lyman Sights, indicating that he was "enclosing, herewith, a full size layout of our carbine. We look forward to the opportunity of cooperating with you in the development of optional sighting equipment for this new product . . . [and] would appreciate your opinion as to the most favorable location for the scope base screws." Ultimately, Lyman front and rear sights were selected, with the receiver drilled and tapped to accept Weaver-type scope bases.

Hunting in Uganda with Pete Kuhlhoff, Tony Henley, and Glen Cottar

Ruger's second African safari, from early March to late April 1961, proved an impressive means of promoting this new .44 Magnum Carbine. Ruger and friend Pete Kuhlhoff were in Kenya and Uganda, with hunters Tony Henley and Glen Cottar. Henley wrote November 15, 1960, to advise the planned itinerary:

Start the safari in Karamojo at the foot of Mt. Debasien, for leopard, possibly lion, roan, buffalo and various species of lesser game. From this area we could also try for greater kudu, if you want to shoot another. We will then drive across Northern Uganda to Lake Albert where we board a launch which takes us 50 miles down the eastern shore of the lake to a good hunting ground for Uganda kob, buffalo, Jackson hartebeeste, leopard, possible lion and the most magnificent Nile perch fishing. Then to what is at present the Semliki Game Reserve for elephant and lion. This area is being opened to shooting on January 1st, so we should be one of the first in. We then move to Lake George for the giant waterbuck and hippo, also possibly a few days in the Kigesse district, if we have had no luck with elephant and lion. We then move either to Lake Mburu for eland, lion, buffalo, leopard and possibly situtunga [antelope], or if you would like to do a special trip to the Sese Islands in Lake Victoria for the very big situtunga?

On this trip we would take a launch to the islands for about a week. The situtunga is a very diffi-

---

Shooting and hunting. At *center*, Ruger showing Mary the fine points of pistol shooting, with a Colt Ace. At *top*, Ruger firing the Hawkeye pistol. *Upper left*, scenes from the National Championships at Camp Perry, in the 1950s. Ruger firing the Blackhawk .357 Magnum, and the William Evans .450/.400 double barrel rifle, at *left*; the rifle itself, at *right*, with Hawkeye pistol and boring and chambering tools. *Below* the early Hopkins & Allen advertisement showing a boy attempting to shoot an apple off head of apprehensive pet dog in the rare hand-cranked .45-70 Lowell Battery Gun in operation; and to the *left*, shooting an original Remington Zouave muzzle-loader.

Checkered Walnut Panels
for **RUGER** Pistol

STURM, RUGER & CO., INC.   SOUTHPORT, CONN., U.S.A.

The Ruger .44 Magnum Carbine

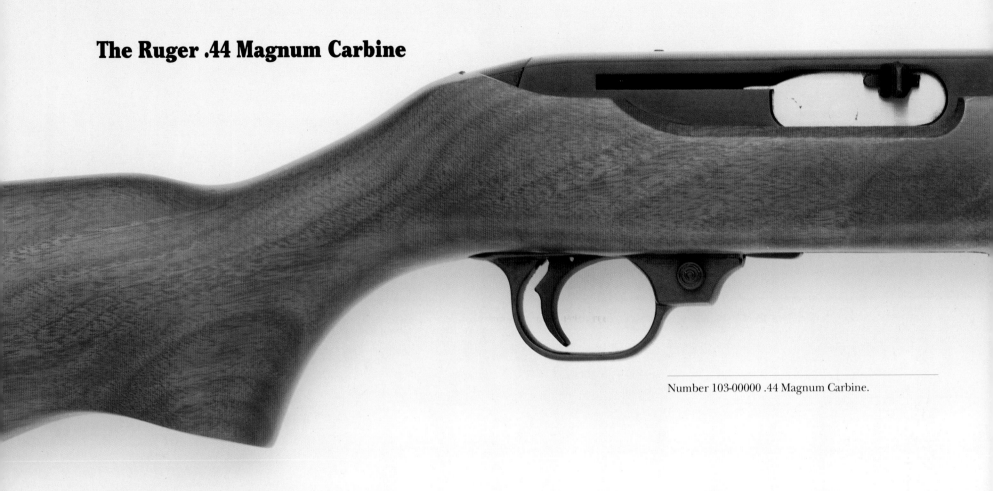

Number 103-00000 .44 Magnum Carbine.

Number 103-00000 .44 Magnum Carbine.

Introduced: 1960. "America's newest game rifle.... Proven on the plains of Africa, the RUGER "Deerstalker" carbine is a technological breakthrough for the benefit of American sportsmen.... proven not only on Whitetails in North America, but on Leopard, Hyena, Wart Hog [*sic*], Topi and many other species in Africa.... developed to provide the sportsman with the best possible rifle for hunting deer and other medium-sized game in brush country."

Serial Numbers: 1 to 8129; 50000 to 138095; prefix introduced 1969, 100-00000 to -99999; and similarly numbered prefix serial range 101-00000 to -02200; 102-00000 to -99999; 103-00000 to -15400.

Total Made Through 1985: In excess of 250,000.

Caliber: .44 Remington Magnum (a few prototypes made in .38-44 Magnum).

Magazine Capacity: 4 in tubular magazine.

Barrel Length: 18¼"; lengthened by ¼" to 18½" from serial number 102-64701.

Rifling: 12 grooves, right-hand twist, one turn in 38".

Markings: See Table of Markings, pages 330–35.

From January 4, 1978 (no. 102-49724) standard warning marking on barrel.

Sights: Folding-leaf rear with reversible U/square notch plate, adjustable for elevation.¹⁄₁₆" wide gold bead front sight. Frame drilled and tapped for scope mounts.

Overall Length and Weight: 36¾", 5 pounds, 12 ounces.

Stocks: American walnut, oil-finished. Offered with Standard, International, and Sporter style stocks, the latter two checkered at the wrist and forend, and fitted with sling swivels and pistol grip caps.

Finish: Blued.

Materials, Construction, and Innovations: Light in weight, short in length, and moderate in recoil. Receiver machined from a billet of hot-rolled chrome-molybdenum steel. Tubular magazine in forend, accessed by aperture on bottom of receiver, foreward of trigger guard. Two-stage trigger pull. Cross-button safety, forward of trigger guard bow; locks sear and hammer.

Gas-operated, using a short-stroke piston, which operates from a small quantity of gas tapped from barrel upon firing. Breech remains in locked position until after the bullet has left the barrel, at which point it opens automatically. Bolt remains open after last shot fired, and until being released by latch ahead of the trigger guard.

Issue Price: $108.00, Standard. $118, Sporter. $128, International (1960).

Engraving: Serial number 12848, with scroll engraving, in the collection of William B. Ruger, Sr.

Price Sheet Listings and Major Production Variations:

44R *Standard Model:* Carbine style stock with barrel band at front of forend; no checkering on stock. Early model with white, ivory-appearing front sight insert.

M44SP *Sporter:* Fluted, semi-beavertail forend to stock; Monte Carlo style butt stock. Checkered stock.

International: Mannlicher style stock, extending to the muzzle, with blued steel forend cap. Checkered stock.

44RS: Standard stock style; peep sight built onto the receiver; sling swivels.

YR25: Commemorative model; last .44 Carbines built; with inlaid stock medallion, scene depicting the gun's 25 years of manufacture; in 1985 Price Sheets.

Warning Series: "Warning" marking on barrel from date and in location as indicated above.

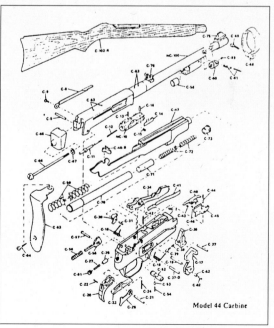

Exploded view of .44 Magnum Carbine.

cult animal to hunt but a very worthwhile trophy. . . .

While on safari, Ruger asked Henley to look for the monument to Sir Samuel Baker, an early English hunter, explorer, and boyhood hero of Ruger's. After several queries and hours of looking, they found it, covered by vines. Nearby was a beautiful country hotel, very English. They made camp at a site where the legendary hunter W.D.M. "Karamojo" Bell had set up one of his camps, as Ruger and Henley were purposely following Bell's trail. They also camped on the southern slopes of Mt. Debasien, where they could see the mountain and the two breast-like smaller peaks, known as "Twin Cones." Henley, Cottar, *et al.*, were photographed on the famous Tsavo Bridge. Many adventures took place in this area as revealed in J. H. Patterson's *The Man-Eaters of Tsavo*. Kuhlhoff wrote the hunt up in the August 1961 *Argosy* ("Rifles and Bullets Safari Tested") and in the 1963 *Gun Digest* ("The Ruger Carbine in Africa").

Ruger found the safari experience fit perfectly into his advertising and promotional plans for the Blackhawk and the .44 Magnum Carbine. In the August 1961 *Argosy*, an ad showed Ruger with a Uganda kob, taken with the .44 Carbine in the Semliki Valley. Still another ad (in the September 1961 *Guns & Ammo*) had an equally delighted Ruger with a warthog, taken near Lake Albert. Both ads began with the legend: "Proven on the

plains of Africa, the RUGER 'Deerstalker' carbine is a technological breakthrough for the benefit of American sportsmen." The ad also promoted the "matching caliber Super Blackhawk, superbly finished, single-action revolver. . . ."

For Ruger, one unexpected trophy was the coveted Shaw & Hunter, awarded for the finest game animal head taken by any clients in Kenya for the year 1961. The winning head was a record-book reedbuck, measuring an impressive 13⅜".

To Jack O'Connor, May 11, 1961, Ruger recounted his Uganda game bag, taken with the .44 Magnum Carbine:

> . . . one leopard, one topi, one waterbuck, one spotted hyena, three Uganda kob, one bushbuck, two warthogs and two reedbucks. . . . There may be a few other things, but I don't remember them. I would say that on the average, the range for all this shooting would be 75 yds., to 100 yds. In the several instances when we recovered bullets which were the new Remington jacketed soft points, the mushrooming seemed very uniform and the bullet always remained in one piece.

One day the hunters, clients, and some of the safari crew took a motor launch on Lake Albert. While en route, they went through a monsoon rain, just as had Sir Samuel and Lady Baker nearly 100 years before, as recounted in one of Baker's books. The launch, like the "African Queen," took refuge in some calm waters behind a peninsula until the storm blew over. While belowdecks, Ruger lit up a cigarette, and a sick native woman let him know she wanted a smoke. Ruger had been advised not to give anything to begging natives, but he made an exception in this case, lighting the cigarette for the woman first. Then he looked around and saw a half dozen of the boys watching all this—figuring Bwana was finally going soft.

In a letter to Glenn Anderson, Ft. Collins, Colorado, November 16, 1961, Ruger discussed accommodations in Nairobi, Kenya:

> Nairobi is a modern city and I am sure that if you

arrive there with nothing more than a pack of travelers' checks, you could be completely and magnificently outfitted in twenty-four hours' time. All kinds of camp clothes and hunting shoes can be made to order in forty-eight hours at reasonable prices. If I were you, I would plan to arrive in Nairobi approximately four days before the safari starts and this will give you time to round out your outfit. . . . outside of [certain recent American calibers], almost anything else you might need would be available in Nairobi. . . . As to food, the best way to get what you want is to tell [the safari outfitters] your requirements before starting out so that there is a good supply of the things you like while you are in the bush. Of course, your fresh meat will have to be the actual game you shoot and this is generally served in a manner to make it very appetizing to a hungry hunter.

The Hawkeye Single-Shot Pistol

Not one to rest on his laurels, Ruger was ruminating on still another new handgun design, this model another joint design by Ruger and Harry Sefried. The idea of necking-down a magnum cartridge to a smaller bullet for better performance was still alive. This time, it was the .357 Magnum case that was chosen. The concept was revealed in another letter to Judge Don Martin (February 16, 1962):

> . . . just for relaxation during the past few months, I have put a lot of thinking into a single-shot pistol for these new high velocity cartridges—the .22 Remington Jet . . . and the .256 Winchester Magnum which does seem to be the better bet. I understand that Winchester is very happy with the cartridge as far as ballistics go and is only waiting for us to get our gun on the market, which I hope will be next summer. We are just now starting the tooling having spent a surprising amount of time on design of the gun itself. The design is based on a revolver frame just as in the past both Colt and Smith & Wesson have made single-shot pistols using their revolver frames. I think we have a very perfect design mechanically and I believe that in a single-shot these small bore magnum cartridges make some sense, while in a revolver they lead to nothing

but a real Swiss Navy lash-up. Not only that, but I am getting more and more sold on amusement pistol shooting with the new pistol scope sights. Nickl and Bushnell both have them and Litchert has a long eye relief attachment for the Weaver. All these work perfectly and seem to fascinate everyone by the accuracy that can be achieved even by shooters who are not necessarily good pistol shots. An outfit like this, i.e., a big single-shot revolver, is certainly not intended to be a holster gun or a defensive weapon and I am sure no one will buy it except the real handgun enthusiast. This gun is still on the confidential list. Elmer Keith knows about it, but except for him please don't mention it for the time being. . . . I am in good shape except for this little case of rheumatoid arthritis that hangs on. By and large the world has treated me very well and these guns have certainly led to a lot of friendships.

Despite a glowing review in *The American Rifleman,* and a warm welcome from the more sophisticated of handgun shooters, Ruger Hawkeye sales never caught on, and the model became the first Ruger to be destined primarily for the gun collector's shelf. Its sales were discontinued in the mid-1960s after only a few thousand were made.

An In-Depth Look at Ruger
Precision Investment Castings

A scientific, aesthetic, financial, and technological triumph which has been a hallmark of the Ruger saga is the use of precision investment castings. With the founding of Pine Tree Castings in 1963 at the Newport facility, Ruger and his company established the vital bulwark which has proven as important as any of the manufacturing factors in the firm's domination of the firearms field. Says Ruger:

> My business career has been no drudgery whatsoever; long hours, but it was always because I was driven by actual enthusiasm. I suppose you could say investment casting was a good decision! We began our revolvers in 1953 with the idea of using this brand-new technology of forming metal parts by precision investment casting rather than through

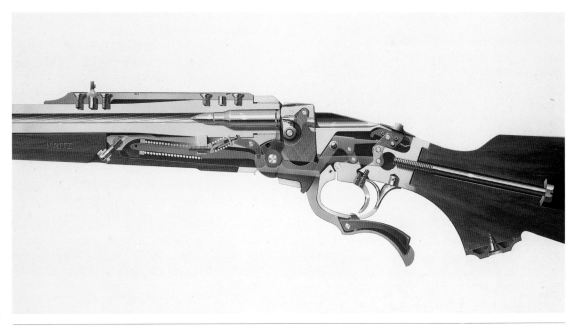

Complex mechanism of the No. 1 Rifle evident from cross-sectional.

forging. It's called "investment" because you enclose [invest] the pattern in the mold and can never use the pattern or the mold again. It was sort of an extravagant procedure, but it turned out to have vast advantages.

> I love to work things out on the kitchen table and give a lot of thought at all times to these matters. But if it weren't for the fact that there are men here who can immediately interpret this and reduce it to scale drawings and practical mechanisms, obviously, we'd have nowhere near the capacity we have at the present time. This engineering and drafting work is really the heart and soul of the whole enterprise.

The problem of producing the frame for the Single-Six revolver brought us to the consideration of the investment casting process. Our prototype frames were actually machined out of solid blocks of steel by Rex King, but even when made from forgings, the machining of those single-action frames is very tricky and requires very special set-ups such as the ball breech area, and configura-tions like the pawl slot are not normally machined by standard tools. So from early on, the thought in the back of my mind was that perhaps that frame could be investment cast.

Of course we were concerned about the average gun buyer's misconceptions as to the strength of such castings as compared to forgings or sintered metal.

Our chrome-molybdenum alloy steel castings would not be weak like pot metal or brittle like cast iron. Special test equipment clearly proved to us that investment cast frames were *at least* as strong as the forged ones we also had made. Besides scientific tests, we clamped some in a big vise and simply beat on them with a sledgehammer! Investment casting was an absolutely ideal way for our small company to proceed in the manufacture of relatively complicated components.

Superiority of the Ruger Lost Wax Process

Investment casting is a subject that sometimes needs some explaining. The process is relatively

The Hawkeye Pistol: Harry Sefried Remembers

The Hawkeye was fathered by Winchester's abortive effort to put the .256 bottlenecked cartridge into a Blackhawk revolver. But unless the chambers were absolutely spic and span, the case shoulder would expand and push forward, and the primer would protrude. Furthermore, if you left any oil in the chamber, on firing the case extended back and locked up the cylinder. We decided that it was a poor cartridge to put in a revolver.

Bill suggested we should try a single-shot pistol. He thought up the artillery-type breech block system. So I worked on that for awhile, and we put a prototype together.

We got a lot better accuracy with the single-shot than with the experimental revolver in .256. This looked interesting enough to try from a production standpoint, especially since we realized Remington was fooling around with the .221 caliber XP100 bolt-action pistol. Our basic pistol was with a rotating breech, short firing pin, and a fairly long hammer fall. We were totally limited to a short cartridge; the .357 and .44 Magnums would have been rather redundant, since those were two of our revolver chamberings.

Unfortunately, the limitations of the cartridge, that diminutive .256 caliber, sort of killed the Hawkeye project before it got started. Mike Walker of Remington (who designed their single-shot XP 100) and I used to kid each other that we had managed to come out with the two least popular pistols in the history of handguns.

new. It began in World War II, I would say, as a commercial manufacturing process; although it is a very old art, sometimes referred to as "lost wax." Investment casting is simply a technique for producing castings out of the highest strength alloys there are; and this means not only alloy steels and stainless steels, but such exotic materials as Stellite. When they are produced by this method, castings are *as strong as or even stronger than the comparable component made as a forging.*

There's no questioning the fact that our parts are the strongest in the firearms field today, or in history—and every qualified engineer knows it. We've pioneered the use of these castings, and we have rightfully been extremely proud of that.

We are probably the only American firearms manufacturer that makes its own castings,[1] and the Pine Tree division is on the threshold of becoming a major commercial foundry, as well as simply producing our own parts requirements.

I am very happy about our New Hampshire project—it's a thing I have wanted to do for a long time, and it is really a refreshing experience to find such a friendly reception from people in Newport and throughout the State.

Technique of Making Investment Castings[2]

The process begins with the wax patterns dies, very much like a plastic injection mold. [The] wax injection presses begin the process. We have to make a wax pattern for every casting that we propose to produce, so in reality what is happening . . . is that we are producing wax patterns in the same quantity that we will subsequently produce castings. The pattern must be attached to rods of wax by using the wax itself as an adhesive, by means of a hot "butter knife," and these groups of patterns attach to rods, which are more technically referred to as gates and runners, forming the entire interior of the mold that we will subsequently make to cast these parts. These rows of completed trees often assume abstract shapes that you can read any way you'd like. Some even seem like miniature apartment houses.

As the wax trees come into the mold room, the first operation at producing a mold is a dip into a slurry of zircon flour and colloidal silicon, which serves as the beginning of the mold that will be built up in layers by subsequent dips. The first coat is of zircon sand in a fluid air bed. The molds are built up by a long series of dips in a refractory material, thus producing a shell mold strong enough to withstand molten steel that will subsequently have to be poured into it.

When the shell mold has been built up so that it achieves the proper thickness, it now begins to look like a bit of a Mayan sculpture, but we pay no attention to it as that. It's just waiting to dry out adequately to begin to be able to stand the application of really high heat. A cutaway [see illustration] shows how the wax patterns are completely surrounded or "invested" by the shell mold.

The furnace melts the wax from the molds. When the molds come out of the furnace, they are practically free of wax. Electric induction furnaces melt the steel. The molds are again heated to get out the last of the wax before casting, and to bring the molds up to an ideal temperature to ensure that the casting will have perfect detail and sharp edges.

The operator watches the steel with his optical pyrometer, the purpose of which is to bring the steel up to the correct temperature and then to have it poured quickly. This is the climax of the whole process.

Molds come out of the furnace, and are very promptly and quickly set into position onto sand beds so they are ready and in position for the foundrymen with ladles to then pour as quickly as possible. Speed is critical in order to ensure that there is a minimum exposure of the molten steel to oxygen. This part of the job takes a lot of training, experience, and teamwork—like a championship football team. The steel must be poured into the molds and covered as quickly as possible. These red-hot molds are handled with a good deal of proficiency and care. One might think this is a risky operation, but it works perfectly.

When these molds are cooled off enough, they must be exposed to the air. They are placed on a rack and sit in a blast of air for cooling purposes. After all that work of making the molds, now they must be destroyed with an air hammer to get the contents out. The tree of steel components is then ready to go to the abrasive saws where the parts will be separated from the gates and runners. So this process transforms the wax patterns into steel component parts.

Although the castings look like finished parts, they are in fact far from finished. For this purpose, we have hundreds of machine tools in our factories, and long sequences of machine operations [have]

The Ruger Hawkeye Single-Shot Pistol

Number 1 Hawkeye Single-Shot Pistol.

Number 1 Hawkeye Single-Shot Pistol.

Miniature .22 Standard and Hawkeye pistols, in 1/3 scale, from a series of twelve each, by David Kucer. One of the first of the .22 Standards was presented by The Ruger Collectors' Association to William B. Ruger, Sr. The .22 pistols were cased in "salt cod" boxes with miniature instruction sheets.

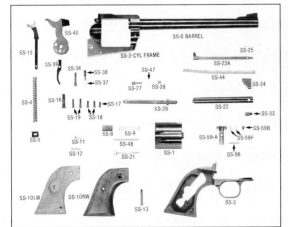

Exploded view of Hawkeye Single-Shot Pistol.

Introduced: 1963, made only through July 1964. Sporadic shipments continued through the early 1970s. "A New Super Velocity Single-Shot Hunting Pistol. . . . Never in the history of shooting has a handgun delivered so much energy at such long range with so much accuracy. . . . Not every pistol shooter can tax the accuracy of a Hawkeye, but there's a challenging new type of shooting waiting here for the man who can."

Serial Numbers: 1-3296; experimental numbers X1 to X13 also produced (in August–September, 1962).

Total Made: 3,075.

Caliber: .256 Winchester Magnum center fire. Two experimental pistols known in caliber .221 Fireball.

Barrel Length: 8½". One experimental .221 Fireball pistol-carbine built with 16" barrel and fixed shoulder stock.

Rifling: 6 grooves, right-hand twist, one turn in 14".

Markings: See Table of Markings, pages 330–35.

On left side of receiver:

STURM, RUGER & CO.
SOUTHPORT, CONN. U.S.A.

On left side of barrel:

RUGER *HAWKEYE.*
WIN. .256 MAG. CAL.

Trademark to right of marking with encircled R trademark marking.

S proof mark on top of barrel at breech.

Serial number stamping on right side of frame.

Sights: Micro rear sight, click adjustable for windage and elevation. Baughman-type front sight, mounted on ramp. Barrel drilled and tapped for scope mounting.

Sight changed to Ruger anodized aluminum rear, in serial range 1100 to 1700.

Overall Length and Weight: 14½"; 45 ounces.

Grips: American walnut, oil-finished, with trademark medallion inlays.

Finish: Blued, with anodized aluminum alloy grip frame.

Materials, Construction, and Innovations: Although appearing to be a revolver, the single-shot Hawkeye pistol is quite different. The breechblock is manually rotated to load a single cartridge directly into the barrel.

Chrome-molybdenum steel frame; Ruger-patented frame-ribs protect rear sight. Unbreakable steel music wire coil springs; no leaf springs. Grip frame of aluminum alloy, with modifications to allow for wide trigger. Manually operated breechblock, breech lock, and extractor.

The hammer cannot be cocked, or the trigger pulled, until the rotating breech is locked into firing position. The pistol may then be cocked for firing. As the trigger is pulled, the sear moves into a notch on the breechblock, preventing the block from rotating open on firing. The ejector engages the rimmed .256 cartridge case.

Issue Price: $87.50 (1963).

Engraving: No factory-engraved examples were built.

Price Sheet Listings and Variations:

RH28 *Type I:* Steel ejector rod housing, Micro rear sight.

Type II: Aluminum alloy ejector rod housing, alloy rear sight (unmarked).

Type III: Aluminum alloy ejector rod housing, Micro rear sight.

Type IV: Steel ejector rod housing, aluminum alloy rear sight (unmarked).

A variation noted at about number 1500 (but found earlier than that number, though assembled later) is replacement of the spring-loaded breechblock stop by a pressed-in pin.

to be performed before at least these major components can be called ready for assembly to finished firearms. Because this process opens up so many design possibilities, it makes it possible for a shooter to find, in a sporting goods or gun store, better quality, at a lower price, and a more interesting variety of firearms.

The Marvels of Best Quality Castings

The investment casting technique pointed directly toward the production of the particularly advanced actions, like the single-shot, a design which has incorporated into it details which would have been really impractical, and impossibly costly by conventional machining.

This is especially true of some of the internal surfaces which control the extraction cycle and which require little internal recesses that are practically hopeless to perform or to produce as machine cuts, but which are perfectly straightforward when they're formed as part of an investment casting. Actually, there are many refinements of the design of this thing. We have cast-in radiuses which distribute stresses perfectly, whereas in machining alone there would be the tool marks themselves which are always the beginning of heat treatment cracks.

Thus, thanks to investment castings, we have been able to do everything we wanted to do. Whereas, if you think it over, you will see that guns designed forty or fifty years ago, in an effort to be machinable and straightforward from a production point of view, used something like a tubular re-

---

The old and the new. The Model 1903 Springfield rifle and the Springfield Armory assembly room (*top left*) contrast to Sturm, Ruger precision investment casting operations in Newport and the foundry, established in the mid-1980s, in Prescott, Arizona. Robin's egg blue parts are the waxes, made by injection molding. Raw cast parts in gray; finished parts either bright stainless, colored (such as the Vaquero frames), or blued. Stripped GP100 revolver (introduced 1985) shows advantages of designing with available investment casting technology. Note how many intricate shapes, cuts, and curves appear on the castings right out of the mold. A tremendous savings in materials and labor result, and designers are given far more flexibility to design formerly "unmachinable" components.

ceiver. That was not itself an improvement, that was simply a means to an end. The use of simplification of parts where they needed some extra stud or excessive metal or some difference in sections, this had to be achieved by adding on components or attaching things, by brazing, or some other way of creating a total component. It really is not as good as having it all one piece; that is to say, integral. We have been able to design rifles and handguns in which the scope base was integral, which just makes much more logic from the shooter's point of view.

Another industry which relies heavily on precision investment castings is aerospace: The turbine blades on a jet engine are the perfect example of a widely common use. Probably turbine blades are all made by investment castings. They have to be from many logical points of view, because they're made of tremendously hard heat-resistant alloys, all virtually unshapable. Everybody that is flying today is riding on investment castings.

Pine Tree Castings

Without question we have used investment castings more extensively than any other gunmaker in history. From the very outset I disclosed that and emphasized it. To some extent I think that made us not a little controversial, maybe somebody thought that was not as good as all-milled parts. In my view that is the ultimate, quintessential expression of an ignorant person. And then in a childlike faith in forgings and bar stock, people never understand that these may be faulty, unless due care was exercised throughout the manufacturing process. Anyway, I knew then that there was a stigma in some circles to the word "cast," so I decided not to hide it, to come out with it, to say what castings were, at least as far as our products go.

Then I noticed Weatherby rifles were very strong in those days and I saw a Weatherby rifle that had a telltale purple bluing. One of the things we had heard was that the average investment casting doesn't give you a nice dark blue. In no time at all, like a day, they can turn purple. We struggled to get rid of that. It was a ghastly kind of color, neither this nor that, and I didn't know what the cause of it was. The bluing people didn't know. We came up with all sorts of theories, and finally it occurred to me to

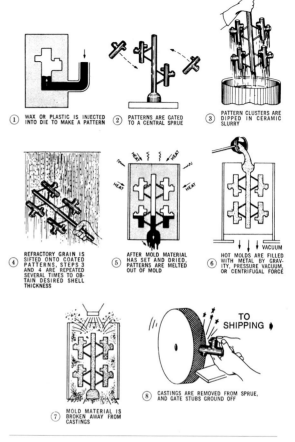

① WAX OR PLASTIC IS INJECTED INTO DIE TO MAKE A PATTERN

② PATTERNS ARE GATED TO A CENTRAL SPRUE

③ PATTERN CLUSTERS ARE DIPPED IN CERAMIC SLURRY

④ REFRACTORY GRAIN IS SIFTED ONTO COATED PATTERNS, STEPS 3 AND 4 ARE REPEATED SEVERAL TIMES TO OBTAIN DESIRED SHELL THICKNESS

⑤ AFTER MOLD MATERIAL HAS SET AND DRIED, PATTERNS ARE MELTED OUT OF MOLD

⑥ HOT MOLDS ARE FILLED WITH METAL BY GRAVITY, PRESSURE VACUUM, OR CENTRIFUGAL FORCE

⑦ MOLD MATERIAL IS BROKEN AWAY FROM CASTINGS

⑧ CASTINGS ARE REMOVED FROM SPRUE, AND GATE STUBS GROUND OFF

TO SHIPPING

The investment casting process, reproduced from "Utilization of Investment Castings," a seminar presented at Rock Island Arsenal, Rock Island, Illinois, January 25, 1977, by Joseph N. Internicola, Kenneth L. Herrick, and Stanley B. Terhune.

---

go to the Battelle Memorial Institute, private researchers in Columbus, Ohio. It didn't take them long, and in a few weeks they came back with a full report. The cause of the purpling was the silicon in the steel; it has to be maintained at a very low level to avoid this, so that was then reported to the foundry. They weren't all that happy about that. The fact is, silica is often added to castings because it makes the steel (as it's being poured) go into the crevices of the die more accurately. But thereafter we had to minimize the use of it.

So, here's this Weatherby, purple as hell, and I knew it was a cast receiver. Yet Roy Weatherby himself would never, ever say anything about that. In fact I was talking to Bud Waite [a Weatherby employee, later with *The American Rifleman*] and he said, "Yes, we do that," and we asked Roy about it. By his response we knew Roy was using cast receivers.

Educating the Public on Castings
Look at the number of pages devoted to the many hundreds of machining steps on the Model 1903 Springfield receiver: That's a long involved exercise and it's got to be extremely time intensive. I think we can do some interesting comparisons to show how that technology has changed. It is important, as is the fact that most Americans have little appreciation of how things are made. That is partly because more and more people are in service-type jobs.

Understanding how a product gets to be and how it comes to look like it is from the raw material is something which is totally lost on most Americans. That sense of all the thought that has to go into *making* anything mechanical—not just "Oh, I've got a great design here," but "I've got a great design I can actually manufacture"—is part of what we want to convey.

Unquestionably, the general public has no fundamental insight about product manufacture whatsoever. I just wish somehow we could educate them, but it's like trying to turn the Queen Mary around with a rowboat. There's so much to it when you really experience manufacturing. For the public, there probably never can be an insight; people are so, you might say, abstracted from the whole industrial scene.

The Russian inventor and designer Mikhail Kalashnikov was truly impressed by the cast slide for our P85 pistol [visiting America, as a guest of Ruger, in 1992]. Seeing a cast part and realizing how much of it is shaped in the casting process, and then looking at the finished piece and realizing how close this is to the casting is a revelation. If somehow we can convey a little bit of that, I think we will have done something really useful in conveying what this company is about.

I think to really make this point stick, there has to be some real evidence that the casting's metallurgical quality does not suffer. That's easily demonstrated—a steel investment casting is not like a piece of cast iron that will crack when you drop it on a concrete floor. It's steel, just as a forging is, but the casting has absolutely uniform grain structure, as opposed to the stresses that heavy drop-forging can create. If you tell people what you are doing and why, you are definitely better off.

The problem that Winchester had when they introduced the post-1964 Model 70 was one of perception. All of the things they did in terms of using stampings instead of forged parts or machined parts was perfectly acceptable from the strength standpoint, but from an aesthetics standpoint, the customers balked. I used to get the idea that our use of castings compromised our image of quality among some ignorant shooters; but over many years I gradually got the feeling it was no longer a serious influence. It's funny how the rest of the world has been so slow to move on investment castings—probably because the expense of getting up a foundry is enormous, or because some parts can't be cast, or just because they're already financially committed to their obsolete designs and machinery. Maybe it's a combination of all these reasons. They can always come to us for castings!

The 10/22 Carbine
The 10/22 Carbine was another joint project combining the talents of Harry Sefried and Bill Ruger, as well as Doug McClenahan. Designs were begun as early as the late 1950s, the rotary box magazine inspired by one of Bill's favorites, the Savage Model 99 rifle. Ruger was anxious to give the word to Jack O'Connor (March 25, 1964):

I have just received this proof of our new catalogue page and rush it to you herewith, because I hope you are going to be somewhat intrigued by our efforts to make a .22 rifle which avoids all the usual banalities—I am also sending this folder to other publications today and this represents our first release of information concerning this. I really think we have been successful in this and from a techni-

cal point of view, the new 10/22 is one of the best things we have done. We are planning to show the gun at the N.R.A. Show, but will not announce it in our advertising until June. Will rush-rush a sample as soon as possible, but at the moment have only three pilot guns which we are still tuning. Production guns are very near at hand, we should begin shipments early in May, but I hope to get a sample to [you soon].

The New York Times's Outdoor Editor, Oscar Godbout, was so impressed with the 10/22 that he wrote Ruger in appreciation of the "new .22 self-loader. . . . A typical Ruger gun; distinctive, ingenious and well made. Make sure, when you're ready to announce something that is news, to phone, write, send smoke signals, send a runner with a cleft stick, anything."

Godbout's faith in the new .22 was well placed. The 10/22 became one of the best-selling .22 rifles in history, and remains one of the most popular of all Rugers. It has become the favorite of small-game hunters, tin can "plinkers," and has won numerous matches in which speed, reliability, and accuracy are paramount. Over 3 million have been sold in less than 30 years.

The No. 1 and No. 3 Single-Shot Rifles
Ruger's views on single-shot rifles are those of a longtime aficionado dedicated to one of the most traditional of firearms:

Single-shots are a marvelous type of rifle. You can't

Two favorite rifles of two magnates. Long Island Railroad president Austin Corbin's Model 1886 Winchester, from a group of Winchesters custom built for his use at Corbin Park. Wild boar, elk, and whitetail deer were maintained in Corbin's own game preserve. Tin with inscribed lid a cigar humidor from Corbin's private railroad car. Corbin was one of the first to help rescue the North American bison from extinction. Park superintendent and naturalist Harold Baynes sits in cart drawn by bison. No. 1 Rifle in .270 caliber, a favorite of Bill Ruger, engraved by Alvin A. White; the other side with gold inlaid script WBR monogram.

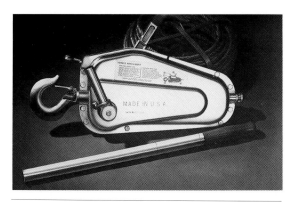

Winch-Hoist, made by Sturm, Ruger & Co.

shoot very fast, but you can shoot well, and they're certainly handy and light and dandy. When all is said and done, they are among my real favorites in firearms. The Alexander Henry is, of course, very similar to the Sharps, but more refined. The Henry is the rifle that started a whole train of good British single-shots. The British had a lot of them, as well as the Americans, and there is, of course, the Scottish Farquharson.

When I started thinking about the No. 1 rifle, the Farquharson was sort of a natural one to begin on. The big thing about these single-shot rifles is you just don't have so much of the gun constituting the action, thus the compact action shortens the overall length. Anyone who likes rifles appreciates these qualities as well as that special atmosphere about a single-shot. It may not be for everybody, but it's certainly very important to a lot of people.

Ruger No. 1 rifles, with their elegant lines, have always been a favorite of custom engravers and gunmakers. From *top*, by contemporary masters Alvin A. White, John E. Warren, and Paul Lantuch. The *top* rifle a factory sample, number 956, in .308 caliber, with 22" barrel; one of the '21 Club' group of rifles. The Creedmoor rifle (named after the famous Long Island rifle range), number 2374, with 34½" barrel, .45-70 caliber, made for *Gun Digest* editor John T. Amber, and featured on the publication's 1969 cover. *Bottom* rifle number 132-35920, in .30-06, with 22" barrel. Except for the Creedmoor, which was stocked by John Warren, the rifles have factory walnut stocks.

Our rifle, of course, is more sophisticated than the Farquharson, and has a very potent ejector of our design. I wanted a hammerless action with a dropping block, but the available interior space of the Borchardt-type action did not permit the inclusion of the trigger and other features which we felt were required. I must say I am pleased that so many of the world's truly great hunters have taken to the No. 1 rifle.

Master gunsmith and stockmaker Lenard M. Brownell, one of the hunters on an O'Connor-Ruger British Columbia hunt in the fall of 1963, played a key role in the design of the stocks for the No. 1 and in setting up the factory woodworking operations. He spelled out his hopes and ideas for the project in a January 17, 1964 letter to Ruger:

[I've] been getting a little impatient lately thinking about the single shot so was tickled to get the plans [you sent to me].

Although I have gone over them and find a few things I'll comment on, if it were to come out just as drawn it would be everything I've hoped for and more. I think this exceeds, by far, anything you have brought out to date and should find acceptance among a lot of shooters. After studying your plans and drawing pictures, I've noticed that some of my ideas after being played with revert back pretty much to what you have, although I had started to change some dimension or line.

My end conclusion is that you and I are quite in agreement on liking the English styling. Most of my experimenting was only slightly away from that but in the direction of what has become known as the "classic style." The reason being, I keep wondering if a little compromise to suit what domestic shooters are more used to, would not be more readily accepted by them. What people refer to as good classic styling as done by Monty Kennedy, Shelhammer and myself, is really only European slightly modified to better use of scope sights which are used almost exclusively by my customers.

. . . Do you propose two grades of these or two styles? This rifle has so many possibilities as to good styling, it will be hard to settle on just one. . . .

You said . . . the stock lends to manufacturing simplicity. This surprises me as it has some very nice features that a lot of so called custom stockers would fall flat on. One being the cute little shelf on under side of forend. . . .

You don't show much detail on a scope mount. How I would like to see a pair of integral dovetails, either both on the barrel or one on the top of receiver and one on the barrel. . . . With no bases necessary, you eliminate loose screws, makes for low mounting and if you produced scope rings, you would have that market about sewed up.

I hope this is material that may be of some help. You aren't in need of much from the looks of things.

Brownell became a valued member of Ruger's staff, and his practical eye and fine hand helped in creating guns with handsome, elegant, and (where possible or appropriate) classical stocks. Everyone said in 1966 that it was crazy to bring out a rifle that could only fire one shot before reloading, and that nobody would want one in the age of "firepower." Once again, Ruger was right, they were wrong, and the No. 1 has come to symbolize the classic appeal of Ruger firearms to many shooters.

Mary Thompson Ruger

Throughout these early years, Mary Ruger was a positive force. Mary was a true Southern belle and was immensely charming, witty, and bright. She could size people up readily, and handily, and was the source of sound business advice and insights into dealing with others. She had a magical way with people, and could inspire or cajole the best out of them. Stories about Mary are legion, and a selection reveals her multifaceted character and personality.

While accompanying an entourage of approximately a half dozen from the factory on a 1962 visit to Governor John A. Notte of Rhode Island, the Governor unguardedly confessed, prodded by Mary's coaxing, that he got a lot of his ideas by

The Ruger 10/22 Carbine

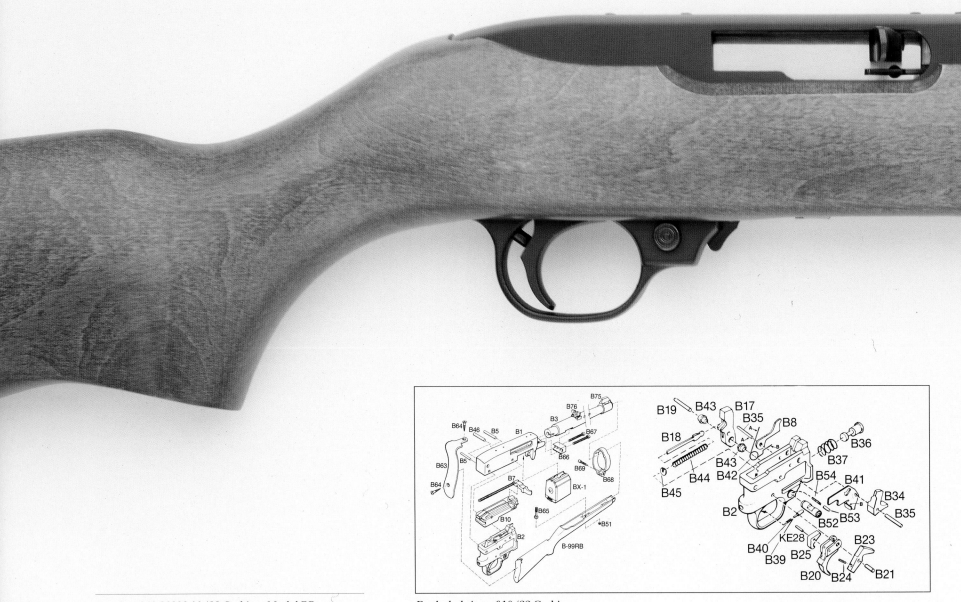

Number 240-26293 10/22 Carbine, Model RB.

Exploded view of 10/22 Carbine.

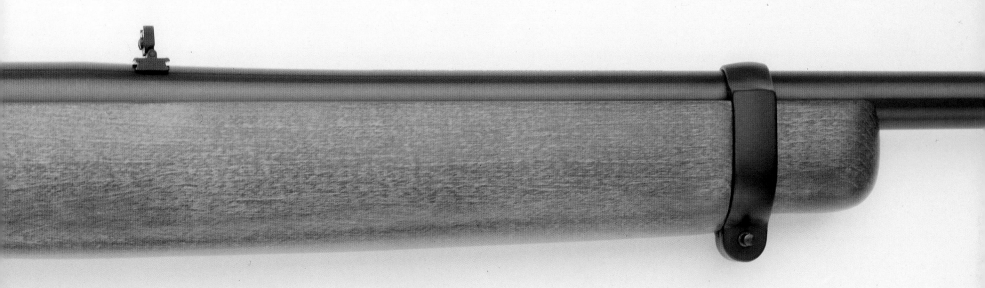

Introduced: 1964. "There is no finer 22 rimfire than a Ruger 10/22 autoloading carbine. . . . built to high-power rifle standards. . . . engineered to appeal to every shooter who appreciates exceptional quality and performance. Everything . . . is made better than it needs to be—full use is made of modern materials whenever they provide unique advantages and yet the finest of steel and walnut remain wherever required by tradition or function. . . . originality designed with sound engineering. Its smooth, handsome finishes, racy lines, perfect balance, and superb accuracy, make this new RUGER an approach toward perfection."

Serial Numbers: 1 to 200850; prefixes (began 1969) of 110-00000 to -99999, and similarly numbered serial prefixes 111-, 112-, 113-, 114-, 115-, 116-, 117-, 118-, 119-, 120-, 121-, 122-, 123-, 124-, 125-, 126-, 127-, 128-, 129-, and commencing anew with 230-, 231-, 232-, 233-, 234-, 235-, 236-, 237-, 238-00000 to -22094 (through 1993).

Production began in Southport, and manufacture was moved to the Newport factory in 1970, from serial number 110-25722.

Total Made Through 1993: In excess of 3,055,000.

Caliber: .22 Long Rifle.

Magazine Capacity: 10, in patented rotary detachable box.

Barrel Length: 18½".

Rifling: 6 grooves, right-hand twist, one turn in 16".

Markings: See Table of Markings, pages 330–35.

On left side of receiver (five variations known, differing in details as the R *marking):*
**RUGER MODEL 10/22 CARBINE [trademark] R
.22 LR CALIBER**
Serial number on left side of receiver near barrel breech.
On top of barrel (early production lacking **INC.***):*
**STURM, RUGER & CO., INC.
SOUTHPORT, CONN. U.S.A.**
Trademark and **RUGER** embossed on bottom of box magazine.
From approximately January 4, 1978 (serial range 117-00027), standard marking on barrel:
   U indicating guns used for demonstration or samples; suffix to serial number.
   S indicating surface blemish; suffix to serial number.
   D indicating duplicate serial number.

Sights: Fold-down, folding-leaf sporting rear, adjustable for windage and elevation. Gold bead front, dovetailed onto base integral with barrel, and adjustable for windage. Variations noted in front sights, particularly in blade size and profile.

Initial sights supplier was Lyman (and so marked on rear blade, with triangular pointer below curved sighting notch), from 1964–75, and again during part of 1977; sights by former Lyman employee William Renals (marked with an R on either end of base) from 1976 (except for part of 1977, and post 1992). The Renals sight blade has two types of notches, and can be rotated for choice; imprinted at center with a white diamond motif. Present production sights by Weimann Brothers Manufacturing.

Overall Length and Weight: 37", approx. 5 pounds.

Stocks: American walnut, originally issued without checkering, and with carbine barrel band. As walnut increased in price, switch made to birch (serial range 119-70067 to 121-50355), and finally to maple. Variations evolved of sporter style (fluted forend, sharply curved pistol grip, Monte Carlo comb, checkered, no barrel band), Sporter SP (classic profile, checkered forend and grip, and no barrel band), International (1964-70; Mannlicher style with forend cap; standard plain, deluxe checkered), laminated (introduced 1986; birch wood in multiple, ofttimes colorful, layers, supplied in blanks by Rutland Plywood Co. and termed by that firm "Stratabond").

Stock production originally by subcontractors, the S. E. Overton Co., with checkering done at the Ruger factory. The company woodworking shop began operations in 1971. Thereafter all stocks produced in-house.

Finish: Blued. Anodized aluminum receiver, trigger assembly (and barrel band, when present). Aluminum buttplate, anodized, used through 1976. Anodized aluminum alloy finish changed to teflon-coating, c. 1970. Stainless barrels satin finished.

Materials, Construction, and Innovations: Built from integrated subassemblies: trigger housing contains entire ignition

system, with high-speed swinging hammer (insuring shortest possible lock time), barrel secured to receiver by unique dual-screw dovetail system (providing exceptional rigidity and strength, and contributing to accuracy). Energy dissipating bolt. High-impact 10-shot rotary magazine with sturdy alloy stainless steel lips and ramps to guide cartridge into chamber. Cast aircraft aluminum alloy receiver and trigger housing. Positive bolt lock.

General Electric Celcon buttplate introduced in 1976 (116-38021 to -39625 serial range). Rubber buttpad used on deluxe sporters after c. 1989.

Issue Price: $54.50 (1965).

Engraving: Limited number factory engraved. Serial 111-08857 engraved and inscribed for presentation to Bart Skelton, son of writer "Sheeter" Skelton, on order from Stephen K. Vogel; at the same time, no. 111-08883 done for author; scroll embellishment on receivers by Denise Thirion, of A. A. White Engravers, Inc.

Price Sheet Listings and Major Production Variations:

10/22-R: Standard Carbine, walnut stock (first listing, 1965, through 1980 price sheets; returned to sheet 1987–89).

10/22-SP: Sporter style stock (from 1966–79 price sheets).

10/22-SPC: Sporter, hand checkered (from 1967–68 price sheets).

10/22-X: International (Mannlicher) style stock (from 1966–69 price sheets).

10/22-XC: International, hand-checkered (from 1967–69 price sheets).

10/22-SPCC: Canadian Centennial.

10/22-SPCCC: Canadian Centennial, checkered.

10/22-RB: Standard model, birch carbine stock (from 1980 price sheet to date).

10/22-DSP: Deluxe checkered American walnut stock (from 1980 price sheet to date).

K10/22-RB: Stainless barrel, birch carbine stock (from 1992 price sheet to date).

10/22-RBI: Standard model, with International full stock (from 1994 price sheet).

K10/22-RBI: Stainless barrel, with International full stock (from 1994 price sheet).

Matching .44 Carbine: Serial numbers 89000 to 92304 were special group of 10/22s to match .44 Carbine serials.

Liberty Series: On left side of barrel of 1976 production:

MADE IN THE 200th YEAR OF AMERICAN LIBERTY. Within serial range of approximately 115-42738 to 116-46233 (103,495 total, approximately 69,342 Carbines and 34,153 Deluxe Sporters).

Warning Series: Warning marking adopted approximately January 4, 1978, in serial range and with legend as indicated above.

Carbines:

Laminated Stock Series, Carbines: Begun within serial range 128-3384 to -95152, with a three-colored stock layered in red, blue-gray, and green ("green camo"). Only about 3,000 made of the first production.

In 1988 a second series begun, ordered by distributor Faber Brothers, Inc., and often termed the "FBI" gun (after the buyer, *not* the Federal Bureau of Investigation). The stocks colored reddish-brown, light-walnut, and tan ("desert camo"). Marked FBI 00000 to 01500 (on right side of receiver), and within serial range 230-53911 to -60408.

Kittery Trading Post issue: celebrating the firm's 50th anniversary. Marketed through Shawmut Distributors, parent organization of Kittery. 104 rifles only; with porcelain medallion

inlay on right side of stock, and accompanied by "Certificate of Ownership." Within serial range 230-72795 to -76409 and 231-06515 to -06529.

Other special issues or orders were filled for Faber Brothers, Badger, Dixie, FBF (Baker), Shawmut, Burney, P & B, Russell, Sportsman's Supply, Jerry's Sports, Point, Simmons, Western-Hoegee, Williams, all Ruger distributors. Late in 1991, Wal-Mart stores ordered a stainless 10/22, with laminated stocks. Negotiations on this order, for 10,000 units (serial range within 234-45400 to -93663), involved William B. Ruger, Sr., J. Thompson Ruger, and Sam Walton. The design featured a sling of black nylon with a RUGER patch stitched in red, and Uncle Mike's deluxe swivels. The Wal-Mart variation has since been repeated in large quantities.

A natural style laminate was ordered by All Sports, CSI, and Henry's, in 1993. Total order was 4,000.

Total color range of laminated stocks to date: green camo, desert camo, tree-bark camo, two-tone brown, walnut-red-green, olive camo, and natural.

Code numbers for laminated stock 10/22s, to date: **RB-Z, RB-ZS, RB-DZ, RB-BBZ, RB-BZ, RB-DZII, RB-TBZ, RB-BOZ,** and **DSP-TBZ** (deluxe) **RB-NZ** (Standard).

Silencer-Adapted Carbines for Law Enforcement and Military Use: Carbines with silencer attachments have been supplied for these specialized uses. Suppressors manufactured and fitted by SWD Company, Atlanta.

MSP (Military and Special Purpose): Suppressors also fitted by Sionics, Inc., and its replacement firm, Military Armaments Corporation. Sturm, Ruger sales of such arms have included shipments to Springfield Armory and Rock Island Arsenal, and other sites. Fingergroove sporters also supplied to Rock Island, with Bushnell scopes; the whole given a camouflage

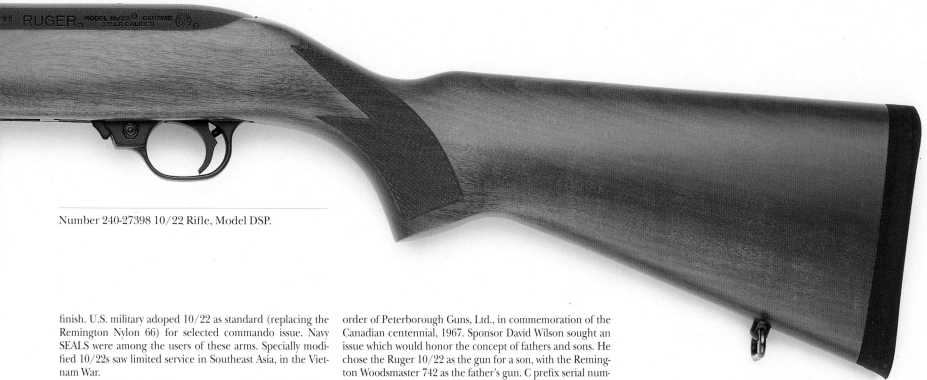

Number 240-27398 10/22 Rifle, Model DSP.

finish. U.S. military adoped 10/22 as standard (replacing the Remington Nylon 66) for selected commando issue. Navy SEALS were among the users of these arms. Specially modified 10/22s saw limited service in Southeast Asia, in the Vietnam War.

Some of these special-issue arms were fitted with a device to secure the bolt closed, and some had folding stocks, and other special features.

Sporter Models:

Fingergroove: Pronounced stock styling with fluted, beavertail forend, Monte Carlo comb, sling swivels, pistol grip cap (with white and black trademark), and plastic buttplate (embossed with trademark); introduced early in 1966, and first advertised in the February issue of *The American Rifleman.*. Stock made by S. E. Overton Co., based on drawings and specifications supplied by Ruger. Serial range from 43908 through 110-78890. Available checkered or non-checkered (only about 500 made of the former, within the range 64513 to 158480).

Canadian Centennial: A variation of the Fingergroove Sporter, made in checkered and plain versions; approximately 4,400 made (within range 79000 to 118000). Made on

order of Peterborough Guns, Ltd., in commemoration of the Canadian centennial, 1967. Sponsor David Wilson sought an issue which would honor the concept of fathers and sons. He chose the Ruger 10/22 as the gun for a son, with the Remington Woodsmaster 742 as the father's gun. C prefix serial numbers, from C1 on up. Buttstocks inlaid with silver centennial medallion. The top of the Ruger's receiver roll engraved with a centennial motif. The Remington and Ruger were cased together. Ruger stocks either checkered (3,025) or plain (1,399).

The Deluxe Sporter: Stock built in the Newport factory, with checkering as a standard feature. More refined stock style than that on the "fingergroove." With sling swivels. Serial range began with 110-90067. Buttplate changed from plastic to rubber in 1987 (transition within the range 128-64738 to -69029).

The Laminated Sporter: 1990 edition of 796, made on order of Faber Brothers, Inc. Black on black lamination of the "Tree-Bark style"; without checkering. Within serial range 223-15878 to -19491.

The International Sporter: Mannlicher style stock, first advertised in *The American Rifleman*, February 1966. Pistol grip cap

of black, with white inlay, impressed with black-outlined trademark; sling swivels; blued steel forend cap; barrel band not turned down. Within serial range 46077 to 110-12551. Made in both checkered (two variations identified, known as 1-Point and 2-Point) and plain versions (serial range 59636 to 110-12475).

Note: From March 14–21, 1987, Chief A.J. (John Huffer) set the world aerial target record by shooting 40,060 2½" cube wood blocks with the Ruger 10/22—without a single miss. He also set the world's one-day record, 8,900 blocks, without a miss. A total of eighteen 10/22s were used in the record, with ammunition supplied by Hansen Cartridge Co. Copper commemorative plaques were made for each of the 18 10/22s used in the event, and were inset on the stocks, but this is not a factory issue.

watching the Jack Paar TV show. While the Governor was being presented an inscribed Ruger .44 Magnum Carbine, everybody was photographed taking turns sitting in the Governor's chair.

Another time, when at the Ritz-Carlton Hotel in Boston on a holiday weekend, the Governor stopped by for a drink. He wanted to leave to prepare an address to the Rhode Island Assemby the next morning about raising taxes. Mary not only managed to persuade him to stay, she convinced him *not* to go before the assembly, *nor* to raise taxes! She was a woman ahead of her time.

When the new Southport post office building was opened—a building which, as confirmed by the postmaster, owed much of its existence to the explosion of mail to and from Sturm, Ruger and Company—the Rugers stood in the lobby. Pointing to President Kennedy's portrait on the wall, Mary said to Bill: "That should be your picture up there!"

One time, coming home in a snowstorm from

At *center*, the Thompson family home, Greensboro, where Ruger developed many of the details of the Ruger machine gun before working at the Springfield Armory and Auto Ordnance. *Top left*, Ruger with first whitetail deer, taken at King and Bartlett camp, in Maine; to *right*, testing of the .44 Magnum Carbine, in New Hampshire; *below*, Stan Terhune and George Hamilton, setting up Pine Tree Castings, 1963. *Below*, the Rugers on the day of their remarriage, 1957 (10 years after divorce). Family portrait taken soon after move to Center Street home, Southport; to *left*, May Ruger by Christmas tree; *below*, Stan Terhune and wife Carolyn. Hamilton children, *bottom left*, Scott, Perry Ann, and Tom (destined to be bass guitarist of the celebrated rock and roll band Aerosmith). *Lower right*, Bill Ruger, Jr., with Stone sheep trophy from British Columbia hunt, 1963; other trophies taken were grizzly bear and two mountain goats. Walter Berger, *far right*, beneath alluring photograph of Mary. XK120 Jaguar a Ruger favorite, Mary at the wheel. *Beneath*, candid shot of daughter Molly, Ruger with grandson Alex Vogel. Ruger by swimming pool, and the Rugers together on spring day by lilacs, both photographs taken at Southport home. Antelope hunt picture from Wyoming, 1955.

---

a New Year's Eve party at about 3 A.M., Ruger fell asleep at the wheel of their Jeep, and ran into a snowdrift. This woke him up, and he looked to check on Mary's condition. "Bang, all of a sudden, when I looked over at the passenger seat, Mary wasn't there! I was befuddled! Trying to reconstruct the evening, I got out of the Jeep. The drifts were some six feet deep. All of a sudden I heard a voice in the distance: 'I'm coming! I'm coming!' There was Mary; she'd somehow managed to fall out of the car, and Providence must have been watching, because nothing happened to her."

When Ruger mentioned with some concern to Mary that Harry Sefried had a habit of going into the model room and tinkering with the development of prototypes, she simply said that was Harry's way of doing things, and Bill had to expect someone creative like Harry to do things his own way, and not to try to change him.

Her mischievous nature was evident when she would tease Ruger by saying she would leave her estate to the animal rights fund-raisers, fully knowing how he felt about those activists. Her pet cats and dogs were liberally catered to with doting affection, and they never wanted for fresh meat or fish.

The Ruger marriage could at times be rocky; and though they were divorced in 1947, the couple remarried in 1957.

Mary was also a person of real strength; generous, caring, and devoted to her family. The Rugers' bond was one of enduring respect, matching intellects, and a mutual love which stood the test of time. All too soon, she passed away in 1994.

"Quality is to a product what character is to a man."

—Sign in Lenard Brownell's office
at the Newport factory

Early in the 1960s, Carl Wesselhoft, Ruger's brother-in-law, who worked the thirteen southeastern states for Sturm, Ruger from 1973 to 1991, was on a New England hunting trip with writer Robert Chatfield-Taylor, John T. Amber, Ruger, and others. One night single-shot rifles became the subject of such a heated discussion that Ruger finally said in desperation, "I will build a single-shot rifle so you guys will shut up!" That was the first indication to Carl that Ruger was thinking about making what became the No. 1 rifle.

I first visited Bill Ruger in Southport, and later went hunting as his guest in Newport, when the No. 1 rifle was introduced. There was a spot I walked to in the forest, where the wild boar were likely to be, and I tested the new Ruger with a single-shot kill—just as the rifle was designed to do.

When I stayed at his Southport home, on Center Street, it was like being in a private art gallery. I was so taken by his collection of paintings that the experience launched my own collecting in that area. Not only did I have one of those visits with Bill that you can't forget; I left his mansion house a determined and dedicated art collector. As it turned out, in later years we sometimes bid against each other at auctions! Which no doubt annoyed him a bit—since he started it all!

—Robert E. Petersen,
Founder and Chairman
Petersen Publishing Company

About collecting, Ruger wrote to Lindley Eberstadt, Edward Eberstadt & Sons, New York (June 2, 1966):

"I wish I had more time to think about collecting. The only thing I am collecting now is small green steel engravings of the Presidents."

The Ruger No. 1 Single-Shot Rifle

Number 133-19491 No. 1 Single-Shot Rifle, .300 Winchester Magnum, with 26" barrel.

Introduced: First shipment, September 1966; initial advertising, 1967; "A more efficient long range rifle.... the single-shot action is approximately 4½" inches shorter than that of a standard length bolt action ... the single-shot may have a longer barrel than the bolt gun, if they are both to be of the same overall length. As a result, the single-shot will deliver increased velocities from modern magnum cartridges.... This modern classic puts to a true test the skill and marksmanship of the hunter."

Serial Numbers: *No. 1 Rifles:* Marked on the left side of the bottom of the frame, beginning with 1 to 8437. Prefix added to numbering in 1968, beginning with 130-00000, up to -49998, 131-00000 to -54116, 132-00000 to -99999, 133-00000 to -13007 (through 1993). Not all serial numbers used, occasionally on early production.

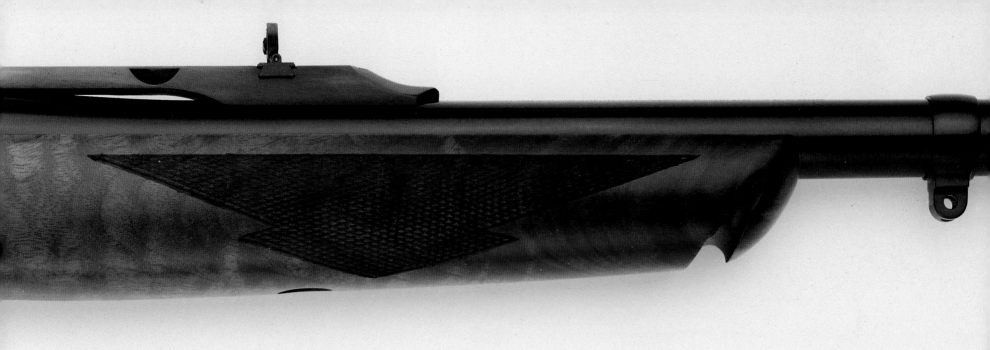

Total Made Through 1993: In excess of 180,000.

Calibers: .218 Bee, .22 Hornet, .222 Remington, .223, .22 PPC, .22-250, .220 Swift, 6mm PPC, 6mm Remington, .243 Winchester, .257 Roberts, .25-06, .270 Winchester, .270 Weatherby Magnum, .280, 6.5 Remington Magnum, 7 x 57mm, 7mm Magnum, .30-06, .300 Holland & Holland, .300 Weatherby Magnum, .300 Winchester Magnum, .308 Winchester, .338 Winchester Magnum, .375 Holland & Holland Magnum, .38-55, .404 Jeffrey, .416 Remington Magnum, .416 Rigby, .45-70, .458 Winchester Magnum.

Barrel Lengths: Initially introduced in 22", 24", and 26". A-type (lightweight) in 22". D-type (heavyweight) in 24". B-type (medium weight) in 26". A limited number of rifles built with special barrel lengths. 20" barrel introduced with International Model in 1983.

Rifling: Right-hand twist; number of grooves and pitch varies according to caliber; 6 grooves, one turn in 14", generally employed.

Markings: See Table of Markings, pages 330–35.

On top of barrel through c. 1976:

STURM, RUGER & CO. INC., SOUTHPORT, CONN. U.S.A.
Differences will be noted in the refinement of the roll dies.

Calibers roll marked *on left side of barrel breech.*

SAFE *on upper tang* through nearly all of production; for a short time in early series, s was employed.

Some hand-markings also evident internally *on stocks, forearm hangers, and early breechblocks.*

Sights: Folding-leaf open sights dovetailed onto barrel quarter rib. Dovetail style gold bead front sight. Front sight ramps of early rifles slotted for hood, a feature discontinued in 1968; early barrels protrude further beyond sight band. Scope ring apertures machined onto barrel ribs on all models, except IV. Scope rings themselves show evolutionary changes.

Overall Length and Weight: Vary from approx. 7¼ pounds for models 1-A, 1-S, and the No. 1 International, up to approx. 9 pounds for the model 1-V. Overall length for a 22" barrel rifle at 38½".

Stocks: American black walnut; checkered pistol grip and forend. Deluxe stock with polyurethane finish. Some variations noted in checkering patterns observed on buttstock, on Alexander Henry style forearm, and on beavertail forearm. Steel pistol grip caps show variation in company trademark stamping, with the first variant a more delicate stamping than a deeper and somewhat larger later stamping. Buttpads evolved from the early style with differences in center reinforcement and contours of the edges.

Finish: Blued.

Materials, Construction, and Innovations: Investment cast steel frame; steel trigger guard and barrel rib or sight blocks cut for patented Ruger scope rings. Steel finger lever. Douglas barrels through c. 1973; thereafter by Wilson Arms Co., until manufacture assumed by Ruger. Variations also evident in construction detailing of the finger lever, forearm hanger.

Combines beauty, elegance, and strength, with compactness and accuracy, and the challenge of single-shot marksmanship and sportsmanship. Selective ejection. Shotgun style safety on upper tang. Investment casting technology for frame, loading lever, and selected parts. The ultimate evolution of the single-shot rifle.

Issue Price: $280.00 (1967).

Engraving: Early presentation rifles, known as the "21 Club" series, made in a quantity of 35, including the following writers, Warren Page, John T. Amber, Charles Askins, Roger Barlow, Pete Barrett, Pete Brown, Elmer Keith, Pete Kuhlhoff, and Jack O'Connor, each of whom received an engraved rifle with a game scene on one side and a gold inlaid monogram of the writer's initials on the other; this series embellished by Alvin A. White. Serials 9 and 16 were made for Herb Glass. Most of the remaining rifles bore inscriptions only. The "21 Club" rifles were in single digit up to four digit serial numbers. Serial numbers 270 and 956 engraved for William B. Ruger, Sr., by Alvin A. White. The Creedmoor rifle, serial number 2374, was the first elaborately embellished factory deluxe No. 1. Engraved, gold inlaid, and stocked by John Warren, this 34½" barrel rifle had been inspired by the Creedmoor target rifles of the 1870s and 1880s. It was featured on the color front and back cover for the 1969 edition of *The Gun Digest.* In honor of Amber's 25th anniversary as editor of *The Gun Digest,* a second Creedmoor No. 1 was built, engraved by Lynton McKenzie and Winston Churchill, fitted with a 34" barrel, and chambered in .45 caliber; serial number, 130-06888. The rifle was completed in June 1975. The "Ruger North American" series was introduced in 1985, with the announced issue to be 21 rifles, each honoring a major species

of North American big game, and each elaboratedly engraved, gold inlaid and cased, and accompanied by paintings depicting wildlife scenes which in turn were embellished on the matching rifle. The first of the series was donated by the company to the Arms and Armor Department of The Metropolitan Museum of Art, for a fund-raising auction held by Christie's, 1985. The second completed was of a mountain lion theme. Factory engraved rifles are rare; non-factory engraved rifles, usually custom-stocked as well, have challenged the artistry and craftsmanship of engravers and gunmakers worldwide. A rifle by Heym of Germany, number 43503, is in the collection of William B. Ruger, Sr.

Serial number 132-35920 engraved and gold and silver inlaid for William B. Ruger, Sr., by Paul Lantuch.

Price Sheet Listings and Major Production Variations: Initially issued in five versions, which evolved by 1970 into the following advertised designations: First sales were special order with barrel length and weight, sighting equipment, and forend variations.

1-A, *The No. 1 Light Sporter:* In .243, .270, .30-06 calibers, with 22" lightweight barrels, Henry style forends, and open sights.

1-B, *The No. 1 Standard Rifle:* In .22-250, 6mm, .243, .25-06, .270, 7mm Magnum, .30-06, and .300 Magnum, with 26" medium barrels, semi-beavertail forends, and Ruger rings for scope sights.

1-H, *The No. 1 Tropical:* In .375 H & H and .458 Winchester Magnum, with 24" heavyweight barrels, Henry forends, and open sights. Later referred to as Tropical Rifles.

1-S, *The No. 1 Medium Sporter:* In 7mm Magnum, .300 Magnum, and .45-70, with 26" medium barrels, Henry forends, and open sights.

1-V, *The No. 1 Special Varminter:* In .22-250, .25-06, 7mm Magnum, and .300 Magnum, with 24" heavyweight barrels, semi-beavertail forends, and target scope mounts.

In **1981** a sixth designation was added:

1-AB, *The No. 1 Standard Light Sporter:* In .223, .270, 7 x 57mm, and .30-06, with 22" lightweight barrels, semi-beavertail forends, and Ruger rings for scope sights. Discontinued in **1983,** the same year in which the No. 1 International was announced **(1-RSI).**

1-RSI, *The No. 1 International:* In .243, .270, 7 x 57mm, and .30-06, with 20" lightweight barrels, Mannlicher style forend, adjustable folding-leaf rear sight on quarter rib, with ramp front sight base and dovetailed gold bead front sight. Approximately 7¼ pounds.

Liberty Series: Rifles made in 1976 roll marked on the left side of the barrel, adjacent to forend: **MADE IN THE 200th YEAR OF AMERICAN LIBERTY.**

Warning Series: Warning marking adopted approximately January 4, 1978, in serial range and with legend as indicated above.

NRA Hunt of a Lifetime Rifle: 1977, built in 7mm Remington Magnum caliber, as part of the *American Hunter* magazine "Hunt of a Lifetime Sweepstakes." 104 rifles of this model were made, and a total of 99 were awarded. Each rifle is roll marked on the right side of the frame: THE AMERICAN HUNTER/NRA [trademark] NRA/1977 HUNT OF A LIFETIME. The serial numbers were NRA 1 to NRA 104.

Lyman Centennial Rifle: 1978, in .45-70. 101 sets built in Grade I and 1,000 in Grade II. Grade I rifles were hand engraved, with custom stocks, 28" D weight barrels, and tubular 4X Lyman Century scopes; serial numbers L-001-1878 to L-101-1978. The Grade II featured a photo-engraved frame, and bore serial numbers L-78-0001 to L-78-1000. A unique William Lyman Commemorative cased rifle was also made, preceding the Grades I and II. The elaborate set was displayed at the 1978 NRA show in Salt Lake City, and was sold at auction to benefit the NRA.

California Highway Patrol: 1981, built in a quantity of 1,820, chambered for .357 Magnum, in 1-A configuration, and without a special serial range. The series was sold by *A.P.B.* magazine, a publication of the California Highway Patrol. Roll marked on the left side of the frame was LIMITED EDITION beneath the flying wheel CHP trademark.

One Shot Antelope Hunt: Roll marked on left side of frame with event logo, and inscription: *One Shot/Antelope Hunt/ Lander, Wyoming.* Roll marked on right side of frame with

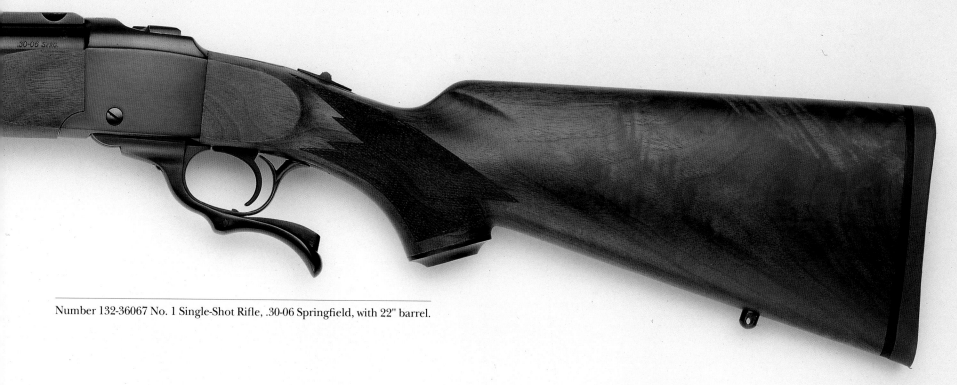

Number 132-36067 No. 1 Single-Shot Rifle, .30-06 Springfield, with 22" barrel.

name of shooter, his team, and a serial number. Limited numbers made for participants only. Introduced c. 1978.

Guns Magazine *25th Anniversary:* Engraved by Ray Viramontez, stocks by Al Lind, gunsmithing by Buzz Huntington; 24" Shilen barrel, 7mm R.C.B.S. caliber; built in 1981. English walnut stock of exhibition grade. Right side of breech with *Guns* logo, Ruger trademark, and inscription. Left side with inscription: **25 YEARS 1955–1980.** Donated by *Guns* as part of a fund-raising project for the 1984 U.S. Olympic Shooting Team.

Safari Club International: 1982, 60 No. 1 Tropical rifles commissioned, in .375 H & H Magnum, with 24" heavy barrels. Frames were etched and gold finished with scrollwork and the SCI logo on the right side, and scrollwork and an inscription on the left: *Safari Club International /Limited Edition /1 of 60.*

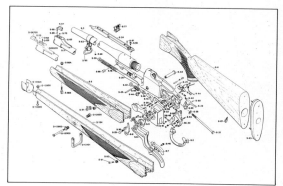

Exploded view of No. 1 Single-Shot Rifle.

The Ruger No. 3 Carbine

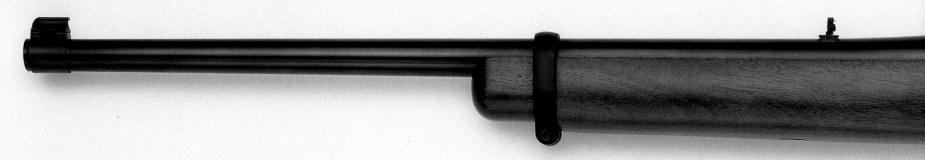

Introduced: 1973. "A Modern Rifle in the Classic Style. The Same Strong, Rugged Action as the Ruger No. 1 Rifle, with an American Style Lever."

Serial Numbers: 130-50000 to -70344. *Note: From 1980 serial numbers intermix with No. 1 Rifles.*

Total Made Through 1986: In excess of 30,000.

Calibers: .45-70, .22 Hornet (discontinued 1982), .30-40 Krag (discontinued 1978), .223 Remington (1978–85), .375 Winchester (1979–80), .44 Magnum (1981–86). Other calibers include: .375 (1979–83).

Barrel Length: 22".

Rifling: Right-hand twist standard; grooves and pitch vary according to caliber, *e.g.:* .45-70: 8 grooves, one turn in 20". .223: 6 grooves, one turn in 10". .22 Hornet: 6 grooves, one turn in 16".

Markings: See Table of Markings, pages 330–35.

On top of breech:

RUGER [banner motif]
No. 3

On top of barrel, after January 1, 1978, from serial range approximately 130-65000:

Before using gun-read warnings in *instruction manual* **available free— from Sturm, Ruger & Co., Inc. Southport, Conn. U.S.A.—**

Caliber and **SR** proof monogram *on left side of barrel at breech.*

Serial number *on left side of bottom of receiver, adjacent to front of finger lever.*

SAFE *on upper tang.*

Sights: Early production, folding-leaf Lyman sporting rear, adjustable for elevation and windage; gold bead undercut style front sight, on blade dovetailed onto barrel band. Later production of Ruger rear and front sights, with latter straight-cut. Some overlap occurs. 16" sight radius.

Number 132-32726 No. 3 American Single-Shot Carbine, .223 caliber, with 22" barrel.

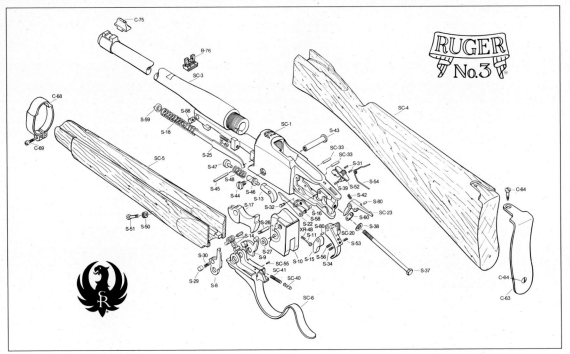

Exploded view of No. 3 Single-Shot Rifle.

Overall Length and Weight: 38½", approximately 6 pounds (.45-70).

Stocks: Polyurethane-finished American walnut, 13⅜" length of pull, 1½" drop at comb, 2½" drop at heel.

Finish: Blued.

Materials, Construction, and Innovations: Winchester Low Wall style trigger guard-finger lever, carbine style stock, barrel band forend attachment, and curved buttplate.

Issue Price: $165.00 (1973).

Price Sheet Listings and Major Production Variations:

Type **1A:** *Early Production,* built in 1973, serial range 130-50001 to -51500. Barrel not drilled or tapped for scope mountings. Round top buttstock, aluminum alloy buttplate, Lyman rear sight with white triangle sight point; undercut front sight. Catalogued in calibers .22 Hornet, .30-40 Krag, .45-70 Government (production primarily the latter). *Note:* Some early carbines (number 130-50100 or before) have non-slotted pivot pin for finger lever (as on pre-1973 No. 1 Rifles); approximately 10 or less built.

Type **1B:** *Later Production,* built from late 1973–75, same as above, but drilled and tapped for scope mounts, which could be purchased from the company as an accessory item. Serial range 130-51500 to -55000.

Type **2:** *1976 Production, Liberty Models,* marked on left side

of barrel: **MADE IN THE 200th YEAR OF AMERICAN LIBERTY.** Otherwise same as **Later Production, Type I** carbines. Buttplate changed to Celcon (plastic) as the year progressed. Serial range 130-55000 to -60000.

Type **3:** *1977–1984 Production, Post-Liberty Models,* 1977 and early 1978 production has a combination of **Type IB** and **Type 2,** and is termed **3A:** assembled from pre-Liberty parts and are pre-"Warning." Flattop buttstock adopted, Ruger sights replacing Lyman sights. Serial range 130-60000 to -66000. Some intermingling of features.

Late 1977 production includes the "Warning" barrel marking, and some rifles in the 130-62000 to -65000 range will include that roll die.

Type **3B:** *From late 1978 through end of production, "Warning Models,"* feature "Warning" barrel marking, drilled and tapped barrels, Celcon buttplates, Ruger sights. Serial range from 130-65000, and including all 131- and 132- prefix carbines.

Viper Simulator: **3A** Tracer Trainer, built on the No. 3A action, for U.S. military training with tracer ammunition. The action was installed in a rocket launcher to train the operator under simulated tactical situations, at reduced cost. Serial number range 132-39000 to -57000. Approximately 1,400 produced.

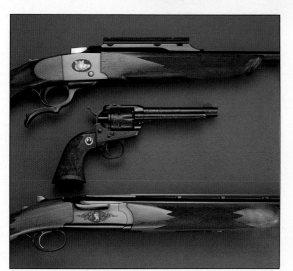

Presentations from a grateful Bill Ruger to his old friend Bill Lett; each inscribed and each with serial number 24. The Single-Six and No. 1 Rifle by Alvin A. White; the Red Label 20 gauge by Leonard Francolini.

Letter to Judge Don Martin, June 4, 1959— A Working Holiday in England

I have been in England and Europe for the past seven weeks on a combination vacation and business trip. My wife went with me and we traveled luxuriously on the Cunard line. In London I made friends with all the leading gunmakers and got invited to a fascinating dinner given by the "Gunmakers Company." This is the sort of ancient guild of London gunmakers and it is the organization which runs the London proof house today. It was a strictly formal occasion, requiring me to rent a suit of tails, and given in one of the old guild halls in the old part of London. The ancient usages and rituals involved in this dinner are still maintained in full force and the atmosphere was practically medieval. They were a wonderful bunch of people and the eight course dinner was accompanied by a different wine with every course—a very interesting experience. My invitation came from the director of Holland & Holland, Malcolm Lyell, and in the course of my stay in London, I not only made his acquaintance, but also that of Vernon Harris of Rigby and Harry Lawrence of Purdey's.

Over on the continent, I went through the

Ray Viramontez at his engraving vise, the Blackhawk embellished by Charles Jerred, the burins from his workbench, and the envelope showing his signature scroll device. Single-Six engraved in Spain, a 1956 Ruger brochure announcing revolvers which were customarily engraved by Jerred, a former L. C. Smith Gun Company engraver. Aluminum grip frames inscribed through anodized finish. Rifle engraved for William B. Ruger, Sr., as a sample, by Alvin A. White; serial number 956. Writer remembers calling on Ruger and Ed Nolan to discuss engraving program for the No. 1 rifles, representing A. A. White Engravers, Inc. Throughout company's history, Ruger concentrated on developing his product line, instead of becoming involved in often time-consuming demands for custom hand-embellishments. "Not one penny spent on meaningless ornamentation," read a 1970s Ruger M77 rifle advertisement.

F.N. [Fabrique Nationale, Herstal, Belgium] plant, which is really tremendous. They have 12,000 employees, 8,000 working on firearms and ammunition and the balance on motor scooters. They were making all the Browning stuff, Mauser and a great many military automatics and light machine guns—a really dynamic outfit. At the other end of the scale, I saw the Hammerli plant in Lenzburg, Switzerland, and there, of course, fine craftsmanship applied to specialized automatic weapons was the order of the day.

Ruger also looked into several investment casting firms, and had a list of several West German contacts to work from. His list, supplied by the German-American Trade Promotion Office, also bore names of shotgun and combination rifle makers, and manufacturers of sport rifles, small bore rifles, and even alarm and starting pistols.

Ruger's Plans for a Factory in Puerto Rico, 1957–60

A nearly forgotten letter reveals the scope of the founder's plans for expansion. In March of 1957 Ruger wrote to Manuel E. Benitez, of the Economic Development Administration, New York, that "We have reached the point where we are, virtually, convinced that our proposed manufacturing subsidiary in Puerto Rico would be successful. We must, of course, make a personal visit to Puerto Rico, and we must develop more of a detailed picture of how our operation would be arranged but on the basis of the very considerable information you have given us, we are very optimistic. I am most anxious to visit the Island and plan to do so early in April."

In February of 1960 he wrote to friend Wilson Rood, of Santuce, Puerto Rico: "I am writing to ask if you think you would be interested in heading-up a Puerto Rican plant for us. We are just

about set to go ahead, if we can get the right people. If you are interested let me know and we can go into details." And in March of 1962 Ruger wrote Rood, indicating the idea had not been forgotten: "Our plans for a Puerto Rican operation were derailed last year, but the program is far from a dead issue. We have an investment casting expert working for us here as a metallurgist and it is quite possible that we will find the additional engineering talent we need in the near future." The site was slated for San Germán.

In the end the rapid expansion of the Newport and the Southport operations dominated company time, and Puerto Rico remained on the shelf, forever.

Ruger Knives

Using castings from the Pine Tree division, Sturm, Ruger briefly experimented with hunting knives in the 1960s. Chrome-molybdenum 4140 and beryllium copper alloy steels were used. Some of the blades were marked 4140, but that was the extent of the markings. Although prototypes were polished to varying stages of manufacture, no complete knives were ever made. The beryllium blades were virtually impossible to break, but the project was dropped when it was learned that a poisonous gas was given off by the beryllium copper in the polishing process.

On creating something new, Ruger wrote to friend Roger Barlow (March 3, 1966):

"Whenever anything really great is created, it is the outcome of someone's real convictions. The corollary of this would be that an attempt to please the majority can only produce an Edsel."

CHAPTER IV

"Build Your Car . . . House . . . Rifle the Way You Want It"

The Ruger Style
1967–1972

B ill and Mary Ruger are on their honeymoon, a grand tour of Europe, from May to August 1938. At peak rush hour, smack in the middle of London's Piccadilly Circus, Bill spots a sleek, racy, strikingly beautiful, obviously high-performance car. It is light blue in color, with a gentleman operator at the wheel. Ruger weaves and dodges through the fren-

---

Ruger's enchantment with cars rivals his dedication to guns. Early influence evident from framed photograph of his father and party in immaculate new open touring car. Boyhood engine designs at *lower right.* Ruger in his first sports car, an MG, at *top left,* which was followed by stream of high performance machines by Jaguar, Ferrari, Bentley, Bugatti, Rolls-Royce, numerous American classics, and the Ruger Sports Tourer. The Ruger won its class on first entering of Mt. Equinox Hill Climb event. Old friend Luigi Chinetti, Sr., (in crash helmet) and with associates at 1972 LeMans 24 Hour race (to *right* of early auto technical book). Formula I World Champion Phil Hill and racer-commentator Sam Posey at same LeMans event (*lower left*). Indianapolis 500 pit pass pin from time when Ruger considering purchase of Meyer-Drake company, manufacturers of the Offenhauser engine. *Bottom left,* honeymoon pictures, 1938, with Renault used to drive around continental Europe. At *top center,* Bill, Jr., award-winning Cadillac coupe, on display at Meadowbrook, Michigan, event; later won again at Pebble Beach Concourse, 1994. Not pictured, Ruger, Sr., favorite contemporary passenger car, the BMW.

---

10. 1968
M77 Bolt-Action Rifle
11. 1970
Ruger Sports Tourer Car
12. 1971
Security-Six Double-Action Revolver

---

zied traffic, reaches the car, peers down at the debonair driver, and asks, "What kind of car is this?"

"It's a Bugatti."

The name, like an incantation, awakens a passion from Ruger's childhood, one derived from his love of things which combine beauty and mechanical complexity. As with the guns which have absorbed his attention for the past several years, Ruger's deep interest in cars is based on an appreciation of their artistry, craftsmanship, history, mechanics, performance, and romance. Although several years will pass before it finds an outlet in his creative impulses, the memory of the Bugatti will be a partial impetus to the automotive equivalent of the Ruger Super Blackhawk revolver: The Ruger Sports Tourer.

"When I have a subject at hand, I study it profoundly. Day and night it is before me. My mind becomes pervaded with it. Then the effort which I have made is what people are pleased to call the 'fruit of genius.' It is the fruit of labor and thought."

—Alexander Hamilton

Sturm, Ruger Diversifies

With several models of pistols, revolvers, and rifles in production—and more in various stages of development—Bill Ruger considered diversifying his product line. Drawing on his longtime interest in fine automobiles, in 1965 he undertook the design and construction of a working prototype of a luxury touring car.

Ruger described his rationale in a 1975 case study of Sturm, Ruger prepared by the Harvard Business School:

> I've always been interested in cars and motorcycles since I was young. I've tinkered around with a number of cars including Jaguars, Rolls-Royces, and Ferraris. In the process, I noticed that there was a lot of overlap between guns and cars among purchasers. I felt that a well-known reputation for quality and engineering design in guns would be useful in selling a particular type of car; hopefully the name Ruger would correlate the two. I also felt I had some insight into what people would like to have in cars. I thought we could come up with a beautifully engineered car that we could sell at a profit.

Ed Nolan, then Ruger's Vice President of Marketing, told the Harvard case writer:

> Bill has a love for engineering and design in everything, particularly cars. When we used to go to lunch, and I would stop for gas, Bill would get out and look underneath the cars on the racks. After he bought one Bentley, I remember he set up a guy in a garage to work on it. We would go to lunch and then stop by the garage afterwards; Cal [the mechanic] always kept a second slide board and before you knew it, Bill had his coat off and was banging around underneath the car and talking about it for hours with Cal. I started taking work with me to lunch because I knew we would wind up at the garage.

The Ruger Sports Tourer, as it was called, was described in the Harvard study as a sports-touring car with a soft top and body styling similar to the 1929 vintage Bentley. However, it used a modern, 427 V-8 Ford engine, sophisticated Monroe shocks, Bendix brakes, and a double-walled fiberglass body. Ruger's intent was to sell his cars, on a limited basis, at a price of approximately $12,000–$13,000. Two prototypes of the Ruger Tourer were built, costing some $400,000 for design and development. They were exhibited at the New York Automobile Show in 1969 and 1970, and were written up favorably in a number of car magazines.

Ruger to Luigi Chinetti, Sr., April 7, 1965

I am writing on the subject we have discussed previously—the possibility of having an engine built by Ferrari for our Vintage Sports Car.

I have been doing some more thinking about this and wonder now if it might not be more agreeable to Ferrari to sell us the 5 litre V-12, which I assume is similar in layout to the 330-GT. This would eliminate the work of designing a brand new engine and perhaps with this extra business, the factory would have some advantage in the form of lower production costs on this large motor.

I wonder if you would refer this subject to the factory—I think that we could use as many as 500 of these engines per year, depending on the price.

Although Ruger spent eight years attempting to bring the Tourer to production, in the end he scrapped the project. As he told the Harvard case writer:

> I really felt this car would sell but unfortunately we got a very ambiguous market reception. Then there was also a mechanical problem in the steering which caused the car to drift. This blasted some confidence in the car. We finally decided to abandon the program in 1973.

On Cars, Guns, and Engineering

Cars and guns are art forms, but ones with an engineering or scientific component, unlike painting pictures or making sculptures. When you design something—a utilitarian object—it's got to represent technology as well as art. It's acquired all the accumulations of tradition. It has to look a certain way. The variations in cars—and it's always been this way—really come out quite small when you look at them in broad perspective. They all have four wheels, they all have hoods out front, they all have a feeling of motion and power. That general envelope dictates a lot about the drivetrain and the other more technical characteristics.

So it is with firearms, yet I've always felt that the soul of the true gunmaker can be seen in the artistry of his firearms and their functional elegance.

On His Automotive Inspirations

W. O. Bentley certainly has to be given an exalted position in the panoply of automobile engineers. The more you read about him, the more you see that. Bugatti, I think, was a bit more of a showman and a bit more capricious, a more bohemian sort of artist than Bentley, but he certainly did create machines that worked well, and he showed great independence of thought. On this side of the Atlantic, the man who appeals to me most is Harry Stutz and his successor in the Stutz Motor Car Company, Frederick Moskovics. And then, above all, Frank Lockhart, my great, great, great boyhood hero—killed going for the land speed record in the Stutz Blackhawk Special, back in April 1928. Lockhart was the Lindbergh of the racetrack. He was running with an intercooler at Indianapolis two years before those other S.O.B.s figured out what he'd done. He invented it, at twenty-three years old! And I think of Birkigt of Hispano-Suiza. Marc Birkigt was also a great gun designer. He designed lots of aircraft machine guns and feeding mechanisms for fighter planes and so on and so forth. Interesting people . . .

On Eminent Automotive Designers

They have several common traits: a fair amount of technical knowledge and engineering insight, mechanical instinct, a degree of sophistication, I suppose. Somewhat competitive in their sphere, wanting to design the best thing of its kind, and probably putting that ahead of making money. They were not often the financial beneficiaries of their own good works. I can't believe that any of them became as rich as Henry Ford. Perhaps it's the basic faith of engineers who are primarily inter-

For
1970...

The "Ruger Cars" brochure; reverse with technical identification; obverse with statement and details as follows:

Ruger Cars

The Ruger Car is designed as a machine for travel which completely transcends the vagaries of fashion: it is a permanent possession, like a good shotgun, a fine saddle, or a handmade fly rod. The long term economy and logic of this Ruger Concept never fails to impress the astute judge of value. All the performance and luxury of the new Ruger can be protected for years to come because it is mechanically accessible and because it is built of time-tested materials: the stainless steel exhaust system, the heavily chromium-plated brass and bronze hardware, the corrosion proof fiber-glass body and fenders, the fine woolen carpeting and the genuine leather upholstery. The Ruger Car is designed to combine extreme durability with the highest standards of performance, luxury, and safety available today.

Luxuries and Necessities

The body shell with firewall back is, except for the doors, a one piece fiber glass moulding, with steel reinforcement. The doors, two in front, one in the rear, are basically aluminum castings. The radiator shell is plated brass, the engine hood is aluminum.

All external surfaces of the body except the hood and fenders are covered with Naugahyde, available in a choice of color. The interior and seats are upholstered entirely with genuine leather, and best quality cut pile woolen carpeting.

The windshield is made from Triplex laminated electrically heated safety glass, mounted in all brass, chrome-plated frame.

The two-speed electric windshield wipers are specially designed to sweep a wide area.

The solid walnut instrument panel carries the individual, internally-illuminated Smith's instruments, comprising tachometer, speedometer with trip mileage, oil temperature, oil pressure, water temperature, ammeter, fuel supply, and clock, plus conveniently sited switches.

The front seats are individually adjustable fore-and-aft and for back angle. The rear seat is comfortable for two adults and may be readily removed to provide additional luggage accommodation.

Comprehensive all weather equipment includes a hot water heater with thermostatically regulated control and two speed blower. Detachable side windows are provided and are designed to be stowed in a locker behind the back seat when not in use.

The folding top is lightly constructed and can be easily lifted manually. A top boot and tonneau cover are provided.

Lighting equipment consists of two 7" sealed beam headlights, parking lights, turn signals, backing lights, tail lights, brake lights, illuminated rear license plate, and interior lighting under the cowl. Heavy gauge wiring throughout, and all circuits provided by fifteen fuses and a circuit breaker.

The car in concept conforms to all applicable U.S. Motor Vehicle Safety Standards.

Ruger Cars Division
STURM, RUGER & CO., INC.
SOUTHPORT, CONN., U.S.A.

Dave Davis on Bill Ruger

I met Bill Ruger at a cocktail party given by *Road & Track* magazine in connection with the 1970 New York Automobile Show, where Bill was showing the Ruger Special. I approached him with some caution—he does not look like anyone you'd slap on the back—introduced myself, and said I greatly admired his work. He smiled and said that he had enjoyed my work, too. The ice was broken. We have been friends ever since.

My first experience with a Ruger firearm was on a trip to Carroll Shelby's ranch at Terlingua, Texas, in the middle sixties. Carroll had been a great racing driver and was the creator of the Shelby Cobra. We flew to Texas from Los Angeles in the old DC-3 that he'd purchased from the Hearst family. Among the goods and chattels crammed into the airplane were a half dozen Ruger .44 Carbines and what seemed like a lifetime supply of ammunition. I so enjoyed the little Ruger .44 in the west Texas desert that I immediately bought a full-stock version for my deer-hunter father. Soon after that I purchased a Number One single-shot rifle in 7 mm Remington magnum, and I was a Ruger aficionado from that day onward. I own a couple of dozen Rugers at this writing, and that thirty-year-old single-shot is still my favorite and the hunting rifle I use most often.

Bill Ruger is equally durable. He has changed little or not at all in the twenty-five years of our friendship—still tough, occasionally irascible, and always gracious. He keeps track of the lives of countless friends and acquaintances, and always has something pertinent to say about my life or my business when we speak, sometimes after a six-month hiatus. Illness has slowed him down but not dulled his edge. His incredible talent as a designer and engineer still shines forth. I'm in awe of his abilities, but, in truth, asked to comment about the man, what comes immediately to mind are all the good times, the laughs, the ad-

ventures. We have shared a lot of good meals and at least as many bottles of whiskey, and Bill has introduced me to a crowd of similarly inclined people who also became friends of mine: the late John Amber, Bill Ruger, Jr., collector Knox Kershaw, and gunamker Lenard Brownell, to name a few.

First and foremost among those adventures, for me, has to be the Ruger Special. It is a splendid replica of a Bentley LeMans car, fitted with Bill's ingenious fiberglass version of the original patent-leather Van den Plas coach work, powered by an enormous Ford 427 cubic-inch stock-car-racing engine. It defined fun in automotive terms. It was fast and beautiful, and both prototypes look as good today as they did in 1970. Taken by some mad impulse, Bill loaned me the yellow Ruger in the early spring of 1971, and I drove it for about two months, including a wonderful New York–Detroit night run with a friend riding shotgun. My companion that night was a quiet, gentle man who had never experienced a fast open car on a cold night. I told him to dress warmly. He thought that meant a poplin raincoat. He was nearly dead when I had to stop somewhere in central Ohio to check him into a motel to thaw him out. I couldn't understand it. I was prepared to drive that car to California or beyond. It is a great pity that Bill never completed his program to put that great machine on the market.

I once asked Bill to describe his favorite breakfast, and he said, "My favorite breakfast is at Claridge's in London. They make the finest oatmeal porridge I know. I eat that oatmeal with plenty of Devonshire cream and butter and salt and pepper, and I send down for every English-language newspaper available. That to me is an excellent breakfast." I, on the other hand, have rich memories of breakfasts at Bill's house with five or six other guests. John Amber, of *Gun Digest,* in his carelessly tied dressing gown, his pacemaker showing. Gough Thomas, the great English shot-

gun authority and writer, accompanied by his wife, who was determined to go for a morning walk in the freezing New Hampshire rain. Bill, holding forth at the head of the table, plates heaped with food coming and going all around him. That's my idea of a fine breakfast.

—David E. Davis, Jr., Editor and Publication Director, *Automobile Magazine*

ested in building the very best, as opposed to building the best business proposition.

Ruger's Favorite Cars

In terms of absolute excitement and mechanical performance, the Ferrari Daytona will beat the Bentley any time. On the other hand, if you have any interest in history or mechanical development, the Bentley remains fascinating because it was so far ahead of its time. But the Daytona is a tremendous automobile. It's just no use to compare cars of that sort.

Part of the joy of driving a car is also the designer's thinking, and to relate that to the period of today. Driving a modern car like the Daytona, it's fascinating to see how successful that design is in the context of today and how it surpasses practically everything of the old Bentley. But I get the same joy out of the old Bentley because in its time it was the Daytona.

On Building the Ruger Sports Tourer

The main reason I decided to build our own ideal car was that I was going to try to create something I thought perfect from every point of view. I think that the best of old cars in one way or another had shortcomings and that the best of modern cars, in one way or another, were not my ideal. I was really trying to get everything into one car. I always had a preference for the appearance of cars, the general atmosphere of the car. Our style embodied less of an aerodynamic thing and more of a powerful mechanical thing, say typical of the cars built in the late 20s and early 30s. At the same time, I've known that the performance of these early cars was not in comparison to what modern engineering could achieve.

So the whole objective with us at the beginning of this program was to see whether or not we could have a modern car in the earlier format of appearance: the ladder-type frame, perhaps with a torsional extender added, the solid axle, the engine set well back. The general layout of the car to be reminiscent (or even precisely the same) as the sort of car that Bentley built. Put it this way: I love the

A view of the Southport Tool Room. Surface gauge for scribing dimensions and indicator surface gauge for checking parts for flat and parallel shapes, positioned on surface plate, *left to right in foreground*. These gauges directly in front of Rockwell tester for determining steel hardness. Tall devices at *right* are gauges for measuring height, in place on surface plates. At *left background*, cylinder grinder for inside and outside surfaces. Ninety-degree-angle irons in *right foreground*. Small vertical device at *center* a surface gauge. At *right background*, a turret lathe. The wooden box at *right* contains a 6" sine plate for inspection use.

Tool Room at the Southport factory, established in 1959. Rotary table, primarily for machining on model parts, in *foreground;* parts can be set up here, then put in place beneath any of the three Bridgeport vertical milling machines. Honing machine in background to *right* of center Bridgeport. At *left* in background, cut-off band saw, for cutting off pieces of steel. Surface grinder in background, to *right* of Bridgeport vertical miller at *left*. Sandblast machine in *right background*, with small window for observing work in progress. The last product to have been built in prototype form in this room was the P-series centerfire pistol, 1985–87.

old Bentley, but the frame is too flexible, there's too much unsprung weight, there's too much in the way of stiff springs. These things all detract from the use of the car today, and limit its everyday performance. All that is the sort of shortcoming that one might try to improve upon. I wanted the best of the old coupled with the best of the new.

It did represent that sort of thing I personally wanted. The most satisfying thing I think a man could do is to build your house the way you want it, build your car the way you want it, build your rifle the way you want it. It's just the question, really, of whether or not what you like is something that anyone else likes.

A Ride in the Ruger Sports Tourer

A ride in the Ruger is like stepping into the future—and into the past, at the same time. The grill over the radiator is a powerful mesh, unbendable and unbreakable. The running board and suspension have absolutely no give as you step up to climb in. The 425-horsepower takeoff rivals the Ford Shelby Cobra, and the combined engine and exhaust roar produce instant goose bumps from head to toe. The car exemplifies style and solid power, from stem to stern, and its performance is daunting.

On the Specter of Government Intervention

Ruger still regrets that the Sports Tourer never entered into production. The robust car surely would have proven a success, and, as usual, he was ahead of his time.

> It was perfectly clear we could build this car and sell it for a profit. It was fully engineered, we built two prototypes and had all the subcontractors and suppliers ready to go, but then we began to notice the influence the government was taking in the auto industry; safety standards, economy standards, innumerable other standards, all very difficult to interpret or comply with. We kept working with the government, but their answers were never complete. They seemed to be saying, "Do your best, and we'll see what happens."

> There was the ogre of too much government in

it, and this product liability thing was beginning to emerge, so we backed off. A sad thing.

Sturm, Ruger & Co. Goes Public

With the start from Alexander Sturm's original investment of $50,000, and the steadily increasing income from sales, Sturm, Ruger maintained a steady pace on all fronts for the first several years. In 1969, the company made its first public stock offering, resulting in a sale of 330,264 shares at a price of $14 per share. Bill Ruger sold 264,000 of his own shares, while Joanna Sturm, Alex and Paulina Sturm's daughter, sold 66,264 shares. They each realized $13.05 per share. Explaining his decision to a Harvard Business School case writer in 1974, Ruger notes the stock issue was influenced by other alternatives:

> In 1968, I was approached by a major conglomerate who offered me $28 million for the company. At that time I owned 1,320,000 shares or about 80% of the outstanding shares; the other 20% was owned by Joanna Sturm. I considered this offer, which was basically a stock deal and would have been based on bottom line and volume performance for a specified period, but the alternative was to go public. I chose the latter alternative since it enabled me personally to diversify my assets. After the public offering, I didn't have all my own eggs in one basket and I was still free to operate the company with my own philosophy.

One of the critically important tenets of the philosophy which Bill Ruger applied to his company had to do with freedom from debt. Having learned a bitter lesson in over-borrowing from his Ruger Corporation experience, Ruger was determined not to repeat the mistake. Executive Vice President John M. Kingsley, Jr., who joined the company in 1971, told the Harvard case writer:

> We've been fortunate to not have to use any outside financing, and in the future we plan to finance our expansion internally. A key to this will be our ability to manage our inventories more judiciously. I think, however, we can grow and still maintain our net profit margins at about 15% of sales. [This remarkable figure remained constant through the

next two decades, despite the explosion of social costs, inflation, and the general decline of American manufacturing.]

Jack Behn, the Sturm, Ruger Purchasing Agent, provides a lively, behind-the-scenes look at Ruger's attitude toward borrowing:

> The longarm business started to grow, after John Kingsley was there for quite a while. We had dated billings then—"Buy in January and discount in October." In August one year, John went to Bill Ruger on the dated billings, saying we might have to go to the bank to borrow money to fund the accounts receivable for thirty days. Bill said, "If we borrow five cents, you're fired!" John came back to me and said, "What do we have coming that we can put off?" We went through a pile of orders for supplies and machines to find deliveries we didn't need right away, and put off some other things. We got through it all right. John's answer to Ruger had been, incidentally, "If we have to borrow money, I'm not doing my job."

As a public corporation, traded "over the counter" on NASDAQ (National Association of Securities Dealers and Automated Quotation), Sturm, Ruger began issuing the required Annual Reports in 1969. Each contained a detailed statement from Ruger, and each provides not only information about the company's year but also insights into Ruger's manufacturing, marketing, and financial strategy.

From the 1969 Annual Report

In presenting this first full year report to public shareholders, I am particularly gratified that it is a good report, showing that our business growth continued through 1969 and that we enter 1970 well equipped to achieve further progress. Nineteen sixty-nine was the all time record year for Sturm, Ruger & Company in terms of earnings and sales. In fact, we could have made that same comment at any year-end except for four of the past nineteen years.

Thus 1969 can be fairly regarded simultane-

Ruger-owned Mannlicher styled Springfield bolt-action rifles, at *top,* by Griffin & Howe, their serial number 1994; .30-06 with 24" barrel, engraved by Joseph Fugger. Quarter rib with express sights; G & H quick detachable scope mount, Redfield scope. *Bottom* rifle by R. F. Sedgely, Philadelphia; in 7mm, with 20" barrel. Mannlicher style stock long a Ruger favorite. Ruger remembers visiting both shops as a young man; particularly the businesslike approach of G & H. The customer dealt with the salesman in the show-room, and the shop was separate, managed with efficiency and purpose by Seymour Griffin. Note the resemblance to the later Ruger "International" style rifles.

ously as a record year and a routine year for our company. Substantial and uninterrupted earnings, continuously reinvested in the business over a long period of time, have enabled us to grow from a minimum beginning to a role of leadership in an industry composed for the most part of relatively large and well established companies.

Notwithstanding the satisfactory year-end result, 1969 provided management with an interesting mix of problems. We have been, and continue to be, preoccupied in the areas of product engineering, manufacturing methods, and plant expansion. Particularly, in 1969 we dealt quite successfully with problems which were new to us. In the marketing area, our new M77 bolt-

action sporting rifle made its debut at a time when our customers' inventories were high, and they were in effect committed to competitive brands. In addition, we learned that the range of cartridges for which this rifle is made must be increased. As a result, sales of this model in 1969, although substantial, were less than we expected, and we have had to work quickly to turn this experience to advantage in time to benefit 1970 sales. We expect in 1970 to do much better with the M77, as it has been greatly admired by sportsmen as a rifle of exceptional quality, appearance and performance.

In the midyear we were engaged in a close study of our cash position, as we realized that our customers would be taking full advantage of the

extended terms we offer in connection with seasonal products shipped out of season. This meant that most of our accounts forfeited the opportunity to take discounts of as much as 8 percent for early settlements—a first time ever situation which reflects current high interest rates. By careful management of cash resources, we accommodated all concerned and met our September 15 tax obligations without borrowing.

Throughout 1969 we sold our products in a keenly competitive atmosphere through distributors and retailers who in general had substantial inventories of competitive products and who, at the same time, were obviously conscious of high interest rates on borrowings. Toward the end of the year we observed some pessimism in the trade regarding the level of business in the near term, and we have learned that most of our competitors experienced some lessened demand for their products. Accordingly we interpret our own successful performance for the year as a tribute by sportsmen to the performance and superior design of our products.

We have made good progress during these twelve months in the difficult area of product design. Our objectives for future products are clear, but bringing new designs into production is a lengthy and exacting process, often involving problems that are hard to solve. The programs that we are most concerned with, and which will have a considerable influence on our future development, are materializing rapidly. Our new double-action revolver, designed primarily for police service but also correct for target shooting and personal defense, has been named the "Security-Six." It is a genuine advance in the design of this type of firearm and we expect substantial sales, both in the near term and in the future.

Our Pine Tree Castings subsidiary made a handsome contribution not only to consolidated earnings, but to our design and manufacturing potentials as well. The appropriate use of their investment casting techniques, and the integration of these remarkably accurate, high strength components into our more traditional manufacturing methods, account to a large degree for the superiority of our products and our ability to produce them in relatively compact factories. The production capacity of Pine Tree has reached its limit in their present facility, which occupies a portion of the Newport, N.H., plant. During 1968 we engaged the engineering firm of Jackson and Moreland of Boston to prepare a detailed study pointing toward construction of a complete new, separate foundry, expected to cost in the neighborhood of $1,500,000. We have not yet set a date for starting construction, but believe the need for this new capacity will be confirmed by early 1971. In moving Pine Tree to new facilities, the space they presently occupy would become available for Sturm, Ruger & Company's manufacturing activities. . . .

I believe that most of our shareholders are aware that we have designed and built prototypes of a luxury sports car. Our shareholders should understand the rationale behind this engineering effort because it represents what for us may be regarded as an important investment. The Ruger automobile is being built because we know how to do it, we believe there is a demand for it, and we want an additional product line for growth and diversification. The car that we have designed would appeal because of its mechanical quality to a relatively small luxury market composed of automobile connoisseurs. This concept of a specialty car, or the extra quality car, is followed by a number of small and successful producers in the U.S.A., in England and in Europe. The availability of basic components at low cost makes small volume production economically feasible. In our own case, the facilities for production would involve very little actual manufacturing and we have visualized a plant that is more of a warehouse and garage than a factory.

We have brought the automobile program to its present stage through frequent reappraisals and we have come this far because each reappraisal was encouraging but not definitive as to costs and salability. By actually completing two cars we have obtained a great deal of cost and market data. The cars themselves have received rigorous initial testing and they have performed to our complete satisfaction. We are now endeavoring to come to a final disposition of this project. We have several alternatives and all are being thoroughly explored.

Our endeavors in 1969 illustrate, I believe, the capacity of our organization for innovation, competition and growth. Our people are unified by mutually desired objectives, a strong interest in their work, and a sense of continuing achievement.

We are deeply grateful to sportsmen the world over, and to our employees, customers, suppliers, and stockholders, all of whom have encouraged and helped us to do our best.[1]

Jim Sullivan Joins Sturm, Ruger

Most of my background is in military weapons and ammunition. I started with Gene Stoner, and worked for him at Armalite and Cadillac-Gage, in developing and designing. The M16 military rifle (in 5.56mm or .223 caliber) was jointly designed by Bob Fremont and myself. I was also assigned to do the Armalite AR-7 .22 rifle, in which the barrel and receiver unit could take down to fit inside the composition stock. Sean Connery used one in *From Russia With Love*. I was kind of the late arrival with Stoner; and had previously done a stint with Harvey Aluminum on some explosive components.

Things were winding down at Cadillac-Gage on the Stoner 63; Bob and I did that project while Stoner had done the Model 62. The 63 was the second of the 5.56 caliber rifles, and the Marine Corps tested it and recommended it for adoption. But the Army said the Marines should use what the Army was using. Then I ran into Bill Ruger at a meeting at one of the arsenals; the arsenals periodically give briefings to people in the gun industry. Stoner already knew him, and he introduced us.

What followed was correspondence from Ruger, asking if I would be interested in joining him. The program at Cadillac-Gage was about completed; the Army's comment was kind of a death blow to that project. With Stoner's blessing, I took Ruger up on his offer in the summer of 1965. I moved back East to Southport, and was there the full three years, until the summer of 1968.

Creating the M77 Rifle

Sturm, Ruger had already taken a potentially costly gamble in making a single-shot rifle. In undertaking a bolt-action rifle, the company took an even bigger risk. There was no competition for the No. 1 and No. 3 rifles, but there was plenty for the M77. As Ruger recalls:

Maybe we had more to worry about than we realized, but it worked out very well. There has been an immense amount of competition in bolt-action rifles, but I think that our Model 77 has generated a real following today. There was no doubt that having our magnificent foundry and that tremendous ability to produce these intricate and strong castings gave us all the potential that anybody could ask for, and was a real inspiration to the designers.

Jim Sullivan, who joined Sturm, Ruger in 1965, remembers how the Model 77 developed:

My first project was the Model 77 bolt-action rifle. I'm not sure when Ruger decided on a name for this rifle, probably in mid-program. Like many of Ruger's programs, they don't need a name until you know it will go into production. By midway he had settled on the name. The reason he picked the number 77 was obvious, since the Winchester Model 70 and the Remington Model 700 constituted the main competition to the new rifle.

At first, Bill gave me an illustration which showed a gunsmithed Mauser action, with an S-shaped flat bolt handle shape that he liked. And he set the other specifications that he wanted: a tang-mounted shotgun-style safety, which included the locking of the bolt from rotation, a Mauser-type positive cartridge extractor, a swing-open floorplate, and the back of the bolt covered by a screw-on sleeve. As the design progressed, he began to insist on some other details as well. We would add a flange onto the left side of the bolt sleeve, to prevent any gas or blowback from hitting the shooter in the face (in the rare event of a faulty or ruptured cartridge).

One of the unique patentable ideas that Ruger came up with out of the clear blue sky was that slanted stock-to-breech screw that pulls the action down and to the rear when tightened. The value of that in putting the action in a precise place in the stock can't really be overestimated from the standpoint of accuracy. It really anchors the receiver back in to the inletting and nothing is necessary to seat the action, unlike the vertical front trigger guard screw common to most bolt actions. It's completely simple, and yet its importance is indisputable.

This rifle was to utilize investment casting technology from the beginning, including the receiver, and, in time, the bolt. Someone had warned Bill that a bolt built using an investment casting would not last. The Model 70 and 700 bolts are both machined from bar stock. However, the grain structure in bar stock, lengthwise, sets up an ideal fracture point for failure under great stress. This is in contrast to our investment casting, which we determined was much stronger.

When we had sample bolts, we put them through a test along with the Mauser and the Models 70 and 700. This was conducted on a machine, a Tinnius-Olsen dynometer, connected to a hydraulic ram. The printout information told us what force was on the bolt when it finally failed. We were attempting to shear off bolt lugs. Our bolt was stronger, and outlasted any of the others.

Other tests were performed, once we had a completed rifle. One of these was with cartridges in which we drilled holes into the powder chamber, enough to start a good case rupture. We tested these with sheets of paper at the shooter's face position, to see the effect of ruptured cartridges in different positions. It was then that we came up with the bolt flange. This flange served to deal with gas or debris that could come flying back along the left hand lug passageway (which has a full length track); that path is an enclosed channel. There's no ejection port opening on the left hand side. On the right hand side, it was unnecessary to block off that passageway, because the gas dissipates at the breech out the gas port. By having a flange that stopped immediately behind the receiver, and reached across the entire left hand side of the receiver, any gas that came back in the lug track as a result of a defective cartridge reaches that flange and is deflected sideways, protecting the shooter.

A side story on that: To some extent Bill and I had argued over the need of the flange. During the test I was blowing holes through that paper. Ed Nolan was in the process of writing up the brochure announcing the gun, while I was still doing the test firing in the range. He needed an answer on that safety feature right away. I was testing other bolt-actions along with the M77, and started showing the paper test cards to Nolan. He said, "I don't need a long-winded explanation; just give me a simple explanation." Jokingly my answer was, "We are as bad as the worst of them." After we had developed this system, before the first rifle was sold, my answer became, "We are as good as the best of them."

The requirement for integral scope bases was important. We went through the various types; Bill wanted the rings to be secured by a thumb screw. This had to be attractive, and very strong, and mounted as low as possible. A scoped bolt-action has a different problem than many other rifles, since the bolt itself, as you withdraw it, has to pass over the top of the buttstock. So you cannot raise the stock, but a scope is invariably higher than iron sights would be, and if the shooter brings the stock correctly up to his face, he can't see through a high-mounted scope without straining upward. So one of the things that he insisted on was that the entire scope mount end up with the lowest possible center line. At the time the rifle came out, I believe it was the lowest of any factory scope mounts.

Then for a little bit, while working on the details of the M77, I joined with Larry Larson, doing the finishing touches on the No. 1 Rifle, to work in the scope mount on a quarter rib, so that that scope system would fit both rifles. Again as a first on any American production rifles, we were able to produce the patented Ruger scope bases as part of the rifle's receiver or rib, instead of the separate screw-on bases that all the competition used, which were constantly working loose and destroying accuracy.

Lenard Brownell was involved in the stock styling for the M77. I designed a stock, but it was primarily for dimensioning and the inletting. Len didn't take any exception to that, but boy did he laugh when he saw my stock design! He was given a free hand in doing a proper stock, fortunately for all. Len, easily one of the best stockmakers in the world at the time, had been hired about when I was. His task was to set up production stockmaking with classic styling and lines.

Bill said about the pistol grip's shape and profile: "I want that thing to look like a Polish girl's ankle." He meant a big, thick, husky thing. That's one of the things that Len really hooted over. Of course, Bill knew that lots of Polish girls have beautiful, graceful ankles.

From the 1970 Annual Report

Our moderate increase of 15 percent in sales and 13 percent in earnings in 1970 was achieved in a year of numerous frustrations and problems. The demand for sporting firearms was affected adversely by the prevailing pessimism of 1970, and we kept our shipments going only by utmost care in coordinating production with our jobbers' very specific requirements. This was in contrast to the previous year, when we couldn't seem to make sufficient quantities of any model to satisfy demand.

At the same time, start-up difficulties in the production of our newest products were so time-consuming that these new models contributed virtually nothing to sales. The new models that I refer to are our Security-Six police revolver and our new "Magnum"^{2} size M77 sporting rifle. We expected them to produce substantial additional sales volume during 1970 and, indeed, our customers were ready and waiting. Accordingly, this benefit to sales will have to be deferred to 1971, and the only satisfaction to be derived from work done in 1970 on these models is that they are now solidly in production.

The fact that our sales and earnings for 1970 came to an all-time high without the help of the new products is really an indication of the good reputation that our older products have among shooters and sportsmen. It is also a testimonial to the adaptability and flexibility of our operating management who were called on late in the year

to make many additions and changes to their production schedules.

On the other hand, our delayed production of newer models reflects the extra burden on management arising from an enlarged line-up of products. Each new firearm in itself is a complex manufacturing task. It requires additional technical and logistical capacity in the management group, as well as the development of experience in new jobs at all levels in the factory.

Having seen the need to strengthen our manufacturing management during 1970, we were happy to be able to employ John A. Clements as General Manager of our Newport Division. He was formerly Vice President in charge of Manufacturing at New Hampshire Ball Bearings, Inc. in Peterborough . . . With Michael J. Horelik in charge of Southport manufacturing facilities and Mr. Clements in Newport, I believe that we have established a logical basis for the future development and enlargement of our production capabilities.

As to physical plant, we have, in the course of 1970, made numerous refinements and additions to many categories of processing equipment. Various plant rearrangements have been completed to make more efficient use of floor space. To illustrate the variety of such improvements, in Newport we relocated and enlarged our polishing room, installed Teflon coating facilities, built a new spray area for the finishing of

Hunting worldwide, with trips in North America, and to Iran and Africa. *Top*, Ruger .44 Magnum Blackhawk, one of the first revolvers designed specifically for hunting. Jack O'Connor with mountain goat, directly under pistol grip cap of Model 77 in .308 caliber used by Australian professional hunter to take over 15,000 stags, buffalo, and other game. Under buttstock, Marty Talbot in Kenya, with her faithful Bearcat; to her *right*, Ruger's old friend and hunting companion, Robert Chatfield-Taylor. Iranian guides admiring Ruger No. 1 Rifle with International stock. Pack train pictures from Yukon expeditions. At *right*, Bill, Jr., on his British Columbia hunt, with bighorn sheep, 1964.

THE WILDERNESS
OF THE
UPPER YUKON

CHARLES SHELDON

The Ruger M77 Bolt-Action Rifle

Number 773-07599 M77 Bolt-Action Rifle, .270 caliber, with 22" barrel.

Introduced: 1968. "The World's Leading Hunting Rifle. . . . a hunter's rifle in which correct design and careful attention to detail in every step of manufacture have resulted in superb performance. . . . [built] for accuracy, strength and reliability [and for] lightness, low recoil effect, and smoothness of operation. . . . not a penny spent on meaningless ornamentation."

Serial Numbers: 1 to 3189. 70-00000 to -99999; and similarly numbered serial prefixes 71-, 72-, 73-, 74-, 75-; prefix 76 not used; 77-, 78-, 79-. New prefix series began with 770-00000 to -99999; and similarly numbered serial prefixes 771-, 772-, 773-00000 to -29824 (through 1992).

Total Made Through 1990 [serial list shows 1992]: In excess of 1,087,000.

Calibers: *Short Action* (introduced 1968), .22-250, .220 Swift, 6mm Remington, .243 Winchester, .250 Savage, 6.5mm Remington Magnum, .284 Winchester, 7mm/08 Remington, .308 Winchester, .350 Magnum, .358 Winchester.

Long Action (a.k.a. Magnum Action), (introduced 1970, beginning with serial range no. 70-22198), .257 Roberts, .25-06,

.270 Winchester, .280 Remington, 7 x 57mm Mauser, 7mm Remington Magnum, .30-06 Springfield, .300 Winchester Magnum, .338 Winchester Magnum, .416 Taylor, .458 Winchester Magnum.

Magazine Capacity: Hinged floorplate, staggered integral box magazine, holding 5 rounds for all calibers, *except* 4 rounds for .220 Swift, and 3 rounds in the 6.5mm Remington Magnum, 7mm Remington Magnum, .284, .300 Winchester Magnum, .350 Magnum, .416 Taylor, and .458 Winchester Magnum.

Barrel Lengths: Light 22" Sporter version most common, 18½" light (International stock), 24" light, 24" medium, 24" heavy, 26" heavy, varying in use based on calibers, stock styles, and action sizes.

Rifling: Right-hand twist standard; number of grooves and pitch varies according to caliber.

Markings: See Table of Markings, pages 330–35.

On left side of receiver:

RUGER M77 R

Serial number *on left side of receiver at breech.*

On top of barrel (before January 1, 1978):

STURM, RUGER & CO. INC., SOUTHPORT, CONN. U.S.A.

On top of barrel, after approximately January 1, 1978:

Before using gun-read warnings in *instruction manual* **available free— from Sturm, Ruger & Co., Inc. Southport, Conn. U.S.A.—**

Caliber and **SR** proof monogram *on left side of barrel, usually at breech.*

S *on upper tang,* indicating safety position.

Sights: Integral scope mount grooves on receivers, for 1" Ruger scope rings (made in high base and standard base heights), provided in a gray or red cloth drawstring bag. Early production "round top" long action receivers drilled and tapped to accommodate standard scope mounts. All other actions subsequently built with integral Ruger scope bases. Some variations of both action lengths fitted with open sights: rear fold-down sporting style, on contoured ramp (secured to barrel by two screws); front sight blade slides into ramp flat (on top of barrel band) and is secured by spring plunger.

Overall Length and Weight: *Short Action,* 42" (22" barrel); approx. 6½ pounds (.243 Winchester).

Long Action, 44⅜" (24" barrel); approx. 8¾ pounds (.458

Winchester Magnum).

Action length difference approx. ½".

Stocks: American walnut, checkered and polyurethane-finished, with rubber buttpad and composition pistol grip cap inset with white and black or brown trademark. Length of pull, 13¾", drop at comb, 1⅜", drop at heel, 2⅛". Quick-detachable sling-swivel studs.

Buttpads: Early pattern, with rounded edge, marked **PAD BY MERSHON;** succeeded by square-edge Ruger pad of similar reddish coloration; then a somewhat darker colored pad; at 73- or 74- prefix, a brown pad; then changed back to reddish. Trademark in relief on pad.

Finish: Blued. Dull finish changed to high polish, in late 70-prefix series rifles, both Short and Long Action.

Materials, Construction, and Innovations: Heat-treated chrome-molybdenum steel used in the investment cast receiver and bolt, and other major parts. Thick receiver walls; short and long action receivers. One-piece bolt, with two long and massive locking lugs. Integral bolt handle acts as third locking lug. External Mauser-type extractor. First models had

Number 772-19910 M77 Bolt-Action Rifle, .30-06 caliber, with 22" barrel.

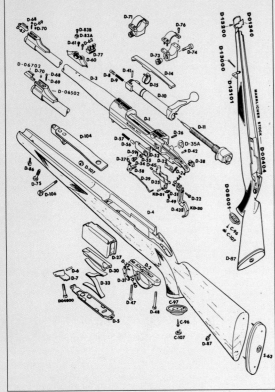

Exploded view of M77 Bolt-Action Rifle.

angular "flat" bolt handle; later changed to rounded type. Patented guide lug on bolt for smooth bolt travel. "Classic" style stock design. Integral scope mount bases on receiver. Hinged, quick-release floorplate. Aluminum alloy floorplate and trigger guard, except on special order or for the **77RSC** .458 Winchester Magnum. Steel trigger, adjustable. Sliding tang safety. Patented Ruger angled bedding system.

Issue Price: $175.00, M77RS; $160.00, M77R (1969).

Engraving: Limited number of sample floorplates done by A. A. White Engravers, Inc., as company samples, and a limited number of floorplates engraved on long-service rifles presented to employees, e.g., on serial number 70-23679: *To Walter E. Berger From William B. Ruger To Commemorate 20 Years of Work and Friendship in Sturm, Ruger & Co., 1950-1970.* Serial number 78-15396, a .308 with International style stock, gold inlaid and engraved for William B. Ruger, Sr., by Paul Lantuch. Serial number 67215, in .458 Winchester Magnum, also for Ruger, Sr., by Lantuch.

Catalogue and Price Sheet Listings:

77R: Standard rifle, no sights, receiver machined for Ruger scope rings, both action lengths.

77RS: With iron sights and receiver machined for Ruger scope rings, both action lengths, including .458 Winchester Magnum.

77RSC: Primarily .458 Winchester Magnum, and a few .416 Taylor, Magnum Action, Ruger scope rings, 24" heavy barrel. Steel floorplate and trigger guard. Stock of Circassian walnut, with wide stock forend. Barrel secured in stock with barrel band and an extra screw attachment through forend into barrel. Flat steel bar hooked over recoil lug, running forward, forming further recoil lug in barrel channel; bolt through stock, behind recoil lug.

77RSI: International model, with Mannlicher style stock; 18½" barrel, with scope rings and iron sights.

77S: With iron sights, scope rings not provided.

77ST: Round top receiver, drilled and tapped for screw-on

mount scope bases (e.g., by Weaver or Redfield); with iron sights. Known as the Round Top Model.

77V: Varmint rifle, no sights, receiver machined for scope rings, heavy 24" barrel (.22-250, 6mm, .243, .25-06, .280, .308), or 26" heavy barrel (.220 Swift). Drilled and tapped for target scope blocks. Intended primarily for silhouette shooting.

77PL: Round top receiver, without iron sights.

Barreled Actions: Codes **77RBA, 77RSBA,** and **77RSBA .458 Magnum,** advertised as "available in all calibers and configurations."

Major Production Variations: Early production rifles were of the Short Action, with flat style bolt handle, without serial prefix markings, without bolt guide, stock wood on right side lacking downward profile cut (discontinued approximately serial range 70-07000 to -08000), Ruger scope rings, no sights; aluminum floorplate; reddish-colored American walnut stock of light grain, handsomely finished and contoured; rounded-edge Mershon buttpad with Ruger medallion inset; black pis-

tol grip caps with white and black trademark medallion inlays. Dull finish; some receivers with purplish coloration.

Flat Bolt: Angular, square, or "dogleg" bolt, first type handle, found on early Short Action rifles, and limited number of Magnum Action rifles.

Hollow Bolt: Second style of bolt handle, found on Magnum Action rifles only.

Round Bolt: Standard style used on Short Action after Flat type and on Long Action after Flat and Hollow types.

Other variations noted by collectors include Drilled Extractor (early Long Actions), Bolt Guide (metal piece dovetailed onto body of bolt, for support and smoothness; not present on earliest Short Action rifles), D-rifles (D stamped as prefix or suffix to serial number, indicating number duplication), Round or Narrow Forend, Square or Wide Forend, Integral-Base Receiver or Round Top Receiver, Non-Warning guns, Magnum Action, Short Action, Prefix and Non-Prefix rifles, wide groove or standard groove receiver top serrations.

Liberty Rifles: Made in the bicentennial year, with roll mark: **MADE IN THE 200th YEAR OF AMERICAN LIBERTY.**

Warning Series: Warning marking adopted approximately January 4, 1978, in serial range and with legend as indicated above.

.416 Taylor: Limited quantity chambered for caliber designed by Robert Chatfield-Taylor (whose personal rifle bore serial number 70-71644).

111

gun stocks, and installed new tape-controlled equipment for automated machining of gun stocks. In Southport, we have added a second story to our office wing thereby obtaining about 2500 sq. feet of additional office space—the first addition to our Southport office area in over ten years. At the close of 1970, Sturm, Ruger's plant facilities were probably adequate to accommodate the growth in arms production that we anticipate through 1972, but this may be true only if in 1972 our Pine Tree subsidiary vacates the space that it occupies in the Newport factory, as is now planned.

Throughout the year we continued, and in fact increased, our efforts in the product design and market research area. New product development work is well ahead, and future products are moving into the production tooling phase. We have maintained close liaison with influential sportsmen, retailers and wholesalers, and have obtained a continuous monitoring of the performance and salability of our products in a highly competitive market.

An effort to understand our customers is, of course, not a new development—but during 1970 we were able to get more data and do more analysis than previously because of the effectiveness and efficiency of Hawkeye Communications, our in-house communications division. In cooperation with our Director of Sales, Edward P. Nolan, Hawkeye not only prepared our advertising for the year, but arranged surveys which have at low cost provided us with valuable summaries of our retailers' point of view. Hawkeye has also been invaluable to us as a means of gathering and interpreting news regarding consumer safety and protection, product liability, conservation, and other matters which relate to future responsibilities and opportunities. . . .

We have deferred further action on the Automotive Program primarily because of the inroads on management time that this program will require and the uncertainties regarding the market

during 1970 for a car priced in the $13,000 range. I do not think that we have lost anything by this delay.

Pine Tree Castings Corp. . . . recorded unconsolidated sales of $1,324,000, comparable to $1,312,000 in 1969. Toward the end of the year, there was an increasing volume of new business from outside sources, although Sturm, Ruger's requirements for alloy steel investment castings continue to represent the major part of Pine Tree's business. Ultimately, we hope that these proportions will be reversed and to this end we are actively soliciting orders from new customers, primarily in the New England states. Pine Tree's efficiency as a producer has been amply demonstrated and, with the inevitable growth of their market, it is reasonable to expect our subsidiary to become of still greater importance to us. Our plans for building complete new facilities for Pine Tree remain the major near-term program of the company.

To put the year 1970 into a proper perspective, I would say that these foregoing activities show us to have been heavily engaged in the conduct of our arms business at existing levels while, at the same time, we have been deeply involved with implementation of our plans for the future growth of this business.

The Security-Six Line of Double-Action Revolvers

Ruger knew that if he wanted a complete line of firearms, a double-action revolver was an absolute necessity. Why not go head-on with Colt and Smith & Wesson, and offer a modern, up-to-date alternative? Both companies were using complicated and relatively fragile systems which had seen little improvement since the original designs of the late nineteenth century. Only moderate "fine tuning" had been done in the twentieth, and their manufacture was straight from the "hammer and forge."

Ruger noted that the manufacture of double-action revolvers "is, of course, far more difficult than that of single-action revolvers, with which we were so familiar. The first years of manufacture were full of problems, though the guns all turned out well. Now, with our experience and with far better machinery, the picture is bright indeed."

Harry Sefried remembers the early years:
Bill Ruger and engineer Henry Into were a mismatch made in hell. Henry was so anxious to prove literally that Bill's ideas would not work, that they were almost working against each other. This was as compared to a feeling of accomplishment from teamwork, like Jim Sullivan would get. Henry seemed to have the idea that if he didn't think of it, it wouldn't work. He was a very good designer, and did a very nice job on one version of a double-action setup. But then he claimed it wouldn't work, and he was right! It took me about two weeks to make it work after he left (to take a job at Colt's) working with Bill. We had to abandon the complex series of levers that Henry created to come up with a really workable design. Not only did the new double-action work, but it was relatively easy to manufacture.

For a six-month period in 1966 that job was given to Henry, who did a great many styling outlines, and laid out a very nice double-action system, under Bill's guidance. I recall one of the things we tried was a roller bearing on the hammer pivot. The double-action system proved a very smooth and efficient design.

We jumped from the .44 Magnum Carbine project to the 10/22 and the Security-Six, which came about from a project of about 1966, when we had Doug McClenahan (who subsequently left and founded Charter Arms, which made compact double-action revolvers of his design). Doug was then working on the 10/22 or some other project, and we also had Henry there at the time.

Henry had been given a project on the Single-Six, to see if he could design an updated version, and he was the first guy to get the assignment to work on what became the New Model single-action series. It was an important project, because Bill wanted to modernize the single-action line, eliminating the safety notch and the loading notch. We had the program well thought out as to what we wanted to do, but the limited trigger travel of the single-action revolver made this a *very* tough nut to crack.

The single-action designs Henry was working on hit a dead end, because he was attempting extremely long leverages. That is to say, the blocking bar system, to prevent discharge of the cartridge except by the trigger being pulled, required that you retract the hammer in some way as the Smith & Wesson does mechanically, with a long trigger stroke. The method that Into tried was a rebounding hammer. That's when I sent the gun with a rebounding hammer to the H. P. White Laboratory, and through high speed movies they found we got pierced primers and interference with cylinder rotation on the .357. So the blocking bar system wouldn't work if it didn't have a way to get the bar off the hammer.

We put Henry onto the double-action project, and abandoned the single-action for awhile. That was the start of the Security-Six. Henry made this very nice double-action mechanism. Then he tried to put together a hinged trigger guard, with a key at the front end, and a lock at the rear (or vice versa). Bill wanted to do that so he could maintain a solid frame; no weakening side panel like the competition and no screws, and with the double-action mechanism mounted on the trigger guard which would be inserted and keyed up in there, without screws or delicate parts.

Henry again ran into a common designer's problem. In this case, he simply decided it was an impossibility. He made a layout to show it would not work, and he couldn't get the parts up there the way Bill wanted it. The project deteriorated into a contest to prove he was right and Bill was wrong. As Bill said, if some of these people who worked so hard to prove it didn't work had worked half as hard to prove the idea would work, it might well have worked.

I think that's one of the reasons Bill and I got along so well, because instead of stating an idea was impossible, I'd flesh it out and show that it had such merit that was adaptable to the space in the mechanism that we had.

Henry seemed to be incapable of that. There was a certain amount of animosity there, butting heads against Bill, so I suggested Henry take an opportunity at Colt's and recommended him for that. I finished off Bill's double-action idea, with a key in the front and a snap in the back, which worked, and devised a system to lock the cylinder in place with a couple of little balls, to anchor the cylinder and let it rotate freely.

The double-action came out quite well. We made several modifications to the grip's backstrap, adapting and improving upon the dozens and dozens of styling layouts that Into made. We changed the backstrap to a more standard contour, and ended up with a solid frame and trigger guard with trigger and transfer bar and all these parts anchored in such a way that you simply put in the trigger housing and the gun was ready to work. For the first time, a complex double-action revolver had the tool-free takedown system commonly found on automatic pistols, which made cleaning and maintenance literally "a snap."

Bill and I had several patents together on the Security-Six. I made a few contributions and he had the basic idea of how he wanted it to work. We ended up with a sturdy and highly pragmatic revolver, accepted by police departments even as conservative in weapons procurement as the N.Y.P.D.

From the 1971 Annual Report

Our consolidated income statement for the year ended December 31, 1971 shows a decline in net income from the previous year, although sales volume increased. Sales of $13,318,892 during 1971 resulted in a net income of $1,462,317 while sales of $12,789,781 in 1970 yielded a net income of $2,226,322. Accordingly, 1971 achieves the distinction of being one of the very few years in our 21 year history when a decline in net income occurred. I personally derive very little satisfaction from the fact that our margins are still respectable when compared with the inadequate profits earned by American business in general.

Having had an exceptional profit record in the past, and having unlimited confidence in the future, the onset of a downtrend, or the occurrence of a less successful year, is an irritating disappointment. It was, in fact, apparent early in the year that profits were declining. Very little analysis was needed to see that in the case of new firearm products and facilities, production increases were not materializing as rapidly as overhead costs. This was essentially a startup situation arising out of a major expansion of our facilities, product line and organization.

I believe it is true that our product design effort over the past few years has been so successful, and our sales potential therefore so much greater, that we tended to outgrow our manufacturing and management resources. We began late in 1970 with a program to enlarge our production engineering and supervisory staff—an obvious preliminary to any successful increase in the factory work force. As a result, the total number of employees has grown significantly through 1971, and we have acquired many people with valuable experience at all levels. At the end of the year, the Company's employment roll totalled slightly over 500 for the first time in its history.

In September 1971, we were particularly fortunate in obtaining the services of John M. Kingsley, Jr. as Executive Vice President. Mr. Kingsley, who is 40 years of age, has had extensive experience both in finance and in industry. He is a graduate of the Harvard Business School as well as a Certified Public Accountant. Mr. Kingsley's financial and management experience has already proven to be of great value to us, and his presence is welcomed throughout the Company.

In July 1971, William B. Ruger, Jr. was made a Vice President of the company and assumed responsibility for manufacturing operations in the Southport plant. Mr. Ruger, who is 32 years of age, attended Harvard College, and received the A.B. degree in 1961. He has been employed in engineering work by the Company since 1964,

Griffin & Howe custom-stocked Winchester Model 70 used by Ruger on Uganda safari, 1961; serial number 368050, .375 H & H caliber. The M77 in .458 caliber, gold inlaid by Paul Lantuch, in commemoration of the rifle as the 1,000,000th M77 rifle manufactured (in less than 20 years!).

and has been familiar with the work in Southport since his school days.

On April 1, 1971, G. R. ("Dick") Shaw joined the Company as a marketing consultant. Mr. Shaw had previously been the Executive Vice President of the W. R. Weaver Company, the largest American manufacturer of telescopic rifle sights. His extensive knowledge of the firearms industry makes him an invaluable addition.

During the year, we have continued our past policy of continually striving to develop new products which will enable us to maintain our position in the very competitive firearms industry. During the year a new sporter version of the 10/22 was introduced which has been enthusiastically received by the market. 1971 also saw the final development of the Number 3 single-shot rifle and the Ruger Old Army [percussion revolver]. . . . Both of these two products should be available to the market early in 1972. . . . The appeal of these two products is romantic and historical; although their design incorporates a great deal that is applicable from modern engineering techniques, these are old-fashioned weapons, built in response to an ever widening interest in the use of such arms for both target shooting and hunting.

In contrast, we have also continued the work of grooming our ultra high performance M77 rifle to expand its appeal in the market for purely modern firearms. We have made the M77 available in a form which permits the use of proprietary mounts for telescopic sights, as an alternative and in addition to our basic M77 which is designed to receive our own very popular and exclusive mount.

During 1971 we were much encouraged to observe a marked increase in sales of the M77 and believe that it is now well established as a market leader in a highly competitive field.

A major revision of our Bearcat revolvers also materialized during 1971, this being the replacement of aluminum alloy with chrome-moly steel in the manufacture of the frame.

In addition to product developments which were actually announced or put on the market during the year, our engineering efforts continued on many additional and significant products for the future. Some of this engineering was on basic new firearms products, but a great deal of effort was also devoted to refinements and new features for future incorporation into our older models. Our product engineering work during 1971, as in previous years, has proceeded toward longstanding and clearly perceived objectives—i.e., significant products in every major segment of the small arms market. . . .

On April 1, 1971, Pine Tree Castings Corporation, formerly a wholly owned subsidiary, was merged into the Company and now operates as a division [in order to streamline administrative practices]. During the year, this division achieved the highest level of production and sales since its founding in 1963. Continuing attention is being focused on further developing the commercial business which is potentially available to this division, but which only materialized slowly during 1971. While there was no major increase in the physical plant of either Pine Tree or the Company's other two plants, plans are being finalized to significantly increase present Pine Tree capacity. During 1971 we reconsidered our virtually completed plans for a large new Pine Tree facility . . . which was to be located on a site about five miles from our present plant. We have instead designed additions to our present site which will achieve the same results more economically, and construction is planned for the summer of 1972. This should enable Pine Tree to continue to meet, for years to come, the growing demands of Sturm, Ruger for high quality alloy steel investment castings as well as to develop outside commercial business. . . .

In last year's report, I commented that we had deferred activity on our automotive program because of the pressures imposed by our firearms business. During 1971 the situation with the car remained substantially unchanged although one of the prototype automobiles is in England for the purpose of exploring the possibilities of participation in this project with a qualified British or European manufacturer. There are no active negotiations proceeding at the present time, but we have observed a continuing strong interest in the cars that we have designed and have also noted evidence of substantial growth in the sales of luxury cars in this price category. We intend to continue to study the commercial possibilities of this product and remain optimistic about its future possibilities.

In looking at 1971 from the perspective of today, I believe substantial progress was again made toward increased earnings capacity from a more diversified product line. Inadequate production, which was the primary cause of our setback in earnings, is the type of problem that we can most certainly solve.

In Pursuit of Perfection

A strong vision of the innate rightness in a product, coupled with the engineering skills and plant equipment to accomplish it in real-life manufacturing, have been the driving forces behind Sturm, Ruger's quality. Bill Ruger knew what the customer wanted because he knew what *he* wanted—and he accepted no compromises in delivering the goods. Again, the memories are Jim Sullivan's:

On Larry Larson's No. 1 stock design, we had to deal with the draw screw that comes through the buttstock and holds it solid against the steel action. For some reason Bill changed his mind on where the head of that screw would come out on the butt. He changed it after the casting of the steel receiver was already done. So Larry made the new change with the angled stock screw; it would then intersect the boss that was already cast into the steel receiver, since it was drilled and tapped anyway. Looking at the back end you couldn't tell that the angle of the screw was not on the same angle as the boss. However, the angle of the two was not going to be parallel. This bothered Bill; and every day for a week, he would come in and tell Larry "we're going to have to change the angle on the boss." But every day Larry would talk Bill out of the change; no one else could see that angle difference, only Bill. The next day Bill would be right back in there, and Larry would talk him out of it again. For a whole week this went on. After Bill had left, we'd just laugh.

In the end, Bill prevailed. And of course that's one more reason why the Ruger products are superior. When you worry about details like that, it shows up in many ways.

The general routine was that Bill would come in every day to work with the engineers. These were intensely concentrated sessions, which could go on for hours and hours. Everybody got their share. Sometimes this would go on for a month at a time. Bill would usually come in and catch everybody before they went out for lunch. If it was the bolt-action, I had it for about a month, if it was the single-shot, it was Larry's turn. If it was the Security-Six, it would be Harry's. Whoever's turn it was, we called it being "in the barrel."

One time, Bill brought down the first wax pattern of the receiver casting for the bolt-action. He left it on my desk to see if I had any comments. I was clumsy enough to knock the end of the tang off. When he came in he noticed I had broken the tang. At first he was really upset, but then he was looking at the underside, and noticed it was thin there.

"Here's why it broke there, it's thin."

"Yes, but Bill this is wax, not steel."

Then an argument started. Bill wanted to change the tang design, and I didn't. Everyone was getting ready to leave for lunch, and were over at the corner closet, putting on their coats. Larry and Harry et al., they were all listening to us argue. Bill finally got so angry, he just crushed the whole receiver. You dared not laugh when he was really angry. But I couldn't help it. The others had all turned away, and they were all laughing so hard you could see them all shaking. Generally he would kind of put his head down and concentrate on something so hard that he might not see you laugh.

However, without a doubt, the best sense of humor, the sharpest wit of all of us, was his.

From the 1972 Annual Report

Consolidated operating results for the year ended December 31, 1972 showed net sales of $16,182,972 and net income after taxes of $2,129,324 equivalent to $1.29 per common share. Comparable figures for 1971 were net sales of $13,318,892, and net income after taxes of $1,462,317 equivalent to $0.89 per common share.

In reviewing the year from my particular point of view, I regard 1972 as another year of intense effort and important progress although we did not achieve the sales and profit goals set up at the beginning of the year. Our sales and profit expectations for each ensuing year are actually derived from carefully considered sales forecasts developed by our sales department, and detailed operating budgets prepared on the basis of these sales forecasts. We believe that the preparation of these budgets, and then the achieving of them, is the true test of managerial expertise in a company such as ours; but this is rendered very difficult by the continued physical growth of our factories, the acquisition of new personnel, and the start-up problems associated with new firearms designs.

It is gratifying to note that considerable progress has been made by the Newport Plant towards reaching the goals set out for it. It is also significant to note that the dollar volume and units produced by the Newport plant increased approximately 50 percent during 1972. Essentially, 1972 marked the fourth full year of operation for the Newport plant. It is confidently expected that in 1973 the Newport plant will make an even more significant contribution to corporate profits.

The foregoing comments of course point to our manufacturing capacity as the limiting factor in our sales for the year, and this is, with a few ex-

The 1,000,001st M77, relief engraved and gold inlaid by Paul Lantuch. Grizzly bear from trophy taken by Ruger in the Yukon, 1963. Narwhal tusk discovered by Adolphus W. Greely Arctic Expedition, on June 29, 1882, in remains of an Eskimo camp, on interior of Grinnell Lane, near Discovery Harbor and Lake Hazen. The 25-man Expedition was lost and abandoned for three years; finally rescued by a U.S. Navy Relief Expedition. The Narwhal, or "sea-unicorn," a nearly extinct species of whale. The tusk, measuring 84⅞", with largest circumference measuring 8¼", later presented to Senator William E. Chandler by a member of the Greely party; was on display at the Senator's hunting lodge for many years.

ceptions, the reality of our situation. The demand for our entire range of firearms continues to be highly gratifying. Those products which have achieved market leadership continue to grow in popularity, while our newer products appear to be rapidly gaining the recognition we hope for.

Our products are engineered and produced to the highest possible standards of quality and performance. It is, therefore, not surprising that we have a growing share of the market for firearms, and that we have enthusiastic supporters among all categories of users.

Our identification with quality manufacturing and unique engineering capability is the result of twenty years of constant effort. In 1972, approximately 20 percent of our sales were derived from products which have been introduced since

1967. We think the company has also gained the good esteem of its customers for our policy of never marketing firearms made by other producers. In recent years, many of the old, established, American arms manufacturers have become importers and distributors of foreign manufactured firearms.

Two of the Company's longstanding objectives have been to broaden and diversify its line of products to include firearms of all basic types for both law enforcement and sporting purposes, and concurrently to make improvements, if possible, in the existing product line. During 1972 several product engineering programs were completed and production begun which signified the attainment of both of these goals.

Specifically, 1972 marked the completion of development and beginning of production of the "New Model" series of Single Action Revolvers. This development assures our leadership in this category of products and gives us a unique competitive advantage. Full details on this new product are contained subsequently in this report. . . .

During 1972 the major additions to our Newport facilities, referred to in previous reports, were substantially completed. . . . This additional floor space, increasing the total available from approximately 76,000 to 100,000 square feet, will be used primarily by our Pine Tree Casting Division, although the Newport firearms manufacturing capacity will also benefit. While this additional space was of no benefit to us in 1972, it will of course make a real contribution to production in 1973. During the year we invested over $1,200,000 in additions to property, plant and equipment.

During 1972 a great deal has been said and heard about "firearms legislation." The potential impact upon the Company by anti-firearms legislation is a matter of concern to all those who have a stake in the future of Sturm, Ruger & Company, Inc. This is a subject that has been with us for many years, and it is well known that substantial Federal gun control laws have been in effect since the 1930's with periodic updating and substantial strengthening in 1968.

The next legislation that might be enacted would set up criteria for quality and safety in firearms construction, and by this means deprive the market of certain new handguns designed primarily for concealability and cheapness—the "Saturday Night Special." A law of that kind would perhaps be a theoretical step in the right direction, but it would not, as we understand the proposal, affect our high quality handguns all of which are relatively large in size at the present time. In a longer term view it is, as usual, more difficult to be specific.

In conclusion, 1972 in my opinion has been a significant and on balance a successful year. While the record earnings of 1970 were not surpassed, great progress was achieved in improved operating performance. Most important of all, I feel that 1972 was a year during which a management team was assembled which should enable the Company to achieve the ambitious goals and objectives which have been set out for 1973. It is important to realize that your Company has now reached the point where it has almost six hundred employees, in contrast to less than three hundred at the end of 1967. With the enthusiasm and support of all my fellow employees, I look forward with confidence and anticipation to 1973 and the future.

Developing the Export Department: Charles Rogler Remembers

I was always active in shooting, was a member of the University of Iowa Shooting Team for four years, and was an All-American all of that time. In 1949 I won the National Collegiate Rifle Championship. One of my records, set with a Ruger .22 Standard pistol, lasted eighteen years.

When I started my export business, I called Bill Ruger. He was very polite, and told me to drop over whenever I was near Southport. Two days later I hopped in my car and drove there from Hamilton, New York.

I can still remember that red barn building complex. Bill had a big rolltop desk in his little office upstairs. He always liked those historical things, and that desk had belonged to Chauncey Depew, U.S. Senator from New York and president, New York Central Railroad. Of course, Bill was quite an impressive individual, and he wasn't suffering from arthritis at that time. He was good-looking, very tall, and had a resonant, commanding voice.

Immediately he liked the fact that I was not only a "gun person," but had used his pistol competitively. He was interested in working something out, and told me that he was hiring a man from Winchester to join the company—that was Ed Nolan. So I was a protégé of Bill even before Ed came into the picture.

I made an arrangement where I would travel abroad, and send Ed the orders. Then he would prepare the documentation and ship out the product, reserving for me a reasonable commission. The first order I wrote was in Guatemala, for 25 pistols. However, it took Ed 18 months to deliver! I sent him a very nasty letter, as to how did he expect me to support myself with that kind of delivery. Generally speaking, the demand has always been such that the factory could never make the guns fast enough, except for a couple of periods. Under-spaced and under-capacity has always been a problem. It was very frustrating to me, to go to small stores and usually not see any Rugers. The market then was dominated by Smith & Wesson, Colt, Winchester, and Remington.

Finally the big light came at the end of the tunnel when the company opened the New Hampshire operation, and we finally began to get good deliveries.

By mid-1960, I had travelled almost all of Central and South America and had visited France, Germany, and England. I would go to those countries while living in the U.S. I used to go to shooting tournaments all over the world, which

The Ruger Security-Six, Police Service-Six, and Speed-Six Double-Action Revolvers

Number RDA-00038 Security-Six Revolver, with 4" barrel.

Exploded view of Security-Six Revolver.

Introduced: 1971. "The first fundamental improvement in double-action revolver design in more than a half-century. . . . both reliable and durable, correctly designed, and perfectly mated to the .357 Magnum, .38 Special and 9mm Parabellum cartridges, with the structural strength to withstand the firing of many thousands of rounds under the most rugged conditions. . . . consist of a series of integrated sub-assemblies based

upon the design requirements of strength, simplicity, and ease of maintenance."

Serial Numbers: 150-00000 to -99999; and similarly numbered serial prefixes 151-, 152-, 153-, 154-, 155-, 156-, 158-, 159-, 160-, 161-, 162-00000 to -42687 (through 1988).

Total Made Through 1985: In excess of 1,210,000. The Security-Six Model last appeared in the 1985 price sheet, and the Service-Six and Speed-Six last appeared in the 1988 price sheet. The Ruger GP100 Model superseded these models totally, as evidenced by the 1988 catalogue and the 1989 price sheet.

Calibers: .38 Special, .357 Magnum (.38 Special interchangeable), 9mm Parabellum. Some export models for British .38/200 (.38 S & W) cartridge.

Number of Chambers in Cylinder: Six.

Barrel Lengths: 2¾", 4", 6".

Rifling: 5 grooves, right-hand twist; one turn in 18¾".

Markings: See Table of Markings, pages 330–35.

After approximately January 4, 1978, marking standard on left side of barrel:

BEFORE USING GUN-READ WARNINGS IN
INSTRUCTION MANUAL AVAILABLE FROM
STURM, RUGER & CO., INC.
SOUTHPORT, CONN. U.S.A.

On left side of barrel, at breech, Sturm, Ruger & Co. proof marking.

Sights: Ruger adjustable rear, for windage and elevation. Front sight ⅛" wide, and serrated. Service-Six and Speed-Six had fixed sights.

Overall Length and Weight: 9¼", 33½ ounces (4" barrel).

Grips: Checkered walnut. Optional plain Goncalo Alves grips, with trademark medallion inlays, introduced in the 1985 catalogue, for the Security-Six (in either semi-target or target style); also in 1985, checkered Goncalo Alves grips adopted for the Service-Six and the Speed-Six (option of rubber grips available for either model; and standard in the Models RDA-34HP, -36P and GA-34HP, -36P of the Security-Six).

Finish: Blued, or stainless steel.

Materials, Construction, and Innovations: Major parts of heat-treated chrome-molybdenum steel. Integral unit of the barrel, sighting rib, and ejector rod housing. Unbreakable steel music wire coil springs. Solid frame, without sideplate. Quick takedown, can be accomplished with a coin. Firing pin, spring-loaded, secured in frame. Can be fired only when trigger in rearward position. Hammer cannot be cocked when cylinder is out of the frame; nor can the cylinder be opened when the hammer is cocked. Major components fabricated from precision investment cast steel.

Half-moon clips permit using the 9mm Parabellum in revolvers chambered for that cartridge.

Design and performance features, and reasonable pricing, led to adoption by many police departments and U.S. and foreign government and law enforcement agencies.

Issue Price: $89.00 (1971).

Engraving: Milestone Security-Six stainless serial number 1,000,000 donated to the National Shooting Sports Foundation, and auctioned off to help fund NSSF shooting education programs. Featured in the company's 1985 catalogue. Speed-Six serial number 150-01563 gold inlaid and engraved by Alvin A. White, for William B. Ruger, Sr., with Albrecht Dürer style dragon motif.

Price Sheet Listings and Major Production Variations:

Security-Six, Blued, Model 117, .357 Magnum, adjustable sights, square butt:

RDA-32: 2¾" barrel, semi-target grips.

RDA-34-H: 4" heavy barrel, semi-target grips.

RDA-34-HT: 4" heavy barrel, target grips, white outline rear sight, red-insert ramp front sight.

RDA-34-HP: 4" heavy barrel, with checkered rubber grips, white outline rear sight, red-insert ramp front sight (new in 1985).

RDA-36: 6" barrel, semi-target grips.

RDA-36-T: 6" barrel, target grips, white outline rear sight, red-insert ramp front sight.

RDA-36-P: 6" heavy barrel, checkered rubber grips, white outline rear sight, red-insert ramp front sight.

Security-Six, Stainless steel, Model 717, .357 Magnum, adjustable sights, square butt:

GA-32: 2¾" barrel.

GA-34-H: 4" heavy barrel.

GA-34-HT: 4" heavy barrel, target grips, white outline rear sight, red-insert ramp front sight.

GA-34-HP: 4" heavy barrel, rubber grips, white outline rear sight, red-insert ramp front sight.

GA-36: 6" barrel.

GA-36-T: 6" barrel, target grips, white outline rear sight, red-insert ramp front sight.

GA-36-P: 6" barrel, rubber grips, white outline rear sight, red-insert ramp front sight.

Police Service-Six, Blued, checkered walnut grips, square butt, fixed sights:

Model 107

SDA-32: .357 Magnum, 2¾" barrel.

SDA-34: .357 Magnum, 4" barrel.

Model 108

SDA-84: .38 Special, 4" barrel.

Model 109

SDA-94: 9mm, 4" barrel.

Police Service-Six, Stainless steel:

Model 707

GF-34: .357 Magnum, 4" barrel.

GF-34-P: .357 Magnum, 4" barrel, checkered rubber grips (new 1985).

Model 708

GF-84: .38 Special, 4" barrel.

GF-84-P: .38 Special, 4" barrel, checkered rubber grips (new 1985).

Speed-Six, Blued, checkered walnut grips, round butt, fixed sights; 2¾" barrel revolver weighs 31 ounces, and measures 7¾" overall length:

Model 207

SS-32: .357 Magnum, 2¾" barrel.

SS-32-P: .357 Magnum, 2¾" barrel, checkered rubber grips with finger grooves (new 1985).

SS-34: .357 Magnum, 4" barrel.

Model 208

SS-82: .38 Special, 2¾" barrel.

Model 209

SS-92: 9mm, 2¾" barrel.

Number 158-40693 Speed-Six Revolver, in stainless steel.

SS-94: 9mm, 4" barrel.

Speed-Six, Stainless steel, checkered walnut grips (unless otherwise indicated), round butt, fixed sights:

Model 737

GS-32: .357 Magnum, 2¾" barrel.

GS-32-P: .357 Magnum, 2¾" barrel, checkered rubber grips with finger grooves (new 1985).

GS-34: .357 Magnum, 4" barrel.

Model 738

GS-82: .38 Special, 2¾" barrel.

Model 739

GS-92: 9mm, 2¾" barrel.

Warning Series: Warning marking adopted approximately January 4, 1978, in serial range and with legend as indicated above.

Special Issues Include:

Minneapolis Police Commemorative: 415 revolvers, built in 1978. Models **GA-32-T, GA-34-T,** and **GA-36-T.** Marked on topstrap with the seal of the City of Minneapolis, and date June 5, 1878. On left side of frame: **MINNEAPOLIS POLICE 1978 COMMEMORATIVE.**

Minnesota Conservation Officer: 315 revolvers, built in 1978. Models **GA-32-T, GA-34-T,** and **GA-36-T.** Marked on topstrap with the organization's badge, and **MINNESOTA CONSERVATION OFFICER.** On left side of frame: **M.C.O. 1979 SPECIAL EDITION.**

Police Marksman Association: 1000 cased sets of **KRH-44** Redhawk and **GA-36-T** stainless Security-Six; built in 1980. Marked on top of each frame with the PMA logo, matching last five digits of the serial number. Roll marked on left side of each frame: **POLICE MARKSMAN ASSOC.**

South Dakota Peace Officers Association: 200 revolvers, built in 1980. Models **GA-32-T, GA-34-T,** and **GA-36-T.** Marked on left side of frame **1931 - SOUTH DAKOTA PEACE OFFICERS - 1981.** On topstrap **50 YEAR ANNIVERSARY SDPOA,** within an encircled star motif, and accompanied by **1 of 200.**

Alabama State Trooper: 659 cased revolvers, built in 1981. Model **GS-32;** etched with trooper logo and series number and **ALABAMA STATE TROOPER ASSN. 1981 LIMITED EDITION** on the backstrap.

Sunnyvale Department of Public Safety: 200 cased revolvers, built in 1981. Model **GA-36-T;** star motif on topstrap.

R.C.A. Government Model: Approx. 200 **SS-84L** and **SS-32L,** built in 1981. Fitted with lanyard loops, these Speed-Six revolvers were of a pattern made on U.S. government contract. Excess guns sold to the Ruger Collectors Association.

Government of India, Border Security Force: Approximately 30,000 **SDA384L,** .380 caliber rimmed cartridge, with lanyard loop. 20,000 shipped 1983–84, additional 10,000 revolvers shipped 1985–86.

Easy takedown of Security-Six series revolvers.

The Security-Six, heralded as the most advanced of double-action revolver designs. The large spring-loaded plunger below and behind the trigger is the key to its tool-free disassembly. This allows most working parts to be removed in one unit out the bottom of the revolver, for easy maintenance and ultra-rugged solid-frame construction, unlike revolvers with frame-weakening access via removable sideplates.

presented a prime opportunity to show off Ruger products.

Sturm, Ruger was growing so fast that their accounting had trouble keeping up with the pace. Controller Walt Berger was extremely busy and the arrangement with Ruger was based on the best they could deliver for me. After a while Ed said he just didn't have the time to take care of the export paperwork. In the early 1960s he said they would ship me consignment guns, and I could pay when I was paid. Our arrangement was

based on mutual trust, and we didn't have a written agreement.

There was as much as $60,000 or $70,000 on consignment at any one time. Finally the company decided to treat me as a regular distributor. We made arrangements for payment terms, and I've always felt Sturm, Ruger was completely fair in every respect.

I remember Bill saying that when John Kingsley came in, he had incorporated some new accounting strategy and systems that modernized

the whole paperwork process. Bill once said that John recommended they buy a lot of gunstock wood before the end of the fiscal year, and things like that would save them a lot of money.

Steve Vogel, Bill's son-in-law, was setting up an export department, from Southport, and the arrangement was that he got involved with larger government projects, and some house accounts, like New Zealand, Australia, England, and Italy. Other than that I handled the commercial export sales.

Our first big order was for something like 6,000 Speed-Six revolvers for the police of Colombia. This was before 1970. S & W had the market in double-action revolvers. I went to see the Colombian Chief of Police, Henry García. I had an appointment, and went to his office in Bogotá, at 10 A.M., and they kept me waiting there till 4 P.M. It seemed like cab drivers, and everybody else was seeing him, and finally his secretary told him that I had been waiting all day.

Chief García had never heard of Ruger guns, whereas S & W and Colt had been around for over 100 years. I gave him my talk about the features that I liked on our double-actions. I could say all of this with expertise, as a knowledgeable shooter. He kind of shuffled his shoulders, and I knew that I wasn't getting anywhere.

Then I happened to notice a plaque on his desk which said Henry García, President of the García Lorca Society.

"Do you know García Lorca?"

"Yes, I know most of his poems by heart."

"Which is your favorite poem?"

"'The Unfaithful Wife.' Would you like me to recite it for you?" I could recite that poem beautifully, and had had some coaching from some well-known poets. When I finished my recitation, he called up his wife and asked if we could go out to dinner that night. We became great friends.

So I invited García to Southport, and we went out on Bill's yacht, the *Titania*. Steve Vogel and I entertained him, shooting off the stern and so forth. I wish I could say it was my expertise in firearms that got the order, but it was my knowledge of the poetry of García Lorca.

I always found Bill to be very bold and innovative. He didn't care if the competitors were in the business 100 years or more before him.

That sideplate on the S & W double-action was an absolute nightmare. I was showing the Thai police the difference between our revolver and the S & W. And you know, once you get that sideplate off the S & W, you can never get it back right. Also in the process the heads of the screws can be all stripped, and you might also damage that tight-fitting sideplate.

Another highlight of our export business was when we set up an assembly operation to make the Security-Six, with the Industrial Militarie, in Bogotá, Colombia. We used to send them the castings, cylinders, and other components, and set them up with a complete buffing operation, jigs, and fixtures. We also sent some of our people there to teach them how to do the gunsmithing and assembly. We had a similar operation in Caracas, Venezuela, called the Cavin Company. They had special roll marks with their names, for both operations.

Unfortunately when Sturm, Ruger stopped making the Security-Six line, the company stopped making those castings. The Colombians and the Venezuelans had spent so much down there for the tooling and so forth, they didn't want to retool for the new model. These are true rarities—Rugers not made in the U.S.A.

The Ruger Armorers School

In 1973, Stephen Vogel took on the responsibility of establishing the Ruger Armorers School, to provide a training program for law enforcement and government agencies, domestic and foreign. In a generally five-day-long course, students learn the care, repair, and maintenance of Ruger law enforcement-oriented products, from factory experts. The fundamentals of Ruger police and military arms are explained and demonstrated, in their construction and function, assembly and testing, all to specifications of the factory.

Day one is a general orientation, with a tour of the Newport factory, including manufacturing departments, the proof and function firing test ranges, and the investment casting facility. Day two is classroom instruction on safety, function, assembly and disassembly, and studies in detail of interior components and their functioning, replacing, and fitting. Days three to five cover product troubleshooting, and offer extensive question and answer sessions.

Excepting transportation, lodging, and meals, the training is free of charge. The number of students per class is limited, to provide the most intense training. The classroom at the Newport factory comfortably accommodates approximately two dozen students.

A demonstration in one of the on-site classes, described by Chris Pollack in *S.W.A.T.* magazine's November 1987 issue, reveals the kind of abuse the Ruger double-action police revolvers handily survive. Factory representative Mike Moore:

. . . took one of the Service-Six .357 Magnum revolvers . . . and subjected it to tremendous abuse. Mike began by firing six rounds of Federal Magnum ammo, then throwing the gun the length of the range. He walked to the end of the range, picked the gun up, and threw it against a concrete block wall. Then, instead of carrying it back, he threw it again.

The range walkways are asphalt with desert gravel and sand in between. Sometimes the gun landed on the asphalt, sometimes in the sand. Each time the gun got back to the center of the range, he'd check it for function by cycling the trigger six times, then load six more rounds of magnum ammo and fire it. . . . Everybody present was given the opportunity to abuse it. After each toss, the cylinder still rolled free and the action actually got smoother the more we fired it. . . . I do not believe any other double-action revolver will take this sort of punishment and continue to function. . . .

After many trips across the asphalt, the cylinder was gouged, the muzzle crown had a bad case of road rash and the front sight was so disfigured that it wasn't much use when shooting. But, the only thing that broke was the grips. The screw . . . eventually gave out. Mike taped them back on and kept on firing.

As a final test, we brought a truck onto the range, put the Ruger in front of the tire, and peeled out over it—twice. The gun was tossed about thirty feet and had a layer of burnt rubber on it, but it kept functioning, perfectly. I then fired fifty rounds of Federal .357 Magnum ammunition through it without a hitch. . . . Abusing your revolver like this will void the warranty, but now I understand why Ruger has no 'authorized service centers.' Civilian guns in need of repair must be returned to the factory. With more than a million and a half Security-Six type revolvers in circulation, the factory double-action service department is one man in a small office!

School dates are announced periodically, and the company has literature explaining enrollment, details of the course structure, and the products covered. The school has graduated thousands of students from around the world, at classrooms conducted at the Newport facility, and on-site around the U.S. and worldwide.

Early in the 1990s, the company's Law Enforcement Sales Division set up a college credit option with the New Hampshire Vocational Technical College in Claremont, an institution which is accredited by the New England Association of Schools and Colleges.

At about the same time, Sturm, Ruger set up the Ruger International Law Enforcement Exchange Fellowship (RILEEF), to promote an exchange of ideas between law enforcement agencies, as well as education and comprehension on police matters, on a worldwide basis. The first fellowship recipient was Captain Mikhail Trusov of the Moscow Police Department. His visit to the U.S. began in November 1992, and was completed in February 1993.

In some areas, American manufacturers still set the standards for the rest of the world.

When I was in prep school with Tom Ruger at Salisbury, Bill Ruger came to one of the parents' day functions. That evening there was a dinner in which the school put its best foot forward in every respect. All through this event, Mr. Ruger had a dry cleaning tag attached to his jacket, right on the sleeve.

My mother remarked that only Bill Ruger

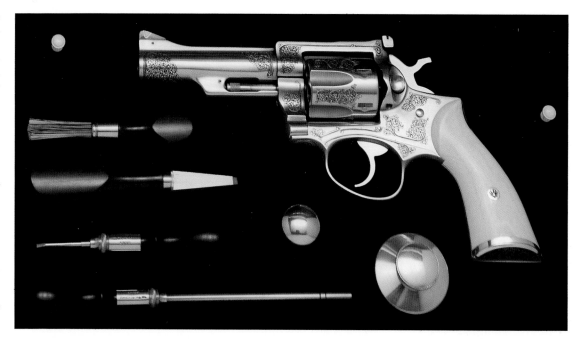

Another millionth milestone, serial number 1,000,000 of the Security-Six, donated by Sturm, Ruger & Co., in 1981 for the benefit of the National Shooting Sports Foundation's programs of conservation and safety education in thousands of schools. Engraved, gold inlaid and fitted with ivory grips and silver buttcap; front sight with ivory insert. Rare use of red Ruger logo, inlaid on left grip panel. Butt marked with number 159-99999. Revolver realized $20,300. Embellishments by Paul Lantuch; case by Fred Wenig; interior custom-fitted by Marvin Huey; accessories by Mike Marsh.

could have gone through that entire day and evening, with that cleaning tag, and maintained his innate dignity.

—Herb Glass, Jr.

Late Night Sessions with Bill Ruger: Rex King Remembers

Back in those days, after-hours work was likely to be once a week on the average, and would vary anywhere from an hour to five hours. Once we were working until midnight making the investment casting die for the No. 1 Rifle receiver. My assistant toolmaker, Jimmy Poleio, was right there with me. We worked overtime every night for about two weeks, just to make the master, till about eight o'clock, and the last night we worked on it was until 12 midnight. Then we were another week to a week and a half on making the die itself. Ruger himself would work later than the rest of the shop, anyhow.

After the regular working hours, I was in the tool room, and sitting on the edge of the desk, talking with Bill. He was pretty excited about getting the double-action revolver going, but he hadn't as yet designed it. He wanted to know how we could go about inserting the sideplate and getting the real hairline fit. With standard manufacturing equipment there was no easy way we could ever do it. That's when I suggested to him that we try to utilize a solid frame, similar to the single-actions, with a separate trigger guard, which he subsequently did. He took to that idea right away, and could see the advantages. He had a little question in his mind about the design, as to how he was going to have the trigger and the cylinder latch and all that involved. But we were able to do it, and that evolved as one of the greatest advances in the double-action revolver design.

Robert M. Lee, Founder, Hunting World, Visits Sturm, Ruger

Back in the 1950s, my old friend Jack O'Connor phoned and said that he would be in New York shortly, and wondered if I would like to accompany him on a visit to Bill Ruger, in Southport, Connecticut.

I had never met Bill, who, even at that time, was famous among designers and producers of sporting arms. But I certainly looked forward to meeting the man who created many new and novel methods of manufacturing designed to simplify and reduce costs without sacrificing functional reliability, longevity, and accuracy. The guns were also good-looking, which, of course, contributed to their success.

However, in the back of my mind, and as a purist, I was skeptical about the use of stamping and investment casting in the manufacture of fine firearms. Nevertheless, I welcomed the opportunity to visit Bill in the company of my great friend Jack.

We drove to Southport and arrived at the Ruger plant in the early afternoon. Bill greeted us warmly and showed us around. As a matter of fact, it was my very first visit to a gun factory of any kind. I was certainly impressed by the array of machinery and by the manufacturing process; but more than anything, I was impressed by the creator.

Bill was at his charming best and laid out an excellent foundation which justified the reasoning behind his pioneering manufacturing methods.

Although precision investment casting certainly was not new, it was most uncommon in the arms industry and I believe that Bill was the first entrepreneur to use this process for the manufacture of sporting arms in the United States. I had heard some rumors about investment casting being used before in Europe, but these were merely rumors. The use of stamping, however, was common in the production of World War II small arms and especially in the production of submachine guns—proving its worth not only as a cost-saving method but also as a good means of weight reduction without loss of structural integrity.

Bill invited us to his palatial home after our visit to the factory and I was impressed by his collection of early blackpowder double rifles. Here again, Bill was a man of vision. In those days, the blackpowder double rifle was not yet a collector's item, but I well remember him saying: "Someday these old blackpowder doubles will become very much sought after, and valuable." He was indeed a prophet. I remember that the decor of his living room also complemented his personality. There was a glass-top coffee table with an array of antique guns displayed beneath the top.

Bill outlined a number of his future plans to us for the production of exciting new handguns and rifles.

I engaged Bill in a conversation comparing the traditional methods of machining a receiver from forgings as opposed to his method of investment casting. I had always had qualms about using investment casting in a receiver since I associated casting with brittleness. Bill explained the merits of investment castings to me, and I became convinced that the end product was as strong as, and often better than, the traditional machine forging.

I never did agree with the enclosed bolt face design that was then very much in vogue, having been introduced by Remington on its Model 700 rifle. I much preferred Mauser breeching, featuring the controlled round feed. Incidentally, I am delighted to see that Ruger M77 Mark II rifles have gone "back to the future" with that system.

My first meeting with Bill Ruger left me with the impression that here was a true, classic American entrepreneurial engineer and inventor, a man of tremendous charm and obvious integrity. Over the years, it has been my privilege to meet with Bill on many occasions. I have always been amazed by his enthusiasm and by his uncanny ability to produce a seemingly never-ending flow of excellent new products. The latest Ruger M77 Mark II Magnum and Express rifles [introduced 1990–92] are very close indeed to high-quality custom-built rifles that cost three or more times their price. The lines are "pure classic"—a true reflection of the maestro's vision.

We formed a 10-year club in the company's 10th anniversary year, and we would hold formal dinners annually. Early photographs show the men wearing shirts, ties, jackets, and there was a decent menu, with wine. There was no rough stuff or uncivilized behavior at these events. The first of these dinners was organized by Bill, Jr., and was at the Shakespeare Restaurant, in Milford. They were also held at the Stratford Motor Inn. There was a bar, and a yard of beer.

We also held wonderful family picnics and get-togethers, which went on for years, and finally ended about 1962. There were some overtones of unionization in those days, that always cast a shadow over these outings, as though the company was trying to be friendly artificially. In many respects, in modern times, unions have outlived their usefulness; the Government often has attempted to assume that role.

—William B. Ruger, Sr.

"Fundamentally Correct Classical Concepts"
The Old and the New
1972–1975

*E*verything we did at Sturm, Ruger was new. During the time I was there, we did more products development and released more new products than anyone else in the business. Everything we worked on was designed for ease of quality manufacturing and designed with investment casting in mind, to get the optimum use of that capability. There were also projects for upgrading guns and updating them. It was fun. I enjoyed it all the while I was there.

I used to tell Larry Larson that I occasionally had dreams—nightmares, actually—that the old man had died and that he had hired a medium so he could tell me what he wanted from the other side! A very interesting man to be around, and very interesting to talk to.

"Old model" Ruger Single-Six engraving samples, "old model" Super Blackhawk, and Old Army. Single-Six set engraved by Jerred in contrasting styles; numbers 5119 and 5105. Super Blackhawk by Denise Thirion, number 4806. The stainless steel Old Army percussion revolver engraved by Paul Lantuch. Three-screw frames of the cartridge revolvers were replaced in 1973 on the New Model revolvers by two-pin frames, and adoption of the revolutionary patented "transfer bar" safety system. Another Ruger first for single-action revolvers. Even the name "transfer bar" is a Ruger innovation, describing perfectly the function of a part that transfers the blow of the hammer to the firing pin only when the trigger is pulled.

---

13. 1972
Old Army Blackpowder Revolver
14. 1973
New Model Single-Six Single-Action Revolver
15. 1973
New Model Blackhawk Single-Action Revolver
16. 1973
New Model Super Blackhawk Single-Action Revolver

I miss Mr. Ruger terribly; he was an S.O.B. to work for, but he knew what he wanted. There were no ifs, ands, or buts about it. Fortunately I have a pretty good mechanical mind, and after awhile I could read what he wanted almost without him having to say it. I still consider him a friend. I also miss the company on occasion, I really do. We engineers who worked there are like graduates of the "Ruger Engineering School," and are very proud of it.

—Roy Melcher

"We loved a great many things—birds and trees and books and all things beautiful, and horses and rifles and children and hard work and the joy of life."
—Theodore Roosevelt, *An Autobiography*

The Old Army Blackpowder Revolver: Harry Sefried Remembers

Bill and I were both interested in antique blackpowder guns, and my own favorite was the Rogers & Spencer. Bill had several percussion revolvers in his collection, including the prettiest little Remington Pocket Model, on which he had styled the Ruger Bearcat.

He said it would be nice to make a percussion revolver that was a really good shooter, and as close to indestructible that could be made, with all the usual features. With the advances in our investment

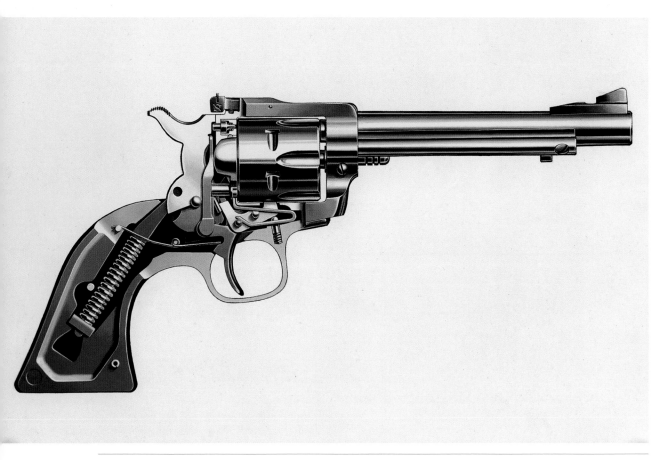

nice big hammer for positive ignition and we even investment cast the cylinder as well. In other words, we combined all the features for which investment castings were perfect, on a frame natural for the .44 caliber. We called the caliber ".44," but it's technically a .457, since we used our .45 caliber revolver barrels.

We finished the design, and it sat there for awhile, while we were preoccupied on other projects. After a couple of years, Larry Larson went over the possibilities to prepare for production.

The gun was of incredible strength, as Bill always insisted. I decided the logical way to test these was to do so with Bullseye smokeless powder—definitely *not recommended* to the public! I'd stoke the cylinders up, and pop the cap. You can't, however, ignite Bullseye with the spark from a percussion cap going through a tiny little hole in a blackpowder cylinder nipple. We opened these up, and boy, we were getting ignition! We found we couldn't get enough Bullseye in to blow the cylinder. Even if not filled up, we could not blow it with Bullseye powder! (Again, not to be tried at home!)

The only criticism I've ever heard of that gun was that there were certain calibers that were considered more accurate than our .44. But it has won blackpowder matches across the country. The Ruger Old Army does have a very good reputation for strength, accuracy, and practicality. It performed well, and was eminently worthy of wearing the Ruger label.

Transfer bar design, as developed for the New Model Single-Six revolver. The bar is the vertical member in front of the hammer, connected to the arm extending rearward from the top of the trigger. In this position, the hammer cannot contact the firing pin, which can be seen resting partially in the frame and partially in a recess cut into the hammer face. Compare with black-and-white cutaway photographs and cross-sectional painting of New Model Super Blackhawk. This patented design has been used on all Ruger single-actions since 1973.

casting program, we had come to a point where we could do just about anything. Having that process in mind left the way wide open for a lot of innovative design work.

I started off with a clean sheet of paper. None of this stuff of no topstrap, like the Colt percussion revolvers, or simply duplicating an antique design. This sturdy revolver would be basically a Super Blackhawk in percussion, to utilize Blackhawk components as much as possible—grips, gripstraps, etc.

One of the details we wanted was no screws (since, for one thing, they always shot loose in the percussion revolvers of the 19th century), except for attaching the grip frame and securing the hammer, trigger, and cylinder stop within the frame. I worked that linkage, using the rammer and base pin to secure the cylinder, a coil mainspring system, and a number of other innovations. The fired gun could be cleaned up easily, especially when we came out with a stainless steel version. We wanted a

Creating the Single-Action Transfer Bar System: Bill Ruger Remembers

Ruger again surprised the shooting world in 1973 with the announcement of a revolutionary new operating mechanism for its Single-Action revolvers; a system which even General Hatcher thought "cannot be utilized in the conventional type of single-action revolvers." None of the dozens of Colt-type single-actions on the market even incorporated a fully automatic safety system until Ruger engineers patented it in 1973. *The American Rifleman* called it "a brilliant concept in design and engineering. . . . It is the safest single-action revolver to date."

Carrying the hammer resting on a live round (in any original Colt-type single-action revolver like the Ruger Blackhawk) is the same as carrying a percussion gun with the hammer resting on a capped nipple, and for the past 150 years the assumption has been that the owner has better sense than to carry a gun that way. Normal procedure with a single-action revolver is, and has been from the beginning, to carry the gun with the hammer down on an *empty* chamber. Do that and there is no way a blow on the hammer, no matter how hard, can produce a discharge. In the 100 years or so that single-action revolvers have been in use, thousands upon thousands of users have followed this generally accepted safety procedure; and remember, the Colt single-action was for a very long time a standard handgun of the U.S. Army.

In the middle of our customary heavy workload of research and development, the 1968 gun laws came along, which had import limitations, and size and import criteria. There was a point system to qualify a gun for importation. And that's where a "drop test" first evolved and that's where we thought we might not pass it. I think by that time we ourselves were wondering what this meant, since we didn't think the gun (Ruger "old model" single-action revolver) was not safe. We felt really that if there was to be some standard requirement, it would be best if we conformed. Anyway, that was the whole atmosphere, the evolution of the (1973 Ruger New Model) design linking the transfer bar to the trigger as we do.

What I liked in particular was the way in which I

Oil portrait of Indian chief, by Charles Bird King. Old Army revolver with etched decoration, part of presentation set to William B. Ruger from Ruger Collectors Association, cased with knife and accessories. Full stock sporting rifle by English gunmaker William Moore, of style brought by English adventurers for their hunts or explorations in the West; serial number 360; .64 caliber. Remington Pocket Revolver, converted from percussion to metallic cartridge; a mechanical and stylistic influence on the Ruger Bearcat revolver. The solid frame of the Remington percussion revolvers was also an influence on the design of the Ruger Old Army. Rugged stainless steel construction would have been ideal for the hard usage firearms endured in hands of Indians.

The Ruger Old Army Revolver

Number 140-00001 Old Army Revolver.

Number 1 Old Army Revolver, in stainless steel.

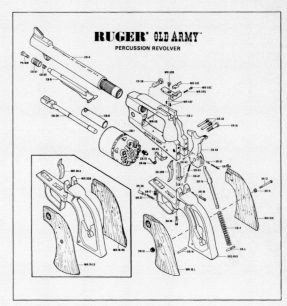

Exploded view of Old Army Revolver.

Introduced: 1972. "The finest percussion revolver ever made . . . [integrating] modern mechanical features with the beautiful lines of the classic cap-and-ball models. . . . one of the most accurate cap-and-ball revolvers available in America today."

Serial Numbers: *Blued,* 140-00000 to -46841 (through 1981); serial numbers intermix with stainless steel revolvers from 1982 (with prefix 145-).

Stainless Steel, 1 to 7790. 145-00000 to -68310 (through 1993; intermixed with blued from 1982).

Total Made Through 1993: In excess of 120,000.

Caliber: .45 cap-and-ball, bore of .443", groove of .451", with suggested bullet diameter of .457" (pure lead, either ball or conical). Uses standard #10 percussion cap and blackpowder charge.

Number of Chambers in Cylinder: Six.

Barrel Length: 7½".

Rifling: 6 grooves, right-hand twist, one turn in 16".

Markings: See Table of Markings, pages 330–35.

After approximately January 23 (serial range 140-34882) and February 11 (serial range 145-08142), 1978, standard marking on top of barrel:

Before using gun-read warnings in *instruction manual* **available free—from Sturm, Ruger & Co., Inc. Southport, Conn. U.S.A.—**

On cylinder periphery, marked twice within border motif (scarce stainless variation with backward cylinder markings, serial range approx. 1500 to 2000):

BLACK POWDER ONLY

Sights: Target rear, adjustable for windage and elevation; ⅛" wide flattop Baughman type ramp front sight (changed after serial range approximately 140-00800 to pointed profile), with blued steel blade. In 1994, traditional fixed sights also introduced.

Overall Length and Weight: 13½", 2⅞ pounds.

Grips: American walnut; rosewood grips also used.

Finish: Blued, or satin-finished stainless.

Materials, Construction, and Innovations: The most advanced blackpowder revolver ever made.

Chrome-molybdenum steel, or corrosion-resistant stainless steel. Unbreakable steel music wire coil springs. Stainless steel nipples. Adjustable rear sight, and ramp front.

Cylinder pin secured by large pin laterally through frame lug; one-half twist allows pin to be removed forward, after loading lever has been dropped; lever comes out at the same time, for easy cleaning and quick reassembly. Cupstyle loading lever latch secures lever from movement, when engaging the barrel catch, and cannot unlatch during recoil.

Six holes at rear of cylinder serve as ratchets for revolving from chamber to chamber. Safety recesses between each chamber, for resting the hammer nose. Nipples deeply set into cylinder, to prevent cap fragments from flying loose. Designed to permit dry-firing, since the hammer face clears the nipple by .005" when hammer fully downward.

Investment cast frame, cylinder, hammer, and loading lever.

Nipple wrench supplied with each revolver.

Issue Price: $115.00 (1972), $167.50 (stainless, 1976).

Engraving: A pre-production blued sample engraved with scrollwork and borders; brass grip frame; barrel address marking on side of barrel. Engraved by Denise Thirion. Inscribed revolver presented to Valmore Forgett of Navy Arms Company, "a valiant competitor," by William B. Ruger, Sr. (serial number 59). Serial number 48484 engraved for William B. Ruger, Sr., by Paul Lantuch.

Price Sheet Listings and Major Production Variations:

BP-7: Blued steel, anodized aluminum grip frame; built up through approx. serial range 140-07700.

BP-7B: Brass Grip Frame, Wide Trigger. Approximately 1200 blued revolvers built in this variation, serial range 140-00000 to -04750.

BP-7F: Blued steel, with fixed sights.

KBP-7: Stainless steel, with adjustable sights.

KBP-7B: With brass grip frame.

KBP-7F: Stainless steel, with fixed sights.

Liberty Series: Barrels of Old Armys built in 1976 marked

MADE IN THE 200th YEAR OF AMERICAN LIBERTY

Liberty Year Revolvers Without Liberty Marking: Within serial range approximately 145-00000 to -00300.

Warning Series: Warning marking adopted in serial ranges and with legend as indicated above.

Special Issue Revolvers:

National Muzzle Loading Rifle Association: Serial range 140-14000 to -14100. Identified by an N.M.L.R.A. logo on the grip panel.

Ruger Collectors Association: Serial range 1500 to 1599, - **RCA** - marked on the topstrap and a star motif preceding the serial number.

Ruger Collectors Association: Second series, serial range 145-01401 through -01600. Total of 201. Engraved RCA logo and intertwined RCA monogram on topstrap; standard with an eagle marked before the serial number, on grip frame butt, and on right grip panels (some few variations observed, including with **U.S.** marking). Barrels with Liberty marking, and these 201 revolvers were the last of the 1976 Rugers so marked.

Note: total of eight revolvers embellished with etching, arranged by James M. Triggs.

Cross-sectional of the New Model Super Blackhawk Revolver.

these really fundamentally correct classical concepts, and the same feeling comes along periodically, maybe not in connection with the whole complete firearm, but in some aspect of gun design.

There are still many customers who prefer the "old model" (pre-1973) Rugers. We have reports of both new and second-hand "old models" bringing higher prices than the list price of our New Model. Firearms appeal to a variety of people in a variety of ways. In one sense, people want the most modern performance they can get . . . there's immense appeal in progress and I think our New Model fills that type of demand. On the other hand, there are shooters with a kind of antiquarian interest or historical sensitivity . . . and you see this typified by the great popularity of muzzle-loading guns and shooting which certainly relates to the continuing appeal of our older model . . . and the old Colts. You know, way back in the 1930s Elmer Keith wrote, "The single-action is not obsolete and never will be."

It is very difficult to apportion the work on the New Model single-actions. Larry Larson was particularly active on this, over a period of years. While I regularly came to him with concepts, and worked with it on the drawing board to test the possibilities of these ideas, he carried on a major portion of the work. It is impossible at this point, or even at the time, to really say who should take credit for any one phase of the design work. And for that reason Larry and I have appeared as co-inventors on the various patents associated with the New Model.

We're conscious that the possibility exists of someone being injured by a product we make, usually by misuse or just plain carelessness. Also, it occurred to me that the operational characteristics of our "old model" single-actions were quite different from the operational characteristics of the New Model single-actions, so perhaps there was a need to make sure that this was clear in the minds of all owners. That is, that they can distinguish one model from the other and understand the mechanical differences and the effect of those differences; because, of course, there are things that you can do with the New Model that are not good practice with the "old model." To that end, we embarked on a widely publicized campaign to re-educate shooters

saw, by luck, the method of interlocking the opening of the loading gate with the cyclinder latch—because now, releasing the cylinder so that it could be spun for loading was done properly for the first time in history. You opened the gate and the locking bolt was retracted, by extremely simple means. We tried to do that previously with a lot of cams, unlikely mechanical motions and so on. We had some system, I can't really rehash it all, there were so many varieties. Two or three people were struggling with this, good designers, over a period of several years all in all. Sometimes we just gave up, and

sometimes someone would say, "I think I've got an idea," and I'd say, "Go ahead and spend another month on the board. Maybe it will happen."

There would always be some empty area on the drawing where we couldn't figure it out. And then I also tied the opening of the gate in with the position of the hammer. We couldn't open the gate unless the hammer was down. That really made the gun super safe. Now you didn't need to know anything. It would be safe. The only thing you ever could do to make it fire was to pull the trigger all the way, from full cock. I thought this was one of

about safe handling practices with older firearms, regardless of manufacturer, which is still going on as we speak.

The Ruger New Model Single-Actions from the 1972 Annual Report

Throughout 1972, a tremendous amount of engineering and production effort went into the final design of, and production tooling-up for, the New Model Ruger single-action revolvers. This program is of major importance to the future of the company, and of universal interest to sportsmen the world over.

The original Ruger Single-Six mechanism was hailed as a significant advance in single-action design when first introduced. These revolvers became the basis for a Ruger line that maintained commanding popularity in the market for 20 years. The Ruger single-action line occupies position number one in the market.

All these superior features are retained in the New Model line, plus a number of unique improvements, notably an entirely new mechanism which provides the user with reliability, durability and convenience never before realized in arms of this type. The result is the finest single-action revolver made.

The New Model Single-Six is already in production. Shipment of the New Model Blackhawks and Super Blackhawks will follow later in 1973. All are built far better and stronger than need be. As is true of all Ruger firearms, the New Model series represents exceptional value.

Everything new in the New Model line is a plus for the sportsman and a major step forward in the development of handguns. Transfer bar ignition system, gate-controlled loading and interlocked gate, transfer bar, and hammer functions are typical of the innovative Sturm, Ruger thinking. The new revolvers have only two hammer positions: all the way forward and fully cocked. With the transfer bar system, pivoted at its lower end to an arm of the trigger, any possible connection between the hammer and the firing pin has been removed. The hammer surrounds but cannot touch the firing pin and the revolver can be carried with all six chambers loaded. Unless the trigger is held to the rear as the hammer falls, the transfer bar will automatically lower, preventing the revolver from firing.

From the 1973 Annual Report

The Company achieved both record sales and net income during 1973. Consolidated net sales amounted to $19,541,773 and consolidated net income after taxes amounted to $2,674,370 which was equal to $1.62 per share of common stock outstanding. While these results are gratifying and represent a 21 percent increase in sales and a 26 percent increase in net income over the comparable amounts in 1972, there is in my opinion, room for further improvement. . . .

1973 was a productive year in many aspects. We have clearly established the company as a major producer of sporting rifles, and every model we make has attained a gratifying acceptance or outright preference among the most knowledgeable users. Our penetration of the police market with our double action revolvers has been encouraging and growing. The New York City Police have approved our Police Service model, for example, and we have sold these outstanding products in several foreign countries for government use after their stringent tests. Our single-action revolvers, the "Single Six" and "Blackhawk" models, . . . remain as the acknowledged sales leaders in this category, and their technical leadership was further enhanced early in 1973 with the adoption of our new internal mechanism. . . . Foreign demand for our products has risen sharply, and foreign competition has diminished.

Intensive effort and a great deal of time were spent during the past year on our two new products, namely the Mini-14 Police Carbine and the Over-and-Under Shotgun. At the present time production of both . . . are in the pilot plant stage, and it is our intention that limited quantities of both guns will be available for sale during 1974. To further this program, a small addition was made to the Newport plant which will be devoted totally to these two new products during 1974.

For the longer term, detailed plans have been drawn for a major addition adjacent to the present Newport plant. In preparation for this development, we built a bridge across the Sugar River, which divides our Newport property, thus securing access to land which will accommodate our needs far into the future. This new facility, scheduled for completion late in 1974, should provide adequate space for production quantities of both the Mini-14 and Shotgun in 1975.

While our major attention during the past year has been directed toward pursuing the Company's basic business, . . . a substantial effort has been made to identify other business opportunities which would provide the Company with more diversification. This search is continuing and will ultimately enhance our growth potential.

As a partial step in this direction, Pine Tree Castings Division finished 1973 with a record level of outside orders. Our long term goal is to have Pine Tree Castings achieve a significant position as a producer of high quality investment castings for industry. . . .

In closing, I must concur with what many economists have already written about 1974, namely that never have there been more uncertainties. Despite this, I am confident and optimistic about the future. The last several years have seen hard work and planning by all the people of our Company, and we are now in a solid position to respond effectively to opportunities or problems, as they may appear in the future.

The Ruger New Model Single-Six Revolver

Number 62-00001 New Model Super Single-Six Revolver.

Number 262-66968 New Model Single-Six Revolver, in stainless steel.

1993). Colorado Centennial Commemorative, numbers 76-00000 to -15888.

Total Made Through 1993: In excess of 1,057,000.

Calibers: *New Model Super Single-Six:* .22 Long Rifle, with extra cylinder in .22 Magnum.

   New Model Single-Six Convertible: .22 Short, Long, Long Rifle, standard with extra cylinder in .22 Magnum.

Number of Chambers in Cylinder: Six.

Barrel Lengths: 4⅝", 5½", 6½", 9½".

Rifling: 6 grooves, right-hand twist, one turn in 14".

Markings: See Table of Markings, pages 330–35.

After December 29, 1977 (serial range 65-96958) marking standard on left side of barrel:

Before using gun-read warnings in *instruction manual* available free— from Sturm, Ruger & Co., Inc. Southport, Conn. U.S.A.—

Sights: Rear sight click adjustable for elevation and windage, and protected by integral frame topstrap ribs. Patridge type ramp front sight. Fixed sight models introduced 1994, in .22 Long Rifle.

Overall Length and Weight: 9⅞", 31½ ounces (4⅝" barrel, .22 L.R.); 14⅞", 38 ounces (9½" barrel, .22 L.R.).

Grips: Walnut grips with trademark medallion inlay. Goncalo Alves grips first listed in 1988 catalogue. Rosewood grips first listed in 1994 catalogue.

Finish: Blued. Anodized aluminum grip frame and ejector rod housing on blued revolvers. Satin-polished stainless steel introduced 1974 catalogue.

Materials, Construction, and Innovations: Hardened chrome-molybdenum alloy steel cylinder, trigger, and transfer bar. Unbreakable steel music wire coil springs. Two frame pins enter from the left side, serving as the hammer pivot and the trigger/cylinder bolt pivot, both interlocked by internal action components; will not work loose under extended shooting. On cocking hammer, transfer bar moves up into firing position, between face of the hammer and the firing pin. It remains there only if the trigger is pulled.

Introduced: 1973. "The result of many years of intensive analysis and development effort, [the New Model Single-Six] makes firearms history from any point of view. This remarkable new (U.S. and Foreign patents pending) revolver successfully combines, for the first time, the traditional appearance, handling and simplicity of the single-action with the durability and convenience of the most advanced double-action mechanism. . . . This new Ruger revolver is, without

question, the most durable single-action ever produced. [It is], in every respect, a thoroughbred single-action revolver."

Serial Numbers: 62-00000 to -99999; and similarly numbered serial prefixes 63-, 64-, 65-, 66-, 67-, 68-, 69-; then begin new prefix sequence 260-, 261-, 262-00000 to -65843 (through

Loading accomplished by simply opening the patented loading gate, which cams the cylinder bolt down and releases the cylinder to turn freely clockwise. On closing of the loading gate, the cylinder bolt returns to its locked position, securing the cylinder. Conventional loading or "half-cock" notch therefore is unnecessary.

Hammer and loading gate are interlocked, so that on cocking the hammer, the gate cannot be opened. When the hammer is down, the gate is free to open, thereby preventing the hammer from being cocked.

Unloading is achieved by simply opening the loading gate and using the ejection rod to remove cases or cartridges.

The patented transfer bar, used for the first time in history in a single-action revolver, acts as the medium to transfer energy from the falling hammer to the firing pin, and thereby to the cartridge for firing. The hammer therefore does not touch the firing pin, which is of the floating type, mounted in the cylinder frame.

The transfer bar is pivoted (at lower end) to the trigger. Thus the transfer bar is only in its upward or firing position when the trigger is held in its rearmost position. The firing pin will not move forward unless the transfer bar is in its upward position and has been struck by the hammer.

When the hammer is down, the transfer bar's top interlocks with the face of the hammer, so that the trigger cannot be pulled until the hammer has been drawn to the rear. The hammer has only two positions: all the way forward or cocked all the way back. No longer necessary are the usual "safety notch" or "half-cock" notches found in all other conventional single-action revolvers.

In an unprecedented test of durability, Ruger New Model Single-Six revolvers were tested with over 100,000 dry-firings—without a single parts breakage, breakdown, or wear of any kind. Most revolvers are sold with extra cylinders, chambered for .22 Magnum. Cylinders can be changed quickly, without special tools.

The frame design includes the sight-protecting Ruger integral frame ribs. Easily adjusted rear sight, improved Patridge type front sight, and a wide, non-serrated trigger contribute to the New Model's accuracy and performance.

New Model grip frame differs from the "Old Model."

Quoting from the factory press release, of January 1, 1973: Viewed from any standpoint—appearance, durability, smoothness, accuracy, balance, convenience—the Ruger 'New Model' Single-Six is unquestionably the finest single-action revolver ever manufactured.

Issue Price: $95.00 (1973).

Engraving: None by the factory.

Price Sheet Listings and Major Production Variations: *First listing, January 2, 1973 Price Sheet*, all with click adjustable rear sight, ramp front sight:

New Model Single-Six, blued, walnut grips:

SR5: 5½"barrel

SR4X: 4⅝" barrel, with .22 WMR extra cylinder

SR5X: 5½" barrel, with .22 WMR extra cylinder

SR6X: 6½" barrel, with .22 WMR extra cylinder

SR9X: 9½" barrel, with .22 WMR extra cylinder

New Model Super Single-Six Convertible, Blued, walnut grips:

NR5: 5½", .22 WMR cylinder, click adjustable rear sight, ramp front sight, with ribbed topstrap protecting rear sight; **NR6:** (6½" barrel).

Listing changed March 19, 1973: All revolvers listed as *New Model Super Single-Six Convertible, Blued* (following remain listed in Price Sheets to date, except not present in 1986 price sheet):

NR4: 4⅝" barrel, .22 WMR cylinder, click adjustable rear sight, ramp front; **NR5** (5½" barrel); **NR6** (6½" barrel); **NR9** (9½" barrel).

Note: New Model Super Single-Six, Blued, 1975 only Price Sheet lists separate category, **S4, S5, S6,** and **S9,** same as above, but *without .22 WMR extra cylinder.*

Note: New Model Super Single-Six, Blued, 1986 only Price Sheet lists separate category, **SSR4, SSR5, SSR6, SSR9,** also *without .22 WMR extra cylinder.*

New listing in **1994** price sheet, *New Model Single-Six Convertible, blued,* with fixed sights:

NR5F: 5½" barrel, blued, with extra Magnum cylinder; **NR6F** (6½" barrel).

New Model Super Single-Six Convertible, stainless steel, 1974 only:

KNR4: 4⅝" barrel, with .22 WMR cylinder, click adjustable rear sight, ramp front sight; **KNR5** (5½" barrel); **KNR6** (6½" barrel); **KNR9** (9½" barrel).

Stainless Steel, 1975 price sheet to date:

KNR5: 5½" barrel, with .22 WMR cylinder, click adjustable rear sight, ramp front sight; **KNR6** (6½" barrel).

1975 price sheet also listed:

New Model Super Single-Six: **KS5:** 5½" barrel, click adjustable rear sight, ramp front sight, .22 L.R. cylinder only; **KS6** (6½" barrel).

High Polish Finish, new listing in **1994** *price sheet:*

GKNR5: 5½" barrel, click adjustable rear sight, ramp front, extra Magnum cylinder, high gloss polish; **GKNR6** (6½" barrel).

Single-Six Convertible, with fixed sights, new listing in **1994** *price sheet:*

GKNR5F: 5½" barrel, polished stainless steel, extra Magnum cylinder; **GKNR6F** (6½" barrel).

Liberty Series: Barrel roll marking on revolvers built in 1976: **MADE IN THE 200th YEAR OF AMERICAN LIBERTY.**

Warning Series: Warning marking adopted in serial range and with legend as indicated above.

Colorado Centennial Model: Serial numbered from 76-00000 to -15888; 6½" barrel; stainless steel and blued combination; rosewood grips. **1876 - COLORADO - 1976** on grip frame. Left side of **1876 * COLORADO CENTENNIAL * U.S. BI-CENTENNIAL * 1776.** Majority of barrels did not include the **Liberty Series** marking, since production was done in 1975. Roll engraved non-fluted cylinders (historical-motif design by James M. Triggs). Walnut case with lid inscription and medallion inlay.

Kalispell Gun Show Model: 100 KNR6 revolvers, to commemorate the 25th anniversary of the Kalispell, Montana, Gun Show, 1983. Serial range approx. 69-94301 to -94400. Commemorative markings on interior and exterior of walnut case lid.

.32 H & R Magnum A Centerfire Magnum on the New Model Single-Six Frame

Introduced: 1984. "The .32 H & R Magnum cartridge, recently introduced by the Federal Cartridge Corporation, is a modern, compact cartridge, the muzzle energy and velocity of which exceed those of the .38 Special cartridge. Combined with Ruger's famous New Model Single-Six revolver, this new cartridge is a hard-hitting small game, varmint, and target load which brings the new Ruger Single-Six SSM revolver into a class with the powerful, larger centerfire models and bridges the gap between the .22 Long Rifle rimfire and the .38 Special High Velocity +P centerfire cartridges.

"Specifications . . . are almost identical to those of its proven .22 rimfire counterpart, with only those modifications necessary to adapt to the centerfire cartridge. The Single-Six SSM revolver will also handle the .32 S & W and .32 S & W Long cartridges."

Serial Numbers: 650-00000 to -33570 (through 1993); Standard model.

610-00000 to -05202; Convertible model.

Total Made Through 1993: In excess of 16,000.

Barrel Lengths: 4⅝", 5½", 6½", 9½".

Rifling: 6 grooves, right-hand twist, one turn in 14".

Markings: As on the New Model Single-Six of contemporary manufacture; caliber marking on right side of the frame.

Overall Length and Weight: 9⅞", 31½ ounces (4⅝" barrel).

Issue Price: $205.00 (1985).

Price Sheet Listings and Major Production Variations (from 1984 Price Sheet to date):

SSM-4: with 4⅝" barrel.

SSM-5: with 5½" barrel.

SSM-6: with 6½" barrel.

SSM-9: with 9½" barrel.

The Ruger New Model Blackhawk Revolver

Number 32-00001 New Model Blackhawk Revolver.

Number 36-00001 New Model Blackhawk Revolver, in stainless steel.

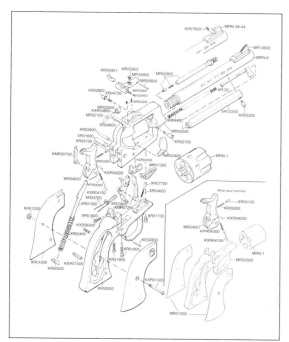

Exploded view of New Model Blackhawk and Super Blackhawk Revolvers.

Introduced: 1973. "The revolver that brought the traditional single action into the 20th century . . . incorporates innovative design features to a degree hunters and outdoorsmen will not find in any other single action revolver . . . When you understand the logic of this thoroughbred Ruger New Model Blackhawk design, you will agree that it could have been made only by people who know, through personal experience, just what real firearms progress is all about."

Serial Numbers through 1993: *.357 Magnum (and .38 Special), 9mm:* 32-00000 to -99999; and similarly numbered serial prefixes 33-, 34-, 35-, 36-, 37-00000 to -30015.

Barrel with warning roll marking began with serial number 34-06874.

.30 U.S. Carbine: 51-00000 to -36645. Barrel warning roll marking began with serial 51-13066.

.41 Magnum: 41-00000 to -33954; 46-00000 to -99999, serial numbers intermix with .45 caliber Blackhawks, from 1981 (*q.v.*). Barrel warning roll marking began with serial number 41-17490.

.45 Colt, .45ACP: 46-00000 to -99999, and similarly num-

bered serial prefixes from 47-00000 to -55235; serial numbers intermix with .41 Magnum Blackhawks, from 1981. Barrel warning roll marking began in January, 1978, with serial number 46-42174.

Total Made Through 1993: In excess of 1,160,000.

Calibers: .357 Magnum (.38 Special interchangeable), .41 Magnum, .45 Colt, .45ACP, .30 U.S. Carbine. The following calibers available as convertible models, with extra cylinder calibers listed in parentheses: .357 (9mm Parabellum), .45 Colt (.45ACP; discontinued c. 1983).

Number of Chambers in Cylinder: Six.

Barrel Lengths: 4⅝", 5½", 6½", 7½", varying based on calibers.

Rifling: .357 Magnum and .45 Long Colt: 6 grooves, right-hand twist, one turn in 16".

.30 Carbine, .41 and .44 Magnum: 6 grooves, right-hand twist, one turn in 20".

Markings: See Table of Markings, pages 330–35.

After approximately December 28, 1977, marking standard on left side of barrel (see above for serial ranges):
Before using gun–read warnings in *instruction manual* available free— from Sturm, Ruger & Co., Inc. Southport, Conn. U.S.A.—

Sights: Rear click adjustable for windage or elevation, protected by integral topstrap ribs. Front sight of Patridge type, mounted on ramp.

Overall Length and Weight: 10⅜", 40 ounces (4⅝" barrel, .357 Magnum); 13⅛", 40 ounces (7½" barrel, .45 Colt).

Grips: Walnut grips with trademark medallion inlay. Goncalo Alves grips first listed in 1988 catalogue. Rosewood grips first listed in 1994 catalogue.

Finish: Blued. Anodized aluminum grip frame and ejector rod housing on blued revolvers. Satin-finished stainless steel introduced 1974 catalogue.

Materials, Construction, and Innovations: Larger component parts used in the New Model Blackhawk revolvers, to accommodate centerfire cartridge pressures. Identical materials and innovations as detailed in New Model Single-Six, *q.v.*

Convertible models in the New Model Blackhawk series were identified by an X within the catalogue and price sheet identification number.

Issue Price: $180.00 (1973).

Engraving: Serial number 35-45040 gold inlaid in art deco motif for William B. Ruger, Sr., by Paul Lantuch.

Price Sheet Listings and Major Production Variations:
30 Carbine:
   BN31: 7½" barrel, blued.
   KBN31: 7½" barrel, stainless steel (1974 only).
.357 Magnum:
   BN34: 4⅝" barrel, blued.
   BN36: 6½" barrel, blued.
   Note: If catalogue code includes an **X**, above models ac-

companied by extra cylinder in 9mm Parabellum (available 1973 to date).
Stainless Steel, introduced 1974:
   KBN34: 4⅝" barrel.
   KBN36: 6½" barrel.
   KBN34X and **KB36X:** manufactured, but not catalogued; approximately 300 made, in stainless steel.
   GKBN34: 4⅝" barrel, high gloss finish (introduced 1994).
   GKBN36: 6½" barrel, high gloss finish (introduced 1994).
.41 Magnum:
   BN41: 4⅝" barrel, blued.
   BN42: 6½" barrel, blued.
Stainless Steel (1974 only):
   KBN41: 4⅝" barrel.
   KBN42: 6½" barrel.
.45 Long Colt (available 1973 to 1982; 1986 to date):
   BN44: 4⅝" barrel, blued.
   BN45: 7½" barrel, blued.
   Note: If catalogue code includes an **X**, above models accompanied by extra cylinder in .45ACP (1973 through 1982 only).
   BN455: 5½" barrel, blued, introduced 1993.
Stainless Steel, 1992 to date:
   KBN44: 4⅝" barrel.
   KBN45: 7½" barrel.
High gloss finish introduced 1994:
   GKBN44: 4⅝" barrel, high gloss finish.
   GKBN45: 7½" barrel, high gloss finish.
   Arizona Rangers: .45 Colt, 4⅝" barrel, stainless steel grip frame, walnut grips with trademark medallion, marked on top of barrel: **ARIZONA RANGERS.** Rangers logo and profile of Arizona state border marked on topstrap. Serial range within 46-44228 to -44550, with Ranger numbers from 001 to 304.
   Buckeye-Ruger 10mm/.38-40 Convertible: A 6½" convertible model (**S3840**) with cylinders chambered for 10mm Auto and .38-40, built for distributor Buckeye Sports Supply, and marketed exclusively by them. All-steel grip frame, bright blue finish, Goncalo Alves grips. Serial number range 611-00000 to -06199.
   Liberty Series: barrel roll marking on revolvers built in 1976:
MANUFACTURED IN THE 200th YEAR OF AMERICAN LIBERTY.
   Warning Series: Warning marking adopted in serial range and with legend as indicated above.
   The Buckeye .32 New Model Blackhawk: A 6½" convertible New Model Blackhawk with cylinders chambered for .32-20 and .32 H & R Magnum, built for distributor Buckeye Sports Supply, and marketed exclusively by them. **S32X.** Approximately 5,200 produced.

The Ruger New Model Super Blackhawk Revolver

Number 81-00001 New Model Super Blackhawk Revolver.

Number 85-00001 New Model Super Blackhawk Revolver, in stainless steel.

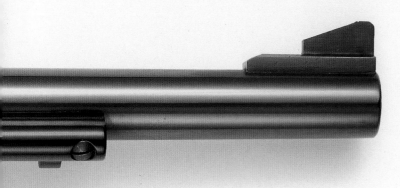

Introduced: 1973. "One of the world's truly great handguns. . . . widely regarded as the finest, most advanced single-action revolver ever produced. Exactingly designed and built to take advantage of the power of the 44 Magnum cartridge . . . [and] provides the hunter and explorer with a capability for special situations."

Serial Numbers Through 1993: 81-00000 to -99999; and similarly numbered serial prefixes 82-, 83-, 84-, 85-, 86-00000 to -64126.

Total Made Through 1993: In excess of 647,000.

Caliber: .44 Magnum (.44 Special interchangeable).

Number of Chambers in Cylinder: Six.

Barrel Lengths: 4⅝", 5½", 7½", 10½".

Rifling: 6 grooves, right-hand twist, one turn in 20".

Markings: See Table of Markings, pages 330–35.

After January 3, 1978 (serial range 82-27536), marking standard on left side of barrel:

Before using gun-read warnings in *instruction manual* available free— from Sturm, Ruger & Co., Inc. Southport, Conn. U.S.A.—

S proof mark stamped on back of cylinder.

Front of cylinder engraved by electric pencil with last three digits of serial number.

Sights: Rear click adjustable for windage and elevation; Patridge style ramp front.

Overall Length and Weight: 13⅜", 48 ounces (7½" barrel).

Grips: Oil-finished walnut with trademark medallion inlay. Goncalo Alves or laminated grips used in some later production.

Finish: Blued, high polish. Stainless steel revolvers with satin finish; later joined by high polish gloss.

Materials, Construction, and Innovations: Non-fluted cylinder, with squareback "Dragoon" style trigger guard in most versions.

Hardened, chrome-molybdenum steel used for cylinder frame, cylinder, trigger, and transfer bar. Steel grip frame. Frame reinforcements include integral ribs to protect rear sight. Unbreakable steel music wire coil springs. Wide, deeply serrated hammer spur. Wide trigger, at first smooth, then changed to grooved. Stainless steel introduced for major internal components in 1983.

Issue Price: $135.00, S47N (1975).

Engraving: Serial number 83-80502 gold inlaid and engraved for William B. Ruger, Sr., by Paul Lantuch.

Price Sheet Listings and Major Production Variations:

Blued:

S458N: 4⅝" barrel (introduced 1994).

S45N: 5½" barrel (introduced 1987).

S47N: 7½" barrel (first variation, introduced 1973).

S410N: 10½" barrel (second variation, introduced 1979; code discontinued 1983).

S411N: 10½" barrel (new code adopted 1984).

Stainless Steel:

KS458N: 4⅝" barrel (introduced 1994).

KS45N: 5½" barrel (introduced 1989).

KS47N: 7½" barrel (introduced 1983).

KS410N: 10½" bull barrel; improved target sights; ejector rod and housing lengthened one inch for improved ejection (introduced 1983).

KS411N: 10½" bull barrel (introduced 1984).

GKS458N: 4⅝" barrel, high gloss polish (introduced 1994).

GKS45N: 5½" barrel, high gloss polish (introduced 1994).

GKS47N: 7½" barrel, high gloss polish (introduced 1994).

Liberty Series: Barrel roll marking on revolvers built in 1976:

MANUFACTURED IN THE 200th YEAR OF AMERICAN LIBERTY. Sometimes termed 3rd Variation.

Warning Series: Warning marking adopted in serial range and with legend as indicated above.

1st Variation: Old Model style cylinder, counterbored. Smooth trigger.

2nd Variation: Non-counterbored cylinder. Grooved trigger.

3rd Variation: Revolvers made in 1976, with Liberty roll marking on barrel.

4th Variation: As above, but with Warning barrel marking.

5th Variation: Catalogue code **S410N,** 10½" barrel.

6th Variation: Catalogue code **KS47N,** made of stainless steel, excepting blued front sight blade, and rear sight.

7th Variation: Catalogue code **KS410N,** as above, but with 10½" barrel.

8th Variation: Catalogue code **KS411N,** 10½" bull barrel, new target sights, lengthened ejector rod and housing.

Special Editions:

Have been introduced by various organizations or companies, among them: Mag-Na-Port (including the Mark V and the Tomahawk), the Michigan Association of Chiefs of Police, the Foundation for North American Wild Sheep, Handgun Hunters International, and the International Handgun Metallic Silhouette Association.

Ruger Collectors Association Tomahawk, 90 **S47N,** made in 1978, for the RCA Tomahawk motif on the hammer and topstrap, and the Mag-Na-Port logo. Tomahawk and the RCA number marking beneath loading gate. Metalife SS finish; Mag-Na-Port recoil reduction barrel vents. Packaging of a suede pistol rug marked with the Mag-Na-Port tomahawk.

From the 1974 Annual Report

1974 net sales of $22,335,652 established a record for the Company in dollar terms. In actuality these record sales were a disappointment in that they were generated by shipments of virtually the same number of units as 1973. Net income after taxes amounted to $2,226,406 equivalent to $1.35 per common share. These amounts are net of LIFO adjustments of $720,000 and $0.44 per share respectively.

The year has been a difficult one for the management of the Company because of material shortages and the continuous increase of all manufacturing costs. . . . The value of in process inventories . . . has increased greatly, and this reflects to a considerable degree the buying policies required to minimize problems caused by uncertain deliveries of vital materials and supplies. Regardless of this enlarged inventory, production and shipments have been frequently interrupted during the year, and the problem of balancing the inventory is made practically impossible.

At the beginning of the year, the prices for our various firearms were reviewed and many increases established. We are conscious of competition and do not like to raise prices, but by midyear the need for further increases was apparent as it was again by the end of 1974. Looked at from this distance, we see now that the unusually sharp increases we were forced to announce were in reality long overdue. Our hourly employees received major increases in 1974 and the cost of all supplies, materials and services advanced more than we have ever previously experienced.

The demand for all our products was at record levels all through the year, and it is literally true that the Company could have substantially increased sales if production had been forthcoming. Although our hopes for near-term production increases were disappointed, long-term plans achieved real progress. Construction of a new 60,000 square foot factory building in Newport, New Hampshire has been substantially completed, giving us now a vastly increased production potential.

The special emphasis we have placed on the development of Police and Military products has yielded encouraging results particularly in foreign markets. The Mini-14 Carbine and the Security-Six Revolver have been demonstrated to many Government officials abroad, and significant orders have been received. We regard this business as a valuable and logical outlet for our engineering expertise and an important profit potential far into the future.

Our sporting firearms are in stronger demand than ever, but I regard this not as the evidence of a rapidly increasing market but of an increased recognition of the desirable qualities we have built into our products. We remain aware of the possibility that restrictive or prohibitory legislation could curtail this market.

Legislation of this kind cannot achieve its announced objective which is the curtailment of crime. Firearms have an important and legitimate use in the lives of a major segment of the American public, and furthermore, symbolize for millions of Americans the meaning of personal freedom and responsibility. If modern society cannot resolve issues such as this by more direct, effective, and equitable means, the future of all business, not merely the arms industry, is indeed in doubt.

The sober tone of this report does not mean that we are discouraged. Although we are small, we are strong. We see problems as challenges, and throughout the Company there is a strong faith in the continued success and marketability of our outstanding products.

From the 1975 Annual Report

Behind these figures there is the planning and activity of all the people constituting the Company over the period of 12 months. Throughout the entire year, the objective has been to run the Company in accordance with the budgeted plans set up in the Fall of 1974. This has meant a sharp focus on current operations, particularly in the area of production management and cash management. In the Fall of 1974 we were much concerned about liquidity. The Company has never in its 26 years of operation had to resort to bank borrowing. We concluded that if at the present time borrowing became necessary we would have to be reflective of poor management or the appearance of adverse fundamentals in our business. By detailed study and projections of future cash positions, we were able to avoid borrowing and to reestablish our normal liquidity. In effect, we reduced inventories while at the same time increasing shipments.

Much of the improved production performance was due to appear anyway as the result of visible improvement in management efficiency and in the productivity of factory personnel. Throughout the year of 1975, we also realized the benefit of substantial capital equipment additions. Early in 1975 our new 60,000 square foot building in Newport was completed, and by the end of the year we had transferred to this new building manufacturing and assembly operations sufficiently to vacate 20,000 square feet in the main plant building which could then be made available to the Pine Tree Castings Division. The process of enlarging and re-arranging the Newport manufacturing facilities is a continuous one. This work has to be done in a way that never creates an interruption in our flow of production. This enlargement of our facilities has been an extremely interesting planning problem as it must accommodate the production of new firearms products which will be put into production in the near future, but also the steadily increasing market for those which are already being produced. For example, our Security-Six Revolver over a pe-

New Model Super Blackhawk with relief carved ivory grips, gold inlaid and low relief engraved. Turquoise buttcap to each grip, mounted in silver; .44 Magnum, serial number 83-80502. Art nouveau motifs gold inlaid on New Model Blackhawk; carved horn grips; number 35-45040; .357 Magnum caliber. Both revolvers embellished for William B. Ruger, Sr., by Paul Lantuch.

riod of 6 or 7 years has been accepted throughout the world as a basic police and personal defense weapon and although production has increased many times over in this period, we have yet to produce enough to match demand. Throughout 1975 we responded to a continued heavy demand for our Single Six and Blackhawk single action revolvers. These two products together with our 44 magnum carbine and our 22 automatic target pistols are made in our Southport Plant where there has been no physical expansion but immensely improved efficiency to account for a record-breaking production year.

Notwithstanding the success of our handgun business, we are especially gratified by the continuing increase in sales and production of our sporting and military shoulder weapons. Our sporting rifles taken as a group, [sic] appeal to all the major segments of the market and are distinguished by both design and performance. This must account for the growth of this segment of our business and confirms the correctness of plans we have made in the past and encourages us in the developments which are now in progress. Our AC556 military carbines have been demonstrated in a number of foreign countries and significant sales have been made. The new plant in Newport was planned particularly as the locale for our forthcoming production of shotguns. Our shotgun program received a much increased effort during 1975 and we feel that the engineering phase is substantially completed. Much equipment has been installed for the production of this model and early manufacturing operations were started.

Low relief etched and gold inlaid New Model Blackhawk, with Sturm, Ruger & Co. trademark in gold on top of backstrap. Ebony grips, with turquoise buttcap to each, mounted in steel and silver. For William B. Ruger, Sr., by Paul Lantuch; serial number 46-58769. Cutlery handled Bowie knife, with etched blade; by Manson, Sheffield.

To summarize these comments: I think that all the major functions of a firm such as ours . . . have interacted very successfully to produce an ideal year of progress. The performance of all the people in the Company has steadily increased in effectiveness and the esprit de corps and cooperation which is [sic] evident among the people of both our plants must represent some ideal of industrial life.

However, the year 1975 confirmed that we are still threatened by the possibility of additional firearms legislation. In previous reports to stockholders, I have repeatedly stated our position on this subject. During the course of 1975, I have frequently participated in the public discussion of this subject. This includes attendance at the conference on the forum of handgun controls sponsored by the U.S. Conference of Mayors, television interviews, and testimony before Congress. In all of this I have been supported and helped by members of our organization who are in fact long-time students of this subject.

We know there is no meaningful correlation between handgun ownership and crime statistics, but the polemics of the debate are so confusing to the public, to Congress and even industry itself, that we can only hope that future resolution will respect our American tradition of individual freedom and responsibility. However, I think that during the year 1975 the public seemed to support the old tradition so that even in that respect, the year ended with cause for optimism.

Product Liability Litigation

As with most American manufacturers, product liability lawsuits were virtually unknown at Sturm, Ruger until the mid-1970s. In July, 1976, the company was found liable for injuries sustained during the use of an "old model" Blackhawk in the case of *Day vs. Sturm, Ruger* (Alaska), with an initial award of $2.3 million. The case was remanded for a new trial, but the ensuing publicity

opened floodgates of litigation. Unfairly, the innovative Ruger New Model single-actions, using the patented transfer bar safety mechanism for the first time in any single-action revolver, were used by plaintiffs' attorneys to imply that the pre-1973 "old models" were "defective." This litigation peaked around 1979, and has decreased steadily ever since. Less than 6/100ths of 1 percent of the almost 1.5 million "old models" have ever been involved in any claim of accidental injury, despite millions of users and billions of cartridges fired from them since their inception in 1953.

Nevertheless, the company embarked upon a massive safety campaign to help stop accidents caused by a blow to the hammer if the user failed to take the basic safety precaution of keeping an empty chamber under the hammer. Sturm, Ruger had already run full-page safety advertisements in the 1950s and 60s, but the focus shifted to "old model" single-action safety ads.

In 1976, the company first introduced the "Ruger Practical Holster," designed to shield the hammer from impacts and to prevent the gun falling from its holster (much like the full-flap cavalry holsters of the nineteenth century). In 1977, the company began running full-page warnings entitled "Handle with Care—Old Style Single-Action Revolvers," and in the following year began roll marking Ruger guns themselves with a warning to "read the instruction manual before using"—another industry first.

Later safety ads included the award-winning "Empty Chamber," featuring a $5.00 bill tucked into one chamber of an old-time single-action cylinder as a reminder to keep the hammer on an empty chamber. There was a new run of "A Father's Advice" (a safety poem first published in Ruger advertising in 1965). And, beginning in 1981, the first TV safety spot in the industry advised gun owners that the most important safety measure with a single-action was the empty chamber.

A SYMBOL OF RESPONSIBILITY

With the right and enjoyment of owning
a firearm goes the constant responsibility
of handling it safely and using it wisely.

As of this writing, product liability lawsuits are at a 17-year low. The company has never lost a product liability case involving any other Ruger products. Its defense strategy in product liability cases has set the standard for the industry, and Sturm, Ruger controls its own defense.

In other than product liability cases, Sturm, Ruger has obtained significant judgments against those who wrongfully copied Ruger designs. These include United Sporting Arms of Arizona and Arcadia Machine & Tool Company (AMT). Ruger does not believe the adage that "imitation is the sincerest form of flattery."

William B. Ruger on Firearms Safety

We have become so careful, and so effective in the courtroom, that our product liability has declined. It varies from state to state. Courts always seem to want to go against the defendant and make it a windfall for the plaintiff. Millions! You're lucky when you shoot yourself in the foot in Texas. It's what soldiers used to call the "million dollar wound."

My general impression is that in recent years .22 shooting has seemed to have plateaued while centerfire shooting has increased. Maybe because the cost of .22 ammo has increased while less expensive centerfire ammunition is now more frequently seen on the market. But regard-

less of the type of ammunition used, shooting can be the source of immense pleasure so long as the shooter has a modicum of knowledge and exercises common sense and good judgment.

I once saw a little poem written many years ago by an Englishman on the occasion of giving his son his first shotgun. It made a tremendous impression on me, and we obtained permission to reprint and advertise it numerous times since the early 1960s. Called "A Father's Advice," it explains literally and succinctly the basic rules of firearms safety—never point your gun at anyone, loaded or not; unload it if there's the slightest chance of a mishap; don't shoot where you can't see, and think about what you're doing at all times.

One of our own safety ads, entitled "Handle with Care," said it perfectly—firearms accidents used to be limited to those occasional lapses of common sense for which there is no real protection. Now, some people think that guns, like electric toasters, are meant to be foolproof. That kind of thinking has no place around firearms. There is no such thing as a foolproof gun.

Colts are like collectors' items that you want to put on a shelf. Rugers are like collectors' items that you can shoot; they won't break, and you can still put them on a shelf.

—John R. Hansen, Founder and President
Hansen Cartridge Co.

A serious side of the business. Ruger Vice President and General Counsel Stephen Sanetti, with 5-to-1 scale models of Ruger firearm mechanisms, used to illustrate their functioning. The 1955 Ruger advertisement is a concise statement of the long-standing Ruger philosophy concerning the serious responsibilities that firearms ownership entails, and Ruger has little patience for those few who misuse their right to own its products or who treat them carelessly or improperly. The company has won all of its court trials except for a few "old model" single-action revolver cases (and has won over 80 percent of those). Accidents and lawsuits have been declining since the late 1970s, which is precisely what the company intends.

Ruger Mini-14 rifle and Red Label Over-and-Under shotgun prints were among the first of over a dozen such creations by artist Jim Kritz. Steve Vogel discovered Kritz, when Vogel was seeking a talented cross-sectional artist due to Jim Triggs' glacially slow pace in producing his excellent, badly needed illustrations. Kritz had a long and distinguished pedigree of intricate cutaways of complex engines for Avco-Lycoming, and was a prize-winning graduate of Los Angeles's Art Center. He had also created airplane interiors for Boeing and automotive exteriors and interiors for General Motors, as well as any number of other projects in industrial design.

As a teenager growing up in California in the 1950s, Kritz admired a friend's Colt Frontier Scout .22 single-action revolver, a product inspired by Ruger's success with the Single-Six. Kritz could not afford the Colt, and one day he went into a gunshop. The dealer showed him a used Ruger Single-Six: "Here's a better gun than the Colt, better designed, won't break, and it's accurate."

Kritz bought the Ruger for $50, and fell in love with it. The pistol was not only beautifully made, but, "unlike the Colt, you could hit something with it. I fell in love with Rugers. The dealer also showed me a picture of Bill Ruger with his Jaguar XK120, a car that I dreamed of owning. I fantasized then that I might someday meet Mr. Ruger. That was in 1960."

In 1982, Kritz did meet Ruger, and it was at Ruger's request. He had seen Kritz's complex drawings of the Mini-14, and wanted to meet the artist and order more of his work: "When I was introduced to Mr. Ruger, I felt I was meeting more than a gunmaker or manufacturer; I was meeting a fellow artist."

Kritz made over a dozen complex cross-sectional illustrations for Sturm, Ruger, and remembers Ruger himself as "like all of us, he's a Dr. Jekyll and a Mr. Hyde. Sometimes he was a bit irascible, but I always felt that this was an expression of his impatience for people who didn't do their jobs up to the standards of perfection that he held for everyone, particularly himself. I noticed he truly cared about his workers. Once we were going through the foundry in Newport, and everyone who looked up from their machines or whatever they were doing, to say hello to Mr. Ruger, were responded to by his greeting and calling each one by his or her first name. He would talk to them as if they were a member of his family. Ruger is definitely not like the usual corporate executive, where you would rarely see the chairman or founder, especially on the factory floor.

"That same evening, at dinner at his house in Newport, with Bill, Jr., Stan Terhune, and others, Mr. Ruger was talking about the workforce, and concerned about details of their well-being. My boyhood wish to meet Mr. Ruger came true, and I was not disappointed."

CHAPTER VI

"A Unique Niche"

A Full Line of Products
1975–1982

A s we went along in our research and development programs, it was evident that Bill was filling niches. In other words, the .22 autoloading pistol, that first gun, was like Henry Ford's Model T. It was mechanically unique, aesthetically pure, had a competitive price, and was a line-leader that started the ball rolling superbly.

Then Bill filled another niche: people had the old Colt single-actions, but they didn't want to shoot them. So he brought out the Single-Six, and the company virtually had that market to itself. Next was the larger caliber line of single-actions. They, too, were unique, and he brought them out before Colt revived their line in 1955.

The .44 Magnum Carbine was another step in the niche direction—there was no light rifle in that caliber for deer and other brush-hunting. The 10/22 Carbine and the No. 1 and No. 3 Rifles established two more niches. The former, an ultra-reliable "plinker"; the latter, elegant rifles for the connoisseur.

When he branched out into the M77 rifle, the company went up against the Model 70 Winchester and the Model 700 Remington, which were dominating that market. Ruger felt that the Model 70 had lost a great deal of its character by the ill-fated redesign in 1964. He captured a niche with a top quality bolt-action.

The Security-Six double-action line was another

---

17. 1975
Mini-14 Rifle
18. 1977
Over-and-Under Shotgun
19. 1979
Redhawk Double-Action
Revolver
20. 1980
The *Titania*–A Ruger-
Designed Yacht
21. 1982
Mark II .22 Pistol
22. 1982
Ranch Rifle

---

head-on collision, this time mainly with S & W and Colt. It was simpler, stronger, and more easily maintained.

The Old Army immediately put us in the forefront of advanced, high tech, yet traditionally styled black-powder percussion revolvers.

Bill continued to fill those niches, and to a great extent the Mini-14 and the Over-and-Under Shotgun did it again. There was certainly nothing like the Mini-14, and the Remington 3200 had been discontinued, so there were no American-made over-and-under shotguns.

Bill obviously had this thought of broadening the scope of Ruger products. I don't really think that anyone else had the vision or the capacity to share that thought or ambition.

By 1982 we had a full line of single-action and double-action rimfire and centerfire revolvers, a solid line of rifles in most calibers, updated the self-loading .22 target pistol and the original single-actions, created the big Redhawk .44 Magnum double-action, produced two shotguns, and had added the Ranch Rifle to the Mini-14 line. We were on the verge of getting into the 9mm centerfire, double-action autoloading pistols—which was a major step toward making Ruger an even more comprehensive market leader.

Ruger was spread all over the place, and had achieved what no American gunmaker in history had

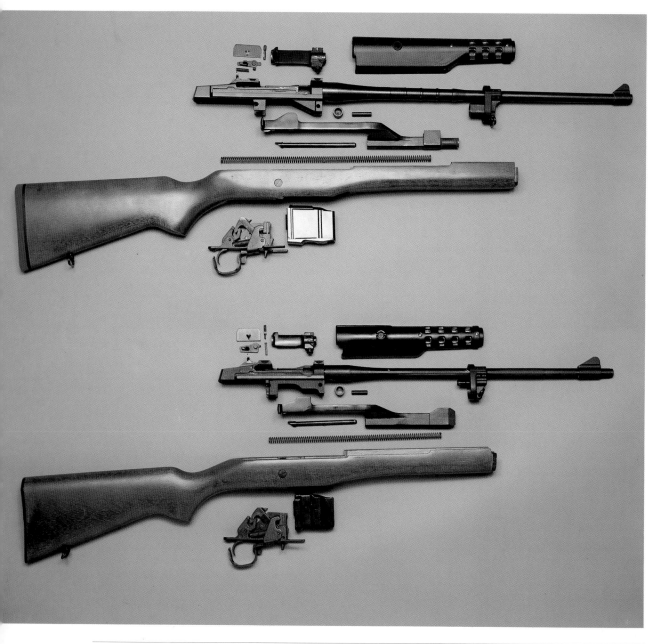

Comparison of the Ruger Mini-14 in .223 caliber (at *bottom*) and the .308 caliber XGI (see page 175), which has not yet been produced for sale.

"I think that, as life is action and passion, it is required of a man that he should share the passion and action of his time, at peril of being judged not to have lived."

—*Oliver Wendell Holmes, Memorial Day, 1899*

Ruger on the Mini-14 Rifle

I was at the N.R.A. show, standing by our booth along with some other people. We were quite busy, as always, and we had just then been getting well into the design of the Mini-14, and had even made some prototypes. It was not on the market, at that point. But the famous Ordnance Colonel Studler came along and shook hands. "How are you?" "Fine," etc.; he had another man with him, probably a neighbor or something. Both were dressed in civilian tweeds, and so I said, "It occurs to me, we're doing something you might be interested to know about; a miniaturized M14 to take the .223 cartridge." I tell you the reaction on the Colonel's face was electrifying. He said, "What?" I said, "Just like the M1; but it's scaled way down in proportion to the M14 as the .223 is to the .308 or .30-06." He said, "Oh, what have you done with it?" I said, "Well, nothing at this point. We're just finishing up the tooling" and so on. He said, "You haven't shown it to the government?"

He seemed to be utterly stunned by this concept as though he wished he had done it—because if he had done it the Army would never have had to revolutionize their thinking. It was a great wrench for them to give up that M1 Garand principle to go to the futuristic M16.

I have often said—and I know I am correct here—if we had brought the Mini-14 out five years earlier it would have become the standard Army rifle. I used to hand it to some old Marines I knew and they'd pick it up, bang, bang, just like it was the M14 and slap it open, slap it shut. You could shoot it all day long. Of course that was the fatal flaw of the M14: The Army was looking for a full-power fully automatic handheld weapon. They really wanted it to do everything, which it just couldn't do. They didn't see that. I saw them demonstrating that M14 when it first came out, at an Army Ordnance meeting in Springfield. We went out to Quabbin Reservoir for a major demonstration. Here's the poor bastard trying to shoot an M14, with all kinds of strange stocks they were trying, in order to reduce that heavy recoil. On full automatic, one burst at 700 rounds a minute employing a 20-shot magazine knocked him all over, and the barrel ended up pointing straight up! If you have a light rifle and a heavy recoil impulse, you're not going to be able to control the gun. That was so simple. It was a tough day for the Army, anyway. They then demonstrated a .308 caliber Vulcan [high-speed aircraft machine gun, designed on the Gatling Gun principle] and that didn't work. They couldn't get a single shot off, while the audience waited 20 minutes.

The Ruger Mini-14:
Jim Sullivan Remembers

The Mini-14 was a project developed at Southport. From the very beginning the rifle was to be of 5.56 caliber, sort of a reduced, scaled down version of the M14, but not exactly.

Bill wanted proportionally longer locking lugs. And to achieve this required different enough geometry so that the magazine follower ended up with an extension. To do all of that and to get it to operate reliably and to feed correctly meant we couldn't simply scale it down from the schematic concept of the M1 and the M14. The Mini-14 is quite a different rifle, and much of the geometry is different. Part of that is again due to some of the opportunities and limitations of investment castings.

Again, Len Brownell did the stock, and I furnished him with the inletting drawings. Originally, there were no sheet metal inserts into the stock, which the bottom of the receiver drops into. Those reinforcements were added after I left. The gas system was also changed from my original design.

Harry Sefried and Roy Melcher did some changes on the Mini-14 in its evolution.

The right hand lug originally had a stem with a roller on it to reduce friction; this was a squared off stem, a locking piece engaged by the operating rod. Bill thought that, like the roller on the M14, this would be a great idea. But it interfered with the timing of the bolt closing and loading cartridges into the chamber, and it took up space better used to power a strong extractor spring, to reliably throw empty shells out of the chamber. Otherwise, you'd have to have a very small extractor spring there. It robs you of room for the good strong spring necessary for positive cartridge case extraction when the rifle is used extensively.

Bill eliminated the use of the roller shortly after the Mini-14's introduction. If anything, its functioning improved. We also changed the bolt hold-open device to one more readily operated. Even this was changed once again (after I left the company) to a much neater design. Ruger never sits on his laurels.

I only worked on the semiautomatic Mini-14. Harry Sefried did the full auto AC556 with a three-shot burst feature. I kind of scoffed at the idea: "Who the hell would want this?" Yet, it was one of the features most favorably commented on, and the later U.S. Army M16s featured a similar device. . . . I was sure wrong, wasn't I?

Sullivan's Takedown Surprise

The takedown on the M1, M14, and Mini-14 are all the same: you swing open the trigger guard and then you can remove the trigger mechanism. In all three guns there is a tab that snaps into a detent. The act of doing that binds the whole gun together. I had stupidly designed the tab wrong, and on the first model it didn't work properly. It kept breaking off after just a few cycles of shooting. I was in the process of test-firing that prototype, and rather than redesign the tab and get a new trigger guard made, I kept firing the rifle with my middle finger pressing up hard against the bottom of the trigger guard, holding the whole gun together. Bill happened by and saw that I was shooting the prototype. He hadn't fired

it yet, and he wanted to. I said, "Fine," and I tried to say, "This is broken off and you have to hold your finger up under the trigger guard or the whole gun will come apart."

He interrupted my instructions with a stern, "I know how to fire a gun!" I'd insulted him by telling him anything about a gun. He took over, fired one shot, and the gun just fell apart in his hands!

You can imagine the sequence: The guard swung open, the whole trigger mechanism came crashing down, the barrel and action jumped up and fell out of the stock. He looked completely startled. The range master and I just roared; it was just so funny. Bill half laughed, and was half angry. He's good at laughing at himself at the same time he's yelling at you. . . .

From the 1976 Annual Report

It is apparent from our 1976 year-end financial statements that the Company has had another year of substantial growth and progress. In terms of earnings, sales and physical volume of output, we have achieved substantial increases over the year before. These results confirm my belief that we are proceeding through a logical program of corporate development based upon plans that were made and actions taken in the past. For many years, we have planned and engineered the firearms products and production facilities which would open up to us all the major segments of the sporting and police markets, and it is apparent now that we are beginning to reap the harvest of work done in previous years. Although our product design has been a major preoccupation throughout 1976, the development of our production facilities has been most emphasized and accounts to a large degree for our advances in sales and earnings. I think it should be a source of satisfaction to our shareholders to know that the Company's physical plant has been tailored as perfectly as it is to perform its special functions. Both our Southport and Newport operations are housed in modern, well-built factory buildings and both plants are equipped with every conceivable aid in the way of machinery and equipment for high volume, high quality precision production.

As I observe the unrelenting inflation in the cost of factory equipment, I cannot help but appreciate the fact that we have these hundreds of machine tools and their support equipment in place and paid for, as the cost of duplicating this kind of facility, now or in the future, would be staggering. These plants are today the means by which we maintain our competitive position in a highly competitive market. They are an asset not only on the balance sheet but in real life enabling us as they do to offer real values to the hundreds of thousands of people who each year buy our firearms, productive employment to our 1,000 or so employees, and directly and indirectly significant support to the communities in which they are located.

In the course of 1976, we continued to make plant improvements. The capacity of our Pine Tree Castings Division was increased approximately 46%. As our foundry operations were able to expand physically into space provided by major plant rearrangement, Pine Tree also made substantial acquisitions of new equipment for both production and quality control and must now represent one of the largest investment castings facilities in the country.

In the Spring of the year, we began construction of an extension to our woodworking plant in Newport, enlarging this building from floor space of about 20,000 square feet to something over 41,000 square feet. This building is well equipped with the most modern machinery for the manufacture of gunstocks, and in its enlarged form, provides us with an efficient, integrated facility for the complete production of gunstocks on a scale to meet the requirements of the foreseeable future.

These additions to and rearrangements of plants have been approximately timed responses to the growing market for our products. Although the future is always uncertain, there is every present indication that the future demand for our products not only will justify these investments in plants but will require additional capacity which is already being planned. I am particularly encouraged by the fact that our sales increases have not required massive advertising and sales expense but appear to have been realized as a consequence of a growing regard for our products in the market place. The users of Ruger products, whether sporting, police, or governmental agencies, both of the U.S.A. and abroad, have sent us a steady stream of complimentary letters, and this flow of customer reaction has been, in fact, so marked during 1976 as to indicate clearly the expanding and good reputation of the Company. Especially encouraging has been the purchase of our police revolvers and AC556 carbine by police departments throughout the U.S.A. and in numerous foreign countries. We are relatively new in these markets, which have long been dominated by well-entrenched competitors, so that progress has been slow. During 1976 more and more of these departmental purchases have recognized the superiority of our product with the resulting increase in this part of our business. However, our police business is still small as a percentage of our total. The principal significance of our 1976 performance in this area is that we now have a real beginning in a phase of our marketing which ought to increase steadily in importance.

During the year 1976, we became aware that many consumers had heard rumors of our efforts to develop a new over and under shotgun. It is true that this program has absorbed a great deal of our time and energy during the past year and we have, in fact, virtually completed the required production facilities. . . .

The only essentially adverse development during the year has been the emergence of the product liability issue as a major corporate problem. Although this problem was perceived during 1974 and 1975 its true dimensions were not clear until the verdict rendered in the Day case in Fairbanks, Alaska. The principal problem introduced by this case was the award of approximately $2,895,000 as punitive damages. It is to us an incomprehensible and shocking verdict and although it is being appealed, it has spawned a number of similar cases, almost all of which involved our old model single action revolvers. . . . These revolvers have always been regarded as a perfect example of a classical type, and manufactured to a high level of quality. The awarding of punitive damages in connection with a product of this quality was astounding.

We are now engaged in a vigorous effort to defend ourselves in all these cases, and our attorneys are generally hopeful of a favorable outcome. . . .

In the final analysis, the resolution to this problem will emanate from the American public itself, and my faith in the common good judgment provides the basis for my belief that at some time in the future, the application of punitive damages in product liability suits will either be eliminated or restricted by the courts or by Congress itself.*

The good sense of the American people when they are in full possession of the facts surrounding any issue seems to have been demonstrated over the last year in relation to the matter of gun control. The public has been exposed to this debate and now seems to have signified that it has no interest in the proposition that it surrender its right, constitutional or otherwise, to own and bear firearms.

In case my view of this situation seems overly optimistic, I should add that all business today is dealing with new and unexpected problems—

---

*As enacted in the mid-1990s.

far and away more time consuming for management than the work of regular operations and competition.

Although our problems may be somewhat unusual, we have the means and the organization to deal with them. This will take continued effort and dedication, but I am confident that the Company will prevail and prosper.

Ruger on the Mini-14 in France

That was an interesting little period. I used to go over to Paris to meet with Henri Guyot, head of the Technical Branch of the French National Police. He had written to ask if we made a carbine for police use that they might like, and the letter was mislaid—I didn't get it until sometime after. I wrote hastily to say I was sorry we were slow in the reply. The next thing was, we were invited over to show the rifle to them and it developed into a real great friendship. They used to have a marvelous conference table, in a comfortable room, all laid out with drinking water, cigarettes, pad and pencils, adjutants all around the place, and a bar. After an hour's talk we'd all stop and have a drink and then go back to the table. The French know how to do these things. It's called "civilization."

So they wound up buying a good many of the carbines, and we sold large quantities to the government of Peru or Ecuador. I made Stephen Vogel take "Skeeter" Skelton with him because he was good at speaking Spanish, and we made a few sales. We lost out in Nicaragua, lost out in Zaire. Stephen went down to the Gulf Coast a lot of times. I often thought he went down there to drink with some British Army officers. He was having all the good times while I was doing all the hard work!

From the 1977 Annual Report

The Company's somewhat lower earnings in 1977 were caused by logistical and technical manufacturing problems which prevented us from achieving our production goals. Our broader product line and increased production facilities have presented challenging questions for our manufacturing organization. Many of these questions are already answered, and we have reason to expect increasingly profitable operations from our newly enlarged facilities.

In the areas of marketing, product development, and financial management we have had a highly successful year, and there is no question that the Company is in a stronger competitive position than it was a year ago.

Our new Over and Under Shotgun was announced in April 1977, marking the beginning of an era in which we produce leading products in the three major areas of the small arms market: rifles, handguns, and shotguns. This new Shotgun has been in product and process development for many years and we expect to effect substantial shipments to our distributors in 1978. We had expected shipments early this year, but have delayed full scale production to achieve certain product and production refinements. We are very pleased with the results, because the aesthetic correctness and the many technical advances embodied in the design of this new Over and Under Shotgun have been quickly recognized by the shooting press and the sporting goods trade. The enthusiastic reaction of those who have seen and used the first few guns makes us very optimistic about our entry into this major market area.

In 1977 our Mini-14 underwent a number of design revisions for simplified manufacture and increased utility. This product has reached a high level of development, and has been adopted by police forces in the United States and abroad, in addition to having increasingly strong acceptance in civilian markets.

During the past year, we have completed major engineering work on future developments for double action revolvers for police, military, and civilian use, and have improved and refined the manufacture of our current line of Security Six revolvers. We have a strong civilian demand for these revolvers, and have obtained encouragingly expanded business with police and government agencies, the latest being a major sale to the U.S. Government.

Our M77 bolt action rifle has attained tremendous public acceptance, surpassing in unit sales many of its old line competitors. We consider this an important achievement for a product that has been on the market such a relatively short time.

Our various other products, also, continue to enjoy a demand exceeding supply. In response to this and to accommodate new products we went forward with the construction of additional floor space which enlarges our new plant building in Newport. That building was finished in 1974 and provided 60,000 square feet. It was expected at that time that we would make additions in the future. This need came around perhaps more quickly than we expected, and a 50,000 square foot addition is now being completed. This will give us the floor space which we estimate is needed for production of a considerably larger volume than we are currently achieving, and should permit sustained output on an uninterrupted and continuous line basis. We believe we have designed a plant facility which is in proportion to long-term demand for our products and one which will enable us to produce them with utmost efficiency. To develop maximum utilization of this new facility is, in fact, a principal objective of our production management effort.

During the year 1977, we began a series of advertisements which emphasize the proper use of firearms, and strongly state the necessity of a shooter's thorough understanding of the mechanical characteristics of the particular firearm he is shooting. This is a somewhat controversial approach to the goal of firearms safety, because it is unprecedented in the history of the industry. We realized this as we undertook this advertising campaign, and we are certain that we are fundamentally right. There has been an overwhelmingly favorable reaction from shooters throughout the nation, as they see the Company take the

The Ruger Mini-14 Rifle

Number 187-00001 Mini-14 Rifle.

Schematic view of folding stock assembly; for sale only to military, law enforcement, and other government agencies.

Exploded view of Mini-14 Rifle.

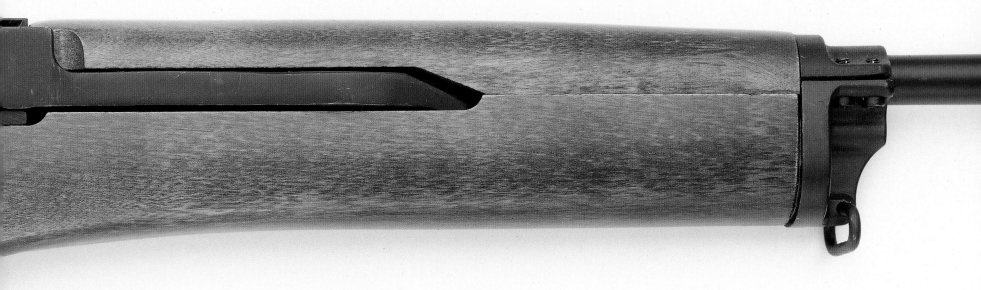

Introduced: 1975 (prototypes completed and tests conducted from 1971). "A Rugged, Compact .223 Semi-Auto . . . The Smallest of Powerful Small Arms. . . . embodies the proven engineering ideas and superior materials that are standard in all Ruger products. . . . Ranchers and outdoorsmen will recognize the advantages of this small, reliable autoloader. . . . ideal for carrying in a saddle scabbard, pickup truck, camper, or afoot. . . . Ideal for law enforcement and sporting use."

Serial Numbers: *Mini-14, for commercial sale:* 180-00000 to -60000 range; and similarly numbered serial prefixes 181-, 182-, 183-, 184-, 185-, 186-00000 to -31116 (through 1993).

AC-556 Law Enforcement and Military Rifles: A few prototype full automatic AC-556 rifles built, with prefix B180. Highest number B180-00205. Full production began with 190-00000 up to -19999; and similarly numbered serial prefixes 191-00000 to -13000 range, 192 prefix began in 1986 after change in BATF regulations regarding fully automatic weapons. Mechanism not interchangeable with commercial Mini-14s.

Total Made Through 1993: In excess of 656,000, excluding Ranch Rifles and full-automatic, AC-556 selective fire rifles.

Caliber: .223.

Magazine Capacity: 5, in spring-fed staggered detachable box magazine. 10- and 20-round magazines were available for brief periods as accessory item. 10-round no longer offered from 1979 listing; 20-round no longer listed from 1989. 30-round limited to law enforcement and government sales.

Barrel Length: 18½".

Rifling: 6 grooves, right-hand twist, one turn in 10"; after 1988 twist changed to one in 7"; in mid-1994 twist changed to one in 9".

Markings: See Table of Markings, pages 330–35.

On top of back of receiver:

RUGER

MINI-14 R

CAL. .223

Serial number *on left side of receiver, near breech.*

Box magazine embossed *on base* with trademark and:

RUGER

mini-14

After January 1, 1978 (serial range 181-07488), marking standard on left side of receiver at rear:

BEFORE USING GUN-READ WARNINGS IN
***INSTRUCTION MANUAL* AVAILABLE FREE FROM**
STURM, RUGER & CO., INC.
SOUTHPORT, CONN. U.S.A.

Trademark *to left of bottom two lines of marking,* as is **R** registration stamping.

Sights: Peep rear, blade front. One minute of angle click adjustments; except in the Ranch Rifle, which has Ruger integral scope bases and flip-up auxiliary rear sight.

Overall Length and Weight: 37¼", approx. 6.4 pounds.

Stocks: American hardwood; lined in steel at stressed and high-temperature areas.

Finish: Blued. Brushed stainless steel added to the line in 1979.

Materials, Construction, and Innovations: Stainless steel or chrome-molybdenum steel. Investment cast frame and bolt; stamped trigger guard. Unbreakable steel music wire coil springs. Originally equipped with wooden hand guard, to protect hand from moving operating rod; later changed to reinforced fiberglass.

Created to use Garand breechbolt locking principles, but a completely fresh design. Fixed piston gas system, with self-cleansing moving cylinder. Powder particles which have not burned are automatically vented from system. Before bolt unlocks, the gas pressure drops to negligible level. Firing pin retracts mechanically during initial unlocking movement of rotating bolt. Capable of being field-stripped in seconds to eight basic subassemblies, without tools. Stock reinforced with steel liners, at points of stress and heat. *Note:* Ranch Rifle (*q.v.*) is equipped with patented Ruger scope mounting system, side ejection, and recoil buffer system to protect scope.

Issue Price: $200.00 (1976).

Engraving: serial number 187-10132, engraved and gold inlaid by Paul Lantuch for William B. Ruger, Sr.

Price Sheet Listings and Major Production Variations:

Blued Steel:

    Mini-14/5: Standard model, 5-round magazine.

    Mini-14/5F: Standard model, 5-round magazine, with

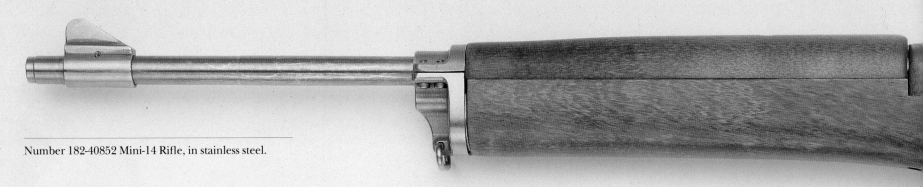

Number 182-40852 Mini-14 Rifle, in stainless steel.

folding buttstock (introduced 1982; restricted to law enforcement sales only in 1990).

Mini-14/5R: 5-round magazine, with integral dovetails on receiver to accommodate Ruger 1" scope rings (introduced 1982 and advertised as the Ranch Rifle, *q.v.*, page 153).

Stainless Steel:

K-Mini-14/5: Standard model, introduced 1979; 5-round magazine.

K-Mini-14/5R: Ranch Rifle, first listed 1985; 5-round magazine, with integral dovetails and Ruger 1" scope rings (**Ranch Rifle,** *q.v.*, page 153).

K-Mini-14/5F: 5-round magazine, with folding buttstock (introduced 1982 and listed through 1989).

K-Mini-14/5RF: With folding buttstock (listed 1986 through 1989; **Ranch Rifle,** *q.v.*, page 153).

Pre-Production Prototypes and Pilot Productions Models:

Southport Mini-14 Rifle, First Production Model: 1,000 rifles. 180- prefix serial numbers. Differ from Newport Model primarily in details of sights, particularly due to the sporting style gold-bead front sight on the Southport production. Larger, external bolt hold-open device and slimmer forend.

1st Newport Model: 180- prefix serial numbers. Stamped, external bolt hold-open lever.

2nd Newport Model: 181- and higher prefix serial series, with smaller bolt hold-open and deeper forend.

The Mini-14/5: Standard Model Mini-14, with 5-round magazine; all Mini-14s with 181- prefix and later have smaller bolt hold-open button and deeper forend.

Mini-14R: Ranch Rifle features integral scope mount apertures on the receiver, for Ruger 1" rings, and a folding peep sight near rear of receiver. A composite-material hand guard shields the hand from the operating rod. Side-ejection and patented recoil buffer protects low-mounted scopes.

.222 Caliber Mini-14 Rifles: Same as commercial .223 caliber Mini-14, except for caliber. Largely manufactured for export sales, primarily for France. Offered domestically, 1983–84, code **Mini-14/5R.222.** The .222 production was a caliber variation of the Ranch Rifle, and was serial numbered from that series.

Warning Series: Warning marking adopted in serial range and with legend as indicated above.

Special Issues:

Oklahoma Highway Patrol, 1,300 rifles with 18½" barrel, flash hider, fiberglass hand guard, recoil pad, and combination bayonet lug and front sight. **O.H.P.** behind rear sight on receiver. Sold directly to the State of Oklahoma, for service issue; 1979.

Oklahoma Highway Patrol, 300 rifles as above, but not bearing the **O.H.P.** marking. For sheriff's departments and local police; 1979.

Arizona Highway Patrol, 676 rifles with 18½" barrel, stainless steel, rubber buttpad, wooden hand guard. Roll marked **ARIZONA HIGHWAY PATROL** on right side of barrel. Arizona logo on bolt slide. Registration number roll marked on top of rear of receiver; 1980.

Military and Police Rifles

Full automatic and selective fire, these rifles restricted in sale to government and law enforcement agencies. Sale strictly controlled by federal, state, municipal, U.S. Department of State, and foreign firearms laws. Fully automatic military and police rifles are identifiable from the flash suppressor at the muzzle, bayonet lug mounting, and selective fire switch. The **AC-556** has a three-position selector switch for firing semiautomatic, 3-shot burst, or fully automatic. The folding stock fully automatic version, the **AC-556 GF,** was designed for "aircraft and helicopter operations, patrol vehicles, dignitary pro-

tection and many other applications where a high rate of accurate fire combined with compactness and short overall length are required." 30-round magazines, 37¼" length for the standard wood stock version (weight 7 lbs., 7 oz.), and 39¼" for the folding stock when opened (28⅞" when stock closed; weight 7 lbs., 15 oz.). Cyclic rate of fire: 750 rounds per minute. Both rifles available in stainless steel, with K prefix before catalogue code. **AC-556K** the same as above, but with 13½" barrel. **KAC-556K** is the stainless steel version.

Mini-14 GB Government Model: Semiautomatic only; not sold commercially. The GB suffix denotes the flash suppressor and lug for the U.S. "government bayonet." Heat-resistant ventilated fiberglass hand guard. 20-round magazine. 6⅞ pounds (with loaded magazine). 30-round magazine optional for government sales only. Catalogue and Law Enforcement/Military model codes:

Mini-14/20 GB: blued finish

K-Mini-14/20 GB: stainless steel

Mini-14/20 GBF: folding stock, blued finish

K-Mini-14/20 GBF: folding stock, stainless steel

U.S. Department of State: **AC-556** machine guns, issued for embassy security. Approximately 500 guns in service, since 1978. Folding stock model, with two-position selector switch (semiautomatic and 3-shot burst only).

Bermuda Regiment: 500 rifles with 18½" barrels, blued, roll marked with crest of the Bermuda Regiment; 1982.

French National Police (Gendarmie Nationale): Approximately 2,500 rifles, variation of the AC-556 machine gun, with fiberglass hand guard, 18½" barrel, blued, no warning roll mark on barrel, special front sight, gas block with side sling swivel, curved magazine latch, special roll mark. Some with specially checkered stock.

Issue Price: $241.00, AC-556 (1976).

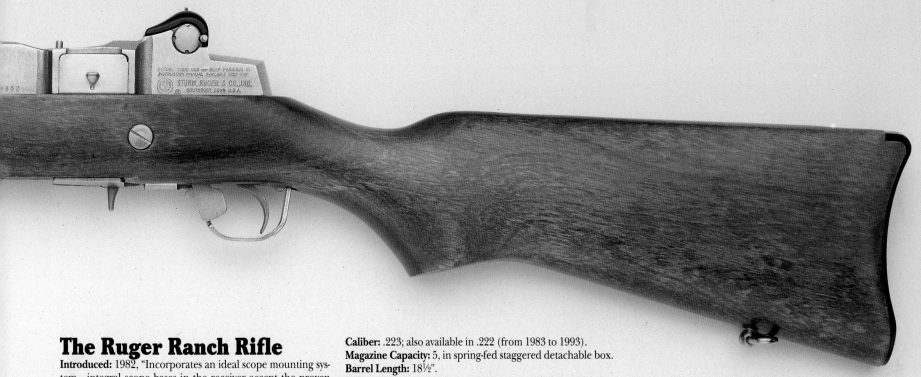

The Ruger Ranch Rifle

Introduced: 1982, "Incorporates an ideal scope mounting system—integral scope bases in the receiver accept the proven solid steel Ruger mounting rings. . . . for correct, comfortable scope use and convenience in carrying. All of the best features of the basic Mini-14 design have been retained in the Ranch Rifle."

Serial Numbers: 187-00000 to -99999; and similarly numbered serial prefixes 188-00000 to -71016 (through 1993).

Total Made Through 1993: In excess of 156,000.

Number 187-26569 Ranch Rifle.

Caliber: .223; also available in .222 (from 1983 to 1993).

Magazine Capacity: 5, in spring-fed staggered detachable box.

Barrel Length: 18½".

Rifling: 6 grooves, right-hand twist, one turn in 10"; after 1989, one turn in 7"; after mid-1994, one turn in 9".

Markings: See Table of Markings, pages 330–35.

On left side of rear of receiver:

> **BEFORE USING GUN-READ WARNINGS IN**
> ***INSTRUCTION MANUAL* AVAILABLE FREE FROM**
> **STURM, RUGER & CO., INC.**
> **SOUTHPORT, CONN. U.S.A.**

Trademark to left of bottom two lines of marking, as is **R** registration stamping.

Sights: Fold-down rear peep sight, blade front sight. Receiver with factory-machined scope mounting system. 1" Ruger scope rings standard accessory.

Overall Length and Weight: 37¼", approx. 6½ pounds.

Stocks: American hardwood, molded sporter-type buttplate, polyurethane finish. Some stocks have curved Celcon buttplate; othrs have rubber recoil pad.

Finish: Blued, or satin-polished stainless steel.

Materials, Construction, and Innovations: Unique new patented buffer system, re-directing and effectively absorbing the shock of the slide block striking the receiver in recoil (to protect scopes). Re-designed bolt; eliminating the old spring-loaded ejector. Modified bolt stop, serving as an ejector, wherein empty cartridges are ejected sideways, to best clear low-mounted scopes. Folding rear peep sight, as back-up for scope. Ventilated glass fibre hand guard.

Issue Price: $345.00 (1982).

Engraving: Serial number 187-10132 gold inlaid and engraved for William B. Ruger, Sr., by Paul Lantuch.

Price Sheet Listings and Major Production Variations:

    Mini-14/5R: With integral dovetails on receiver to accommodate Ruger 1" scope rings.

    K-Mini-14/5R: Stainless steel (first listed 1985); with integral scope bases and Ruger 1" scope rings.

    K-Mini-14/5RF: Stainless steel, with folding stock "for hikers, campers, boaters, pilots, and others when space is at a premium" (1986–1990).

lead in the vitally important area of shooting sports safety.

In the course of the year, we have observed the continued effects of inflation on our costs. We have in the past raised our prices as our only recourse in offsetting higher costs. We are fortunate that our price increases up to this point have been less than the general level of inflation. By far the most rapidly increasing cost has been that of product liability insurance. The premiums for this coverage have advanced so markedly that we wonder whether in the future insurance will be economically possible to obtain, or whether we will have to seek such alternatives as the captive insurance carrier or some form of self-insurance. In any case, the Company reluctantly finds that it must, in part at least, recover the cost of its product liability defenses by raising the prices of its products. We expect the price increases needed to offset this one item to exceed the combined effect of all other inflationary factors now and into the foreseeable future.

I have previously reported that the Company has had some product liability suits filed against it, relating mostly to our old model single action revolvers. . . . The trend of this litigation will be unclear until several key cases, including our appeal of a verdict in Alaska, to its Supreme Court, are resolved. Nevertheless, we remain confident that the Company can continue to defend itself against such claims, and that it will be in an increasingly favorable position in the years to come.

In this message I have mentioned some prominent business difficulties, most of which are shared to a great extent by all of American industry. Nevertheless, I have great enthusiasm and optimism for the future, not only because of our well regarded products and increasing market share, but because of the great confidence I have in the employees of this Company.

From the 1978 Annual Report

I am pleased to report that 1978 resulted in record sales and earnings . . . made possible by the highest production levels in the Company's history as well as a continually greater acceptance of the Company's products in the market place.

On the negative side, these record earnings were achieved from lower operating margins. The lower margins were primarily the result of significant increases in the Company's product liability insurance premiums and concurrent legal expenses. In addition, the Company, like the majority of American manufacturing companies, has sustained continual upward pressure in the cost of all goods and services purchased. To some degree, these increased costs have been offset by increases in the selling price of the Company's products.

I have written in several previous reports concerning the Company's product liability problems. The Company's position with respect to this situation remains unchanged. We believe firmly that the claim that the design of the old model single-action revolver is defective has no merit in fact. . . .

Our federal government Form 10-K Report gives a detailed listing of cases instituted against the Company in 1978 which involved the largest demands for compensatory and punitive damages . . . including the Day case. . . . I would like to emphasize that the Company's ability to internally finance its dating program, which essentially provides extended credit on certain products to its customers, would be severely jeopardized by an unfavorable judgment of the magnitude cited in the Day case. . . .

During 1978 modest levels of production [of the Over and Under Shotgun] were achieved. It continues to be our goal to increase these quantities in order to meet what has been an overwhelming acceptance of this product. . . . We expect the output to grow continuously, and I am

confident that 1979 will see substantial utilization of the physical capacity which we have created for production.

In 1978 extensive development and engineering was completed on a .44 Double Action Revolver [the Redhawk] which will neatly complement the existing Security-Six product line. This new .44 Double Action incorporates significant engineering improvements which should enable the Company to capture a significantly greater segment of the double action market. . . .

While 1978 was an excellent year when measured by almost any financial standards, I cannot help but feel uneasy at the continued erosion of the dollar and the continued expansive monetary policy of the Federal Reserve. Since the Company's export business is less than ten per cent of all its overall business, the weakness of the dollar does not impact our Company as adversely as if it were a multinational corporation. However, taking a broader view, I feel strongly that the dollar must be defended and its position solidified if the U.S.A. is to continue to be one of the dominant factors in the world economic scene. I am dismayed by the continued staggering budgetary deficits which in my opinion are the mainspring of inflation in our country.

1979 is a special year for the Company. It marks [our] 30th anniversary. . . . During these thirty years the Company has grown from its humble beginnings in a "Red Barn" beside the Southport railroad station to a leading producer of quality firearms for sportsmen and law enforcement agencies here and abroad. We now have over a quarter of a million square feet of modern manufacturing facilities and employ over twelve hundred people.

I am proud of what the Company has accomplished. I am thankful to all of those who have helped make the Company grow and prosper. With the continued help and support of all our employees, as well as our friends and supporters in the firearms industry, I look forward to the advent of our fourth decade.

Ruger on the Over-and-Under Red Label Shotgun

Provided good looks, strong components and sensible design features are employed, there is always room to make a few guns profitably. I felt that Americans deserved a good over-and-under shotgun made by Americans. As it happened, our profits have not been significant, but we are now rethinking the entire manufacturing concept of the Red Label, and hope to better the profit picture without changing the gun.

We make the finest pair of shotgun barrels that could ever be built. We put the money into the machine instead of into hand labor. All the old-time great gunsmiths—the men who made the beautiful things—are today building the beautiful equipment to build the beautiful things. Perhaps you could say that, except for engraving, gold inlaying, and elegant finish, using machines you can easily surpass the work of the finest person in terms of truly mechanical movement, the precision of the apparatus. You have to remember—fine watches are not made with files.

Furthermore, it's the design of the gun that gives the clue to answering the question of how to build a double barrel shotgun by machine methods—and yet retain a high degree of craftsmanship and quality construction.

It's a matter of studying the construction of things to see in what way the necessary precision and fit can be really produced on a manufacturing or interchangeable basis. This is an area that requires a strong factory group of highly skilled peo-

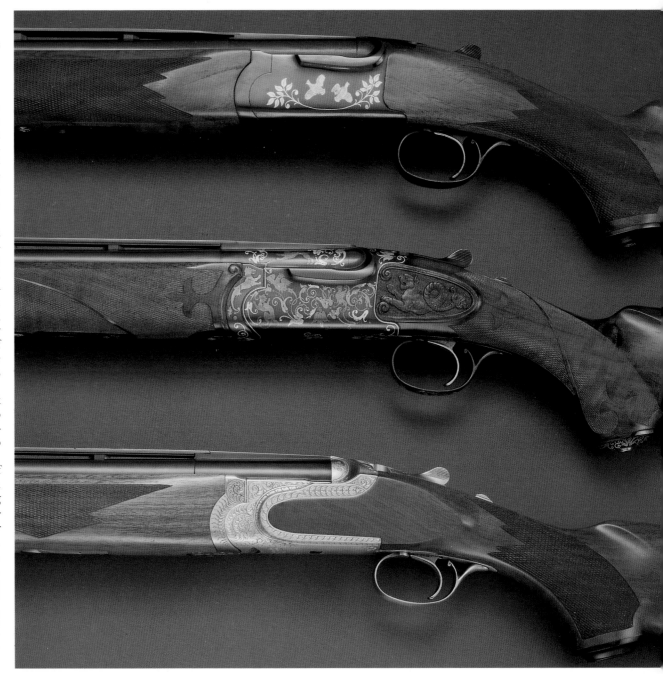

At *top*, the first Ruger Red Label to be engraved, number 81, 20 gauge, gold inlaid for William B. Ruger, Sr., by Alvin A. White. Elaborately decorated Red Label, at *center*, also in 20 gauge, inlaid in multi-colored gold and silver, with carved and checkered stocks; for Ruger, Sr., by Paul Lantuch. Serial number 400-18525. The 12 gauge stainless Ruger Woodside model at *bottom*, covered by 1976 design patent; the gun and engraving introduced in 1995; serial number 410-00016.

The Ruger Over-and-Under Shotgun

Number 400-24311 Red Label Over-and-Under Shotgun, 20 gauge.

Introduced: 1977 (20 gauge); 1980 (12 gauge). "This first Ruger Over-and-Under . . . is a perfectly balanced, plain grade gun of elegant simplicity, combining a classic form and advanced design. By the Ruger definition 'plain grade' means high quality and precision workmanship, with a superior finish to all external metal surfaces. Curved shapes are geometrically accurate and plane surfaces are finely polished. Mechanical joints are fitted to minimum hairline clearances. Guns finished at this level will be designated as being of 'Red Label' grade."

Serial Numbers: 400-00000 to -56304 (through 1993) (20 gauge); 410-00000 to -60380 (through 1993) (12 gauge).

Total Made Through 1993: In excess of 116,000.

Gauges: 20, 3" chambers; 12, 2¾", and (as of 1986) 3" chambers.

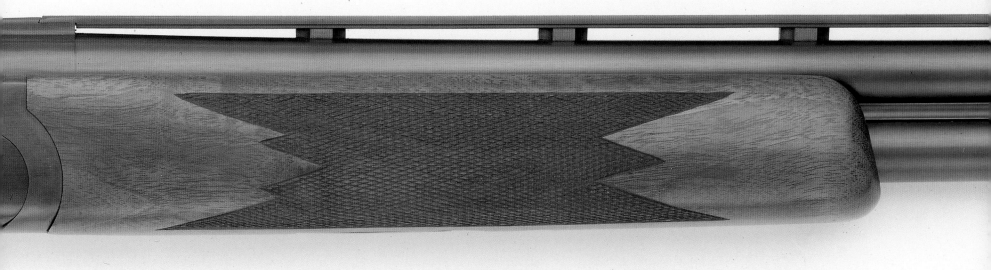

Number of Chambers: Two, superimposed.

Barrel Lengths: 26", 28" (introduced 1982), 30" (latter introduced 1992 with the Sporting Clays Model). Originally equipped with fixed chokes bored improved cylinder/modified, full/modified, or skeet/skeet. Screw-in chokes introduced in 1988, and became standard on all models in 1991.

Markings: See Table of Markings, pages 330–35.

Sights: Gold bead front sight; gold bead middle sight as well on Sporting Clays Model.

Overall Length and Weight: 43", approx. 7 pounds (20 gauge, 26" barrels); 47", approx. 7¾ pounds (12 gauge, 30" barrels).

Stocks: American walnut, pistol grip or English style straight (introduced 1992) buttstock, 14 to 14⅛" length of pull (introduced at 14"), 1½" drop at comb, 2½" drop at heel.

Finish: Blued, or blued with satin-polished stainless steel receiver and forend iron. Earliest stainless steel receiver guns had blued forend iron.

Materials, Construction, and Innovations: 400-series stainless steel receiver, trigger, and forend iron.

Hammer-forged barrels of chrome-molybdenum steel, stress relieved, contour ground, and finely fitted. Silver solder

(*not* soft solder) used in attachment of barrels and rib to the monoblock. Unbreakable firing pins. Dovetailed and free-floating rib aligned automatically and precisely, and silver-soldered to the top barrel.

American walnut stocks, of high quality and straight grain, deep cut checkering (20 lines to the inch). Rubber recoil pad; composition pistol grip cap with trademark inset.

The locking system considered the strongest ever built for over-and-under shotguns.

Reliable single trigger. Rebounding hammers for easy opening. The shotgun must be fully cocked before the hammers can reach the firing pin. Selection of barrel is via the sliding safety; intercepting sears allow for added protection. Barrel side spacers attached by mechanical means; removable if desired.

Note: Ruger barrels are built to allow firing "normal factory steel-shot loads without damage."

Screw-in chokes introduced 1988.

As of 1994, back-bored barrels (.743", 12 gauge; .633", 20 gauge) serve to soften recoil and provide more uniform patterns. Further, the screw-in choke tubes were lengthened to

2⁷⁄₁₆" (12 gauge) and 2" (20 gauge). Full and extra-full chokes became available (1993) as an accessory. These new chokes will not fit earlier shotguns.

Issue Price: $480.00, 20 gauge (1978); $798.00, 12 gauge (1982).

Engraving: On introduction of this new model, presentations were made of the following Red Labels, each with an inscription dated 1978 from William B. Ruger: John T. Amber (400-00009), John S. ("Jim") Carmichel (400-00013), Elmer Keith (400-00015), Alex Kerr (400-00018), Charles A. ("Skeeter") Skelton (400-00022), Pete Brown (400-00023), Peter Barrett (400-00033), John R. Wooters (400-00054), Colonel Charles Askins, Jr. (400-00062), Jon R. Sundra (400-00067), Robert W. Zwirz (400-00080), George W. Martin (400-00081), William H. Jordan (400-00086), Robert M. Brister (400-00087), Gene A. Hill (400-00153), Jerome J. Rakusan (400-00154), Claude H. "Grits" Gresham (400-00155), Robert Stack (400-00157), G. K. deForest (400-00158). The hand engraving was by Bob Kain, with photo-etching arranged by James M. Triggs.

Serial number 400-00081 gold inlaid as a sample for William B. Ruger, Sr., by Alvin A. White.

Serial number 400-18525, a 20 gauge, was gold inlaid and engraved, with carved stocks, for William B. Ruger, Sr., by Paul Lantuch.

A total of 1,000 12-gauge, 3" chamber guns were hand engraved for Ducks Unlimited, featuring the 1934 and 1984 Federal Duck Stamp designs and scrollwork on the receivers. The guns had 28" barrels, with full and modified chokes, and were stocked in extra-fancy American walnut. Each was in a custom leather luggage style case. The series was called the "1 of 1,000" and was embellished for the factory by the Ken Hurst engraving company.

A limited number of 300 12 gauge Red Labels were announced in 1994 as a fund-raising project for Wildlife Forever, a nonprofit affiliate of the North American Hunting Club. Decoration was by photoengraving and selective gold plating.

Griffin & Howe, Inc., made up a special series of Red Labels, with false sideplates, hand engraved lockplates and receivers, and straight English style stocks of select-grain walnut, checkered, and with rubber buttpads. Each gun was custommade for individual clients.

A limited number of Red Labels have been used for presentations to factory employees, on completion of 20 years of service. Customarily the breech is inscribed with a presentation to the recipient, in recognition of "20 years of Faithful Service," or similar legend.

As of 1995, hand engraving available, in established patterns.

Price Sheet Listings and Major Production Variations:
20 Gauge, 3" chambers, pistol grip stocks, blued:
RL-201: "Red Label" in 26" barrels, imp. cyl./mod. (introduced 1977 catalogue and 1978 price lists; through 1981 list).
RL-202: "Red Label" in 26" barrels, skeet/skeet (introduced 1977 catalogue and 1978 price lists; through 1981 list).
RL-200: "Red Label" in 26" barrels, full/mod. (introduced in 1979 Price Lists; through 1981 list).
RL-2006: 20 gauge, 26" barrels, full/mod. (new code, 1982 price list; through 1984 list).
RL-2008: 20 gauge, 28" barrels, full/mod. (1982–1988).
RL-2016: 20 gauge, 26" barrels, imp. cyl./mod. (new code, 1982 price list; through 1988).
RL-2018: 20 gauge, 28" barrels, imp. cyl./mod. (1982–1988).
RL-2026: 20 gauge, 26" barrels, skeet/skeet (1982–1988).
RL-2028: 20 gauge, 28" barrels, skeet/skeet (1982–1983; resumed 1986–1988).

Stainless Steel Receiver and Forend Mounts:
KRL-2008: 28" barrels, full/mod. (1989–1991).
KRL-2016: 26" barrels, imp. cyl./mod. (1989–1991).
KRL-2018: 28" barrels, imp. cyl./mod. (1989–1991).
KRL-2026: 26" barrels, skeet/skeet (1989–1991).
KRL-2028: 28" barrels, skeet/skeet (1989–1991).
KRL-2029: 26" barrels, screw-in chokes; (1989–present).
KRL-2030: 28" barrels, screw-in chokes (1989–present).
KRLS-2029: 26" barrels, English style straight stock (1992–present).
KRLS-2030: 28" barrels, English style straight stock (1992–present).
Note: Sporting Clays Model (**KRL-2036**) added to line in 1994; see pages 264–65.
12 Gauge, pistol grip stocks, blued:
RL-1206: 2¾" chambers, 26" barrels, full/mod. (1982 through 1983).
RL-1208: 2¾" chambers, 28" barrels, full/mod. (1984 only).
RL-1216: 2¾" chambers, 26" barrels, imp. cyl./mod. (1982–1984).
RL-1226: 2¾" chambers, 26" barrels, skeet/skeet (1982–1984).

Number 410-07911 Red Label Over-and-Under Shotgun, 12 gauge, with stainless steel receiver.

RL-1218: 2¾" chambers, 28" barrels, imp. cyl./mod. (1984 only).

Stainless Steel Receiver and Forend Mounts:

KRL-1232: 26" barrels, full/mod. (1985; 3" chambers as of 1986; through 1990).

KRL-1235: 28" barrels, full/mod. (1985; 3" chambers as of 1986; through 1990).

KRL-1230: 26" barrels, imp. cyl./mod. (1985; 3" chambers as of 1986; through 1990).

KRL-1233: 28" barrels, imp. cyl./mod. (1985; 3" chambers as of 1986; through 1990).

KRL-1231: 26" barrels, skeet/skeet (1985; 3" chambers as of 1986; through 1990).

KRL-1234: 28" barrels, skeet/skeet (1986; 3" chambers; through 1990).

KRL-1226: 26" barrels, screw-in chokes (1988–present).

KRL-1227: 28" barrels, screw-in chokes (1988–present).

KRLS-1226: 26" barrels, English style straight stock (1992–present).

KRLS-1227: 28" barrels, English style straight stock (1992–present).

Double Rifle Conversion by Jaeger: Built on the Red Label action, and using original factory stocks, Jaeger manufactured a limited number of double rifles, in .375 H & H Magnum and .45-70. The .375 H & H had 24" barrels, and were regulated using 270-grain factory ammunition. The .45-70 rifles were built in 22" and 24" barrels. Both calibers were regulated at 100 yards. Mounted on the quarter rib was an express sight, with two folding leaves; the front sight mounted on a ramp. Weights were 9 lbs. 8 oz. for the .375 H & H, and 9 lbs. 4 oz. for the .45-70 (24" barrel). For the .375 H & H, quick-detachable mounts were used, accommodating scopes of from 2½ to 8 power. The guns were built to permit use of the original shotgun barrels, simply by exchanging barrels, allowing switching from rifle-shooting to shotgunning, in a matter of seconds.

An *Orvis Special Series* and a *Double Rifle Conversion by Francotte* are two "after-market" versions of the Red Label.

*Note: Sporting Clays Model (**KRL-1236**) added to line in 1992: see pages 264–65.*

*28 Gauge (**KRL-2826 and -2827**) added to the line in 1994, see pages 290–92.*

*Woodside Shotgun (**KWS-1227**) added to the line in 1995, see pages 290–92.*

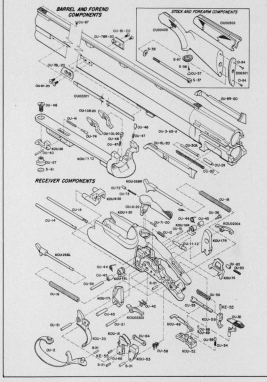

Exploded view of Red Label Over-and-Under Shotgun.

159

Lakeside landscape by Levi W. Prentiss, with Ruger Red Label Over-and-Unders, the stainless steel receiver gun from the Ducks Unlimited series. Holland & Holland 12 gauge hammer gun, number 12576, from a cased set.

1979 marked the completion of the third decade of Sturm, Ruger & Company, Inc. as a manufacturer of high quality sporting and law enforcement firearms. There were many positive aspects to the year, but also unfortunately some troublesome developments.

1979 saw the highest sales and earnings achieved by the Company in its thirty-year history. Sales were $68,856,000 and net income after taxes reached $7,934,000. These are increases of 15.1% and 13.3% respectively over the comparable amounts in 1978.

The year saw the first real production of the Company's Over and Under Shotgun. Production is growing, and we look to this product line as a major growth area. The American Rifleman magazine described it as the over and under shotgun by which all others will be judged in the future.

The Company's latest product, a .44 Double Action Revolver known as the Redhawk,® was introduced at the NRA Show in San Antonio, Texas in May 1979. This product incorporates significant technological advances. Initial reaction to this product has been extremely favorable. A great deal of time and effort was expended in 1979 to organize the manufacturing facilities to produce [the Redhawk]. It is the Company's goal to achieve significant production quantities in the second half of this year.

From the point of view of product development, 1979 can be said to be the time when the Company finally achieved its long-range goal to be a manufacturer of a full line of products covering all the major segments of the sporting and law enforcement markets. It is our intention in the future to develop additional firearms which will complement those in the existing line. In terms of providing products for all segments of the aforesaid markets, it is my belief that the

ple who will not actually be working directly on the guns so much as on the tools that make the guns.

An illustration of the way we make the process economical is the automatic cycling and silver-soldering of the barrel components together by induction means. All this happens very quickly, and it makes a tremendously strong bond, as durable as

there is. And it is accomplished on one automated station. The old laborious hand tinning and old-fashioned soldering hasn't really produced a better product. Now we don't have the problem of solder which will melt in bluing salts. Our material, in fact, is vastly stronger, and the job comes out with great precision.

Company indeed occupies a unique niche in the industry. . . .

[In the course of the year] there have been several . . . groups which have . . . shown an interest in entering into some sort of transaction with the Company. Various formats have been suggested, including the currently popular "leveraged buy out" concept. In addition, there have been discussions concerning the possibility of certain joint venture arrangements. All of these discussions have been preliminary in nature and have represented nothing more than exploratory talks in which the objective of the Company has been to ascertain how the long-term interests of its shareholders might best be served.

Regretably [sic], it has been necessary for several years to report to you on the status of the Company's product liability problems, and this year is no exception. . . .

[With respect to the Day case,] as a result of the Company's appeal to the Supreme Court of Alaska . . . that Court reversed the judgment of the lower Court and remanded the case for a new trial as to comparative negligence and punitive damages. It further directed that, if the jury on a new trial should find that punitive damages should be awarded, "on essentially the same evidence as that presented at the first trial," they should not exceed $250,000. . . .

In addition to the Day case, the Company is a defendant in approximately fifty other lawsuits. . . . In substantially all cases, both compensatory and punitive damages are demanded.

The cases involve primarily our Old Model Single Action Revolvers. . . . Today [our single actions] are beyond question the largest selling Single Action Revolvers in the world.

While the outcome of the pending cases cannot presently be determined, it is my ardent hope that this entire issue will be satisfactorily resolved at some foreseeable future point. To a large extent, the increase of product liability claims against the Company seems to reflect the increase nationally of such claims against all manufacturers and indeed, the national increase in litigation generally. The increasing size of jury verdicts and claim settlements in personal injury cases also appears to be a national phenomenon.

Despite the foregoing problems, I am optimistic as we embark into the decade of the 80's with all its obvious problems. The Company is well positioned in its basic business. In addition, plans are underway to significantly increase the capacity of the Pine Tree Castings Division. This should enable the Company to profitably compete in what I perceive as a growing and exciting market, namely the manufacturing of precision investment castings which have a wide variety of uses in many different industries.

The Redhawk Revolver:
Harry Sefried Remembers

Roy Melcher and I worked together on the Redhawk—with Bill, of course, who laid out for us what he wanted. It was Bill who thought up an extremely ingenious ejector, where the rod was in the center of the cylinder, but it was not in the center of the axis of the frame, a change from the usual double-action revolver geometry. The ejector rod on the Redhawk doesn't rotate axially with the cylinder; it is offset, allowing a thicker frame in that area. Of course, the threads in that area (where the barrel screws into the frame), restrict how much thickness you can have there. But offsetting the ejector rod increased that thickness about 100 percent, effectively doubling the frame's strength. That was a substantial improvement upon all previous revolver designs.

Roy and I worked a new system cylinder latch, which positively locks the cylinder in place when you fire the gun. We departed from the typical fore-and-aft motion of the latch to reengage it; ours pushes in to disengage the cylinder. We decided to try a system whereby we used a little latch in the trigger to pivot the cylinder latch. That way the latch could not move or be disrupted when firing; once it was engaged to the cylinder, it stayed there and was not displaced when you released the trigger.

We were able to work out a system in which we had the ejector rod out there free and unencumbered, not latching to a lug under the barrel, which was always a somewhat fragile point of conventional double-action revolvers. In addition, we worked out a leverage in which we locked the cylinder crane at the front and at the rear. We did not go to a "triple lock" like the old S & W because to put a lock where they put it (other than prove we could do it) wouldn't do anything. Their geometry was not optimal. We locked the crane and cylinder beautifully at the front and at the rear. This gave us an extremely good way to maintain alignment between the cylinder and the barrel, for strength and accuracy. And again, it was a stronger system than their little tab going into an ejector way out on the end of the ejector rod. Ours was a lot more rugged than it needed to be, and would last about indefinitely.

I worked on a little different leverage system for the Redhawk's hammer spring. The S & W system, which has a separate trigger return spring (inside a block that is also the hammer retracting system, when the trigger is released), unnecessarily increases trigger pull and does not give you any additional energy for the hammer fall, which you want to ensure cartridge ignition. The Colt systems had one leg of a flat spring pushing on the trigger for a return spring; and the other leg of that same spring operated the hammer, through a small link. As you pulled the trigger you were also compressing the hammer spring. That has a decided advantage in that you can get a lighter overall trigger pull than with a separate trigger spring, but it still doesn't give the hammer any additional push.

So I worked out a system with a single mainspring operating on two linkages—one to push the hammer forward, the other to return the trigger. As you pulled the trigger you also compressed the hammer spring. This gave us the possibility of a beautifully light trigger pull. Unfortunately, we couldn't take full advantage of this; because even though we could get completely reliable ignition with a double-action pull as low as seven pounds, we didn't think a trigger pull that low was appropriate for an all-around-use revolver. We decided to not go under a nine or ten pound trigger pull, to keep it in the range of conventional double-action revolvers. Our double-action pull still felt very smooth and controllable—the best in the business.

On the single-action trigger pull, of course, you could get just about anything you wanted. That's pretty good, too! Our new linkage system also gave us the possibility of going pretty light on double-action or on the single-action trigger pulls, without having to worry about misfires.

We pretty much went whole hog and decided if we were going to make a big massive beast of a hunting revolver, it would be just that. Sure, it's a heavy gun, but that and its grip shape, patterned somewhat after my old Sentinel revolver, helps make it a relatively "pleasant" .44 Magnum to shoot. No other double-action revolver that I'm aware of is built as ruggedly.

The Redhawk on the Fiennes-Burton Transglobal Expedition: Jeremy Clowes Remembers

Long before I joined the London gunmakers Holland & Holland, I met Sir Ranulph ("Ran") Twiselton-Wykeham-Fiennes, Bt.; we were both on duty in the British Army, on a climbing course in Snowdonia. He subsequently managed to survive a very adventurous life, until in 1973 he set up an office in London for his great venture, christened the Transglobe Expedition.

To quote from his autobiography, *Living Dangerously:*

The expedition we were to attempt involved crossing Europe and the Sahara, descending the Atlantic to its ice-bound extreme, crossing the Antarctic Continent via the South Pole, descending the Pacific from the southern tip to the Arctic, boating over 1,000 miles of the Yukon and Mackenzie rivers, traversing the North West Passage and 500 miles of ice-bound Archipelago to the north, skiing 300 miles over Ellesmere Island ice caps and crossing the Arctic Ocean via the North Pole.

The preparations took seven years during which

time I introduced Stephen Vogel to Ran, and we all had dinner together in London with Molly [Vogel] and Ginnie Fiennes. As a result, Steve decided to donate a Ruger .44 Magnum Redhawk to the expedition which was carried by Ran throughout. On Easter Day 1982, he and Charlie Burton became the first men to reach both poles overland. The expedition was finally completed when they returned to Greenwich, England, on August 4, 1982. The book on the expedition is called *To the Ends of the Earth.* One memorable passage:

We relaxed. Then I saw Charlie stiffen and his eyeballs seemed to grow larger all of a sudden.

"Correction," he said, "we *do* have a visitor."

A large polar bear stepped out from behind my tent. Its front legs were across the guy ropes some three yards in front of us. It licked its lips and impressed me with the length of its long black tongue. The official warning notes came back to me—"Do not allow polar bears to get close." There was not much we could do about that. Without remembering to focus or adjust the shutter speed I took a couple of photographs hoping not to irritate the great beast with the clicks. The bear eyed us up and down for a while then slowly walked away. Like a poodle that barks ferociously once a bulldog has left its immediate vicinity, I began to shout "Shove off" at our visitor when it was well clear of the camp.

Next time we were not so lucky.

Again, the bear moved about by the tents for a while with each of us thinking its movements were the other man working outside. When we twigged and emerged armed, the bear was close by Charlie's tent. We shouted at it and I fired my revolver over its head. All this was studiously ignored.

Charlie's .375 rifle was bolt-action and at the time he had only two bullets. I had plenty of ammunition but my .44 Ruger Magnum revolver had been ridiculed by some Canadians as inadequate for effectively stopping an aggressive bear, so I had little confidence in it. For ten minutes the bear padded about us in a half circle between our ration boxes whilst we shouted abuse in three languages, clashed our pots together and sent revolver bullets past its ears.

After fifteen minutes Charlie lay down on a sledge and took careful aim. I stood behind and to one side and fired off a parachute illuminating flare. The rocket blasted by Charlie's head and struck the snow in front of the bear fizzing brilliantly. This was also ignored and the bear crouched down in the snow facing us, waggling its rear end slightly in the manner of a cat stalking a mouse. It began to approach us.

"If it comes within thirty yards, over that snow dip, I'll fire one shot at it," I whispered to Charlie.

The bear, a beautiful looking creature, continued to advance and I aimed the pistol at one of its front legs [and fired].

The bear stopped abruptly as though stung by a bee, hesitated for a moment, then moved off sideways and away. . . . We followed it to the end of the airstrip where it jumped into the sea and swam across to another floe. Would it have been better to have killed the bear? A dead bear lying beside our camp or even floating in a nearby lead, might attract other visitors. Or should I have left it alone? *How* close should one allow a bear to get? To my mind, no closer than you feel is the distance where, if it does charge, you can shoot it dead with your available firepower before it can reach you. A single raking scratch from the paw of even a dying bear is to be avoided by individuals who cannot be evacuated by any means and whose first aid know-how would be sneered at by the Battersea Girl Guides.

A goodly number of bears wandered across our floe over the weeks ahead and eighteen came up close to our camp. Each one seemed to react differently to our scare tactics. Their visits kept us from being bored. So, too, did the shrinking nature of our floe. Any noise outside the tents had us listening intently. There were many false alarms. One night I awoke in a gale. Amongst the plethora of wind noises I heard a rhythmic scuffling that I was certain must be a bear. It turned out to be merely the sound of my heartbeat against the canvas earflaps of my night cap!

Ran said the Ruger Redhawk never failed to fire—no matter how bitterly cold the temperature.

From the 1980 Annual Report

1980 marked the beginning of the Company's fourth decade . . . and it was a record year for both sales and net income after taxes which were $80.3 million and $8.9 million respectively. These amounts represented increases of 16.7% and 11.9% over the comparable figures for 1979. . . . The increase in sales is a result of both price increases and a higher level of shipments. Particularly gratifying is the increase in the level of sales of the Over and Under Shotgun.

1980 marked the commencement of shipments of the .44 Double-Action . . . Redhawk revolver; . . . it is my hope that in 1981 production of this product will significantly improve so that the very strong market demand . . . can be satisfied.

A great deal of effort has been expended during the past year and continues to be expended in the development of several additional products which I feel will be logical additions to our present line. In my opinion, the Company has never enjoyed a stronger position in the market place with strong demand being recorded for virtually all the Company's products. To meet this demand, the Company has completed a significant capital expenditure program especially with respect to its Pine Tree Castings Division. The capacity of Pine Tree was increased by 50% in 1980. It is hoped that this new capacity will enable not only the demands of Sturm, Ruger to be met, but also enable Pine Tree to become a more significant factor in the investment casting business. It is my feeling that our growth in the investment casting industry constitutes an attractive and important diversification of the Company's business.

As in recent years, I must report to you again regarding the Company's product liability problems. . . . The Company appealed the Day case to the Supreme Court of Alaska which, in opinions dated April 6, 1979 and August 22, 1980, re-turned the case to the Superior Court for a partial new trial on the issue of comparative fault, letting the amount of compensatory damages remain intact. The Supreme Court further ordered a remittitur of the punitive damages (that is, deciding that the original award as to punitive damages was excessive) giving the plaintiff the choice of accepting $500,000 or having a new trial. To date the plaintiff has not responded. The Company intends to file a Petition for Certiorari with the United States Supreme Court once this decision becomes final.

In addition to the Day case, the Company is a defendent [sic] in approximately sixty other law suits in various parts of the United States. As I have reported before, these cases for the most part involve our "Old Model" single-action revolvers. . . . The final outcome of the Day case as well as the other cases cannot presently be determined. . . .

Despite the foregoing problems, I am confident about the Company's future. In my opinion, . . . the Company enjoys a stronger market position than at any time in its history. I foresee a continued growth for the Company in the firearms industry. In addition, we are always evaluating other potential business opportunities.

Down to the Sea Again— The *Titania*

Ruger had decided that his second yacht would be along the lines of the Richard K. Mellon yacht, the *Cassiar,* which he had seen at Woods Hole, Massachusetts. Ruger had met Mellon through an Episcopal minister, The Reverend John Baiz (a Ruger cousin on the Batterman side), whose church in Pittsburgh had a number of prominent Pennsylvanians as parishioners. After Richard K.'s death, Ruger wrote to one of his sons, Richard P., and inquired about buying the *Cassiar.* Mellon replied that it was not for sale, as his mother wanted to keep it.

Robert Derektor's Boat Yard, conveniently located close to Southport in Mamaroneck, New York, was chosen as the builder of the new yacht, to be named after a character from medieval folklore: *Titania.* Ruger himself was the designer, with the drawings and construction executed by Derektor, under the watchful eyes of Lloyd's. After weekly inspections during the 18-month construction period, the yacht earned the coveted Lloyd's Maltese 100A1 rating.*

Bill Harris, the captain of Ruger's former yacht *Island Waters,* commuted to Mamaroneck daily to oversee construction. Ruger himself would go over about twice a week, with new ideas and sketches (Ruger had also been a student of naval architecture, particularly steam-powered launches, in his youth). Derektor was highly opinionated about yacht design, and so was Ruger, whose ideas for deck layout and other matters were logical, and were incorporated by Derektor. A feature of the design was that access for the crew to the engine room, their quarters, and the cockpit was

---

*The Lloyd's Society's Special Survey is a rating body of Lloyd's of London. The Maltese 100A1 rating denotes as follows:

Maltese is a distinguishing mark denoting the ship was constructed under the Lloyd's Society's Special Survey in compliance with the Society's Rules.

100 is a character figure assigned to ships considered suitable for sea-going service.

A is a character letter assigned to ships constructed or accepted into class in accordance with the Society's Rules and Regulations and which are maintained in good and efficient condition.

1 is a character figure assigned to (a) ships having on board, in good and efficient condition, anchoring and/or mooring equipment in accordance with the Rules, and (b) ships classed for special service for which no specific anchoring and mooring rules have been published, having on board in good and efficient condition, anchoring and/or mooring equipment considered suitable and sufficient by the Society for the particular service.

The Ruger Redhawk Double-Action Revolver

Number 500-00001 Redhawk Revolver.

Number 500-00001 Redhawk Revolver.

164

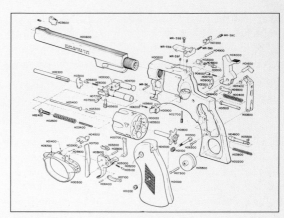

Exploded view of Redhawk Revolver.

Introduced: 1979. ". . . the product of intensive engineering and testing . . . the logical evolution of the now-famous line of Ruger double-action revolvers. . . . With the accuracy and power of the .44 Magnum cartridge well established by the extensive competition in handgun metallic silhouette shooting, the Ruger REDHAWK revolver can be expected to be widely used as a hunting revolver . . . an entirely new firearm, representing the most significant advance in the development of heavy frame double-action revolvers in many decades."

Serial Numbers: 500-00000 to -99999; and similarly numbered serial prefixes 501-, 502-00000 to -96855 (through 1993).

Total Made Through 1993: In excess of 290,000.

Caliber: .44 Magnum (.44 Special interchangeable); later introduced in .357 Magnum (.38 Special interchangable) and .41 Magnum.

Number of Chambers in Cylinder: Six.

Barrel Lengths: 5½", 7½".

Rifling: 6 grooves, right-hand twist, one turn in 20".

Markings: See Table of Markings, pages 330–35.

On left side of barrel:

Before using gun-read warnings in *instruction manual* available free— from Sturm, Ruger & Co., Inc. Southport, Conn. U.S.A.—

Sights: Ruger adjustable rear, for elevation and windage; outlined sighting notch. Interchangeable front sight blades, of varying heights, plastic inserts of fluorescent red or yellow, with later additions of white and sky blue (all four available as Redhawk Colored Front Sight Kit, catalogue **R4S**). Gold bead sight kit an accessory option, steel front with gold bead and matching "V" notch rear sight leaf having white centerline (catalogue **GVBR**).

Overall Length and Weight: 11", 49 ounces (5½" barrel); 13", 54 ounces (7½" barrel).

Grips: Checkered walnut, Magnum style.

Finish: Blued, or satin-polished stainless.

Materials, Construction, and Innovations: Heat-treated A.I.S.I. type 410-series stainless steel or blued chrome-molybdenum steel. Extra metal in topstrap and critical areas below and sur-

rounding the barrel threads. Built without a removable side plate. Frame and cylinder assembly lock directly into frame, at front of the crane, and the rear of the cylinder. Locking notches of the cylinder offset significantly, and not cut into thin part of the walls on chamber centerlines. Unique "single spring" mechanism: hammer and trigger powered by opposite ends of a massive coil spring. Components linking the trigger and hammer to spring transmit energy with minimum friction losses and operate as direct, efficient levers: resulting trigger pull is smooth and promotes precision shooting.

Mechanism, cylinder and crane group, and trigger guard group dismantle into subassemblies in seconds, without tools. Hammer and cylinder interlock, ensuring hammer cannot be cocked when cylinder swung out, or cylinder swung out when hammer cocked.

Integral rib and ejector rod housing on the barrel. Massive (¾" x 20-pitch) barrel thread, resulting in increased wall thickness of the barrel at the breech end. Interchangeable front sight blades, secured by a plunger to the integral sight base. Firing pin mounted in frame, transfer bar ignition system, unbreakable steel music wire coil springs.

Issue Price: $325.00 (1980).

Engraving: Serial number 500-03211 inlaid for William B. Ruger, Sr., by Paul Lantuch.

Price Sheet Listings and Major Production:

Blued Steel:

RH-445: 5½" barrel, .44 Magnum, blued (1984–present).
RH-44: 7½" barrel, .44 Magnum, blued (1986–present).
RH-44R: 7½" barrel, .44 Magnum, with Ruger scope rings (1986–present).
RH-415: 5½" barrel, .41 Magnum (1987–1991).
RH-41: 7½" barrel, .41 Magnum (1987–1991).
RH-41R: 7½" barrel, .41 Magnum, with Ruger scope rings (1987–1991).

Stainless Steel:

KRH-445: 5½" barrel, .44 Magnum (1986–present).
KRH-44: 7½" barrel, .44 Magnum (1980–present).

KRH-44R: 7½" barrel, .44 Magnum, with stainless steel Ruger scope rings (1982 to date).

KRH-355: 5½" barrel, .357 Magnum (1984–1991).
KRH-35: 7½" barrel, .357 Magnum (1984–1991).
KRH-415: 5½" barrel, .41 Magnum (1984–1991).
KRH-41: 7½" barrel, .41 Magnum (1984–1991).
KRH-41R: 7½" barrel, .41 Magnum (1986–1991), with stainless steel Ruger scope rings.

1st Variation: Prototype, pre-production.

2nd Variation: First production, with dubbed ejector shroud.

3rd Variation: Sloping ejector shroud.

4th Variation: **KRH-44R,** narrow barrel rib pattern.

5th Variation: **KRH-44,** with sloped ejector shroud, wide barrel rib pattern, and left hammer pivot tab.

6th Variation: **KRH-44,** with sloped ejector shroud, wide barrel rib pattern, and right hammer pivot tab.

7th Variation: **KRH-44R,** with wide barrel rib pattern and left hammer pivot tab.

8th Variation: **KRH-44R,** with wide barrel rib pattern and right hammer pivot tab.

9th Variation: 5½" barrel **KRH-445,** with left side hammer pivot tab.

10th Variation: 5½" barrel **KRH-445** with right side hammer pivot tab.

11th Variation: Production in .357 Magnum, either barrel length.

12th Variation: Production in .41 Magnum, either barrel length.

practical without their having to go through the main salon. The deck, living quarters, main salon (patterned after the mahogany and birch paneled salon in the famed yacht *Cleopatra's Barge*, built in 1816), and fishing deck were entirely functional and accessible. The yacht also had a striking black aluminum hull and a distinctive profile, as Ruger says, like a "rumrunner of the Prohibition Era."

The *Titania* was finished in November 1979, and would spend its winters based in Palm Beach, its summers in Newport, Rhode Island. It could be seen in attendance at many of the New York Yacht Club annual regattas in the 1980s, and was present, with its owner aboard, as an official N.Y.Y.C. vessel at the 1984 America's Cup races off Newport.

When Ruger sold the boat, in 1993, the brokers, David Fraser, Inc., prepared an elaborate sales monograph, from which the description that follows was drawn:

Type of Vessel: Technically termed a "yacht fisherman," built with an aluminum hull.
Length: 88'
Waterline: 82'
Beam: 20'
Draft: 6'
Engines: Twin Caterpillar 3408 V8 diesels 500 horsepower each, with twin disc 514 3-1 gears. 4" Aquamet 17 stainless steel shafting with 40" x 42" Colombian bronze propellers. All engines constructed to Lloyd's Maltese 100A1.
Speed: 12 knots cruising, 15 knots maximum. Transatlantic capability.
Tanks: 5,100 gallons diesel, 5 tanks. 1,200 gallons water. 35 gpm Racor central fuel filter servicing 275 gallon day tank.
Construction: Heavy-duty welded aluminum with ½" bottom, 1" plating over struts and rudders. Framing all 12" centers, engine room stringers run full length of the vessel. Topsides and decks ¼" aluminum. All surfaces faired with International Microballons and Awlgrip painted.
Electrical: Two Caterpillar 3304 diesels with 50kw Lima brushless alternators. 100 amp shore power isolated transformer with two 50 amp self-autophas-

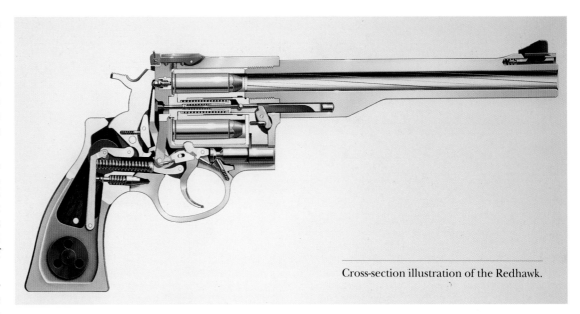

Cross-section illustration of the Redhawk.

ing shorelines. All circuits protected with two sets of circuit breakers with central master switchboard adjacent to wheelhouse.
Accommodations: Three double staterooms aft with two complete heads with showers. Forward, captain's cabin and office, port crew's stateroom, twin bunks, starboard stateroom, one bunk. Head and shower.
Main Salon: Paneled in mahogany and birch, in the elegant fashion of Cleopatra's barge. At the forward end are two buffets, one of which is easily opened for full access to the electrical panel. There is an expandable dining table to seat up to eight. All of the side paneling is removable for access to large storage areas under the side decks. The aft end of the salon has a wet bar and hi-fi equipment, and bookcase.
Aft Staterooms: A short flight of stairs leads down to the afterguard. There are two guest staterooms, port and starboard, with head and shower, and farther aft is the master stateroom, with twin bunks, head, and shower. A short stair leads up to the aft fishing cockpit with a large sliding hatch for excellent ventilation.
Forward: A stair runs from the flying bridge through five levels to the wheelhouse, main salon,

galley, and engine room. The galley is full width with Westinghouse washer and dryer, KitchenAid dishwasher, 17-cubic-foot Foster freezer, six-burner JennAir range, KitchenAid trashmasher with cutting-board top, two full-size self-cleaning Thermodor ovens, the top of which is also a full-size microwave. There are two sinks, one on each side, each with disposal. A dinette seats three, and several lockers allow for storage.
Crew's Quarters: Three private staterooms are forward of the galley. On the starboard side, the captain's cabin and office with sink. On the port side, a head and shower. In the bow, a double stateroom to port; a single stateroom to starboard.
Engine Room: 6' headroom and easy access to all machinery.

"The Old Man and the Sea." How many persons have designed even one gun, car, *and* boat? And how many gun designers are members of the New York Yacht Club? Ruger's boyhood yachting designs at *top right*, precursor of things to come. First yacht, the 95-foot *Island Waters*, with white hull. Yacht with black hull, the 92-foot *Titania*. Late nineteenth-century oil painting, "Centennial Pilot Boat No. 7," by T. E. Baker.

Wheelhouse: Light and airy with large windows and an elevated seat for three for viewing.

Flybridge: Spacious with vinyl top and removable side curtains for plenty of air. A steering station and table seat four. Full seating for 10.

Main Deck: Easy access directly up from the main salon and directly down from the flybridge to the main deck. The deck holds a 17' Mako boat with an 85 horsepower Johnson outboard engine.

Fishing Deck: Directly down from the main deck, and a short step up from the master stateroom, with two sportfishing chairs.

Electronics: Sperry Gyrocompass, Sperry Magnetic compass for backup, and Sperry autopilot. Amot pneumatic throttles and shifter with 3 stations: wheelhouse, flybridge, starboard side. Decca 914 48-mile radar. Sinrad LC204 loran. Northern Singlesideband, Motorola Modar all-channel VHF, Raytheon loud-hailer and auto foghorn, digital rpm gages, pyrometers for both engine exhausts, Datamarine digital depth sounder with flybridge remote, Perko searchlight, RCA remote TV antenna, two Konel 14" rotating windscreens, 10-station ITT telephone system with intercoms compatible with AT&T service, complete bilge alarm system.

Gear: 600' ⅜" galvanized steel anchor chain with 325# anchor Spare 150# Danforth anchor with nylon line and chain. Four backup steering systems including 10' tiller. 5,000-pound hydraulic deck winch and boom for shoreboat. Kidde CO_2 automatic system. Two Lloyd's-approved 1½" bilge pumps to four watertight bulkheads. 10-step Marquipt boarding ladder. Folding door in transom for fish and swim platform. Two 10-ton J. D. Nall circulating water air-conditioning systems with individual heaters in each cabin.

Southern Boating magazine's October 1980 issue admiringly described Ruger's new yacht, featured on the front cover and in a three-page color spread:

One is not overwhelmed by a show of ostentatious opulence; to the contrary, the prevailing tone aboard *Titania* is one of patrician, almost austere, simplicity. . . . underlying all the understated luxury remains the overriding consideration for function. . . . A brass grab rail runs the length of the sa-

lon ceiling (a common-sense safety feature so often either overlooked or intentionally omitted on many yachts). . . . Protection from too much sun is provided by a bimini top which was designed to resemble the top of a Packard phaeton, adding another touch of classic styling to this elegant yacht. . . . *Titania,* in all her quiet beauty and functional simplicity, surely exemplifies the refinement and dignity of a very discriminating owner.

From the 1981 Annual Report

The very gratifying result of the year's operations can be attributed to the ongoing strong demand for our products, together with real effort by management to improve the efficiency and capacity of our manufacturing departments. . . .

Although the year-end figures give no hint, the growth and complexity of our product line has required expansion of our engineering management. This has not been easy to achieve, and during the year the existing management group has spent much of its time on recruiting efforts and the formation of an enlarged organization. We have made some tangible progress, and in the near future we look forward to improved efficiency in both product engineering and manufacturing engineering. The past year is notable also because we have made major investments in computer controlled machine tools, and have almost completed a new engineering office building at our Newport factory. I believe our timing will prove correct—that the computerized equipment we are now acquiring is beyond the experimental or novelty stage, and that an attractive return on investment projection is in reality attainable.

Our product engineering program for the year came through very much on schedule and I am hopeful that the results of these efforts will be visible in 1982. Specifically, the Company has introduced a modernized and upgraded version of our original product, the "Standard Model" .22 caliber automatic target pistol; a new, more

purely sporting version of our "Mini-14" .223 caliber rifle; and a new Ruger "International" Model 77 rifle with design details to suit it for export markets as well as for our domestic market. Furthermore, in numerous detail improvements we have enhanced the present product line, and have work well advanced for additional products and improvements to come.

I am confident that our work in product design is going in the right direction and will form the basis of successful marketing efforts in the next few years. This confidence is largely inspired by strong evidence that owners of our products are unusually loyal. . . .

We have, in fact, developed a rapport with our market, and I include in this category not only users, but our wholesalers and retailers, which must be quite unique in modern business. I think that our entire organization is conscious of this friendship, and with rare exceptions our people do their daily work with the customer in mind. . . .

We are now in the process of introducing a unique conversion kit which upgrades our "Old Model" single-action revolvers. . . . We are offering these kits to owners of these revolvers on a no-charge basis, and I think everyone in the Company is pleased that we are able to do this. We feel that we are in this way further cementing our relationship with owners. This conversion program can, of course, be called a recall and there are, no doubt, plaintiff's attorneys who will attempt to so designate it. The fact remains that there is no design defect in our "Old Model" revolvers, and we are proceeding with this conversion program fundamentally because we think it is good business and because it adds a dimension of safety and convenience to owners who have come to expect the best from our products.

For all the positive factors surrounding our engineering and marketing, we are distressed by the social problems which have attached themselves to us as they have to much other American industry. A great deal of our time and millions of our hard earned assets have been spent annually in fighting product liability litigation. The continual and irresponsible claims for punitive damages in these product liability cases is an absolutely unmeasurable threat, not merely to our Company, but to virtually all of American industry. The abuses (and I call them that very deliberately) that have developed in the product liability trial procedure should be corrected by uniform federal legislation, and we have endeavored with our limited means to call this matter to the attention of every legislator we can reach. . . .

This [is a] national problem which can very properly be regarded as one of the most destructive attacks to date on American industry. Under the present circumstances, all product development and improvement tends to be minimized because no matter how far-fetched the accusation may be, improved products are often held to be evidence that the older product was unsafe. The adverse impact on the liquidity of companies, the cost of their insurance, and the discouragement to new enterprise all combine to hurt industry and to hurt the prosperity of the country to a greater degree than is generally understood. I know of no other country that has product liability procedures as anti-business in effect as the United States.

The strong results we report for 1981 are in my view beneficial as a means of enhancing our prospects for survival. It seems like a bizarre cynicism to have to say that we are working for growth as a means of overcoming the good intentions of our society.

Jack Behn on Working at Sturm, Ruger and Company

I just marvel at the man; he was great to me. We never had a cross word all the time I was there. We used to go to all the gun shows, even before I was working for him. I think he liked that. He figured I was a good dickerer. I will say this too; he gave me a virtual free hand in purchasing. I only went to him when I was in real trouble.

One of the times I well remember—we were having a terrible time getting proof ammunition. This was in .357 or .44 Magnum caliber. Remington and Winchester made these proof loads, but sometimes certain loads were hard to come by. And we did get into some oddball calibers, which only one or the other of the companies would manufacture in small lots. With certain of these calibers there's not enough business in it. However, SAAMI rules say if you brought out the cartridge, you have to supply the proof load.

I went in to Bill in desperation and said, "Look, we've got a problem. I've tried everything and am getting nowhere." Bill got on the phone and said to the president of Remington, "I've got my purchasing agent sitting next to me with tears in his eyes, because he can't get any proof ammunition." With that Remington really started moving, and got shook up a bit. We got it all right.

This is hands-down the best company in the entire history of gunmaking.

Working at Sturm, Ruger: Jim Sullivan Remembers

Working at Ruger was like being in the "Ruger School of Advanced Firearms Engineering and Manufacturing." You'd often get the impression that he just treated us all as kind of beginners; but there were other times when he would give you the benefit of the doubt.

Once Bill was chewing me out for a firing pin that he didn't like. It was unconventional, and was designed partly as a means of leaving out a manufacturing operation. But he was all disgusted, and kind of yelling. This was in the presence of Ed Nolan. Then Ed joined in to say what a crummy design it was. Ruger turned beet red, and yelled at Ed, "Who do you think you're talking to? Jim Sullivan knows 100 times more about gun design than you do. Jim is a red-hot designer who gets real results

fast." Nolan blanched, and turned white as a sheet. Ruger finished by saying "We've got the best design team in the gun business!"

You were expected to argue back if he was wrong. He didn't like yes men; he still doesn't. You had to stick up for what you thought was the better way. On most subjects you'd have to do that. Every detail was discussed, and sometimes it would get pretty stressful. Still, there were limits that Bill put on these things; he wouldn't jump on you for fun. He never had this "big me" and "little you" attitude. And he meant it when he said all this was "a discussion between two professionals."

From the 1982 Annual Report

1982 was a year of marked contrasts as our discordant nation struggled through the worst cycle of pointless pessimism in several decades.

Although sales reached $103 million which is a new plateau and the first time the Company has reached the $100 million level, this was unfortunately accomplished on a slightly lower level of units shipped and accordingly was totally a result of price increases we were forced to initiate to partially cover increased costs and expenses incurred virtually throughout the Company's operations. Net income after taxes declined to $11.3 million or 8.0% below the 1981 figure of $12.3 million as a result of significant cost and expense increases, particularly with respect to "The Ruger Single-Action Conversion Kit" and TV and magazine ads with respect to safety.

However, I want to point out that this backsliding was also due in some degree to production problems and difficult model changeovers. The demand for our products remained surprisingly strong through most of 1982, and it is quite probable we would have had another record year if we had more product to sell. I think it is also quite gratifying to observe that the balance sheet remained strong and shows the characteristic liquidity which has always been a great advantage to us. From all reports, the American arms indus-

Cross-sectional of the MK II Standard pistol.

try has had a poor year and my impression would be that we have outperformed the industry as a whole.

We give a great deal of thought to our position in the arms industry as well as our position in relation to our markets. It is quite possible that in future years there will be some material changes in our marketing and distribution channels. Our product has normally been sold to a substantial number of wholesalers throughout the country, and in turn distributed by them to established licensed local gun dealers and sporting goods stores. Our wholesalers are the principal firms in a category who specialize in sporting goods and equipment of all kinds, and a great many of our customers are also major traditional distributors of hardware and mill supplies for many different types of users. All of these firms stock all brands of firearms and sell them to customers throughout any area they choose and without any territorial franchise limits.

We have been very fortunate throughout the history of our Company in having this network of reliable distributors to provide this ready access

to our ultimate market. We see very worrisome signs, however, that this long established system is changing, and in fact to some extent, has already changed toward a considerably different type of function, probably as a result of the rise of retail chains and discount merchandising. Many of the "old line" hardware firms have disappeared as a result of these changes at the retail level and some of those that remain are doing business much less like traditional wholesalers and more like brokers. Because of this, our potential problem is that of assuring good service to the specialized retailer. These knowledgeable dealers are essential to us in that they are both influential and helpful to the customer.

Another subject directly related to marketing is the question of market share. We could wish that we were functioning, as makers of sporting arms, in a true growth industry but that has not been the case with firearms for many years. Our growth for most of our history has been a matter of struggling for "a larger slice of the pie." This would make little difference to a relatively small company but now that our market share is on the

order of 20%, it is getting increasingly difficult to enlarge and there is even the question of whether we are close to the maximum share we should seek. . . .

There are many more immediately significant matters for us to be continually concerned with. . . . During 1982 we were much encouraged by the improved climate for our Company but the product liability problem will always be a hazard which is immensely difficult to quantify unless some reasonable Federal legislation is enacted, particularly with regard to punitive damages. We were very much encouraged during late 1982 by the defeat of Proposition 15 in California. This proposed restriction on the sale of handguns was a product of some patently fallacious theorizing and was defeated roundly by voters who had no interest in surrendering longstanding constitutional rights for a proposition which could not achieve its stated purpose.

The long term future of private ownership of firearms is difficult to assess, but at least it can be said that as the true causes of criminal activity are understood and identified, the irrelevance of firearm ownership to crime rates becomes apparent to a majority of the people.

The Company had a very productive year during 1982 in its engineering efforts, both as to product design and manufacturing improvements. This is the work that is clearly indispensable to our continued success and I am glad to be able to say that the whole Company seems enthusiastic about the good results they are achieving.

Bill Ruger "in a Trance": Harry Sefried Remembers

I was always amazed by one of Bill's abilities that was a key to his success: He will concentrate on one thing to the exclusion of anything else. When we would be thinking out a mechanical idea, the whole building could have fallen down, and he wouldn't have noticed it. When he was in that mode, he couldn't be interrupted; he wouldn't even hear the phone ring. He sort of lapses into a trance about what he's working on and just ignores everything else. You don't want to disturb him when he's concentrating like that.

When you stop to think about it, the guns and their creation are his life, and he's good at it. He's the best ever, absolutely no question about it.

The Mark II .22 Pistol:
Harry Sefried Remembers

I designed the first automatic bolt lock, which was a major feature of the new design. It automatically locked the bolt open after the last shot was fired, signalling the user to reload. The earlier Mark Is had a bolt lock, but you had to manually engage it by pushing the safety button "on." I built one up in the model shop, just to see if it could be done. I made a horseshoe-shaped linkage (because the button was on the right side of the magazine), inside a slot in the frame, with an external thumbpiece on the left side, where most people's thumbs are, so they could readily lock the bolt open or shut it.

I designed the rigid cartridge magazine feed lips, instead of spring-loaded ones, and found a reliable source for new magazines (a sheet metal specialist). After that the magazine was all set, and we changed the grip frame so the slot for the magazine button (which would automatically actuate the bolt lock when the last shot was fired out of the magazine) would be on the left side of the grip, right near the thumbpiece. Then, when the new pistols came into production, all we had to do was take the new magazine and put the button on the left side, and for the older models, leave it on the right side. The design allowed the buttons to be easily changeable from one side to the other.

Later on, Roy Melcher and Bill got their heads together and they made a double linkage bolt stop, a genuine improvement on the one I made. They got a very nice, convenient, and more reliable operation. In gun design, you often leave an unfinished project that others come back to, with a fresh outlook, and they often end up doing it better.

For what ultimately became the Ruger Mark II pistol, all of these things evolved; the magazine, the bolt lock, and the outside thumbpiece. And some styling changes were worked out as well: flats were milled into the rear of receivers and the ears on the bolt were angled slightly. These weren't really necessary, but they looked good, and they helped to visually distinguish the old gun from the new.

The majority of the Mark II .22 work was finalized 'after I left. By 1982, all of these factors, brought together, made the new Ruger Mark II, and the older Standard pistol, the one that had started the company, was discontinued after a run of over 1,000,000.

The Mark II Autoloading Pistols:
Steve Sanetti Remembers

When the new style .22 autoloading pistols were developed, they were all generically called "Mark IIs." Since we had used the "Mark I" name for all our previous target models of the Ruger Standard pistols, this led to a dilemma—was the target version of these new pistols to be called "Mark III"? The decision was made to use the designations "Mark II Standard" and "Mark II Target," respectively.

The Government Target Model was something else again. The U.S. government approached Steve Vogel with their own specifications for a .22 target and training pistol for the armed forces. It appeared that, with a slightly longer barrel and finer sights, and with an enhanced level of accuracy, our Mark II target pistols could fit the new government specifications. Steve Vogel worked closely with Roy Melcher and Frank Bonaventura, then the Southport plant manager, to develop these guns. A special tight chamber was "roller burnished" in a slightly longer untapered heavy ("bull") barrel, and the sights had to be narrowed somewhat (both front and rear). Rather than spend laborious man-hours targeting these guns, Steve Vogel and Chris Cashavelly developed a new laser sighting system (for which a U.S. patent was granted). It allowed the operator to lock the pistol in a fixture, fire one shot, and turn the sight screws so that the sight-mounted laser would coincide with the point of impact on the target. He would then remove the laser and fire the targeting group This resulted in a tremendous cost saving. The laser was not used for actually sighting the gun, but simply to align the sights on target with only one sighting shot.

It is a great honor to have the Army use our pistols again. They all bear the "U.S." acceptance stamp. The commercial Government Target Model is identical in all respects, except, of course, being made without the "U.S." marking.

The Ranch Rifle:
Roy Melcher Remembers

This project started as an offshoot of a rifle for the French police, who specified an open rear sight mounted on the barrel, and the ability to readily mount a telescopic sight. The first step was to design a receiver specifically for a scope, using aperture mounts cast as part of the receiver. We started out with the regular Mini-14 in mind, as the basic mechanism—with the exception of the sporting style open and scope sights—had been proven pretty thoroughly. We didn't anticipate any problems meeting their requirements. We started testing the gun with scopes, and were pretty surprised!

The development of the Ranch rifle was fun, because it showed us who made strong scopes, and who didn't. The same type Leupold scope had been tested repeatedly on the .458 and .375 Magnums, some of the most heavy-kicking cartridges around. The furthest we ever got until we came up with the recoil buffer was 50 .223 rounds, before the crosshairs parted.

We could not find a scope that would stand up to the G-forces of the slide block impacting on the receiver, although the little .223 cartridge is not exactly known for heavy recoil. Even the best quality Leupold scopes couldn't take the shock, although they lasted the longest. The first thing that would happen is the crosshairs would split from the vibration, and then the lenses would start to loosen. We calculated the acceleration and deceleration velocity of the slide at around 30 m.p.h.; i.e., from 0 to 30 to dead stop in a fraction of a second. It was like hitting the scope with a mallet every time you fired the gun—the bolt flew back and forth at each shot with that much force.

To cushion the blow to the scope, we tried rubber, plastic, and nylon buffers, and we couldn't find anything to stand up to the impact of the recoiling slide. We worked on that over a period of a few months. Bill himself suggested that we should check the design of the 10/22 rifle, which has a

The Ruger Mark II .22 Standard Pistol

Number 18-00001 MK II Pistol.

Exploded view of Ruger MK II Pistol.

172

Introduced: 1982. "Developed as a result of an engineering program to incorporate important mechanical improvements and desirable new features [and are] basically, refinements of the original Ruger Standard and Mark I Target Model pistols. . . ."

Serial Numbers: 18-00000 to -99999; and similarly numbered serial prefixes 19-, 210-, 211-, 212-, 213-, 214-, 215-, 216-, 217-, 218-, 219-00000 to -95550 (through 1993).

When .22 Mark II production was resumed at the Prescott, Arizona, facility, serial numbering began with 218-00000 (early 1992).

Total Made Through 1993: In excess of 1,000,000 (including Mark II Target).

Caliber: .22 Long Rifle.

Magazine Capacity: 10, in spring-fed detachable box.

Larger size button became standard with Prescott production.

Barrel Lengths: 4 ¾", 6".

Rifling: 6 grooves, right-hand twist, one turn in 16".

Markings: See Table of Markings, pages 330–35.

On right side of receiver, standard as illustrated.

On left side of receiver:

Before using gun-read warnings in *instruction manual* **available free— from Sturm, Ruger & Co., Inc. Southport, Conn. U.S.A.—**

Silver trademark motif within magazine base.

Sights: Square notch rear sight dovetailed onto receiver; adjustable for windage. Fixed front sight of wide blade Patridge type.

Overall Length and Weight: 9", 36 ounces (4 ¾" barrel).

Grips: Delrin base material, exceptional impact resistance. Variations include walnut with a red composition insert on back of left grip, walnut thumbrest without trademark medallion, walnut thumbrest, and desert camo laminated with left thumbrest.

Finish: Blued, or satin-polished stainless.

Materials, Construction, and Innovations: Bolt stop to automatically hold bolt in open position when magazine in and last shot fired. May be activated manually at any time by pushing up bolt stop thumbpiece on left side of frame. Bolt may also be closed by pulling it back slightly, then releasing—except with empty magazine inserted. Re-designed magazine, with capacity of 10 cartridges. New magazine latch. New safety, allowing pistol to be loaded or unloaded, or the bolt to be manually operated, while safety is "on"—the sear being locked. Improved trigger pivot retainer.

New trigger manufacturing method for better appearance. Shallow scallops on receiver sides at rear, allowing for better grip on cocking lugs of bolt.

Unbreakable steel music wire coil springs.

Accessories: Supplied with extra 10-shot magazine, and (from 1993) molded, high-impact, lockable composition case, with keys (all variations except the 10" barrel pistols).

Issue Price: $147.50 (1982).

Engraving: Serial number 216-55158 engraved and gold inlaid for William B. Ruger, Sr., by Paul Lantuch; the 2,000,000th Ruger .22 automatic pistol made. Number 19-27605 fitted with special sterling silver sights for Ruger, Sr., by Lantuch.

Price Sheet Listings and Major Production Variations:

MK-4: 4¾" barrel, blued, composition grip panels.

MK-6: 6" barrel, blued, composition grip panels.

Stainless Steel:

KMK-4: 4¾" barrel, composition grip panels (introduced 1984).

KMK-6: 6" barrel, composition grip panels (introduced 1984).

Bolt Stop Thumbpiece: Changed from sheet metal type bent at 90 degrees to serrated, contoured configuration. First appeared on serial no. 19-22967, June 1983.

Stainless Series: Began late in 1983, with serial number 211-00000.

Mainspring Housing: Three main parts cast in a single piece, begun within serial range of 211-26659 to -63924. Either version may be found in subsequent production.

Note: For the Zytel frame 22/45 pistols, see pages 250–51.

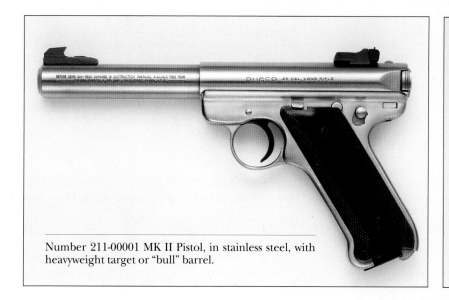

Number 211-00001 MK II Pistol, in stainless steel, with heavyweight target or "bull" barrel.

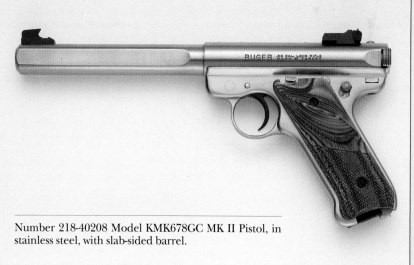

Number 218-40208 Model KMK678GC MK II Pistol, in stainless steel, with slab-sided barrel.

patented pin device in the rear of the receiver. The bolt comes back, and hits that pin, and it redirects the bolt to take the impact "crack" out of the back end. His suggestion gave us the clue to solving that problem. I worked with Jay Jarvis and Bill Spotts on that. That's where the idea of the mechanical recoil buffer came from—it's basically a loose ring with a pin that holds everything in position. When the slide hits the buffer during recoil, it redirects the impact, not necessarily to the same place on the ring each time. There is enough "give" in the ring to remove excess vibration, cushioning the recoil so it doesn't break the scopes. Another patent [was] issued as a result.

The ejector had to be redesigned to throw the fired cartridge cases out of the gun sideways, under the scope. Otherwise, they'd fly up, hit the scope, and bounce back in, jamming the gun. We engineered this as part of the bolt stop. And to say it ejects positively would be an understatement. The Ranch rifle was now fully adaptable to scope use.

Red Labels for the White House

Shortly before leaving office in 1981, President Jimmy Carter called the factory. Secretary Marie Sorge took the call: "This is the White House calling. . . ." The President wanted to speak with Mr. Ruger himself, or one of the company's top executives. None of the Rugers was in town that day, and Marie referred the call to Executive Vice President John Kingsley. The President wanted a Ruger Red Label shotgun, engraved and inscribed as a farewell presentation to Vice President Mondale.

Kingsley then asked the President if the company could, at the same time, prepare a Red Label for the President. His answer was that he would be delighted.

Kingsley and his wife Ines hand-delivered the Red Labels to the President at the White House, on the very day that the Iran hostages were released! The President sent Bill Ruger a handwritten letter, along with a photograph of him with his new prize, expressing his delight with "the

two beautiful Ruger shotguns, which the Vice President and I will be able to enjoy for many years in the future. They certainly live up to their fine reputation." President Carter later visited the company's exhibit at the 1982 SHOT Show, in Atlanta.

The check in payment for his shotgun was made out by Rosalynn Carter.

Harley-Davidson and Others— Deals That Might Have Been: Ruger Remembers

Although I have never owned a motorcycle, they have always fascinated me. Harley-Davidson was a grand old American company, which filled a niche in their way, much as Sturm, Ruger does in ours. Harley-Davidson also represents a technological set of requirements similar to a gunmaker's. Harley is, in fact, a user of castings, and should become a client of our investment casting operations.

In about 1980, we were considering an investment in Harley, which at that time was run by a bunch of caretakers, managers who were, for the most part, purely businessmen, more interested in golf than in the motorcycle and its culture.

I asked a friend who knew the workings of the company to let them know that Sturm, Ruger was an interested buyer. However, at the time there was a leveraged-type buyout going on. Some of the dedicated management people at Harley were in the process of trying to gain control of the company, which was then a subsidiary of AMF. The message came back to me that this buying group would appreciate my laying off, in that my interest might interfere with their deal.

I did so, and since then the company has made a remarkable recovery.

Additionally, over the years Sturm, Ruger & Co. has had the opportunity to purchase Colt, Smith & Wesson, Remington, and Winchester, as well as the Ithaca Gun Co., Weatherby, Maserati, John Rigby and Sons (London), and the Meyer-Drake Company, the latter for manufacturing engines

for the Ruger Sports Tourer. For many years Meyer-Drake built the Offenhauser engines for Indianapolis car racing. John Kingsley observes:

I think the main reason Sturm, Ruger never closed on one of the various acquisition possibilities was the fact that the Company itself was achieving year in and year out a level of profitability which could not be matched by any of the foregoing firms. I remember particularly when we looked at Colt and Smith & Wesson. Their operating results were not comparable to Sturm, Ruger's and it was doubtful that the acquisition of either firm would have resulted in any increase in return on investment to Sturm, Ruger.

To the best of my knowledge, any acquisitions that were being looked at would all be considered as cash transactions, because I do not think Bill Ruger would ever seriously have considered diluting his ownership in the company by issuing stock to complete any kind of an acquisition.

Walter Howe: John Kingsley Remembers

Walter Howe was one of the most brilliant and hardworking persons I ever met. He had a mind like a steel trap, and with the proper education could have been a professor of law at Harvard. He would never ask anyone to do anything he wouldn't be willing to do himself.

It was Walter, former editor of *The American Rifleman*, who set up Hawkeye Communications (1968), our own in-house advertising agency. Walter was probably the leading authority on firearms legislation, and had done an exhaustive study on the subject right after the assassination of President Kennedy.

As manager of the Southport factory (1974 to 1976) he increased our productivity from 200,000 guns a year to 300,000, in the course of about a year's time. He worked himself so hard he had a heart attack. On the other hand, he drove his workers almost as hard as he drove himself. Excellence was expected and demanded at all levels.

After the heart attack Walter was our special projects administrator working from his home, with a phone line to the office. He put together the best firearms market analyses ever compiled, although Ruger was known to say that "market research is a waste of goddam money." Howe retired in 1984.

Ruger on the XGI—A 1980s Project: An Autoloading Mini-14-Based Rifle

When our XGI rifle finally appears, my goal is that it be more accurate than its running mates. It is being designed primarily for the American sportsman, though of course it would have military and police potential, as does the Mini-14. The basics of the new rifle are, of course, there, and when a gun is fundamentally right, its design progresses agreeably so that the major contribution a manufacturer can make is to details. I feel that at this point we are on the verge of perfecting the XGI and won't release it until it is perfected.

Military and police business figures very importantly in our business and future plans. There is increasing interest among foreign and U.S. police forces, not only in our rifles but in our revolvers and autoloading centerfire pistols, and several new developments will be aimed at those already good markets.

The 2,000,000th Ruger .22 pistol made; an MK II, number 216-55158; flush gold inlaid and engraved, the safety set with a garnet; ebony grips. For William B. Ruger, Sr., by Paul Lantuch.

The Turkey Sandwich Episode

I can remember a time, in the late 1970s, when we had a staff meeting up at Pine Tree. It was hot as hell, and we used to have these quarterly staff meetings, presentation, slide show, and so forth . . . though Bill soon got tired of that. In any event, at this one it was after a lunch where we had had turkey sandwiches, and some of them were somewhat spoiled. Bill started to ask Ed Nolan, then the sales manager, questions about marketing. Ed had some solid reference material, prepared by Walter Howe. But Ed made the mistake of not studying this report. Ruger's questions became more and more pointed, and Nolan didn't have all the answers. Ruger absolutely roasted Ed. This became known as the Turkey Sandwich Episode.

—John M. Kingsley, Jr.

From *The New Yorker*, June 1, 1981:
Bill Ruger's office is straight out of the early 1900s. The furniture is dark oak and maple. Wild animal heads stare menacingly from the walls, a rhinoceros and a lion Ruger bagged in Africa. "They weren't endangered when I shot them," says Ruger.—*Forbes*.

That's what *they* thought.

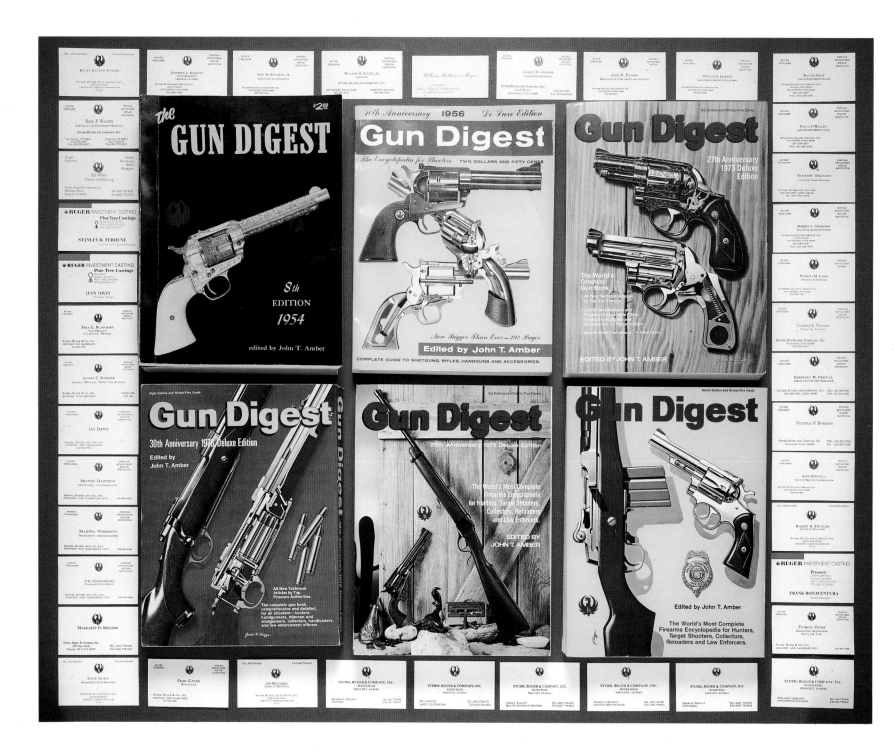

CHAPTER VII

"Innovative Engineering, Traditional Craftsmanship"
1982–1987

Our company is a prime example of an entrepreneur running a business his way, and making it work. Fortunately, guns are a consumer product which evoke a true dedication, an emotion. But increasingly Bill Ruger and the company have had to deal with an anti-business attitude by government, the anti-gun and anti-hunting activists, a hostile media, a seemingly static or shrinking market, and fewer places to use our products.

Sometimes he will be looking at a model he introduced years before, and he'll notice little details; he never forgets, since he has been so deeply involved all along. And he's just as proud of these guns today as he was the day each one was launched.

Bill has that extraordinary, uncanny ability to know what a gun ought to be, and what it ought to look like. Unlike John Browning, who did not make or work from drawings, Bill's precision is partly due to his abilities on the drafting board. Even the most

Sturm, Ruger & Co., Pine Tree Castings, and Ruger Investment Casting business cards with a few of the several covers featuring Ruger firearms and technology. First Ruger *Gun Digest* cover was the deluxe prototype Single-Six, on 8th edition in 1954. Speed-Six commissioned by Bill Ruger; the gold inlaid dragon motif and monogram signature inspired by the art of Albrecht Dürer. On other side of receiver, craftsman Alvin White positioned the dragon's tail to encircle the serial number, 150-01563. Revolver donated by Ruger to Buffalo Bill Historical Center's Winchester Arms Museum, for benefit auction by Christie's, July 5, 1984.

23. 1982
"Old Model" Single-Action Safety Conversion

24. 1983
.357 Maximum Blackhawk Single-Action Revolver

25. 1983
77/22 Bolt-Action Rifle

26. 1985
GP100 Double-Action Revolver

27. 1986
Super Redhawk Double-Action Revolver with **30. 1988** SP101 Double-Action Revolver

28. 1986
Bisley Single-Action Revolvers

minute dimension or shape will not escape his eye. And when he gets onto something, he stays on it relentlessly, and will not compromise on the final product. Of course, we've also got the edge on the competition with our investment casting capability, which we utilize even in the design process—you can't design a practical mechanism unless you know that its components are manufacturable. Like Bill says, "Pretty pictures don't mean a thing."
—Jay Jarvis
Manager, Engineering, Newport facility

"If you would see his monument, look around."
—Epitaph of Christopher Wren,
St. Paul's Cathedral, London

Engineering the Ruger Conversion Kit
A major innovative step toward shooter safety was the 1982 announcement of the Ruger Conversion Kit retrofit for "old model" single-actions. Dropping the patented New Model components into existing "old models" was impossible, since despite outward appearances, the guns are totally different mechanically. But after some hard thinking and concentrated efforts, Ruger was able to engineer yet another, different, transfer bar safety mechanism that could be factory retrofitted into 1953–72 single-actions (and for which

Ruger was awarded still another U.S. patent in 1984). The company heavily advertised the Kit, and continues to do so in many ways, including product catalogues, new gun packaging, and in single-action ads. All known "old model" owners have even been sent free shipping containers and reminders to send their revolvers to Ruger for this free safety conversion. It is the largest and most comprehensive such product safety program ever undertaken in the firearms industry, earning the 1982 "Product Award of Merit" from *American Firearms Industry* magazine and the National Association of Federally Licensed Firearms Dealers.

Ruger on the Single-Action Conversion Kit

There was some urge for us to have the Conversion Kit available—perhaps to answer some of the lawyers. I can't remember exactly what it was, but I had gone around with this conviction or assumption or whatever that I really couldn't expect to do it; it was against nature, because the frame would inevitably have to be altogether different inside (as the New Model frames are, as compared to the "old model") and we just couldn't do it. You'd have a whole new gun, not a retrofit, by the time you were through. So that was the situation for a long while.

But one winter [1979–80] I was down in Florida on the *Titania* and I had a lot of spare time, sitting there on the deck. One day, for some reason or another, I was thinking: Was it really impossible, as General Hatcher had publicly stated, or was there some possibility if I abandoned some basic assumptions and found others that were more productive? And I said, all right; I won't make any rules to myself about what's good enough, or artistic enough, or sturdy enough, or what. I'll just take what I can get and see how it looks.

And by God, it emerged very quickly. I had to make space for a different transfer bar, and instead of having a slot inside the sidewall of the frame, I put a recess in the side of the hammer. I also scaled way down my ideas about what was the necessary thickness and configuration of this vertically moving transfer bar, and that got me pretty close. Then I said, okay, this is a retrofit, a little kit of parts that's basically installed with a screwdriver and will enable you to carry the gun safely with the hammer down. But how am I going to proceed to make it all work?

For that I had to say to myself, it's got to be just right. I can't make a mistake on that, and I think I was right. In any event, this is what happened: The retrofit for "old models" did not have room for that extra added luxury that we have on the New Models where you simply open the gate to load the cylinder. You still have to draw the hammer back to the loading position. But what I did get was the idea for a new transfer bar safety and it was a good one, one that might be worth a little extra attention. I got Roy Melcher to come down to Palm Beach for a few days and get my data; he made two trips like that. And after some considerable struggling, there it was!

You might say it was a relatively simple mechanical objective, but for some reason it was very difficult to comprehend and implement. Virtually on the drawing board, Roy and I designed the final version, the interpretation of how it could happen. It did require a trigger that moved a little more, but still a single-action trigger, not double—not having a full double-action travel between its fully cocked and its hammer down position. So that culminated years of messing around with the single-action retrofit objective. And, we got still another patent for it—none of the many other single-action manufacturers had even thought of something remotely like this.

I am immensely proud of it, and remember—we did this great thing with utterly no government requirement that we do so; no bureaucrat dictating that we must do thus and so. I think it's a great act of faith that we have undertaken to help stop, in some mechanical way, those accidents caused by careless or ignorant use of our older products, which you must remember were of the totally conventional Colt Peacemaker mechanism, perhaps the most famous revolver of all time. I initially contemplated perhaps charging some small amount to at least partially offset the not inconsiderable costs of factory installing this device, but I became convinced to offer it free of charge as a gesture of goodwill to our older customers; and this, of course, was the correct decision.

The Single-Action Conversion Kit: Roy Melcher Remembers

On this project, I worked on everything from Mr. Ruger's original concept: It was my assignment to make it work. This was kind of like building a ship in a bottle. He first discussed the concept with Harry Sefried, who was nearly at the point of retiring due to ill health. So Harry said, "Here Roy, it's yours."

This started out by taking the three frame sizes, and making up a set of parts for each one: the .22 caliber Single-Six, the .357 Magnum, and the .44 Magnum. We then took these parts and found as many different frames as we could possibly find, and put the parts into the frames. We continually made adjustments, and in time came up with a set of parts that would work in each of the various frame sizes. This required months and months of work, and finally we decided that the kits would work but would have to be factory retrofitted.

To check the new system, I had a weight, equal to the weight of the Super Blackhawk .44 Magnum, suspended on a string from the ceiling of the engineering department. I would drop the weight square on the hammer with a primed cartridge case in the chamber. The barrel of the gun was pointing straight down, so the weight hit the hammer perfectly. This far exceeded any blow the hammer could receive in the field. To my great surprise, the gun went off—it was not supposed to, with all our new mechanics!

I did it again, over and over, and every time I did it, the gun went off. We finally found out that when the weight hit the hammer, the impact would propel the trigger rearward, which would carry the transfer bar up just as the hammer bounced slightly away from the frame. When the hammer came down again, it caught the transfer bar between the frame and the firing pin for just a few hundredths of a second, enough to fire the gun. This just proves that not everything that looks good on paper works out in real life.

We then added a lug on the upper periphery of the hammer, below the clearance area for the transfer bar, which meant that the trigger would have to be pulled and held rearward for the transfer bar to be all the way up, and to clear the lug, before the gun would fire. In the event of a sharp blow to the hammer, this lug would contact the transfer bar and keep it from coming up to fire the gun. We never had a problem with it since, but that held things up for some time until early 1982.

The conversion [patent] is in Mr. Ruger's name and my name. Basically, as with every project I worked on, I had a personal interest in each project, and I walked it through all the way.

From the 1983 Annual Report

1983 has been a difficult year for the Company as well as for the entire firearms industry. The downtrend which commenced in 1982 sales volume continued during the past year and for the second year in a row, units shipped were reduced from the previous year.

As a result, sales for the year 1983 were $86.4 million or 16.1% below the 1982 level of $103.0 million. Net income after taxes declined to $10.0 million or 11.5% below the 1982 figure of $11.3 million. This decline in net income after taxes would have been greater except for the fact that the Company's expenses in connection with its Conversion Kit Program were significantly reduced in 1983 as a result of the anticipated aggregate liability being booked in 1982. In addition, 1983 was not encumbered by any significant write off as had been the case in 1982 when the Company's $1 million write off of an

The Sturm, Ruger Safety Conversion advertisement, placed by the company since 1983 in all catalogues, with all new firearms, and in the broadest possible spectrum of publications. Some periodicals, however, due to intolerance of firearms, refused to accept this public-service piece. Those that did run the piece range from virtually all publications in shooting sports, law enforcement, press dedicated to women, outdoor activities, home mechanics, sports, farming, hunting, firearms dealers, hunter safety instructors, and others. It is by all accounts the most widely publicized and longest running firearms safety program in history, and the program continues to this day.

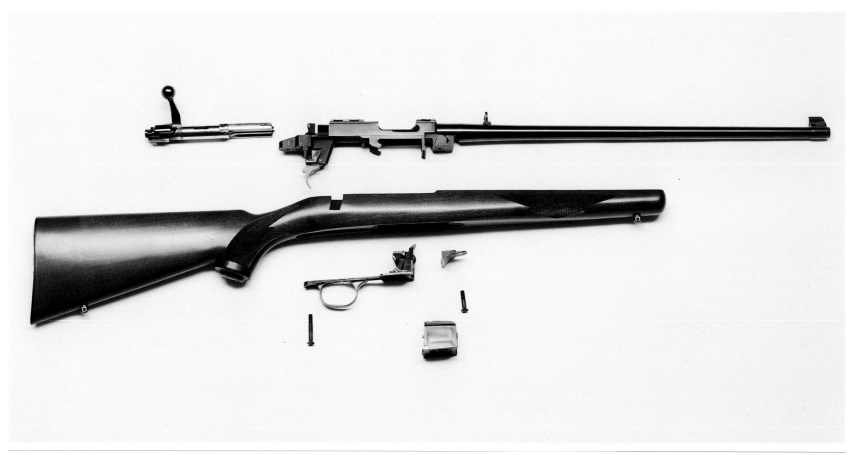

Simplicity of the modular construction of the Ruger 77/22 bolt-action rifle. The model marked the 1983 reintroduction of the high-quality .22 caliber sporting rifle.

independent oil and gas investment occurred. Despite these disappointing financial results, the Company enters 1984 in good financial shape with its liquidity and historically strong balance sheet unimpaired.

Our prime focus at this point is to continue with the Company's program of developing new products to offset the decrease in demand for some of the Company's older products. In line with this, our new bolt-action .22 caliber rifle, the Model 77/22, was introduced to the public at the NRA show in Phoenix in May. The initial recep-

tion of this product was enthusiastic, as we expected it to be, because the 77/22 is by all commonly accepted standards the highest quality rifle of its type on the market and by far the most handsome, although the announced price makes it a notable value. I think this new rifle illustrates our product engineering thinking very clearly. It is designed to be produced largely on computer controlled machines and, of course, makes extensive usage of our increasing investment casting technology.

We expect products produced in this way to

make larger profit contributions and have through 1983 made great progress with the development of other major firearm products which will become part of our sales program in 1984. So much product engineering has been brought to completion, that in the future, I think we will regard 1983 as unique in the engineering history of the Company.

Paralleling this focus on product engineering has been our effort to strengthen our production management organization. The need in 1981 and 1982 was evident when we accepted a certain

180

amount of inefficiency in the interest of maximizing output. It has taken some time to define some room for improvement in this part of our day-to-day activities and to locate the specialized and experienced people who have now joined the Company management staff. Our manufacturing facilities leave very little to be desired, and I believe that now we are addressing ourselves to the interesting problems of exploiting these facilities to their full potential for production.

I am pleased to report that our product liability situation improved somewhat in 1983. We have seen a very real decrease in the number of recent accidents, and I attribute this in no small measure to our ongoing shooter safety warnings and the Conversion Kit Program, in which we have modified approximately 100,000 "old model" single-action revolvers. The sole adverse jury verdict against the Company last year resulted in a finding of 75% fault on the part of the plaintiff and only 25% responsibility allocated to the Company with no punitive damages awarded. This is consistent with our very strong belief that these unfortunate accidents are purely the result of careless firearm handling, and the Company is taking all reasonable measures to promote shooter safety.

However, I continue to feel that the only long-term solution to the product liability crisis faced by this nation lies in the form of fair, nationwide legislation. S.44, the "Kasten Bill," represents the type of reform that is so badly needed if this nation is to remain competitive and have its industrial base restored.

We are happy to welcome Jack S. Parker, retired Vice Chairman of the Board and Executive Officer of General Electric Company, to our Board of Directors, joining us early in 1983. He brings with him a wealth of experience and has already proved to be an invaluable addition.

I would also like to recognize the contribution which has been made to our Company during the last decade by G. Richard ("Dick") Shaw as the Company's field representative in the eleven Western states and Canada. Dick will continue as a Board member, but will curtail his heavy travel schedule.

In summary, 1983 was what I would call a problem year. I like to view it positively in that the Company's position as a leader in the firearms industry remains secure in spite of lower sales. While there are many problems besetting the industry, I can readily perceive of many opportunities which are available. These represent our challenges for the future and the entire Company has responded to these new circumstances in a way that reinforces my faith in our continued success.

The Ruger .357 Maximum Blackhawk Single-Action Revolver: Roy Melcher Remembers

In our design we had stretched both the frame and the cylinder and, using the new, lengthened and beefed-up .357 Maximum cartridge, had a spectacularly performing new revolver, designed for the sport of "metallic silhouette" shooting, where you must knock down heavy steel animal silhouette targets at long range.

The original Remington test ammunition did not present a problem, but when they made a change in the powder, it brought about gas-cutting on the top of the frame. The high pressures and temperatures created an "acetylene torch" effect, eroding the throat of the barrel, and the topstrap of the frame. We tried to correct that for a long time, with little success.

I fired the gun in a cardboard box to collect unburned grains of powder. These grains of powder measured about .0030", and yet the gap between the revolver's cylinder and the barrel was only about .006" to .008". The powder change actually made the pressure curve peak at the barrel gap, forcing those particles out with tremendous force. We felt that we would only be able to deal with this by a system in which the cylinder overlapped the barrel and completely sealed breech, but that

would have been too complex. Try as we might, there was no way we could figure how to make the ammunition work with a conventional revolver, that had to have a space between the barrel and cylinder so it could rotate. The erosion was largely cosmetic, and would go so far and generally stop; but we didn't think this was acceptable on a long-term basis, and it probably was having an adverse effect on the revolver's accuracy. It was one of our few failures.

Fate of the .357 Maximum

After extensive experimentation, the factory released a statement in 1984, which, to date, has been the final word on the subject:

We are disappointed with the [.357 Maximum] cartridge's pressure and its tendency to erode the barrel. We have tried all sorts of approaches to lengthening barrel life and had hoped that the final development of the cartridge would result in lower pressures, but that has not occurred. . . . Like the .44 Carbine, therefore, we will be dropping it from our catalogue this year, but experimentation will continue and the .357 Maximum may resurface.

At our very next gun writers' seminar, we had perhaps twenty of the then-premier American gun writers in attendance. I recited the problems that we were having with the .357 Maximum revolver to get some feel for how the product and this situation were being perceived in the field. One of the most prominent writers who specialized in handgun hunting, Bob Milek, spoke up quite loudly and said, "Bill, you ought to just kill it," which was really rather shocking, coming from him. But under the circumstances, we had reached a dead-end, so we took his advice.

From the 1984 Annual Report

I must report that 1984 has been another somewhat disappointing year for the Company, as well as a difficult one for the entire firearms industry. For the third year in a row, the Company experienced a decline in unit shipments from the previous year, although the drop in 1984 was only nominal versus 1983. Further, in my opinion, this would not have been the case if we had not experienced an assortment of production delays which made it impossible to meet the generally improved demand for the Company's products.

As a result, sales for the year were $89,327,000 or 3.4% ahead of the 1983 level of $86,348,000. Net income after taxes and earnings per share in 1984 declined to $9,190,000 and $2.78 respectively. These amounts were 8.6% below the respective 1983 amounts of $10,048,000 and $3.04 per share.

The primary reason for the $858,000 decrease in net income after taxes on a sales increase of $2,979,000 is the significantly higher overhead cost per unit in 1984 versus 1983. This is the result of accumulating significant overhead costs in inventory in 1983 when production in units exceeded sales in units by a wide margin, and there was a resultant build-up of inventory. In 1984, the reverse was true. In 1984 there was a significant reduction in inventory, and these costs have now been taken out of inventory and made part of the cost of goods sold.

The downtrend affecting our industry, about which I have written often during the last several years, continued in 1984, but I believe that we are now at, or close to, the bottom of the cycle. This contraction in the industry has resulted in a severe financial problem for a number of industry participants, and was undoubtedly brought on by overproduction and a lack of creative product engineering among many members of this industry. This overproduction was so acute in 1983 and 1984 that it caused a partial breakdown of the industry's distribution channels with the result that the Company's sales during this period were adversely affected. During the latter part of 1984, the foregoing conditions appear to have been somewhat rectified. I have noted a decidedly more optimistic atmosphere at the last few trade shows I have attended.

In March, 1984, we reluctantly came to the conclusion that it was necessary to reduce the Company's workforce in order to ensure that the Company's inventory of finished goods would not grow beyond a reasonable point. Accordingly, approximately 13% of the Company's workforce was laid off in early March. Prior to taking this step, the majority of overtime had been eliminated during the preceding six months. This was a very difficult decision to make and was an unfortunate milestone in that it had never been necessary to take this step at any time during the Company's thirty-five-year existence.

As a result of the foregoing, the Company has been able to reduce its inventory of finished products considerably between the end of 1983 and the end of 1984, and has thereby preserved, in our opinion, the long-term security of the Company and its employees.

The reduction of orders received from our distributors during the early 1980s caused us to re-examine our distribution policies. It became apparent that an increasing number of distributors were not fulfilling their basic function of servicing established retail dealers, and in fact, many had become brokers selling to other mail order distributors. Accordingly, on December 1, 1984, Sturm, Ruger established a strict policy that it will only sell to distributors who in turn represent that they will only sell to established retail dealers. By definition a retail dealer is one who has a regular place of business, a State Resale Tax Number (where applicable) and where products are displayed to the shooting public. It is my feeling that by strictly following such a policy, the industry and shooting public will be better served. We have been frequently complimented for this policy provision and have been told that it is typical of our industry leadership.

I am gratified to report that our product liability situation continues to improve. We are now at a seven-year low in pending lawsuits, and we experienced two defense verdicts in the *McGill* and

Baker cases (in Iowa and Idaho) in 1984. The successful 1982 defense verdict in the *Smith* case (Washington) was recently affirmed on appeal. Our conversion program for "old model" single-action revolvers continues, and I am hopeful that badly needed Federal product liability reform legislation will be enacted this year.

On January 2, 1985, the Company purchased the assets of American Metals and Alloys, Inc., for slightly in excess of $3 million. This property consists of an investment casting foundry which has been highly successful in the production of large sized aluminum castings. This acquisition enables the Company to gain a foothold in the non-ferrous investment casting industry. It is my feeling that this will complement our Pine Tree Division's ferrous investment capabilities nicely. During 1985 a strong effort will be made to increase on a profitable basis the sales volumes of both of these divisions.

As we enter 1985, despite the problems reported herein, I remain confident and optimistic about the future. We have a good selection of new products in various stages of development which should provide exciting profit opportunities for the Company. I am speaking specifically of our 77/22, a bolt-action .22 caliber rifle, and the XGI, a Mini-14 in .308 caliber. Following these will be a 9mm pistol which is fully developed and will be in production toward the end of 1985.

We are disappointed that this gun was not in existence in January 1984 when samples were to be submitted for the highly publicized U.S. Army's 9mm test program. In what we consider to be an exceptional engineering and development program, we completed the first 50 prototypes of the new Ruger P85 9mm pistol by midyear 1984. However, it has not been tested because of the Army's policy to refuse tests to late entries. While this is unfortunate in a sense, it detracts very little from the profit potential of this product because it is unquestionably the finest double-action automatic pistol ever made. There will be a large market for it for police and personal defense purposes for many years to come.

The realization of the full potential of these and all our other products will require the full effort of our entire Company, and I look forward to working with all of the employees of the Company to ensure that our goals for 1985 will be met.

The 77/22 Bolt-Action Rifle: Roy Melcher Remembers

Mr. Ruger had talked to me about the Model 77/22 rifle a little bit in 1982. Then I got a telephone call from him, on board the *Titania*, when it was wintering down in Florida (the boat was then usually in Palm Beach). He wanted me to go down to work on the Model 77/22 project, and I thought it would be nice to get down in the sun. Little did I know. . . .

I wound up slaving away for days, and the only time I was out in the light of day was at lunch. During the rest of the trip we were at the dining table on his yacht, concentrating on the receiver details. We were at it from 9 A.M. 'til 9 P.M., working out the style, the integral scope bases, and the casting details. This was the "KISS" principle, trying to keep it as simple and pure in every respect as possible, and yet end up with a classically styled sporting rifle.

Here he was, working like a dog on his yacht, at the age of about 68, suffering from rheumatoid arthritis—which would fluctuate from good to bad, and neither of us enjoying the magnificent weather and that famous Florida sunshine.

From the 1985 Annual Report

Before reporting to you on the 1985 operating results of the Company, I would like to give you a brief overview of what has been happening to the domestic firearms industry during the last decade. Having some knowledge of industry trends will make it easier to assess the position of our Company.

In 1974 the annual production of firearms

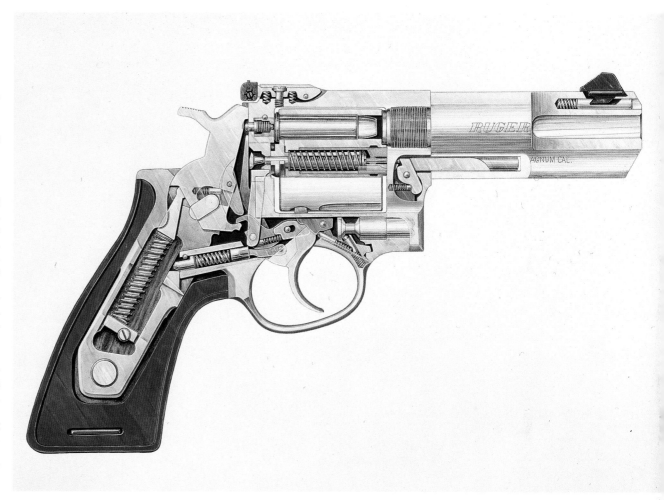

Cross-sectional art of GP100 the work of silver designer and artist Siro Toffolon. Note how there is no grip frame *per se*, but only a "peg" surrounded by a patented rubber-cushioned grip for comfort. It also has Ruger's modular takedown system and double solid frame first introduced in the Ruger Security-Six.

The Ruger New Model Blackhawk .357 Maximum Single-Action Revolver

Number 600-00002 .357 Maximum Revolver.

Number 600-00002 .357 Maximum Revolver.

Exploded view of .357 Maximum Revolver.

Introduced: 1983. "An entirely new version of ... [the] famous New Model Blackhawk revolver, specifically designed as a high performance handgun for sporting use and chambered for the new *.357 Maximum* cartridge being announced simultaneously by Remington Arms Company, Inc. ... [with] a case length that is .315" longer than that of the .357 Magnum cartridge.... For both handgun hunters and metallic silhouette target shooters ... [the] cartridge generates energy levels that put it in the same class with the .44 Remington Magnum cartridge."

Serial Numbers: 600-00000 to -16314.

Total Made Through 1984: 9,500.

Caliber: .357 Maximum. 158-grain semi-jacketed hollow point bullet, with a muzzle velocity of 1,825 feet per second, and 1,168 foot-pounds of energy; at 100 yards the velocity was at 1,381 f.p.s., and 669 foot-pounds, with a mid-range trajectory of 1.7".

Number of Chambers in Cylinder: Six, the cylinder measuring approximately ⁴⁄₁₀" longer than the standard .357 Magnum Blackhawk cylinder.

Barrel Lengths: 7½"; 10½" a bull style barrel.

Rifling: 8 grooves, right-hand twist, one turn in 16".

Markings: See Table of Markings, pages 330–35.

On left side of cylinder frame:

RUGER .357* MAXIMUM CAL.
NEW MODEL BLACKHAWK

*R trademark registration mark

On left side of the barrel:

Before using gun-read warnings in *instruction manual* available free— from Sturm, Ruger & Co., Inc. Southport, Conn. U.S.A.—

S proof marking on back of cylinder, visible on opening of gate.

Sights: Ruger rear sight, adjustable for elevation and windage. Front sight on the 7½" barrel revolver of undercut style. The 10½" revolver's rear sight with a narrow aperture to provide proper sight picture needed with the sight radius and blade widths of the target style front sight used on the longer barrel.

Overall Length and Weight: 13⅞" (7½" barrel), 53 ounces. 55 ounces for 10½" bull barrel.

Grips: Oil-stained walnut with trademark medallion inlay.

Finish: Blued, with high polish.

Materials, Construction, and Innovations: Heat-treated chrome-molybdenum alloy steels and unbreakable music wire coil springs. Steel "Dragoon style" grip frame. Heavy frame construction and extra metal, around the barrel threads and within the topstrap.

Lengthened cylinder and frame to accommodate long cartridge case, as well as lengthened ejector rod and its housing. Wide spur hammer; wide, serrated trigger. The new cartridge and the Maximum's weight and design features combined high performance with noticeably less recoil than commonly encountered with the .44 Magnum cartridge. The flatter trajectory of the .357 Maximum reduced the amount of sight adjustment needed for targets at various distances, as compared to .357 Magnum or .44 Magnum cartridges.

Issue Price: $340.00 (1983).

Engraving: No factory engraved specimens built.

Price Sheet Listings and Production Variations (1983 and 1984 price lists only):

BNM-7: 7½" barrel model.

BNM -10: 10½" heavy barrel model.

Note: Although factory testing included firing "tens of thousands of rounds of commercially loaded cartridges, along with a variety of specially formulated handloads, in several production revolvers," problems subsequently developed with "barrel erosion," as well as erosion of the topstrap. These problems were due to "a new loading of a commercial cartridge," and led to withdrawing the Maximum revolver from the production line. In a letter of April 11, 1983, William B. Ruger, Jr., then Senior Vice President, Manufacturing, noted:

> The Ruger Blackhawk SRM [Sturm, Ruger Maximum] breaks new ground in the use of high pressure, high power revolver cartridges. As in any product at the leading edge of its relevant technology, continued research and product experience leads the way towards higher levels of performance and longevity.

The ammunition erosion dilemma proved unsolvable and the Maximum became one of the few Ruger products to be discontinued.

(pistols, revolvers, rifles, and shotguns) as reported by the Bureau of Alcohol, Tobacco, and Firearms ("BATF") was just under 6 million units. A decade later in 1984 the total of domestic firearms production was 3.9 million units. In short, the domestic firearms industry has contracted by more than 33% during the last ten years. This contraction has impacted all participants in the industry, including Sturm, Ruger. We believe that the reduced demand for firearms is the result of many years of high production in a finite market area, the scarcity of new models, and recently, generally adverse economic conditions in rural areas of the country where much of our market is located. Our own Company has fared comparatively well, but our management feels challenged by this interruption in our growth trend. Accordingly, we have reemphasized the development of new products, and we have also worked hard through operating efficiency to effect economy.

Sales for 1985 totalled $94 million or 5.3% over the comparable figure for 1984. This $4.7 million increase in sales was primarily the result of the Company's acquisition in January 1985 of the assets of American Metals and Alloys. For the fourth year in a row the Company experienced a decline in the number of firearms it has been able to sell. This decline in unit sales was offset to some degree by price increases we were forced to initiate to cover our continuing increase in costs in practically all segments of our operation. Net income reached $9.6 million and $2.89 per share. These figures were 4.3% over the comparable 1984 amounts of $9.2 million and $2.78 per share. 1985's profit margins were aided by the fact that production in units was only nominally ahead of sales in units. In 1984 sales in units exceeded production in units by a wide margin with the result that there was a significant reduction in inventory resulting in costs being taken out of inventory and made part of cost of goods sold. 1985's operations were not so charged due

to the balance between production and sales in units.

During the year a great deal of time and effort has been expended on a number of new products, specifically the GP-100. This will be a series of new double-action revolvers which I feel confident will firmly establish the Company as a leader in this niche of the market. There are several other products which are now taking a good deal of my time and that of our engineering department which I hope will be ready for introduction later in 1986.

I am happy to report that the Company's January 1985 acquisition of the assets of American Metals and Alloys, Inc., has been a successful venture. This operation, known as Unicast, makes large sized aluminum investment castings. It represents what I hope will be the first in a series of acquisitions in the investment casting industry. This is an industry of over $1.5 billion consisting of many segments which are characterized by the use of different materials (ferrous vs. nonferrous) and different applications ranging from relatively simple shapes to highly complex shapes with very exacting tolerances. Our goal is to build the Company's investment casting group both through future acquisitions and internal growth so that it is a significant contributor to the Company's overall earnings within a period of no more than two to three years.

1985 saw the same level of lessened product-related legal activity as I reported to you last year. A number of claims against the Company were summarily dismissed. The Company's experience continues to run contrary to the unfortunate trend of ever-increasing numbers of lawsuits and ever-higher verdicts or settlements.

Despite the Company's generally favorable situation, the unparalleled judicial activism of recent years is continuing. The year saw still further expansion of theories of recovery into the supposedly "deep pockets" of industry, regardless of traditional concepts of fairness, causation, or

fault.

The status of product liability reform legislation is currently somewhat confused, with various alternative systems being discussed. I still feel this is the only long-term solution to an ever-growing national catastrophe, which faces manufacturers with ruin arising from the self interest of lawyers and the inability to obtain insurance.

It is with great sadness that I must report to you the death of Frank L. McCann who has served on the Company's Board of Directors since 1970. He was our close personal friend for more than 35 years and was known and respected by the entire Company. I know I speak for all when I say that we shall miss his wise counsel and friendship.

1985 has been a challenging and somewhat frustrating year. Clearly the basic industry in which we operate is going through turbulent and troubled times and may never return to what it was a decade ago. We will change as a Company to keep pace and to maintain substantial and profitable market share. In addition we will vigorously pursue our investment casting business which we feel is an immense opportunity for future growth.

GP100 Double-Action Revolver: Jay Jarvis Remembers

Bill's idea was to develop a new trigger mechanism and the so-called "peg" frame style, which then allowed us to go to the soft cushion grips. The dashboard on his BMW was an inspiration for the grip styling. We also used the Redhawk's advanced locking system, as well as the Security-Six's modular tool-free takedown. The idea for the interchangeable front sight came from the Redhawk, and was one of Bill's brainstorms. That was a feature easily carried over into the GP revolvers, and was another advancement over the Security-Six series.

The drawings and layouts were made by Larry Larson in Southport. These were then sent to us in Newport. . . . We went through a refining process, checking the layouts, and then built prototypes.

From the time we started to work on the project seriously, beyond an idea and sketches from Bill, to the detailed design, was only about 18 months. It was another probably 9 to 12 months before the GP100 was in production. Considering the variety of projects we had going, that is awfully fast. This was a perfect example of the advantage of our investment casting process. When you have a prototype done, you really have a lot of the production tooling done as well.

We originally started off with a two-piece grip, made in two halves, which was tricky to get to fit and stay together right, being of that soft synthetic rubber material. We had enough problems with the two-piece, so we designed the one-piece grip, and that's what is used on the GP, and the subsequent models of the SP101 and the Super Redhawk.

Only a few parts were used from the Security-Six; all of the major components are unique to the GP100. This was a fresh, new model, and the most advanced revolver ever made. Unfortunately it was overshadowed by the rise in popularity of autoloading pistols in the late 1980s, but is still a great gun for those who prefer revolvers.

From the 1986 Annual Report

Sales for 1986 totalled $87 million or 7.4% under the comparable figure of $94 million for 1985. This $7 million decrease in sales was primarily as a result of the significant reduction in units shipped in 1986 which was only partially offset by modest price increases initiated at the beginning of 1986. Net income was $6 million or $1.80 per share of Common Stock. These figures were 37.5% under the comparable 1985 amounts of $9.6 million and $2.89 per share of Common Stock.

This decrease reflects a decrease in the firearms market which affected the entire industry. We are not sure of the reason for this decline, but certainly it was to some extent brought about by high production over many years without adequate engineering and styling innovations.

Our own Company has maintained product development programs and pushed new products with a real sense of urgency. Nevertheless, in 1986 we could not produce enough of the new products to offset the effect of reduced demand in the firearms market. Our new revolvers and our new P85 9mm pistol have been enthusiastically received by users, and as their production grows, sales and earnings will show major improvement.

It is also satisfying to report that demand for our older sporting firearms products particularly strengthened noticeably in the latter weeks of 1986. Accordingly, I believe our basic firearms market remains strong and continues to provide us with a valuable opportunity for our unique capabilities in engineering and production.

During the year our Company expanded and modified its operations in several interesting ways. Factory operations have been virtually revolutionized by the installation of CNC (computer-numerically controlled) machine tools and ongoing efforts to streamline our production organization. I believe these changes are on a scale that is much larger than any routine update of facilities. We have furthermore, in the nature of an experiment, sited the manufacture of our new 9mm pistol in a new vest-pocket factory in Prescott, Arizona. With this special purpose plant we expect to obtain data on costs, management organization and employee training that will benefit our management of older facilities. Longer term, we hope that this organization created in Prescott will be the basis for expansion, not only of our arms business, but also of our investment casting business in the dynamic Southwest.

The Company continued its efforts to broaden its participation in the investment castings field with the purchase last May of the assets of TiLine, Inc., a titanium investment casting facility in Albany, Oregon. Subsequent to this acquisition, the Company sold a 55% interest in

TiLine, Inc., to Esco, a Portland, Oregon, based company. It was felt that Esco, being in the proximity, would be a more logical candidate to provide day-to-day management, but at the same time would not diminish our involvement in policy or planning. In addition, Esco's general management style and operating policies are quite similar to ours. To date the results of this joint venture appear promising. Manufacturers of jet engines are among TiLine's customers. In our opinion this is a fast growing segment of the multibillion dollar investment castings market.

Regarding product liability matters, the Company continues to vigorously defend its products. There are approximately forty such claims pending. The so-called "absolute liability" types of cases urged by gun control advocates, wherein a properly functioning firearm is claimed to be "defective" because a criminal can misuse it, have quite correctly received widespread disavowal by courts all across the country. Any clear-thinking individual should realize that it is obviously in the best interest of this country to remove all disincentives for safe products and to increase the competitiveness of American goods both here and abroad. Instead, this nation seems caught between a liability crisis (where recovery seems to drift ever toward who can best pay rather than who is at fault), and an insurance crisis (where insurance rates are either usuriously high or insurance is completely unavailable).

Clear and uniform Federal tort reform, including the abolition of the egregious "joint and several liability rule," a uniform statute of limitations, a statute of repose, severe limitation on punitive damages, and a cap on the intangible "non-economic" damages, is vital if America is to maintain any industrial base whatsoever. I for one do not foresee America's survival solely as a "service economy," as some social engineers would have us believe.

It is with great sadness that I must report to you the death of Norman K. Parsells, who served

The Ruger 77/22 Bolt-Action Rifle

Introduced: 1983. "Developed in response to increasing shooter interest in quality, the new Ruger .22 caliber bolt-action rifle tips the scale at just under six pounds and has been designed to provide the small bore shooter with a compact, feather-weight arm that delivers the performance, reliability, and luxury features characteristic of the finest high-powered big-game rifles."

Serial Numbers: 700-00000 to -99999; and similarly numbered serial prefix 701-00000 to -65008 (through 1993).

Total Made Through 1993: In excess of 86,000 (for blued .22 L.R.; does not include stainless steel .22 L.R. or stainless and blued .22 Magnum rifles, *q.v.*).

Caliber: .22 Long Rifle.

Magazine Capacity: 10, in detachable rotary box; not interchangeable with 10/22 carbine; 5-round magazine available as accessory.

Barrel Length: 20".

Rifling: 6 grooves, right-hand twist, one turn in 16".

Markings: See Table of Markings, pages 330–35.

On left side of receiver:

RUGER 77/22 with **R** trademark registration stamp and encircled trademark.

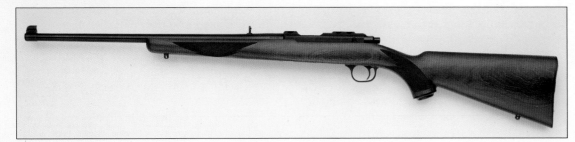

Number 700-00001 Model 77/22 Bolt-Action Rifle.

Number 700-00001 Model 77/22 Bolt-Action Rifle.

On left side of barrel breech:
.22 L.R. CAL.
On top of barrel forward of rear sight:
Before using gun-read warnings in *instruction manual* **available free—from Sturm, Ruger & Co., Inc. Southport, Conn. U.S.A.—**
Serial number *on left side of receiver near barrel breech.*
Sights: With or without folding-leaf rear, gold bead front dovetailed onto integral barrel band. Integral scope mounting bases on receiver, for Ruger 1" scope rings.
Overall Length and Weight: 39¼", approx. 6 pounds.
Stocks: American walnut, checkered, polyurethane finish. Molded nylon buttplate, pistol grip cap. Sling swivel studs.
Finish: Blued; non-glare surfaces on top of receiver.
Materials, Construction, and Innovations: Heat-treated chrome-molybdenum steel. Unbreakable steel music wire coil springs. Investment cast, heavy-duty receiver, with integral Ruger scope mounting system. Military rifle quality bolt assembly; front section non-rotating; locking lugs located at middle of action; rear section of bolt rotates and cams like Model 77 rifle, and its connection to forward part of bolt is a sturdy joint, simple and strong. Bolt locking system engages precision machined surfaces in receiver, behind magazine. 10-round rotary magazine.

Ruger dual-screw barrel attachment system: parts rigidly locked together by two longitudinal screws, via a heavy V-block barrel retainer, pulling barrel tightly into receiver.

Three-position safety. Simplified bolt stop, flush with left side of receiver, and permitting release of the bolt when pressed downward. Crisp, medium-weight trigger pull; non-adjustable trigger. Single strong coil spring, for sear recovery and trigger return. 2.7 millisecond lock time, rivaling that of sophisticated target rifles.

Issue Price: $275.00 (1984).

Engraving: Serial number 700-06182 gold inlaid in art nouveau motif for William B. Ruger, Sr., by Paul Lantuch.

Price Sheet Listings and Major Production Variations:

77/22 Model as introduced, hand checkered American walnut, with scope rings (1984 Price Sheet only, effective December 1, 1983).

77/22-S: Iron sights, scope rings not included (from 1984 Price Sheet through 1988).

77/22-R: No open sights, with 1" scope rings (from 1984 price list to present).

77/22-RS: With iron sights *and* 1" scope rings (from 1985 price list to present).

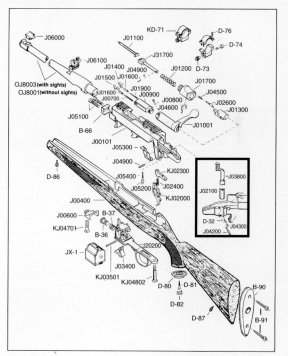

Exploded view of 77/22 Long Rifle and 77/22 Magnum Rifles.

The Ruger GP100 Double-Action Revolver

Number 170-00001 GP100 Revolver, in stainless steel.

Number 170-03963 GP100 Revolver.

Introduced: 1985. "Designed as the ultimate .357 Magnum for police and personal defense use . . . incorporates a number of important new features and improvements (patents pending), and offers a greater degree of accuracy, strength, reliability, and effectiveness than ever before realized in any double-action revolver."

Serial Numbers: 170-00000 to -99999; and similarly numbered serial prefixes 171-, 172-, 173-00000 to -00030 (through 1993).

Total Made Through 1993: In excess of 298,000.

Calibers: .357 Magnum (.38 Special interchangeable).

Number of Chambers in Cylinder: Six.

Barrel Lengths: 3", 4", and 6".

Rifling: .357 Magnum (.38 Special): 6 grooves, right-hand twist, one turn in 18¾".

Markings: See Table of Markings, pages 330–35.

On left side of barrel:

BEFORE USING GUN–READ WARNINGS IN
INSTRUCTION MANUAL AVAILABLE FROM
STURM, RUGER & CO., INC.
SOUTHPORT, CONN. U.S.A.

Sights: Adjustable rear with positive, fine-click settings for windage and elevation; square notch rear sight blade, with white outline. Blade front sight changeable, secured with spring plunger accessed from muzzle; alternate Ruger front sights, varying in styles, heights, and colors.

Overall Length and Weight: 4" barrel: 9⅜", 41 ounces; 3" barrel, with short shroud, 35 ounces; 6" barrel, with long shroud, 46 ounces.

Grips: Patented one-piece Monsanto Santoprene grip, with walnut inserts. Optional grip inserts of high-impact modified resin of G.E. Xenoy. All-wood grips offered as an accessory. Square butt and compact round butt grips available.

Accessory grips in a variety of materials for Ruger handguns, from W. F. Lett Manufacturing Inc., Contoocook, New Hampshire, first listed in the 1991 catalogue, and continuing thereafter.

Finish: Blued, or satin-polished stainless.

Materials, Construction, and Innovations: Ordnance quality 4140 chrome-molybdenum steel, or stainless steel. Heavy, solid investment cast frame; no weakening sideplates. Integral subassemblies, simple takedown, allowing for stripping in seconds, without special tools. Full-length ejector rod shroud, contributing to slight muzzle-heavy balance, helpful in rapid double-action shooting.

Dual cylinder locking system: at rear of cylinder by strong pilot bearing, and at front of crane by locking bolt (engaging a matching slot at front of frame). Transfer bar ignition; floating firing pin; unbreakable steel music wire coil springs.

Grip portion, cast integral with rest of the frame, houses mainspring seat, the trigger guard latch, and the grip panel

Front locking system and ejection rod of GP100 Revolver.

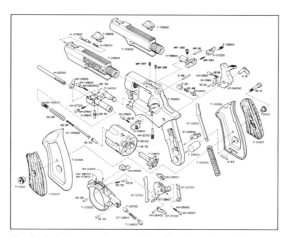

Exploded view and parts identification for GP100 Revolver.

locator. The patented frame extension permits customized wrap-around grip panels, in various shapes, sizes, and materials, for personal taste, as well as the Ruger cushioned grip system.

Wide top rib barrels, with longitudinal serrations for glare-free sighting surface. Cushioned grip panels. Interchangeable front sight system. Square butt and round butt grips available.

Long barrel (ejector) shrouds and short barrel (ejector) shrouds available.

Issue Price: $340.00 (1986).

Engraving: Serial number 170-00777 gold inlaid and engraved for William B. Ruger, Sr., by Paul Lantuch.

Price Sheet Listings and Major Production Variations:

Blued, .357 Magnum, adjustable sights, square butt:

GP-141: 4" heavy barrel, full ejector shroud (first listing, 1986–95).

GP-160: 6" barrel, short shroud (1986–present).

GP-161: 6" heavy barrel, full shroud (1987–present).

Blued, .357 Magnum, fixed sights, round butt:

GPF-330: 3" barrel, short shroud (1989–present).

GPF-331: 3" heavy barrel, full shroud (1989–present).

GPF-340: 4" barrel, short shroud (1989–present).

GPF-341: 4" heavy barrel, full shroud (1989–present).

Stainless Steel, .357 Magnum, adjustable sights, square butt:

KGP-141: 4" heavy barrel, full shroud (1987–present).

KGP-160: 6" barrel, short shroud (1987–present).

KGP-161: 6" heavy barrel, full shroud (1987–present).

Stainless Steel, .357 Magnum, fixed sights, round butt:

KGPF-330: 3" barrel, short shroud (1989–present).

KGPF-331: 3" heavy barrel, full shroud (1989–present).

KGPF-340: 4" barrel, short shroud (1989–present).

KGPF-341: 4" heavy barrel, full shroud (1989–present).

Blued, .38 Special, fixed sights, round butt:

GPF-830: 3" barrel, short shroud (1989–present).

GPF-831: 3" heavy barrel, full shroud (1989–present).

GPF-840: 4" barrel, short shroud (1989–present).

GPF-841: 4" heavy barrel, full shroud (1989–present).

Stainless Steel, .38 Special, fixed sights, round butt:

KGPF-830: 3" barrel, short shroud (1989–present).

KGPF-831: 3" heavy barrel, long shroud (1989–present).

KGPF-840: 4" barrel, short shroud (1989–present).

KGPF-841: 4" heavy barrel, long shroud (1989–present).

1990, 1991, and 1992 Catalogues: Same as 1989 listings, except grip panel inserts available for certain models, made of G. E. Xenoy.

1993 and 1994 Catalogues: Same as 1990–92 listings, except model **GPF-330** discontinued, and the following added:

KGPF-840: .38 Special, stainless steel, fixed sights, 4" barrel with short shroud, round butt.

KGPF-841: .38 Special, stainless steel, fixed sights, but 4" barrel with full shroud, round butt.

Special Issue:

American Handgunner Limited Edition: 1,000 cased 4" blued revolvers, with non-fluted cylinders, full shroud, adjustable sights, gold-filled. *American Handgunner* logo and scroll embellishments. Santoprene grips with simulated ivory inserts, embellished with 10th anniversary scrimshaw logo. 1986.

on the Company's Board of Directors since 1969. He was our close personal friend for more than 35 years and was known and respected by the entire Company. I know I speak for all when I say that we shall miss his wise counsel and friendship. We are fortunate to have obtained the services of Richard T. Cunniff who was elected a Director last December. He is President of Ruane, Cunniff & Co., Inc.

In conclusion, 1986 has been a disappointing year as to profits, but a year when the Company took significant steps to position itself in an evolving business environment. We enter 1987 with a strong balance sheet and a dedicated and able group of employees who I know will enable the Company to meet its goals of preeminence in the sporting and law enforcement firearms field as well as to become a significant and profitable participant in the investment castings industry.

Super Redhawk Double-Action Revolver: Jay Jarvis Remembers

We had originally talked about taking the Redhawk and changing it to the GP100 style grip, and to the GP100 style trigger mechanism. This would essentially be a large .44 Magnum size GP100. But then there were enough Redhawk fans that Bill thought we should come up with a different gun and call it the Super Redhawk.

That was also at a time that we were having some problems in the field with the barrel shank breaking off a few Redhawks, with a combination of extremely rough usage and a phenomenon called stress corrosion cracking. The particular lubricant that we used at that time on the barrel threads at first was the major contributing factor, so that situation basically disappeared once we discovered this

Badges, buttons, and other memorabilia representing international scope of Ruger law enforcement and government sales. Cartridges of most popular calibers for those markets. Old Remington pump-action rifle suggests possible future law enforcement products from Ruger engineers.

and changed lubricants. It's not a safety problem, but certainly was embarrassing! Rather than just redesign the Redhawk, we made the longer extension on the frame and a much longer thread on the barrel, and that enabled us to get the scope rings mounted back on the frame, and not on the barrel. At the same time we scaled up the GP100 trigger mechanism and grip style. Contemporaneously, we solved the Redhawk barrel shank problem and it remains in production.

There's been talk about every year since then as to whether we want to drop the Redhawk, and come out with a shorter barreled Super Redhawk; and perhaps taking the Super Redhawk and shortening the front of the frame, to make up a shorter version. Most of the design work is already complete on a lot of that. Until the latter part of 1994, we were still considering dropping the Redhawk out of the catalogue.

That's the way most of these things happen. They are put aside and revived, and put aside, and revived with revisions, and at some point are evolved into a final concept, on which Bill then makes a decision to go ahead.

I think his approach is a lot different from the way most everyone else does it. Most of our "competition" decide they want something to fill a certain need, and then go into production; the way all industry generally works.

Bill Ruger goes over ideas for a long period of time, evolving and changing them, and has that uncanny sixth sense about what people want, and when to go ahead with a refined product.

SP101 Double-Action Revolver:
Jay Jarvis Remembers

When the GP100 came out there was some concern about discontinuing the Security-Six, because the GP100 might be considered too big. Some thought we could have problems with law enforcement agencies not wanting our new relatively large-framed .357 revolver. But Bill didn't buy that argument at all, and so we dropped the Security-Six as we came out with the GP100.

The SP101 was to be our small-frame revolver, but originally in .38 Special caliber only. It would have the features of the new trigger mechanism, soft rubber grip, and so forth, but would be like a small GP100. That's the way it was designed, drawn up, and originally produced. But it began to be apparent that the model wasn't going to cut it just as a .38. One day in Newport, self-defense guru Massad Ayoob convinced Bill that it would be just fine to sell it as a .357 as long as you said it could only fire a 125-grain bullet. The problem with that was some 125-grain ammo can be just as long as any of the other .357 cartridges. But Bill didn't want to listen to that argument either.

So we then came out with a .357 version which said on the barrel, ".357 Magnum 125-grain ammo only."

It soon became apparent that there might be a problem with the 125-grain bullet if loaded out to the longer length. Finally, we decided to extend the cylinder and frame size about another $\frac{1}{16}$", essentially taking a slice down through the center of the frame and cylinder and lengthening all of the parts which that plane passed through. We stretched it out to make a true .357. We had only made about 3,000 of the 125-grain short-frame revolvers, which made real collectors' items out of them.

To identify the new longer frame ones we put an X for "extended" in the model numbers of the catalogues and price lists. When we made that change we had a lot of parts inventory to use up. We did that, making .22 Magnums, .32 Magnums, 9mms, and .38 Specials that didn't need the extra length. Once that inventory was used up, all of the revolvers were made with the longer frame and cylinder.

The present gun uses all factory .357 Magnum cartridges, without any qualification whatever, and is extremely versatile and popular.

For a while, some SP101s were made with a little round knob for a hammer spur. But that was awkward looking, and only a few went out to law enforcement—another collectors' item. We don't consider such small changes to be significant, but collectors love them!

Bisley Single-Action Revolvers:
Steve Sanetti Remembers

In the early 1980s, we had been receiving many requests from potential customers that "Ruger should make this or that" new product. One of them was that Ruger reintroduce the Colt Bisley revolver. Larry Larson also thought this was a great idea and immediately began sketching numerous drawings. Bill did not like any of the specific grip profiles that Larry drew, and extensively reworked them. One of Larry's other pet goals was to put some engraving onto the cylinder. He asked me to come up with some pictures of some "old time pistol shooters" so he could do some engraving roll mark dies for the cylinder. I found some pictures in Gould's 1890-era book of *Modern American Pistols and Revolvers* and Larry incorporated two of these gentlemen on a roll die with the words "Ruger Bisley" and some relatively elaborate scroll work.

The initial advertisements and promotional flyers for the Bisleys incorporated this engraving. Immediately before the SHOT Show, Bill saw them and decreed that he did *not* like the engravings whatsoever and that they were to be deleted from all production. Some of the early Bisley advertising shows the Bisleys being available both with and without engraved cylinders. Currently, the only versions available do *not* have any engraving on the cylinders.

Another thought was to make the production of the Bisley models relatively simple, unlike the Colts, which were built with different cylinder frames from the Single Action Army revolvers. We were not entirely successful in this, as the Bisley grip frame placed directly onto a previously manufactured New Model revolver created a pronounced hump where the Bisley grip frame met the polished-down area at the rear of the existing gun's cylinder frame.

Many shooters like the grip frame shape and the curved "Bisley" style hammer/trigger configuration of the Ruger. Many believed that we simply copied Elmer Keith's "No. 5" grip design, but I can tell you that these designs are strictly from Larry Larson and Bill Ruger, with a nod to the original Colt Bisley. Nobody copied Keith's design.

One other aside about the Bisley—I took a 10" barreled .44 Magnum prototype up to the Fairfield County Fish and Game Protective Association firing range one Sunday, and entered my very first "bowling pin" match. (Although they were then quite popular, I'd never even seen one up to that time.)

The Ruger Super Redhawk Double-Action Revolver

Number 550-00001 Super Redhawk Revolver.

Number 550-00001 Super Redhawk Revolver.

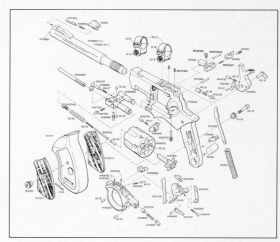

Exploded view and parts identification for Super Redhawk Revolver.

Introduced: 1986. "The ultimate development in a heavy frame .44 Magnum double-action revolver of unusual appeal for today's outdoorsmen, hunters, and metallic silhouette shooters. It has all the mechanical features and patented improvements of Ruger's newest double-action revolvers, the GP100, with a number of important additional features. Unique new Ruger Cushioned Grip panels are anatomically designed to fit the hands of a majority of shooters. The extended frame is designed to accommodate the Ruger Integral Scope Mounting System which positions the scope rearward for superior balance and performance. Interchangeable front sight system. Offered in stainless steel in a variety of barrel lengths. . . . [From] an entirely new generation of Ruger double-action revolvers."

Serial Numbers: 550-00000 to -88134 (through 1993).

Total Made Through 1993: In excess of 86,000.

Caliber: .44 Magnum (.44 Special interchangeable).

Number of Chambers in Cylinder: Six.

Barrel Lengths: 7½", 9½".

Rifling: 6 grooves, right-hand twist, one turn in 20".

Markings: See Table of Markings, pages 330–35.
On left side of barrel:

Before using gun-read warnings in *instruction manual* **available free— from Sturm, Ruger & Co., Inc. Southport, Conn. U.S.A.—**

Sights: Rear sight all steel, adjustable for windage and elevation, with white line outline square notch blade. Ramp front sight base; Redhawk style interchangeable insert sight blades standard. Integral scope mounts; 1" Ruger stainless steel scope rings supplied.

Overall Length and Weight: 13" (7½" barrel), 53 ounces; 15" (9½" barrel), 58 ounces.

Grips: One-piece Monsanto Santoprene, with Goncalo Alves wood inserts.

Finish: Satin-brushed stainless steel.

Materials, Construction, and Innovations: Mechanical design features and patented improvements of the GP100 model (including cylinder/crane locking system, tranfer bar ignition, stainless steel coil springs), with additional details. Massive extended frame, providing substantial bearing surfaces, and relocated barrel threads to allow more than abundant strength and rigidity of barrel mounting. Solid scope mounting surface on exclusive Ruger Integral Scope Mounting System on wide topstrap. Scope mount position permits improved focus and more stable sight picture. Sophisticated open sights. Round barrel with front sight base with insert blades available.

Patented Ruger Cushioned Grip panels: Live rubber grip, with wood inserts, for comfortable, non-slip hold, and cushioning of the shock of recoil. Grip frame design permits use of a variety of custom wood grips.

Low profile hammer spur for improved scope clearance, easy cocking.

Easy takedown for cleaning or field maintenance.

Issue Price: $510.00 (1988).

Price Sheet Listings and Production Variations:

KSRH-7: 7½" barrel model (first published in 1988 price list, but revolvers announced 1986; listing to present).

KSRH-9: 9½" barrel model (first published in 1988 price list, but revolvers announced 1986; listing to present).

The Ruger SP101 Double-Action Revolver

570-00002

Introduced: 1988. "Ruger continues to set the industry standard for small-frame revolvers.... [making] firearm history with the introduction of the SP101 in six-shot .32 H & R Magnum, and five-shot versions in 9x19mm and .357 Magnum. The Ruger double-action revolvers have been widely recognized by knowledgeable police and civilian shooters for their logical design, reliability, exceptional workmanship, and outstanding value.... [they] outshoot and outlast any comparable revolvers made."

Serial Numbers: 570-00000 to -99999; and similarly numbered serial prefix 571-00000 to -61034 (through 1993).

Total Made Through 1993: In excess of 160,000.

Calibers: .22 Long Rifle, .32 H & R, .38 Special, .357 Magnum (.38 Special interchangeable), 9x19mm.

Number of Chambers in Cylinder: Five (.38 Special, .357 Magnum, 9x19mm); six (.22 Long Rifle, .32 H & R Magnum).

Barrel Lengths: 2¼", 3¹⁄₁₆", 4", with full ejector shroud except for .22 Rifle in 4" barrel, made with a short shroud.

Rifling: .22 L.R., .32 H & R: 6 grooves, right-hand twist, one turn in 16".

.357 Magnum (.38 Special): 5 grooves, right-hand twist, one turn in 18¾".

9x19mm: 6 grooves, right-hand twist, one turn in 10".

Markings: See Table of Markings, pages 330–35.
On right side of barrel:
RUGER SP 101 with **R** trademark registration stamp
Caliber marking *on barrel shroud, right side.*
On left side of barrel:
READ INSTRUCTION MANUAL
STURM, RUGER & CO. INC.
SOUTHPORT, CONN. U.S.A.

SR monogram proof stamping *on left side of barrel at breech.*
Trademark stampings *on right side of frame.*
Serial number marking *on right side of frame, above trigger.*

Sights: Fixed, ramp style front sight pinned to barrel.

Overall Length and Weight: 7⅞" (3¹⁄₁₆" barrel); 27 ounces (.38 Special-.357 Magnum).

Grips: Ruger patented recoil-cushioning grip, of Monsanto Santoprene, with inserts of high-impact modified resin of G.E. Xenoy.

Finish: Satin-polished stainless steel.

Materials, Construction, and Innovations: 400-series stainless steel, including most internal parts. Floating firing pin mounted in frame, transfer bar ignition, hammer and cylinder interlock, unbreakable steel music wire coil springs. Exclusive grip design allows for comfortable, accurate shooting, without sapping shooter's endurance. Spurless-hammer version available in .357 Magnum and .38 Special. Cylinder locking notches offset and machined into thick areas of cylinder walls, between chamber centers. Secure locking and alignment of cylinder to frame and barrel at rear (by cylinder pin) and at front of crane (by large latch, spring-loaded). Redhawk system ejection mechanism, with non-rotating ejector rod serving only for ejection. Strong and thick frame under barrel threads, the point of most severe stress.

Issue Price: $370.00 (1989).

Engraving: Serial no. 570-25918 was engraved as a sample for possible sales, on order of William B. Ruger, Sr., embellishments by Paul Lantuch.

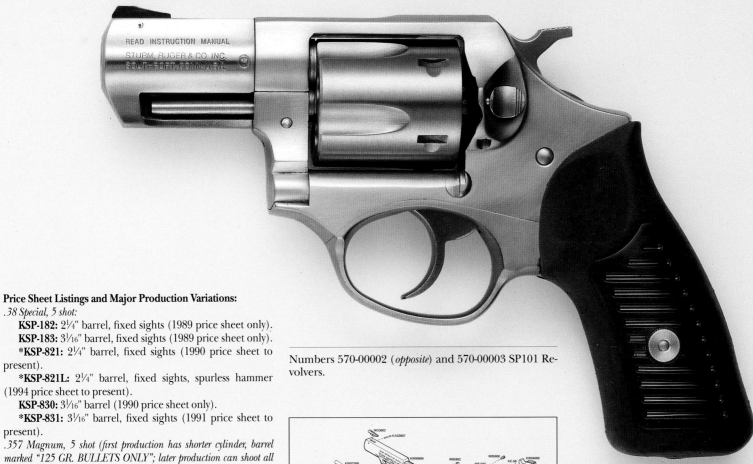

Price Sheet Listings and Major Production Variations:

.38 Special, 5 shot:

KSP-182: 2¼" barrel, fixed sights (1989 price sheet only).

KSP-183: 3¹⁄₁₆" barrel, fixed sights (1989 price sheet only).

***KSP-821:** 2¼" barrel, fixed sights (1990 price sheet to present).

***KSP-821L:** 2¼" barrel, fixed sights, spurless hammer (1994 price sheet to present).

KSP-830: 3¹⁄₁₆" barrel (1990 price sheet only).

***KSP-831:** 3¹⁄₁₆" barrel, fixed sights (1991 price sheet to present).

.357 Magnum, 5 shot (first production has shorter cylinder, barrel marked "125 GR. BULLETS ONLY"; later production can shoot all factory .357 loads):

***KSP-321:** 2¼" barrel, fixed sights (1991 price sheet to present; **x** added to code in 1992).

***KSP-331:** 3¹⁄₁₆" barrel, fixed sights (1991 price sheet to present, **x** added to code in 1992).

***KSP-321XL:** 2¼" barrel, spurless hammer, double-action only (1993 price sheet to present).

9x19mm, 5 shot:

***KSP-921:** 2¼" barrel, fixed sights (1992 price sheet to present).

***KSP-931:** 3¹⁄₁₆" barrel, fixed sights (1991 price sheet to present).

.22 Long Rifle, 6 shot:

***KSP-221:** 2¼" barrel, .22 rimfire, windage adjustable sights (1990 price sheet to present).

Numbers 570-00002 (*opposite*) and 570-00003 SP101 Revolvers.

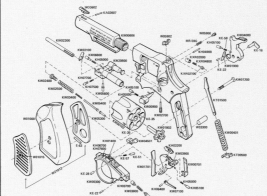

Exploded view and parts identification for SP101 Revolver.

KSP-240: 4" barrel with short shroud, .22 rimfire, windage adjustable sights (1990 price sheet to present).

***KSP-241:** 4" heavy barrel, .22 rimfire, windage adjustable sights (1990 price sheet to present).

.32 H & R, 6 shot:

***KSP-3231:** 3¹⁄₁₆" barrel, windage adjustable sights (1991 price sheet to present).

***KSP-3241:** 4" heavy barrel, windage adjustable sights (1994 price sheet to present).

*Note: As of 1995, *special high-gloss finish* revolvers are identified with the catalogue prefix **G,** and apply to all of the above models marked with an asterisk.

197

After watching the proceedings, and learning that you had to knock the bowling pins completely off the table to score, not just hit them, I took my turn up at the plate. When the whistle blew, I got lucky and the .44 Magnum Ruger Bisley *very conclusively* swept away five bowling pins with five shots. This certainly was in contrast to the effect of the usual 9mms and .45s, which would often simply tip the pins over but not knock them off the table. I can personally attest to the fact that the .44 Magnum Ruger Bisley can quite handily remove bowling pins from the top of any table ever built, even though it was never designed for such an arcane use. I should add that it was also the first .44 Magnum I ever completely enjoyed shooting, that odd-looking grip and comfortable curved trigger really taming its recoil.

From the 1987 Annual Report

I am pleased to report that 1987 was the first year since the beginning of the decade where there was an increase in units shipped over the level of the preceding year. This, coupled with the Company's continued emphasis on cost controls resulted in improved profits and profit margins. Specifically, sales in 1987 were $94.3 million and net income was $8.6 million equivalent to $2.55 per share of Common Stock. In 1986 the comparable figures were sales of $87 million, net income of $6 million equivalent to $1.80 per common share.

This increase in sales is a combination of the general improvement in the demand for firearms throughout the world as well as the success of the Company's engineering innovations and demand for its new double-action revolver, the GP100.

During the year considerable progress has been made to bring the Company's new 9mm pistol, the P85, to full production in the Company's Prescott facility. The demand for this product from commercial and police distributors has been very strong. Enthusiastic response to the P85 from users at various industry shows has also been very encouraging.

In anticipation of continued strong demand for this product, the Company entered into an agreement with Emerson Electric Company at the end of 1987 to take over the remaining forty-six years of a lease between its U.S. Electric Motors Division and the City of Prescott. This lease is for a 200,000 square foot manufacturing facility. The acquisition of the lease on this facility will give the Company all the production facilities that it will need for many years to come.

In conjunction with the anticipated growth of firearms production in Prescott, it is also envisaged that this facility will be the site of another investment casting facility to augment the present facilities in Newport and Manchester, New Hampshire. Initially it is planned that the Prescott foundry will produce aluminum castings to accommodate the demand for this type of product by the many manufacturers located in the growing Southwestern area of this country.

The Company's 45% owned titanium investment casting facility in Oregon has made progress and is rapidly becoming an important supplier of jet engine parts as well as to a growing variety of other industries which use titanium parts.

Last Fall marked an important milestone with respect to the Company's distribution system. It was determined that the Company's position would be enhanced in the ever more competitive firearms industry, especially in the double-action revolver segment which has long been dominated by Smith & Wesson, if the Company's double-action revolvers were carried exclusively by a selected number of distributors. Accordingly it became Company policy to distribute our firearms through a selected group of distributors who would not carry Smith & Wesson revolvers. It was felt that this would increase competition at the retail level by making more Ruger products available to shooters. I felt that this will enable the Company to increase its market share in the double-action revolver segment.

The Company's product liability situation continues to improve. At year's end, there were only 18 "old model" single-action cases, the lowest number in many years. We attribute this to the success of our efforts to remind shooters of the well-known rules for the safe handling of firearms and our ongoing conversion program, now entering its sixth year. Many cases against the Company were summarily dismissed in 1987, and in the two jury trials held last year (*Paisley* in February and *Shields* in September), there were specific findings that the "old model" single-actions were not defective in design. Indeed, the Company has already won yet another "old model" single-action revolver jury trial this year. The Company was also successful in obtaining insurance in excess of its self-insured retentions in 1987.

I am pleased to report that Nils Anderson has been nominated for election to the Board of Directors at the forthcoming Annual Meeting. He brings to the Company many years of experience in a variety of business endeavors.

I look forward to 1988. Last year marked a turning point, not only in our industry, but also in the resurgence of manufacturing in America across a broad spectrum of industries. I, for one, could never believe that it was inevitable that manufacturing and technical know-how had seen its best days in this country and that the economy would be driven to a larger and larger degree by service industries.

The Company, in my opinion, is well positioned as we start the year. It is an acknowledged

---

Ruger Redhawk flush inlaid with gold, silver and copper; ivory grips mounted in gold, with malachite inlaid buttcap; special frost finish; number 500-03211; .44 Magnum. The GP100 flush gold inlaid, number 170-00777; .357 Magnum. SP101 low-relief engraved, as sample for possible sales. Ruger patented paneled cushion grips with Goncalo Alvez inserts. All three revolvers embellished in Renaissance style, for William B. Ruger, Sr., by Paul Lantuch.

The Ruger Bisley Single-Action Revolvers

Number 47-39937 Bisley Revolver, .45 Long Colt, with 7½" barrel.

Number 261-03249 Bisley Revolver, .22 caliber, with 6½" barrel.

New Model Single-Six Frame Series

Introduced: 1985. "An American Tradition Renewed. . . . Now two more thoroughbred models have been added to the line of fine Ruger single-action models—the New Model Bisley Blackhawk and Single-Six revolvers have been subtly modified to adapt the proven Ruger single-action design for precision target shooting, and to suit the most discriminating marksman. . . . [the] marriage of a fine target shooting tradition with a subtly modernized version of the Bisley grip shape which may prove to be just right for many single-action shooters."

Serial Numbers: Shared with Super Single-Six revolvers, beginning in .22 caliber series with serial number prefix range 261-; and continuing within 262-00000 to range -92015 (through 1993).

Also in .32 H & R Magnum series with 650-18600.

Total Made Through 1993: In excess of 8,600 (.22) and 2,800 (.32).

Calibers: .22 Long Rifle, .32 H & R Magnum.

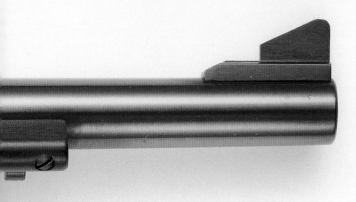

Number of Chambers in Cylinder: Six.
Barrel Length: 6½".
Rifling: .22: 6 grooves, right-hand twist, one turn in 14"; .32 H & R: 6 grooves, right-hand twist, one turn in 16".
Markings: See Table of Markings, pages 330–35.
On left side of barrel:
Before using gun-read warnings in *instruction manual* **available free— from Sturm, Ruger & Co., Inc. Southport, Conn. U.S.A.—**
Sights: Dovetailed rear sight, adjustable for windage, *or* adjustable rear sight for elevation and windage; ramp style blade front sight.
Overall Length and Weight: 11½", 41 ounces.
Grips: American walnut, with trademark medallion inlay.
Finish: Blued.
Materials, Construction, and Innovations: Low hammer profile, smoothly curved, with a deep-checkered wide spur. Strongly curved, wide, smoothly surfaced trigger. Longer grip frame, with distinctive, full shape. Trigger guard of large profile. Straight inside grip profile for firm, comfortable hold. Rear gripstrap screws hidden by grip panels. Non-fluted cylinder to allow for roll engraved Ruger and Bisley names, in a traditional styling.
Issue Price: $258.00 (1986).
Engraving: Roll engraved scene on non-fluted cylinder.
Price Sheet Listings and Major Production Variations* (beginning with 1986 Price Sheet):
  RB22W: .22 Long Rifle, fixed sights (through 1992).
  RB32W: .32 H & R Magnum, fixed sights (through 1992; reintroduced 1994).
  RB22AW: .22 Long Rifle, adjustable sights.
  RB32AW: .32 H & R Magnum, adjustable sights.
  *Code without W indicates revolvers having cylinder with flutes and without roll marking, as noted in 1986 Price Lists. Later Price Lists indicate roll marked cylinders only.

New Model Blackhawk Series

Introduced: 1985. "The frame of the New Model Bisley Blackhawk is identical to the popular Ruger New Model Blackhawk revolvers. The New Model Bisley Single-Six frame is styled after the classic Bisley "flat-top" configuration. Most mechanical parts remain unchanged. . . . These revolvers are, in effect, the target-model versions of the Ruger single-action line."
Serial Numbers Through 1993: *Shared with Blackhawk series as follows:* .357 Magnum: serial range approx. 36-67000 to 37-30115; .41 Magnum, .45 Long Colt: approx. 47-04000 to -55235.
  Shared with Super Blackhawk series as follows: .44 Magnum, approx. 85-05000 to 86-64126.
Total Made Through 1993: .357 Magnum: 5,600; .41 Magnum: 4,400; .44 Magnum: 13,500; .45 Long Colt: 6,700.
Calibers: .357 Magnum (.38 Special interchangeable), .41 Magnum, .44 Magnum (.44 Special interchangeable), .45 Long Colt.
Number of Chambers in Cylinder: Six.
Barrel Length: 7½".
Rifling: .357 Magnum and .45 Long Colt: 6 grooves, right-hand twist, one turn in 16".
  .30 Carbine, .41 and .44 Magnum: 6 grooves, right-hand twist, one turn in 20".
Markings: See Table of Markings, pages 330–35.
On left side of barrel:
Before using gun-read warnings in *instruction manual* **available free— from Sturm, Ruger & Co., Inc. Southport, Conn. U.S.A.—**
Sights: Adjustable rear sight for elevation and windage; ramp style blade front sight.
Overall Length and Weight: 13", 48 ounces.
Grips: American walnut, with trademark medallion inlay.

Exploded view of Bisley Revolver.

Finish: Blued.
Materials, Construction and Innovations: As above, with larger cylinder and frame, to allow for more potent cartridges.
Issue Price: $307.00 (1986).
Engraving: Roll engraved cylinder scene on non-fluted cylinder. Serial numbers 47-05161 and 85-43379 embellished for William B. Ruger, Sr., by Paul Lantuch.
Price Sheet Listings and Production Variations* (from 1986 to date):
  RB35W: .357 Magnum
  RB41W: .41 Magnum
  RB44W: .44 Magnum
  RB45W: .45 Colt
*Code without W indicates revolvers having cylinder with flutes and without roll marking, as noted in 1986 dealer and distributor price lists. Later price lists indicate roll marked cylinders only.

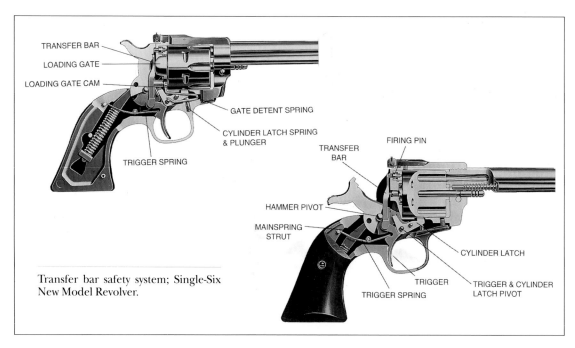

TRANSFER BAR
LOADING GATE
LOADING GATE CAM
GATE DETENT SPRING
CYLINDER LATCH SPRING & PLUNGER
TRIGGER SPRING
TRANSFER BAR
FIRING PIN
HAMMER PIVOT
MAINSPRING STRUT
CYLINDER LATCH
TRIGGER
TRIGGER SPRING
TRIGGER & CYLINDER LATCH PIVOT

Transfer bar safety system; Single-Six New Model Revolver.

worldwide leader in the manufacturing of high quality sporting and law enforcement firearms. In addition it has added to its expertise in the various segments of the investment casting industry which should enable it to become an increasingly important factor in this dynamic, multi-faceted market. Last, but by no means least, the Company has the financial strength to make significant commitments where it views opportunities which will enhance shareholder value.

I look forward to the coming years and thank not only our customers for their support, but most of all the well over one thousand Sturm, Ruger employees, a large percentage of whom have been with the Company over ten years, for their invaluable contributions over the years. They have been an integral part of the Company's success.

Bill Ruger on Computers: Jim Sullivan Remembers

Bill feels vaguely distrustful of computers; he feels that people tend to use them to "do their thinking for them." Although he growls and grumps about the CAD [Computer Aided Design], he still likes it. I suggested once in my last tour of duty with him, "Why don't you bust loose and get us some CAD training and let us get into that a little bit?" That was a "no go"; there was a hrrrumph or two, and that was that. For all of his advanced manufacturing techniques, Ruger products are designed on the boards pretty much as they were almost a half century ago.

He kind of dismisses any suggestion that you've done any purely mathematical analysis; he kind of pooh-poohs it unless you've actually designed and built a real mechanism you can hold and observe. "We make our own principles of physics here at Sturm, Ruger." However, that does not by any means indicate any compromise on safety or durability, or in any other manner or means.

Of course he doesn't mean these things in total, he's just making a point. He's an educated and sophisticated man, and is certainly not ignorant of these things. Just looking at any Ruger gun, or especially picking it up, you know it's been approved by a man who absolutely believes in safety and strength. He just wants people to design it, not machines. After all, a firearm is an intensely personal possession.

The idea that the boss is supposed to be some kind of buddy to all his workers, and be Mr. Nice Guy just doesn't work. There are too many hard business decisions to be made.
—William B. Ruger

Ruger is an icon; he was described once as "the gun owner's guru." All you have to do to appreciate this is see the crowd that he attracts at one of the trade shows. At the NRA show in Phoenix in 1983, when President Reagan was there, Bill Ruger got a bigger ovation than Reagan.
—John M. Kingsley, Jr.

"It's awfully quiet around here, considering the products you make."
—Luigi Chinetti, Sr., champion race car driver and Ferrari importer, on a visit to the Newport factory's Pine Tree Castings operation, 1986

Ruger Bisley .44 Magnum, number 85-43379. Gold inlaid and relief engraved in an art nouveau motif, with browned and blued finish; ivory grips, the American eagle buttcap relief sculpted in silver. Commissioned by William B. Ruger, Sr., from Paul Lantuch, who shows yet another style of embellishment in his repertoire.

CHAPTER VIII

"To Suit Our Own Criteria"

Prescott and the P-Series Pistols
1987–1989

*O*ur centerfire self-loading pistol was under study for many years, but we wanted to make it to suit our own criteria, not to suit someone else's timetable. The U.S. tests were being turned on and off for years, but about two years ago [1985] we seriously decided to go ahead with the pistol's final design anyway. If it came in time for the U.S. trials, that would be good; if it didn't, we still felt that we had the best pistol of its type available and would find a ready market here and elsewhere.

And that's exactly what happened.

—William B. Ruger, Sr.

The Prescott factories; at *bottom right*, the original 10,000 square foot building, later purchased by Ruger distributor, Davidson's. At *left center*, present 205,000 square foot facility. Ruger at *top center* with competitive shooter and early advocate James L. Clark, whose target shooting fame with Ruger pistols and accuracy program actively promote Ruger .22 pistols and the 10/22 rifle. Vertical snapshot at *left* with Jim McGarry, Stan Terhune, Bill Atkinson, and writer/commentator Grits Gresham, at early 1990s SHOT show. Current Board of Directors at *bottom, left to right:* Townsend Horner, Stan Terhune, Nils Anderson, William B. Ruger, Jr. and Sr. (latter next to one of his Duesenbergs), Paul X. Kelley, James E. Service, Richard T. Cunniff; not shown here, John M. Kingsley, Jr. To *right* of Board, Single-Six Ranch, corporate real estate investment and testing facility.

29. 1987
P-Series Pistols

41. 1993
P93 Pistol

44. 1994
P94 Pistol

"We go eastward to realize history and study the works of art and literature, retracing the steps of the race; we go westward as into the future, with a spirit of enterprise and adventure."

—Henry David Thoreau, "Walking"

A Factory in Arizona

The Prescott facility was originally begun by Bill Ruger to occupy himself while spending part of his winters in the relatively mild, dry climate of Arizona, which was beneficial to his by-now severe rheumatoid arthritis. He first hired W. T. "Bill" Atkinson, a renowned barrel maker and rifle and shotgun shooter, to set up a 10,000 square foot operation which would produce the P-series centerfire pistol, already in development at Newport and Southport.

That tiny plant, conveniently located on the edge of the Prescott airport, grew to nearly ninety employees. The first year's production of slightly more than 2,100 pistols in 1987 expanded to more than 30,500 in 1988, and to nearly 85,300 in 1989. In the spring of the latter year the plant moved into a mammoth 200,000 square foot facility on the other side of the airport, the former site of U.S. Electrical Motors, a division of the Emerson Electric Company. The move was set up

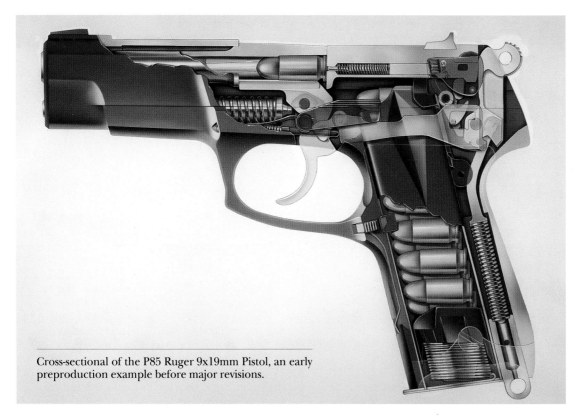

Cross-sectional of the P85 Ruger 9x19mm Pistol, an early preproduction example before major revisions.

room, out of a solid block of aluminum. The first run of guns totalled about ten. I went to Arizona briefly, where they had the little building out on the edge of the Prescott airport. I left the company soon thereafter. (There was a party for me in the front office, in Southport, on my departure. The briefcase they gave me, a black attaché style, has been with me around the world ever since. Some day, I'd like to bring it back.)

Soon, another twenty pistols were built in Prescott. About 200 pistols, the earliest production, were made with a two-piece barrel, the back part cast, the front from cylindrical barrel steel. Some of these were sent out as test samples for writers, who commented less than favorably upon what actually was quite a clever way to make a complicated part. These earliest pistols, for unrelated reasons, were not as accurate as later guns, which unfortunately was a reputation hard to shake.

The P85 at Prescott, Arizona

Stephen K. Vogel, who for many years managed the Ruger export department, was general manager of the Prescott Division from 1988 to 1991. Interviewed in the January 1989 issue of *Shooting Times*, Vogel told the story of the Arizona plant's role in the evolution of the P85, and of Ruger's competition against Beretta and Smith & Wesson for the U.S. military pistol contract:

The P85 was developed in response to potentially large commercial domestic demands, especially law enforcement sales. In addition, the international market was ready for a "new" generation of 9mm pistols.

The PDW [Personal Defense Weapon] . . . testing that resulted in the selection of the Beretta entry as the M9 service pistol was initiated in 1984 . . . the contract award was made in April 1985. Since production of the P85 began in 1986, no candidate pistols were available from Ruger to submit to this test program. P85 test samples were submitted to the Army for evaluation in December 1987, but this second test program was canceled in March 1988.

The P85 test package was submitted to the Army's Aberdeen test facility prior to the due date of August 17, 1988. The package included 30 pistols, 360 magazines, selected spare parts, and associ-

on a long-term lease basis with the city of Prescott.

Although Atkinson wondered at first if the huge new plant would ever be filled up, it took only a few years to put to use all the available space, and the site soon underwent even further expansion. When the Southport factory was phased out (1991), all .22 pistol production was moved to Prescott. There the machines dating from the late 1940s and 1950s, which had been used for the Ruger Standard .22 pistol manufacturing, stand like anachronisms among the state-of-the-art equipment for the P-series pistols, investment casting wax presses, ceramic dipping line, melting furnaces, and space-age vacuum casting equipment for titanium—which give the new plant a twenty-first-century atmosphere.

This virtually self-contained operation starts with ingots of special alloy aluminum, steel, and titanium, and ends up with complex products ready to ship. Sturm, Ruger & Co., Prescott, and Ruger Investment Casting are further examples of Ruger industrial magic.

The P85 Series Pistol: Roy Melcher Remembers

The P85 project was started by Bill Ruger giving Larry Larson and me general directives. Larry did the cosmetics, and I dealt with the mechanism. All we had to do was come up with the finest centerfire autoloading pistol ever made! The layout, drawing, and developmental work, and the prototype parts, were done in Southport, and the pistols were assembled in Newport. The prototype receiver was machined by Alex Santella in the tool and model

ated instruction and maintenance manuals in accordance with the RFTS [Request For Test Samples] issued by the Army in May 1988. Questions were raised by several of the unsuccessful competitors after the 1984 tests were concluded. . . . recent events involving premature failures of the [Beretta] M9 probably influenced the decision to retest the Army pistol.

There is a great deal of bureaucratic inertia that must be overcome in order to select a different pistol. I don't believe the final decision will necessarily reflect the test results—assuming any of the candidate entries successfully pass the evaluation criteria. There are factors other than the actual testing that will enter into making a final decision. The Army will also evaluate the cost proposals submitted by the technically acceptable competitors. If an entry other than the Beretta is considered for selection, the Army has indicated their intention to evaluate the additional costs required to field a different pistol. These costs include new instruction and maintenance materials, potential facility changes for depot maintenance, additional training of combat personnel, the logistics impact of stocking more and different spare parts, etc. . . . these factors could easily outweigh even significant improvements in cost and performance of a different pistol. . . . I expect the P85 will prove to be the top performer during the tests. Hundreds of thousands of rounds of ammunition have been fired in performance testing of many P85s. There has never been a failure of a major component such as the slide, barrel, or frame. In fact, special tests were conducted to demonstrate the inherent safety of this new pistol. In one test, a production weapon was assembled with a standard barrel that had been completely blocked with a steel rod in the bore. The pistol was fired using military high-pressure M882 ammunition. The only damage was a bent extractor that separated from the slide as the case extruded from the chamber. The pistol was field stripped as normal. The barrel wasn't bulged or damaged in any way. The P85 was then reassembled with a new extractor and barrel and test-fired extensively. Although the original barrel would have been serviceable, this pistol was retained in its "as-fired" condition for future use in exhibitions. In another

Relative simplicity of the P85, composed of only 55 parts. A very early P85 Pistol is shown, with a two-piece band, layer slide stop, and other early features, which were later changed (along with other mechanical details).

test, a production slide was modified by removing the entire wall at the right side of the ejection port. Even so severely weakened, the slide showed absolutely no sign of stress when subject to the firing of 2,000 rounds of the M882 ammunition.

The state police of Wisconsin adopted the P85 in 1987. In addition, it has been selected for use by the governments of countries in Central America, Asia, Europe, and the Middle East. The Israeli Air Force, for example, has ordered and received a substantial number of P85s.

The P85 is being considered by numerous domestic law enforcement organizations as well as other foreign government agencies. . . .

[The P85 is competitively priced, at least $100 less than most of the other competitors because] Bill Ruger planned it that way. We have a dedicated facility in Prescott . . . that was designed along with the P85 to assure the most effective product to date would result. Mr. Ruger pioneered the use of precision investment castings in the firearms industry. . . . The Prescott facility is equipped with state-of-the-art computer-numerically controlled machining centers that perform multiple machining operations with a single setup. This requires precise integration of the weapon's design requirements and the

The Ruger P-Series Autoloading Pistols (P85 and Subsequent Models)

Number 300-00001 P85 Pistol.

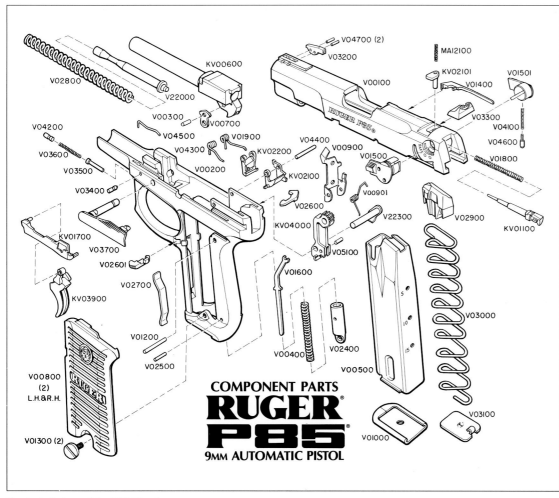

Exploded view of the P85 Pistol.

COMPONENT PARTS
RUGER
P85
9MM AUTOMATIC PISTOL

700,000; *P90:* In excess of 85,000; *P91:* In excess of 22,000.

Calibers: 9x19mm *(P85, P85 Mark II, P89);* 9x21mm *(P89);* .45ACP *(P90);* .40 Auto *(P91).*

Magazine Capacities: 15, in 9 mm, in spring-fed staggered column box. 10-round after September 1994.

    11, in .40 Auto, staggered column box; 10-round after September 1994.

    7, in .45ACP, single column box.

    Magazine loader introduced c. 1989.

Barrel Length: 4½".

Rifling: 9x19mm: 6 grooves, right-hand twist, one turn in 10"; 9x21mm: 6 grooves, right-hand twist, one turn in 10"; .40 Auto and .45ACP: 6 grooves, right-hand twist, one turn in 16".

Markings: See Table of Markings, pages 330–35.

On right side of grip frame:
    BEFORE USING GUN-READ WARNINGS IN *INSTRUCTION MANUAL* AVAILABLE FREE FROM
—STURM, RUGER & CO., INC. SOUTHPORT, CONN. U.S.A.—
Slide marked SAFE on manual safety models; and DECOCK ONLY on decocker models.

Sights: Square notch rear, drift adjustable for windage. Square post front sight. Both with white inserts for rapid target acquisition. Front sight blade quickly removable.

Overall Length and Weight: 7.8", 2 pounds, 9x19mm *(P85, P85 Mark II, P89);* 7.9", 2 pounds, 1.5 ounces, .45ACP *(P90);* 7.9", 2 pounds, 1 ounce, .40 Auto *(P91).*

Grips: Molded G.E. Xenoy high-impact material.

Finish: Originally blued steel slide, sandblasted for matte black finish. Hard-coated aluminum alloy frame, matte black. Both parts glare-resistant overall. Stainless steel versions introduced in 1990.

Materials, Construction, and Innovations: Slide of ordnance quality 4130 chrome-molybdenum alloy steel, or special "Terhune Anticorro" stainless steel, investment cast, and heat-treated for hardness. Aluminum alloy grip frame, investment cast. Designed to be rugged and strong, with ample metal in stressed areas. Unbreakable steel music wire coil springs. Only 52 to 56 individual parts, depending upon model. Disassembly and reassembly possible with minimal, and simple, tools.

    Meets all U.S. military specifications
        designated in the mandatory categories of the Joint Service Operational Requirements, it also includes a number of the Operational Requirements desirable optional features, such as an oversize trigger guard which permits shooting with the gloved hand, a recurved trigger guard bow to accomodate the non-shooting hand in a two-hand hold, a lanyard loop, [originally] fifteen-round magazine capacity, proper functioning with various U.S. commercial and foreign 9mm Luger caliber ammunition, and an expected service life of 20,000 rounds.

Introduced: 1985. "Ruger engineers began the design of the P85 semiautomatic pistol with a clean sheet of paper and an unlimited budget. This fresh start allowed Ruger to incorporate in the P85 pistol the most desirable features and improvements dictated by many years of service experience, without the restrictions imposed by outmoded factories, obsolete machine tools or methods. Throughout the P85 development program, Ruger engineers have taken full advantage of today's advanced technology and sophisticated manufacturing techniques. . . . Rugged, reliable, and simple to manufacture, operate, and maintain."

Serial Numbers through 1993, *P85, P85 Mark II, P89:* 300-00000 to -99999; and similarly numbered serial prefixes 301-, 302-, 303-, 304-, 305-, 307-00000 to -01040; *P90* (.45ACP): 660-00000 to -85009; *P91* (.40 Auto): 340-00000 to -22595.

Total Made Through 1993: *P85, P85 Mark II, P89:* In excess of

Recoil-operated. Tilting-barrel, link-actuated design; barrel and slide locked together securely at moment of firing. Barrel and slide then recoil together for a short distance, locked together. The barrel then tilts downward, unlocking from the slide, allowing full recoil of the slide, and extraction and ejection of the empty cartridge case. Extractor is simple, rugged, strong, durable, and reliable; based on proven design similar to the Thompson submachine gun system.

Loaded magazine can be inserted into pistol whether slide open or closed. Can be loaded or unloaded with safety positioned at "safe." In rapid firing, the magazine can be allowed to drop from its own weight from the grip frame, simply by pressing the magazine release. Magazine with removable floorplate; can be dissasembled without tools.

Firing-pin-blocking safety mechanism, preventing firing pin from contacting the primer until trigger has been pulled fully rearward, while the manual safety is in "fire." When manual safety set in "safe," the hammer and trigger are disengaged entirely, and the hammer is automatically dropped onto the safety's drum, without contact with the firing pin—thereby serving as a decocking lever.

Open-top slide design allows convenient single-loading of cartridge for training purposes, or without magazine. Permits easy and rapid clearing of breech.

Ambidextrous magazine latch and safety (except for the P90), slide stop and magazine latch located within convenient arc of the thumb. Can be comfortably operated without changing handhold while shooting.

Ergonomic grip design; exceptionally tough, and resistant to wear, breakage, and standard lubricants; comfortable, non-slip surface.

Can be field-stripped to five basic subassemblies in seconds, without tools.

Issue Price: $295.00 (1987).

Engraving: Serial numbers 300-16083 and 300-45732 gold inlaid and engraved for William B. Ruger, Sr., by Paul Lantuch.

Price Sheet Listings and Major Production Variations:
9x19mm, Blued:

P85: Standard double-action pistol, 4½" barrel, 15-round, fixed sights, blued finish (first listing, 1987 Price Sheet, through 1990).

P85C: As above, but with case and extra magazine (first listing, 1988 Price Sheet, through 1990).

P85D: 4½" barrel, fixed sights, blued, *decocker-only* model with decocking lever instead of safety lever. Preference of many police departments, since there is no delay of bringing pistol into firing mode. Decocking is achieved by depressing the decocking lever and the pistol returns to the firing position as soon as the decocking lever is released; (1990 listing only). Slide marked "DECOCK ONLY."

P85DC: *Decocker-only* model, as above, but with extra magazine and case (1990 listing only).

P85DA: 4½" barrel, fixed sights, blued, *double-action only*

(1990 listing only). Pistol does not remain cocked between shots; long "double-action" pull required to fire each round.

P85DAC: *Double-action only*, as above, but with extra magazine and case (1990 listing only).
Stainless Steel:

KP85: 4½" barrel, fixed sights (1990 listing only).

KP85C: As above, but with case and extra magazine (1990 listing only).

KP85D: 4½" barrel, fixed sights, *decocker-only* model (1990 listing only).

KP85DC: As above, *decocker-only* model, with extra magazine and case (1990 listing only).

KP85DA: 4½" barrel, fixed sights, *double-action only* (1990 listing only).

KP85DAC: As above, *double-action only*, with extra magazine and case (1990 listing only).
1991 Price Sheet:

P85CMKII: 4½" barrel, fixed sights, *blued* (from 1991 Price Sheet): refinements of changes to the safety mechanism, which

> modify the posititon of the firing pin when locked in the safe position. These changes eliminate the possibility of any transfer of energy from the hammer to the firing pin during the decocking procedure, ensuring the safety of the pistol even in the rare event of a broken firing pin. [1991 Catalogue, p. 14]

With extra magazine and case.

KP85CMKII: As above, in *Stainless Steel.*

KP89DCC: 4½" barrel, fixed sights, stainless steel, *decocker,* with extra magazine and case.

P91DAC: 4½" barrel, fixed sights, blued, *double-action only,* with extra magazine and case.

KP91DAC: 4½" barrel, fixed sights, *stainless steel, double-action only,* with extra magazine and case.
1992 Price Sheet: Standard with 4½" barrel, extra magazine and case.
9x19mm, Blued:

P85CMKII: Ambidextrous safety, and decock lever.

P89DCC: *Decocker-only,* with safety refinement of the P85MKII.
Stainless Steel
9x19mm:

KP85CMKII: Ambidextrous manual safety.

KP89DCC: *Decocker-only* **KP89DC** in Terhune Anticorro stainless, with safety refinement of the P85MKII; available 1991. Terhune Anticorro stainless and 400-series stainless standard in P-series slides and selected parts thereafter, except for blued-finish pistols, which utilize chrome-molybdenum steel slides.

KP89DAC: *Double-action only.*
.45ACP:

KP90C: Manual safety, 7-round magazine.

KP90DAC: *Decocker-only;* 7-round magazine.
.40 Auto:

KP91DAC: *Decocker-only;* 11-round magazine.

K91DAOC: As above, but *double-action only.*

Note: Hard-coated A356T6 aluminum alloy used in grip frames, unless otherwise indicated.
1993 Price Sheet:
9x19mm, Blued, 15-round:

P89: Ambidextrous manual safety.

P89D: Ambidextrous *decocker-only* (**P89DC** in Catalogue).
Stainless Steel:

KP89: Ambidextrous manual safety.

KP89D: Ambidextrous *decocker-only* (**KP89DC** in Catalogue).

KP89DAO: *Double-action only,* stainless steel. Double-action only models made *without* external safety, full-cock hammer position, or decocking lever. Operate similar to a double-action revolver. Firing pin blocked from forward movement by internal safety, until trigger is completely pulled. Spurless hammer.
.45ACP, Stainless Steel, 7-rounds:

KP90: Ambidextrous safety.

KP90D: As above, but *decocker-only* (**KP90DC** in catalogue).
.40 Auto, Stainless Steel, 11-round:

KP91D: Ambidextrous decocker (**KP91DC** in catalogue).

KP91DAO: *Double-action only.*

Note: From 1993 catalogue, but not on price list:

KP88X: Convertible, with two interchangeable barrels (9x19mm and .30 Luger); can be interchanged without tools. New for 1993.

1994 Price Sheet and Catalogue: The most complete list of P-series automatic pistols up to that time *(see also Models P93 and P94, pages TK).*
9x19mm, Blued, 15-round magazine (10-round after September 1994):

P89: Ambidextrous manual safety.

P89DC: Ambidextrous *decocker-only.*
9x19mm, Stainless Steel, 15-round magazine (10-round after September 1994):

KP89: Ambidextrous manual safety.

KP89DC: Ambidextrous *decocker-only.*

KP89DAO: *Double-action only .*

KP89 Convertible: Ambidextrous manual safety, with interchangeable barrels for 9x19mm and .30 Luger.
.45ACP, Stainless Steel, 7-round magazine:

KP90: Ambidextrous manual safety.

KP90DC: Ambidextrous *decocker-only.*
.40 Auto, Stainless Steel, 11-round magazine (10-round after September, 1994):

KP91C: Ambidextrous *decocker-only.*

KP91DAO: *Double-action only.*

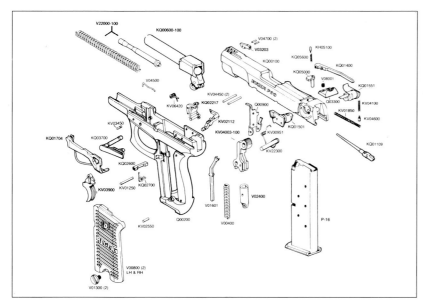

Exploded view of the P90 Pistol.

Number 300-00001 P85 Pistol.

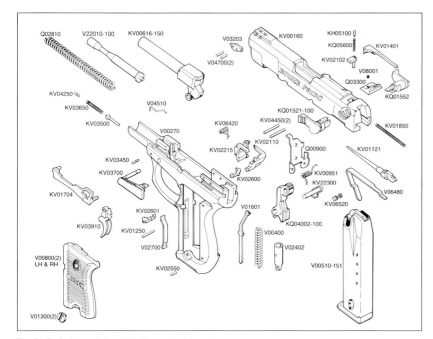

Exploded view of the P91 Decocker Pistol.

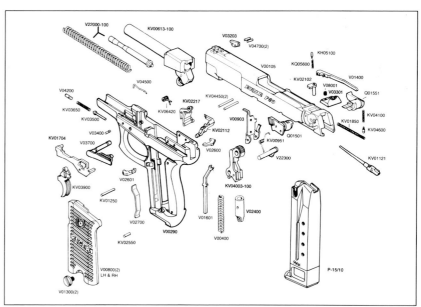

Exploded view of the P89DAO Pistol.

manufacturing facility's capabilities to be successful. Bill Ruger is personally responsible for this. The inspection equipment is both modern and sophisticated. Statistical process controls are being implemented throughout the facility. All of these factors, coupled with a "robust" design philosophy (meaning a design that is easily made), result in an efficiently produced firearm with outstanding performance that costs less.

The SIG/Sauer P226 from West Germany and the Italian Beretta Model 92F appear to be, at this time, the world market competitors of the Ruger P85. Both of these pistols, of course, are at a severe price disadvantage when compared to the Ruger. Neither of the foreign pistols contains all of the advanced characteristics of the P85 design.

I always figured it was Bill Ruger's football and it was his field, and no matter how he wanted to play the game, it was his option. I would get aggravated a lot. For example, on his orders, I spent thirty days making a complete set of layouts of the P85, lowering the centerline of the barrel, bringing it down closer to the top of the magazine by 1/16", even after we had something on paper that we knew would work; but he wanted a new layout. After all this effort, he sat down and looked at it for about five or ten minutes, and he said, "Change it back."

Shortly thereafter I had a stress attack at the factory. I got dizzy and fell out of my chair. Bill was right there; I simply said, "Excuse me; I don't feel so good." He jumped up and stood back, in case I was going to die on him. It turned out that it was aggravated by a sinus infection; but I had to go home and rest.

—Roy Melcher

Ruger P85 number 300-16083, flush gold inlaid in two colors, and engraved in Renaissance style; finished in brown. The back of the frame flush gold inlaid *WILLIAM B. RUGER*. P85 number 300-45732, with relief chiseled, flush gold inlaid, and engraved art nouveau scrollwork. Both pistols with ebony grips and in 9x19mm caliber. Commissioned by Ruger from Paul Lantuch.

Margaret Sheldon's First Meeting with William B. Ruger, Sr.

I well remember the first time I met Mr. Ruger— I had worked for the company for only a short time. Everything was a bustle of activity in anticipation of Mr. Ruger's arrival. The tower called to say that the plane would be landing momentarily and would park just outside the gate. Mr. Ruger had been in the plant for some time before he met with Mr. Vogel, then the Division Manager. Mr. Ruger needed his pen from his office and I was asked to retrieve it. When I presented Mr. Ruger with his pen, I commented how nice it was to have him visiting us. His reply (in his now familiar crusty voice), "I'm not here to visit—I'm here to riiiide herd!!!!" I learned early that his usually gruff exterior camouflaged a witty, sensitive, and unique taskmaster and leader.

The P85 Semiautomatic Pistol: Ruger Remembers

You take some things for gospel only to wake up almost at the edge of some big mistake saying, "Dammit, no, you can't do that." We had a tremendous error in the development of the P85 series pistol and I tell you, it was so embarrassing I was damn well red-faced. We had a thing to block the firing pin if the trigger wasn't pulled, in the manner of most modern autoloading pistols. It was mounted in the frame and as you looked at the static drawings, there it was doing its job, and if you didn't pull the trigger, the firing pin was blocked. What we didn't realize was that if the gun was dropped on the muzzle, the frame containing the firing pin block would be moving forward in relation to the slide and the blocker couldn't block the firing pin, and it could fire. That blocker had to be in the slide with the firing pin, and we promptly put it there. We really caught ourselves just in time—we hadn't shipped any guns. We'd shown some to a few gun writers but we hadn't shipped any.

Tests were then still being performed on the gun. This is when we were getting ready for the U.S. government testing. We hired one of the re-tired old hands from Aberdeen, Otto Hanel, who had done the leg work of the testing on the Beretta M9 pistol, and whatever else was in that competition. He knew the test procedures first-hand. Hanel was retired and was free to function for us as a consultant and was a charming old guy, a real old-time troubleshooter. Everyone in the company liked him. He was out at the Prescott factory. He constructed all the test procedures—cold test, mud test, abusive handling test, accuracy test—just testing these guns exactly as though it was an Aberdeen approved gun. Luckily, it was very easy to fix the firing pin block. In this place for the blocker in the slide, there was a ready way of adding an arm, it had to be there anyway. It just needed relatively little redesigning, and all the production pistols worked perfectly.

Problem Solving

A second-generation Ruger employee, Frank Bonaventura, joined the company fresh out of the Air Force in the 1950s, worked his way up the ladder to Southport plant manager, and by 1992 was manager of the investment casting foundry in Prescott. He knows firsthand about the Chairman's magical knack of problem solving:

> We had a challenging question involving the production of P85 pistol slides, and none of us could come up with a solution. I racked my brain, and discussed this with some of the engineers, and this just plain had us stymied. One Saturday, Bill came into the factory, and I thought it might help to broach the subject with him. He took out a pad and pen and jotted a few things down as I explained this extremely perplexing and frustrating problem. You could almost see the wheels turn, and within 30 seconds flat he had the perfect answer—just straddle mill it. I couldn't believe it . . . just like that. It was truly like a lightbulb, and it went on right before my eyes.

From the 1988 Annual Report

1988 was a year which showed marked improvement over 1987 with increases in both units shipped and produced. The net result was sales of $112,335,000, and net income of $12,657,000, equivalent to $3.77* per share of Common Stock. In 1987 comparable figures were sales of $94.3 million and net income of $8.6 million, equivalent to $2.55 per share.

The Company's results benefited from what I perceive to be a generally stronger market for firearms as well as excellent demand for the Company's new products, especially the P-85. . . . As of this date we have shipped 42,585 P-85's and have a backlog of 94,095 units.

Great amounts of time, effort, and energy were expended in 1988 to make the Company's Prescott facilities fully operational. The second half of the year saw significant production of the P-85 at the Company's original Prescott facility. . . . Concurrently, the 200,000 square foot facility leased from the City of Prescott was refurbished and renovated. By the end of the first quarter, production of the P-85 will be moved into the new facility, and plans are in motion to rapidly expand our production capacity for this product.

In addition, an aluminum investment casting operation has also been located in this facility, with the first castings scheduled to be made by the end of the first quarter of 1989. This in effect will provide the Company with a fully integrated facility equipped with the most modern machine tools available to produce not only the P-85 but other high quality sporting and law enforcement firearms.

It is contemplated further that a titanium investment casting operation will be established in this plant which will enable the Company to

---

*This sum reflects a two-for-one stock split; the 1988 annual report had indicated the dividend at $3.77, per-share earnings prior to the split.

serve the fast growing high tech market in the West and Southwest.

In conjunction with this decision to establish its own titanium investment casting facility, the Company sold its 45% interest in TiLine, a titanium investment casting facility in . . . Oregon.

I am pleased to report that the Company's decision . . . to distribute firearms only through a select group of distributors who would not carry Smith & Wesson revolvers has been eminently successful. I feel that the Company's goal of increasing its market share, especially in the double-action revolver segment, will be realized.

In 1988 the Department of Defense reopened the bidding process for acquisition of a 9mm pistol for the U.S. Armed Forces. The Company has submitted its P-85 in this competition, and I am very hopeful that we will receive a favorable response when a winner is selected late this year. I feel that the P-85 combines all the physical characteristics which are required from the official 9mm pistol for the U.S. Armed Forces and that it will be extremely competitive from an economic standpoint. Intense effort has been expended to insure that all of the Government's qualifications and criteria have been met.

The Company's product liability picture continued to improve in 1988. We obtained a defense verdict in the case of *Iacucci v. Sturm, Ruger* in February 1988, which involved an "old model" single-action revolver. A number of other cases were summarily dismissed, and the number of new cases filed was the fewest in many years. Consequently, at year's end, the number of pending cases was the lowest since 1977. Already in 1989, we have won two jury trials, and the U.S. Supreme Court has finally agreed to hear the constitutionality of punitive damages. Consequently, our liability situation has not been this promising in many years. Of particular interest, our auditors this year have removed the qualification they have previously included in their report on the Company. . . . In other litigation, in January 1988, the Company obtained a $2.8 million

judgment in the case of *Sturm, Ruger v. Arcadia Machine & Tool Company,* in which we proved that A.M.T.'s confusingly similar copy of our popular .22 pistol constituted unfair competition under Federal Law. A.M.T.'s motion for a new trial was denied, and it is uncertain whether they will appeal this decision.

The spectre of increased restriction of the lawful ownership of firearms looms as we enter 1989. Although the Company manufactures no "Saturday Night Specials" or "Assault Rifles" under any accepted definition of these nebulous terms, we are legitimately concerned that efforts to control or eliminate certain types of firearms from lawful channels could either inadvertently or otherwise apply to some of our firearms. We will do all that we can to remind the public of the eternal truth that further restrictions upon law-abiding citizens in the exercise of their fundamental rights to own firearms for legitimate purposes will have absolutely no effect on the plague of drug-related crime. It's time this nation stopped trying to make our honest customers into scapegoats and started coming down hard on the violent few who threaten to destroy our society.

While much progress was made in 1988, I am not unmindful of the fact that our long range goal to broaden the Company's earnings base, so that it is relatively evenly balanced between firearms, investment castings and a third as yet to be specifically identified source, is still to be achieved. Nonetheless, progress is one measure of the success of any organization, and I feel we have made some forward strides this past year, especially in our plan to establish ourselves as a significant factor in the investment casting marketplace. Our goals in 1989, the fortieth year since our founding, are to insure that more progress is made in that direction as well as to maintain our position as the pre-eminent American manufacturer of high quality sporting and law enforcement firearms.

From the 1989 Annual Report

1989 was a significant year for the Company for many reasons, not the least of which was that it marked our 40th anniversary as a high quality producer of sporting and law enforcement firearms.

From a purely statistical standpoint, the year was a tremendous success with record sales and earnings being achieved. Sales reached $133,696,000 and net income was $18,124,000, equivalent to $2.70 per share. In 1988, comparable figures were sales of $112,335,000 and net income of $12,657,000, equivalent to $1.88 per share.

As we entered the year, one of our primary goals was to fully establish the P85 as a leading factor in the commercial and law enforcement 9mm pistol market. I am glad to report that this goal has been achieved. During the early part of the year the production of the P85 was moved into the fully refurbished 200,000-square-foot facility which is leased from the City of Prescott. The demand for the P85 continued throughout the year and remains strong as we enter 1990. Production of this product increased significantly during the year to meet the increasing demand from both commercial and law enforcement markets.

As previously reported, the Company submitted the P85 when the Department of Defense reopened the bidding process for the acquisition of a 9mm pistol for the U.S. Armed Forces. During 1988 and early 1989, the U.S. Army tested several other 9mm semi-automatic pistols, ostensibly to decide whether to continue with the existing supplier's pistol or to adopt a new design. For this purpose, Sturm, Ruger submitted a test package. . . . Other companies did the same. The test procedure was clearly established and involved the firing of tens of thousands of rounds to test all aspects of pistol performance. However, as a result of all this testing, the government decided to continue with the existing supplier, Beretta, and they expressed satisfaction with its performance. The fact remains, however, that the Beretta pistol has a well-documented tendency to have slide fractures—a "catastrophic failure" in which the slide breaks in two, according to government reports. I find the government's decision inexplicable.

The Company has also made excellent progress in establishing a modern investment casting foundry in the new Prescott facility. It presently has the capability of producing high quality aluminum and ferrous investment castings. By mid-year it is anticipated that the titanium foundry currently under construction will also be operational. Upon completion, this will give the Company the unique capability to offer high quality investment castings in many materials to serve the large southwest market.

As has been the case for many years now, there continues to be an ongoing debate concerning the right of responsible citizens to own firearms for legitimate purposes. I know I speak for many people when I say that I deplore the violence and tragedy that is reported so often in connection with the misuse of firearms. However, experience shows the futility of attempting to control the drug and crime problem that plagues the urban areas of this nation through gun control legislation, and this has been for many years the majority view throughout the nation. Congress is supposed to give the gun control issue further consideration this year and allow for some nominal changes. Our prediction is that if there is any congressional action, it will have no material effect on our affairs.

I am glad to tell you that the Maryland Handgun Roster Board has approved all models of Ruger firearms for sale within that state, and has specifically recognized their utility for legitimate and honorable activities by law-abiding citizens. An unlikely source, perhaps, but in these troubled times it is gratifying to see the facts prevail. While much so-called "assault weapon" legislation was discussed last year, none of the Com-

Cross-section from the myriad of publications devoted to the shooting sports and law enforcement, and representative of the responsible use of firearms. Majority of these publications picture Ruger firearms on covers. Among the numerous writers who have covered Ruger products are (from *top left*) Pete Kuhlhoff, John T. Amber, Skeeter Skelton (between Steve Vogel and Jim Triggs), Jim Baker (standing with Ruger), Jeff Cooper, and Charles Askins, Jr. From *top right:* Peter Barrett (in red jacket), filmmaker/writer (*Conversations with Bill Ruger*) Roger Barlow holding rifle and large group of writers at Pine Tree Castings on announcement of Over-and-Under shotgun. Author and Smithsonian Institution curator (Department of Military History, National Museum of American History) Dr. Edward C. Ezell, to *left* of cylinder frame, had begun present book; cut short by Ezell's untimely death in December 1993.

pany's products was the object of any legislative prohibition at any level. This is, of course, as it should be, since throughout our 40-year history we have manufactured nothing but the highest quality firearms for the legitimate sporting, personal protection, and law enforcement markets.

The Company continues to expend considerable time and effort with respect to the product liability situation about which I have previously reported. During 1989, the Company prevailed in three jury trials, as well as experiencing a marked decrease in new cases filed against it. As a result, the number of cases pending against it at year end continued to decline versus the comparable number a year ago. However, the product liability issue is a serious threat, not only to Sturm, Ruger & Company, but to all American enterprise and investment.

In January of this year, the Company filed a registration statement in connection with a proposed secondary offering of shares primarily by me and Joanna Sturm. We are the two largest shareholders of the Company and this proposed sale would simply represent a logical step in diversification for both of us. Since January, the securities market in general has been very unsettled. This, coupled with a decrease in the per share market price of the Company's stock to a level which I deem unattractive, has resulted in the decision to withdraw the registration state-

A few of the celebrities who either owned Ruger firearms or were otherwise associated with the founder or the Ruger firm, over the years. At *top left*, Ruger with President Ronald Reagan and Sturm, Ruger Washington emissary Ron Crawford, at a Washington, D.C., reception. In addition to Presidents Nixon, Carter, Bush, and Reagan, note H.R.H. Prince Abdol Reza, Congressman Cecil King, Hugh O'Brian, Bill Mauldin (cartoonist), Jamison Parker, Fess Parker, Patrick Swayze (in a still from John Milius's *Red Dawn*), the Buffalo Bill Historical Center board of trustees (Chairwoman Mrs. Margaret Coe at front, to *right* of Ruger), and gun-related dignitaries John T. Amber, Peter Barrett, former NRA Executive Vice President Warren Cassidy, Herb Glass, Mikhail Kalashnikov, Jim Rikhoff, and Roy Weatherby.

ment at the present time.

As the Company begins its fifth decade, it is a logical time to ask what the future holds. Obviously no one can answer this question precisely and any response will be no more than one man's "educated guess." Nonetheless, I see the future as one where there will always be room for the manufacturer of high quality firearms for legitimate sporting and law enforcement purposes. I also see an excellent future in the Company's continuing expansion, investment, and commitment to the production of a broad spectrum of high quality precision investment castings applicable to both commercial and aerospace markets.

In January 1990, the Company lost a true friend and counselor with the death of G. Richard "Dick" Shaw. He had served as a Director of the Company since 1973 as well as being a marketing consultant. He had a myriad of friends in the industry as anyone would attest who tried to walk across the convention floor [with him] at any of our trade shows. We will miss him very much and are very grateful to have counted him among our friends.

Ex-Marine Officer R. R. Stutler Appointed General Manager, 1991, Prescott Factory

A Marine veteran of Vietnam and crises around the world, Robert R. Stutler rose through the ranks and retired as a major. He was hired in 1987 by Bill Atkinson to work in assembly, but his talents were quickly recognized by Bill Ruger, who promoted him to run the Prescott facility upon the death of Steve Vogel. During his service, Stutler was on the staff of General P. X. Kelley, commandant of the Marines, who has been on the Board of Directors of Sturm, Ruger since his own retirement.

Stutler's father was a professional gunsmith with a lifetime of hunting and shooting experience. He brought his son up totally dedicated to the shooting sports. At the age of twelve, the boy's picture was in *The American Rifleman*, with an antelope he had shot.

Stutler is representative of the dedication of company employees at all levels. "My dream was to work for Bill Ruger and this company." As General Manager of the Prescott factory, he oversees manufacture of large quantities of units a year, charting production and shepherding output with military precision.

The factory is a model of efficiency and enlightened production techniques. With the state-of-the-art, multi-station CNC machines predominating, at some stations one operator can run as many as six simultaneously. Because of the advanced technology of investment casting, the sophisticated machinery, the totally thought-out product design, and the perfectly coordinated production, the double-shift work force of only 300 can build an amazing number of products.

In the front office are Bob Stutler and his group, and the R & D staff under Bill Atkinson—design engineers like Jim McGarry and Mike Smisko. Strategically placed between McGarry and R & D is Bill Ruger's own office.

While showing the latest prototype rifle, in the final stages of development, the founder remarks that working with McGarry on this project has been "like a great chess game." McGarry will take a cue from Ruger on a design change, then develop as many as three alternatives, expressed in precise terms, from which the best approach can be selected. Working together they have created what will be the newest addition to a line which is the envy of any gunmaker.

In the furthest reaches of the facility is a section set up for part of the Ruger car collection, where Lyle Patterson attends to the Bentleys, Rolls-Royces, Stutzes, Packards, and the Ruger Tourer, working with the same dedication one finds throughout Sturm, Ruger. Patterson can switch from shotgun technology to the most intricate antique automobile engine or chassis in the collection, without skipping a beat. He is one of many who share an interest in fine cars and fine firearms, which have in common many concepts of interrelated mechanisms, functionality, and aesthetics.

The Magazine Capacity Controversy

It was June 9, 1989, and Jay and Barbara Hansen, owners of Hansen & Co., were in Prescott, Arizona, for the wedding of Steve and Molly Vogel's son, Kurt, and his fiancée, Billy Jean. Barbara made Jay promise, before they flew west, that Jay would not get into any discussion with Ruger about a letter he had sent to every member of Congress, regarding regulation of the largest capacity magazines as a substitute for the "assault weapon" bans then being considered. Barbara summed it all up by saying, "There's no damned way I'm going if you do not swear to totally abstain from discussing that subject with Molly's father."

On their arrival at the hotel in Prescott, one of Ruger's people, Bob Thompson, presented the Hansens with an invitation to dine at Ruger's condo in Prescott that evening—with him, Mary, Bill Jr., Charlie Rogler, and some other guests.

Shortly after they all started their first cocktail, Ruger looked at Jay and said something like, "Well, Jay, I suppose a lot of people you know think I'm a horse's ass for my statement on magazine capacity."

Hansen recalls, "Boy, there was silence in that room, I'll tell you. 'Head don't fail me now.'" After contemplating Ruger's statement for a moment, Jay explained that a number of people who visited with Jay periodically "were disappointed about Sturm, Ruger's position on magazine capacity. This was the most diplomatic way I could conceive of at that time to tell him that I and others were unhappy, and yet trying not to personalize it."

Ruger made no reply.

The proposed magazine capacity limitation substitute for so-called "assault weapon" bans was not an idea exclusive to Sturm, Ruger, but had been approved by the 14-member Sporting Arms and Ammunition Manufacturers' Institute (SAAMI). The brunt of the furor over the SAAMI statement, however, was borne by the outspoken Ruger. Among the sentiments voiced in the press is this excerpt from Cameron Hopkins's column in the *American Handgunner*'s September/October 1989 issue:

> I respectfully disagree with Mr. Ruger. The problem with the illegal misuse of firearms is not magazines, it's not guns, it's not caliber, it's not action type. The problem is the criminal. Criminals that steal guns, criminals that waltz through the revolving door of our wrist-slapping court system.

The theory of SAAMI, a group which included, among others, Remington, Winchester, Browning, Mossberg, Marlin, and Smith & Wesson, was that Congress's restricting the magazines to fifteen cartridges would refocus the public debate on limiting firepower rather than on creating lists of "assault weapons" and banning "bad" firearms. The idea was therefore to take a responsible position to head off any further restrictions that might even have banned *all* semiautomatic firearms from civilian possession in the public furor over some widely publicized mass crimes in which so-called "assault weapons" were used. Bill Ruger, as usual, was determined to make his voice heard.

Some gunowner lobbying groups were incensed at this position. The president of the Gunowners of New Hampshire, Alfred Rubega, said gunowners felt "betrayed" by the SAAMI position. There were statements by some that they would no longer buy or sell Ruger firearms. However, sales have risen every year since 1989.

Congress ultimately passed an "Assault Weapon" Ban in 1994. The latter not only banned magazines over ten shots (five shots fewer than conventional practice and the SAAMI proposal), but also banned the manufacture of nineteen groups of military style firearms, which, in effect, banned about 185 self-loading firearms. For these reasons, Ruger opposed the law, even though all Ruger rifles were properly exempted by name as "legitimate sporting firearms." Whether or not those laws will be modified is an open question, but the public's mood, reflected in the November 1994 elections, is clearly against the restrictive gun control theories of certain social engineers.

Recall on the P85 Pistol— a Broken Firing Pin

In 1990, Ruger discovered that if the original P85 firing pin was broken in precisely the right place, the gun might fire when it was decocked. Despite the fact that only one out of 200,000 pistols had malfunctioned, Ruger instituted a recall of all P85 pistols made between 1987 and 1990. The statement published by the company indicated that if "the firing pin is broken, these pistols may fire when the safety or decock lever is depressed . . . [contact the company] and we will schedule your pistol for a FREE factory safety modification to prevent such firing. This offer does *not* apply to P85 Mark II pistols, pistols with an "R" on the manual safety, or any other P-Series pistol." The statement further noted:

> These firing pins are very durable and breakage has occurred only in a handful of cases. In the interest of complete safety, users should *always* point the pistol in a safe direction when decocking. However, the new design components eliminate the possibility of this kind of accidental discharge.

All Ruger P-series pistols produced since 1991 have safety/decocker/firing pin components that preclude this situation, and fortunately, no injuries have occurred that can be traced to a broken firing pin.

The P93 and P94 Pistols: Bill Atkinson Remembers

The P93 and P94 projects were about half done in Newport and half in Prescott, depending on where Bill Ruger was at the time. A lot of work on these pistols was done in Newport, but production was planned to be done in Prescott. The waxes, dies, and castings were adapted and developed in New Hampshire. The idea was to come up with so-called compact and streamlined versions of the P-series, and although they do not have single column magazines, these pistols are about as compact as their basic design permits. They're not small guns, by any means. We just don't make small pistols.

We took the buttresses off the receiver and the slide, to make a smooth surface on the outside. The P89, P90, and P91 all had the original frame with a buttress on the side ahead of the trigger, like a flute on a revolver cylinder. There were a few internal changes as well, to improve smoothness and durability. The first drawings were made in Southport, under Bill's supervision. We added slide serrations in the back for ease of opening. We also extended the front rails of the receiver to allow more surface for the slide to ride on. Bill put a radius on the front of the slide and the receiver. This rounded off the front instead of being blunt and flat like the P89, P90, and P91.

On the P94 we moved the chamber ahead .0047". But basically most of the internal parts are interchangeable between the current P-series pistols. The P93 and P94 frames are the same, except for their length; the latter is a little bit longer. Then we also made the limited production, law enforcement-only P94 Laser sighted pistol, which is another story entirely.

Profusion of Ruger memorabilia, some made for employee Christmas gifts (including mugs, factory-site cup plates, and watches). Many of these items have become collectibles themselves. Majority of staff pictures in this photograph from Southport office, including long-term employee Walt Sych, at *center foreground*, with Bill Ruger, Jr. Early 10-year Club dinner at *left center*. Pictures in *right foreground* taken at December 1994 retirement party for Marie Sorge, secretary to Ruger, Sr., for 17 years, and with the company for 30 years; shown with Maureen Graziano of Marketing Department, Mr. Ruger and John Kingsley. Now retired Corporate Secretary Gloria Biagioni with her successor, Leslie Gasper, at *right center*. Rodeo queens wear custom-made Ruger chaps, perform at Prescott and other rodeos. Pistol with gold inlaid trademark inscribed and presented to Ruger, Sr., from "Everyone at Sturm, Ruger Christmas 1971," number 11-23222.

The Ruger P93 Compact Autoloading Pistol

Number 306-00142 P93 Pistol, in stainless steel.

Introduced: 1993. "Condensed design, expanded performance."

Serial Numbers: 306-00000 on up.

Calibers: 9x19mm.

Magazine Capacity: 15, in spring-fed staggered column detachable box magazine; 10-round after September 1994.

Barrel Length: 3⁹⁄₁₀".

Rifling: 6 grooves, right-hand twist, one turn in 10".

Markings: See Table of Markings, pages 330–35.

On right side of grip frame:

> **BEFORE USING GUN-READ WARNINGS IN**
> *INSTRUCTION MANUAL* **AVAILABLE FREE FROM**
> —**STURM, RUGER & CO. INC.**—

Slide marked DECOCK ONLY on decocker models.

Sights: Square notch rear, drift adjustable for windage. Square post front. White dots on front and rear sights for rapid target acquisition.

Overall Length and Weight: 7⁹⁄₁₀", 31 ounces. Height, 5¾". Width, 1½".

Grips: 6123 Xenoy resin.

Finish: Matte, with satin-polished stainless slide and gray-finished frame.

Materials, Construction, and Innovations: Compact, streamlined configuration.

Built from hard-coated A356T6 aluminum alloy, 400-series stainless steel, and the exclusive Terhune Anticorro stainless steel. 6123 Xenoy resin grip panels. Steel magazines.

Recoil-operated, double-action, autoloading. Quick exchangeable front sight. Tilting barrel, link-actuated.

Issue Price: $520.00 (1993).

Price Sheet Listings and Production Variations:

KP93DC: *Decock-only,* stainless steel, 9x19mm, 15-round (10, as of September 1994), 3⁹⁄₁₀" barrel. Zytel grip frame (listing only). 31 ounces. Tapered-side slide. Introduced in 1993.

KP93DAO: *Double-action only,* spurless hammer, stainless steel, 9x19mm, 15-round (10, as of September 1994). 3⁹⁄₁₀" barrel. Zytel grip frame (listing only). 31 ounces. Tapered-side slide. Introduced in 1993.

Number 306-00142 P93 Pistol, in stainless steel.

The Ruger P94 Autoloading Pistol

Number 308-00142 P94 Pistol, in stainless steel.

Introduced: 1994. "Midway in size between the full-size P-series and the down-sized P93 models. . . . available in six new models . . . from three configurations: Double-Action-Only, Decock-Only, and Manual Safety; and two calibers: 9x19mm and .40 Auto."

Serial Numbers: 308-00000 on up.

Calibers: 9x19mm or .40 Auto.

Magazine Capacity: 15, in 9x19mm, spring-fed staggered column detachable box.

11, in .40 Auto, spring-fed staggered column box. Both changed to 10-round from September 1994.

Barrel Length: 4.2".

Rifling: 9x19mm: 6 grooves, right-hand twist, one turn in 10"; .40 Auto: 6 grooves, right-hand twist, one turn in 16".

Markings: See Table of Markings, pages 330–35.

On right side of slide:

STURM, RUGER & CO. INC.

SOUTHPORT, CONN. U.S.A.

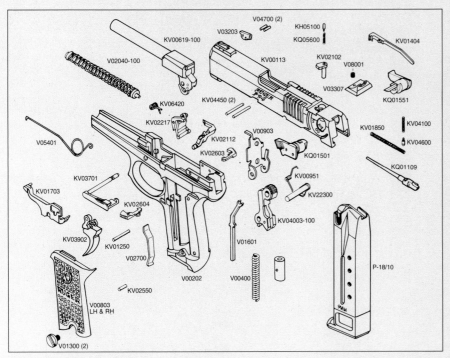

Exploded view of the P94 Double-Action Only Pistol.

Number 308-00142 P94 Pistol, in stainless steel.

On right side of barrel breech:

9x19mm [*proof mark*]

or

.40 Auto [*proof mark*]

On right side of grip frame:

BEFORE USING GUN–READ WARNINGS IN
INSTRUCTION MANUAL **AVAILABLE FREE FROM**
—STURM, RUGER & CO., INC.—

Serial number on *right side of grip frame, above front of trigger guard.*

On left side of slide, depending on model:

RUGER   RUGER   RUGER
P94   P94DC   P94DAO

Slide marked SAFE on manual safety models; DECOCK ONLY on decocker models.

Grips embossed with trademark motif and **RUGER.**

Sights: Square notch rear, drift adjustable for windage. Square post front. White dots on front and rear sights for rapid target acquisition.

Overall Length and Weight: 7.6"; 33 ounces.

Grips: 6123 Xenoy resin.

Finish: Matte, with satin-polished stainless slide and gray frame.

Materials, Construction, and Innovations: Larger than P93, but sharing that model's sleek, streamlined shape.

Built from hard-coated A356T6 aluminum alloy, 400-series stainless steel, and the exclusive Terhune Anticorro stainless steel. Slimmed and checkered 6123 Xenoy resin grip panels. Steel magazines.

Recoil-operated, double-action, autoloading. Quick exchangeable front sight. Tilting barrel, link-actuated. Ambidextrous safety/decocking levers (excepting on double-action only models), and magazine release.

Issue Price: $520.00 (1994).

Price Sheet Listings and Production Variations (* indicates 10-round magazine capacity as of September 1994.):

KP94: 9x19mm, manual safety, stainless, 15-round.*

KP94DC: As above, but *decock-only.**

KP94DAO: As above, but *double-action only.**

KP944: Manual safety, stainless, .40 Auto, 11-round.*

KP944DC: *Decock-only*, stainless, .40 Auto, 11-round.*

KP944DAO: *Double-action only*, stainless, .40 Auto, 11-round.*

P94L*: For law enforcement and military sales only, this advanced design was termed by *Shooting Times* as "the world's first regular-production integral laser handgun. . . . It is an extremely well-thought-out, well-engineered product." The beefed-up forward section of the grip frame holds the laser equipment, powered by five hearing aid batteries. TacStar Industries produces the patented laser system for Ruger. At 75 yards the dot measures 1½"; the red dot will project, and can be observed, to a range of 500 yards, in darkness. The battery supply lasts approximately one hour of continuous usage. To turn the laser on or off, the ambidextrous switch is mounted on the sides of the laser housing, forward of the trigger guard—easily reached by the trigger finger, at the ready for firing. Ruger experiments with laser sights go back to the mid-1980s.

CHAPTER IX

"The Basis of a Free Market Economy"

RGR on the New York Stock Exchange
1989–1992

Y ou need to have a certain work ethic, or modus operandi, to be successful at Sturm, Ruger. Low-key management style happens to be to our taste. Some other company's managers may look flashier, but they do not have the same quality or productivity, nor do any of the other product lines offer equal value.

Everybody works here. A couple of people came here from larger companies, and lacked a certain willingness to roll up their sleeves and do what had to be done. They didn't last long.

Somebody said the Sturm, Ruger table of organization looked like a rake, with Bill the handle, and everybody else the teeth. There are not a lot of fancy offices or big staffs. This starts with Bill himself, who is the mainspring. This was never more dramatically brought home to me than in the spring of 1989, when we looked at purchasing the Colt Firearms Division of Colt Industries. On meeting at the Colt offices, we

---

Specimen stock certificates, with documents and memorabilia from Sturm, Ruger on Wall Street. Delegation of June 20, 1990—when Ruger stock was first listed on the New York Stock Exchange as "RGR"—at *lower right* (positioned vertically) with then-Company Secretary Gloria Biagioni and (*at right*) William B. Ruger, Jr., and stock exchange and investment officials. Dinner in the wine cellar at the '21' Club celebrated the successful completion of a secondary offering of Ruger stock personally sold by Joanna Sturm and Bill Ruger, at $24 a share.

---

31. 1990
M77 Mark II Bolt-Action Rifle
32. 1989
All-Weather 77/22 Bolt-Action Rifle
33. 1990
77/22 Magnum Bolt-Action Rifle
34. 1991
Mini-Thirty Rifle
35. 1992
Super Blackhawk Hunter
Single-Action Revolver
36. 1992
22/45 Autoloading Pistols
37. 1990–1992
Magnum and Express
Bolt-Action Rifles
38. 1992
Mark II Target Bolt-Action Rifle

---

found they had about five people to every one of our delegation, and they were on the verge of bankruptcy.

In this firm the challenge is to be flexible enough to know the nuts and bolts, and to be able, for example, to make a presentation to a security analyst, and give the big picture. It's a challenge we've met, in special stock issues, in June 1990 and July 1993.

The importance of gun expertise, and the tremendously widespread interest in firearms, was even brought home to us while on the "road show" with the stock issues. We often found that after presenting information on the company and why it was an outstanding investment, questions from the interested investors and their agents would quickly turn to guns, like, "When are you going to bring out a 28 gauge?"

—John M. Kingsley, Jr.
Executive Vice President
Sturm, Ruger and Company, Inc.

"There are forms which time adorns, not wears, and to which beauty obstinately clings."
—Lord Byron

(Bill Ruger is the source of this quotation but according to him, it may be spuriously attributed to Byron; Ruger found this quotation engraved on a sterling silver plate that was screwed to the supercharger housing of a 1929 4.5 liter Bentley automobile. Whatever its source, Ruger thought it applied equally to some of the classical firearms and liked it so much he even used it in his advertising.)

From the 1990 Annual Report

Sales for the year 1990 reached the record level of $135.5 million, a slight advance over the old record of $133.7 million reached in 1989. However, net income for 1990 was $13.5 million, the second highest annual result in the history of the Company, as compared to 1989's all-time record of $18.1 million. . . .

Since our annual financial results are so directly affected by market conditions and the way in which we respond to these conditions, it is appropriate at the outset to enlarge upon how we view the Company in its two markets: firearms and, to an increasing extent, precision investment castings.

The strong and increasing interest in autoloading pistols over the last few years seems to us to be a stable and continuing phenomenon. We have responded by augmenting our line of 9mm pistols during 1990, and plan to introduce three new pistols in two new calibers, .40 and .45, in 1991.

We have significantly broadened our line of bolt-action rifles to include firearms made entirely of stainless steel, rifles equipped with fiber reinforced plastic stocks, and new, large, high power rifles of luxury quality. The latter are in a higher price category than any of our previous products, and though we do not expect unit volume comparable to lower priced rifles, we expect ample rewards in profit and prestige.

All these new products have added a considerable increment to the steady sales of our now well accepted lines introduced in earlier years. Further, we have a considerable array of new products in various design phases, for which we have high future expectations.

The Company saw the completion of two sales incentive programs in the first half of 1990. These programs were very successful in increasing market share, maintaining sales volume in difficult market conditions, and reducing a somewhat high finished goods inventory. We fully anticipated the cost of these programs and considered them necessary in 1990. We do not, however, foresee the need for any such program in 1991.

In the past year we have seen a continuing expansion of our . . . investment casting foundry in Prescott. . . . As of mid-1990 [we] began the production of titanium investment castings in an entirely new and completely equipped facility. Our Prescott Foundry Division is one of only eight facilities in the country which has the capability of producing titanium investment castings.

Our Pine Tree Castings Division in Newport . . . and our Uni-Cast Division in Manchester . . . continue to refine their processes and capabilities, and we are making a major effort to place our precision castings in both commercial and aerospace markets throughout the country. We look to our castings divisions as a major diversification, and expect them to provide an increasing portion of net income in the future.

Anti-firearms legislation is always a matter of concern. However, despite a flurry of "gun control" legislation at all levels in 1990, none of the Company's products has been the subject of any legislative prohibition. We continue to work at the national, state, and local level to help point out the fallacy of attempting to control violent criminals by the political expedient of enacting ever increasing controls upon law-abiding firearms owners.

The Company began, voluntarily, offering a free safety modification of its P85 pistols late last year, based on one instance of a broken firing pin, which resulted in a pistol firing when being decocked. Fortunately, no injury occurred because the shooter took the proper care to keep the pistol pointed in a safe direction. A new pistol under development at the time, the P85 Mark II, utilizes a system which prevents such firing, even given the remote possibility of a broken firing pin, and we decided to offer to factory retrofit the new system free of charge to existing P85s. A pretax charge of $3 million was taken in the 3rd quarter of 1990 to cover the anticipated cost of this program, and therefore there should be no further adverse financial effect arising from this program.

In mid-1990 General Paul X. Kelley, USMC Ret., former Commandant of the U.S. Marine Corps and member of the Joint Chiefs of Staff, joined our Board of Directors. General Kelley brings to the Company a breadth of experience which we welcome. As a result, we are all strengthened, and as a Board, possess an enhanced perspective in our guidance of the Company.

In June 1990, a secondary offering of shares in the Company was completed. This offering was mentioned in the 1989 Annual Report but had been postponed at the time the Annual Report was published. The selling shareholders were primarily myself and Miss Joanna Sturm. . . . Our reasons for doing this were primarily to achieve greater diversification of our own personal assets. As a result of this sale, it became possible to have the Company listed on the New York Stock Exchange, where trading commenced in June 1990 under the symbol RGR.

I regret to report the passing of Edward P. Nolan in September 1990. He had served the Company since 1956 in the capacities of Sales Manager, Vice President of Marketing, and Representative in the Northeastern United States. He is missed by all of us in the Company, and by his many, many friends in the firearms industry.

We remain thankful for the successes we have had and grateful in the realization that these successes are the measure of the dedication and conscientiousness of our employees, the loyalty of our customers, the faith of our shareholders, and the friendship of all of them.

From the Press Release When Sturm, Ruger & Co. Went onto the Big Board

June 20, 1990 was a milestone in the company's history. On that date, Sturm, Ruger & Company, Inc., was listed on the New York Stock Exchange. Now known to Wall Street and investors by the ticker symbol "RGR", Sturm, Ruger enjoys the benefits—and responsibilities—that accompany a listing on the Big Board.

On hand for this historic occasion were company officials and guests who were welcomed to the floor by officials of the New York Stock Exchange.

The company listed 6,807,200 shares of common stock.

Said William B. Ruger, Sr., chairman and treasurer: "Listing on the New York Stock Exchange was a significant step for Sturm, Ruger & Company, Inc. It represents the next logical step in a program designed to broaden interest in our stock while at the same time offering our present and potential . . . stockholders immediate access to an efficient, safe, and growing auction marketplace."

When Sturm, Ruger shares began trading on the New York Stock Exchange, it joined a select group of the nation's largest, most important corporations.

These corporations—which comprise the NYSE list—are among the most well regarded, influential, and dynamic in the nation. This does not mean that only very large corporations qualify for an NYSE listing. Size is considered, of course. But in reviewing a company's qualifications, the Exchange also takes into account such factors as profitability, the degree of national interest in the company, its ranking and stability within its own industry, and the prospects for the industry's growth. . . .

Selected longarms from Bill Ruger's collection, with carved walnut nineteenth-century German hunter's bench; *left to right*, Colt Model 1855 revolving rifle, serial number 1419, .36 caliber, six-shot fluted cylinder; Model 1874 Sharps rifle, .40 caliber; Colt Burgess lever-action rifle, number 2285, .44-40 caliber; Springfield Officers Model, dated 1878 on top of breechblock, *SWP/1885* proof marking on left side of stock, .45-70 caliber; Winchester High Wall Single Shot rifle, .45 3¼ caliber, number 2 barrel, hard rubber buttplate, number 82278; Remington-Keene bolt-action rifle, deluxe engraved, .45-70 caliber; Springfield sporter bolt-action, with custom Mannlicher stock, checkered steel buttplate, .30-06 caliber, number 517320. The designer/gunmaker's personal Ruger No. 1 Single-Shot with sling; .270 Winchester caliber, number 270, left side of frame gold inlaid with WBR monogram; Ruger 10/22 with International style stock, number 51896; Ruger XGI number 800-01449, .308 caliber; Ruger 77/22 in .22 Winchester Magnum in *foreground*.

An important benefit of an NYSE listing is the complex system of rules the Exchange has evolved for self-regulation. For example, about eight times a year specialists face a detailed review by the Exchange staff of every trade made during a selected random period. Specialists and the trading in their stocks are also subject to continuous electronic surveillance through the "stock watch" program. Built into the Exchange's vast computer system is a profile of trading activity of every one of the more than 1,600 listed issues. Whenever trading exceeds certain predetermined guidelines, the computer alerts Exchange staff and a floor official may be sent to the individual specialist's post—or the company itself may be called to determine whether it has any explanation for the unusual activity in its stock.

The extensive surveillance of Exchange trading activity is matched by Exchange regulation of its member firms. Exchange rules provide that member firms carrying accounts for customers must have a prescribed amount of capital and must file annually a financial questionnaire based on an audit by the firm's independent public accountants. All customers of member firms must be offered or furnished with a copy of the firm's financial statement once a year. Member firms must also file monthly a Joint Regulatory Report of Broker/Dealer's Financial and Operational Conditions with the Exchange. . . . an NYSE listing encourages a broader stock ownership base. . . . A listing on the Big Board almost invariably brings a company to the attention of investors throughout the United States and around the world. In this country alone, some 3,500 offices and branches of Exchange member firms help publicize and distribute information about listed companies. More than 600 U.S. daily newspapers carry complete or partial stock tables. An estimated 4,000 radio and television stations devote time to stock prices and corporate news.

Another important aspect of the diversification of ownership made possible by an Exchange listing is the increase in interest on the part of financial institutions. As a matter of course, institutional investors gravitate towards NYSE-listed securities. Many of them, in fact, are limited by law or their own policies to listed securities when buying industrial, rail, and utility common stock for their portfolios. The bulk of all institutional equity holdings are in NYSE-listed stocks. In fact, institutions now hold over one-half the value of the shares listed for trading on the Exchange. . . .

Listing on the New York Stock Exchange was a significant milestone for Sturm, Ruger & Company. . . .

M77 Mark II Bolt-Action Rifle

The M77 Mark II contained a number of detailed improvements that Ruger had long been contemplating for the centerfire bolt-action rifle line. The question of a bolt locking safety mechanism had been raised during the mid-1980s. While it was certainly desirable to lock the bolt with the safety so that the bolt handle could not accidentally be raised and cause a misfire, it was also desirable to be able to unload a firearm with the safety "on," even though the theoretical moment of possible firing was very brief (the instant between the time the safety was disengaged and when the bolt handle began to be lifted). Ruger decided to incorporate a three-position safety, and he adopted this completely from the Ruger 77/22 bolt-action rifle.

To prevent the floorplate from accidentally unlatching and dumping cartridges at the shooter's feet during recoil, Ruger developed a patented latch, which, while flush with the front of the trigger guard, operated by pressing forward from the *outside* of the guard, totally eliminating that possibility.

Further, some shooters did not like the plunger style ejector present in the original M77, since it ejected cartridges with some velocity even if the bolt were operated slowly. Ruger had just completed work on the Ranch rifle, which has a fixed-blade-type ejector. By translating that design into the bolt-action rifle, he basically recreated the original Mauser concept.

The first M77 trigger design had a number of possible adjustments. Although the company warned in the instruction manual against any adjustment other than *increasing* the weight of the trigger pull, the screws were there, possibly inviting mischief by some of the more adventurous shooters. An adjustable trigger was considered the mark of a fine rifle when the M77 was introduced in the 1960s.

However, the climate of litigation was very much changed by the mid-1980s. A non-adjustable trigger, operating in conjunction with a three-position safety, and with the capability of unloading the rifle through the hinged floorplate, was desirable from a product liability standpoint. The M77 Mark II features a quality trigger, but it is not adjustable. Like the three-position safety, the trigger design was largely adapted from that on the M77/22. Shortly after its introduction, a new version featuring a very distinctive injection-molded synthetic stock combined with a stainless steel barreled action was introduced as the Ruger "All-Weather" rifle, completing the marriage of the twentieth-century technology and materials to a traditional design.

The Ruger All-Weather 77/22 Bolt-Action Rifle: Jay Jarvis Remembers

There came a point when Bill decided it was time to go to synthetic stocks. The newly developed synthetic materials had great durability and cost advantages over wood stocks and older "plastic" stocks, and especially appealed to shooters who hunted in bad weather. His idea always combined an injection-molded synthetic stock with stainless steel, an industry first. We had talked about this for a couple of years, planning to use the Mini-14 rifle as a logical beginning. We drew up a plastic folding stock for the Mini-14, but this was about when there was concern about so-called "assault weapon" legislation. So Bill suddenly said, "Let's put a synthetic stock on the 77/22." At that time the only molded plastic stock around, outside of the old Savage, was the Remington Nylon 66.

We started drawing this up, working with a very respectable injection molder, and put the drawing into prototype form. In the beginning we worked with Nypro, and with Du Pont on materials. We came up with a finalized design which we then put out for quotations. At some point we gave an order to Hubbell Plastics.

Hubbell then procured the die, and we went ahead using the Du Pont Zytel—their super tough nylon, which is the same material from which M16 buttstocks were made. The most radical thing on the stock, and one that remains controversial, is the butt portion being relieved on the sides—certainly a nontraditional stock style! But we are used to setting styles ourselves, and it is also functional. The scalloped butt is a less costly way of getting the bulk out of the butt end of the stock. To make the normal style of stock out of molded plastic, the mold would require a complex core in the back, vastly complicating manufacture. In the system we used, there is no separate core required, thus the stock is functional as well as stylish.

The inserts on the grip and the forend are there for the same reason. In order to get the mass and bulk out of the plastic, elongated holes are molded into the outside of the stock. To fill up the holes, the inserts were used. They were green at first,

Art nouveau style embellishment flush gold inlaid on Ruger 77/22 rifle (at *left*); gold inlaid scope rings, bolt knob, receiver, trigger guard, frame around magazine, and front barrel band; 20" barrel; number 700-06182. M77 International style rifle, with gold inlaid and engraved floorplate, breech, barrel, scope rings, forend cap, front sight ramp, rear sight, bolt handle, trigger guard, and pistol grip cap (note gold-mounted bloodstone); the serial number, barrel, and receiver markings flush gold inlaid; the bolt handle relief chiseled; 19" barrel; number 78-15396. Engraved receiver and bolt handle on Mini-14 Ranch Rifle, with gold inlaid markings on breech; 18½" barrel; number 187-10132. Commissioned by William B. Ruger, Sr., decorated by Paul Lantuch.

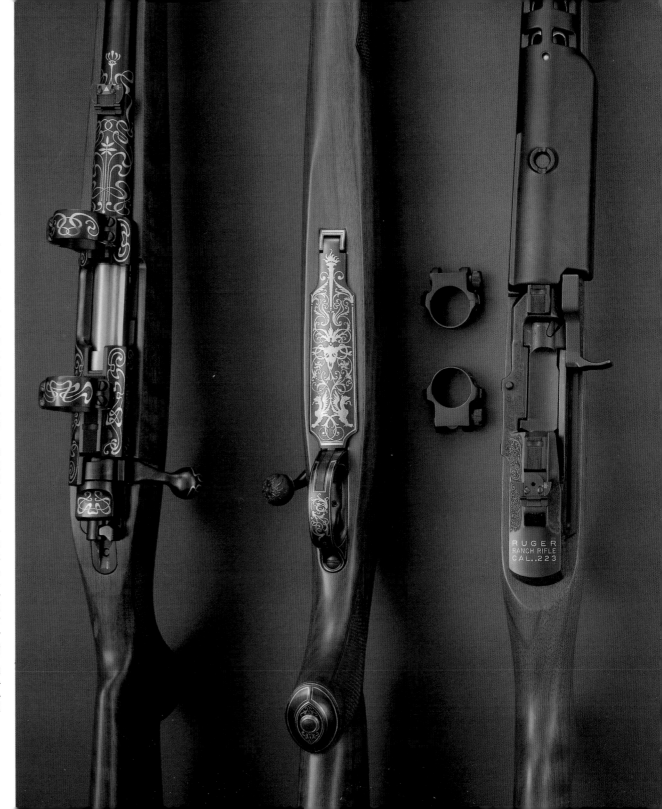

The Ruger M77 Mark II Bolt-Action Rifle

Number 780-00560 M77 Mark II Ultra-Light Bolt-Action Rifle, .223 caliber, with 20" barrel.

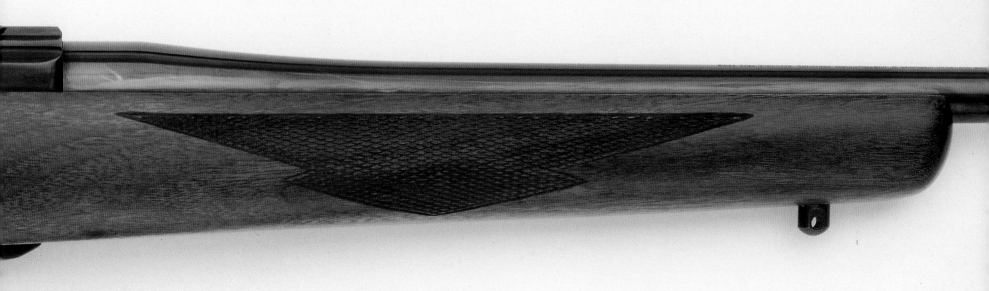

Introduced: 1989. "The perfect hunting rifle. . . . an evolutionary design based on Ruger's experience making millions of sporting rifles. . . . a handsome utilitarian rifle. . . . Crisp positive ejection, handsome design, and famous Ruger strength have made the Mark II a classic."

Serial Numbers: 780-00000 to -99999; and similarly numbered serial prefix 781-, 782-00000 to -02684 (through 1993).

Total Made Through 1993: In excess of 190,000.

Calibers: .223, .22 PPC, .22-250, .220 Swift, 6mm Remington, 6mm PPC, .243 Winchester, .257 Roberts, .25-06, 6.5 x 55 Swedish, .270, 7 x 57mm, .280 Remington, 7mm Remington Magnum, .30-06, .308, .300 Winchester Magnum, .338 Winchester Magnum, .458 Winchester Magnum.

Magazine Capacity: 4-round (3 in Magnum calibers). Hinged floorplate, secured with patented latch; staggered integral box magazine.

Barrel Lengths: 18", 20", 22", and 24", depending on variation. 26" in Target rifle.

Rifling: Right-hand twist standard. Number of grooves and pitch of rifling varies according to caliber.

Markings: See Table of Markings, pages 330–35.
Approximately midway on top of barrel:
Before using gun-read warnings in *instruction manual* **available free— from Sturm, Ruger & Co., Inc. Southport, Conn. U.S.A.—**

Sights: Integral scope base mount on receiver, for Ruger 1" steel scope rings.

Open iron sights on some variations.

Overall Length and Weight: International Rifle at approx. 6¼ pounds, overall length (with 18" barrel) of 38½".

Ultra Light rifle at approx. 6 pounds, overall length (with 20" barrel) of 40¾".

Target rifle at approx. 9¾ pounds, 26" barrel, overall length of 46¼".

Stocks: American walnut. All-Weather rifle in Zytel polymer. Target rifle in laminated wood.

Finish: Blued, or stainless steel. Target rifle with Ruger's own target-gray antireflective finish.

Materials, Construction, and Innovations: 3-position safety. Non-rotating Mauser-type extractor. Controlled round feeding. Fixed-blade ejector. Right-handed action standard, with left-handed available in major long-action calibers (.270, 7mm Remington Magnum, .30-06, and .308).

Target rifle featuring Terhune Anticorro stainless steel in the bolt and action; barrel in 410 stainless steel. Target rifle with two-stage trigger; free-floating hammer-forged barrel. Resin-filled laminated stockwood; forend wide and flat-bottomed.

Issue Price: $531.25, M77R and M77 RP MK II; $587.00, M77RS MKII (1990).

Price Sheeting Listings and Major Production Variations:
Blued (first listed in the 1989 catalogue and Price Sheet as):

77R M77 MKII: Receiver with integral dovetails to accommodate Ruger steel rings. Scope rings are included (no sights) (Price Sheet); the catalogue listed the rifle available only in .223 Remington caliber, with 20" barrel, overall length 39¾". Weight, approx. 6 pounds 7 ounces, catalogue number **M77 MK II RL.**

The 1990 Price Sheet carried a table of six available versions, in calibers .223, 6mm, .243, .308 (7.62mm), and the new **Ruger Magnum** (see page 238) in .375 H & H and .416

Number 780-52520 M77 Mark II Bolt-Action Rifle, .30-06 caliber, with 20" barrel.

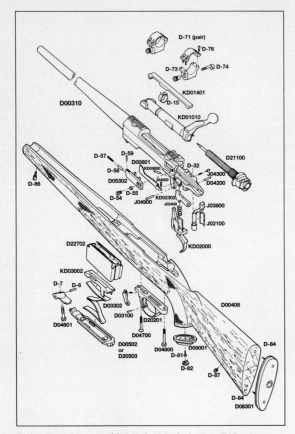

Exploded view of M77 Mark II Bolt-Action Rifle.

RUGER M77 MARK II: models by caliber, catalogue number, and barrel length

Caliber	M77R MKII	KM77RP MKII	M77RS MKII	KM77RSP MKII	M77RSI MKII	M77RL MKII	M77LR MKII	KM77VT MKII
.223	22"	22"	-	-	-	20"	-	26"
.22 PPC	-	-	-	-	-	-	-	26"
.22-250	22"	22"	-	-	-	-	-	26"
.220 Swift	-	-	-	-	-	-	-	26"
6mm Rem.	22"	-	-	-	-	-	-	-
6mm PPC	-	-	-	-	-	-	-	26"
.243 Win.	22"	22"	22"	22"	18"	20"	-	26"
.257 Roberts	22"	-	-	-	-	20"	-	-
.25-06	22"	-	22"	-	-	-	-	26"
6.5x55 Swedish	22"	-	-	-	-	-	-	-
.270	22"	22"	22"	22"	18"	20"	22"	-
7x57mm	22"	-	-	-	-	-	-	-
.280 Rem.	22"	22"	-	-	-	-	-	-
7mm Rem. Mag.	24"	24"	24"	24"	-	-	24"	-
.30-06	22"	22"	22"	22"	18"	20"	22"	-
.308	22"	22"	22"	-	18"	20"	-	26"
.300 Win. Mag.	24"	24"	24"	24"	-	-	24"	-
.338 Win. Mag.	24"	24"	24"	24"	-	-	-	-
.458 Win. Mag.	-	-	24"	-	-	-	-	-

Variations of the M77 Mark II Bolt-Action Rifle, from the 1995 catalogue.

Rigby. The catalogue code numbers of rifles in these calibers offered a total of 17 variations, broken down as follows.
.223, 6mm, .243, .308 (7.62mm):

77MKIIR: Receiver with integral dovetails for Ruger steel rings, no open sights.

KM77MKIIRP: As above, of stainless steel, and with All-Weather Zytel stock.

M77MKIIRS: As above, except also fitted with open sights.

M77MKIIRL: Ultra-Light, 6 lbs., with black forend tip.

M77MKIIRLS: As above, but with 18½" barrel, and open sights.

By the 1991 Price Sheet, the options had been developed noticeably further, with new calibers added to the above of .270,

.30-06, 7mm, and .300 Magnum. The left-handed bolt-action (**77LRMKII**) was featured on pages 1, 4, and 5 of the 1991 Catalogue: " . . . the long-awaited left-handed version of the M77 Mark II. . . . in several popular calibers . . . not just a modified right-handed version, but a true mirror image rifle designed and built as a left-handed firearm from concept to packaging." Ejection port, safety, bolt handle, extractor, and bolt stop all located on correct side of rifle for left-handed shooters.

By the 1992 price sheet, the options had expanded still further (although some versions of the original M77 bolt-action rifle were still carried in the line). The Ruger Express rifles, **77RSEXP,** were first listed in 1992.

The 1993 price sheet had a considerably expanded listing, and offered the 6.5 x 55 Swedish among its total of 18 Mark II calibers, not counting the four Express calibers and the two in the Magnum.

The 1994 price sheet and catalogue presented the most exhaustive options in the history of the company, in lists and descriptions so detailed that the catalogue table on page 5 is illustrated with all available options, except for barreled actions (**77RBAMKII:** all calibers, no open sights; **77RSBAMKII:** all calibers, with open sights).

233

The Ruger All-Weather 77/22 Bolt-Action Rifle

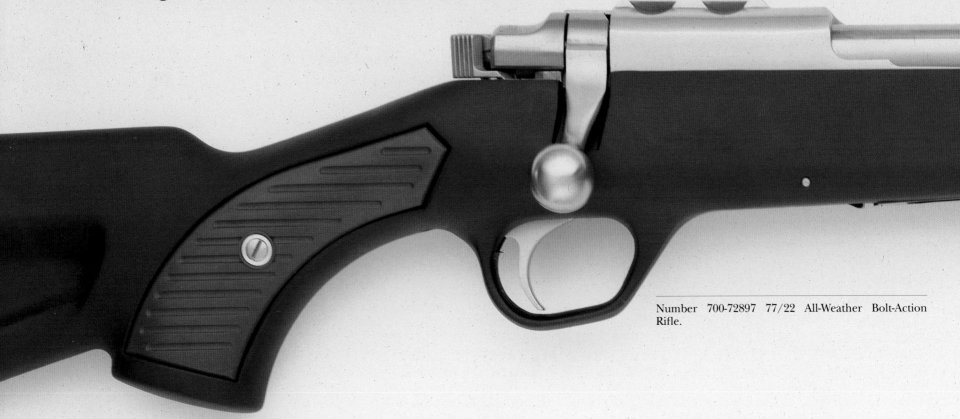

Number 700-72897 77/22 All-Weather Bolt-Action Rifle.

Introduced: 1989. "The first factory, all-stainless steel, bolt-action .22 with a high-strength, injection-molded all-weather stock."

Serial Numbers: 701-00000 to -65008 (through 1993); serial numbers intermixed with 77/22 .22 L.R. and Magnum rifles.

Total Made Through 1993: In excess of 30,000 (for .22 L.R. only; for figures for stainless steel and blued .22 Magnum All-Weather.

Calibers: .22 Long Rifle or .22 Magnum.

Magazine Capacity: 10, in rotary detachable box (.22 L.R.), 9-round capacity for the .22 Magnum.

Barrel Length: 20".

Rifling: .22 Long Rifle, 6 grooves, right-hand twist, one turn in 16"; .22 Magnum , 6 grooves, right-hand twist, one turn in 14".

Markings: See Table of Markings, pages 330–35.

On top of barrel:

Before using gun-read warnings in *instruction manual* available free— from Sturm, Ruger & Co., Inc. Southport, Conn. U.S.A.—

Sights: Folding sporting style open rear, with blade front. Integral scope bases, patented Ruger Scope Mounting System; 1" scope rings.

Overall Length and Weight: 39¼", 5 pounds, 12 ounces.

Stocks: High-strength, injection-molded Zytel polymer, black, with green or black inserts in forend and grip areas.

Finish: Satin-polished stainless steel.

Materials, Construction, and Innovations: Du Pont Zytel injection-molded stock, 6/6 glass-fiber reinforced nylon. Slip-resistant, grooved side and forend panels of chemical and impact resistant G.E. Xenoy 6123, a modified resin. Heat-treated

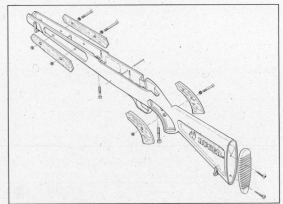

Exploded view of synthetic stock for 77/22 All-Weather Bolt-Action Rifle.

234

Number 701-74959 77/22 All-Weather Bolt-Action Rifle, with black stock panels.

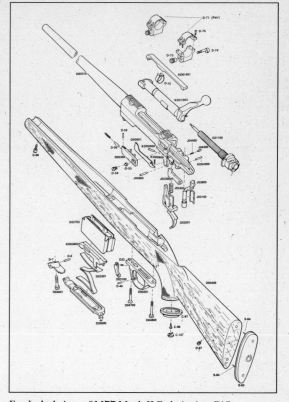

Exploded view of M77 Mark II Bolt-Action Rifle.

ordnance quality 400-series stainless steel. Light in weight and resistant to extremes of weather.

Other performance features of the barrel and action as detailed for the Model 77/22, see page TK.

Issue Price: $300.00 (1989).

Price Sheet Listings and Production Variations:

Blued:

77/22RP: No open sights, with 1" scope rings (1989 price sheet through 1992).

77/22SP: Iron sights, scope rings not included (1989–1991).

77/22RSP: With iron sights *and* 1" scope rings (1989–1993).

Stainless Steel:

K77/22RP: No open sights, with 1" scope rings (1989 to present).

K77/22SP: Iron sights, scope rings not included (1989–1991).

K77/22RSP: With iron sights *and* 1" scope rings (1989 to present).

K77/22RMP: In .22 Magnum, with 1" scope rings (1990 to present).

K77/22RSMP: In .22 Magnum, with iron sights *and* 1" scope rings (1991 to present).

On Friday, January 2, 1992, Jack Behn retired from Sturm, Ruger. From the original Ruger Corporation days, his family-owned firm, H. J. Behn & Co., Inc., had been a supplier; Jack called regularly as a salesman, and friend. In 1969, when his company was sold, Behn was appointed Sturm, Ruger's Purchasing Agent. Besides being a gun, car, and watch collector, Behn was a machinist, and fully understood manufacturing techniques and innumerable related subjects. Over the years, this depth of knowledge and experience saved the company untold millions in costs, and untold hours in design and production time. Quoting Harry Sefried: "Jack could tell us designers to change a part a certain way, which would permit use of a stock type of fixture, screw, or bolt, whatever. He also knew processes like castings and cold-forming, and other significant time and cost savers." At *center, left to right,* Behn, Mike Horelik, Ed Nolan, and Hugh O'Brian (TV's Wyatt Earp). Sequence in cold-formed scope ring clamp to *right* of .22 Standard pistol frame. Comic M77 "best quality" rifle, a good-natured gift from Newport factory personnel chiding his exactitude. Behn with wife Lou, flanked by the Rugers, Sr. and Jr., at retirement party, attended by nearly 100 suppliers (all of them friends), relatives, and Ruger company employees.

which did not prove to be popular. But we soon went to black and also have a very attractive wooden insert, the latter available from Lett Mfg. Co. This practical rifle is unmistakably a Ruger.

77/22 Magnum Bolt-Action Rifle: Jay Jarvis Remembers

When the 77/22 was first drawn up and designed, it was only made with a receiver to accommodate the .22 Long Rifle cartridges. I had suggested many times to Bill that we at least build this long enough for the .22 Magnum, because it was not of that much greater length, and it would not change the appearance or configuration of the rifle that much. It was clear that the gun would certainly be strong enough.

But at that time, Bill's feelings were that "the .22 Magnum was dead." He'd been hearing that from various sources. But I hadn't been out of Winchester too long at that point [Jay left Winchester in 1981 and came to Ruger in October of that year], and kept reminding him that we had sold a lot of .22 Magnum rifles and ammunition.

Finally he did agree to make the necessary changes, which we could readily change by altering the waxes and thereby the castings. However, we still had to develop a rotary magazine which would accommodate the longer Magnum cartridge length. That was a very difficult thing to draw and lay out. However, once it was laid out and a prototype made, you could see what was working and what was not, and we made the required adjustments.

There were other changes we needed to deal with, like the trigger guard, the magazine aperture, and so on. The next problem was getting the synthetic stock to take the new magazine. We needed a new set of cores for the bottom of the mold, and again we worked with Hubbell, the stockmakers. We came up with a way of having interchangeable cores, so that by changing those you could run either the .22 Long Rifle or the .22 Magnum stock, and applied for a process patent.

From when we decided to go ahead [1989] to the time of completion, it only took us about a year. The difficulty was basically a magazine problem.

The rest was relatively easy and a matter of simple layouts, making the drawings, and producing a couple of new castings, and was very straightforward once the magazine was finalized. It's this kind of fast-track but solid engineering approach that lets Ruger get new products to market quickly, instead of the years it generally takes the competition.

From the 1991 Annual Report

I am pleased to report that the operating results for 1991, after a slow first six months, turned out quite satisfactorily, especially when viewed in light of the grim economic news emanating from many quarters of the economy. Specifically, in 1991, sales totaled $136.8 million, net income $14.6 million, and earnings per share $2.17. Sales were the highest ever achieved and exceeded the previous record of $135.5 million reached in 1990. The net income and earnings per share were both the second highest achieved in the Company's history. Comparable figures for 1990 were sales of $135.5 million, net income of $13.5 million, and earnings per share of $2.01.

1991 was a landmark year in the Company's history in that the decision was made to close the Company's Southport, Connecticut manufacturing facility. This facility had been in continuous operation for over thirty years and was the main-spring for the Company's expansion during the 1960's and 1970's. However, during the last decade, there had been a gradual reduction in the demand for the products produced by the Southport plant. These were primarily Single-Action Revolvers and .22 caliber Autoloading Pistols. This situation, coupled with the fact that the Company has ample manufacturing floor space available in both Newport . . . and Prescott . . . dictated that this move be made. The Company will continue to produce Single-Action Revolvers in Newport . . . and Autoloading Pistols in Prescott . . . to accommodate a continued demand for these products, albeit at a lower level than existed a decade ago.

Decisions such as the foregoing are never easy, especially when there is a history of a long relationship with a loyal group of men and women whose efforts were so vital in helping establish the Company as the leading manufacturer of small arms during this period. I acknowledge with great thanks and appreciation their collective efforts. Nonetheless, these decisions, hard as they are, must be made if a Company is to survive, prosper, and grow in what is becoming an increasingly more competitive global market place. However, Southport will remain the site of the Company's Headquarters.

There has been much discussion recently about the "global nature" of the marketplace and America's ability to compete successfully in this marketplace. Concurrent with this discussion has been increasing evidence that America has been losing its leadership position as a manufacturer in many industries, most notably steel, automobiles, and electronics. Many causes for this decline have been articulated and many remedies proposed.

As the Founder and Chief Executive of the Company which has grown over the last forty plus years to a preeminent position in its industry, I would like to make a few observations. America has been declining as a manufacturing economy, and this trend cannot be observed without concern for the future.

American manufacturing needs more support and less antagonism from Government. American politics being what they are, it is doubtful that there will be any improvement in the foreseeable future, but our shareholders in particular should take every opportunity to influence change.

There are certain areas that, as a result of various factors which have evolved over the past decade, have become virtual millstones on the backs of American manufacturing companies attempting to compete in the global market or even survive profitably in the domestic market. I

refer particularly to the areas of medical insurance, workers' compensation insurance, and product liability costs. Volumes have been written with respect to each of these areas with a multitude of, to date unsuccessful, solutions having been proposed. . . .

Taking the three foregoing areas, your Company, with annual revenues of $136.8 million, spent approximately $14 million or 10.2% of each sales dollar to cover these costs. These figures in no way convey the distraction product liability claims impose on management and the amount of management time which has to be spent in the course of defense. This is particularly frustrating in view of the fact that these suits are frequently spurious, make exaggerated claims, jeopardize the livelihood of employees, and have the effect of throwing cold water on the production and sale of products which are needed and wanted, as well as affect the productive impulses that are the basis of a free market economy. Our Company is typical of thousands which labor under these handicaps. It is almost sickening to hear political candidates offering such placebos in their campaign speeches as "Soaking the Rich" and/or meaningless tinkerings with tax rates.

To summarize the foregoing, I believe in Corporate responsibility, and so does our whole Company, but the time has now come when the Government and particularly Congress should be concerned about Government responsibility.

On a more positive note I am glad to report that during 1991 and into early 1992, we have introduced new products and model variations to appeal to our ever more demanding and diversified customer base. The new P90 and P91 pistols, in .45 and .40 caliber, in both standard, decock-only, and double action only models are perfect examples of this sort of product enhancement. Our new "22/45" pistol combines the grip angle and magazine latch of the famous Government .45 automatic with the proven Ruger Mark II ac-

The Ruger 77/22 Magnum Bolt-Action Rifle

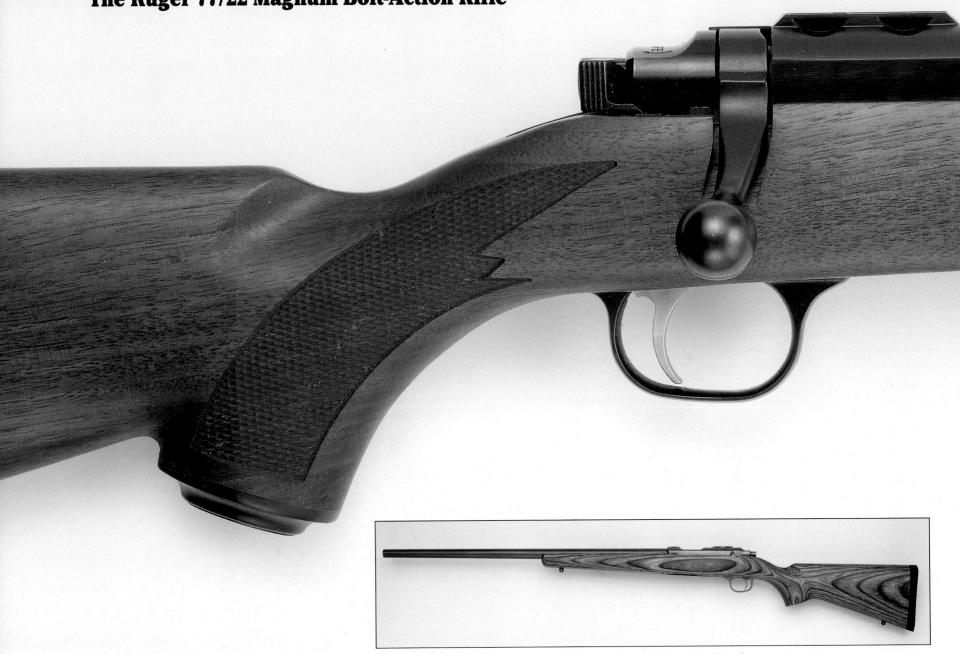

Number 701-75979 77/22 Magnum Bolt-Action Rifle, with laminated stock.

Number 701-77643 77/22 Magnum Bolt-Action Rifle.

Introduced: 1990. "Fast handling, slim, and lightweight, the Ruger .22 Magnum Rimfire is the logical first choice of serious target and varmint shooters who seek uncompromising performance in their small-caliber rifle. . . . a shooter's gun that provides the best of both possible worlds: Big-bore construction and a practical, flat-shooting, small-bore cartridge."

Serial Numbers: 701-00000 to -65008 (through 1993); serial numbers intermixed with .22 L.R. and other .22 Magnum 77/22 rifles.

Total Made Through 1993: In excess of 35,000.

Caliber: .22 Magnum.

Magazine Capacity: 9, in rotary detachable box.

Barrel Lengths: 20", 24" (Varmint model).

Rifling: 6 grooves, right-hand twist, one turn in 14".

Markings: See Table of Markings, pages 330–35.

On top of barrel:

Before using gun-read warnings in *instruction manual* available free—
    from Sturm, Ruger & Co., Inc. Southport, Conn. U.S.A.—

Sights: Open iron sights, or built for scope use only. In either case, 1" Ruger Scope Rings accompany all rifles.

Overall Length and Weight: 20" barrel rifles measure 39¼" overall, and weigh approx. 6 pounds. Laminated stock Varmint or Target Model measures 43¼" overall; weight of approx. 7 pounds, 8 ounces.

Stocks: American walnut, Zytel polymer (see **All-Weather 77/22,** pages TK), or laminated.

Finish: Blued steel, or antireflective satin-finished stainless steel.

Materials, Construction, and Innovations: Same technical features as detailed for the Model 77/22 Bolt-Action Rifle (see page 234), with added advantage of the flat-shooting and more powerful .22 Magnum cartridge. Slim stock profile; big-bore rifle feel, appearance, and quality. 9 rounds rotary magazine. Also available in the Zytel-molded, stainless steel, All-Weather model (see page 231).

Variation made of Terhune Anticorro Stainless Steel, with

heavy barrel and antireflective gray finish, and laminated stock, for match or varmint shooting; joined the line in 1994.

Issue Price: $382.75 (1990).

Price Sheet Listings and Production Variations:

Stainless Steel, with All-Weather Stocks (from 1991 price sheet):

    K77/22RMP: Without open sights (September 1991 to present).

    K77/22RSMP: With open sights (December 1991 to present).

Blued with Walnut Stocks:

    77/22RM: Blued, for scope use, American walnut stock (1990 to present).

    77/22RSM: Blued, open iron sights, American walnut stock (1990 to present).

Terhune Anticorro Stainless Steel, Laminated Stocks:

    K77/22VBZ: Heavy barrel; with target-gray antireflective satin finish, for scope use (1994 to present).

tion, all in a package constructed of the latest polymers and stainless steel alloys. New Model "Hunter" Single-Action revolvers allow easy scope mounting on these big-bore revolvers, and "Competition" model .22 caliber pistols permit efficient optical sight use without cumbersome "after market" mounts. On the long gun scene, our new Sporting Clays and English Field model shotguns have a lighter, trimmer feel for the discriminating shooter. Our 10/22 is now offered in a stainless steel barreled version, as is our new M77 Mark II Varmint rifle (with a special laminated stock). Finally, our Palma Match rifles are being produced in very limited numbers for the U.S. Shooting teams, an honor heretofore bestowed on Government armories and specialized target rifle craftsmen.

Besides these, we have many new products under development, and it gives me an immense sense of pride and accomplishment to see our product line continually expanding in depth and breadth. In addition, the Company's foundry in Prescott . . . continues to add new customers and I anticipate will soon become an important contributor to the Company's earnings.

It gives me great satisfaction that no additional anti-gun (actually, anti-gun owner) legislation of any significance to the Company was enacted in 1991. Across the nation, there is a great feeling of support for the right of law-abiding citizens to keep and bear arms for legitimate purposes, yet a small but influential group of urban elitists continues to demand that their view of society and their failed ideas of so-called crime control be imposed upon all of us.

Perhaps the worst manifestation of this was the enactment of a law in Washington, D.C. that will hold the manufacturers of nine specified "assault weapons" absolutely liable for any criminal misuse of their products. This is despite the fact that the sale of guns in the District has been illegal for over 10 years, and there is therefore no way for any manufacturer or dealer to avoid liability short of totally ceasing to sell guns outside Washington where it is perfectly legal to do so.

Although none of the Company's products are on this so-called "assault weapons" list, we testified against this law during the United States Congressional District of Columbia Subcommittee hearings in November, and will continue to battle this blatantly unconstitutional deviation from accepted law in every possible way. The responsibility for the criminal misuse of a firearm belongs on the criminal, period.

Most gratifying to me is the fact that we enter 1992 in strong financial condition with an expanding product line which is well accepted by the consumer. We will continue to endeavor to maintain our position as the finest manufacturer of small arms as well as endeavor to expand our investment casting capabilities.

I am proud to report that in February 1991, William B. Ruger, Jr. was elected President of the Company. He has had twenty-seven years of service with the Company and is well grounded in every aspect of the Company's operations.

I would like to note the retirement of Stanley Terhune as a Vice President. He has been associated with the Company for thirty years and has been instrumental and an industry leader in developing the Company's investment casting capabilities, especially as they have been utilized in the production of high quality firearms. I would like to express my appreciation for his invaluable contribution during his many years of service. I am happy to report that he will continue as a member of the Board of Directors and will maintain his association with the Company as a consultant.

No report would be complete without acknowledging the loyal and dedicated service of our fourteen hundred plus employees. Without them, there would be no report to write. I look forward to the challenges and responsibilities in the years to come.

William B. Ruger, Jr., Appointed President: Memo of February 5, 1991

William B. Ruger, Jr. has been appointed President of Sturm, Ruger & Company, Inc., and will report to me in my continuing capacity as Chairman of the Board of Directors and Chief Executive Officer of the Corporation.

He will be directly and specifically in charge of all operational matters of the Corporation, except for firearms engineering and development, which I shall continue to direct personally.

His responsibilities include the operations of all firearms manufacturing divisions, and all foundry divisions whose officers and managers will report to him.

Further, his responsibilities will encompass the marketing, legal, and financial areas, whose officers and managers will report primarily to him, but also to me and to the Board of Directors, as the circumstances may require.

I believe, as does the Board of Directors, that the appointment of William B. Ruger, Jr., as President of Sturm, Ruger & Company, Inc., is a correct and logical step in the evolution and continuity of the management of our Company, and will well serve present needs and provide for the attainment of future goals.

—William B. Ruger, Sr.
President

The Ruger Mini-Thirty Rifle

Ruger had long sought additional export markets for the Mini-14 sporting rifle, and was disappointed when the rifle did not seem to catch on as a prominent military or police rifle to the degree that he had expected. One of the reasons for this was that many foreign countries used the 7.62 x 39mm cartridge, instead of the .223. C. E. "Ed" Harris, formerly of *The American Rifleman*, was then working in quality control in New Hampshire, and was also quite a fan of this cartridge. Harris and Ruger steered each other toward bringing out a slightly larger version of the Mini-14 in this cartridge. Thus the Mini-Thirty. Steve Sanetti remembers:

The receiver is slightly wider to take the .30 caliber magazine, and the gas block is slightly larger. Curiously, the Mini-Thirty was never made in the original Mini-14 "Garand" receiver-sighted version, but only in the more civilized "Ranch Rifle" version, with a fold-down auxiliary peep sight, recoil buffer, recoil pad, scope bases, and so forth. It was marketed as the "world's most perfect deer rifle," and it was John Nassif's idea (then advertising manager) to add a short range cartridge comparison table in its advertising (which continues to this day in our catalogue) illustrating why this is such a good short range deer hunting rifle.

Mini-14 and Mini-Thirty rifle magazines are not interchangeable, and some confusion was engendered at first, since both magazine bases were originally labeled "Mini-14." A lot of effort was spent issuing warning stickers and instructional manual inserts explaining the differences between the two magazines and why, like any rifle, the correct magazine had to be used for proper functioning. The Mini-Thirty featured the fixed-blade ejector of all the Ruger Ranch rifle series, and ejected cartridges *very* vigorously out the right side, often landing thirty feet or so from the rifle! The engineers put an eccentric opening where the bolt lock pivots, to slow down the empty on its exit from the gun.

From the 1992 Annual Report

1992 was a banner year for the Company. The results were particularly gratifying in light of the poor economic news from so many segments of the economy during 1992. Specifically, sales of $156.1 million and net income after taxes of $22.2 million, equivalent to $3.29 per share, were record figures for the Company. The previous high for sales was 1991 when they reached $136.8 million, and the earnings record was previously established in 1989 when net income reached $18.1 million, equivalent to earnings per share of $2.70.

More details will be found further on in this report, but I would like to draw attention to the virtual flood of liquidity to be seen in our balance sheets. The recent improvement in cash and short-term investments, from $9 million on December 31, 1990 to $31.4 million on December 31, 1992, is a gratifying vindication of the truth that a manufacturing business such as ours can grow steadily over a period of years without recourse to debt. A day may come when some outstanding business opportunity will suggest a change in this strategy. Such occasions have occurred in the past. Until then, our engineering expertise and resources will produce opportunities, growth, and profits in the fields where we are now established.

In 1992, we introduced a substantial number of new products in both our handgun and long gun categories, further enhancing their appeal to both sporting and police markets. Our whole product line has been favored with strong demand which reaches us via thousands of well established retailers and our strong network of national wholesalers. The new products I refer to were in production by the end of 1992 and are all shown in our 1993 consumer's catalogue.

New product development work goes on continuously in this Company, and several important new products are nearing the announcement stage and will certainly be publicized within the next few months. Product development is more than a marketing necessity to us. We regard it essentially as an opportunity, because it certainly produces a direct response in the form of additional demand for our product line, and because it is so essentially straightforward for us to put these new products into production with our modern manufacturing techniques and our easily expanded capacity.

With respect to the investment castings market, the results in 1992 were mixed. Pine Tree Castings, which is the Company's oldest casting division, enjoyed record sales and earnings on its

outside business. The Uni-Cast Division, which is primarily tied to the defense industry, experienced a poor year with a reduction in sales and an operating loss for the year. Progress with respect to the newest casting division, Ruger Investment Casting, located in Prescott, Arizona, has been disappointingly slow. While sales to outside customers increased significantly, various start up and operating problems continued to plague the division, resulting in its operating loss for the year. Over the long term we continue to be enthusiastic about the prospects of Ruger Investment Casting, especially its ability in titanium investment castings. In my opinion there are any number of exciting and potentially profitable markets for titanium investment castings, both within and outside the firearms field.

The Company will continue to attempt to become a more significant factor in the investment castings industry as well as looking at other business opportunities which will broaden the earnings base in a logical way. This ongoing effort to enlarge the scope of our business obviously incurs extra time and thought as well as a growth of management and operating personnel. It has often been said at this Company that our management layer is extremely thin. (A famous consultant once stated of Sturm, Ruger & Company that management was so thin that it was barely visible.) Within the Company we often recognize the necessity of additional help, but we also enjoy the variety of responsibilities and challenges which a thin management imposes on the various individuals.

There have from time to time been questions about management succession in Sturm, Ruger & Company, and we are all conscious of the need that the Company continue to prosper regardless of the inevitable changes that time produces.

We have, I believe . . . a depth of understanding of our business which protects our creativity in the future. Our management organization is unanimous in its feeling that talent needs to be

The Ruger Mini-Thirty Rifle

Number 189-00001 Mini-Thirty Autoloading Rifle.

Introduced: 1991. "Big-bore performance in a compact, light-weight, self-loading sporting rifle. . . . slightly larger than the . . . Mini-14 Ranch Rifle and is chambered for the 7.62 x 39mm cartridge. . . . a perfect medium-sized hunting combination. . . . a superb rifle for extended carry and walks in deer country. . . . authoritative power with light recoil, allowing for quick recovery."

Serial Numbers: 189-00000 to -59348 (through1993).

Total Made Through 1993: In excess of 59,000.

Caliber: 7.62 x 39mm.

Magazine Capacity: 5, in spring-fed staggered detachable box. Not interchangeable with Mini-14 magazine.

Barrel Length: 18½".

Rifling: 6 grooves, right-hand twist, one turn in 10".

Markings: See Table of Markings, pages 330–35.

On left side of rear of receiver:

BEFORE USING GUN-READ WARNINGS IN
INSTRUCTION MANUAL **AVAILABLE FREE FROM**
STURM, RUGER & CO., INC.
SOUTHPORT, CONN. U.S.A.

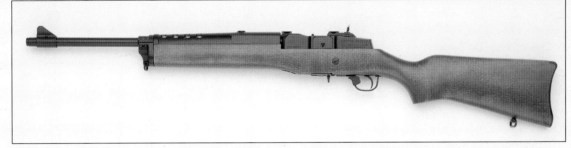

Number 189-00001 Mini-Thirty Autoloading Rifle.

Trademark *to left of bottom two lines of marking*, as is **R** registration stamping.

Sights: Folding peep rear, blade front. Receiver with factory machined scope mounting system. 1" Ruger scope rings standard accessory.

Overall Length and Weight: 37¼"; approx. 6⅞ pounds.

Stocks: American hardwood; lined in steel at stressed and high-temperature areas.

Finish: Blued, or brushed stainless steel.

Materials, Construction, and Innovations: First American rifle in this mid-sized caliber.

Stainless steel or chrome-molybdenum steel. Investment cast frame and bolt; stamped trigger guard. Fiberglass hand guard.

Gas-operated, the mechanism developed from the highly successful Mini-14 and the Ranch Rifle.

Issue Price: $504.50, blued; $552.50, stainless (1991).

Production Variations: *Mini-Thirty:* Blued (from 1990).

K-Mini-Thirty: Stainless steel (from 1991–present).

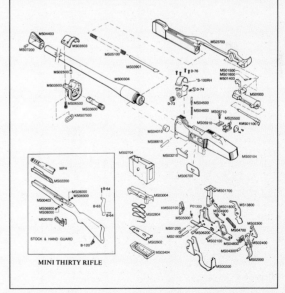

Exploded view of the Mini-Thirty Autoloading Rifle.

Some of the finest American-made (1920s–50s) Griffin & Howe custom rifles, from the Bill Ruger collection; from the *top*, Mauser square bridge action, .350 Magnum caliber, with integral rib extending length of the 24½" barrel; oil-stained French walnut stock with horn forend and steel pistol grip cap; engraved and checkered steel trapdoor buttplate; serial number 8598 (G & H number 517); oval silver escutcheon, inlaid on bottom of buttstock, engraved: L.B.M.; built for L. B. Maytag (of the washing machine family), in anticipation of an African safari, on which he never went. .35 Remington caliber Mauser square bridge action rifle; G & H number 1153; express sights graduated for 50 and 200 yards; 24½" barrel of Poldi Anti-Corro steel; floorplate gold inlaid with MS monogram within gold oval; silver's style buttpad on oil-stained walnut stock; horn forend and steel pistol grip cap; Joe Fugger engraved. G & H number 716 square bridge Mauser action rifle in .416 Rigby caliber; with Poldi Anti-Corro steel barrel; oil-stained French walnut stock; silver oval inlaid on bottom of buttstock; horn forend cap and steel pistol grip cap; silver's buttpad; sling swivels. *Bottom* rifle G & H number 1753, Mauser action in .35 Whelen, with Poldi Anti-Corro steel barrel; 26" barrel; double-set triggers; profusely engraved, with TCF monogram on trigger guard; Camp Fire Club of America logo on floorplate; fitted with G & H quick detachable scope mounting system; oil-finished walnut stock with horn forend cap and rubber buttpad; made for Thomas Florich, an expert handloader and friend of Bill Ruger.

American-made firearms once set the standard for the world; the Ruger Magnum and Express rifles are as close to these as possible in factory production rifles.

recognized throughout the workforce, and that engineers and planners need an environment which expands their potentials and fields of interest. We are continually alert to bring exceptional new people into the organization.

To refer to specific and ongoing problems and to disturbing events, I can relate a mixture of news. The overall number of product liability claims against the Company continues to drop. Furthermore, there are currently only nine "old model" single-action revolver cases pending, which represents a 17-year low. This dropoff in the number of claimed accidental discharges is especially gratifying to me. If the minuscule percentage of people who misuse our products would simply use them with the care and respect that we put into them, the way the vast majority in fact use them, there would be no accidents to fuel the anti-gun few, who believe that common sense can be legislated.

It is still too early to tell what firearms legislation will be pushed in Congress this year, but I hope and believe that the ground swell of revulsion felt by the law-abiding community over the actions of murderous drug thugs will not be wrongly and unconstitutionally misdirected at lawful firearms owners. In many respects, the Bill of Rights could be the greatest casualty of the urban drug wars if this whole topic is not subjected to some highly critical thinking before we plunge ahead and "do something" about guns and society in general.

In the course of 1992, the Company suffered several losses that hurt us deeply.

James Triggs died after many years of association. He was a gifted artist and illustrator who made many valuable contributions to the Company.[1]

Hal Seagraves was one of the early directors of the Corporation and remained in that position for many years. He was also the Company's patent attorney, a lawyer, a hunter, a philosopher, and an arms expert. He retired from our board at an advanced age in 1981 and passed away in January 1993.

In January 1993 Tom Ruger died at the age of 48 after a gallant six-month battle against leukemia. Tom's association with the Company began almost thirty years ago. During the intervening years he was involved with production management at our Newport firearms facility and during the last fourteen years was Vice President of Marketing. He had the unique ability always to look at the bright side of every situation, and his friends both within and outside the industry were countless. While perhaps I cannot be an impartial reporter in this case, I know I speak for all my associates at Sturm, Ruger when I say that his death leaves a deep void at the Company, and he will be sorely missed.

I will close by looking to the future and saying that I truly believe it holds promise. There will be problems as well as opportunities, but with the focused attention, energy, and determination of the men and women who constitute Sturm, Ruger, I know we can meet the challenges and capitalize on the opportunities which lie ahead.

The Ruger Super Blackhawk Hunter Single-Action Revolver: Steve Sanetti Remembers

The massive Super Blackhawk Hunter was one of the last of the Southport projects. Frank Bonaventura had received some samples of various laminated wood stocks, via Jack Behn, from Bill Lett. One of the colored laminated pistol grip panels was sort of a gray-appearing laminate, perfect for the new revolver, then under development, which was subsequently termed the "Hunter."

Ruger had pioneered integral optical scope base systems on the Redhawk (barrel) and the Super Redhawk (frame). Bill Ruger Jr.'s concept was to beef up the single-action New Model Super Blackhawk barrel and give it a solid rib large enough to accommodate cuts for the Ruger scope base system. The threads of the barrel were also changed to mate with similar coarse threads in the cylinder

frame, in order to provide a stronger support, much as was done when the Redhawk was introduced.

The interchangeable Redhawk front sight blade kit was also incorporated into the Super Blackhawk Hunter, as was the longer "full-length" ejector rod system of the then-defunct .357 Maximum. Stainless steel was regarded as the best material for a gun likely to be used in adverse hunting conditions.

The trigger guard could originally have either the rounded or the square back, with the rounded design eventually emerging. Bill Ruger entrusted Chris Cashavelly to do most of the design work, since this revolver required some heavy engineering right after the time both Larry Larson and Roy Melcher had left. I remember Chris repeatedly bemoaning his fate—"I'm not a gun designer; I'm a draftsman!" But he was drafted and his considerable talents well utilized to come up with this excellent revolver, and he became a designer after all. Soon after, he again graduated—to become a retiree.

The Ruger 22/45 Autoloading Pistols: Steve Sanetti Remembers

This project was designer Jim McGarry's first with Sturm, Ruger. He had come to us because he was intrigued with the idea of designing in the firearms field—his training and experience had been as an engineer specializing in the design of medical instruments, and he also had extensive experience working with plastics and plastic model-making. As with most Ruger staff, he also had an abiding interest in firearms.

With the increasing acceptance of polymer frames in pistols, Bill Ruger assigned Jim to see if he could utilize a synthetic frame for our long-lived .22. The pistol had already been updated (to the Mark II), but Bill was concerned about competition from imports as well as less expensive American-made plastic-framed .22s. Bill and Jim liked the feel of the original Colt .45 Model 1911 grip frame, and decided early on that the pistol would have that basic configuration.

The complexity of manufacturing each gun rivals, and sometimes exceeds, the evident technical and performance features of the finished product.

For example, the plastic frame for the 22/45 autoloading pistol had to be designed for the practical attachment of internal parts. The function of crosspins which could be used on the steel-framed .22 Mark II autoloader had to be duplicated by other means in the plastic-framed 22/45, to avoid cracking the plastic under the stress of moving steel parts. The plastic molding had to be adapted to accommodate springs, and to enable attachment of metal parts, some of which required re-design. Two steel shims were required in the plastic frame for its attachment to the tubular steel receiver at both front and rear.

It was Jim's idea to eliminate the separate grip panels, and he figured out how to mount the very strong recoil spring mechanism into the plastic frame. We felt if the pistol had a 1911 style grip frame, it ought to have a 1911 style magazine release button, rather than the heel-mounted release of the Mark IIs. After quite a bit of effort, Jim was able to make that happen. The long "foot" of the 22/45 magazine is necessary in order to retrieve and insert magazines into the grip, since the original style would not work with the newly shaped .45 style grip frame.

Magnum and Express Bolt-Action Rifles

Early in the 1990s, Bill Ruger's interest in classic Griffin & Howe sporting rifles was revived, and with it his interest in making a top quality big-game bolt-action sporting rifle, derived from the Ruger M77 Mark II. It was Ruger who insisted that the new rifles use barrels containing an *integral* quarter sighting rib, made right from the barrel itself, even though the bar stock for these barrels was very hard to obtain and they took approximately seven hours *each* to produce! The first group of rifles was completely ruined when the machinists who normally threaded round barrels neglected to pay attention to the position of the quarter ribs. The result was barrels with ribs which lined up on the receivers at every position of the clock except 12!

The Express and Magnum rifles were given an enthusiastic reception. Finn Aagard, a former

The Ruger New Model Super Blackhawk Hunter

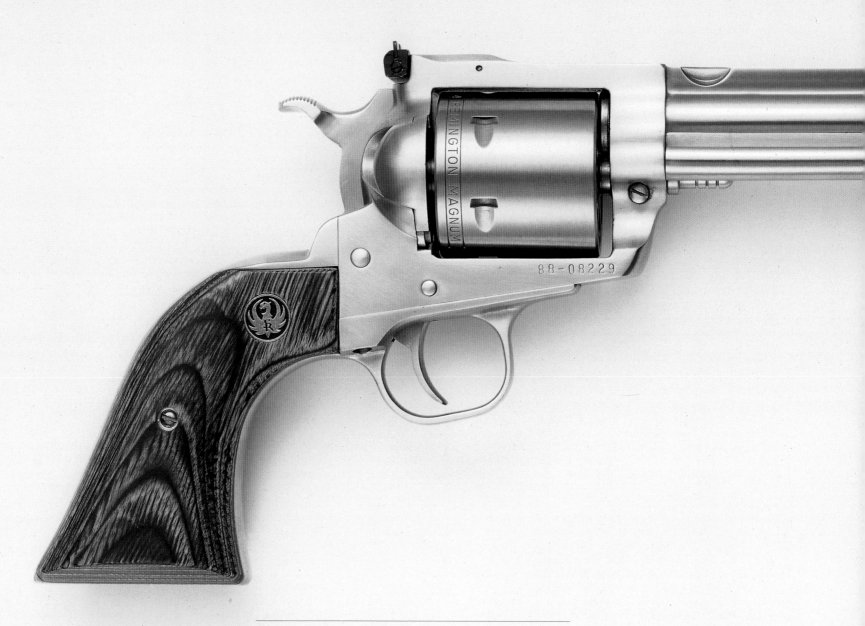

Number 88-08229 New Model Super Blackhawk Hunter Revolver.

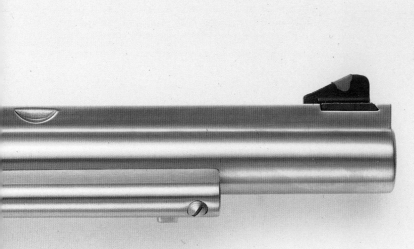

Number 88-08229 New Model Super Blackhawk Hunter Revolver.

Introduced: 1992. "[To] merge the traditional single-action revolver with a heavy ribbed barrel machined for Ruger scope rings. . . . the only single-action ready to use today's superior optical sights."

Serial Numbers: 88-00000 to -08812 (through 1993).

Caliber: .44 Magnum (.44 Special interchangeable).

Number of Chambers in Cylinder: Six.

Barrel Length: 7½".

Rifling: 6 grooves, right-hand twist, one turn in 20".

Markings: See Table of Markings, pages 330–35.

On left side of cylinder frame:

RUGER* .44 MAGNUM CAL
NEW MODEL *SUPER BLACKHAWK*

*R registered trademark stamping

On left side of barrel:

Before using gun–read warnings in *instruction manual* **available free—from Sturm, Ruger & Co., Inc. Southport, Conn. U.S.A.—**

Repeated twice peripherally on breech end of cylinder:

.44 REMINGTON MAGNUM

Serial number *on right side of front of cylinder frame.*

Sights: Click adjustable rear sight for windage and elevation,

ramp front sight, with interchangeable nylon inserts (in blue, orange, yellow, or ivory), or steel with a gold bead. 9½" sight radius.

Barrel with integral full-length solid rib, factory machined for 1" Ruger scope rings.

Overall Length and Weight: 13⅝" and 52 ounces.

Grips: Laminated wood, with trademark medallion inlays.

Finish: Satin-polished stainless steel.

Materials, Construction, and Innovations: 400-series stainless steel, rugged construction, heavyweight ribbed barrel machined for scope mounting, sophisticated open sights, non-fluted cylinder, laminated grips, Ruger transfer bar ignition system and loading gate interlock. Low and wide hammer spur and wide trigger in stainless steel grip frame.

Issue Price: $479.50 (1992).

Production Variations:

KS47NH: 7½" barrel, Ruger scope rings, stainless steel, first listed in the 1992 price sheet and catalogue, and continuing to present.

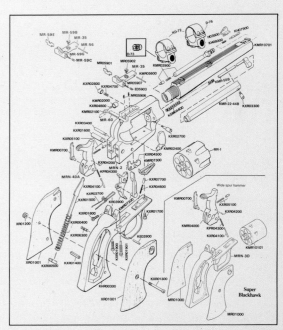

Exploded view of the New Model Super Blackhawk Hunter Revolver.

professional hunter in Kenya, wrote up the Magnum in *The American Rifleman* as "a big brute of a rifle designed for taking the world's largest game under the toughest field conditions the hunter is likely to encounter . . . a great rifle, and I do believe Ruger has done it again."

Ruger Mark II Target Bolt-Action Rifle: Jay Jarvis Remembers

Our development of the Mark II Target Rifle came after we had been selected to make the prestigious Palma Match special rifle—which was based on a precision trigger mechanism that Bill Atkinson came up with. We had met with NRA Palma Team Shooters George Tubbs and Mid Thomkins, and talked about the stock, and they had given us a sample, along with their requirements for the Match gun. Jim Carmichel, shooting editor of *Outdoor Life*, and an accomplished target shooter, was also involved in this project.

We came back, with the requirements they gave us, and drew up the stock, coming up with an adjustable comb, adjustable recoil pad for length, a track in the forend for a variety of accessories (such as palm rests), and the Atkinson trigger mechanism. The Palma rifles were not laminated, but were made from conventional walnut.

We made up a small quantity of these sophisticated and highly accurate rifles for the Palma team. From that project we developed our first purpose-built Target Rifle. This used Bill Atkinson's trigger mechanism, with a much simplified stock over the Palma. The stocks of these were laminated wood, the heavy barreled action of stainless steel.

The stock is a typical target stock, closest to the old Winchester Model 70 match rifle stock, but the design was an outgrowth of the Palma Rifle project. It was the first time we mated a laminated stock to a stainless steel rifle.

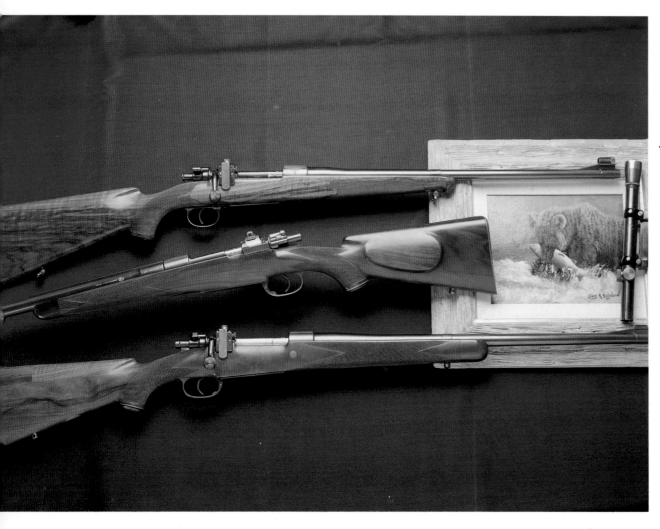

More influential classics from the Ruger Collection, by Griffin & Howe; from *top*, Springfield action rifle, G & H number 7, in 7mm caliber; 23" barrel; oil-stained walnut stock, with Schnabel forend; horn pistol grip cap; scroll and border engraved action, barrel, floorplate, trigger guard, and checkered trapdoor buttplate. L. B. Maytag rifle at *center* in .350 Magnum (also illustrated, page 244); classic G & H style cheekpiece, wrist and forend. *Bottom* rifle G & H number 1302; in .375 H & H Magnum; 24½" barrel; oil-stained select walnut stock.

What the well-equipped sportsman would confront the bear with in the 1930s; these could also serve him well today, both as "shooters" and as investments.

Baron Meets Baron: Jay Hansen Remembers

In May of 1989, Sam Cummings, founder of Interarms and a leading international firearms dealer, gave me a call, and said he would be in the area in a few days, and asked would I be able to see him.

Sam appeared on a Friday evening, and explained that he had been up to see the people at Smith & Wesson, which was then for sale. He thought it would be interesting to own his own gun company, from the "big four." Cummings also mentioned that he had been looking a little bit at Colt as well, with the same thought in mind. We had lunch the next day, and after lunch determined that Ruger would be in his Southport office. After lunch Cummings and I met with Ruger at the plant, and spent the entire afternoon there. They did most of the talking.

It was a unique experience, with the Baron of gunmakers meeting the Baron of international gun and ammunition merchants.

That evening, after a break, Cummings and I were Ruger's guests at one of his favorite restaurants in the area, Le Chambord. The discourse continued.

It was a somewhat guarded conversation, as both of them in a sort of apprehensive way seemed to have a very high regard for each other. They didn't seem to want to let any really interesting cats out of the bag.

Ruger, of course, spoke about (and early in the day had shown Cummings) one or two of his new rifles with high-tech stocks and stainless steel parts. Cummings talked about some new things he would be importing, explaining that in that year he would be importing between 300 and 400,000 new guns. Ruger boasted that year he would be making something like double that number.

There was some talk about older collectible guns, which they both had an obvious love for.

Although I have known Sam Cummings casually for many years, I somehow hadn't noted that he didn't drink. This caused minor discomfort at supper, and I thought he cleverly defused the issue by simply having a couple of drops of wine, dribbled into the bottom of his wine glass, which

he, of course, never did drink.

The single greatest impression I formed from witnessing this get-together, and being part of it, was the obvious respect these two men have for each other, regarding their different but monumental achievements within the firearms industry.

In retrospect I feel that I witnessed two great shamans quietly interacting in my presence.

A letter of appreciation was sent from President George Bush to Bill Ruger, Jr., for the gift of two deluxe shotguns. Bush sent Bill, Jr., still another letter to stress how he fully enjoyed shooting the guns, and showing it off to friends:

> This past week I went to Texas for my annual quail hunt. We were in birds the whole time. One of the 3 hunters was [Senator] Al Simpson of Cody. I told him of your recent visit to the Oval Office and of those 2 special 12 gauge guns. . . .
>
> I love hunting. I love beautiful shotguns and these 2 specially crafted Rugers will be on display after I'm gone. Before then I'll try to reach out and touch a duck with all of them if I ever get the chance. . . .

When the first of the two 12 gauge shotgun receivers was completed, by engraver Paul Lantuch, Steve Sanetti was admiring his handiwork, but noticed what appeared to be scratches on the upper tang. Carefully looking at that detail revealed that Lantuch, who had come to America with his family from Lithuania, had minutely engraved the words "Today Bagdad—tomorrow Kremlin. Free Lithuania now, George—help us!" Needless to say, this receiver was *not* used on the shotgun presented to the President.

A second gun was made for presentation, which was intended for field shooting. Later, President Bush learned of the inscription on the first shotgun receiver, had a hearty laugh, and requested to purchase it as a memento. That tiny

legend, to the naked eye just some scratches, remains to this day on that receiver owned by the President. In the meantime, the plea for freedom for Lithuania, to the surprise of millions, and the delight of Paul Lantuch, came true.

Presidential attitudes on guns can be gleaned from a meeting between Ruger and President Ronald Reagan, when both were attending a black-tie dinner in Washington, D.C. Sturm, Ruger capitol representative Ron Crawford introduced Reagan to Ruger, and when the latter noted, "You know, Mr. President, we also made a gun for President Carter," Reagan didn't miss a beat—he replied "Oh, I didn't know he could shoot!"

Bill Ruger, Jr., at the White House with President George Bush

Late in 1991, Sturm, Ruger & Co. presented two deluxe Ruger Over-and-Under shotguns to President George Bush. The first of the two guns was brought to the White House by Bill, Jr., and straightaway he was asked by the President about his old friend John Kingsley, who had known the Bush family since childhood.

"He's back at the office, Mr. President. Somebody has to work!"

The President said he felt the gun was too beautiful to shoot. Bill's reply was: "I would think that a few Presidential scratches might enhance its value, and most importantly give you some pleasure. This would be our hope." Later Bill, Jr., received a letter written on Air Force One, revealing how much the President was enjoying his Rugers.

The Ruger 22/45 Pistol

Number 220-14291 22/45 Autoloading Pistol.

Introduced: 1992. "Designed for those who prefer the handling characteristics of the venerable 1911 Government Model, this rimfire pistol features a grip angle and magazine latch virtually identical to the 1911 Model .45 ACP. . . . grip frame of Zytel, a super tough, fiberglass-reinforced, lightweight composite. . . . the perfect plinking pistol, an inexpensive way to practice, or an accurate small game hunting sidearm. . . ."

Serial Numbers: 220-00000 to -36560 (through 1993).

Total Made Through 1993: In excess of 36,000.

Caliber: .22 Long Rifle.

Magazine Capacity: 10, in spring-fed detachable, single column box, with prominent "foot." Not interchangeable with Standard or Target Model Mark II magazines.

Barrel Lengths: 4¾" standard, 5¼" target tapered, and 5½" bull.

Rifling: 6 grooves, right-hand twist, one turn in 16".

Markings: See Table of Markings, pages 330–35.

On left side of the barrel:
—BEFORE USING GUN-READ WARNINGS IN *INSTRUCTION MANUAL*—
AVAILABLE FREE FROM: STURM, RUGER & CO., INC.
SOUTHPORT, CT. U.S.A.

Slight variation noted on bull barrel pistol.

Trademark *on back of bolt.*

Sights: Square notch rear, click adjustable for windage, elevation (Target models only). Patridge type blade front.

Overall Length and Weight: 8¾" and 28 ounces (4¾" barrel); 9½" and 35 ounces (5½" bull barrel).

Grips: Grip frame of Zytel composite material.

Finish: Brushed stainless steel.

Materials, Construction, and Innovations: 400-series stainless

250

Exploded view of the 22/45 Autoloading Pistol.

steel, with the bolt and lockwork of blued chrome-molybdenum steel. Grip frame material with innovation of the fiberglass-reinforced, light-weight Zytel composite.

1911 Government Model .45ACP grip angle and magazine latch for the .22 L.R. caliber. Aluminum trigger. Choice of barrel types, weights, and sights. Push-button magazine release.

Issue Price: $280.00, KP-4; $330.00, KP-514 and KP-512 (1993).

Production Variations, First listed in the 1993 Price Sheet, and continuing to 1995:

KP4: Standard Model, 4¾" barrel, fixed sights.

KP514: Target Model, 5¼" barrel, adjustable sights.

KP512: Bull Barrel Model, 5½" barrel, adjustable sights.

Number 220-00225 22/45 Model KP512C Autoloading Pistol.

The Ruger Magnum Bolt-Action Rifle

Number 780-57436 Magnum Bolt-Action Rifle, .375 H&H Magnum caliber, with 22" barrel.

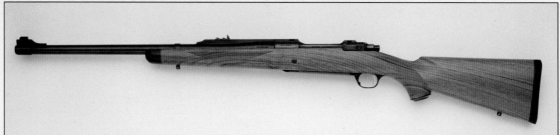

Number 780-57436 Magnum Bolt-Action Rifle.

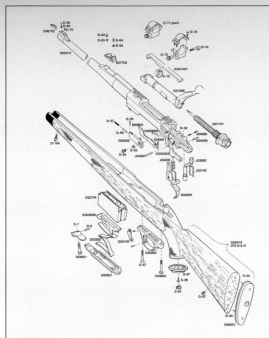

Exploded view of the M77 Mark II Express and Magnum Rifles.

Introduced: 1990. "Custom features, reasonable cost, and exceptional finish detail put the Ruger Express and Magnum rifles in a class by themselves. The Ruger Magnum Rifle continues the tradition of beautiful, powerful rifles; a tradition begun in the great game areas of Asia and Africa."

Serial Numbers: Initially made within the 780- prefix serial range of the Model 77 Mark II rifles. After a few hundred Magnum rifles built, numbering began in 1991 with 750-00000.

Caliber: .375 H & H Magnum, .416 Rigby.

Magazine Capacity: 3-round for .416 Rigby; 4-round for .375; steel hinged floorplate and trigger guard; staggered box magazine.

Barrel Length: 23" with matted quarter rib (.375 H & H); 24" with matted quarter rib (.416 Rigby).

Rifling: .375 H & H: 6 grooves, right-hand twist, one turn in 12"; .416 Rigby: 6 grooves, right-hand twist, one turn in 14".

Markings: See Table of Markings, pages 330–35.

On left side of receiver:

RUGER R MAGNUM

Serial number, *on left side of receiver, at breech.*
Caliber marking and proof mark, *on left side of barrel, at breech. On top of barrel, forward of barrel band (moved c. 1994 to forward of barrel rib and behind barrel band):*

STURM, RUGER, & CO. INC., SOUTHPORT, CONN. U.S.A.

SAFE with directional arrow, *on top of breech of bolt.*

Sights: V-notch rear express sights; one stationary, two folding and drift adjustable for windage; blade front sight; neatly mat-

ted quarter rib. Breech machined for 1" ring Ruger scope mounts.

Overall Length and Weight: Approx. 43⅞" and approx. 9¼ pounds (.375 H & H); approx. 44⅞" and approx. 10¼ pounds. (.416 Rigby).

Stocks: Polyurethane-finished Circassian walnut, checkered, with black composition forend cap. Live rubber recoil pad; steel pistol grip cap, inset with brass trademark. Studs for sling swivels. Length of pull, 13½"; drop of comb, 1⅞"; drop at heel, 2⅛".

Finish: Blued.

Materials, Construction, and Innovations: The first true "Magnum" length action from Ruger. Barrel and sighting rib machined from single steel bar; folding-leaf express sights. Special receiver and bolt measuring approximately ⁷⁄₁₆" greater in length than standard .30-06 breech; locking area and receiver front increased in length, for further strength. Hardened alloy steel floorplate (with protected latch to prevent accidental dumping of cartridges in recoil), trigger guard, and pistol grip cap. Three-position safety. Crisp trigger. Available in two classic cartridges.

Issue Price: $1,550.00 (1990).

Production Variations:

77RSM: .375 H & H and .416 Rigby (from 1990 price sheet through 1992).

77RSMMKII: .375 H & H and .416 Rigby (from 1993 price sheet to present; .404 Jeffrey advertised in 1994, but not produced).

The Ruger Express Bolt-Action Rifle

Number 780-77833 Express Bolt-Action Rifle.

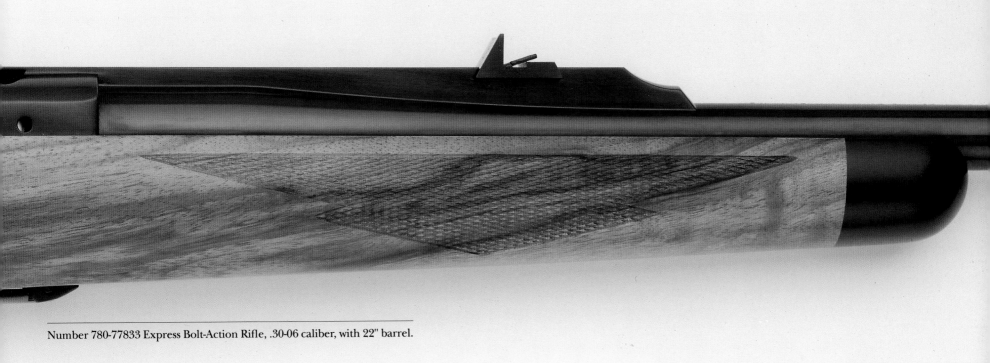

Number 780-77833 Express Bolt-Action Rifle, .30-06 caliber, with 22" barrel.

Introduced: 1992. "Stunning in performance and elegant of design, the Express Rifle is a quick-handling, practical firearm for those who appreciate the extra dimensions a finely crafted tool adds to the hunting experience.... the Express and Magnum rifles share features normally found only on custom rifles built without regard to cost."

Serial Numbers: Initially made within the 780- prefix serial range of the Model 77 Mark II rifles. After a few hundred Express rifles built, numbering began in 1991 with 760-00000.

Caliber: .270, .30-06, 7mm Remington Magnum, .300 Winchester Magnum, .338 Winchester Magnum.

Magazine Capacity: 4-round for .270 and .30-06; 3-round for remaining calibers. Steel hinged floorplate and trigger guard; staggered box magazine.

Barrel Length: 22" with matted quarter rib.

Rifling: .270, .30-06, .300 Winchester Magnum, .338 Winchester Magnum: 6 grooves, right-hand twist, one turn in 10".

7mm Remington Magnum: 6 grooves, right-hand twist, one turn in 9.5".

Markings: See Table of Markings, pages 330–35.
On left side of receiver:

RUGER M77 R MARK II

Serial number, *on left side of receiver, at breech.*
Caliber and proof marking, *on left side of barrel, at breech.*
On top of barrel, forward of rib:
STURM, RUGER, & CO. INC., SOUTHPORT, CONN. U.S.A.
SAFE with directional arrow, *on top of breech of bolt.*

Sights: V-notch express rear, with one stationary, the other folding and drift adjustable for windage; neatly matted quarter rib. Blade front sight mounted on ramp. Breech machined for Ruger scope mounts, with 1" rings standard.

Overall Length and Weight: 42⅛" and approx. 7½ pounds.

Stocks: Polyurethane-finished French walnut, checkered, with black composition forend cap. Live-rubber recoil pad. Steel pistol grip cap, inset with brass trademark. Studs for sling swivels. Length of pull, 13½"; drop of comb, 1⅞"; drop at heel, 2⅛".

Finish: Blued.

Materials, Construction, and Innovations: The Deluxe version of the Long Action Model 77 Mark II. Barrel and sighting rib machined from single steel billet; folding-leaf express sights. Standard length Ruger Model 77 action. Three-position safety. Mauser-type extractor. Controlled round feeding. Hardened alloy steel floorplate, trigger guard, and pistol grip cap. Secure floorplate latch. Crisp trigger.

Issue Price: $1,550.00 (1992).

Production Variations:

77RSEXP: First listing, 1992 Price Sheet; in calibers .270, .30-06, 7mm, .300 Magnum. The rifle was initially known as the Deluxe and, within a year after introduction, became known as the Express.

77RSEXPMKII: Listing from 1993 price sheet to date; 1993 listing in calibers .270, 7mm, .30-06, .300 Magnum caliber .338 Winchester Magnum added in 1994.

255

The Ruger M77 Mark II Bolt-Action Target Rifle

Number 781-22626 Model 77 Mark II Bolt-Action Target Rifle.

Number 781-22626 Model 77 Mark II Bolt-Action Target Rifle, .308 Winchester caliber, with 26" barrel.

Introduced: 1992. "A true out-of-the-box precision rifle incorporating the most desirable custom features with fine Ruger craftsmanship and value. . . . features a *new* Ruger two-stage trigger system. . . . stainless steel action [with] a heavyweight, 26-inch free-floating, stainless steel barrel with a special matte finish . . . resin-filled laminated wood . . . stock."

Serial Numbers: Within range of 781-00000 on up; serial numbers intermixed with the M77 Mark II rifle.

Calibers: .223, .22 PPC, .22-250, .220 Swift, 6mm PPC, .243 Winchester, .25-06, .308.

Magazine Capacity: 4-round; steel hinged floorplate and trigger guard; staggered box.

Barrel Length: 26".

Rifling: Right-hand twist standard. Number of grooves and pitch of rifling varies according to caliber.

Markings: See Table of Markings, pages 330–35.
On left side of receiver:

RUGER M77 ʀ MARK II
Serial number, o*n left side of receiver, at breech.*
Caliber and proof marking, *on left side of barrel, at breech.*
On top of barrel, midway:

**Before using gun-read warnings in *instruction manual* available free—
from Sturm, Ruger & Co., Inc. Southport, Conn. U.S.A.—**

Sights: Integral base receiver, 1" Ruger steel scope rings. No open sights.

Overall Length and Weight: 45⅞", approx. 9¾ pounds.

Stocks: Heavy laminated wood, beavertail forend, rubber buttplate, sling swivel studs at butt and forend.

Finish: Satin-finished matte stainless.

Materials, Construction, and Innovations: 400-series stainless steel, including barrel. Two-stage trigger system, for reliability and accuracy. Heavyweight, free-floating barrel, hammer forged. Resin-filled laminated wood stock. Dimensionally stable in all weather conditions, while retaining handsome wood grain and color. Flat, wide, forend for benchrest shooting.

Issue Price: $665.00 (K77VBZMKII) (1993).

Production Variations:

M77NVMKII: As listed in the 1992 catalogue, page 4; initially in calibers .22-250, .220 Swift, .25-06, .223, .243, and .308.

KM77VTMKII: As listed in the 1993 and 1994 catalogues, and pictured on page 2 (1993) and page 5 (1994). In price sheet as code **K77VBZMKII** (1993) and as code **K77VTMKII** (1994). The 1993 and 1994 price sheets listed the additional calibers .223 and .22 PPC.

Top left, the Cathedral Arms apartments, Ocean Avenue, Brooklyn, New York, birthplace of William B. Ruger; ten-year-old Buddy in bathing suit standing at *right,* next to the Dutch Reformed church. Ruger residence at Albemarle Terrace, to *left* of polar explorer Frederick A. Cook visiting Brooklyn, with Ruger's grandfather William Batterman, and other dignitaries, c. 1908; Buddy with his pony to *left* letter of Alexander Hamilton High School Rifle Team, of which he was captain. Portrait of Ruger by western artist Bob Harris. Street scene of Albemarle Terrace, *left center, above* 412 Stuyvesant Avenue apartment, and 1943 picture of Bill Lett, stop-motion photographer Harold Edgerton, and Bill Ruger at Auto-Ordnance. *To right,* Stamford Achievement Test by Ruger, 1927.

Left center, pensive Ruger photographed at in-laws' home, Greensboro, c. 1938; *below,* façade of Gage & Tolner restaurant, Brooklyn; *beneath,* May Ruger with her baby son. Factory *below* Ruger and Packard car was the Truitt Manufacturing Co., Greensboro, where Ruger worked as a machinist, c. 1938. *Bottom center,* H. Peter Kriendler of '21', with Bill Ruger and old friend Ted Rowe, president of Sigarms USA; Molly in riding clothes. Rock band Aerosmith album cover beneath Cape Buffalo bronze by Robert Glen; *center* of portrait, Ruger nephew Tom Hamilton, the group's bass player. Engineer Jay Jarvis *beneath* Aerosmith cover, and to *right* of Bill Ruger, Jr., Reeves Callaway's 1995 SuperNatural LM race car at Le Mans, partially sponsored by Bill Ruger. Factory view with Bill Ruger superimposed by *Business Week* at the Southport plant, c. 1963. At *bottom,* Mary, Molly, and Tom, c. 1960. Ruger granddaughter Vicky in orange slacks at Easton, Connecticut, private shooting range, *above* photo of Ruger with Wilhelm Kuhnert painting of Cape Buffalo (to *left* Mini-14 firing-pin investment casting, twisted 360 degrees in test—and unbreakable). Ruger's Newport secretary Carol Twyon at her desk, to *left* of another picture of Callaway SuperNatural LM, *above* that is group photograph taken at Wave Hill, New York, on occasion of fiftieth anniversary dinner honoring Luigi Chinetti's first victory (1932) at Le Mans twenty-four-hour race. *Beneath,* Ruger with friend Bob Lee, founder of Hunting World, Inc., discussing rifle for Lee's 1995 sheep-hunting expeditions to Mongolia. To *right* of serial no. 203 .22 Standard Pistol (originally shipped to heavyweight boxer Gene Tunney and later presented to filmmaker and adventurer Peter Gimbel). His Highness the Sultan of Oman, with a Security-Six revolver in holster; Maynard Dixon's "Cloud World" *below;* and Steve Vogel with son Alex and singer Hank Williams, Jr., on the *Titania.* Kurt Vogel near *bottom right center,* above deer-hunting photograph with Bill Lett (at *right* in red jacket).

Bill Ruger with Tom Brokaw at *top right;* best footage of interview not used; it was too convincing for program's antigun agenda. Dave Davis's portrait *above* American Driver, and cartoon by Bob Dearden, for many years head of Ruger Service Department. *Top right,* Robert Chatfield-Taylor with Eleanor and Jack O'Connor on Canadian big-game hunt. Russian explorer Dr. Misha Malakhov with Ruger All-Weather M77 MK II, customized by Dan Cullity for trek by Malakhov and Canadian Richard Weber on foot crossing the North Pole, from February to June 1995. To *right* of Buffalo Bill portrait, trade publication article announcing Gerald R. Bersett's appointment as Sturm, Ruger & Co. president, 1995. *Lower far right,* Bill Ruger, Jr., in Gasoline Alley at Indianapolis 500 race, early 1960s. His Newport secretary Sandra Brown at far *lower right;* note Mini-14 bolt, the casting tested by 360-degree twisting—without breakage. Ruger orchestra, beneath gillie with stag shot by Ruger in Scotland. Black-and-white picture superimposed on Ruger orchestra, Ruger secretary Mildred Keller and Larry Colman, a public auditor from the early period of Sturm, Ruger.

CHAPTER X

"Preserving a Way of Life"
1992–1993

I was a city boy that wanted to be a cowboy, or explore Africa or the North Pole. . . . Really a pathetic example of a child born in the wrong place."

Ruger, however, found his right place in the Connecticut River Valley, known as Gun Valley for the once great armsmakers who used to thrive there. Remington and Winchester have now been sold off, and Colt's is in Chapter 11 bankruptcy. But Southport, Conn. based Sturm, Ruger continues on, booking a handsome $15 million in profits, or $2.17 a share, on [1991] revenues of $137 million. And with a five-year average return on equity of $19.2%, the company ranks 82nd on this year's [Forbes] Up & Comers list. . . .

Steering clear of Saturday night specials and thin-margined government deals, he has aimed his pieces at gun enthusiasts—hunters, target shooters and collectors—who buy as much for esthetic as security reasons. And while the company does sell to police departments, those deals are made on a city-by-city and state-by-state basis. Hence the company has never become reliant on a single contract.

39. 1992
Sporting Clays
Over-and-Under Shotgun
40. 1993
Vaquero Single-Action
Revolver
41. 1993 (see pp. 220–21)
P93 Pistol
42. 1993
New Bearcat Single-Action
Revolver

Today, Sturm, Ruger depends upon collectors for its business as much as hunters. Issuing four or five new firearm varieties every year, Ruger is confident that customers will continue to buy to add to their collections. . . . [Further] Ruger [has] a bit of cachet as a prestige firearm. Innovations in design and ballistics help keep that image. . . .

Over the past ten years Sturm, Ruger's stock price has more than quadrupled. . . . The company has also paid out almost $14 [million] worth of dividends over that period. Ruger . . . believes shareholders have better use for the company's extra cash than he does.

Along with his family, Ruger still owns 43% of Sturm, Ruger's shares, worth over $100 million. And Ruger recently named his 53-year old son, William Ruger, Jr., president of the company. Still, he insists he has no plans for stepping down. "Retire?" Ruger says with a laugh, "I've never done a goddam day's work in my life."

—Forbes, *November 9, 1992,*
"The 200 Best Small Companies"

The national championship Ruger Women's Sporting Clays Team, with their champion, Tom Ruger; as featured in the November 1991 issue of *Town & Country*. From *left,* Barbara Schaefer, Parker Gentry, Nina Craig, Susie Clarke, and Denise Herman.

"If we did all the things we are capable of doing, we would literally astonish ourselves."
—Thomas Edison

Red Label Sporting Clays Over-and-Under Shotgun

Tom Ruger was an active shooter, and was particularly dedicated to sporting clays. This relatively new shooting sport, unlike conventional skeet or trap shooting, which is shot on a fixed layout, has been described as "golf with shotgun." The shooter travels through woods and fields to at least ten different stations, to shoot at clay targets launched from hidden locations, and no two courses are exactly alike. The growth of this sport in the U.S. almost exactly coincided with the introduction of the Ruger Red Label shotgun, the only American-made over-and-under at the time.

When the Ruger Women's Sporting Clays Team, then one of the most respected names in competitive shooting, asked Ruger engineers for certain modifications to the Red Label shotgun, they found the company more than willing to help. The requested features were designed to place the shotgun at a more competitive level in the rapidly growing world of sporting clays shooting. The changes included elimination of the center barrel spacer, a slightly longer barrel for easier follow through, "back boring" of the chambers, and relieved forcing cones in order to reduce perceived recoil. A second sighting bead was also put on the barrel rib. Considered, but not adopted, was a different, non-snagging recoil pad. Dave Tilden, manager of Ruger's Newport firing range and a world-class skeet and sporting clays shooter, worked with the engineers and had a hand in the gun's final design. These various adaptations emerged as the Ruger Sporting Clays Model.

The Jack Behn collection of Ruger firearms, all different models bearing the primary serial number 95, with the collector himself holding the Super Redhawk presented on his 20th year (a long-standing tradition at Sturm, Ruger). Gold Hamilton railroad watch was a retirement gift from Sturm, Ruger. Behn attended the Ruger booth at all of the NRA annual meetings and shows from 1955 to 1991 and his association with Ruger goes back to even before Bill Ruger met Alex Sturm. At time of photograph, Red Label 28 gauge and Woodside shotguns had not yet been shipped. Not only a collector's dream, this assemblage illustrates the substantial diversity in Ruger firearms from 1949 to 1994.

J. Thompson (Tom) Ruger

John Kingsley first met Tom Ruger in the spring of 1971, the first time Kingsley went to Newport. Tom had recently joined the Company on a full-time basis and was working in the Production Department of the firearms facility:

I really got to know Tom well when he came to Southport at the beginning of 1979, as Vice President of Marketing. Like anyone who had the pleasure of knowing Tom, I have many fond memories. Probably more than almost anybody I knew, Tom squeezed every ounce out of life and as some people said when he died at age forty-eight, he really lived a life that would have taken ninety years for most people to live.

He was the eternal optimist and one of his favorite expressions was "No problem."

Like others, there were times when I would momentarily be annoyed with Tom because perhaps he had not done the "homework" which he had been asked to do. This notwithstanding, it was impossible to be angry with Tom for any length of time.

Tom was one of those few people in life who exuded charisma. I can still picture him—whether it was arriving in the Company's offices, or at a trade show, or entertaining distributors—with his effervescent presence as the focal point.

Tom's funeral underlined the tremendous impact which he had on so many people. The Episcopal church in Southport, across the street from the Ruger family home, was overflowing. People from all walks of life, including some who had lost their jobs when the plant closed, were present to bid him a sad farewell.

I think it is fair to say that everyone who had the privilege of knowing and working with Tom feel as I do: His presence is sorely missed, and rarely a day goes by when he is not remembered. It is still difficult to reconcile the fact that he is no longer with us.

There's one thing about Dad. He might be cantankerous and have a bit of a boisterous side; but if he wasn't making guns, he'd probably be making cars, machines, or some other useful product. And he'd be just as successful, and just as cantankerous. He just wants everything to be done in what he regards as the right way; and depending on your performance, you're either a hero or an idiot.

—Tom Ruger to Jim Kritz, 1988

From the 1993 Annual Report

1993 was a record year for the Company by any standard. Sales were $194.2 million and net income after taxes was $32.8 million, equivalent to $2.44 per share. Comparable figures for 1992 were sales of $156.1 million and net income after taxes of $22.2 million, equivalent to $1.65 per share. The per share figures have been adjusted to reflect the two-for-one stock split in May, 1993. All of the 1993 figures represent records for the Company and surpass by a comfortable margin the previous record figures achieved in 1992. . . .

These record results were achieved as a result of strong demand for virtually all of the Company's firearms products in each of the major market segments it serves. . . . In my opinion, the fact that the Company is the only one in the industry which produces products in each major market segment gives it a distinct competitive advantage, and we are working to enhance that advantage. 1993 saw the introduction of several new products including a new compact 9mm pistol, a new 77/22 Varmint rifle, and a new fixed-sight version of the New Model Blackhawk single-action revolver called the Vaquero. In addition, we have made gratifying progress in the development of new firearms which should be of considerable importance to us in 1994 and thereafter.

This development program provides a diversi-

The Ruger Sporting Clays Over-and-Under Shotgun

Number 411-02037 Sporting Clays Red Label Shotgun, 12 gauge.

Introduced: 1992. "Using the experience of [the firm's] world-class sporting clays team, Ruger has produced the ultimate Sporting Clays shotgun. . . . designed to take the brunt of [competition] punishment. . . . a live-rubber recoil pad, special chokes and its 7¾-pound weight help absorb the 12 gauge recoil, while the pistol-grip, two-bead sighting system, and reduced-weight 30-inch barrels help increase success."

Serial Numbers: 411-00000 on up.

Gauges: 20 or 12, 3" chamber, modified, improved cylinder, and skeet and skeet chokes—all employing interchangeable tubes. Full and extra-full Sporting Clays chokes available. Sporting Clays chokes do not interchange with other models of Red Label shotguns.

Number of Chambers: Two, superimposed.

Barrel Length: 30".

Markings: See Table of Markings, pages 330–35.

Sights: Gold bead at middle and muzzle of barrel.

Overall Length and Weight: 47", approx. 7 pounds (20 gauge); 47", approx. 7¾ pounds (12 gauge).

Stocks: Oil-finished walnut, checkered, pistol grip. 14 ⅛" pull, 1½" drop of comb, 2½" drop of heel.

Finish: Blued, with polished stainless steel receiver and forend mounts.

Materials, Construction, and Innovations: Single sighting plane preferred by Sporting Clay shooters. An elegant gun, of rugged construction. Reduced-weight barrels, back-bored to .743". 30" barrel length contributes to accuracy, and follow-through. Two-bead sighting system. Wide choice of special screw-in chokes (of stainless steel); with special 2⁷⁄₁₆" taper, to soften recoil. Pistol- grip stock; live-rubber recoil pad.

Issue Price: $1,285.00 (1992).

Engraving: From 1995, hand engraving available.

Production Variations:

KRL-1236: 12 gauge (first listed in 1992 price sheet and catalogue, and continuing to present).

KRL-2036: 20 gauge (first listed in 1994 price sheet and catalogue, and continuing to present).

fication of products which should enhance and protect our volume of sales a long way into the future. One of the major developments of 1993 has been our new emphasis on law enforcement business. We've been fortunate in being able to add to our organization a well proven network of police sales and service specialists. Our "P" series pistols . . . have been recognized widely in the civilian market so that we are now probably the largest maker of that category of firearms. During 1993 there was a visible increase in the usage of these arms by law enforcement organizations. With our new and more specific focus on police markets, we are optimistic about the prospect of enhanced sales in that sector. We have, furthermore, produced specialized firearms for police use which will be available for delivery during 1994, particularly our new police carbine and a new police submachine gun. These products also have substantial export potential. All during 1993, we actively pursued the sale of our police pistols in several export markets, and we are working against worldwide competition in several countries where major purchasing programs are being implemented.

In July 1993 there was a registered secondary offering of two million shares of Sturm, Ruger Common Stock through an underwriting syndicate headed by A.G. Edwards & Sons, Inc. and Morgan Keegan & Company, Inc. I was the selling stockholder and did this as part of my estate planning and to concurrently provide a greater degree of diversification in my personal holdings. Nonetheless, I remain the largest individual stockholder in the Company, and together with other members of the Ruger family and through voting agreements, still own or vote 31% of the Company's Common Stock after this offering.

The advantage of this secondary offering is to provide a much greater liquidity in the Company's shares for present as well as potential stockholders. . . .

We recognized [in 1993] the necessity of a substantial increase in investment casting capacity. Plans were underway by year-end to approximately double the capacity at our Prescott facility, and we are also studying the means for enhancing production at our New Hampshire facility. Now that these steps are being taken, I think we have made a major improvement in our growth potential.

1994 marks the 45th anniversary year of the Company and naturally invokes a certain degree of nostalgia when I think of the ground that has been covered and the progress which has been made.

Nonetheless, my focus, as well as that of management, remains firmly fixed on the future. All of this planning for the future is stimulating to me as I observe the enthusiasm with which top management embraces these extended objectives and starts the task of making it all happen. The loyalty and effort demonstrated by our whole organization is inspiring, and I believe I am correct in saying that they are unstintingly helping to make us recognized as a premier American manufacturing organization.

The Vaquero Single-Action Revolver: Stan Terhune Remembers

Even the *Wall Street Journal* was writing about a new category of shooting sport—western-style "action shooting"—which developed in the 1980s and continues to grow today. With the distinct interest generated by these cowboy shoots, we recognized that the standard Blackhawk was not being used. Because it had an adjustable sight, it couldn't be shot in the traditional matches, which required original-type equipment with styling from the nineteenth century.

In the Vaquero project, one variation had to simulate a traditional "case-hardened" colored cylinder frame, with the balance of the revolver blued. Bill had asked our Newport metallurgist, Doug Fay, and myself to experiment with different finishes for these new single-actions. It was a matter of developing an acceptable color that didn't require the standard procedure of color case-hardening which used intense heat and then quenching. With our tremendously strong steels, we did not need to case-harden for durability; all we wanted was the color simulating that traditional mottled look.

The rest of the project was just to get out the product, which we came to call "the gun that would have won the West." When we had a design and production print, we had the investment casting die changed to eliminate the adjustable rear sight apertures.

The amount of time from the original idea, to the drawings, to the first prototypes, and to production was only a matter of about four months, which shows how fast we can move. The first time we exhibited the Vaqueros was at the distributor show in Denver, early December, 1992.

The response to this revolver has been as tremendous as any product the company has come out with in my memory. It was instantly and enthusiastically accepted.

The only criticism we heard on the first showing of the stainless steel version was that the finish was like other stainless steel guns, sort of satiny, rather than having the appearance of a nickel-plated Single Action Colt. That satiny finish didn't do it; we worked on that until the gun division perfected the current polish. So now the stainless model has the appearance of the classic nickel-plated versions. We actually have to tell people it's not plated. The only difference you can tell between a nickel finish and our stainless is a slight nuance of color; one is more silvery than the other. But the only time you can see the difference is by putting them side by side. And with our special polish, there is no problem of flaking, a distinct weakness with nickel plating. It's a special process, unique to Ruger.

Our technological skills got us into production quickly, and show the magic of precision investment casting. The Vaquero was another triumph

Frederic Remington Cavalryman painting, with Ruger Vaqueros and a Bisley: "The guns that would have won the West." Ruger is a keen aficionado of Western art, much of which adorns the various company offices.

The Ruger Vaquero New Model Single-Action Revolver

Number 55-00225 Vaquero Revolver, .45 Long Colt, with 7½" barrel.

Number 55-41465 Vaquero Revolver, .45 Long Colt, with 4⅝" barrel, in stainless steel.

Introduced: 1993. "Evocation of the Old West. . . . Unique in strength and design yet classic western in style . . . a fixed sight version of the . . . New Model Blackhawk. . . . destined to become an instant legend . . . the gun that would have won the West."

Serial Numbers: 55-00000 to -10037 (by beginning of 1993).

Calibers: .44-40, .44 Magnum (.44 Special interchangeable), .45 Long Colt.

Number of Chambers in Cylinder: Six.

Barrel Lengths: 4⅝", 5½", 7½".

Rifling: .44-40, .44 Magnum: 6 grooves, right-hand twist, one turn in 20"; .45 Long Colt: 6 grooves, right-hand twist, one turn in 16".

Markings: See Table of Markings, pages 330–35.

On left side of barrel:

Before using gun-read warnings in *instruction manual* **available free— from Sturm, Ruger & Co., Inc. Southport, Conn. U.S.A.—**

Sights: Open, fixed: notched topstrap rear and blade front.

Overall Length and Weight: 10¼", 39 ounces (4⅝" barrel, .44-40); 13⅛", 41 ounces (7½" barrel, .45 Long Colt).

Grips: Two-piece rosewood, with trademark medallion inlays.

Finish: Blued, with "color case" frame; or high-polish stainless steel.

Materials, Construction, and Innovations: Polished stainless steel, or blued and "color case" simulated finish on hardened chrome-molybdenum steel.

Single Action Army look-alike, at reduced cost from the Colt, and with patented transfer bar ignition system and loading gate interlock. Steel coil springs of unbreakable music wire quality, rather than ancient, breakable flat springs. Calibers include potent .44 Magnum, which is not available in the Colt Single Action Army or in Single Actions by most contemporary makers. Polished stainless steel finish closely resembles antique nickel finishes, but cannot chip, peel, or flake.

Issue Price: $394.00 (1993).

Engraving: No engraved examples have been factory produced to date.

Price Sheet Listings and Major Production Variations:

.45 Long Colt (introduced 1993):

BNV44: 4⅝" barrel, blued and color case finish.
BNV455: 5½" barrel, blued and color case finish.
BNV45: 7½" barrel, blued and color case finish.
KBNV44: 4⅝" barrel, high-gloss stainless steel.
KBNV455: 5½" barrel, high-gloss stainless steel.
KBNV45: 7½" barrel, high-gloss stainless steel.

.44-40 (introduced 1994):

BNV40: 4⅝" barrel, blued and color case finish.
BNV405: 5½" barrel, blued and color case finish.
BNV407: 7½" barrel, blued and color case finish.
KBNV40: 4⅝" barrel, high-gloss stainless steel.
KBNV405: 5½" barrel, high-gloss stainless steel.
KBNV407: 7½" barrel, high-gloss stainless steel.

.44 Magnum (introduced 1994):

BNV475: 5½" barrel, blued and color case finish.
BNV477: 7½" barrel, blued and color case finish.
KBNV475: 5½" barrel, high-gloss stainless steel.
KBNV477: 7½" barrel, high-gloss stainless steel.

A small cross-section of articles on Sturm, Ruger. Due largely to its steady and solid debt-free success, the newsworthiness of its engineering-driven product philosophy, and Ruger's willingness to speak plainly about controversial issues, the company and its founder have received more such publicity since 1949 than any other firearms firm, in the general media as well as in sporting firearms and other gun-related periodicals.

Model Single-Six and New Model Blackhawks, Bearcat production was halted; but demand for the discontinued revolver remained strong.

In the early 1990s, some thought was given to producing a smaller "kit gun" type .22 revolver for campers and outdoorsmen where size and weight were at a premium. The .22 caliber version of the SP101 was viewed as too heavy. A lightweight experimental version of the New Model Single-Six was tried, with a three-inch barrel and an aluminum alloy cylinder frame. This did not meet with the approval of either Bill Ruger, Sr. or Jr., although Frank Bonaventura spent a considerable amount of time with the Southport engineers developing it. The next step was to see if a version of the "old model" Single-Six retrofit could be used in the Bearcat. While it was quickly determined it could not, it also became apparent that a scaled down conversion might be possible to use. At the same time, Bill Ruger decided that the New Bearcat would also be more versatile if it also accepted a .22 Magnum cylinder, which necessitated a longer cylinder and frame.

The smaller size of the Bearcat, and the more intricate workings of the internal mechanisms, made all this more difficult, but it had advanced to the point where the New Bearcat revolver was announced early in 1993, and a few thousand guns were shipped. Problems immediately surfaced with the timing of the .22 Magnum cylinders, which have since been recalled. The entire New Bearcat project is on hold pending re-engineering in order to better time those cylinders. We hope to get back on track, but the complex engineering of small mechanisms can be pretty difficult. In the meantime, we announced the availability of a newly designed safety retrofit for the original (1958–73) Bearcats, which were only made with .22 Long Rifle cylinders. This has proceeded independently of the ups and downs of New Bearcat production.

for us. This company just gets stronger and stronger.

The New Bearcat Single-Action Revolver: Steve Sanetti Remembers

Requests consistently came from shooters that we reintroduce our smaller Bearcat revolver, which had been out of production for many years. The model did not share many production processes with the "old model" Single-Six, and none with the New Model. In 1973, when the patented transfer bar safety system was utilized in the innovative New

Sturm, Ruger Business and Market Share

When John Kingsley joined Sturm, Ruger, he was aware of the firm's steady business rise and could see its impressive potential. Kingsley originally met Bill Ruger late in 1969. The next year Kings-

Catalogues, annual reports, and "The Art of the Rifle" advertisement show the rich, evocative style of Ruger marketing literature. 1982 catalogue, known to collectors as the penultimate Ruger "road map" due to fold-up nature, used for annual catalogues from 1949 to 1983. Staple-bound booklet format standard for catalogues since 1984. "The Art of the Rifle" one of the most popular of advertisements; painting by W. R. Leigh. Grizzly bear painting by Carl Rungius, which, like much artwork adorning Ruger publications, is owned by William B. Ruger, Sr.

ley, representing the investment banking firm of F. S. Smithers & Co., contracted to set up a budget system and develop better financial controls. He was then spending a day a week in Southport. After assuming the position of Executive Vice President, Kingsley set as a goal, "the concept of developing a tripod of earnings—with firearms as the first leg, outside investment castings the second, and a third leg . . . yet to be determined."

As Kingsley recalls:

During general discussions about the future course of the company, I remember saying to Bill that if he were interested in simply building up volume and becoming a conglomerate, the company could reach sales of $100 million in no time at all. One must remember that this was the early 70s when conglomerates were becoming somewhat of a financial fad. I said to Bill, and he agreed, that the company's and shareholders' best interest would be served by building growth internally, and if an acquisition were made, it would have to fit in with the company's general line of expertise, which I said was "precision metal manufacturing."

Sturm, Ruger's growth from 1971 to 1994, concurrently with increases in sales, margins, and net income as a percent of sales, has been far in excess of the norm for American manufacturing companies. In good years, our net income after taxes, as a percent of sales, was from 15 percent to 20 percent, and that has enabled us to finance our growth internally. This is particularly remarkable when you look at product liability, medical and workmen's compensation expenses, and utility costs. Look at those as a percent of sales: In 1970, our total bill for insurance was $20,000. Consider that $20,000 as a percent of $13 million, and you come to an infinitesimal figure. Social benefits at the same time also amounted to an insignificant percentage. You now [1994] look at product liability as 4 percent—and sometimes as much as 6 percent—of sales! Social benefit costs have also risen. Today our portion of social security, medical, and utility costs, is much more significant. We have been able to maintain our margins due to increased productivity and intelligent manufacturing methods, and by constantly monitoring overhead costs.

Published production figures of domestic units of firearms released from the Bureau of Alcohol, Tobacco and Firearms, which are a year behind (for confidentiality reasons), are quite revealing: In 1974 the total U.S. production was at 5.8 million units, while Sturm, Ruger & Co. production and sales were 395,000 units. There was a subsequent industry decline to 4,889,000 in 1977, with an upswing in 1980 to 5.6 million units produced. From 1980 to 1986, total U.S. firearms production decreased to a low of 3,040,000 units. But Sturm, Ruger's production in 1986 *increased* to 437,000 units, markedly counter to the trend. We never re-

The Ruger New Bearcat Single-Action Revolver

Number 93-00504 New Bearcat Revolver.

Introduced: 1993. "The 'Cat is back! And the 'Cat is better than ever because now the 'Cat can change its spots! . . . *two* cylinders, one specifically engineered to handle the .22 WMR Magnum cartridge."
Serial Numbers: 93-00000 on up.
Calibers: .22 Long Rifle, extra cylinder in .22 Magnum.
Number of Chambers in Cylinder: Six. Non-fluted cylinder.
Barrel Length: 4".
Rifling: 6 grooves, right-hand twist, one turn in 14".
Markings: See Table of Markings, pages 330–35.
On left side of barrel:
> STURM, RUGER & CO., INC. [LO- .22
> SOUTHPORT, CONN. U.S.A. GO] CAL
> READ INSTRUCTION MANUAL

Caliber marking on cylinder periphery at breech, both sides: **.22 L.R.** *or* **.22 WIN. MAGNUM CAL.**
Serial number *on right side of frame.*
Sights: Open, fixed.

Overall Length and Weight: 8⅞", 23 ounces.

Grips: Rosewood, with trademark medallion inlays.

Finish: Blued, or bright stainless.

Materials, Construction, and Innovations: Blued model of chrome-molybdenum steel. Bright model in polished stainless steel. Both types including precision investment cast frame.

Lengthened frame and cylinder, over the original Bearcat. Stainless steel introduced for the New Bearcat, as well as the patented transfer bar ignition system, and the extra cylinder in .22 Magnum.

Issue Price: $298.00, blued; $325.00, stainless (1993).

Engraving: Bear and cougar motif roll engraved on cylinders, with **RUGER/BEARCAT** marking.

Price Sheet Listings and Production Variations:

SBC4: In blued chrome-molybdenum steel.

KSBC4: In polished stainless steel.

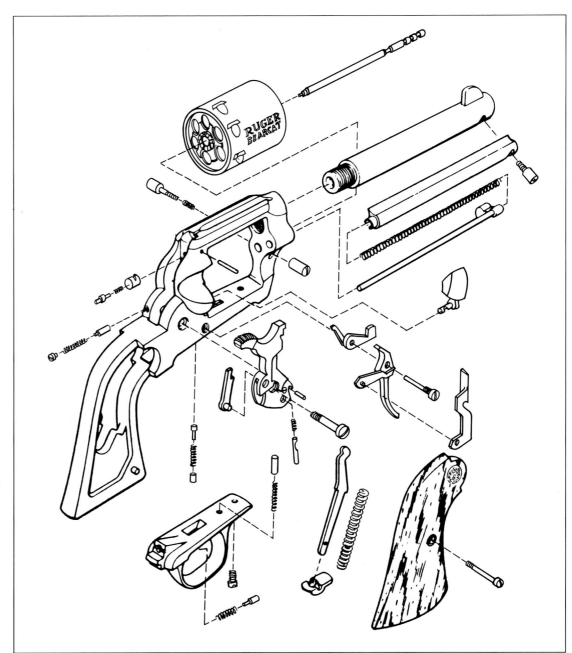

Exploded view of the New Bearcat Revolver.

273

ported an annual loss during this period, even though some of our small competitors went heavily into the red or even went bankrupt or out of business. 1992 domestic production was 4,030,000, and we made and sold 629,000 units.

The bottom line is that Sturm, Ruger's phenomenal growth has come at the expense of other companies in what has basically been a declining or static industry. As I say this [1994], however, the entire industry and our company are experiencing a phenomenal across-the-board increase in demand for all kinds of firearms: rifles, shotguns, pistols, and revolvers. The future is anyone's guess.

A Win-Win Situation

My industrial and corporate background is from the executive management level at United Technologies. I left because I was impressed by the *modus operandi* at Sturm, Ruger. The Chairman wants this company to be a win-win situation for everybody: The employees should be happy, management ought to be happy, and the customers will be happy. We will change the product or production or whatever else, so that our operation is fair to all. Sixty percent of our employees in Newport have been with the company for ten or more years. We have developed a solid relationship all around, and if there is a problem, we solve it; we do not institute temporary patches and hope the problem might fix itself, or just go away. We don't impose on our employees. Bill Ruger has a marvelous way with words, and can dictate a memo off the top of his head that the employees can understand, that will deal per-

Miscellany of just a few corporate, marketing, product, and safety awards and other tokens of recognition presented to the company, and its founder, over the years. Photograph of Ruger with Hank Williams, Jr., taken on presentation of Blackhawk revolver, in appreciation of donation made by popular singer to the Buffalo Bill Historical Center's firearms museum. Profusion of awards unequaled by any other firearms firm or industry figure in like period.

fectly with whatever the situation is at hand. There is that turn of phrase, just the right word, for which he is justly recognized. He has a perfect knack to communicate.

He has a way of giving us so much to do, so much to choose from, to get the job done. The way he presents this prods your interest, intrigues you, makes you want to do the project, and to get it done, and to do it right.

The fact that we have never borrowed money is important; this allows the managers to do their job, without having to worry about collecting money to meet the payroll, or take care of harrying bankers. He has dispensed with the perennial receivables problem, so we can concentrate on achieving our goals in manufacturing, engineering, and marketing. This has taken the burden off us as manufacturers; we don't have to take our eyes off the ball.

Further, we have so many employees in Newport, over 1,200 of them [1994], and such a continuing demand for production, that in 1987 we instituted a quarterly bonus program. The system worked so well that it is still in effect, and the factory production employees—who work on piece rate—can get as much as an additional $2,000 a year. If they miss more than a certain number of work days in a quarter, that employee misses out on the bonus for that period. Our attendance record is outstanding, and the teamwork here has got to set a standard hard to equal by any factory in the U.S.A.

All you have to do is look at our parking lot: Nearly everyone has a new or recent-year car, van, or truck, and if not new, at least the vehicle is in top condition.

Our employees are happy, management is happy, and our customers are happy.

—Erle Blanchard
Vice President, Controller
Newport facility
[1983–1995]

Teamwork

Al Scribner,* Production Manager of the Newport facility, rose to the position of manufacturing manager in his thirty-seven-year career at the Heald Division of Cincinnati Milacron Co., Worcester, Massachusetts. For a year after his 1991 retirement he remained with the company as a consultant, to smooth the transition. Soon thereafter he got bored, and decided to get back into the industry. He had known Bill Ruger for years, and had gone hunting with him from time to time. One evening at dinner, Scribner mentioned his plans to Ruger. Ruger said he wanted him to come work at Sturm, Ruger in Newport, and that's what happened:

I wouldn't have done this for anyone in the world but Bill Ruger. We talk about three times a week when he's not in Newport, and much more than that during the warm weather months, when he's usually here. He's always thinking of ways to improve our production, and the latest addition that will be finished in March 1995—65,000 square feet—is exactly on schedule. We made a deal with the contractor to remove 200 truckloads of rocks and dirt from the site, per day, and they maintained that pace right up to the concrete-pouring stage.

We're the eighth largest industrial employer in the entire state, and growing. Everybody here knows his or her job, and they do it with dedication and enthusiasm. This job sure beats retirement.

Over Al Scribner's desk is a framed statement of the Sturm, Ruger approach to production:

Together
Everyone
Accomplishes
More
WORK

*Al Scribner died January 28, 1996.

CHAPTER XI

"Our Responsibility for the Future"
1994–1995

It has always surprised and saddened us how much time and effort has gone into both sides of the "gun control" debate. Accidents with firearms are at an all-time low, and the violent crime rate of most segments of society is comparable to that of England, except for one demographic group—young, urban males. The curious thing is that most of them are not even legally permitted to possess any gun, due to age, local law, prior convictions, drug history, and the like. We do not, legally cannot, and don't want to sell our products to this group, yet their almost total societal breakdown is blamed by some upon law-abiding citizens many miles away who comply with the law and who choose to own firearms for lawful purposes. Over 99 percent of all firearms, including handguns, are never misused, but that's certainly not the impression conveyed by the contemporary media, which vio-

Cross-section of Sturm, Ruger memorabilia, with company advertising, manuals, and other publications, done in a consistently attractive, no-nonsense style, format, and content. Photographs at *top* show Armorers' School in session, an early 10-Year Club dinner, Ruger at bench with Mini-14 and speaking with Walter Berger, scenes from Pine Tree Castings, and law enforcement use of the Mini-14. Red booklet at *lower right* gives Ruger's vision for the future of a responsible firearms industry in sometimes turbulent society.

43. 1994
77/22 Hornet Bolt-Action Rifle
44. 1994
P94 Pistol (see pp. 222–23)
45. 1994
MP9 Submachine Gun
46. 1995
28 Gauge Over-and-Under Shotgun
47. 1995
Woodside Over-and-Under Shotgun

lently depicts guns in prime time "entertainment" and later denounces them on the news.

When people ask me questions like, "What's wrong with a waiting period?" I reply, "It depends on who's doing the waiting." You could require Bill Ruger to wait five years between gun purchases and you still have done exactly nothing to reduce violent crime; and, of course, the drug traders do no waiting at all. When people state that "the only purpose of a gun is to kill people," they are in effect calling the owners of guns "murderers"; and they wonder why so much passionate resistance is offered against repressive gun laws by the average shooter! As seen in countless editorials, cartoons, and TV shows, gun owners are the last remaining group that it is permissible to slanderously stereotype—the "redneck blaster." Gun owners are sick to death of this.

It amounts to a cultural clash, in which city dwellers (who rarely see guns used in other than an anti-personnel context), and the media (also located in the cities), seem to think that if only their less-sophisticated country cousins will stop being so obstinate and give up this "obsolete" right to own firearms, violent criminals in their cities will be disarmed. Sport shooting or admiring a collectible firearm is inconceivable to this group. For their part, the suburban and rural firearms owners, the vast majority who fire billions of rounds annually without untoward harm *to anyone, don't understand why they just can't be left alone to enjoy their own lifestyle, which rarely includes violent crime. The great grassroots resistance to additional gun control laws comes from this group, not the manufacturers, as is commonly (and wrongly) supposed.*

Hopefully, this book will help explain the allure of quality firearms to some in the former group who will keep an open mind. Firearms and their owners are part of our culture, for good and for bad. The great question for the future is how we can preserve the rights of the law-abiding majority while addressing the criminal misuse of firearms, in a rational, responsible fashion. For our part, we have continually urged the safe, responsible use of firearms by those who choose to own them, and zero tolerance for those who misuse this precious right.

—Stephen L. Sanetti
Vice President,
General Counsel
Sturm, Ruger and Co., Inc.

"Experience should teach us to be most on our guard to protect liberty when the Government's purposes are beneficent. Men born to freedom are naturally alert to repel invasion of their liberty by evil-minded rulers. The greatest dangers to liberty lurk in insidious encroachment by men of zeal, well-meaning but without understanding."
—Louis D. Brandeis, *Olmstead* v. *U.S.*

"There's always an easy solution to every human problem—neat, plausible, and wrong."
—H. L. Mencken

Firearms in America—the 1990s

The 1990s are proving to be a watershed period in the history of firearms in America. For a number of years it seemed the shooting and gun-owning public was in for a problem-free period,

at least while Republicans were occupying the White House. Ronald Reagan and George Bush seemed generally to be aware that tinkering with gun laws was not good politics, nor did it make much sense. However, due to some outrageous crimes by a few psychopaths, and the accompanying media hysteria, even Presidents Reagan and Bush succumbed on occasions to fuzzy thinking. As a consequence, President Bush submitted to pressure on "assault rifles" and former President Reagan eventually endorsed the "Brady Bill."

Then along came a Democratic President, Bill Clinton, supposedly a moderate or centrist, who appointed to his cabinet, staff, and miscellaneous departments a collection of self-proclaimed "policy wonks"—most of whom had severe restrictions on firearms ownership clearly positioned in their collective sights.

The first two years of the Clinton regime raised such a furor among the public (on any number of subjects) that the fall 1994 elections deposed some of the most powerful figures in Congress, and left in its wake a Republican-controlled House and Senate. The President, meanwhile, has endeavored to make the public think that he belongs within the mainstream population—even to the point of going duck hunting once a year (claiming someone else shot the duck!).

While it presently is uncertain whether the anti-firearms policies of the Clinton administration will be rolled back, only time will tell. In the meantime, all Ruger firearms are selling at the fastest and most voluminous rate in the company's history.

In contrast to 1949, the strength of the firearms field in the mid-1990s is astounding. There are innumerable periodicals on firearms, National Rifle Association membership is at a peak (over 3,600,000), hunting and shooting clubs are flourishing, the numbers and activities of hunting preserves are at an all-time high, there are more firearms collectors groups than at any

time in history, and hunting alone generates $40 billion in the U.S. economy, with some 20 million licensed hunters. Even extremely expensive international big game adventures, such as African safari hunting, are at an all-time record popularity with sportsmen.

Further, the 10 percent excise taxes on new firearms and ammunition sales, as well as license fees, are vital revenue sources for the programs of state and federal fish and wildlife agencies and firearms safety programs, and hunting plays a critical role in the conservation of wildlife and of state and national parks. The breadth and scope of gun-related interests go far beyond what most people could imagine, even among firearms professionals.

There are also numerous enthusiasts whose firearms interests are of the closet variety, who prefer not to reveal their inclinations unless addressing others of like enthusiasm. Many are professionals—lawyers, doctors, businessmen, and the like—who have avoided becoming embroiled in bitter and oftimes nasty debates with unyielding and frequently insulting adversaries. Yet they, too, love and appreciate fine firearms. This interest rests deep within the American character.

Certainly a pivotal institution with far-reaching impact on the shooting sports has been Sturm, Ruger & Co. As a designer, gunmaker, manufacturer, marketer, and technical innovator, Ruger has led the firearms field toward the twenty-first century. The string of Sturm, Ruger successes has influenced and inspired the work of other gun designers and manufacturers. There are more companies manufacturing firearms, ammunition, and accessories at this time than in any other decade in the twentieth century. Gunmakers, sportsmen, target shooters, collectors, and their representative groups are offering the public an unprecedented array of educational programs aimed at purifying the shooting sports and stressing firearms safety, while at the same time educating all who will listen to, read about, and observe the exciting and glamorous world of good quality firearms.

Ruger's predominant role in all of this, not only on a national but an international scale, is revealed in many ways. Reference to the list of company firsts (pages 00) documents the firm's multi-faceted dominance. The company's "red book," *Firearms Ownership in America—Our Responsibility for the Future*, is generally accepted as the finest publication on this subject to date, and is available to anyone on request, free of charge. Company catalogues, manuals, spot-TV public service messages, and advertising in periodicals stress safety and responsibility more strongly than has any other gunmaker in history.

In effect, the frontal attacks on guns, gunowners, hunting, and the shooting sports have galvanized the field as never before. And Sturm, Ruger occupies a pivotal leadership role in a massive, ongoing counterattack. To quote industry analyst George Rockwell, a former executive of both the Remington Arms Company and U.S. Repeating Arms (Winchester licensee):

It always seemed to me that Bill Ruger was about a decade ahead of the rest of us in the gun industry. In 1949 when I assembled his auto .22 pistol (before its introduction) the "sheet metal" technology appeared revolutionary and it was many years before his competitors picked up on it. That production lead has continued to this day when he is way out in front with his titanium technology.

Ruger can not only *design* superb guns, but can also do the process engineering to enable low-cost domestic production. Ruger's record of a profit every year and of never borrowing a penny stands unequalled in the annals of gunmaking, and his has become the most profitable gun company in history.

The Ruger brand is sold only to a few distributors, who are compelled to meet rigid requirements. Year after year the dealer associations vote Sturm, Ruger their "Supplier of the Year." When other manufacturers were courting the big discount chains, Bill stayed loyal to the independent dealer. With his competitors encouraging cut prices

at retail, Ruger's widely published suggested retail prices in advertisements and catalogues *discouraged* price reduction. Dealers were able to make a modest profit on Ruger guns.

Recognizing the dealer's difficulties in stocking telescope bases and rings for many different rifles, Ruger built-in the base on Ruger rifles and included the rings in the Ruger box. This insured that the proper base and rings were always available for the dealer to complete the sale of the Ruger rifle. The high quality of Ruger guns has always attracted the dealer because "they don't come back for repairs."

Ruger has always had great faith in his convictions. As a pioneer in investment casting, he constructed his Pine Tree Castings operation with a capacity nearly seven times his own needs at that time, figuring that he would sell the excess capacity until he grew to consume it himself. Even today, the company is once more significantly increasing the size of the investment casting divisions.

Ever one for new technology, Ruger is benefiting from the technological fallout from his lifelong interest in high-performance cars. The new strides in titanium metallurgy have brought him a close association with the Callaway racing engine and car company. In addition he is making oversize "Great Big Bertha" club heads for Callaway Golf. This technology suggests uses for ultra-light, ultra-strong materials like titanium aluminides and other composites that might be applicable to guns or other high-tech products.

And as a manufacturer who is also a leader in promoting the responsible use of firearms, Ruger has no equal.

The Challenge of Contemporary Gunmaking

Conceiving, designing, and manufacturing a firearm clearly presents a series of monumental steps in creating most new products in this increasingly complex field. Ruger, more than anyone else, knows how challenging the process is—as he learned not only from creating some forty-five new models since the .22 Standard in 1949, but even in projects pre-dating World War

II. For other than the most basic of designs, the entire gunmaking process has a complexity of nothing less than mind-boggling proportions.

Trying to enter the field as a manufacturer today is asking for the most severe regulation and interference by federal and state government agencies, to the point that even individual custom gunmakers feel themselves under siege. These concerns are in the broad range of licensing and recordkeeping (required of the maker, the distributor and dealer, and the consumer), the environment, liability and insurance, and the manufacture of a product that some politicians, activists, and others would like to outlaw entirely.

Ruger's domination is evident in any number of ways, not the least of which is the body of work presented here, and in company catalogues over the years. Consider some of the mechanical terms the firm has added to the gunmaker's lexicon: "transfer bar" (New Model Single Actions), "single spring" (Redhawk), "Ultra Light" (M77), "All-Weather" (77/22), "pivotless trigger" (P85), "gas block" (Mini-14), "interceptors" (Red Label shotgun), "integral sight ribs" (Super Blackhawk), "V-block barrel" (10/22), "Alexander Henry forend" (No. 1 Rifle), "integral Ruger scope bases" (M77, M77 Mark II, and No. 1), "round-top" action (M77), "angled bedding" (M77, No. 1), "front sight kit" (Redhawk), "single-action safety conversion" ("old model" single-action), "dual crane lock" (Redhawk), "tool-free takedown" (Security-Six), "push button cylinder latch" (Security-Six), "offset ejector" (Redhawk), "non-rotating ejector" (Redhawk), "extended frame" (Super Redhawk), "integral barrel rib" (M77 Mark II Magnum), "combination bolt lock/ejector" (Ranch Rifle), "flapper" (.44 Carbine), "loading gate interlock" (New Model Single-Actions), "self-tightening loading lever latch" (Old Army), "universal revolver handle" (GP100), "revolver frame integral scope mounts" (Super Redhawk), "no-dump floorplate latch" (M77 Mark II), and "integral laser" (P94L).

The manufacture of firearms has historically and traditionally occupied a pivotal, pioneering role in American industry. Under the leadership of Ruger, gunmaking has been revitalized and has, in some ways, reassumed a dominant place in contemporary American industry and technology. This is particularly true in the area of precision investment casting. Sturm, Ruger occupies a singular position at the forefront of that far-reaching technology. Quoting from a Ruger factory brochure:

> [Investment casting is] an inspiration to designers, allowing the most intricate parts to be manufactured at reasonable cost. Investment casting allows engineers and designers to build parts the way they should be built, instead of building them as well as the budget will allow.

Still another factor in the now thriving firearms industry is that guns are a vital component in the basic American concept of freedom. Both Bill Ruger, Sr., and Bill, Jr., have often stated that the more the gun issue is aired, assuming the facts to be accurate, the more the public, the press, and even politicians will agree with the concept of punishing the criminal, rather than flailing away at an inanimate object. Part of the strength of Sturm, Ruger is that the founder and management are firearms experts and devotees of the shooting sports. Since the beginning the firm has thoroughly cooperated with—and heartily encouraged—the corps of gun writers and magazines who, in turn, have strongly influenced the public.

The evolution of marshaling a response to

Alexander Pope's *trompe-l'oeil* "After the Hunt," with Remington Bronco Buster number 31 (Henry-Bonnard Bronze Foundry cast), and Woodward and new Ruger Woodside over-and-under shotguns. The 12 gauge Woodward once owned by 1930s bandleader Paul Whiteman, a member of the Philadelphia Gun Club and a dedicated trap shooter. Woodside from early production of that model.

pressure against guns and hunting represents one of the most powerful groundswells in modern times. The relatively minute cadre of elitists who decry firearms and hunting have utterly failed to comprehend that they are confronting the most basic, captivating, and time-honored of sporting instincts, and the prejudice against these interests—no matter how powerful the press thinks it is—is not about to destroy a dedicated sport and hobby which generates, in grassroots America alone, *billions* in annual business.

Typical of the evolution of education on firearms in contemporary American culture is an exchange between Stephen Sanetti and historian William Manchester, author of *The Last Lion, The Arms of Krupp,* and several other landmark books. A letter signed by Manchester appeared in the December 20, 1994, *New York Times,* attacking firearms manufacturers like Colt, Winchester, Remington, and Sturm, Ruger for placing "vast bribes . . . into the pockets of members of Congress," manipulating the NRA, willingly profiting from the carnage in the streets, and so forth. A two-page letter from Sanetti to Manchester corrected the numerous errors, and enclosed four decades' worth of Ruger advertisements stressing firearms safety, personal responsibility, and a copy of Ruger's now well-known "red book." In response, Manchester sent Sanetti a conciliatory letter, noting that:

> . . . there was research done, alas, but not by me. . . . I had to delegate some of these chores. . . . The enclosures which you sent me are excellent. I wish they could have the widest possible audience. Certainly they reveal your firm to be highly responsible and aware of the problems which may, and alas do, arise. I remain deeply troubled over the proliferation of small arms in this country and the extraordinary death toll which is a consequence. I have had many other letters in response to my own, several of them supportive of your view. If you have any other thoughts on responsible gun control, I shall be most grateful if you could share them with me.

Civil discourse is the first step toward understanding. As Ruger's "red book" states, "The fact is that neither the proponents of or those against additional firearms regulation are the enemy—*the violent criminal is the enemy of civilization,* and it is time that decent citizens toned down the rhetoric against each other."

The Long Island Railroad Incident

On December 7, 1993, Colin Ferguson undertook a murderous rampage on a Long Island Railroad train, using a Ruger P89 pistol that he had acquired in California (a state with some of the strictest gun control laws, including a background check) and had illegally transported into New York (another state with very strict laws), in violation of numerous federal, state, and local laws. Some of his victims filed suit against Sturm, Ruger & Company on the mere basis that it had manufactured the firearm that Colin Ferguson had criminally misused. As of the time this book was written, one of these cases had been summarily dismissed, the judge restating unanimous legal precedent on this issue:

> . . . to impose a legal duty here would create limitless liability. This would be inappropriate because as noted above, the gun/ammunition manufacturer has no control over the actions of a criminal whose goal might be to randomly kill or seriously injure innocent people. [*Forni v. Ferguson et al.,* Supreme Court of New York, Manhattan County, No. 132994/94, August 2, 1995, page 11.]

This judgment is fully in accord with statutes and court decisions in more than twenty-eight states. The responsibility for the criminal misuse of a firearm belongs solely with the criminal.

"Gun Maker on Mayhem: This Is Not Our Doing"— William B. Ruger, Jr., in *The New York Times*

On one of the rare occasions when it was not blatantly biased on the gun issue, *The New York Times* of March 19, 1994, carried an interview with Bill Ruger, Jr., on the responsibilities of firearms manufacturers in an age of rampant crime:

I don't want to sound crass or oversimplify things when so many people are dying out there in the streets. But the firearms business is not the place to put the blame. Gunmaking has been an honorable and important business in this country for a long, long time. It's a cliché but it's still true; people kill people, not guns.

To find the real answers to why there are deaths, we must look first at what is happening in American society, not at the firearms business. Why have we lost our moral compass and become so lawless? This is not something you can blame on a company like Sturm, Ruger. This is not the fault of the American gun industry. Just because guns exist does not mean people have to kill.

The people who focus on gun control have got it all wrong. They are frustrated—we all are frustrated—but the quick fix they want just doesn't exist. They need to face reality. Criminals will always get guns.

The gun industry has always urged gun owners to handle firearms with care, and suicides are certainly beyond our control. Guns are a matter of individual responsibility. You keep coming back to the fact that people kill people, not guns.

We're one of the manufacturers that have gone out of the way to make a point of this and to live up to it. We don't stamp out 'Saturday night specials' in some back room. America is a place of great diversity, and the gun industry is especially diverse and individualistic. People do their own thing. In any case, in this country you have the constitutional right to make a gun and to buy a gun, however it's made. That's not debatable.

Of course we're concerned any time one of our guns shows up on a crime report. But passing more gun laws is not going to stop such crime or criminals. As long as criminals are around, they'll have guns.

The people who are demanding more laws to control guns should instead be demanding more laws to control thugs. [We should] do more to put criminals behind bars and keep them there. But be-

yond that, I'd look toward making the American family stronger. And then I'd call on television to stop glorifying gun violence. Most of us don't even make the guns that are glorified the most—the assault-type weapons and the like. . . . The importing of cheap foreign guns comes close to violating trade-dumping laws. But, frankly, it's difficult to complain because then you're asking for more Federal intervention in the firearms industry. As for the bullets, in response to public pressure, there's been an effort to withdraw some of them from the market, except for sales to the police. [We have made some high-capacity magazines that we] sell . . . only to police officers. Someone who is not a police officer can buy one made elsewhere, but we can't do anything about that. What we can do is be a responsible firearms manufacturer ourselves. And we believe we are.

77/22 Hornet Bolt-Action Rifle

Ruger and his factory engineers had frequently considered manufacturing a .22 Hornet caliber 77/22 bolt-action rifle, but it seemed to be out of the question, primarily due to the expense of investment casting the specially lengthened and otherwise altered receiver. However, based on experience gained with the development of the .22 Magnum receiver, the Ruger engineers became convinced they could make a .22 Hornet at a reasonable price.

In contrast to the 77/22 rifle, the barrel for the Hornet had to be threaded into the receiver. Overall, the rifle is an enlarged centerfire 77/22, which includes a larger size (but smaller capacity) rotary magazine—a challenging engineering assignment, but ultimately completed successfully.

Jay Jarvis remembers the evolution of this hot new rifle:

For a long time we talked about having a small, centerfire version of the 77/22, like the small Sako action, and one of the cartridges that would be in that short action would be the venerable old .22 Hornet. The .22 Hornet was a cartridge that Bill would

mention frequently, and we had even made some No. 1 rifles in that caliber. It's a great varmint cartridge, with sufficient accuracy and power for 150-yard shots, but with a relatively quiet report and mild recoil.

We still talk about doing that multi-caliber small action, but in the meantime, Bill decided to go ahead with basically a lengthened version of the 77/22 rifle chambered for the .22 Hornet.

That's an easy thing to do, basically stretching it, because of the casting operation. However, the challenging part was developing the rotary magazine, which is even more difficult than in .22 Magnum. We spent a long time on the drawings and the prototypes. It took about a year to complete everything, and get into production. Bill has always liked rotary magazines; you can see a rotary feed in his 1940 machine gun, and in the old Savage 99 he first converted as a young man.

The Hornet rifle, which was featured on the cover of our 1994 catalogue, has proven to be very popular. Over half of our 77/22 production for 1995 will be in .22 Hornet. It's been a fine seller, more so than most people thought it would be.

I've worked closely with Bill Ruger for thirteen years and I still can't figure out how he does it! In fact, I keep telling everybody that if he'd asked me what I'd thought about a lot of projects that turned out successfully, I would have told him he was crazy. Yet we're increasing our production every year.

MP9 Submachine Gun: Steve Sanetti Remembers

In 1985, Bill Ruger told Jay Jarvis and myself to fly up to Diemaco in Ontario, Canada, to meet with Uziel Gal (a fine gentleman and respected designer) and Itzaak Yaakov (a retired Israeli general) to view the prototypes of a gun they had developed and wished to sell to the company. Diemaco, their tool room, couldn't export fully automatic firearms under Canadian law, so they were looking for an American source to produce this submachine gun. Bill Ruger was quite anxious to obtain another product for prospective law enforcement and military sales.

Jay and I made the trip, fired the prototypes, examined the guns in detail, and reported to Bill

Ruger that the design seemed very practical and in fact highly desirable.

Negotiations began to acquire the rights to the gun, termed the "Model 201." Meanwhile, they obtained permission from the BATF to manufacture additional prototypes in the United States. These were much improved over Uzi's original 1950s-era gun. As Uziel Gal himself said, "As I got older, I learned a few things." When we reached an agreement, these prototypes were transferred to us. They were two semiautomatic and two fully automatic versions.

Bill Ruger, himself a former machine gun designer, decided that additional engineering work remained to be done to even further improve these guns. A firing pin block and a bolt lock were added, the entire lower portion of the receiver was made of synthetics, the magazine was given a pronounced rake backwards to improve straight-line feeding into the chamber, and many other detail changes were made. However, the end product still resembles the original 201 gun we purchased, and law enforcement production began in 1995. Many government agencies have expressed an interest in it. This will be another small, but significant prestige market for the company. Remember, from his earliest designing in the 1930s Bill Ruger had hoped to sell a machine gun to the U.S. Government—over fifty years later, it's finally happening.

From the 1994 Annual Report

I am pleased to report that 1994 was another record year for the Company, even though the advance was small. Specifically, sales were $196.4 million, net income after taxes $34.0 million and earnings per share $2.53. Comparable figures for 1993 were sales of $194.2 million, net income after taxes of $32.8 million, equivalent to $2.44 per share. This record performance reflects increased production in 1994, since unlike 1993, the Company entered the year with virtually no finished goods inventory.

While 1994 was a record year from a statistical point of view as noted above, it was much more

significant from another point of view. The major significance of 1994, in my judgment, was that it saw substantial progress in increasing the Company's capacity not only in the firearms segment but also in the investment casting side of the business.

With respect to the firearms segment, ground was broken and substantial progress made in completing a 65,000-square-foot building addition to the Company's Newport, New Hampshire manufacturing facility. This represents the Company's first addition to manufacturing space since the acquisition of the Prescott, Arizona manufacturing facility in September, 1987. Upon its completion, which is expected towards the end of the first quarter of 1995, the Company will realize a substantial increase in its capacity for the continued production of high quality firearms.

Concurrent with this building addition in Newport, the Company is also increasing its capacity to produce the P-Series pistols at its Prescott facility, but this has not required a building addition.

This increased capacity should enable the Company to increase its share of the domestic firearms market. . . . The fact that the Company is the only American producer of firearms in all four market segments . . . puts it in an advantageous position to fulfill the demand for its products.

[Concurrently] there is a continued emphasis on new product development, and 1994 was no exception. 1995 will see the introduction of the Ruger Woodside Shotgun . . . and lightweight 28 gauge shotguns, as well as the 10/22 International Deluxe Sporter Carbine and two new models of the [Ruger] 77/22 [bolt-action rifles].

With respect to the Company's investment castings operations, work is well underway to double the capacity of the Ruger Investment Casting facility in Prescott. . . . This increased capacity will be used to satisfy internal demand for

firearms parts and also to satisfy demand from the golf industry calling for the production of metal woods made from titanium. As announced recently at the PGA Show in Orlando, Florida, the Company has entered into an agreement with Callaway Golf to produce their "Great Big Bertha" clubs in titanium.

For many years, I have written that one of the Company's long-range goals . . . has been to substantially increase revenues and earnings from the investment castings areas, thus in effect broadening the Company's earnings base. I sincerely think that the foregoing provides such an opportunity.

1994 saw the implementation of two significant pieces of anti-gun legislation. The "Brady Law" mandates that the . . . [22] states that did not have waiting periods or purchaser background checks prior to the retail purchase of a handgun, begin doing so. While supporters of this law proclaim its success due to stopping some small number of retail purchases by prohibited individuals, this is accomplished by the background check (which can be performed quite quickly, and which we have long supported), rather than the arbitrary waiting period. As expected, enactment of this law has had no significant impact upon sales.

None of the Company's currently manufactured firearms were banned by the "assault weapon" provisions of the "Crime Bill" enacted in September—indeed, all our long guns were exempted by name as "legitimate sporting firearms." As further mandated by the "Crime Bill," we have secured BATF approval for, and are producing, 10-shot magazines for our pistols. While "sporting purposes" is just one legitimate criterion for lawful firearms ownership, it was somewhat gratifying to see the Company and its products recognized (even by promoters of these wrongly directed gun control laws) as what we proudly are—"Arms Makers for Responsible Citizens." . . .

The Ruger 77/22 Hornet Bolt-Action Rifle

Number 701-70528 77/22 Hornet Bolt-Action Rifle.

Introduced: 1994. "A classic cartridge in a classic firearm. . . . a pioneer cartridge that introduced extended-range small-bore varmint shooting to American hunters. . . . the first high-velocity load specifically designed for small game hunting. . . . [in the] new 77/22 with a slightly lengthened receiver."

Serial Numbers: Initially marked with serial numbers from the Model 77/22, beginning with the 701-73700 range. Soon thereafter the model was assigned the individual range from 720-00000 on up.

Caliber: .22 Hornet (centerfire).

Magazine Capacity: 6, in rotary detachable box, not interchangeable with other 77/22 magazines; 45/100" longer than the .22 Magnum magazine, and ⅕" longer than the .22 Long Rifle magazine.

Barrel Length: 20".

Rifling: 6 grooves, right-hand twist, one turn in 14".

Markings: See Table of Markings, pages 330–35.

On top of barrel, forward of rear sight:

Before using gun-read warnings in *instruction manual* available free— from Sturm, Ruger & Co., Inc. Southport, Conn. U.S.A.—

Sights: Integral scope bases for patented Ruger Scope Mounting System, furnished with 1" Ruger scope rings. Also available with scope bases, rings, and folding-leaf rear sight, adjustable for elevation, and bead front sight.

Overall Length and Weight: 39½", approx. 6¼ pounds.

Stocks: Oil-stained American walnut, with checkered wrist and forend.

Finish: Blued.

Materials, Construction, and Innovations: A compact rifle that bridges the gap between .22 rimfires and the larger .223 class. Investment cast receiver and bolt, of chrome-molybdenum steel. Popular, accurate, and efficient .22 Hornet caliber, rotary box magazine, crisp trigger pull, fast lock time, integral scope mounts. Technical details shared with 77/22 rifle (see page 282), but with action ½" greater in length than 77/22 in .22 rimfire calibers. Threaded barrel, rather than the standard 77/22's clamp-in system. Bolt release on left-hand surface of tang, rather than on left side of receiver as in Model 77/22s in rimfire.

Issue Price: $452.00, without open sights; $469.00, with open sights (1994).

Price Sheet Listings and Production Variations:

    77/22RH, without open sights.

    77/22RSH, with open sights.

The Ruger MP9 Submachine Gun

Number 450-00513 MP9 Submachine Gun.

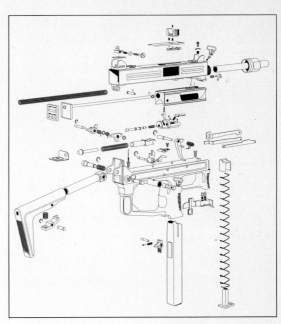

Exploded view of the MP9 Submachine Gun.

Number 450-00513 MP9 Submachine Gun, with stock extended.

Introduced: 1994. "Ruger has a reputation for building high-quality weapons, and I believe the MP9 will follow in that tradition. The gun will function well in police SWAT operations, dignitary protection, high-risk warrant service, or any other close-quarter situation. And one final thing that will make many of us happy: It is made in the U.S.A. by American workers." Sgt. David Spaulding, *Police* magazine, May 1994.

Serial Numbers: 450-00000 on up.

Caliber: 9x19mm.

Magazine Capacity: 32, in spring-fed detachable, double column box. For government and law enforcement use only.

Barrel Length: 6⅓".

Rifling: 6 grooves, right-hand twist, one turn in 10".

Markings: See Table of Markings, pages 330–35.

Sights: Peep rear sight adjustable for windage; 50- and 150-meter apertures. Protected post front sight; adjustable for elevation. Scope mount adapter bases on top of receiver, front and rear, of dovetail Weaver type.

Overall Length and Weight: 14⅚" (22" when stock extended); 5.94 pounds.

Stock: Molded Zytel; folding, telescoping. Length of pull, 16"; drop at heel, 1⅜".

Finish: Nonreflective blued steel parts. Zytel in matte black. Folding buttstock of anodized aluminum alloy.

Materials, Construction, and Innovations: A compact personal defense law enforcement and military weapon that allows controlled full-automatic fire, in either its compact or extended-stock models.

Rectangular receiver, of alloy steel. Barrel of heat-treated chrome-molybdenum steel. Fiberglass-reinforced molded Zytel handle. Buttstock of cast aluminum alloy.

Blowback, hammer fired, firing from a closed bolt. Selective fire, semi- or full-automatic. 600 rounds per minute cyclic rate. Top-mounted cocking handle, slotted to allow for sighting. Barrel secured at front of receiver by large nut. Three-position fire selector. Sliding button-type safety on receiver; separate trigger-actuated firing pin block.

Field-stripping via pressing of detent, and unscrewing of barrel nut, releasing the barrel. Push-out pin permits receiver top to be hinged upwards, allowing access to bolt and bolt operating spring. Single spring and guide rod, which goes through corner of bolt. Termination of spring guide in square plate and buffer of hard rubber, inside receiver at rear. Hood over chamber mouth, for feeding control.

Plastic pistol grip and magazine housing, grooved at front. Slight tilt to magazine, which improves feeding. Patented compact stock design allows for accurate shooting with stock extended or closed.

Product liability cases have continued [their steady decrease in number,] and the one jury trial held in 1994 resulted in a complete defense verdict in favor of the Company. Some attempts were made to resurrect the legally discredited theory of imposing "absolute liability" upon firearms manufacturers for intentional criminal misuse of their products, but they have universally failed and will continue to fail if the idea of personal responsibility for one's own actions retains any validity whatsoever.

Looking towards the future, I must say that I was extremely gratified with the results of last November's elections. For too long, in my opinion, there has existed what amounts to an adversarial relationship between the Government and the private sector. It is generally overlooked that it is the private sector which adds value and creates the jobs and opportunities which provide most Americans with a high standard of living, especially in contrast with the majority of the world's population. I hope that a return to more traditional values on the part of the Government, will, if not result in a partnership between the public and private sectors, at least reduce the level of antagonism. In summary, I as well as my associates are proud of the fact that Sturm, Ruger provides over 1,900 jobs for people in four different communities and that all this has been accomplished by hard work and ingenuity without a dime of subsidy from "Uncle Sam."

1994 marked the forty-fifth year of the Company's existence. While this is a significant milestone and much has been accomplished, it is more important in my opinion to think of the future. I am keenly aware of the axiom that companies must grow and keep pace with the times or they become moribund and eventually expire. Besides new products, a company needs new people and new ideas. In conjunction with this, one of the most important goals for 1995 will be to recruit new members for management. I look forward to being part of this process.

The Ruger 28 Gauge Over-and-Under Shotgun

Tom Ruger had longed for a 28 gauge shotgun in the Ruger line for many years. Although a prototype was made of a 28 gauge on the 20 gauge frame, Bill Ruger decided that an entire redesign would be required, so the frame would be more correctly sized to the slender 28 gauge barrels. This was accomplished in 1994, and two of the first production models were engraved in time for display at the 1995 SHOT Show.

Jay Jarvis was directly involved in the 28 gauge's evolution:

Early in the history of the Over-and-Under, we had made up some prototype double rifles in .45-70 caliber, using the shotgun receiver. Those were demanding because of the difficulty of regulating double rifle barrels, for accuracy. They did demonstrate the strength of the basic shotgun design.

The 28 gauge is a particularly striking example of the advantages of investment casting. The gun was a scaled down Red Label, squeezed down as much as we were able to do. Changes had to be made in the receiver, and in a new monoblock, a new receiver tang, new forend iron, buttstock, forearm, and top lever. We did use the same rib material, and some internal parts, but that's about it. Thus the job required all new casting dies, except for a few small parts. Considering the design cycle, we had to compress the existing configuration to the diminutive 28 gauge size. We had to be down to at least about 6 pounds to be successful, and that's about what the guns came in at (depending on the density of the stock wood). This is truly a new gun.

The project required about two years to complete, and we weren't able to make guns in 1994 as we should have. Better to get it right than in a hurry!

We could have gone a bit lighter, by thinning out on the sides, but it's hard to get Bill to go to anything lightweight. He wants his guns to be rugged. It remains to be seen what kind of volume we'll have with this pretty little gun.

We're even in the process of putting a little .410 together right now. It is necessary to check out the center of impact on the barrels, to see if the angles are right, and we should have that built within the next few days. All the parts we developed for the 28 will work for the .410, with the exception of the necessary barrels, and some other relatively minor changes. This will complete our over-and-under shotgun gauge selection; but it's not the end of our shotgun development, by any means.

The Ruger Woodside Over-and-Under Shotgun

Although the design patent for the Woodside design was issued in October of 1976 to Bill Ruger and Larry Larson, nothing but a handful of prototypes was built until production began in 1994. The Ruger patent had expired by then.

One of the prototypes had been handsomely engraved, and became the cover for the first company catalogue issued under the title *The Ruger Collection*, in 1995. Its scroll embellishments were the inspiration for the four sample Red Labels engraved for exhibit at the 1995 SHOT Show in Las Vegas: two in 28 gauge (⅛ and ⅜ scroll pattern), one in 20 gauge (⅛), and one in 12 gauge (⅜).

Jay Jarvis tells the story of the Woodside, and related Rugers:

This was originally drawn up and five guns were made, around 1980. The engraved sample gun on the cover of our 1995 catalogue is one of the original five. Bill has talked about making that style of gun since I came here in 1981. He made the decision in 1994. "By God, now we're going to make them; let's do it!" At first it was called the Gold Label. In fact, originally there was to be a Red Label, Blue Label, and Gold Label. The blue would have been a blued gun, engraved. The Gold Label was to be the open-sided, Woodside gun, with a stainless steel breech, engraved. And the Red Label was to be the plain, blued field gun.

The only changes we've made are that the wood panels on the frame sides were shortened about ¾" from the originals. We have also changed the early guns which don't have this, but they eventually will.

Further, we've eliminated a relief cut on the top of the frame. That's being filled in coming back from the monoblock and the receiver as a radius, instead of having a step. The first 28s looked like they were bent because of that "D" shaped relief cut. It was caused by the way we had brought the receiver depth down, and had changed the lines enough so that from the side the gun had a "bent" look.

To fix that, we eliminated the "D" on the 28 gauge, and after making up a sample, we concluded that it looked better than it did with the "D," plus it got rid of the optical illusion. So then Bill thought we ought to do that on all the shotguns. We had not made many castings on the Woodside, so we went back and changed the frame, dropping the "D." And I expect we'll do that on everything at some point.

There've been a number of changes on our shotguns over the years. One of the most significant was going to Ralf Dieckmann's patented "easy-open" design. That change had to be put in to the Woodside receiver and tang castings, and has been done. The wood panel was shortened, and we decided to go with a Circassian walnut stock, which makes a beautiful gun.

The Ruger 9mm Police Carbine and the Ruger Model 96 Lever-Action Carbine

Clearly indicative of Ruger's unending fascination with technology and design and his restless creative urges are the new autoloading and lever-action firearms in development as this book nears completion. The 9mm Police Carbine reflects Ruger's continuing dedication to the development of law enforcement firearms. And the Ruger Model 96 is an offshoot of his affection for the Savage Model 99 rifle, truly harking back full circle to his early experiments at converting the lever-action Model 99 to an autoloader.

We never had this idea that the company would be where we are today. It just wasn't anything we could imagine. We knew we had a good job, and we wanted it to continue. The earliest guys coming in after World War II were used to layoffs, of-

ten finding that a company didn't need them anymore. At Sturm, Ruger you got a solid job, and if you performed, you could make the best money in manufacturing in the entire state [Connecticut].

I remember when the new factory in Southport was opened in 1959; a luncheon reception was held at the Fairfield Hunt Club. However, visitors were not permitted through the factory; the closest they could get was walking by a glassed-in area, and peering into the general work space. Ed Nolan was a stern disciplinarian, and even turned down some of his old friends from Winchester ("Come on Ed, let us have a look!").

At first we thought, "What are we going to do with all this space?" That first spring, Ruger already added to the front of the factory. The following spring, a building was put up in the parking lot. The next space added was to the shipping area. Then we expanded upstairs a few years later.

Lacey Place eventually became so crammed full of machines you barely could get a fork lift in most of the factory. And I remember many nights when Bill would come out at 10:30, during the second shift. He would say, "Do you think we're really doing this the best way?" He wouldn't even have had any dinner.

I don't think there's any place in the world I could have worked where I could have a more interesting and exciting job than right here.

—Frank Bonaventura
Manager
Ruger Investment Castings

Sturm, Ruger in the Middle East: Jeremy Clowes Remembers

While with Holland & Holland, I met Stephen Vogel, at the Exposition de la Chasse et Tir in Copenhagen. Sturm, Ruger was interested in the M77 rifles to be marketed for stag hunting in

Scotland, but for various reasons, that never developed substantially. Our next meeting was at the Nikko Hotel, when the same international trade show was held in Paris. Steve asked me if I had any good contacts in a particular Gulf country as he knew they were considering placing an order for the police for a considerable number of rifles and revolvers. I told him that I did and we walked away from the wretched hotel, crossed the Seine, and had an excellent lunch at a very small and insignificant restaurant now, sadly, no longer in business. When he had told me what he knew I said that if he would like to come out to the Gulf with me the following week, I thought there was a very good chance the Minister of the Interior would see us. He said he would certainly be prepared to give it a shot. Afterwards Steve told me he had heard that line so many times before that he didn't think there was one chance in ten of our seeing the Minister. But in any event, we made our plans and I went out ahead of him.

Before Steve and I made our first visit together to the Gulf, he had been to Oman and was very taken with Arabia. Steve had an adventurous flair, and a genuine talent for dealing with potentates, military, law enforcement, and colonial types.

In 1976 I first went to Dubai and with the assistance of a great friend of mine, who had served in both the Trucial Oman Scouts and the Abu Dhabi Defense Force. I was seen by the rulers of four of the seven Emirates that go to make up the United Arab Emirates. I was also extremely fortunate in meeting Colonel E. B. Wilson, who had been seconded from the Trucial Oman Scouts, together with his Intelligence Officer, Charles Wontner, to form the Abu Dhabi Defense Force for His Highness Sheikh Zayed, Ruler of Abu Dhabi and President of the United Arab Emirates. By the time I met him he was Director of Sheikh Zayed's Royal Stables and very kindly had me to stay when I went to Abu Dhabi and extended his hospitality to Stephen when he came

The Ruger 28 Gauge Over-and-Under Shotgun

The Ruger Woodside Over-and-Under Shotgun

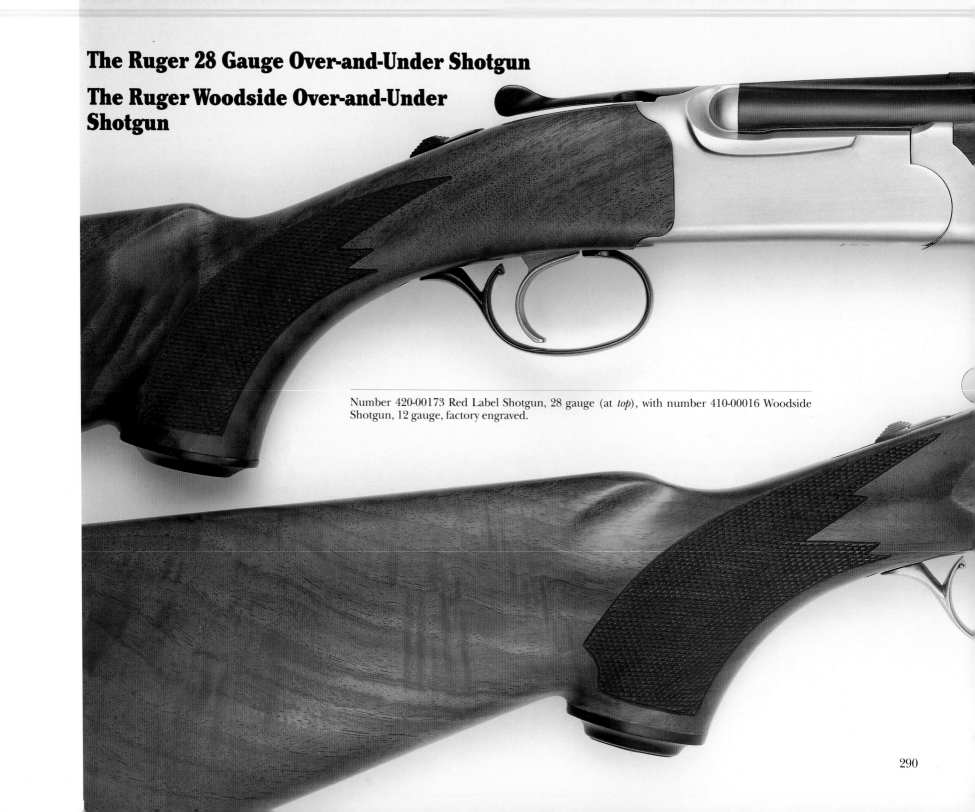

Number 420-00173 Red Label Shotgun, 28 gauge (at *top*), with number 410-00016 Woodside Shotgun, 12 gauge, factory engraved.

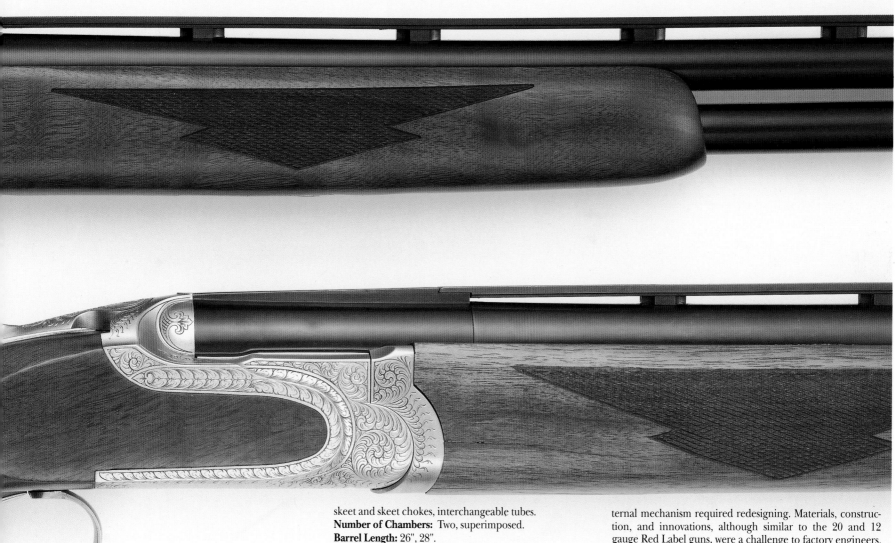

28 Gauge Over-and-Under Shotgun

Introduced: 1994.
Serial Numbers: 420-00000 on up.
Gauge: 28, 2¾" chamber, modified, improved cylinder, and skeet and skeet chokes, interchangeable tubes.
Number of Chambers: Two, superimposed.
Barrel Length: 26", 28".
Markings: See Table of Markings, pages 330–35.
Sights: Gold bead front.
Overall Length and Weight: 43", approx. 5⅞ pounds (26" barrel, English stock); 45", approx. 6⅛ pounds (28" barrel, pistol grip stock).
Stocks: Oil-finished walnut, checkered, pistol grip. 14 ⅛" pull, 1½" drop of comb, 2½" drop of heel.
Finish: Blued, with satin-polished stainless steel receiver and forend mounts.
Materials, Construction, and Innovations: Due to the reduced scale and size allowed by 28 gauge cartridges, much of the internal mechanism required redesigning. Materials, construction, and innovations, although similar to the 20 and 12 gauge Red Label guns, were a challenge to factory engineers. Comparison of the full-size photography of the 28 gauge should be made with the 20 and 12 gauge guns, on pages 155 and 290–91.
Issue Price: $1,157.50 (1994).
Engraving: Hand engraving available on special order, in established patterns, and custom-made designs.
Price Sheet Listings and Production Variations:
    KRL-2826: 26" barrels, pistol grip stock.
    KRL-2827: 28" barrels, pistol grip stock.
    KRLS-2826: 26" English straight stock.
    KRLS-2827: 28" English straight stock.

RUGER OVER & UNDER SHOTGUNS
with screw-in chokes: Red Label and Sporting Clays Models

Catalog Number	Gauge	Chamber	Choke*	Barrel Length	Overall Length	Length Pull	Drop Comb	Drop Heel	Sights**	Approx. Wt. (lbs.)	Type Stock
KRL-1226	12	3"	F,M,IC,S+	26"	43"	14 1/8"	1 1/2"	2 1/2"	GBF	7 3/4	Pistol Grip
KRL-1227	12	3"	F,M,IC,S+	28"	45"	14 1/8"	1 1/2"	2 1/2"	GBF	8	Pistol Grip
KRLS-1226	12	3"	F,M,IC,S+	26"	43"	14 1/8"	1 1/2"	2 1/2"	GBF	7 1/2	Straight
KRLS-1227	12	3"	F,M,IC,S+	28"	45"	14 1/8"	1 1/2"	2 1/2"	GBF	7 3/4	Straight
KRL-1236	12	3"	M,IC,S+	30"	47"	14 1/8"	1 1/2"	2 1/2"	GBF/GBM	7 3/4	Pistol Grip
KRL-2029	20	3"	F,M,IC,S+	26"	43"	14 1/8"	1 1/2"	2 1/2"	GBF	7	Pistol Grip
KRL-2030	20	3"	F,M,IC,S+	28"	45"	14 1/8"	1 1/2"	2 1/2"	GBF	7 1/4	Pistol Grip
KRLS-2029	20	3"	F,M,IC,S+	26"	43"	14 1/8"	1 1/2"	2 1/2"	GBF	6 3/4	Straight
KRLS-2030	20	3"	F,M,IC,S+	28"	45"	14 1/8"	1 1/2"	2 1/2"	GBF	7	Straight
KRL-2036	20	3"	M,IC,S+	30"	47"	14 1/8"	1 1/2"	2 1/2"	GBF/GBM	7	Pistol Grip
KRLS-2826	28	2 3/4"	F,M,IC,S+	26"	43"	14 1/8"	1 1/2"	2 1/2"	GBF	5 7/8	Straight
KRLS-2827	28	2 3/4"	F,M,IC,S+	28"	45"	14 1/8"	1 1/2"	2 1/2"	GBF	6	Straight
KRL-2826	28	2 3/4"	F,M,IC,S+	26"	43"	14 1/8"	1 1/2"	2 1/2"	GBF	6	Pistol Grip
KRL-2827	28	2 3/4"	F,M,IC,S+	28"	45"	14 1/8"	1 1/2"	2 1/2"	GBF	6 1/8	Pistol Grip

*F-Full, M-Modified, IC-Improved Cylinder, S-Skeet. +Two skeet chokes standard with each shotgun.
**GBF-Gold-Bead Front Sight, GBM-Gold-Bead Middle

Variations of the Over-and-Under Shotguns.

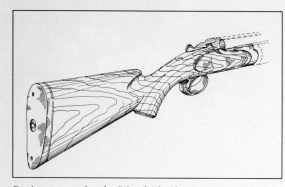

Design patent for the Woodside Shotgun.

Woodside Over-and-Under Shotgun

Introduced: 1995.
Serial Numbers: 430-00000 on up, 12 gauge.
Gauges: 20 gauge, 2¾" and 3" chambers, and 12 gauge, 3" chambers: modified, improved cylinder, and skeet and skeet chokes, interchangeable tubes.
Number of Chambers: Two, superimposed.
Barrel Lengths: 26", 28", 30".
Markings: See Table of Markings, pages 330–35.
Sights: Gold bead front, or gold bead at middle of barrel, and at front.
Overall Length and Weight: See chart.

Stocks: Polyurethane-finished Circassian walnut, checkered, pistol grip. 14⅛" pull, 1½" drop of comb, 2½" drop of heel.
Finish: Blued, with satin-polished stainless steel receiver and forend mounts.
Materials, Construction, and Innovations: Distinguished by a unique stock design, with the buttstock extending forward into the receiver as side panels, inletted as elegant and graceful cutouts. Quoting from the 1995 catalogue:

This precisely sculptured and elegantly curving fit of wood to metal is efficiently accomplished by Ruger's superior manufacturing methods. Close examination of the fit between the

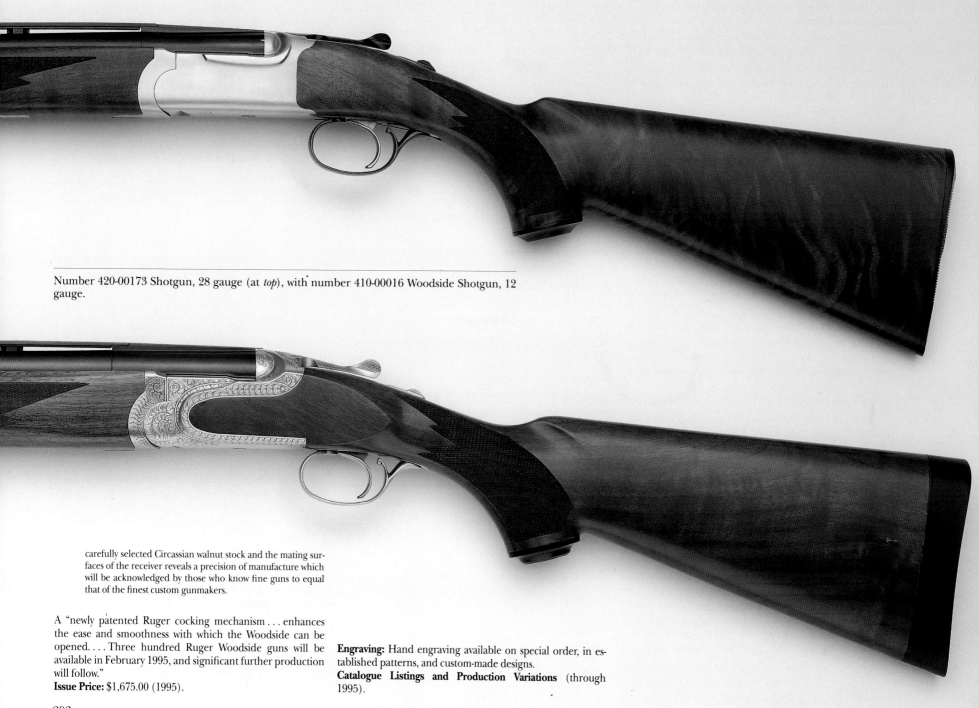

Number 420-00173 Shotgun, 28 gauge (at *top*), with number 410-00016 Woodside Shotgun, 12 gauge.

carefully selected Circassian walnut stock and the mating surfaces of the receiver reveals a precision of manufacture which will be acknowledged by those who know fine guns to equal that of the finest custom gunmakers.

A "newly patented Ruger cocking mechanism . . . enhances the ease and smoothness with which the Woodside can be opened. . . . Three hundred Ruger Woodside guns will be available in February 1995, and significant further production will follow."
Issue Price: $1,675.00 (1995).

Engraving: Hand engraving available on special order, in established patterns, and custom-made designs.
Catalogue Listings and Production Variations (through 1995).

out. Colonel Charles Wontner afterwards commanded the Royal Guard for a number of years.

We had a very good initial meeting and were received most favorably by the Minister who instructed that trials be carried out by the Police. As a result, a sizeable quantity of AC556K rifles and Speed-Six and Security-Six revolvers were supplied. The rifles could still be seen being carried by the Police at the airport over 15 years later, and when I asked if we could supply some more was told that they did not require any as the ones they had were still working perfectly.

Over the years Ruger firearms have been supplied to most of the Gulf States, all subject to U.S. State Department approval, of course. Given that in summer in the Gulf the temperature can reach 112–115 degrees Fahrenheit, with almost 100 percent humidity, Ruger "All Weather" rifles have been very popular with their unbreakable stocks and ease of maintenance. We have also supplied senior officers in the military and police with firearms for their personal use, but overall licensing procedures for the general public are very strict.

Ruger and Glass

Herb Glass, antique arms dealer and collector, and Honorary Firearms Curator-consultant to the West Point Museum, first met Bill Ruger at the 1953 NRA Show in Washington, D.C. Glass looks back on over 40 years:

> Bill Ruger was then "the new man on the block," with his $37.50 .22 pistol, underselling everyone and making him some money that, in those days, he sorely needed (he once told me that due to innovative methods of manufacture, each gun cost him a hell of a lot less!).
>
> I was introduced to Bill by General Merritt Edson, then NRA Executive Vice President, who said I could advise Bill well on his new baby—the Single-Six. At that time I was a top-ranked pistol shot and adviser to Colt's. I can still see this tall, rumpled, studious professorial type walking around the show

One time while visiting with Bill at his Newport residence, I introduced him to a friend, remarking how Ruger ran a "lean, mean, fighting machine." To which Ruger shot back, "What's this 'mean' stuff!"

—Ted Rowe, President
SIGARMS, Inc.

The growth of our Company parallels the growth of the nation.

—William B. Ruger, Sr.

The Sturm, Ruger Cash Position

I think we are the exception rather than the rule—although Microsoft has higher profit margins than Ruger now; they have revenues of $5 billion annually, and make 25 percent after taxes. They have a $1 billion war chest! At present (1993) our retained earnings are a debt-free $71 million, with margins in the 16 percent range, easily the best in the entire firearms industry. To my knowledge the only other major gunmaker carrying no long-term debt is Marlin. Relative to the size of business, and working capital requirements, this is a nice position to be in.

—John M. Kingsley, Jr.

with his tool room Single-Action revolver. We discussed it and I made suggestions, followed up by my letters to him.

We became firm friends almost immediately, with Bill visiting my house and shop in Bullville, New York (for martinis and a square meal), and my wife Viola and me visiting him in a converted barn.

He discussed many of his pistols with me; in fact, the latest I evaluated was his first 9mm autoloading pistol.

I remember when he decided to make the first .44 Magnum single-action, which I had encouraged. One day I called for a progress report and he told me that a few tool room guns were made, were proof tested, and functioned beautifully—but, "the damned things won't shoot!" I asked him what he meant, and he said they couldn't keep them in a "water bucket," with 10" groups at 25 yards. I asked if these were shot in a machine rest (in those days they weren't made for that caliber). So I asked how he was doing the testing. His reply was they had the best shots in the company doing the shooting.

I suggested he bring a .44 Magnum prototype over and let me try it; he left for Bullville immediately, arriving at my range by about 3 that afternoon. We put targets up right away, and I fired six shots: four 10s, a close 9 and a 7 that I called because of flinching. Excluding the 7 the group measured about 3½". If held properly, the guns *could* shoot—and could shoot with accuracy. Martinis were next, and Willy went home the next morning a happy gunmaker.

I later suggested that the space from the back of the trigger guard to the front strap was too close, leading to recoil-caused skinned knuckles. I loaned Bill a Colt Second Model Dragoon trigger guard, backstrap, and grips, which he later incorporated in the .44.

We spent a lot of time together socially, and went on several hunting trips—including the "Rocky Mountain Safari," which was published in my magazine *The American Gun*.

Many, many times Bill and I would get fed up with the tension of business and he would call, or I would call, and we would head for Blue Mountain, and climb those New Hampshire hills all day, with a small pistol, a knife, a tin can for making tea, and a can of beans or a sandwich. We would sit around a campfire like a couple of mountain men, and just look at the sky. Some days we climbed and walked ten or fifteen miles. In those days Bill could run like a gazelle, and even though I've been a jogger for years, he could outrun me up and down those inclines with incredible strides.

In my opinion Bill is definitely the twentieth-century equivalent of Samuel Colt, with the incisive mind of the Colonel, and with a charming personality, and a marvelous sense of humor. He is always a delight to be around.

Unlike most arms makers of our time, Bill is deeply knowledgeable of the history of firearms, and of the people who used them as far back as the seventeenth century. I have spent hours with executives of competitive companies, and in almost every case, their knowledge *might* go back fifty years or so.

This background has permitted Ruger to create, and advertise, imaginatively, to his advantage. Forty years ago Colt, S & W, and others were ignoring him—as one Colt executive told me: "He will lose his shirt making Single-Actions." Today Ruger's firm is the undisputed leader in the industry, and due to one man, the twentieth-century Samuel Colt: Bill Ruger.

Ruger and the Marlboro Man: Tom Pew Remembers

"I want to hear an idea for Ruger advertising I haven't heard before, that in your opinion will really do something for our sales, galvanize things, move us forward with a new approach." Bill Ruger fixed me with his eye in one of those opening challenges I'd often heard before, but had never entirely gotten used to.

A discussion of ideas—not just advertising ideas—with Bill Ruger has implicit in it one of those warnings that appears in another guise on all packets of American-made cigarettes: *"Responding in a way that hasn't been carefully considered, or is trite, can be hazardous to your intellectual self-esteem."*

"I do have such an idea," I answered after some consideration, "and it would 'galvanize' interest in our ads and boost sales, in my opinion, but I know you won't go for it."

"What do you mean, 'I won't go for it?' " he shot back immediately, ever so slightly mocking my "go for it," an expression he obviously didn't care for.

"I'll damn well 'go for it,' as you put it, if it does what you say it will do, if it has any merit on its own," he continued. Then the intimidating

scowl broke into a smile, and he pressed, "Come on, Tom, let's hear your idea and I'll let you know what I think."

"Bill, there's only one firearm designer and manufacturer today with a name that stands out like Colt, Browning, or Winchester. And only 'our name' is alive and sitting across the table from me, challenging me to come up with a single idea that will put a kick we haven't previously considered into our advertising."

He was staring at me now with a quizzical look, so I continued immediately:

"You know, Bill, there are a lot of people out there who love and use firearms who don't even know you're alive, who don't even know how all of this happens," I said with a sweep of my hand over the large table we worked at: a table that's always covered with springs, firing pins, slides, bolts, barrels, and stacks of drawings, ads, art books, automobile books, and gun books. A table that is a constantly changing collage of his passions, and everything Bill Ruger does is done with passion. Sometimes, that passion can have a way of searing everything that gets close to it.

"I've got the 'Marlboro Man' of firearms sitting across the table from me," I continued. "Let me use your photograph, your signature, a personal appoach from you in our ads, and we'll see some galvanizing in our sales. We'll see some increase in response to our product because what we have in you is rarely seen behind any product today."

There was a long pause, as I watched the idea turning over in his mind, and then:

"You were right this time, Tom; that's an idea that might work, but it's not an idea for me. I'm not going to do it. Let's leave that for Lee Iacocca."

Up until that time, although nothing akin to my suggestion appeared in ads, a personal statement written and signed by Bill Ruger and his photograph always appeared on the opening page of the annual catalogue. A statement that

talked about the dedication of the Ruger employees and love for the shooting sports as well as beautiful mechanical design, and it came from the heart.

In the next catalogue he instructed me to take it out with a terse, "Let's let the product sell itself." It has, and it will. It just resonates with the American tradition.

Samuel Colt, William B. Ruger, and the American System of Manufacture

To a professional historian like myself it seems only natural that Sturm, Ruger and Company would start out in Southport, Connecticut, and eventually establish its largest manufacturing facility at Newport, New Hampshire. Both communities are contiguous to an area of New England that was once known as Gun Valley and Precision Valley. I refer, of course, to that span of the Connecticut River that extends from Middletown and New Haven, Connecticut, in the south to Springfield and Windsor, Vermont, in the north. Southport and Newport lie at the southeastern and northeastern extremities of this region. It was here, in the Connecticut Valley and its neighboring areas, that one of the most important manifestations of America's Industrial Revolution occurred. What began in the 1790s with Simeon North, Eli Whitney, and the Springfield Armory eventually became home to Colt, Smith & Wesson, and Winchester. Today Sturm, Ruger and Company has supplanted the valley's venerable "big three" as the nation's leading arms maker.

When Larry Wilson and other contributors to this book refer to William B. Ruger, Sr., as a "modern-day Samuel Colt," they do so for good reason. Ruger's enterprises, most notably Sturm, Ruger and Company and Pine Tree and Ruger Investment Castings, represent a significant late-twentieth-century refinement and extension of what in the nineteenth century was called the

American system of manufacture. Coined in 1855 by a British military commission who visited the United States in search of new equipment for the Enfield Armory, the term refers to the manufacture of firearms (and later, consumer durables like sewing machines, typewriters, bicycles, motorcycles, and automobiles) with functionally interchangeable parts. Before leaving the United States, these British visitors ended up purchasing more than $107,000 worth of arms-making machinery, fixtures, and gauges and acquiring the services of James H. Burton and a number of other skilled American machinists to install them at Enfield. These purchases marked an important watershed: They represented one of the first significant large-scale transfers of American technology to Europe (before it had been the other way around), and they also signaled the beginning of an enormous international trade not only in firearms, ammunition, and arms-making equipment after the Civil War but also in consumer durables. Indeed, the source of America's twentieth-century reputation as a technological society is to be found in the nineteenth-century

From *top*, Alexander Henry single-shot rifle. Presentation Sharps Model 1874 Sporting Rifle, silver plaque on cheekpiece inscribed *Awarded/to/William Caughey/The best Shot in/Sharps Rifle Guard/At their first Annual/Target Excursion/Nov. 2, 1858;* engraved by the Gustave Young shop. Ruger Red Label shotgun presentation inscribed on bottom of the receiver *To:/Alexander A. Vogel/With Love/From His/Grandfather/William B. Ruger,* gold inlaid and engraved by Paul Lantuch; 12 gauge, serial 410-23922. Holland & Holland double barrel rifle, .300 H & H Magnum rimless cartridge, number 35217. Westley Richards drop-lock double barrel rifle, .318 rimless, from the armory of H.H. Maharajah Holkar, of Indore, number 17692. The Ruger No. 1 Single-Shot rifle, serial 270, made for William B. Ruger, and embellished by A. A. White. Set of double rifle barrels from a Holland & Holland back action hammer double rifle, number 17437, with WBR initials on the silver oval inlay on bottom of the buttstock, .240 Magnum flanged caliber. The Ruger shotgun does not look at all out of place in such estimable company.

saga of machine-made firearms with interchangeable parts. More so than the textile mills of Lowell, Massachusetts, or the nation's burgeoning trunkline railroads, this was the high technology production system of antebellum America that Europeans found most novel, lusted after, and unabashedly transferred to their own countries and, subsequently, around the world.

I wonder what Samuel Colt would think if, not unlike Mark Twain's Connecticut Yankee, he could somehow be beamed forward (rather than backward) in time to inspect Ruger's Newport plant today. Total amazement, highly likely; admiration, to be sure. A direct genealogical connection exists between the Connecticut Valley arms-making community of the nineteenth century and the Sturm, Ruger enterprise of today. Enter the stock-making shop at Newport and one immediately understands why. There one finds several banks of multispindled computer-controlled woodworking machines that expeditiously turn, inlet, checker, and finish gun stocks (and other wooden products). Although these machines operate at much higher speeds and perform more functions with greater precision than their nineteenth-century precursors, they nonetheless exhibit many of the same mechanical principles embodied in Thomas Blanchard's classic woodworking machines (introduced at the Springfield Armory in the early 1820s) and their improved and updated all-metal successors that the Ames Manufacturing Company of Chicopee, Massachusetts, sold to the British government in 1855. A stroll through the Ruger machine shop at Newport elicits similar comparisons, though, to be sure, significant differences exist between the speedier, more accurate, and versatile CNC machines used today and their belt-driven, mechanically controlled ancestors from the mid-nineteenth century.

What is completely new and different—and would doubtless astound Colt because it differs so dramatically from the traditional forging/

machining sequences employed at his Hartford factory—is the method of casting metal components employed by Sturm, Ruger and Company. Called investment casting, it represents a level of precision foundry work that could only be dreamed of by Colt and his nineteenth-century contemporaries. Of all the advanced techniques employed at Ruger, this is the one that gives the firm a special edge over competitors in design, productivity, and overall quality, strength, and performance.

The significance of William Ruger and his standing as the twentieth century's most celebrated inheritor and proponent of the American system, however, is not to be found solely in the beautifully designed products that issue from his factories. Writers and commentators often miss the point that Ruger's genius extends well beyond his ability to envision and design stylish, durable, and affordable firearms. It resides, in fact, at a number of different levels. Early on Ruger appreciated the need to employ state-of-the-art technologies like investment casting to achieve the production of high quality yet affordable products. He also recognized the need to be flexible in the market and to seek out niches that gave his firm competitive advantages. Above all, he surrounded himself with extremely talented people who, like Stan Terhune, Harry Sefried, and Jack Behn, possessed the ability, commitment, and enthusiasm to grab hold of Ruger's oft-demanding projects and push them to successful completion. Behind all great leaders stand skilled associates, and Ruger is no exception. Indeed, he clearly excels in this category. What is more—and as many attest—over the years he has maintained an unusually close relationship with people on the shop floor. As Ruger well knows, CEOs have to be tough-minded and keep their eye on the bottom line, but they also have to instill loyalty and respect in their workforce. The low labor turnover rates at the Newport plant, and indeed throughout the Ruger

enterprise, certainly corroborate this point.

Ultimately, however, it is the combination of all these qualities, coupled with his appreciation and use of art and history in conceptualizing new product designs, that speak most eloquently to William Ruger's success as an industrialist. He is, to be sure, an American original, fully deserving comparisons with Samuel Colt, Henry Ford, and other captains of American industry.
—Professor Merritt Roe Smith, Ph.D., Director
Program in Science, Technology, and Society
Massachusetts Institute of Technology

Author to William B. Ruger, Sr.: "Do you collect Rugers?"

Ruger's facetious response: "Are you joking? I sell every one I can!"

CHAPTER XII

"That Was My Dream":
Ruger Remembers

Collage representing diversity of Ruger company, personal and industry associations; *top left*, May Ruger with daughter-in-law Mary, seated at Southport patio. At *left*, Ruger old-timers Kirk Timm, Jack Behn, and Walt Sych, at trade show. Ruger-sponsored race driver Johnny Unser with Ruger and Tom Pew, at 1993 Loudon Indianapolis car race; *above* photograph of Ruger and Stan Terhune with Petersen Publishing founder Robert E. Petersen, Ken Elliott, and Steve Ferber, founder of Acqua-Field Publications. Ruger with son Tom, candid moment at Southport office. *Top center*, company board of directors, 1993; *above* photograph by niece Cameron Brauns of the Rugers at final Christmas together, 1993. Ruger and Kalashnikov discuss new Ruger 22/45 pistol. *Below*, Ruger, Jr., to *left* of Tom Ruger and Jim Carmichel, at 75th birthday party, Cody; limited edition Ruger commemorative cartridges at *left*, custom made for 75th birthday. *Above* cartridge box, Ruger with stockbroker-gun collector John R. Woods, also at Cody party. To *left* of box, Sturm, Ruger poster celebrity and professional guide Kelly Glenn. To *left and below*, Kurt and Billy Jean Vogel wedding portrait, the Sturm, Ruger factories; Ruger, Sr. and Jr., with Stephen Sanetti on secondary stock offering "road show" of spring, 1993. Ruger with Prescott plant manager, Robert Stutler. Sanetti, Gloria Biagioni, Erle Blanchard, and John Kingsley, Jr., at *lower right*, with snapshot of Chickie Ruger and daughter Adrienne. Black-and-white pictures of the six grandchildren, at young age. Jet-black cat Ruger's favorite, Checkers (on Douglas chair); yellow cat, Keto, the gifted vermin-hunter from Ruger's Southport home. Cartridges are all those for which Ruger firearms are chambered, represent broad range and uses of Ruger products.

"To bear up under loss, to fight the bitterness of defeat and the weakness of grief, to be victor over anger, to smile when tears are close, to resist evil men and base instincts, to hate hate and to love love, to go on when it would seem good to die, to seek ever after the glory and the dream, to look up with unquenchable faith in something evermore about to be, that is what any man can do, and so be great."

—Zane Grey

We have manufactured over fourteen million firearms since 1949 and in the course of doing that, I think we have acquired a real insight into the reasons why people buy guns and why guns appeal to people, aside from a purely utilitarian objective of self-defense or whatever. There's a much deeper significance and appeal to firearms, and you have only to look back to the collections of arms and armor in the great museums of the world to realize that this is a vast category of human creativity. The manufacture of firearms has a strong historical interest and says a great deal about the nature of people's psyches or mentalities. Weapons have always been the kind of possession which was valued above almost anything else—weapons of any sort, and, in our time, particularly firearms.

Howard Chappel, the famous archaeologist and historian of small boat construction, commented in the foreword to one of his landmark volumes that, of all the possessions recorded by civilized human beings, those that seem to be the most valued are guns and boats. And I think that's true.

—*William B. Ruger, Sr.*

"Never Worked a Day in My Life"

At his age and station in life, Ruger could easily retire: surrounding himself with his collections of paintings, sculpture, books, sport and vintage cars, firearms, and houses; relaxing with friends, family, and his myriad admirers. But "retirement" isn't in his vocabulary. And though he once remarked to *Forbes* magazine that he'd never worked a day in his life, in fact, there are more Ruger projects in the works now than in his entire career. At seventy-nine, his vision for his company—and for the future of the firearms industry on which he has left such an indelible mark over the past forty-six years—continues to be penetrating and incisive.

In the twilight of a brilliant career, he is still the bold spokesman for his chosen field, taking on the press, testifying before Congressional committees (having done this three times), preaching the Gospel of personal responsibility

Trompe-l'oeil paintings so cleverly done that the pictures have fooled the eye of visitors to Ruger's Southport office for many years; by D. Scott Evans. Ruger .22 Standard pistol, relief chiseled and engraved for Ruger by Paul Lantuch (from the 1 of 5,000 Signature series, first of the stainless steel Ruger .22 pistols); serial number 17-02953; faceted and fluted; the magazine base inlaid with jade, set in silver.

that is summed up in one of his favorite creeds: "To ride, shoot straight, and speak the truth. . . ."

Bill Ruger's lifelong fascination with machines, technology, and invention—and with firearms in particular—has taken him from an unsettled boyhood in Brooklyn to the highest echelons of American industry. Beginning as a largely self-educated teenager working alone to create a sophisticated .30 caliber machine gun, his versatility and brilliance built a transcontinental industrial empire employing nearly 2,000 workers at five locations, producing almost a million firearms per year. The ancient precision investment casting method, which Ruger developed into a space age process, has placed his foundries in constant demand from manufacturers in fields as diverse as aerospace, automobiles, medicine, and golf.

In the entire 600-year history of firearms, no one has achieved such absolute mastery of the art, craft, science, mechanics, business, tradition, and romance of gunmaking as has William Batterman Ruger. Not Oliver F. Winchester, not Eliphalet Remington, not Horace Smith nor Daniel B. Wesson, not the Mauser brothers, not John M. Browning, and not even that benchmark against whom success in the gun business is traditionally measured, the pioneering entrepreneur ("America's first tycoon") Colonel Samuel Colt.

The Ruger legend is all the more remarkable because it spans a period during which America's industrial base has been shrinking; when pundits have relegated the country to a service economy; and when media and activist pressures against firearms and hunting have reached peak levels. Yet even as the market shares of other major gun firms have decreased, Ruger's continues to increase—to the point where, in 1994, it approached 20 percent of the total number of firearms made in the U.S.A. Further, only Ruger, of all the world's manufacturers, designs, engineers, *and* builds a complete line of rifles, shotguns, pistols, and revolvers. There is a Ruger gun for virtually every sporting, personal defense, military, and police purpose. This unprecedented, unequalled, and unsurpassed line is manufactured entirely in Ruger factories, *in America*. And the whole phenomenon sprang literally out of nothing a scant forty-seven years ago.

As if this weren't enough, Bill Ruger's achievements transcend the domains of guns and machines, and enter the realm of art. Like the automobiles of Ettore Bugatti, or the architecture of Frank Lloyd Wright, or the haute couture of Karl Lagerfeld, the guns of Ruger have their own style, their own magic: All are unmistakably, quintessentially, inexorably, and completely identifiable as *Rugers*.

On the Appeal of Firearms
and on His Favorite Ruger Gun

Like boats and cars, guns are among the objects of this world that people live to acquire. They are not just utilitarian. Our company's balancing act has been to put that appeal into these products, and at the same time make sure they are priced so that a fair number of people can afford to go out and buy them.

A lot of people out there want to go shooting, but they don't buy a new gun; they buy a secondhand one. Probably a lot of those guns are in perfectly excellent condition. The manufacturer's point of view may be that shooting is not as strong as it was, but perhaps people are just buying old guns with which to pursue their sport.

In some respects, I think my favorite Ruger is the first gun we produced, the Standard .22 pistol, which we still make in slightly changed form. For sentimental reasons it means a great deal in my life, and I often think back to the days when it had a very small beginning. We struggled to complete the engineering on that and then to bring it into production. I'll look back at it sometimes, recalling the design work that went into it, and think to myself, "You were better then than you realized," at least in strict terms of firearms design.

We see this intense public firearms interest exhibited in our case today, because while many of

Back to the beginning: nostalgic *trompe-l'oeil* painting by James Triggs: depicting the historic red barn complex (main building predates Revolutionary War), prototype of the first Ruger sporting arm, portraits of the founders in daguerreotype format, and the now-famous company "red eagle" trademark. When the trademark was first designed, there was some concern that the SR monogram was too similar to the logo used by the New York *Social Register*, well known to Sturm. No comment was ever made by that publication, or by anyone else, over the years. The two fields of endeavor may not appear to overlap that much anymore, but there has always been a sustained interest in firearms among the wealthy (though often concealed for reasons of "political correctness").

the guns that we make and sell are used for hunting or self-defense purposes, the majority seem to be used very little or not at all. Of all the millions of firearms we have made, I think that you could find about half looking exactly as they did the day they were shipped; they have been a kind of "background possession," acquired by a type of person who simply wanted to have one. We see these guns from time to time and are much impressed by the little use they have had. Others, of course, are used heavily, but I would say that simply the collecting of a prized, precision-crafted, mechanical device certainly motivates a great deal of arms ownership.

Further, there is the investment aspect, proven to be highly productive in the last fifty years. Certainly firearms as investments have been spectacu-

Reverence for the past: a pair of Durs Egg over-and-under flintlock pistols, with set of Wogdon dueling pistols; both sets complete with cases and accessories; double barrel shotgun by London gunmaker James Purdey, all representing best quality English gunmaking of the early 1800s. The Alfred Jacob Miller watercolor from expedition in the West with Scottish Lord William Drummond Stewart, 1837.

lar, like many other types of valuable human possessions. I'm speaking of works of art and paintings, sculptures, old cars—almost every category of collectible object has proven to be a tangible investment. These often are much more successful investments than many securities. Some people have attempted to protect their wealth with gold, and in a world which may be in the future incapable of producing some of this beautiful stuff, possession of things like firearms and antique cars may be as good as gold.

On Arms Collecting

My interest in firearms is as a shooter and a collector, and I became a collector during my teenage years, when guns were not expensive. I saw them as an immensely interesting category of mechanisms which appealed to a young person with that type of aptitude and interests, and so I became an arms historian in a limited way. That, combined with an interest in making things, is what led me to becoming an engineer working on the design and manufacture of firearms. This company is just a natural out-

growth of all that because by 1949, after my work during World War II, I was equipped with the experience and the insights needed to successfully start a company of this sort. But all through this company's original conception, even in its current philosophy, runs that thread of the arms collector, an insight into what the market asks of the firearms it's interested in. To the degree that we've been able to respond, or have been successful in giving our guns the attributes people like, we ourselves succeeded in business and become stronger as the years go by.

The ownership of firearms is not inspired simply because one needs a weapon, stemming from the age-old need to throw a stone or a javelin or project something to kill some threatening animal or person. It's a combination of the symbolic, practical, and aesthetic. A modern firearm is tremendously powerful and accurate and does something which is unique and very impressive. It has an appeal to people that is a mixture of that ancient ability to extend one's own physical force and strength, together with the aesthetic aspect of a work of art. It is an area where you are able to understand the beauty of how a thing is shaped in connection with the purpose it is there for. You can see in firearms the appeal of beautiful racing cars or great motorcycles, and you can see in them the same appeal as you see in beautiful oil paintings. Consider paintings by Frank Tenney Johnson or Frederic Remington—why is it that these appeal to me? It's fundamentally an appeal that's identical to the one you have with firearms.

I have been interested in (and on the Board of) the Buffalo Bill Historical Center, Cody, Wyoming, for many years. It was inspired, primarily, by the local history of William F. "Buffalo Bill" Cody, but basically it shows the history of America, and its marvelous arms collection is one of its many interesting features. The museum's display of arms will illustrate to any person, whether or not he or she is familiar with this subject or has any interest in it, the extent and scope of involvement firearms have had in our culture.

The collecting of utilitarian or mechanical things like cars and guns is different from collecting art, because collecting cars and guns essentially involves observing technical evolution. The history

Alexander Henry sporting rifle cased set, number 1950, .50 caliber. The lock from the William Moore fullstock sporting rifle, number 360. The influence of Alexander Henry features can be seen in some of Ruger's designs.

of firearms parallels the history of industrial development and the rise of precision manufacturing throughout Europe and America in the eighteenth century. Even in the earliest part of firearms history the mechanisms then in use required precision fabrication. These guns were handmade and required extreme skill in the use of the primitive tools then available.

The beginning of the machine tool industry was made possible by the demand for accurate machine tools for the firearms industry throughout New England. These same tools were subsequently used

for all kinds of manufacturing. The mechanical engineering, the inventiveness and ingenuity of the early gunmaker and designer can be seen in the hundreds, if not thousands, of gun mechanisms which intrigue collectors today.

As for collecting art, my pictures reflect history that I like, particularly periods of social history in Europe and the United States and, even more particularly, pictures of Western life. I've got some paintings that reflect Africa and hunting there: African animals, the scenery, the history. But my interest in collecting guns and cars has been primar-

ily to discover the best that's been made in the past. When they're great, I find myself in love with them and want to own them.

The Ruger art collection, now boasting more than 215 paintings and about two dozen drawings, rivals that of most museums. Concentrating primarily on American artists, the range is wide, although emphasizing the nineteenth and early twentieth centuries: Winslow Homer, Alexander Pope, Frederic Remington, Charles Marion Rus-

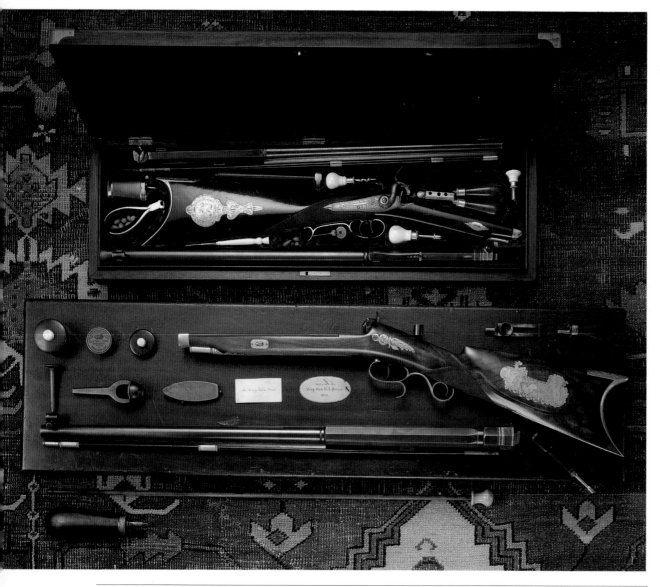

Best quality hand-built Massachusetts cased rifles, that at *top* marked by Whitmore, and gold inlaid, signed N. WHITMORE in gold cartouche on rifled 24¾" barrel breech; maker's cartouche of silver on 22¹³⁄₁₆" smoothbore barrel; .41 caliber percussion; brassbound mahogany and rosewood case. Presentation, cased and unmarked Whitmore sporting rifle, .45 caliber; the oval lid plaque of German silver, engraved: "Presented to/Brig. Gen. R. A. Peirce./1865." Whitmore was one of the most distinguished of mid-nineteenth-century riflemakers; he also built silver-mounted target rifle for presentation to President Ulysses S. Grant.

sell, Christian Schussele, Oscar E. Berlinghaus, Alfred Jacob Miller, Oliver LaFarge, Arthur Fitzwilliam Tait, Albert Bierstadt, Frank Tenney Johnson, Carl Rungius, Jasper Francis Cropsey, Levi Wells Prentiss, Dennis Malone Carter, William Herbert Dunton, Astley David Montague Cooper, Frederick Judd Waugh, Alfred Thompson Bricher, Carle J. Blenner, Martin Johnson Heade, and more.

Ruger on Firearms Technology and Engineering

We've never really been completely absorbed with any technical progress just for the sake of change. We like to build a handsome, accurate, practical firearm for the person who likes to shoot, one that embodies all the required mechanical refinements without slavishly following what others think of as current fashion. In doing so, more often than not, we've set the standard for our industry in terms of practical mechanical engineering.

On Fine Gun Craftsmanship

I believe there has been a resurgence of good craftsmanship in the world of firearms, and the evidence is clear. We have more highly talented stockmakers, metalsmiths, and engravers than we have ever had. These are craftsmen who are working in the classic fashion and doing great things. Forty-five or fifty years ago, there were only a handful of fine gunsmithing sources, such as Griffin & Howe. Today there are literally dozens of first-rate gunmakers. I think that what it really comes to is that there never was, and there never will be, a period when great workmanship isn't admired.

The question of how to build a complex gun like an over-and-under shotgun by machine methods, while still retaining a high degree of craftsmanship and quality of construction, can only be addressed by an integrated design process; one in which the design engineers work hand in glove with the production staff.

Our end product is, in fact, vastly stronger than that from the old hand-fitting shops, and the job comes out with much greater precision.

Manufacturing and Marketing Philosophy

We are absolutely committed to the idea that we are

going to make the best firearms money can ever build. That's always been the goal. Now, that doesn't necessarily mean engraving and gold inlays; but it does mean machinery that can be depended on, that will perform reliably, have immense endurance, strength, and so forth. It is a fact about us that the management of the company today is in the hands of the people who started it. It's a management where the engineering side predominates. You know, some managements will be oriented financially or oriented on marketing. I think it's true that ours is oriented from an engineering point of view.

We've been engineering our products so that they can be brought to the shooter to deliver outstanding performance and at the same time be produced economically.

Too many top executives in the gun manufacturing field aren't really familiar with the products their company is producing. It's not just in the gun world, but in many areas where executives ought to be immensely involved and concerned with the products that they're producing, they're really only interested in the bottom line, the profit at the end of the year. It's absolutely the wrong way to get there. Everybody wants profitability, but how can you evaluate a product that you don't even understand? Again, there are many different ways of approaching good product design, and the right way is to have the object of building an outstanding product efficiently.

I would say that the real key to our philosophy is that we don't make anything that we wouldn't use personally. I could honestly say that I built these products so that I could use them. There was a day when I always went hunting with a Mannlicher, which I like immensely (I have four of them). But there were certain things about it that I didn't like, and I used to use other rifles—Winchesters, Remingtons, all of them. In one way or another, there was something about each and every one that I liked a great deal and then again something I didn't like. So, I had that great pleasure of being able to bring everything that was good together for myself, on the theory that if I could honestly evaluate this thing as having achieved what I wanted it to be, then I would have a product that was worth marketing. In

other words, I would say that these products that we make—and I refer to every one of them—are products which I personally like enough so that I would buy one even if they were made by a competitor.

On the Firearms Industry

Maybe the American gun manufacturers will get healthy again. It seems to me they did some brilliant engineering after World War II and then stayed with those designs too long. It's as though a car company didn't change models for fifteen years. Or they make a new product that doesn't quite appeal to the shooter in the way they've become accustomed. The manufacturer is then producing a gun that is competing against their old gun.

We ourselves were guilty of some of the same overdue engineering. We had a record year in 1981 and then experienced the general falling off in the demand for firearms that the whole industry was experiencing in the mid-80s. The failure of good product engineering to appear at that point made the whole situation worse. Any imaginative designer should be able to produce a new firearm with some new advantages or capabilities that excite people into wanting it. Fortunately, we had a lot of brand-new products in the early engineering stages throughout the 1980s, so we weathered this period far better than most; in fact, some famous old line gun companies went into the red or went completely under. We never did.

The No. 1 single-shot rifle has been a great embellishment to our product line. It was a crazy idea in the first place, trying to sell a single-shot rifle to a generation of World War II veterans trained to appreciate rapid-fire. When we started that gun in the 1960s, the interest in firearms was so much more up-front than it has been lately. We tried it, and the rifle was a great success. We had a receptive atmosphere, a willingness to try anything. Today companies are much more cautious, but I'm happy to say that people still seem to enjoy the pleasure of precision rifle shooting.

We want to know what people like. I used to be able to say to myself that if I like them, I know perfectly well at least half the shooters will. Today, I'm so much older than most of our market that I'm not so confident. I like to find out as far as I can

what people think, which is about all market research can do.

We now have a bigger market share than we ever had in the past, so we are very conscious of a ceiling that may be imposed by the market. I've been feeling that way to an extent we never would have dreamed of when we were small. Then, there was plenty of room for us to grow if we had a good idea. Today, we've got to make a concerted effort to show even a small percentage increase.

I would say that we are probably going to continue to grow, but it will be a growth based on real engineering, product improvement, and cost reduction, taking market share from less competitive companies.

Today there are disincentives—things holding back national industrial development. Industry has been declining in America in a way that ought to alarm all Americans, make them wonder what the hell we are doing wrong. And it isn't what the Japanese are doing or what competitors are doing: It's what we are doing to ourselves.

A piece in a recent issue of *The Wall Street Journal* talked about our shortage of engineers. The best brains in the country are going into the legal profession. And they shouldn't. They should be going into engineering. These lawyers are symptomatic of a society that can't get along with itself, evidencing a breakdown of ethics. People don't know fair behavior from bad behavior. You can't run a country by law alone. The people have to be of a common mind about a lot of values. We have all the best brains wrangling disputes to the point where we are really pirating each other; finding excuses and causes for making money out of real or imagined disputes. We can't afford this continual drain upon our national resources to the enrichment of lawyers.

Jobs are important: The way the country is run today—with government intrusion and overcontrol—there is great incentive not to hire people. Remember that; it's true. When you hire people today you are virtually marrying them. They can quit anytime but you can't fire them without risking a lawsuit or some intervention from a government bureau. On top of that are all the incidental costs industry must shoulder like medical care,

workers' compensation, and so on. Sometimes we have conferences here on how to get more production. And when I am told that we really need more people, and I find myself sometimes saying, "I don't want to do it that way. Let's improve efficiency with equipment; make it more capital intensive. Maybe we should have a machine for every job." In other words, today there is no incentive to hire people. It's a losing deal for everyone, and those who deplore industry had better wake up. We can't grow this nation employing everyone in hamburger stands.

On Sturm, Ruger & Co., Inc., and American Industry

Product development is more than a marketing necessity to us. We regard it essentially as an opportunity, because it certainly produces a direct response in the form of additional demand for our product line, and because it is so essentially straightforward for us to put these new products into production with our modern manufacturing techniques and our easily expanded capacity.

Examples of this are our new M77 Magnum and Express rifles, which will intrigue a lot of hunters—particularly those who have some idea what African hunting is like and those hunting in big-game areas here in North America. These beautiful and sophisticated guns will certainly tell the world that we are a rifleman's company.

America has been declining as a manufacturing economy, and this trend cannot be observed without concern for the future. American manufacturing needs more support and less antagonism from government. American politics being what they are, it is doubtful that there will be any improvement in the foreseeable future. There are certain areas that, as a result of various factors which have evolved over the past decade, have become virtual millstones on the backs of American manufacturing companies attempting to compete in the global market, or even survive profitably in the domestic market. I refer particularly to the areas of medical insurance, workers' compensation insurance, and product liability costs. Volumes have been written with respect to each of these areas, and a multitude of, to date unsuccessful, solutions have been proposed.

On the Right to Own Firearms

I'm a manufacturer because I grew up with a fascination for firearms, as well as other mechanical types of things—cars and so on. In the case of firearms, I became aware that there were also legal issues involved. The right to own firearms, while it was referred to in the Constitution, was often challenged or there were attempts to modify it. This always bothered me, even as a child. I couldn't understand why anyone would want to try to make a simple mechanical object into a form of contraband, or how that could serve a social purpose. I've always thought about this question and have heard these arguments pro and con. I'm really a student of this and will say that the whole discussion is academic. In essense, the Bill of Rights should not be challenged. If we do not, under the existing phraseology of the Constitution, have a genuine right to own and carry firearms, then I say no other part of the Constitution is worth a damn either. If you destroy the Second Amendment you have destroyed a major thread of life through the whole Constitution. And even the early framers of the Constitution warned against that—not to weaken it by modifications all the time or by trying to make it say what a few people want it to say. The document says what it says. "The right to bear arms shall not be infringed." If you can't live with that, then you shouldn't be trying to be an American citizen—that should be something else, by definition.

A constant problem the industry has is that you can't compromise with gun prohibitionists. Every time you concede an inch, it's a wasted concession. That is my view. These people are not interested in rational discourse on how society can best control violent criminals. They simply hate guns, and a complete elimination of these inanimate objects is their actual goal. That is a really shocking and divisive end, in my opinion.

I think what is often lost sight of today is that the Constitution is there to protect the citizen from the government. It is the bulwark that sustains the liberties we are so used to having and that sometimes we are not even aware of. If it were not for the Constitution there would be no fixed points as to our social rankings: our relationship with one another, our relationship to the government, the amount of private interest we give up in the interest of cooperating with each other. We talk about a zoning law—it's giving up the right to do absolutely anything with your property but it means that the man across the street can't do something that's going to make his place ugly to you. So, everything is conditioned to a degree and certainly we have given up a lot of freedom to the Constitution and it in turn limits the government as to what it can do to us and we need that. Governments are instinctively, automatically, and inevitably tyrannical. There is no question about it.

Another thing that ought to be said is about the Bill of Rights and its whole purpose at the time it was written. All those founding fathers who prepared these amendments to the Constitution or additions to it specified ways in which they reassured the thirteen colonies that they were not bartering away fundamental liberties. In other words, the Bill of Rights enlarged on the original concept of the Constitution and made it much more concrete. This gave the document that force which it still has today, and people who talk about doodling with this thing or making it say what they want it to say are the very ones we should regard as dangerous and wrong to listen to. That some don't understand what they are doing only makes matters worse. These people can't leave well enough alone, and they can't enjoy a great beautiful thing without trying to spoil or tinker with it.

Firearms Legislation

Like alcohol in the 1920s and 30s, and drugs in the

Single-shot rifles abound in Ruger's collections. At *bottom*, a presentation Sharps Model 1874 Sporting Rifle, with engraved silver plaque inscribed to William Caughey. Sharps Borchardt single-shot rifle at *center*, with gold inlaid monogram and hard rubber side panel mount. Ruger No. 1 Single-Shot rifle, serial 270, in .270 caliber, one of the "21 Club" rifles, made for William B. Ruger, and engraved and gold inlaid by A. A. White. Daniel Moore, a leading firearms inventor and gunmaker, active in the third quarter of the nineteenth century, drew the color print of his breechloading rifle designs in the 1860s. He is one of the thousands of American gunmakers who have subsequently faded into obscurity.

1960s to the 90s, restricting guns and trying to strangle and lawsuit the industry to its knees have the unintended effect of contributing greatly to the market. When Presidents Reagan and Bush were in office, shooters, hunters, and arms devotees relaxed, knowing that both were friendly to their interests. But when the Clinton people took office the reaction to their pronouncements against guns (and often against gun owners) was electrifying: Sales of all kinds of firearms, ammunition, and accessories soared to unprecedented levels, and continue to escalate. With the Republican-dominated Congress elected in the fall of 1994, the possibility exists that these substantial sales will abate. But that is unlikely. There will still be certain politicians pointing the finger at what they claim to be (even though their statements are patently untrue) the "easy availability of guns" as a major reason for rampant crime. Their comments more accurately reflect an attempt to use the firearm as a smoke-screen for the complete and utter failure of an avalanche of social experiments, engineering a seemingly endless array of one abject failure after another. Total "gun control," it seems, is the only one of their experimental projects which has not had the chance to be tried and ultimately to fail, like all the rest.

There's a sudden decrying about crime, which in fact is decreasing in most demographic groups. However, there are always those who use the fear of crime to capitalize on their own ends. This is symbolic of a certain elitist urban distaste for all gun owners. But when the public discusses and thinks about the issue, people realize there's no direct connection between the availability of guns to law-abiding citizens and crime, and that they don't want to lose the right of choice, should they need a firearm for any lawful purpose. The Brady Bill and the 1994 Crime Bill went through because the public by and large doesn't give a damn about "assault weapons," even though that is a totally false issue.

"Monarch of the Glen" oil painting by an unidentified English artist. Alexander Henry single shot at *top*, with Daniel Fraser side-lever, and Ruger's own No. 1 Rifle, serial 270. The "call of the wild" is still a powerful lure, even to the most urbane city dweller.

But trying to ban conventional handguns, rifles, or shotguns would be quite another matter.

Gun crimes are not my fault. If I had any sense of being in the wrong business, I wouldn't be in it. People use all sorts of tools to display antisocial or criminal behavior and it doesn't necessarily say anything about the morality of the manufacturer—despite the misrepresentation of some false-thinking people. The idea that you can correct these crime situations by "gun control" is a joke; worse still, a hoax. Most violence today is criminals killing criminals; hardly the group calculated to obey complex and costly-to-administer gun laws.

Because of the general breakdown of law and order, people feel helpless without a way to defend themselves. That's the essential psychology of it—and it's valid. The Constitution accepts it and you have a situation that even existed in colonial times: isolated people, no police force nearby. People have to be in a position to defend themselves. There could always be a robber or a criminal coming around and even today in remote parts of the country there are insane murders.

The presence of guns kept responsibly in a household hinders crime rather than provoking it. The fact that there are firearms in so many households is a huge deterrent to crime. And, if you ask me, the deterrent theory is the only one that makes sense—and that means more jails, three strikes and you're out, and so on. Since a tiny number of repeat felons commits the vast majority of violent crimes, it seems to me that the most efficient "preventative" action society can take against violent crime is their swift, certain incarceration.

Personal Responsibility

In an age when many firearms manufacturers are divisions of giant global conglomerates, with faceless boards of directors who are embarrassed (but not to the point of failing to line their pockets) by the fact that their companies produce guns, Ruger has been outspoken in defense of firearms manufacture, private gun ownership, and the Second Amendment to the United States Consti-

tution.

He has confronted the pundits and has—perhaps most important—advocated safe and sane practices with his customers, in his advertising, in his product literature, in his packaging, and in special publications created by Sturm, Ruger. All, as he points out, without any governmental requirements that he do so.

Best Friends Can Hurt the Most

It is because of their redeeming social values that guns are still in the country. You can say that there's no redeeming social value attached to the illegal use of drugs or the possession of a live hand grenade, but in the right to bear arms, there is the right to defend oneself—a God-given right, not just constitutionally given.

I often think sometimes our best friends don't really express themselves too well. That was certainly true one night at a formal dinner of the Safari Club of New York, where a film was being shown, beautifully done in color. There were some celebrity types stalking leopard. The hunters were in hides and blinds, and the pictures were simply magnificent. Beautiful animals, climbing into a tree. Then there appeared a damn human being, lurking, really appearing to assassinate this animal. You watched this movie and you hated hunting by the time you were through with it.

The audience was sitting there watching what appeared to be an unfair advantage, and it went over like a lead balloon. Now, I am the staunchest supporter of hunting. The sport becomes a powerhouse when you make the tremendous effort required in a fair-chase hunt. And the question, the challenge for yourself, is whether or not you can do this. With some of the dangerous game, your courage enters into the equation. That's when there is an emotional content, when the experience overcomes an event which otherwise might appear to some to be a cold-blooded act.

I'm quite disinterested in the person merely making the kill, or the person after the kill. On the other hand, what is important is: the hunter making the stalk, camp life, the wilderness, all that which is a part of the associated excitement of a hunt.

You can't expect to shoot game every time you

come out. There's more to it than that. If the hunter had the chance to shoot something every time he or she went outside the house, there wouldn't be any sport to that. Hunting isn't just killing an animal. Hunting is hunting. The killing part wouldn't have any meaning if there was no hunting and no effort. It's an easy thing to see: If you presented a hunter with a ready-made kill, he wouldn't want it. It's the hunt that counts. Killing animals at the end is simply making the hunt complete. If you keep doing this, you'll see the real pleasure from it is really the work you're doing all day. Perhaps, some hopes you have, some efforts you're making to find your game and then get it. But it certainly isn't a matter of just getting it easily or for sure.

A Historic and Respected Tradition

I always wanted to do it my way, and I wanted to do it in the most historic and respectable product line in the manufacturing business: gunmaking, the most prestigious and fascinating business in the world. It used to be that no commoner would have dinner with the King, but the Royal Armorer was invited to dine with him on a regular basis.

Rightfully, Samuel Colt, Eliphalet Remington, Oliver Winchester, and Daniel B. Wesson were recognized in their day as national heroes. They were at the forefront of America's international dominance of the industrial revolution (the *American* system of manufacture), and the defense of the nation. The sporting arms industry today stands as a relatively small but highly competent, committed, dynamic, and innovative segment of America's industrial base.

Gunmaking and the Future of America

We've gotten so diverse that it's difficult to come to any consensus—or to accept any established values. Large masses of new people coming into the country, and lots of "modern" ideas are affecting the thinking of people who don't think much. Now we see all this confusion. You see lots of children with parents who aren't qualified to be parents. They can't help their own children. Think back to the time around the Civil War when the biggest inheritance a family could give was the gift of literacy, and the schools taught reading, writing, and the corresponding brain function, *thinking*. In the year 1855, the U.S. spent more on elementary school books

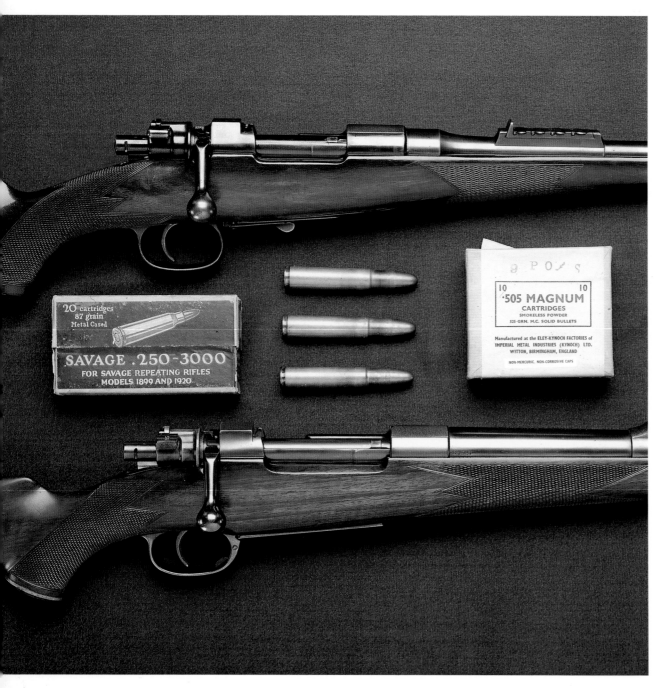

than the whole rest of the world put together.

So the country is in a frustrating situation. In my case, the country has been good to me. I am happy doing what I am doing, but I think that's why the situation worries me so much. I see how valuable it is for these historical American standards to continue, yet they seem destined to oblivion. Or all of it will become some giant corporation, an anthill type of society, regimented, and people will be unhappy. And they'll have all manner of material goods, but you reach a point when they don't do a damned thing for you.

Things to Do and Getting the Job Done

The reality in my life is now. I can't go on forever. When I was younger I never felt that way, and I even find myself evaluating ideas in terms of whether or not I'll be around to see if they bear fruit.

But I see some issues today that need correct decisions, and we need to try to make them. Although I won't be around to see the results of some actions taken today, I still hope for the continuation of the American way of life. We as a nation have corrected some of our injustices, and we have expanded our concepts of democracy, but at a price. It would be marvelous to know that these changes did not end up spoiling the traditional liberties and tolerance for diverse individualism that mark us as Americans.

Into the Future

When the time comes, Bill Jr. can run the company. He grew up with Sturm, Ruger & Co.,

All rifles are *not* the same. Mauser flat bridge action sporting rifles in sharply contrasting calibers: at *top*, .250-3000, with short Oberndorf-made action, number 106138; express sights graduated for 100, 200, 300, 400, and 500 yards; 22½" barrel; varnished walnut stock with cheekpiece; horn forend cap and pistol grip cap; composition buttplate. *Below*, a magnum-length .505 Gibbs rifle by George Gibbs, Saville Row, London; serial B7527; express sights on 22" barrel graduated for 100, 200, and 300 yards; oil-stained walnut stock, without cheekpiece; silver's style buttpad; case-hardened steel pistol grip cap. One for small game, up to deer; the other, for the very largest and most dangerous game— "the ones that fight back."

310

which is only ten years younger than he is. Bill Jr. knew them all and, except for his parents, he was there before anyone else: Alex, Paulina and Joanna Sturm, Justin and Katherine Sturm, Walt Sych, Walter Berger, Ed Nolan . . . all the writers and everyone else who played a role in the history of the company from the beginning. Further, Billy has that incisive Ruger brain, is highly educated, is an engineer and designer in his own right, is a hunter and shooter, and knows every operation in the factory. In effect, next to his father, Bill Jr. and Walt Sych are the longest-term employees.

Whoever is in charge, the backup is unquestionably the finest and most capable galaxy of talent ever assembled to operate a firearms business—with a momentum of orders and performance equally unparalleled.

Daughter Molly has her parents' charm, wit, brain, and style, and though she is not active in the Sturm, Ruger enterprises, certainly knows the business, and could well assume a vital role. And in the wings are grandsons Kurt and Alex Vogel and Charlie Ruger, granddaughters Vicky Roberts (at the Southport office, and a Sturm,

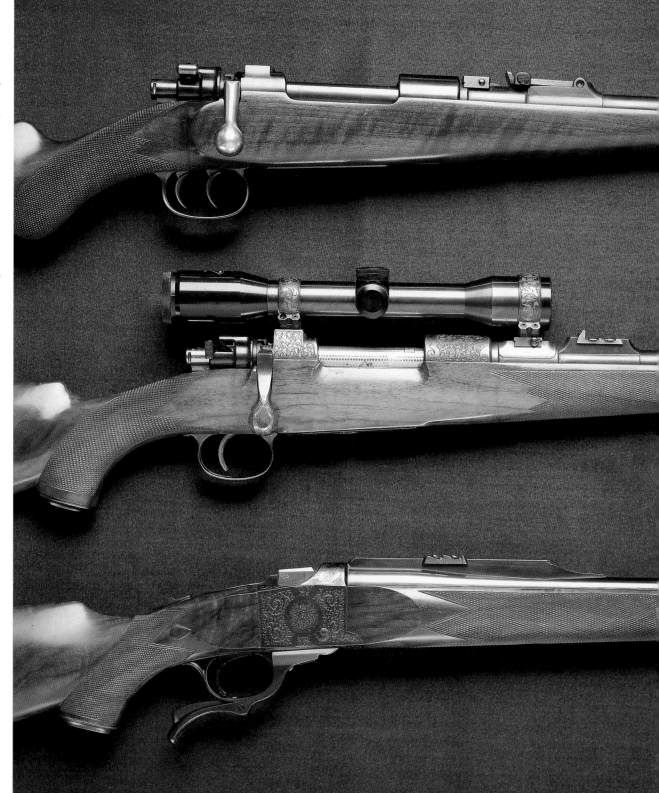

One of the joys of rifle making is to start with a quality product and watch a custom gunsmith turn it into a uniquely personal expression of craftsmanship and individuality. From *top*, square bridge Mauser sporting rifle, of Oberndorf manufacture, number 7544, 24" barrel with military style rear sight; quick detachable scope mount; oil-finished walnut stock with cheekpiece; checkered composition buttplate. John Rigby & Co. custom square bridge Mauser sporter, number 57695; 23½" barrel; 7 x 57 caliber; profusely engraved. Gold stock oval inscribed RICHARD E. QUILLMAN; Swarovski scope; varnished walnut stock with horn forend and grooved buttplate. Ruger No. 1 Rifle; inscribed on 22" barrel: "Stocked and Engraved by Holland & Holland Ltd." .222 Remington caliber; number 3721; commissioned by William B. Ruger, Sr. Removable front sight blade with pivoting cover; oil-finished French walnut stock with leather covered buttpad and horn cap on beavertail forend; gold stock oval engraved WBR; presented by Ruger to his friend Gus Pabst.

First of the "Ruger No. 1 North American series" cased sporting rifles; number 131-12873, .30-06 caliber, 22" barrel; Northern California English walnut stock, oil-finished. Presented by William B. Ruger, Sr., to the Department of Arms and Armor, The Metropolitan Museum of Art, New York, for the October 8, 1985, Christie's benefit auction. Of the 147 lots, including guns by Colt, Winchester, S & W, Remington, Marlin, and others, this rifle realized the record price in the event: $57,200. In fitted trunk style oak and leather casing by Marvin Huey; sheep motif from painting by Gary R. Swanson, "Rocky Mountain Bighorns." Engraving and gold inlaying by Franz Marktl; accessories by Mike Marsh. The sale raised over $250,000, which was devoted to refurbishing the museum's arms and armor galleries. Historically, fine firearms have always been considered works of art. Closely examining this rifle will verify that they indeed are.

Ruger expert in her own right) and Amy and Adrienne Ruger (experts in fine and decorative arts), and four great-grandchildren.

It's interesting about families. There are so few, you know, that go on for generations, one accomplishing more than the next; it doesn't happen much. Family succession may have had its best chances back in the days when there was a real authority and children were trained to take a place and regard it as an obligation, whether they were supposed to be a prince or a king, or whether they were supposed to simply be perpetuating some family business. Today that just doesn't exist. I think that perhaps between Bill Jr. and myself and my grandchildren you see more of the seeds of old-fashioned dynastic attitude than anywhere.

The Titanium Connection

The New York Times, October 5, 1994, ran a feature story—"New Looks on Links: Very Big is Beautiful"—in which one of the illustrations featured the Callaway Warbird "Great Big Bertha" driver, "whose head is made of titanium and its shaft of lightweight graphite." To be more specific, as revealed in the detail of the picture, the head is made of *Ruger* titanium, and is so marked.

Ely Callaway says: "We know what a golfer wants. . . . The point is that we'll go to whatever costs it takes to bring them what they want. The equipment industry is fundamentally a low-cost emphasis industry, but we are not. We are a high-cost operation because we know that if the cost produces the degree of satisfaction in the profit, we will sell it."

These high-tech golf clubs are the latest in a long line of outside castings sales, and are symbolic of the extraordinary potential for Ruger Investment Castings beyond the firearms field. While the core business will always be firearms, the possibilities for outside growth of specialty foundry orders, using Ruger foundries' expertise as suppliers of precision investment castings to a wide range of outside businesses, seems bright.

With Rugers you can lose them, break them (though that's difficult to do), maybe even wear them out (about impossible), but there's more where they came from.

—William B. Ruger, Jr., then President, to Darby Anderson, son of friend and Board member Nils Anderson

Bill Ruger and I go back to when I first started Navy Arms Company, in the late 1950s. In the beginning we both had many discussions on the production of firearms using at that time non-traditional methods, primarily investment castings. We both were pioneers in the field and I still treasure a Ruger Old Army, serial number 59, with the inscription: *To Val Forgett, a Valiant Competitor, from Bill Ruger.*

Ruger is cut from the same cloth as Samuel Colt and John D. Rockefeller. These were people of vision who made things happen. The world is filled with "going-to-dos" and "should-have-dones," but Bill did it all. He put together an industrial complex utilizing state-of-the-art technology that other companies were unwilling to try, or, more specifically, didn't have the inspiration, vision, and energy to accomplish.

Many gunmaking companies are run by executives who have no idea what the product should be like, or how to make or market it. Ruger's expertise is comprehensive, including what will appeal to the public. He has given them what they want at a price they could afford, and in the process built a business that is as important in the firearms field today as any of the old established companies throughout the world.

That was his dream, and he had the ability and true grit to make it come true.

—Val Forgett, President, Navy Arms Company

Ruger doesn't go out of the way to tell people what business he's in. "Either they hit me about gun control, or they waste my time telling me how much they think they know about guns."

—*Daily News*, New York

. . . the arms industry has seen nothing quite like Bill Ruger since the days of Sam Colt. Ruger is like Colt in many ways, and totally opposite in others; but perhaps the way Ruger is most like Colt is in the way his product reflects his own personality. It is impossible to separate the company from the man; they are the same, and the story of one is the story of the other.

But in order to understand the stylish "Ruger look" of his products, one must take into account his family's artistic heritage, his cultured family life, and his early exposure to New York's art treasures. From this budded his appreciation for well-designed automobiles and boats and just about anything else that represented clean, efficient design and good workmanship.

In time, this sense of style and good taste was to become the hallmark of a Ruger firearm.

—Jim Carmichel, Shooting Editor
Outdoor Life

Epilogue

For those who think that, at eighty, Bill Ruger is through, washed up, or ready to retire: look out! His mother lived to ninety-four; Aunt Clara to one hundred and one! Ruger is still at it—hard—and will be until he drops. As he says: "When you rest, you rust; and I don't intend to rust." There are new models in the works, about which he insists, "Don't put them in this book; save them for the next edition!" There are old cars to buy, paintings to enjoy, books to read, guns to design, new techniques and innovations

in the factories and the investment casting foundries, new markets to explore, more new firearms to design, and more mechanisms to invent.

The old lion remains active, either in his lair or on his rounds, and there's a bit of the old fox in him, too. Physical condition notwithstanding, *Ruger is at his peak, NOW!* And the company that he and young Alex Sturm founded in 1949 is poised to go on to even greater accomplishments. What greater legacy can a man leave to his family, his business, his customers, his industry, or, indeed, to his country?

Southport office of William B. Ruger, Sr., paneled in oak, and completed in 1959 at the time company moved main factory to the Lacey Place address. To *left* of Remington oil (over New York *bon vivant* Chauncey Depew's antique rolltop desk), bronze sculpture of safari hunter awarded on induction of Ruger to Hunting Hall of Fame. To *right*, Outstanding American Handgunner award, presented to Ruger in 1975. Equally coveted Shaw & Hunter trophy in *foreground*. Book and long gun cases, desk, and worktables collecting place for memorabilia and pictures. Author first visited office in 1966, to discuss engraving projects with Ruger and Ed Nolan, then Vice President of Marketing. Office designed to permit easy access to tool room and engineering-drafting department. Scale model of Ruger Brothers sailing ship, the *Theodore Ruger*, beneath oil painting by Frank Tenney Johnson. Oil at *right* also by Johnson; *above* bronze by Clark Bronson. African trophies from 1958 and 1961 safaris; bighorn sheep from British Columbia hunt of 1963. Rowland Ward record book reedbuck mysteriously fell off wall the moment professional hunter Tony Henley visited office! Oil at *center*, "Indian Scout," by Frederic Remington, signed, and dated "Fort Reno, I.T. '88."

Sporting, target, and military rifles from the Ruger collection. Books on subjects ranging from accounting, engineering, manufacturing; antique, vintage, and modern guns to cars, boats, Africana, Americana, Western history, the British Empire, and hunting. *Lower* cabinets filled with prototype and early production Ruger handguns, accessories, memorabilia, and literature.

315

Ruger niece Cameron Wesselhoft Brauns seated in main drawing room of Ruger family home, Southport. Portfolio-sized books (to *right* of desk) on hunting and exploring in Africa and Asia; other titles cover broad array of subjects. Elephant tusks, kudu, and Cape buffalo from African safaris; at *right* in cabinet the .470 Evans used on elephant, rhino, and Cape buffalo hunts. Drafting set acquired by Ruger in 1930s, used well into the 1960s. Pistol cabinet contents illustrated on page 54. N. C. Wyeth painting in *left foreground;* A. F. Tait at *right background.* Sculptures by Chiparus and F. Preiss. The Rugers collected Victorian paintings and decorative arts long before these were fashionable. For many years Mary Ruger maintained her own antiques business, headquartered in the red barn complex. Southport residence interior decorated by the Rugers, working with interior decorator Margo Marston. This room, in particular, is quite evocative of Sagamore Hill, Theodore Roosevelt's Oyster Bay, Long Island, residence.

Front parlor of Ruger Southport residence; portrait of Ruger ancestor William Turner Perry, c. 1860. Portraits of grandparents Julius and Adelheid Ruger, done in pastel, by Julius. Martial pistol from Ruger collection, by R. Johnson, Middletown, Connecticut; dated 1842. Legend carved and gold-leaved on mantelpiece coincidentally identical to that on mantel of distinguished English industrialist and munitions magnate Sir William Armstrong, at Cragside, his estate in Ellswick, near Newcastle.

Appendixes

Serial Numbers by Year for All Models

These figures are approximate estimations only. *The serial numbers shown for each year should not be considered as the absolute first firearm shipped for the given year. Throughout Sturm, Ruger's history, it has often been the case that blocks of serial numbers were set aside and actually produced at a later date—thus disrupting the continuity of the serial numbers. Within a block of fifty serial numbers, it is possible to have shipping dates within a three- to five-year time frame.*

There have also been times when firearms were put into storage for a year or so, and then shipped as needed. Or, with the case of multiple models made within one prefix range, one model configuration may be produced at one time, another model produced at another time, then both (or many) configurations at the same time. This makes it very difficult to pinpoint exact serial numbers for certain models, at any one time. Depending upon the popularity of a particular model, there may have been stock which was produced one year, but not shipped until the following year, which causes an overlap *of serial numbers. Note also that not all numbers were used.*

Therefore, the only way to verify a serial number is to contact Sturm, Ruger's Serial Number Department. They can usually furnish details regarding shipping date and model configuration, but do not give out customer information for reasons of confidentiality. This service is provided at no cost; simply call or write to the company, with the serial number and appropriate description.

PISTOLS 1949–1958

RIMFIRE PISTOLS	1949	1950	1951	1952	1953	1954	1955	1956	1957	1958
Standard Automatic & Mark I - .22 Caliber	1	2416	11597	32905	49019	68958	97358	115523	128244	148222
Mark II - .22 Caliber										
22/45 - .22 Caliber										

PISTOLS 1959–1970

RIMFIRE PISTOLS	1959	1960	1961	1962	1963	1964	1965	1966	1967	1968	1969	1970
Standard Automatic & Mark I - .22 Caliber	169400	179712	194484	217767	239621	250296	276308	406740	436226	463239	10-00001	10-38890
Mark II - .22 Caliber												
22/45 - .22 Caliber												
CENTERFIRE PISTOL												
Hawkeye Single Shot					1	3104						

PISTOLS 1971–1982

RIMFIRE PISTOLS	1971	1972	1973	1974	1975	1976	1977	1978	1979	1980	1981	1982
Standard Automatic & Mark I - .22 Caliber	10-75016	11-26288	11-72924	12-22449	12-81988	13-48646	13-99097	14-69121	15-36233	16-06785	16-82937	17-70981
Mark II - .22 Caliber												18-00001
22/45 - .22 Caliber												

PISTOLS 1983–1993

RIMFIRE PISTOLS	1983	1984	1985	1986	1987	1988	1989	1990	1991	1992	1993
Standard Automatic & Mark I - .22 Caliber											
Mark II - .22 Caliber	18-50048	19-31711	211-13150	212-08560	212-91364	213-90898	214-85593	215-61938	216-68349	217-48014	219-35050
22/45 - .22 Caliber										220-00001	220-18560

PISTOLS 1987–1993

CENTERFIRE PISTOLS	1987	1988	1989	1990	1991	1992	1993
P85 - P85 Mark II - P89 - 9mm	300-00001	300-02509	300-33209	301-34818	302-27586	303-65769	304-16318
P94 - 9mm Caliber							
P93 - 9mm Caliber							306-00001
P90 - .45 Caliber					660-00001	660-27550	660-52347
P91 - .40 Caliber						340-00001	340-11615

319

SINGLE-ACTION REVOLVERS 1953–1960

SINGLE-SIX - .22 CALIBER	1953	1954	1955	1956	1957	1958	1959	1960
Standard Model	1	50	10734	31857	55346	88245	122480	151189
Lightweight				200001	203787	209565	212367	
Magnum							300001	305543
Super Single-Six								
SINGLE-SIX .32 CALIBER								
SSM								
S32X								
BLACKHAWK - .357 MAGNUM CALIBER			1	1737	7318	11676	18688	25734
BLACKHAWK - .30 CALIBER								
BLACKHAWK - .357 MAXIMUM CALIBER								
BLACKHAWK - .41 MAGNUM CALIBER								
BLACKHAWK - .44 MAGNUM CALIBER				1	741	5996	14258	22232
BLACKHAWK - .45 CALIBER								
SUPER BLACKHAWK - .44 MAGNUM CALIBER							1	1521
SUPER BLACKHAWK HUNTER - .44 MAGNUM CALIBER								
BLACKHAWK - SPECIAL MODEL - S3840								
OLD ARMY CAP & BALL								
BP7 - Blued								
KBP7 - Stainless Steel								
BEARCAT - .22 CALIBER						1	F483	X454
VAQUERO - .45 CALIBER								

SINGLE-ACTION REVOLVERS 1961–1971

SINGLE-SIX - .22 CALIBER	1961	1962	1963	1964	1965	1966	1967	1968	1969	1970	1971
Standard Model	171403	187367							20-00001	20-39803	20-77705
Lightweight											
Magnum	318696	331116	351442	380392	409921	434541	475650	490279	824407		
Super Single-Six				500001	502608	517860	528826	547679	566735	60-13852	60-52410
SINGLE-SIX .32 CALIBER											
SSM											
S32X											
BLACKHAWK - .357 MAGNUM CALIBER	34325	39490	43698	52569	60373	73551	87269	108764	30-00001	30-24975	30-81253
BLACKHAWK - .30 CALIBER								1	50-00001	50-05980	50-13531
BLACKHAWK - .357 MAXIMUM CALIBER											
BLACKHAWK - .41 MAGNUM CALIBER					1	3820	6781	12272	40-00001	40-03451	40-13852
BLACKHAWK - .44 MAGNUM CALIBER	26680	28515									
BLACKHAWK - .45 CALIBER											45-00001
SUPER BLACKHAWK - .44 MAGNUM CALIBER	6222	7659	11089	14492	18629	22308	26448	33350	80-00001	80-13363	80-27910
SUPER BLACKHAWK HUNTER - .44 MAGNUM CALIBER											
BLACKHAWK - SPECIAL MODEL - S3840											
OLD ARMY CAP & BALL											
BP7 - Blued											
KBP7 - Stainless Steel											
BEARCAT - .22 CALIBER	5600	17468	23688	35373	53805	65810	80330	93810	112456	90-09801	91-00051
VAQUERO - .45 CALIBER											

SINGLE-ACTION REVOLVERS 1972–1982

SINGLE-SIX - .22 CALIBER	1972	1973	1974	1975	1976	1977	1978	1979	1980	1981	1982
Standard Model	21-16995	21-53819									
Lightweight											
Magnum											
Super Single-Six	60-81278	62-00001	62-60261	63-31002	64-22659	64-94851	65-94609	66-72106	67-44104	68-25002	69-15052
Colorado Centennial					76-00001						
SINGLE-SIX .32 CALIBER											
SSM											
S32X											
BLACKHAWK - .357 MAGNUM CALIBER	31-10018	31-41551	32-33639	32-66489	33-03854	33-51451	34-06008	34-59110	35-07904	35-55902	35-93851
BLACKHAWK - .30 CALIBER	50-19180	50-22983	51-02629	51-05293	51-07169	51-10260	51-12751	51-14066	51-18652	51-22408	51-26197
BLACKHAWK - .357 MAXIMUM CALIBER											600-00001
BLACKHAWK - .41 MAGNUM CALIBER	40-18305	40-22301	41-01845	41-04914	41-07462	41-12333	41-17490	41-18701	41-28751	.41 Caliber Blackhawks	
BLACKHAWK - .44 MAGNUM CALIBER											
BLACKHAWK - .45 CALIBER	45-13201	45-21804	46-03651	46-11051	46-19874	46-30801	46-41751	46-43201	46-52451	46-63651	46-85751
SUPER BLACKHAWK - .44 MAGNUM CALIBER	80-41701	80-57651	81-12401	81-32451	81-61051	81-93201	82-27551	82-82146	83-41251	83-90986	84-43801
SUPER BLACKHAWK HUNTER - .44 MAGNUM CALIBER											
BLACKHAWK - SPECIAL MODEL - S3840											
OLD ARMY CAP & BALL											
BP7 - Blued	140-00001	140-04259	140-13723	140-20404	140-26251	140-30204	140-34506	140-39651	140-44201	140-46573	BP7 serial
KBP7 - Stainless Steel					145-00001	145-01204	145-07934	145-15890	145-20194	145-24880	145-33428
BEARCAT - .22 CALIBER	91-25001	91-46701	91-62904								
VAQUERO - .45 CALIBER											

SINGLE-ACTION REVOLVERS 1983–1993

SINGLE-SIX - .22 CALIBER	1983	1984	1985	1986	1987	1988	1989	1990	1991	1992	1993
Standard Model											
Lightweight											
Magnum											
Super Single-Six	69-95871	260-23867	260-44317	261-10138	261-33448	261-70551	261-97610	262-24203	262-41476	262-56030	262-67559
SINGLE-SIX .32 CALIBER											
SSM		650-00001	650-03481	650-16439	650-18601	650-29596	650-30100	650-31950	650-32150	650-32447	650-33400
S32X						610-00001					
BLACKHAWK - .357 MAGNUM CALIBER	36-22705	36-39399	36-66388	36-73330	36-82139	36-95212	37-01082	37-09149	37-17217	37-20595	37-24885
BLACKHAWK - .30 CALIBER	51-29276	51-31564	51-31871	51-32406	N/A	51-33082	51-33728	51-34204	51-35161	51-35525	51-36300
BLACKHAWK - .357 MAXIMUM CALIBER	600-00550	600-07734									
BLACKHAWK - .41 MAGNUM CALIBER	were produced in the same serial number ranges as the .45 Caliber Blackhawks from 1981 to present										
BLACKHAWK - .44 MAGNUM CALIBER											
BLACKHAWK - .45 CALIBER	46-88051	46-98221	47-03176	47-06112	47-15050	47-26050	47-30119	47-32217	47-38759	47-43043	47-52283
SUPER BLACKHAWK - . 44 MAGNUM CALIBER	84-77993	84-98349	85-03813	85-43060	85-65531	85-85102	85-92143	86-15257	86-35272	86-42411	86-51210
SUPER BLACKHAWK HUNTER - .44 MAGNUM CALIBER										88-00001	88-04710
BLACKHAWK - SPECIAL MODEL - S3840								611-00001			
OLD ARMY CAP & BALL											
BP7 - Blued	numbers intermixed with KBP7 serial numbers beginning in 1982										
KBP7 - Stainless Steel	145-46522	145-50008	145-51681	145-52645	145-55577	145-57569	145-60386	145-63537	145-65870	145-66177	145-66292
BEARCAT - .22 CALIBER											93-00001
VAQUERO - .45 CALIBER											55-00001

DOUBLE-ACTION REVOLVERS 1972–1982

	1972	1973	1974	1975	1976	1977	1978	1979	1980	1981	1982
SECURITY-SIX, POLICE SERVICE-SIX & SPEED-SIX	150-00001	150-35383	150-64961	151-21780	151-76180	152-61012	153-60425	154-63332	155-76844	156-94383	158-12020
GP100											
REDHAWK									500-00001	500-03611	500-19388
SUPER REDHAWK											
SP101											

DOUBLE-ACTION REVOLVERS 1983–1993

	1983	1984	1985	1986	1987	1988	1989	1990	1991	1992	1993
SECURITY-SIX, POLICE SERVICE-SIX & SPEED-SIX	159-45126	159-81307	160-58768	161-80082	161-84833	162-39887					
GP100				170-00001	170-18081	170-40819	171-33130	172-00859	172-30612	172-49299	172-73459
REDHAWK	500-50567	500-90245	501-30534	501-78855	501-80232	502-24545	502-49301	502-73151	502-77177	502-85090	502-89051
SUPER REDHAWK					550-00001	550-05951	550-23061	550-47261	550-58827	550-62620	550-74392
SP101							570-00001	570-38900	570-59251	570-89156	571-10044

RIFLES 1961–1970

CENTERFIRE RIFLES	1961	1962	1963	1964	1965	1966	1967	1968	1969	1970
.44 Carbine	1	1339	65061	85111	94131	104345	113049	126443	133089	100-08901
Number One							1	2231	5885	130-00001
Number Three										
Mini-14										
Mini-14 Ranch										
Mini-Thirty										
M77								1	1912	70-14532
M77 Mark I										
M77 Magnum										
M77 Deluxe										
RIMFIRE RIFLES										
10/22				1	453	22906	77384	131304	186076	110-20100
77/22										
77/22 Hornet										

RIFLES 1971–1982

CENTERFIRE RIFLES	1971	1972	1973	1974	1975	1976	1977	1978	1979	1980	1981	1982
.44 Carbine	100-20629	100-31220	100-41326	100-50238	102-04751	102-16701	102-33708	102-50001	102-61388	102-77350	102-90046	103-01400
Number One	130-01681	130-03843	N/A	130-05203	130-12779	130-17490	130-40795	131-19270	131-46676	132-01360	132-07159	132-25986
Number Three			130-50000	130-51170	130-54210	130-55139	130-60511	130-65671	130-70344	No. 3 Rifle serial numbers intermixed		
Mini-14				180-00001	180-05101	180-28282	180-59251	181-07488	181-48351	181-84879	182-45601	183-03581
Mini-14 Ranch												187-00001
Mini-Thirty												
M77	70-23555	70-45045	70-67406	70-87509	71-28501	71-75101	73-38101	73-05351	73-92701	74-65901	75-42703	75-32589
M77 Mark I												
M77 Magnum												
M77 Deluxe												
RIMFIRE RIFLES												
10/22	110-64595	111-16200	111-95550	113-04149	114-17146	115-32735	116-25017	117-36100	118-42599	119-59923	121-03969	122-74713
77/22												
77/22 Hornet												

RIFLES 1983–1993

CENTERFIRE RIFLES	1983	1984	1985	1986	1987	1988	1989	1990	1991	1992	1993
.44 Carbine	103-08524	103-11110	103-13722								
Number One	132-34077	132-39043	132-54434	132-73032	132-76167	132-79519	132-83110	132-87029	132-92985	132-95719	132-99165
Number Three	with No. 1 Rifle serial numbers										
Mini-14	183-40455	184-17175	184-26063	184-95448	185-14140	185-50455	185-56556	185-81009	186-05029	186-18250	186-20065
Mini-14 Ranch	187-02611	187-13218	187-27226	187-50919	187-59308	187-70033	187-84127	188-01157	188-30499	188-50902	188-66901
Mini-Thirty					189-00001	189-15143	189-17652	189-25005	189-38805	189-51041	189-52528
M77	77-50834	77-68636	79-78671	770-12293	770-31006	771-32711	771-94356	772-67360	773-20200	773-27997	
M77 Mark I							780-00001	780-07233	780-27295	780-76042	781-31006
M77 Magnum										750-00001	750-00359
M77 Deluxe										760-00001	760-00503
RIMFIRE RIFLES											
10/22	123-72025	123-80636	126-47192	127-68583	128-38014	129-20927	230-25136	232-10200	233-58183	234-83683	235-10632
77/22		700-00001	700-20951	700-36350	700-47010	700-65369	700-72100	700-84304	701-05515	701-32515	701-36115
77/22 Hornet											

SHOTGUNS 1974–1983

	1974	1975	1976	1977	1978	1979	1980	1981	1982	1983
RED LABEL - 20 GAUGE					400-00001	400-01853	400-09852	400-22235	400-28112	400-32690
RED LABEL - 12 GAUGE									410-00001	410-01798

SHOTGUNS 1984–1993

	1984	1985	1986	1987	1988	1989	1990	1991	1992	1993
RED LABEL - 20 GAUGE	400-38820	400-39749	400-40924	400-42027	400-43521	400-44182	400-48177	400-52607	400-54366	400-55323
RED LABEL - 12 GAUGE	410-02005	410-02259	410-13523	410-20357	410-28802	410-31103	410-38277	410-47506	410-49785	410-54176

SUBMACHINE GUNS 1974–1983*

	1974	1975	1976	1977	1978	1979	1980	1981	1982	1983
AC556	190-08182	N/A	190-08209	191-00002	191-00042	191-02307	191-03711	191-03956	191-09317	191-10317
MP9										

SUBMACHINE GUNS 1984–1993*

	1984	1985	1986	1987	1988	1989	1990	1991	1992	1993
AC556	191-11214	191-12814	191-13005	192-00343	192-00827	192-01000	192-01050	192-01110	192-01180	192-01211
MP9										450-00001

*Presented together due to selective fire, full-automatic capability.

Sturm, Ruger & Co., Inc., Firsts

This list documents the "firsts" of William B. Ruger and Sturm, Ruger, achievements unrivaled by any firearms manufacturer of the post-World War II period:

- First major U.S. firearms manufacturer founded following World War II (1949).
- First major U.S. firearms manufacturer to utilize pressed and welded steel grip frame components (1949).
- First .22 caliber pistol in which the bolt moved inside tubular receiver and sights remained stationary when firing (1949).
- First major U.S. firearms manufacturer to utilize precision investment casting for major components (1949).
- First firearms company to utilize all coil springs in Colt-type single-action revolver mechanism (1953).
- First large-scale production of improved Colt-type single-action revolver (1953).
- First firearms company to use nylok on screw threads to prevent loosening of screws (1955).
- First full-page safety advertisements (1955).
- First rifle chambered for the .44 Magnum cartridge (1960).
- First U.S. single-shot .256 Magnum pistol (1963).
- First U.S. firearms manufacturer to establish its own precision investment casting foundry (1963).
- First detachable rotary .22 caliber magazine (1964).
- First to produce a modern single-shot centerfire rifle (1966).
- First to reintroduce "classic" stock styling to bolt-action rifles (1968).

- First U.S. rifle manufacturer to incorporate integral scope mounting bases into rifle receivers (1968).
- First modern U.S. firearms manufacturer to produce an automobile (1969).
- First to develop a revolver made of integrated sub-assemblies that could be quickly dismantled without the use of tools (1972).
- First to design a "cap-and-ball" blackpowder revolver with "modern" improvements such as adjustable sights, coil springs, and stainless steel parts (1972).
- First to utilize the transfer bar ignition system and loading gate interlock safety mechanisms in single-action revolvers (1973).
- First single-action revolver manufacturer to offer a protective-style holster (1976).
- First to publish product-specific safety warnings in firearms and outdoor magazines (1977).
- First company to state that "free instructions for all model . . . firearms are available upon request" in all product advertising (1977).
- First company to roll mark safety warnings directly onto its firearms (1978).
- First U.S. hammer forged chrome-molybdenum steel shotgun barrels (1979).
- First quick replaceable interchangeable front sights for revolvers (1979).
- First double-frame cylinder lock (double-action revolvers) (1979).
- First offset ejection rod (double-action revolvers) (1979).
- First "single spring" double-action revolver mechanism for both hammer and trigger (1979).

- First company to produce televised firearms safety messages (1981).
- First (and only) company to offer free factory safety retrofits for "old model" Colt-type single-action revolvers (1982).
- First revolver chambered for the .357 Maximum cartridge (1983).
- First revolver grip frame specifically designed to accept cushioned synthetic grips (1985).
- First complete firearms line produced by a single manufacturer (1987).
- First revolver made with integral scope bases in the frame (1988).
- First "all-weather" .22 rifle to utilize a synthetic stock and stainless steel construction (1989).
- First U.S. manufacturer to sponsor women's sporting clays championship team (1989).
- First firearms manufacturer listed on the New York Stock Exchange (1990) (excluding any manufacturers like Winchester, Remington, and Colt, all of whom have been represented as divisions of larger corporations).
- First U.S. rifle chambered for 7.62 x 39mm cartridge (1991).
- First firearms made with proprietary alloy Terhune Anticorro stainless steel (1992).
- First pistol with integral housing for laser sight (1993).

Glossary

(Note: Many of these terms are never used by Sturm, Ruger and Co., but are included because they have become part of arms collector terminology.)

Accessories: listed on factory catalogues and brochures with 00- prefix.

Barreled Actions: listed in factory catalogues and brochures with 91- prefix.

"Bird": Sturm, Ruger trademark.

Brass Frame: factory installed single-action revolver grip frame of brass; marked "MOB3."

Changes of 1962: production changes in cylinder frame, grip frame, ejector rod, and other parts on Ruger "Old Model" single-action revolvers of that period.

Chrome Gun: "Old Model" Super Single-Six revolvers chrome-plated, 1964–65. Extremely rare.

Custom: special features on Rugers, which are out of the ordinary, and non-standard-production. Ruger does not have a full-time custom shop, at this writing.

D-Guns: with **D** marking to indicate duplicate serial number.

Dragoon: the squareback trigger guard configuration of the Ruger Super Blackhawk revolvers; nickname denoting similarity to Colt "Dragoon" models produced in late 1840s and into the 1850s.

Dual-Tone: Combination of two color finishes on some Lightweight Single-Six revolvers. Aluminum-colored cylinder frame; black-colored grip frame.

Eagle: Sturm, Ruger and Company trademark; may be red, black, or silver. Also "hawk" and "bird."

Factory: original or authentic Ruger material; also referring to Sturm, Ruger and Co., Inc.

Flatgate: early "old model" Single-Six revolvers having flat loading gates, and bearing serial numbers lower than the 61000 range.

Flattop: frame configuration for early (pre-1962) "old model" Blackhawk revolvers in .357 and .44 Magnum calibers. Topstrap of the cylinder frame lacks raised protective shoulders as found on later revolvers.

Hawk: Sturm, Ruger and Company trademark. Also "eagle" and "bird."

Long Frame: first "old model" Super Blackhawk revolvers having somewhat longer grip assembly than would become standard. Grip panels stamped with a **C** inside.

Model Number: four-digit internal factory designation, the first two identifying a particular gun type, the second two the particular model. Beginning late in 1991 the model number has been printed on the end label of shipping boxes.

New Model: single-action Rugers made *after* introduction of patented new design in 1973. Incorporate transfer bar ignition and loading gate interlock. Identified by "New Model" marking on left side of frame.

"Old Model": all single-action Rugers made 1953–72 *before* introduction of New Model design in 1973. Sometimes called "three screw" models after the hammer, trigger, and cylinder latch screw heads visible on right side of frame. Functionally identical to Colt Single-Action revolvers, with improvements such as frame-mounted firing pin and all coil spring mechanism.

Parts Bin: referring to the use of parts, and their generally chronological storage and usage.

"Phoenix": one of the names used by collectors in referring to Sturm, Ruger and Co., Inc., trademark.

Post-Warning: reference to Ruger firearms made after January 1, 1978, bearing the "warning" roll marking to "read the instruction manual." Sometimes alluded to disdainfully as the "idiot" variation by collectors.

"Pre-Graffiti Variation": reference to "warning" marking on Ruger firearms built after January 1, 1978. Reflects the disdain of some for this inscription.

Pre-Warning: reference to firearms built before January 1, 1978, when Ruger introduced the "warning" markings to "read instruction manual before use."

Receivers: frames of all firearms, which require serial number markings. Factory catalogue number RO (receiver only) identifies receivers on hand primarily for replacement and repairs to customer firearms. Not sold separately.

Red Barn: original Sturm, Ruger and Company factory, in Southport, where firearms were made from c. 1949–59.

S-Gun: a variation of the Lightweight Single-Six, and of certain other models. Also used as an indication of surface blemished guns, when marked adjacent to serial number.

Super: nickname for the Super Blackhawk, either "old model" or New Model.

Tri-Color: combination of three-color finish on some Lightweight Single-Six revolvers. Aluminum-colored cylinder frame, black anodized grip frame, brownish "hard coated" cylinder.

Two-Tone: combination of finish on the Lightweight Single-Six revolvers. See "Dual-Tone."

U-Gun: **U** marking an indication of guns used as demonstrators or sales samples, and stamped adjacent to serial number.

"White Box" Super: special design of packaging for early "old model" Super Blackhawk casing, to replace losses from the case-making source (original to be of mahogany, until fire destroyed the source's factory). c. 1960.

WMR: abbreviation refering to the .22 Winchester Magnum Rimfire cartridge.

XR-3: grip frame standard from 1953 to 1963, on "old model" single-action Rugers.

XR-3RED: redesigned grip frame design, in use 1963–1973 on "old model" single-action Rugers.

Table of Markings

RIM-FIRE AUTO-LOADING PISTOLS

RUGER 22/45   .22 CAL. LONG RIFLE
                    TARGET

RUGER MK. II
.22 CAL. LONG RIFLE

COMPETITION TARGET MODEL

—BEFORE USING GUN - READ WARNING IN INSTRUCTION MANUAL—
AVAILABLE FREE FROM STURM, RUGER & CO., INC., SOUTHPORT, CONN. U.S.A.

All Pistols

GOVERNMENT TARGET MODEL

RUGER .22 CAL. LONG RIFLE
         MARK II TARGET

All Target and Bull Barrel Models.

—BEFORE USING GUN - READ WARNING IN *INSTRUCTION MANUAL*—
AVAILABLE FREE FROM: STURM, RUGER & CO., INC. SOUTHPORT, CT. U.S.A.

5-1/4 and 6-7/8 Target Barrel Pistols

22/45 Models

DOUBLE-ACTION REVOLVERS

RUGER® *Redhawk*®
Receiver, right side

SUPER REDHAWK
Receiver, right side

RUGER GP100®
Barrel, right side

RUGER SP101.
Barrel, right side

RUGER
Receiver, left side

Receiver, right side

.38 SPECIAL CAL.
GP100 Barrel, right side

.38 SPECIAL CAL.
SP101 Barrel, right side

.357 MAGNUM CAL.
SP101 Barrel, right side

.44 MAGNUM CAL.
SUPER REDHAWK Barrel, right side

.44 MAGNUM CAL.
REDHAWK Barrel, right side

BEFORE USING GUN–READ WARNINGS IN *INSTRUCTION MANUAL* AVAILABLE FREE FROM
——— STURM, RUGER & CO., INC. SOUTHPORT, CONN. U.S.A. ———

REDHAWK and SUPER REDHAWK Barrels, left side

STURM, RUGER & CO., INC.
SOUTHPORT, CONN. U.S.A.
GP100 Barrel, left side

STURM, RUGER & CO. INC.
SOUTHPORT, CONN. U.S.A
GP100 Barrel, left side

STURM, RUGER & CO. INC.
SOUTHPORT, CONN. U.S.A.
SP101 Barrel, left side

BEFORE USING GUN–READ WARNINGS IN
INSTRUCTION MANUAL AVAILABLE FROM
GP100 Barrel, left side

READ INSTRUCTION MANUAL
SP101 Barrel, left side

CENTER-FIRE AUTO-LOADING PISTOLS

Model designation on left side of slide; maker name and address on right; caliber on barrel breech; warning on right side of grip frame; safety on left side of slide at rear.

RUGER P85®

RUGER P85-MK II®

RUGER P89

RUGER P89M

Chicago Police Pistols

RUGER P89DC

RUGER P89DAO

RUGER P90

RUGER P90DC

RUGER P91DC

RUGER P91DAO

RUGER P93DC

RUGER P93DAO

RUGER P94

RUGER P94DC

RUGER P94DAO

STURM, RUGER & CO. INC.
SOUTHPORT, CONN. U.S.A.
P90, P91, P93, P94, and Early P85 Models

STURM, RUGER & CO., INC.   (TERHUNE
SOUTHPORT, CONN., U.S.A.   ANTICORRO)
P85, P85II and P89 Models

S
P89, P90, P94 Safety Models

.30 LUGER
Convertible Cylinder

.40 AUTO

.45 A.C.P.

9mm x 19

9mm x 21

T.C. POLIS
Turkish Police Pistols
Slide, left side, at front

SAFE
P85, P85II Safety Models

DECOCK
ONLY
Decocker Models

BEFORE USING GUN – READ WARNINGS IN
INSTRUCTION MANUAL AVAILABLE FREE FROM
—— STURM, RUGER & CO., INC. ——

All Pistols

331

BOLT-ACTION RIFLES
(All caliber markings on left side of barrel at breech)

22 L R
77/22 and 10/22

22 WIN MAG R F
77/22

22 PPC
M77 MARK II

22 HORNET
77/22

220 SWIFT
M77 MARK II

22-250 REM
M77 MARK II

223 REM
M77 MARK II

243 WIN
M77 MARK II

257 ROBERTS
M77 MARK II

300 WIN MAG
EXPRESS RIFLE, M77 MARK II

338 WIN MAG
EXPRESS RIFLE, M77 MARK II

6mm PPC
M77 MARK II

6mm REM
M77 MARK II

6.5 X 55mm
M77 and M77 MARK II

30-06 SPRG
EXPRESS RIFLE, M77 MARK II

308 WIN
M77 MARK II

404 JEFFERY
MAGNUM RIFLE, M77 MARK II

416 RIGBY
MAGNUM RIFLE

458 WIN MAG
M77 MARK II

7mm-08 REM
M77

BEFORE USING GUN-READ WARNINGS IN *INSTRUCTION MANUAL* AVAILABLE FREE FROM STURM, RUGER & CO., INC. SOUTHPORT, CONN. U.S.A.
77/22, top of barrel

BEFORE USING GUN-READ WARNINGS IN *INSTRUCTION MANUAL* AVAILABLE FREE FROM STURM, RUGER & CO., INC., SOUTHPORT, CONN. U.S.A.
M77 MARK II, top of barrel

7mm REM MAG
EXPRESS RIFLE, M77 MARK II

7 X 57
M77 MARK II

7.62 PALMA MATCH

RUGER ALL-WEATHER 77/22
Stainless, left side of receiver

RUGER 77/22
Blued Models, left side of receiver

RUGER M77
Left side of receiver

RUGER M77 MARK II
M77 MARK II Receiver, left side for R.H. action, right side for L.H. action, EXPRESS RIFLE, left side of receiver

RUGER. MAGNUM
MAGNUM RIFLE, left side of receiver

SAFE)
EXPRESS RIFLE, MAGNUM RIFLE, M77 MARK II R.H., 77/22, top of bolt sleeve

SUBMACHINE GUN
Markings on Left Side of Receiver

RUGER

RUGER
MP9

SEMI
AUTO   SAFE

AUTO-LOADING RIFLES

RUGER®
RANCH RIFLE
CAL. .223

MINI-14 RANCH, top rear of receiver

RUGER•
MINI THIRTY
CAL. 7.62 x 39

MINI THIRTY, top rear of receiver

RUGER
AC-556•
CAL. .223

MINI-14 SELECT FIRE, top rear of receiver

STURM, RUGER & CO., INC.
SOUTHPORT. CONN. U.S.A.

44 CARBINE, top of barrel; RUGER. 10/22, top of barrel
(not currently used)

BEFORE USING GUN — READ WARNINGS IN
***INSTRUCTION MANUAL* AVAILABLE FREE FROM**

10/22, top of barrel

RUGER
MINI-14•
CAL. .223

MINI-14, top rear of receiver

—RESTRICTED LAW—
ENFORCEMENT/GOV'T
—USE ONLY 91494—

MINI-14 LAW ENFORCEMENT/GOVERNMENT. Front left side above serial no. Marking required by BATF after 9/1494

STURM. RUGER. SOUTHPORT. CT.—RESTRICTED
—LAW ENFORCEMENT/GOV'T USE ONLY 91494—

MINI-14 20 round and 30 round magazine right side. Marking required by BATF after 9/14/94

 STURM, RUGER & CO., INC
SOUTHPORT, CONN. U.S.A.

MINI-14 and MINI-THIRTY, left rear

RUGER® MODEL 10/22® CARBINE ®
.22 LR CALIBER

Left side of receiver

S
←

MINI-14, right side of safety, no longer used

(SAFE

M77, Mark II, C.H.. top of bolt sleeve

SHOTGUNS

SKEET

SKEET

Fixed Choke Model; 12 and 20 gauge, right side of mono block

S   **B**
         T

12, 20 and 28 gauge, top tang

FULL

MOD.

Fixed Choke Models; 12 and 20 gauges; right side of mono block

STURM. RUGER & CO., INC.
SOUTHPORT, CONN.
U.S.A.

12, 20, and 28 gauge, bottom of receiver

20 GA. 3" CHAMBERS

Left side of mono block

IMP. CYL.

Fixed Choke Models; 12 and 20 gauges; right side of mono block

MOD.

12 GA. 3" CHAMBERS

Left side of mono block

SKEET

Fixed Choke Models; 12 and 20 gauges; right side of mono block

IMP. CYL.

Fixed Choke Model; 12 and 20 gauge, right side of mono block

12 GA. 2 3/4" CHAMBERS

Left side of mono block

MOD.

Fixed Choke Models; 12 and 20 gauges; right side of mono block

FULL

Fixed Choke Models; 12 and 20 gauges, right side of mono block

SINGLE-ACTION REVOLVERS

STURM, RUGER & CO. INC. ®.22
SOUTHPORT, CONN. U.S.A. CAL
BEARCAT Barrel, left side

RUGER NEW BEARCAT®
Left side of receiver just below cylinder opening

RUGER .22 CAL.
NEW MODEL SINGLE-SIX®
Single action cylinder frame, left side just below cylinder opening

RUGER.32 H & R MAG.
NEW MODEL *SINGLE-SIX*®
Adjustable rear sight .22 Cal. receiver, left side just below cylinder opening

RUGER.32 CAL. CONVERTIBLE
NEW MODEL *BLACKHAWK*®
Adjustable rear sight cylinder frame. Marking indicates two cylinders fitted to the cylinder frame; left side of receiver, just below cylinder opening

RUGER.44 CAL. CONVERTIBLE
NEW MODEL *BLACKHAWK*®
Adjustable rear sight cylinder frame, left side just below cylinder opening

RUGER.30 CARBINE CAL.
NEW MODEL *BLACKHAWK*®
Adjustable rear sight cylinder frame, left side just below cylinder opening

RUGER.38-40 & 10 MM CONV.
NEW MODEL *BLACKHAWK*®
Adjustable rear sight cylinder frame, left side just below cylinder opening

RUGER.357 MAGNUM CAL.
NEW MODEL *BLACKHAWK*®
Adjustable rear sight cylinder frame, left side just below cylinder opening

RUGER.41 MAGNUM CAL.
NEW MODEL *BLACKHAWK*®
Adjustable rear sight cylinder frame, left side just below cylinder opening

RUGER.44 MAGNUM CAL.
NEW MODEL *SUPER BLACKHAWK*®
Adjustable rear sight cylinder frame, left side just below cylinder opening

RUGER.45 CALIBER
NEW MODEL *BLACKHAWK*®
Adjustable rear sight cylinder frame, left side just below cylinder opening

RUGER VAQUERO
.44 MAG. CAL.
Fixed rear sight cylinder frame, left side just below cylinder opening

RUGER VAQUERO
44-40 WIN. CAL.
Fixed rear sight cylinder frame, left side just below cylinder opening

RUGER VAQUERO®
.45 CAL.
Fixed rear sight cylinder frame, left side just below cylinder opening

10 MM AUTOMATIC
Circumference of cylinder between latch cuts and back of cylinder

.32 H&R MAGNUM CAL.
Circumference of cylinder between latch cuts and back of cylinder

.22 WIN. MAGNUM CAL. ® .22 WIN. MAGNUM CAL. ®
Circumference of cylinder toward rear

.44 REMINGTON MAGNUM
Circumference of cylinder between latch cuts and back of cylinder

RUGER
HUNTER
SUPER BLACKHAWK
Hunter cylinder frame ass'y, on top strap of cylinder frame

.22 MAG.
BEARCAT .22 Mag Marking plate installed on Bearcat roll mark when marking Magnum cylinder

.38-40 WINCHESTER
Circumference of cylinder, between cylinder latch cuts and back

.44-40 WINCHESTER
Circumference of cylinder, between latch cuts and back

.44 REMINGTON MAGNUM

BEFORE USING GUN–READ WARNINGS IN *INSTRUCTION MANUAL* AVAILABLE FREE FROM STURM, RUGER & CO., INC. SOUTHPORT, CONN. U.S.A.

All single action cylinder frame barrel assemblies except the Old Army black powder, on left side of barrel

.22 L.R.   .22 L.R.

BEARCAT 22 Cal. Cylinder (Long Rifle). Circumference of cylinder and forward of cylinder latch cuts. .22 L.R. is removable so .22 Mag can be installed for marking the Magnum cylinder

BUCK EYE Emblem, on top of frame

READ INSTRUCTION MANUAL
BEARCAT cylinder frame barrel assembly. On left side of barrel under co. name marking

Bisley Cylinder, .22 CAL., .32 CAL., .357 CAL., .41 CAL., .44 CAL., & .45 CAL. Circumference of cylinder just forward of latch cuts

SINGLE-SHOT RIFLES
(All caliber markings on left side of barrel at breech)

RUGER No.1
Top of receiver

RUGER No.3
Top of receiver

218 BEE
NO. 1

222 REM

225 WIN

264 WIN MAG

270 WIN
NO. 1

284 WIN

280 REM
NO. 1

250 SAVAGE

25-06 REM

6.5mm REM MAG

7.62 X 39

7 X 65R

45-70 GOVT
NO.1

300 H & H MAG

.30 CARB.
NO. 1

35 WHELEN

357 MAG
NO. 1

350 REM MAG

358 WIN

375 H&H MAG
NO. 1

38-55 WIN
NO. 1

416 REM MAG
NO. 1

44 REM MAG
NO. 3.

30-40 KRAG
NO. 1

STURM, RUGER & CO. INC.
SOUTHPORT, CONN. U.S.A.
NO. 1 receiver, at bottom in front of lever, no longer used

STURM, RUGER & CO. INC., SOUTHPORT, CONN. U.S.
NO.1 - No longer used, top of barrel

SAFE
No. 1, Top of tang

OLD ARMY REVOLVERS

FOR BLACK POWDER ONLY
Circumference of cylinder just forward of latch cuts

FOR BLACK POWDER ONLY

RUGER OLD ARMY ®
Left side of receiver just below cylinder opening

BEFORE USING GUN-READ WARNINGS IN *INSTRUCTION MANUAL* AVAILABLE FREE FROM
STURM, RUGER & CO. INC., SOUTHPORT, CONN. U.S.A.
Top of Barrel

SELECTED FINANCIAL INFORMATION 1949–1958

($000 OMITTED)	DECEMBER 31									
	1949	1950	1951	1952	1953	1954	1955	1956	1957	1958
BALANCE SHEET										
NET ASSETS										
Current Assets	$16	$51	$117	$166	$169	$296	$479	$885	$1,220	$1,279
Less: Current Liabilities	8	19	54	76	126	173	254	392	486	481
Net Working Capital	8	32	63	90	43	123	225	493	734	798
Property, plant, equipment, net of depreciation	18	26	24	27	54	71	76	95	86	409
Other Assets	1	13	15	24	98	66	118	119	66	77
TOTAL NET ASSETS	$27	$71	$102	$141	$195	$260	$419	$707	$886	$1,284
CAPITALIZATION										
Installment contract payable	$0	$0	$0	$0	$45	$25	$5	$0	$0	$0
Preferred stock	40	40	40	40	0	0	0	0	0	0
Common stock	10	20	20	20	20	18	20	20	20	20
Retained Earnings	(23)	11	42	81	130	217	394	687	866	1,264
TOTAL CAPITALIZATION	$27	$71	$102	$141	$195	$260	$419	$707	$886	$1,284
INCOME DATA										
Net Sales	$29	$206	$368	$427	$535	$802	$1,297	$1,849	$2,509	$2,562
Net Income (loss) after taxes	(23)	38	37	41	49	114	165	327	460	448
Net Income as a % of net sales		18.4	10.1	9.8	9.2	14.2	12.7	17.7	18.3	17.5
Net Income as a % of total capitalization		53.5	36.3	29.1	25.1	43.8	39.4	46.3	51.9	34.9
CAPITAL EXPENDITURES										
Plant & Equipment	$7	$5	$8	$4	$10	$17	$25	$37	$11	$335
Special tools	11	10	8	11	25	27	41	26	25	34
TOTAL	$18	$15	$16	$15	$35	$44	$66	$63	$36	$369
Depreciation and Amortization	1	8	18	11	8	27	61	46	47	47
Dividends Paid:										
Preferred (A)	0	$4.8	$2.4	$2.4	$0.6	$0.0	$0.0	$0.0	$0.0	$0.0
Common	0	0.2	3.3	0.0	0.0	0.0	15.0	33.7	31.2	50.0
		$5.0	$5.7	$2.4	$0.6	$0.0	$15.0	$33.7	$31.2	$50.0
Dividends paid as a % of net income	0	13.2	15.4	5.9	1.2	0.0	9.1	10.3	6.8	11.2

NOTE:
(A)   Amounts shown in dollars only from 1949 to 1958.

SELECTED FINANCIAL INFORMATION 1959–1968

($000 OMITTED)	DECEMBER 31									
	1959	1960	1961	1962	1963	1964	1965	1966	1967	1968
BALANCE SHEET										
NET ASSETS										
Current Assets	$1,792	$1,689	$1,790	$2,246	$2,379	$2,770	$3,634	$3,912	$5,098	$6,036
Less: Current Liabilities	530	366	334	472	512	565	761	610	773	981
Net Working Capital	1,262	1,323	1,456	1,774	1,867	2,205	2,873	3,302	4,325	5,055
Property, plant, equipment, net of depreciation	395	613	679	592	776	855	1,033	1,341	1,964	2,412
Other Assets	86	100	109	206	347	361	410	515	257	355
TOTAL NET ASSETS	$1,743	$2,036	$2,244	$2,572	$2,990	$3,421	$4,316	$5,158	$6,546	$7,822
CAPITALIZATION										
Common stock	20	20	20	20	20	20	20	20	20	1,651
Retained Earnings	1,723	2,016	2,224	2,552	2,970	3,401	4,296	5,138	6,526	6,171
TOTAL CAPITALIZATION	$1,743	$2,036	$2,244	$2,572	$2,990	$3,421	$4,316	$5,158	$6,546	$7,822
INCOME DATA										
Net Sales	$2,938	$2,742	$2,581	$3,474	$3,713	$4,121	$5,797	$6,023	$7,595	$9,068
Net Income (loss) after taxes	527	393	305	448	509	551	1,001	1,033	1,362	1,401
Net Income as a % of net sales	17.9	14.3	11.8	12.9	13.7	13.4	17.3	17.2	17.9	15.4
Net Income as a % of total capitalization	30.2	19.3	13.6	17.4	17.0	16.1	23.2	20.0	20.8	17.9
CAPITAL EXPENDITURES										
Plant & Equipment	$33	$183	$50	$41	$169	$115	$261	$417	$0	$0
Special tools	17	77	71	55	70	58	24	44	0	0
TOTAL	$50	$260	$121	$96	$239	$173	$285	$461	$620	$686
Depreciation and Amortization	$58	$57	$59	$187	$71	$94	$103	$154	$231	$248
Dividends Paid:										
Common (A)	$75	$100	$100	$119	$119	$125	$125	$125	$125	$125
As a % of net income	14.2	25.4	32.8	26.6	23.4	22.7	12.5	12.1	9.2	8.9
PER SHARE DATA: (B)										
Earnings						$0.05	$0.08	$0.08	$0.10	$0.11
Dividends						$0.01	$0.01	$0.01	$0.01	$0.01

NOTES:
(A) Amounts shown in dollars only.
(B) Information on per share basis from 1964 onward. In 1968 an audit was performed retrospective to 1964 for the purpose of the initial public offering of common stock in 1969: All earnings per share data adjusted to reflect a 2 for 1 stock split in June 1981, June 1989, and May 1993.

SELECTED FINANCIAL INFORMATION 1969–1978

($000 OMITTED)	DECEMBER 31									
	1969	1970	1971	1972	1973	1974	1975	1976	1977	1978
BALANCE SHEET										
NET ASSETS										
Current Assets	$7,700	$8,920	$9,711	$11,835	$13,501	$12,909	$18,083	$22,021	$25,344	$30,727
Less: Current Liabilities	1,246	635	505	1,650	1,832	1,130	3,497	3,890	3,164	3,453
Net Working Capital	6,454	8,285	9,206	10,185	11,669	11,779	14,586	18,131	22,180	27,274
Property, plant, equipment, net of depreciation	2,666	2,702	2,874	3,625	4,391	6,096	7,125	8,435	9,470	9,730
Other Asset— Net (B)	366	395	433	461	225	141	(97)	114	32	280
TOTAL NET ASSETS	$9,486	$11,382	$12,513	$14,271	$16,285	$18,016	$21,614	$26,680	$31,682	$37,284
PRODUCT LIABILITY ACCRUAL	0	0	0	0	0	0	0	0	0	0
CAPITALIZATION										
Common stock	$1,651	$1,651	$1,651	$1,651	$1,651	$1,651	$1,651	$1,651	$1,651	$1,651
Retained Earnings	7,835	9,731	10,862	12,620	14,634	16,365	19,963	25,029	30,031	35,633
TOTAL	9,486	11,382	12,513	14,271	16,285	18,016	21,614	26,680	31,682	37,284
TOTAL CAP. & PROD. LIAB.	$9,486	$11,382	$12,513	$14,271	$16,285	$18,016	$21,614	$26,680	$31,682	$37,284
INCOME DATA										
Net Sales	$11,090	$12,789	$13,319	$16,183	$19,542	$22,336	$33,776	$45,456	$48,069	$59,835
Net Income (loss) after taxes	1,960	2,226	1,462	2,129	2,674	2,226	4,424	6,305	6,240	7,007
Net Income as a % of net sales	17.7	17.4	11.0	13.2	13.7	10.0	13.1	13.9	12.9	11.7
Net Income as a % of total capitalization	20.7	19.6	11.7	14.9	16.4	12.4	20.5	23.3	19.7	18.8
Capital Expenditures	582	387	566	1,186	1,365	2,354	1,797	2,319	2,199	1,392
Depreciation and Amortization	329	350	395	435	599	649	768	1,009	1,165	1,132
Dividends Paid	297	330	330	372	660	495	826	1,238	1,238	1,404
Dividends as a % of Net Income	15.2	14.8	22.6	17.5	24.7	22.2	18.7	19.6	19.8	20.0
PER SHARE DATA: (A)										
Earnings per common share	$0.15	$0.17	$0.11	$0.16	$0.20	$0.17	$0.33	$0.48	$0.47	$0.53
Dividends per common share	0.02	0.03	0.03	0.03	0.05	0.04	0.06	0.09	0.09	0.11

NOTES:
(A)   All per share data adjusted to reflect 2 for 1 stock split in June 1981, June 1989, and May 1993.
(B)   Net of deferred income taxes payable.

SELECTED FINANCIAL INFORMATION 1979–1988

($000 OMITTED)	DECEMBER 31									
	1979	1980	1981	1982	1983	1984	1985	1986	1987	1988
BALANCE SHEET										
NET ASSETS										
Current Assets	$37,022	$44,461	$56,385	$67,415	$69,780	$73,468	$70,217	$69,869	$66,086	$57,718
Less: Current Liabilities	3,572	6,579	10,293	12,535	9,739	10,776	9,619	14,875	10,830	12,734
Net Working Capital	33,450	37,882	46,092	54,880	60,041	62,692	60,598	54,994	55,256	44,984
Property, plant, equipment, net of depreciation	10,422	13,749	14,473	15,605	15,657	15,962	18,103	18,014	19,545	21,318
Other Assets—Net	1,269	2,117	2,472	2,296	2,473	2,696	4,527	12,728	11,652	11,137
TOTAL NET ASSETS	$45,141	$53,748	$63,037	$72,781	$78,171	$81,350	$83,228	$85,736	$86,453	$77,439
PRODUCT LIABILITY ACCRUAL	1,987	3,777	2,825	4,133	6,080	6,674	9,731	12,133	10,256	13,870
CAPITALIZATION										
Common stock	1,651	1,651	3,303	3,303	3,303	3,303	3,303	3,321	3,340	3,361
Additional paid—in capital	0	0	0	0	0	0	0	695	1,391	2,115
Retained Earnings	41,503	48,320	56,909	65,345	68,788	71,373	70,194	69,587	71,466	58,093
TOTAL	43,154	49,971	60,212	68,648	72,091	74,676	73,497	73,603	76,197	63,569
TOTAL CAP. & PROD. LIAB.	$45,141	$53,748	$63,037	$72,781	$78,171	$81,350	$83,228	$85,736	$86,453	$77,439
INCOME DATA										
Net Sales	$68,856	$80,337	$95,472	$103,043	$86,348	$89,327	$93,953	$87,041	$94,288	$112,335
Net Income (loss) after taxes	7,934	8,881	12,305	11,325	10,048	9,190	9,555	6,026	8,550	12,657
Net Income as a % of net sales	11.5	11.1	12.9	11.0	11.6	10.3	10.2	6.9	9.1	11.3
Net Income as a % of total capitalization	18.4	17.8	20.4	16.5	13.9	12.3	13.0	8.2	11.2	19.9
Capital Expenditures	2,078	5,185	2,889	3,550	2,468	3,084	4,768	2,677	4,859	5,189
Depreciation and Amortization	1,386	1,858	2,165	2,418	2,416	2,779	2,627	2,766	3,328	3,416
Dividends Paid	2,064	2,064	2,064	2,889	6,605	6,605	10,734	6,633	6,671	26,030
Dividends as a % of Net Income	26.0	23.2	16.8	25.5	65.7	71.9	112.3	110.0	78.0	205.7
PER SHARE DATA: (A)										
Earnings per common share	$0.60	$0.67	$0.93	$0.86	$0.76	$0.70	$0.72	$0.45	$0.64	$0.94
Dividends per common share	0.16	0.16	0.16	0.22	0.50	0.50	0.81	0.50	0.50	1.94

NOTE:
(A)   All per share data adjusted to reflect 2 for 1 stock split in June 1981, June 1989, and May 1993.

SELECTED FINANCIAL INFORMATION 1989–1993

($000 OMITTED)	DECEMBER 31				
	1989	1990	1991	1992	1993
BALANCE SHEET					
NET ASSETS					
Current Assets	$62,451	$66,424	$76,950	$85,504	$106,149
Less: Current Liabilities	12,289	13,863	16,039	18,451	24,645
Net Working Capital	50,162	52,561	60,911	67,053	81,504
Property, plant, equipment, net of depreciation	24,830	27,560	25,876	25,200	28,139
Other Assets—Net	13,032	12,983	13,135	13,481	15,797
TOTAL NET ASSETS	$88,024	$93,104	$99,922	$105,734	$125,440
PRODUCT LIABILITY ACCRUAL	16,375	15,112	15,533	16,009	17,051
CAPITALIZATION					
Common stock	$6,723	$6,732	$6,726	$6,726	$13,452
Additional paid—in capital	2,156	2,377	2,283	2,283	2,283
Retained Earnings	62,770	68,883	75,380	80,716	92,654
TOTAL	71,649	77,992	84,389	89,725	108,389
TOTAL CAP. & PROD. LIAB.	$88,024	$93,104	$99,922	$105,734	$125,440
INCOME DATA					
Net Sales	$133,696	$135,483	$136,781	$156,075	$194,199
Net Income after taxes	18,124	13,514	14,572	22,151	32,789
Net Income as a % of net sales	13.6	10.0	10.7	14.2	16.9
Net Income as a % of total capitalization	25.3	17.3	17.3	24.7	30.3
Capital Expenditures	8,205	7,070	2,991	3,451	7,291
Depreciation and Amortization	4,225	4,340	4,675	4,127	4,352
Dividends Paid	10,085	7,401	8,075	16,815	14,125
Dividends as a % of Net Income	55.6	54.8	55.4	75.9	43.1
PER SHARE DATA: (A)					
Earnings per common share	$1.35	$1.00	$1.08	$1.65	$2.44
Dividends per common share	0.75	0.55	0.60	1.25	1.05

NOTE:
(A) All per share data adjusted to reflect 2 for 1 stock split in June 1981, June 1989, and May 1993.

SELECTED STATISTICAL INFORMATION Year Ended December 31, 1994

	NEWPORT	PRESCOTT	SOUTHPORT	PINE TREE	RIC	UNICAST	TOTAL
ACREAGE BY PLANT (IN ACRES) (1)	126.00	14.16	2.73	Included w/ Newport	15.84	6.00	**164.73**
FLOOR SPACE (SQUARE FEET) (1)	193,482	109,000	33,000	91,442	95,000	35,000	**556,924**
NUMBER OF EMPLOYEES	883	357	52	311	246	56	**1,905**
CONSUMPTION OF:							
fuel oil (gallons)	128,851			130,678			**259,529**
natural gas (cubic feet)		376,643	29,949		225,986		**632,578**
propane (gallons)				572,827		73,611	**646,438**
methanol (gallons)					4,800		**4,800**
LUMBER:							
stocks (cubic feet)	110,517						**110,517**
grips (cubic feet)	515	119					**634**
CONSUMPTION OF: (2)							
steel (tons)	1,040.00	60.00		999.38	548.66		**2,648.04**
titanium (tons)					23.99		**23.99**
aluminum (tons)					161.30	24.14	**185.44**
AMMUNITION USED FOR PRODUCTION (ROUNDS)	3,901,012	2,512,469					**6,413,481**
KILOWATT HOURS OF ELECTRICITY	11,543,730	9,348,000	400,769	14,109,004	5,680,019	2,121,000	**43,202,522**

(1)   Prescott Gun and Ruger Investment Casting total acreage equals 30 acres and 204,000 square feet of floor space.
     By April 1995 an addition to the foundry of 17,070 square feet was completed, resulting in a total of 221,070 square feet for the entire Prescott facility.
     The square feet indicated above for Newport and Pine Tree, respectively, do not include a 64,700 square foot addition to the Newport Firearms facility, completed in July 1995.
(2)   Pine Tree and Ruger Investment Casting submitted usage in pounds that were converted to tons (2000 lbs per ton) and rounded to the second decimal. Newport and Prescott steel usage is for raw barrel steel only. Information is unavailable as to total pounds of steel used for all individual gun parts. Many of these components are produced by the company's foundries.

Sturm, Ruger & Co. Board of Directors and Officers 1949–1995

1949–1951

Directors: William B. Ruger, Alexander McCormick Sturm, Norwick R. G. Goodspeed. The original incorporators were: Edward G. Riggs, Huntley Stone, Norwick R. G. Goodspeed, Alexander McC. Sturm, and William B. Ruger. The original stockholders were Sturm, Ruger, and Goodspeed. Date of incorporation was January 7, 1949, at Bridgeport, Fairfield County, Connecticut, approved January 12, 1949.

The certificate of organization established the amount of authorized capital stock at 5,001 shares: 4,000 preferred stock at $10 each, and 1,001 shares of common stock at $10 each. The full amount of invested dollars was $50,010. Stock breakdown was as follows:

Alexander McC. Sturm, Cranberry Road, Westport, Connecticut: 4,000 shares of preferred stock, and 999 shares of common stock.

William B. Ruger, Judd Road, Easton, Connecticut: 1 share of common stock.

Norwick R. G. Goodspeed, Birch Road, Fairfield, Connecticut: 1 share of common stock.

The location of the firm's principal office in Connecticut was at Railroad Place, Fairfield. This document was dated February 2, 1949, and was received for record March 7, 1949, by the assistant town clerk of Fairfield, at 9:20 A.M.

The certificate of organization of Sturm, Ruger & Co., Inc., was received and placed on file for record with the Office of Secretary of State, the State of Connecticut, on March 3, 1949.

The first meeting of the incorporators and subscribers to the capital stock of Sturm, Ruger & Co., Inc., was held at Pullman and Comley, 886 Main Street, Bridgeport, Connecticut, January 21, 1949, at 4 P.M. Present were Alexander McC. Sturm, William B. Ruger, and Norwick R. G. Goodspeed. Alexander McC. Sturm was elected chairman of the meeting, by unanimous vote, and Norwick Goodspeed was selected as secretary. Among business transacted was the recording of bylaws for regulating the affairs of the corporation. These bylaws were discussed, motioned for acceptance, and adopted unanimously.

Directors were elected, and the issuance of stock certificates was authorized. The meeting was then adjourned.

The first meeting of the Board of Directors of Sturm, Ruger & Co., Inc., was held at Pullman and Comley, immediately after the initial meeting of incorporators and subscribers to the capital stock. All three directors were present. Sturm was elected Chairman of the Board, and Goodspeed elected Secretary. Among business transacted was that the bylaws were to be incorporated into the minute book of the corporation, approved, and adopted. The following officers were elected:

William B. Ruger, President
Alexander McC. Sturm, Vice President and Treasurer
Norwick R. G. Goodspeed, Secretary

A corporate seal was adopted, and a copy of the seal was made on the minutes' margin.

Further voted was that the Treasurer be authorized to deposit the corporation's fund into an account to be opened at the Black Rock Bank and Trust Company and that arrangements be made with the bank for use of the account as provided by the bylaws of the corporation. It was further voted that the Vice President of the corporation be authorized to engage William B. Ruger in a contract of employment, as General Manager of the corporation, for a one-and-a-half-year term, with the salary at $6,000 per year.

It was further resolved that the Vice President of the corporation be authorized to engage William B. Ruger in an agreement to assign to the corporation all his patents, patent applications, inventions, and licenses owned by him, or to be invented, owned, or acquired by him, while in employment with the corporation, on consideration of $10,000 par value of the common stock of the corporation, the stock to be issued at the time a common stock dividend was declared—but not to be done until the corporation received $50,000 in gross sales, and that the corporation would have a current ratio of two-to-one after such dividend had been paid; however, the stock issue would not be made if the common stock dividend was not achieved within five years of the assignment's execution.

Among other resolutions were that the salary of

$3,000 per year would be paid to the Vice President of the corporation. And that the salaries of Sturm and Ruger would not be increased until issuance to Ruger of his stock interest or until expiration of five years from date of the authorized patent assignment, whichever would be sooner.

At a special meeting of the Board of Directors, November 1, 1950, among resolutions was that directors of the company be authorized to issue 999 shares of the company's unissued authorized common stock, nonassessable and fully paid, in the sum of $9,990 to Ruger, for the previously noted patent application (serial no. 707773, the Ruger Automatic Pistol, assigned to the corporation under contract of February 2, 1949).

Increases voted at a special board meeting of June 1, 1950, in the salaries of Sturm and Ruger, to $12,000 per year and $19,000 per year, respectively, were duly ratified. The increases took effect on July 1, 1950, to be drawn on discretion of the respective officers from time to time. A dividend of 6 percent was declared from the company's net earnings on the preferred capital stock as accumulated between January 1, 1949 through December 31, 1950, the sum being $4,800, and the dividend for payment to preferred stockholders, November 1, 1950. A further dividend was authorized of 10 cents a share (1%) on the common stock outstanding, including the 999 shares authorized to be issued that day, the total amount of $200; that dividend for payment November 2, 1950, to stockholders on record November 1, 1950.

Chronicle of Directors and Officers

Per Minutes*

January 1, 1949
Operations Began

January 12, 1949
Incorporation of Sturm, Ruger & Company,

approved by State of Connecticut
Directors:
    William B. Ruger
    Alexander McC. Sturm
    Norwick G. R. Goodspeed
Officers:
    William B. Ruger, *President*
    Alexander McC. Sturm, *Vice President, Treasurer*
    Norwick G. R. Goodspeed, *Secretary*

Principal Office of Corporation: Railroad Place,
    Village of Southport, Town of Fairfield, CT

1951
    Alexander Sturm Deceased

1953
    Norwick Goodspeed Departed

January 27, 1953
    Paulina Sturm Deceased

March 23, 1953
Directors:
    William B. Ruger
    Norman K. Parsells
    Hal E. Seagraves
Officers:
    William B. Ruger, *President, Treasurer*
    Olga M. Selleck, *Secretary*

June 30, 1956
Officers:
    William B. Ruger, *President, Treasurer*
    Michael J. Horelik, *Vice President*
    Walter E. Berger, *Secretary*

June 26, 1968
Directors:
    William B. Ruger
    Norman K. Parsells
    Hal E. Seagraves
    Lester A. Casler

August 12, 1968
Officers:
    William B. Ruger, *President, Treasurer*

Michael J. Horelik, *Vice President*
Edward P. Nolan, *Vice President*
Walter E. Berger, *Secretary*

February 26, 1969†
Incorporation of Sturm, Ruger & Company, Inc. in
    State of Delaware
Directors:
    William B. Ruger
    Norman K. Parsells
    Hal E. Seagraves
    Lester A. Casler

March 1, 1969
Officers:
    William B. Ruger, *President, Treasurer*
    Michael J. Horelik, *Vice President–Manufacturing*
    Edward P. Nolan, *Vice President–Marketing*
    Walter E. Berger, *Secretary and Controller*

March 24, 1970
    Richard B. Kilcullen to Board
    William B. Ruger, Jr., to Board
    Frank L. McCann to Board

March 24, 1970
    Norman K. Parsells, *Assistant Secretary*

November 2, 1970
    John M. Clements, *Vice President–Manufacturing,*
    Newport

June 19, 1971
    Stanley B. Terhune, *Vice President–Engineering,*
    PTC Division
    George B. Hamilton, *Vice President–Sales and*
    Administration, PTC Division

July 19, 1971
    Michael Horelik Departed

August 17, 1971
    William B. Ruger, Jr., *Vice President–*
    Manufacturing, Southport

September 13, 1971
    John M. Kingsley, Jr., *Executive Vice President*

April 18, 1972
    John M. Kingsley, Jr., to Board
    Townsend Hornor to Board

July 17, 1972
    Robert O. Kenney, *Assistant Controller‡*

July 31, 1973
    Walter E. Berger Deceased

August 22, 1973
    Robert O. Kenney, *Secretary and Assistant*
    Controller

1974
    Lester A. Casler Deceased

June 3, 1974
    William B. Ruger, Jr., *Senior Vice President*
    Walter J. Howe, *Vice President–Manufacturing*

January 1, 1975
    Arnold Rohlfing, *Vice President–Communications*

January 10, 1975
    Stanley B. Terhune to Board

December 19, 1975
    John Clements Departed

December 31, 1975
    Arnold Rohlfing Departed

March 25, 1977
    Richard B. Kilcullen Departed from Board

March 8, 1978
    G. Richard Shaw to Board

November 1, 1978
    Walter J. Howe Reassigned–Special Products
    Administrator

December 31, 1978
    Edward P. Nolan Retired

February 14, 1979
J. Thompson Ruger, *Vice President–Marketing*

November 9, 1981
Hal E. Seagraves Retired from Board

December 31, 1982
George Hamilton Retired

January 5, 1983
Jack S. Parker to Board

August 22, 1984
Robert O. Kenney Deceased

September 14, 1984
Gloria M. Biagioni, *Secretary*

(before) January 16, 1986
Frank L. McCann Deceased

June 19, 1986
Norman K. Parsells Deceased

(before) October 21, 1986
Jack S. Parker Left Board

December 1, 1986
Robert J. Cataldo, *Assistant Controller*

December 16, 1986
Robert T. Cunniff to Board

July 14, 1987
Nils Anderson, Jr., to Board

February 1, 1989
K. Michael Wellman, *Group Vice President–Castings Divisions*

January 1990
G. Richard Shaw Deceased

April 24, 1990
General Paul X. Kelley to Board

May 21, 1990
William B. Ruger, *Chairman, Chief Executive Officer*
Gary W. French, *President*

January 10, 1991
Gary W. French Departed

February 16, 1991
William B. Ruger, Jr., *President*

August 28, 1991
Robert J. Cataldo Departed

January 31, 1992
Stanley B. Terhune Retired as Officer; Remains on Board

July 14, 1992
Admiral James E. Service to Board

January 31, 1993
J. Thompson Ruger Deceased

March 11, 1993
Stephen L. Sanetti, *Vice President, General Counsel*
Erle G. Blanchard, *Vice President, Controller, Newport*

March 29, 1993
K. Michael Wellman Departed

June 30, 1994
Gloria M. Biagioni Retired

October 25, 1994
Leslie M. Gasper, *Secretary*

July 18, 1995
William B. Ruger, Jr., *Vice Chairman and Senior Executive Officer*

August 1, 1995
Gerald W. Bersett, *President and Chief Operating Officer*

Currently (as of May 1, 1996):
Directors:
William B. Ruger
William B. Ruger, Jr.
John M. Kingsley, Jr.
Townsend Hornor
Stanley B. Terhune
Richard T. Cunniff
Nils Anderson, Jr.
Paul X. Kelley
James E. Service
Officers:
William B. Ruger, *Chairman, Chief Executive Officer*
William B. Ruger, Jr., *Vice Chairman, Senior Executive Officer*
Gerald W. Bersett, *President, Chief Operating Officer*
John M. Kingsley, Jr., *Executive Vice President*
Stephen L. Sanetti, *Vice President, General Counsel*
Erle G. Blanchard, *Vice President, Controller*
Leslie M. Gasper, *Secretary*

* Minutes may not contain specific date of event; event may be referred to as having occurred prior to meeting date.
† First Annual Report published for year 1969.
‡ Listed as such per Minutes, but not listed in Annual Report for corresponding year(s).

344

Number of Employees per Year 1949 –1994*

The Ruger Collectors' Association, Inc.

1949 —	not available	1965 —	153	1981 —	1,514
1950 —	27	1966 —	209	1982 —	1,488
1951 —	27	1967 —	280	1983 —	1,386
1952 —	25	1968 —	333	1984 —	1,211
1953 —	30	1969 —	376	1985 —	1,374
1954 —	40	1970 —	397	1986 —	1,147
1955 —	62	1971 —	508	1987 —	1,228
1956 —	81	1972 —	585	1988 —	1,405
1957 —	88	1973 —	684	1989 —	1,553
1958 —	90	1974 —	773	1990 —	1,578
1959 —	92	1975 —	927	1991 —	1,410
1960 —	104	1976 —	1,107	1992 —	1,549
1961 —	105	1977 —	1,172	1993 —	1,719
1962 —	113	1978 —	1,222	1994 —	1,904
1963 —	130	1979 —	1,299		
1964 —	134	1980 —	1,415		

Although cofounded by the late Stephen K. Vogel, the Collectors' Association is an independent association of Ruger collectors, not affiliated with or sponsored by Sturm, Ruger and Company. The organization's beginning in 1975 quickly mushroomed into the largest collectors' group of its kind in the United States, with membership surpassing by far the combined totals of the Colt, Winchester, Smith & Wesson, and Remington associations.

The RCA publishes a quarterly bulletin, known as *The Ruger Collectors' Journal,* and regularly displays at the NRA shows. From time to time issues of Ruger firearms have been made, which were purchased by the RCA, and offered to its members. Current RCA headquarters are at P.O. Box 240, Greens Farms, Connecticut 06436.

---

*1950 –1965: *average of the number of employees during the year;* 1966 –1994: *number of employees at year-end.*

Notes

Chapter I: "We've Got to Learn Sometime"

1. Bannerman's was located at 501 Broadway, New York City.
2. Both guns were purchased from Anthony Fiala's Safari Outfits Store in New York City.
3. One book that made a particularly strong impression was W. W. Greener's *The Gun and Its Development*.
4. Hatcher discussed a variety of topics, including primer-type activation for rifles, in which setback of the cartridge primer upon firing supplied the energy to automatically unload, recock, and reload the rifle. He also went over the mechanics of gas-operated guns and the general principles of automatic weapons.
5. Their first home was on Sigourney Street; the second on Woodbine.
6. Fred Goat and Company was located at 314 Dean Street in Brooklyn, New York.
7. According to Ruger, "In those days, it was still a tiny little company making a .22 caliber automatic pistol designed to compete for the Colt Woodsman pistol market at a much lower price."
8. Ruger and Cook met at offices in the Irving Trust Company building at Wall Street and Broadway in New York City; Auto-Ordnance's factory was in Bridgeport, Connecticut.
9. William J. Helmer, *The Gun That Made the Twenties Roar*, N.D.
10. The building, at 1437 Railroad Avenue, had been used for automobile brakelining manufacture.

Chapter II: "A Clean Sheet of Paper"

1. The basic process involves creating an exact-size model of the part out of wax, "investing" (coating) it in a ceramic slurry that hardens into a mold, melting the wax out of the mold, and pouring molten alloy steel into the void where the wax was. When the steel cools and hardens, the mold is broken apart, revealing the steel part, a virtual duplicate of the wax model.
2. Jack Behn got for Bill Ruger the desk calendar sheet from Peterson's widow for the day in 1995 when Ruger called. On it was written: "Bill Ruger called about the .44 Magnum. I told him nothing."
3. Type of firearm an outdoorsman packs in his "kit" for informal target shooting, shooting small game for food, and self-defense.

Chapter III: "The Risks of Competition"

1. Thompson Center set up its own casting foundry a few years after Ruger's remarks were made.
2. From the film *Conversations with Bill Ruger*, produced in 1975 by Roger Barlow.

Chapter IV: "Build Your Car . . . House . . . Rifle the Way You Want It"

1. Ruger traditionally has concluded his annual report remarks with a statement in appreciation of the loyalty and performance of his employees and suppliers, and the patronage of his customers and stockholders. In the present text, most of these have been deleted for the sake of brevity.
2. Now called the Long Action. True Magnum actions would not appear until 1992.

Chapter IX: "The Basis of a Free Market Economy"

1. When Triggs was sick and bedridden for six years, Ruger kept him on the payroll and maintained his health insurance, even though Triggs could perform only sporadic, but still superb quality, work for the company.

Bibliography

Adams, Henry. *The Education of Henry Adams, An Autobiography*. Boston and New York: Houghton Mifflin Company, 1918, 1946 edition.

Anonymous. *Textbook of Small Arms*. London: H.M. Stationery Office, 1929.

Askins, Charles. *Unrepentant Sinner*. San Antonio: Tejano Publications, 1985.

Boddington, Craig. *Safari Rifles*. Long Beach, California: Safari Press, 1990.

Burke, Ronnie. *Ruger Model 77 Bolt Action Rifles*. Broken Bow, Oklahoma: Ron Burke Publications, 1983.

Carlyle, Thomas. *Sartor Resartus*.

Carmichel, Jim. *Jim Carmichel's Book of the Rifle*. New York: Outdoor Life Books, 1985.

Clayton, Joe D. (John T. Amber, editor). *Ruger No. 1 Rifle*. Southport, Connecticut: Blacksmith Corporation, 1983.

Dougan, John C. (John T. Amber, editor). *Know Your Ruger Single-Action Revolvers 1953–63*. Southport, Connecticut: Blacksmith Corporation, 1981.

———. *Know Your Ruger Single-Actions: The Second Decade 1963–73*. Chino Valley, Arizona: Blacksmith Corporation, 1989.

———. *Compliments of Col. Ruger*. El Paso, Texas: Published by the author, 1991.

Helmer, William J. *The Gun That Made the Twenties Roar*. Highland Park, New Jersey: The Gun Room Press, 1969.

Hiddleson, Chad. *Encyclopedia of Ruger Semi-Automatic Rimfire Pistols 1949-1992*. Iola, Wisconsin: Krause Publications, 1993.

Hogg, Ian V., and John Weeks. *Pistols of the World*. Northfield, Illinois: DBI Books, 1982.

Hounshell, David A. *From the American System to Mass Production, 1800–1932*. Baltimore and London: The Johns Hopkins University Press, 1984.

Keith, Elmer. *Elmer Keith: His Life Story "Hell, I Was There!"* Los Angeles: Petersen Publishing Co., 1979.

Lewis, Jack. *The Gun Digest Book of Single Action Revolvers*. Northfield, Illinois: DBI Books, 1983.

Long, Duncan (Larry Combs, editor). *The Ruger "P" Models*. El Dorado, Arizona: Desert Publications, 1993.

———. *The Ruger .22 Automatic Pistol Standard/Mark*

I/Mark II Series. Boulder, Colorado: Paladin Press, 1988.

Lueders, Hugo A. *Ruger Automatic Pistols and Single Action Revolvers with Check Lists*. Houston, Texas: Published by the author, 1978.

————. *Ruger Automatic Pistols and Single Action Revolvers Book III*. Houston, Texas: Published by the author, 1982.

Munnell, J.C. *Ruger Rimfire Handguns 1949–1982*. McKeesport, Pennsylvania: 1982.

Nordenholt, George F., Joseph Kerr, and John Sasso. *Handbook of Mechanical Design*. New York and London: McGraw-Hill Book Company, Inc., 1942.

O'Connor, Jack. *Complete Book of Shooting*. New York: Outdoor Life Books, 1982.

Roberts, Joseph B., Jr. *Ruger*. Washington, D.C.: National Rifle Association of America, 1990.

Sturm, Alexander. *From Ambush to Zig Zag*. New York: Charles Scribner's Sons.

————. *The Problem Fox*. New York: Charles Scribner's Sons, 1941.

Twiselton-Wykeham-Fiennes, Sir Ranulph. *Living Dangerously*. New York: Macmillan, 1987.

Wallace, Captain W.B., ed. *Text Book of Small Arms*. London: H.M. Stationery Office, 1904.

Workman, William E. *Know Your Ruger 10/22*. Southport, Connecticut: Blacksmith Corporation, 1986.

————. *The Ruger 10/22*. Iola, Wisconsin: Krause Publications, Inc., 1994.

————. *The Sturm, Ruger 10/22 Rifle and .44 Magnum Carbine*. Boulder, Colorado: Paladin Press, 1988.

Periodicals

Ayres, B. Drummond, Jr. "Gun Maker on Mayhem: That Is Not Our Doing," *The New York Times*, March 19, 1994. Based on interview with William B. Ruger, Jr.

Bailey, Harold L., Jr. "Lenard M. Brownell, 1922–1982: A Custom Gunmaker," *Bulletin of the American Society of Arms Collectors*, 1990.

Carmichel, Jim. "30 Years of Rugers," *Outdoor Life*, August 1979.

Cary, Lucian. "Pistols in a Woodshed," *True*, February 1954.

Davis, David E. "Cogito Ergo Zoom, American Driver, What Kind of Car Is This?," *Automobile*, November 1988.

Delfay, Robert T., "An Exclusive Interview with Bill Ruger," *SHOT Business*, March/April 1994, vol. 2, no. 2.

Johnston, Gary Paul. "The Ruger Light Machine Guns," *Gun World*, January 1996.

Koller, Larry. "Safari in the Rockies," *The American Gun*, Winter 1961.

Kuhlhoff, Pete. "The Man Behind the Ruger Gun," *Argosy*, August 1956.

————. "Rifles and Bullets Safari Tested," *Argosy*, August 1961.

————. "The Ruger Carbine in Africa," *The Gun Digest*, 1963.

Latham, Sid (photographer), Larry Koller, editor. "The Target Guns of Bill Ruger," *The American Gun*, Spring 1961.

Lindsay, Merrill K. "Harry Sefried Inventor/Collector Extraordinaire," *Guns*, August 1978.

Pearce, Lane. "Shooting for the Contract, Ruger's P-85," *Shooting Times*, January 1989.

Ruger, William B. "Semi-Automatic .250-3000," *The American Rifleman*, December 1943.

Sharfman, Bill. "William B. Ruger, A Lifetime of Enthusiasm for Engineering," *Automobile*, November 1988.

Triggs, James M. "William B. Ruger, A Personality Profile," *Arms Gazette*, August 1977.

Trueblood, Ted. "The Maverick Gunmaker and His Greatest Gamble," *True*, May 1966.

Warner, Ken. "'Any Great Artist Could Do It. . . . ' The Remarkable Career of James M. Triggs," *The Gun Digest*, 1992.

Articles from periodicals by the following corps of writers on the shooting sports:

Finn Aagard, John T. Amber, Colonel Rex Applegate, Dave Arnold, Colonel Charles Askins, Massad F. Ayoob, Jim Baker, Roger Barlow, Peter Barrett, Bob Bell, E. G. "Red" Bell, Jr., James W. Bequette, David Biser, Craig Boddington, L. P. Brezny, Robert M. Brister, Pete Brown, Robert Brown, Nelson Bryant, Jerry Burke, Warrent W. Buttler, Bill Bynum, Chuck Campbell, Jim Carmichel, Lucian Cary, Russ Carpenter, Chris Christian, Wiley Clapp, Steve Comus, Jeff Cooper, John Crowley, Gene B. Crum, Charles Dees, Joseph F. Delaney, Pete Dickey, Ray Dowling, Ken Elliott, Tom Ellis, Sam Fadala, Denny Fallon, Scott Farrell, J. Wayne Fears, Tom Ferguson, Tom Fulgham, Gene Gangarosa, Galen L. Geer, Dean A. Grennell, Crits Gresham, Tom Gresham, John Guthrie, Ed Hall, Mark Hampton, Walt Hampton, D. W. "Denny" Hansen, Paul Hantke, C. E. Harris, Mark Harris, John Haviland, Chad Hiddleson, Cameron Hopkins, Jerry Horgesheimer, B. R. Hughes, R. W. Hunnicutt, Frank James, Rick Jamison, William S. Jarrett, Norman E. Johnson, Gary Paul Johnston, Sonny Jones, William H. Jordan, Harry Kane, Richard W. Kayser, Ron Keysor, Elmer Keith, Neal Knox, Peter J. Kokalis, John Kronfeld, Pete Kuhlhoff, John Lachuk, H. Lea Lawrence, Tim Leary, Jerry Lee, Jack Lewis, Jan M. Libourel, Sheila Link, Evan P. Marshall, George Martin, Edward A. Matunas, Gila May, Richard Metcalf, Robert Milek, Al Miller, Nigel Milner, Jack Mitchell, Terry A. Murbach, Harold Murtz, George Nonte, Bill Norton, Bill O'Brien, Jack O'Connor, Ludwig Olson, Jim Ottman, Warren Page, William F. Parkerson III, Aaron Pass, Tom Paugh, Lane Pearce, Charles E. Petty, Dave Petzal, Chris Pollack, D. K. Pridgen, Dennis Prisbrey, Ralph F. Quinn, Clair Rees, Walter L. Rickell, Ed Sanow, David Scovill, Ross Seyfried, Robert T. Shimek, James Shults, Tom Siatos, Layne Simpson, Nick Sisley, Gary Sitton, Bart Skelton, Skeeter Skelton, Vince Sparano, Sgt. Dave Spaulding, Nick Steadman, Kevin Steele, Bob Steindler, John Sundra, Hal Swiggett, John Taffin, Turk Takano, Joseph Tartaro, John Taylor, Larry Teague, Bryce Towsley, Ted Trueblood, Stan Trzoniec, Wayne VanZwoll, Michael L. Venturino, M. D. Waite, Richard Williams, Todd Woodard, Jim Woods, Don Zutz, and Bob Zwirz.

Articles from periodicals, company instruction manuals and advertising, catalogues, brochures, annual reports, quarterly reports, interviews with present and past employees, vendors, writers, friends, and members of the Ruger family.

Acknowledgments

To William B. Ruger, Sr., who has made available a profusion of records, files, firearms, and artifacts, and cooperated fully with extensive interviews, enduring the author's queries with patience, insight, humor, and candor. Without his cooperation, editorial insight, and encouragement this book could not have been done.

To William B. Ruger, Jr. (for numerous assists and insights), to Mrs. Stephen K. Vogel (Molly; for a wealth of photographs and recollections), to Cameron Wesselhoft Brauns (for early material from the Center Street attic, and her kind hospitality), to Adrienne Ruger (for information on the art collection), and the complete Ruger family, for their cheerful and generous cooperation.

To the members of the Board of Directors, Sturm, Ruger and Company, Inc., for their individual contributions, and especially to Stanley B. Terhune, for his recollections on the evolution of the Pine Tree and Ruger investment casting operations.

To Stephen L. Sanetti, Vice President, General Counsel, for his perceptive assistance, technical and textual consultation, and unstinting support. And to his assistants Phyllis Garber and Fran Pczonka.

To John M. Kingsley, Jr., and staff, for extensive and detailed insights on the company's financial history, and for allowing access to photographs taken by J.M.K., Jr., during his twenty-three years at Sturm, Ruger. Liz Fogerty compiled statistics on the Sturm, Ruger factories, similar to those published by Winchester Repeating Arms Co. on its 50th Anniversary in 1916.

To Erle G. Blanchard, Al Scribner, Robert R. Stutler, Frank Bonaventura, and Leon Davey for guidance on the factories and the complexities of firearms and investment castings production. Each had their own assistants who also contributed.

To Ruger engineers, past and present, for their insights and commentary on this critical aspect of the Ruger phenomenon: Harry H. Sefried II, Jay Jarvis, Ted Andress, Robert Davis, Bill Atkinson, Jim McGarry, Mike Simsko, Richard Holmes, Jim Sullivan, Lawrence L. Larson, Chris Cashavelly, and Roy Melcher. To Alex Santella for his insights into the Tool Room and production equipment, Southport, and for assistance in the photography of that site.

To Walter Sych, Manager, Law Enforcement Sales, for recollections of his lifetime at Sturm, Ruger, and for the morning spent reminiscing at the original "red barn" factory site.

To Thomas W. Pew, Jr., and his staff at Merlin, for color transparencies and access to their extensive files, and to Tom for rekindling the project when it seemed that the book was nearly dormant.

To retired employees Gloria Biagioni, J. H. Behn, Rex King, W. J. Howe, and Carl Wesselhoft, for their recollections of participating in building the Ruger enterprise.

To Kimberly Pritula and Victoria Vogel Roberts and staff, of the Sturm, Ruger Export Department, for researching numbers and production data, and for double-checking the technical sections on all models.

To Lynn Merrill, Robert Anderson, Richard Beaulieu, Dennis Veilleux, Robert Wood for special assistance at the New Hampshire facility.

To Charles Rogler and Jeremy Clowes, of the Export Department, for their memories from many years of service in the challenging and often complex world markets.

To Maureen Graziano, Paula O'Malley, Linda DeProfio, and Nicole Barrett, for assistance in researching the Ruger advertising and illustrative materials, published articles on Ruger firearms, and other material.

To Leslie Gasper, Carole Markland, Betty Camp, Shannon Psotka, Lou Dicso, and Ken Siwy at the Southport office, for assistance ranging from verifying and completing the Chronicle of the Board of Directors to making sure the author did not miss lunch to numerous other necessary tasks.

To Marie Sorge, Carol Twyon, and Margaret Sheldon, Mr. Ruger's secretaries in Southport, Newport, and Prescott, who followed up on innumerable requests and kept an avalanche of information directed at the author, wherever he was.

To Joseph Molina and his staff at JMPR, whose communication skills have joined with those of Simon & Schuster in the promotion of this book.

To Professor Merritt Roe Smith, Massachusetts Institute of Technology, for his helpful suggestions, from a reading of the entire manuscript, and for his observations based on a thorough tour of the factory

Photographic Notes

and foundry complex in Newport. And to Stephen L. Sanetti, Alison Smith, Richard Alan Dow, Mrs. Stephen K. Vogel, and Cameron Wesselhoft Brauns, for reading the manuscript and making their own observations and suggestions.

And finally to Michael V. Korda, David Wolfe, the late Dr. Edward C. Ezell, Paul McCarthy, Angus Cameron, and Richard Alan Dow. This book began when Michael Korda asked to meet William B. Ruger, Sr., to discuss the possibilities of a Simon & Schuster book. We met the founder at his Southport office, in the spring of 1978, and quickly learned that Bill Ruger had himself been thinking about such a volume . . . but he was then still too procccupied with gunmaking, and other matters, to give the subject much thought. Some years later, Dave Wolfe, publisher of *The Rifle, Handloader,* and other magazines, and founder of Wolfe Publishing Co., began encouraging Ruger to do the book. Transcripts of recorded interviews done by Wolfe proved a vital resource. Finally, in 1992, Ruger was ready to begin, but I was then overcommitted on a number of projects and was unable to fit the Ruger schedule.

At about that time, Dr. Edward C. Ezell, Curator, Department of Military History, National Museum of American History, Smithsonian Institution, was arranging for a visit to the U.S. by Mikhail Kalashnikov, ultimately made possible by the generosity of Bill Ruger. The pivotal event of Kalashnikov's tour was the reception at the NRA Show in April 1993. Soon thereafter Ed Ezell began the Ruger book. His several weeks of meetings and research, at Southport and Newport, resulted in transcripts of a number of interviews and the assembling of key early drawings, correspondence, and other documents. That summer Ed Ezell took a leave of absence from the museum, for health reasons, and to concentrate on the Ruger project. Sadly, terminal cancer prevented Dr. Ezell from writing more than drafts of what became the genesis of Chapter I; he died in December 1993.

Meanwhile, Bill Ruger maintained his usual demanding pace, and the book lay dormant for the next few months. At the NRA Show in Minneapolis, the following April, a seemingly innocuous lunch between Tom Pew and the writer led to mention of "the book." I was now ready to consider such a daunting task, and said so. When Tom relayed this, Ruger's rejoinder was "Well, goddammit, why didn't he tell me that. . . . " After some preliminary phone visits, we met during the Winchester Club of America annual gun show in Cody, Wyoming, on June 25th. During a 2½ hour luncheon meeting (during which we were too absorbed to have any lunch), we made an agreement to resume where we had left off so many years before. Plans for the book became more serious after the author met with Michael Korda on July 20th. The first sit-down interviews and research at Newport began on the very next day. A few days later, all of Ed Ezell's work was hand-delivered to Newport by Mrs. Virginia Ezell.

Peter Beard and Allan Brown collaborated on taking the majority of color transparencies. Brown was responsible for the technical execution, using a 4 x 5 and 8 x 10 Combo View Camera, with Kodak Ektachrome film (either daylight for outdoors or tungsten for studio work). The exposed film was developed in the laboratory of R. J. Phil, East Hampton, Connecticut. Peter Beard was responsible for creative design and layout for nearly all of the non-technical color illustrations. His collage style allowed for the use of an enormous number of individual images.

Other photographs were taken by Porter Gifford, Douglas Kirkland, Jim Kritz, Capitol Photo (Steve Madwed and George Szilagyi), Cameron Wesselhoft Brauns, Richard Beaulieu, and John M. Kingsley, Jr.

Index

Note: Page numbers in *italics* refer to illustrations.